POP CULTURE
RUSSIA!

Upcoming titles in ABC-CLIO's series

Popular Culture in the Contemporary World

Pop Culture Latin America! Media, Arts, and Lifestyle, Lisa Shaw and Stephanie Dennison

Pop Culture India! Media, Arts, and Lifestyle, Asha Kasbekar

Pop Culture Japan! Media, Arts, and Lifestyle, William H. Kelly

Pop Culture Israel! Media, Arts, and Lifestyle

Pop Culture Korea! Media, Arts, and Lifestyle

Pop Culture Scandinavia! Media, Arts, and Lifestyle

Pop Culture Caribbean! Media, Arts, and Lifestyle, Brenda F. Berrian

Pop Culture France! Media, Arts, and Lifestyle, Wendy Michallat

Pop Culture Ireland! Media, Arts, and Lifestyle

Pop Culture Australia! Media, Arts, and Lifestyle

Pop Culture UK! Media, Arts, and Lifestyle, Bill Osgerby

Pop Culture West Africa! Media, Arts, and Lifestyle, Onookome Okome

Pop Culture Germany! Media, Arts, and Lifestyle, Catherine Fraser

Pop Culture China! Media, Arts, and Lifestyle, Kevin Latham

POP CULTURE
RUSSIA!

Media, Arts, and Lifestyle

Birgit Beumers

A B C CLIO

Santa Barbara, California   Denver, Colorado   Oxford, England

Library of Congress Cataloging-in-Publication Data
Beumers, Birgit.
Pop culture Russia! : media, arts, and lifestyle / Birgit Beumers.
    p. cm. — (Popular culture in the contemporary world)
Includes bibliographical references and index.
ISBN 1-85109-459-8 (hardback : alk. paper) — ISBN 1-85109-464-4 (ebook) 1. Popular culture—Russia (Federation)—History. 2. Popular culture—Soviet Union—History.
3. Mass media—Russia (Federation)—History. I. Title. II. Series.
DK510.762.B48   2005
306'.0947—dc22
2004026959

08   07   06   05 | 10   9   8   7   6   5   4   3   2   1

This book is also available on the World Wide Web as an eBook.
Visit abc-clio.com for details.

ABC-CLIO, Inc.
130 Cremona Drive, P.O. Box 1911
Santa Barbara, California 93116-1911

Text design by Jane Raese

This book is printed on acid-free paper.
Manufactured in the United States of America

Contents

Preface   ix

Acknowledgments   xi

Chronology of Events   xiii

Introduction   1

After the Revolution, 1
After World War II, 3
After the Thaw, 6
After Brezhnev, 9
The New Russia, 10
References, 12

1   The Media   13

The Broadcasting Media, 13
   Television, 13
   Radio, 46
   Internet, 49
The Print Media, 51
   Newspapers, 51
   Journals, 57
A-Z, 63
Bibliography, 69

2   Visual Culture   71

The Cinema, 71
   Feature Films, 71
   Animation, 99
Visual Arts and Crafts, 104
   Art Movements, 105
   Crafts, 108

Architecture, 112
    Urban Design, 112
    Churches and Icons, 123
A-Z, 128
Bibliography, 133

3 Performing Arts 134

The Theater, 134
    Drama Theater, 135
    Puppet Theater, 160
Estrada and Popular Entertainment, 168
    Staged Estrada, 169
    Anecdotes and Jokes, 173
The Circus, 182
    A History of the Circus, 182
    Choreographed Acrobatics and Clowns, 186
A-Z, 192
Bibliography, 198

4 Music and Word 199

Jazz and Rock, 199
    The Beginnings of Jazz and Rock Music, 199
    The Bard Movement, 202
    Rock Underground, 207
Pop Culture, 228
    Rock Meets Pop, 228
    Estrada and Pop Music, 236
Youth Culture and Language, 243
    Youth Jargon and Slang, 245
    Swearing, 246
Musicals, 246
    Nord-Ost: The First Russian Musical, 249
    Soviet Musicals—The Revival? 253
A-Z, 255
Bibliography, 262

5 Popular Entertainment 263

Sports, 263
    Olympic History, 264
    Olympic Glory, 264
    Team Sports, 268
    Individual Sports, 278

Winter Sports, 286
Chess, 291
Pulp Fiction, 292
Publishing, 292
Best Sellers, 295
Detective Stories, 298
Soap Operas, 305
Crime Serials and Serial Crimes, 305
Crimeless Serials, 309
A-Z, 309
Bibliography, 314

6   Consumer Culture   316

Advertising, 316
Product Advertising, 320
Investment and Banks, 325
Social Advertising, 329
Leisure, 330
Restaurants, 330
Eating and Drinking, 335
Clubs and Bars, 337
Games, 342
Relaxation and Holidays, 343
Celebrations, 350
Public Holidays, 351
Religious Holidays, 352
Rites and Rituals, 354
Fashion, 356
Haute Couture, 359
Fashion Design, 363
A-Z, 367
Bibliography, 370

Glossary   373

Index   377

About the Author   400

Preface

Popular Culture Russia! is designed to offer an introduction to some of the developments in popular culture in the New Russia. There are some excellent studies on popular culture in Soviet Russia, such as Richard Stites's *Russian Popular Culture* (Cambridge University Press, 1992). There are also collections of essays on aspects of contemporary culture; I should mention here Adele Barker's *Consuming Russia* (Duke University Press, 1999) and Nancy Condee's *Soviet Hieroglyphics* (BFI/Indiana University Press, 1995), which are groundbreaking and tackle aspects of popular culture previously not part of critical discourse. Dmitri Shalin's *Russian Culture at the Crossroads* (Westview Press, 1996), Nicholas Rzhevsky's *Modern Russian Culture* (Cambridge University Press, 1998), and Catriona Kelly's and David Shepherd's *Russian Cultural Studies* (Oxford University Press, 1998) are most valuable collections on Russian culture.

This book attempts to chart the development of popular culture in Soviet Russia in broad terms, in order to set the backdrop for a detailed exploration of popular culture under Gorbachev, Yeltsin, and Putin. I have clearly not covered everything but have selected what seems to be most representative of the fast development of contemporary culture in Russia. I could not even claim that I have covered the most important trends, figures, and events—only history will reveal that.

Acknowledgments

I should like to express my gratitude to the British Academy for funding my research trips to Russia during 2002 and 2003.

I should like to thank Nadia, Polina, and Glasha for making me feel at home in the popular jungle of Moscow; Svetlana Kriukova and Svetlana Khokhriakova for their help in locating articles and pictures; Tamara, Masha, and Sasha at the Golden Mask for sorting me out whenever I got stuck; Tanya Tkach and Tanya Kuznetsova for helping me in Petersburg. Special thanks for help with illustrations to Galina Butseva of *Kommersant* for her incredible patience with the photo selection and to Irina Kaledina for her help with pictures. Sharon Daugherty and Anna Kaltenbach at ABC-CLIO have been the most competent editors any author could wish for.

My sincere thanks to Gordon McVay for reading various drafts of the manuscript, to Barbara Heldt and Gerry Smith, and to Simon Mason for his patience and his invaluable suggestions.

This book is for my mother, who supported the most extravagant endeavors of her quirky daughter and even read Russian pulp fiction!

Transliteration

Transliteration from the Cyrillic to the Latin alphabet is a perennial problem for writers on Russian subjects. I have followed the Library of Congress system without diacritics, but I have broken from this system in several instances to make it more user-friendly:

- when a Russian name has a clear English version (for example, Maria instead of Mariia, Alexander instead of Aleksandr);
- when a Russian name has an accepted English spelling, or when Russian names are of Germanic origin (for example, Yeltsin instead of Eltsin, Eisenstein instead of Eizenshtein);
- when a Russian surname ends in -ii or yi, this is replaced by a single -y (for example, Dostoevsky instead of Dostoevskii); this also applies to names ending in -oi. All Christian names end in a single -i (for example, Sergei, Yuri);

- when "ia" and "iu" are voiced (at the beginning of a word and when preceded by a vowel), they are rendered as "ya" and "yu" (for example, Daneli*ya*, *Yu*ri); a voiced "e" becomes "ye" (for example, Yefremov); and "ë" is rendered as "yo" (for example, Kiselyov);
- when a soft sign has been omitted in an ['ev]-ending, this has been replaced with an "i" (for example, Vasiliev).

I have adhered to some commonly used spellings for Russian names and words (for example, *banya*, *stilyaga*, Nevsky Prospekt, Utesov, Beria).

In the main text, soft signs have been omitted; they have been kept for transliterated Russian titles, which follow Library of Congress without breaking from the system in the above cases. Titles of films, television series, and books are given in their accepted English version, followed by the Russian original in parentheses. Names of rock groups, radio stations, television programs, and newspapers are given in Russian, followed by their English meaning.

Birgit Beumers
Bristol, July 2004

Chronology of Events

1985

10 Mar	Chernenko dies (general secretary of CPSU since the death of Andropov on 9 February 1984)
11 Mar	Gorbachev confirmed as general secretary
28 Mar	death of painter Marc Chagall
04 Apr	death of filmmaker Dinara Asanova
16 May	announcement of antialcohol campaign
11–12 Jun	announcement of "acceleration" (*uskorenie*) of scientific and technological progress
21 Jun	A. N. Yakovlev as secretary for propaganda in the CC
24 Jun	announcement of perestroika
16 Jul	Shevardnadze as minister of foreign affairs
Jul	Avtograf participates in Live Aid concert for famine relief in Africa
Aug	moratorium on nuclear tests (until February 1987) 12th International Youth Festival, Moscow
27 Sept	Nikolai Tikhonov retires as chairman of Council of Ministers and is replaced by Nikolai Ryzhkov (head of UralMash)
2–5 Oct	Gorbachev on state visit to France
19–21 Nov	Ronald Reagan and Gorbachev meet in Geneva
24 Dec	Yeltsin as first secretary of the Moscow Party Section, replacing Viktor Grishin

1986

Jan	television program *Dvenadtsatyi etazh* starts
24 Jan	Alexander Vlasov as minister of interior affairs

11 Feb	exchange of Anatoli Shcharansky in Berlin
20 Feb	Mir launched
25 Feb–6 Mar	27th Congress of the CPSU
Mar	Melodiya releases Beatles album
20 Apr	death of playwright Alexei Arbuzov
26 Apr	fire in reactor at Chernobyl
May	new logo for *Vremia*
05 May	Sviatoslav Fyodorov opens a center for microsurgery on the eye
13–15 May	Fifth Congress of the Filmmakers' Union
19 May	Anatoli Dobrynin recalled as ambassador to the USA after 24 years in office
30 May	Account 904: benefit concert for Chernobyl victims
14 Aug	law permitting cooperatives
06 Oct	Garri Kasparov becomes world chess champion
11–12 Oct	Reagan and Gorbachev meet in Reykjavik
17 Oct	death of football coach Boris Arkadiev
12 Nov	opening of Soviet Foundation of Culture
19 Nov	individual work permitted
03 Dec	Gorbachev meets with the creative intelligentsia
05 Dec	Theater Union formed
08 Dec	death of the dissident Anatoli Marchenko
23 Dec	Andrei Sakharov returns to Moscow from exile in Gorky (Nizhny Novgorod)
29 Dec	death of filmmaker Andrei Tarkovsky

1987

Jan	start of "experiment" in theater management
12 Jan	death of theater director Anatoli Efros
26 Jan	release of Abuladze's film *Repentance* and Iuris Podnieks's documentary *Is It Easy to Be Young?*

19 Feb	rehabilitation of Boris Pasternak
08 Mar	television show *Do i posle polunochi,* hosted by Vladimir Molchanov (closed June 1991)
25 Mar	death of animator Ivanov Vano
28 Mar–1 Apr	Margaret Thatcher on state visit in Moscow
22 Mar	Gorbunov Culture Palace: concert of Young Musicians for Peace (with DDT, Nautilus, ChaiF)
23 May	space link on television (*tele-most*)
May	Voice of America officially transmits in the USSR
28 May	German aviator Matthias Rust lands a Cessna plane on Red Square
June	"market socialism" announced
	Theater der Welt, Stuttgart: theaters of Anatoli Vasiliev and Oleg Tabakov participate
25 Aug	decree on AIDS
02 Sept	first exhibition of Marc Chagall
13 Oct	chess championship: Garri Kasparov beats Anatoli Karpov in Seville
21 Oct	Yeltsin criticizes Gorbachev and Ligachev
24 Oct	death of footballer Nikolai Starostin
Oct	split of the Moscow Art Theater
Nov	television program *Vzgliad* starts
Nov	exhibition of avant-garde and Socialist Realist painting at the Tretiakov Gallery, Moscow
11 Nov	Yeltsin removed from post as Moscow party chief
30 Nov	Mikhail Shatrov's *The Peace of Brest* opens at Vakhtangov Theater
12 Dec	Nobel Prize for Literature to Joseph Brodsky
17 Dec	death of actor and comedian Arkadi Raikin

1988

05 Jan	control of psychiatric clinics moved from Ministry of Interior to Ministry of Health
06 Jan	name of Brezhnev removed from towns and squares
08 Jan	perestroika of the press: increased print runs of the journals *Druzhba narodov* and *Novy mir*, the newspapers *Moskovskie novosti* and *AiF*, and the weekly *Ogonyok*
28 Jan	end of *beriozka* (foreign currency) shops
04 Feb	rehabilitation of the anti-Stalin opposition (1938)
06 Feb	nuclear test in Semipalatinsk
17 Feb	suicide of musician Alexander Bashlachev
28–29 Feb	pogrom against Armenians in Sumgait
15 Mar	first Salvador Dali exhibition in Moscow
04 May	nuclear test in Semipalatinsk
7–9 May	demonstrations in Moscow
16 May	Soros begins support
17–23 May	Pepsi Cola advertisements with Michael Jackson broadcast
29 May–2 Jun	Ronald Reagan in Moscow
03 Jun	Sajudis, Lithuanian independence movement
07 Jun	first auction of modern art by Sotheby's
13 Jun	Rehabilitation of Lev Kamenev, Karl Radek, Grigori Zinoviev (Stalin opposition of 1930s)
23 Jun	demonstrations in the Baltic states against their annexation in June 1940 by the USSR
17 Sept	premiere of Viktiuk's *The Maids*
Nov	refugees from Armenia and Azerbaijan
29 Nov	jamming of Radio Liberty and Radio Liberty Europe stops
07 Dec	earthquake in Spitak, Armenia
30 Dec	death of poet and dissident Yuli Daniel

1989

12–19 Jan	census
19 Jan	first Malevich exhibition
23 Jan	earthquake in Tadjikistan
28 Jan	society "Memorial"
31 Jan	first McDonalds opens in Moscow
15 Feb	removal of troops from Afghanistan
09 Mar	"April" union of writers for perestroika formed
26 Mar	election for delegates for the Congress of People's Deputies
April	exhibition of Andrei Shemiakin
02 May	death of Veniamin Kaverin
23 May	death of theater director Georgi Tovstonogov
May	theater director Yuri Liubimov receives back Soviet citizenship
25 May–9 Jun	First Congress of People's Deputies
27 May	death of poet Arseni Tarkovsky
June	pogroms in Fergana
12–15 Jun	Gorbachev on state visit in West Germany
02 Jul	death of Andrei Gromyko
04 Jul	first exhibition of Vasili Kandinsky
4–6 Jul	Gorbachev in France
10 Jul	miners' strike (Kuzbass)
15–16 Jun	civil war in Abkhazia
24 Sept	emergency power to Gorbachev for 18 months to ensure transition to market economy
6–7 Oct	Gorbachev in GDR
2–3 Dec	George H. W. Bush and Gorbachev meet in Malta
01 Dec	Gorbachev visits the pope
12–24 Dec	Second Congress of People's Deputies

14 Dec	death of Andrei Sakharov

1990

01 Jan	*Tele Sluzhba Novosti* starts
17 Jan	exhibition of Russian artists in emigration at the Russian Museum, Leningrad
15 Feb	fire destroys the House of Actors in Moscow
10 Feb	pogroms in Dushanbe (Tajikistan)
11 Mar	Lithuania declares independence (Vitautas Landsbergis as president)
12–15 Mar	Third Congress of People's Deputies, which elects Gorbachev as president; formation of the Green movement and of the LDP (Liberal Democratic Party) under Zhirinovsky
10 Apr	Helicon Opera opens
16 Apr	Gavriil Popov elected mayor of Moscow (chair of Mossovet)
01 May	calls for Gorbachev's resignation (May Day parade)
03 May	death of orthodox patriarch Pimen; succeeded by Patriarch Alexei II (7 June)
11 May	death of writer Venedikt Yerofeyev
16 May–2 Jun	First Congress of People's Deputies of the RSFSR
23 May	Anatoli Sobchak elected mayor of Leningrad (chair of Lensovet)
29 May	Yeltsin elected chair of the Supreme Soviet of the RSFSR
30 May–3 Jun	Gorbachev in the USA
2–13 Jun	28th Congress of the CPSU
11 Jun	miners' strike, Kuzbass
15 Jun	Igor Silayev as chair of the Council of Ministers of the RSFSR
17 Jul	death of writer Valentin Pikul
20 Jul	death of filmmaker Sergo Paradjanov

13 Aug	rehabilitation of writers Vladimir Voinovich, Lev Kopelev, Vasili Aksyonov, Alexander Solzhenitsyn
15 Aug	death of rock singer Viktor Tsoy
23 Aug	Gorky renamed Nizhny Novgorod
22 Aug	radio station Echo Moscow goes live
09 Sept	Father Alexander Men murdered
Oct	Nobel Prize for Peace to Gorbachev
16 Oct	reform program of "500 days"
24 Oct	nuclear test in Novaya Zemlia
26 Oct	USSR borrows money from international funds
07 Nov	attempt on Gorbachev's life
23–25 Nov	Congress on Chechen independence
30 Nov	double-headed eagle as emblem for the Russian Federation
01 Dec	ration cards on food (vouchers)
17–27 Dec	Fourth Congress of People's Deputies (USSR)
20 Dec	Shevardnadze resigns as foreign minister
21 Dec	newspaper *Nezavisimaya gazeta* launched
27 Dec	7 January (Christmas) as official holiday

1991

03 Jan	beginning of diplomatic relations with Israel
09 Jan	*Vzgliad* removed from air
7–13 Jan	clashes in the Baltic States between Russian and national groups; Vilnius television tower seized by Russian forces
02 Feb	Radio Russia banned from union frequency
08 Feb	Leonid Kravchenko as head of VGTRK
19 Feb	Yeltsin requests Gorbachev's resignation on television
01 Mar	strike in Kuzbass
	Andrei (men's magazine) launched
07 Mar	Gubenko as minister of culture

13 Mar	Erich Honnecker (GDR) on visit to USSR
17 Mar	referendum on USSR
22 Mar	New Opera opens under conductor Yevgeni Kolobov
28 Mar	Third Congress of People's Deputies of the RSFSR fraction (party) of Rutskoy formed 31 May
02 Apr	price rise
09 Apr	Georgia independent
19 Apr	40-hour working week, 24 days of holiday entitlement
29 Apr	earthquake in Georgia
06 May	KGB of RSFSR formed
13 May	Russian TV (RTR) begins transmission
15 May	no tax on sales
21–26 May	Fourth Congress of People's deputies (RSFSR)
12 June	Yeltsin elected president of the RSFSR
8–9 Jun	Chechen National Congress
17 Jun	Union treaty with nine former Soviet republics
28 Jun	Union for Economic Support (SEV) disbanded
01 Jul	Warsaw Pact disbanded
01 Jul	unemployment benefits available
04 Jul	privatization of apartments possible
10 Jul	bodies of the last tsar's family exhumed
17 Jul	G7 in London
29–31 Jul	visit of George H. W. Bush
19–21 Aug	August Coup (GKChP). Gorbachev held at Foros. Coup by Vice President Gennadi Yanayev, Vladimir Kriuchkov (KBG), Valentin Pavlov (PM), Boris Pugo (Interior), Dmitri Yazov (Defense), Vasili Starodubtsev (Peasants' Union), Alexander Tiziakov (industry), Oleg Baklanov (security council).
22 Aug	tricolor as flag of Russia (Yeltsin)

23 Aug	companies move from union to Russian responsibility and gain economic sovereignty
24 Aug	Gorbachev resigns as head of CPSU, which is prohibited
	Pravda closed
30 Aug	nuclear polygon closed by Kazakh president Nursultan Nazarbayev
05 Sept	Sverdlovsk renamed Ekaterinburg
06 Sept	Dudayev seizes power in Chechnia
07 Sept	independence of the Baltic states—Lithuania, Estonia, Latvia—recognized
06 Oct	Igor Talkov killed in Petersburg (anti-Communist songs)
07 Oct	USSR in International Monetary Fund (IMF)
12 Oct	death of sci-fi writer Arkadi Strugatsky
autumn	Leningrad renamed St. Petersburg
28 Oct–13 Nov	Yeltsin authorized by Fifth Congress of People's Deputies of the RSFSR to form a government
01 Nov	COMECON dissolves Council for Mutual Economic Assistance (also CMEA)
14 Nov	Novo-Ogarev: union with Azerbaijan, Kazakhstan, Kyrgyzstan, Tajikistan, and Turkmenistan
08 Dec	CIS treaty at Belovezhsk: Russia, Belarus, Ukraine
14 Dec	Gagarin Party I
25 Dec	Gorbachev resigns; Yeltsin is president of the Russian Federation

1992

01 Jan	economic shock therapy (Yegor Gaidar); free prices (not fixed by state); inflation: 110 RR for one U.S. dollar, rises to 140 (March) and 334 (October)
18 Jan	Ziuganov forms Popular Patriotic Forces
Jan	Black Sea Fleet on Crimea: question of allegiance

12 Feb	Vice President Rutskoy suggests agrarian reforms
01 Mar	Dzhokhar Dudayev seizes television center in Grozny
31 Mar	Federation treaty (except Chechnya and Tatarstan)
April	Congress of People's Deputies
07 May	end of state monopoly on spirits
08 May	death of puppet theater director Sergei Obraztsov
15 May	Treaty on collective security with Kazakhstan and other Central Asian republics
01 Jun	Gavriil Popov resigns as mayor of Moscow and is succeeded by Yuri Luzhkov
15 Jun	Yegor Gaidar as acting prime minister
01 Oct	voucher privatization begins
14 Dec	Chernomyrdin prime minister

_1993_

06 Jan	death of dancer Rudolf Nureyev
16 Mar	war between Georgia and Abkhazia; Sukhumi seized by Abkhazian forces
20 Mar	special presidential rule (decree)
23 Mar	Khasbulatov calls for impeachment of Yeltsin
	600 Seconds removed from air
3–4 Apr	U.S.-Russian summit in Vancouver, British Columbia
25 Apr	referendum supports Yeltsin
24 Jul	monetary reform: bills from 1961–1991 out of use
31 Aug	Soviet troops withdraw from Lithuania
01 Sept	Rutskoy estranged from president
05 Sept	death of spy thriller and detective writer Yulian Semyonov
15 Sept	Michael Jackson in Moscow
18 Sept	Gaidar rejoins government
21 Sept	Yeltsin dissolves parliament

22 Sept	parliament appoints Rutskoy as president
3–4 Oct	storm on White House: Rutskoy and speaker Khasbulatov
Oct	*600 Seconds* closed completely
19 Nov	death of filmmaker Leonid Gaidai
11 Dec	patriotic song by Mikhail Glinka as new national anthem
12 Dec	parliamentary elections: LDPR 23%, Vybor Rossii 15.5%, CPRF 12.5%, Union and Accord 7%
12 Dec	referendum ratifies Russian constitution

1994

13 Jan	Bill Clinton on state visit
06 Mar	death of filmmaker Tengiz Abuladze
11–13 May	Yeltsin visits Germany
23 May	*Burnt by the Sun* wins Grand Prix in Cannes
27 May	Solzhenitsyn returns to Russia
May	*Cosmopolitan* launched
07 Jun	attempt on Berezovsky's life
11 Jun	fight against pyramid schemes (MMM)
16 Jun	Gaidar resigns as deputy PM
10 Jul	Leonid Kuchma elected president in Ukraine; Alexander Lukashenka in Belarus
19 Jul	civil war in Chechnya
July	G7 in Naples
July	MMM collapses
26 Sept	Cathedral of Christ the Savior to be rebuilt
04 Oct	premiere of Vladimir Mashkov's *A Fatal Number*
05 Oct	miners' strike: unpaid salaries
11 Oct	roble crash (one U.S. dollar from 3,000 to 3,900 RR)
17 Oct	death of Dmitri Kholodov (*Moskovsky komsomolets*)
20 Oct	death of filmmaker and Oscar winner Sergei Bondarchuk

29 Nov	ORT as 51% state-owned shareholding company
11 Dec	Russian army into Chechnya

1995

01 Mar	murder of television presenter and ORT head Vlad Listiev
27 Mar	Oscar for Best Foreign Language Film for Nikita Mikhalkov's *Burnt by the Sun*
05 Apr	Tretiakov Gallery reopened after refurbishment
12 May	foundation of the party Nash Dom– Rossiya (Our House, Russia [NDR])
27–28 May	earthquake on Sakhalin
09 Jun	Black Sea Fleet divided between Russia (80%) and Ukraine (20%)
14–20 Jun	Chechens take hostages at Budenovsk
15–17 Jun	summit at Halifax
11 Jul	Yeltsin in hospital: heart attack
13 Jul	state prosecutor against NTV for interview with Basayev and program "Kukly"
26 Oct	Yeltsin suffers second heart attack
	Iversk Gates open on Red Square
autumn	release of Rogozhkin's *Peculiarities of the National Hunt*
17 Dec	parliamentary elections: NDR, Chernomyrdin: 10%; CP, Ziuganov: 22%; LDPR, Zhirinovsky: 11%; Yabloko, Yavlinsky: 7%

1996

09 Jan	Ministry of Foreign Affairs handed from Kozyrev to Primakov
16 Jan	Seleznyov (Communist Party) as chairman of the Duma
17–19 Jan	Chechens seize Turkish ship
28 Jan	death of poet and Nobel Prize winner Joseph Brodsky
28 Feb	RF member of European Council

15 Mar	release of Sergei Bodrov's (Sr.) *Prisoner of the Mountains*
29 Mar/2 Apr	union agreements with Belarus, Kazakhstan, and Kyrgyzstan
21 Apr	death of Dudayev; succeeded by Zelim Khan Yandarbayev
27 May	ceasefire in Chechnya
02 Jun	Yakovlev beats Anatoli Sobchak in election as mayor of St. Petersburg
11 Jun	terrorist attack on Tulskaya metro station and trolleybuses near Rossiya Hotel and Alexeyevskaya metro
16 Jun	presidential elections (69.8% participation): Yeltsin 35%, Ziuganov 32%
June/July	S. Lisovsky and A. Evstafiev caught in the act of removing cash from the House of Government, arrested; Chubais accused of embezzlement, but cleared; Barsukov (KGB) and A. Korzhakov (bodyguard) fired as they ordered the arrest of Yeltsin aides
03 Jul	second round of presidential elections: Yeltsin with 53.7% (Ziuganov 40%)
10 Jul	death of musician Sergei Kuryokhin
25 Jul	death of composer Mikhail Tariverdiyev
July	premiere of Yuri Butusov's *Waiting for Godot* with Khabensky and Trukhin
05 Aug	Chechen rebels retake Grozny
31 Aug	Lebed and Aslan Maskhadov sign peace accord
17 Oct	General Lebed resigns
20 Oct	Rutskoy elected governor of the Kursk region
30 Oct	Berezovsky as deputy of Presidential Security Council
5 Nov–23 Dec	Yeltsin undergoes heart by-pass operation and leaves Chernomyrdin in charge
23 Nov	death of composer Edison Denisov

01 Dec	troops withdrawn from Chechnya

1997

01 Jan	new criminal code
27 Jan	Maskhadov elected president of Chechnya
31 Jan	Bodrov's *Prisoner* released in USA
25 Feb	death of writer and dissident Andrei Siniavsky
21 Mar	Yeltsin and Clinton meet in Helsinki
12 May	peace agreement with Chechnya
17 May	release of Balabanov's *Brother*
26 May	Union charter with Belarus (effective as of 11 June)
09 Jun	TV Center founded for the 850th anniversary of Moscow
12 Jun	death of poet and bard Bulat Okudzhava
18 Jun	death of writer and dissident Lev Kopelev
23 Jun	*Novye izvestiya* opened after editor Golembiovsky removed from office by investor LukOil
27 Jun	end of civil war in Tajikistan
21 Aug	death of circus director Yuri Nikulin
26 Aug	Kultura opens as television channel of VGTRK
27 Dec	New Opera opens its new building in the Hermitage Gardens, Moscow

1998

1 Jan	denomination of the ruble
04 Jan	*Streets of Broken Lights* starts on TNT
23 Mar	Yeltsin sacks cabinet; Kirienko replaces Chernomyrdin as prime minister (24 April)
17 May	General Lebed elected governor of the Krasnoyarsk region
17 Jul	interment of the tsar's family in Petersburg
03 Aug	death of composer Alfred Schnittke

17 Aug	"default" (devaluation of ruble): 90-day moratorium on bank transactions
23 Aug	Yeltsin sacks cabinet; Chernomyrdin replaces Kirienko as interim PM; Chernomyrdin twice not confirmed as PM by government
24 Aug	first issue of *Vogue*
1–2 Sept	Clinton in Moscow
11 Sept	Yevgeni Primakov replaces Chernomyrdin
06 Oct	death of actor Rolan Bykov
Sept	British hostages Camilla Carr and John James freed from Chechen captivity (held since July 1997)
26 Oct	100th anniversary of the Moscow Art Theater
29 Oct	Inkombank bankrupt
20 Nov	Russian Parliament member Galina Starovoitova murdered

1999

20 Feb	premiere of *The Barber of Siberia*
18 Mar	release of Rogozhkin's *Checkpoint*
24 Mar	North Atlantic Treaty Organization (NATO) bombs Yugoslavia
29 Mar	Putin as head of FSB (Federal Security Bureau)
12 May	Yeltsin sacks cabinet; Sergei Stepashin replaces Primakov as prime minister
15 May	impeachment vote against Yeltsin fails
19 May	Stepashin confirmed as PM
22 June	Andreyev Bridge moved from Luzhniki to Neskuchny Garden
07 Aug	beginning of Second Chechen campaign (war)
09 Aug	Stepashin dismissed; succeeded by Vladimir Putin (16 Aug)
29 Aug	formation of SPS (Soyuz pravykh sil, Union of Right Forces) under Sergei Kirienko, Boris Nemtsov, Irina Khakamada
31 Aug	bomb explosion in Okhotny Ryad shopping mall

08 Sept	bomb in Moscow apartment block in Pechatniki
13 Sept	bomb in Moscow apartment block on Kashirkoye Chausee
24 Sept	formation of Unity party (Edinstvo) under I. Shoigu
20 Sept	death of Raisa Gorbacheva
Oct	premiere of the musical *Metro*
19 Dec	Duma elections: CPRF, Ziuganov 24%; Unity, Shoigu 23%; OVR, Primakov, Luzhkov 13%; SPS, Yabloko, Zhirinovsky bloc
31 Dec	Yeltsin resigns, leaving Vladimir Putin as acting president

2000

02 Jan	*Kamenskaya* starts on NTV
15 Jan	Radio Liberty correspondent Andrei Babitsky disappears
19 Jan–25 Feb	Andrei Babitsky held hostage in Chechnya
20 Feb	death of Anatoli Sobchak
09 Mar	death of Artyom Borovik (journal *Sovershenno sekretno*) in a plane crash
Mar	Grishkovets at the Golden Mask Festival, Moscow
26 Mar	Putin elected president
28 Mar	Oscar to Alexander Petrov for best animation for *The Old Man and the Sea*
30 Mar	release of Kachanov's *DMB*
01 May	*Criminal Petersburg* starts on NTV
11 May	search of Media Most (NTV) offices
11 May	release of Balabanov's *Brother 2*
17 May	Mikhail Kasianov as prime minister
24 May	death of actor, director, and head of Moscow Art Theater Oleg Yefremov
02 Jun	death of eye-surgeon Sviatoslav Fyodorov

2–5 Jun	Clinton in Moscow
13 Jun	Vladimir Gusinsky arrested for embezzlement
12 Jun	Akhmad Kadyrov designated president of Chechnya
15 Jun	death of playwright Grigori Gorin
Jul	raid on Media Most offices
08 Aug	bomb explosion in Pushkin Square pedestrian subway
12 Aug	explosion on the *Kursk* submarine
25 Aug	death of filmmaker and scriptwriter Valeri Priyomykhov
27 Aug	fire on Ostankino television tower
09 Sept	Sergei Dorenko sacked from ORT
Sept	Berezovsky under pressure to surrender ORT shares
17 Nov	GazProm settles share issue with Media Most
20 Nov	death of animator Viacheslav Kotyonochkin
07 Dec	death of children's writer Boris Zakhoder
Dec	Soviet national anthem reintroduced

2001

21 Feb	arrest of Anna Politkovskaya
Mar	cabinet reshuffle
04 Apr	NTV journalists strike; new management
18 Apr	premiere of Serebrennikov's *Plasticine*
10 May	release of Bodrov's (Jr.) *Sisters*
Oct	Masiania launched on mult.ru
19 Oct	premiere of *Nord-Ost*
28 Oct	death of filmmaker Grigori Chukhrai

2002

Jan	TV6 closes
14 Mar	release of *War*
Mar	premiere of *Dracula* (musical)

06 Apr	release of *Anti-Killer*
21 May	premiere of *Notre Dame de Paris*
09 Jun	riots after soccer match Russia-Japan
Aug	Russian military helicopter crashes in Chechen minefield: 115 dead
20 Sept	death of Sergei Bodrov Jr. and his film crew
04 Oct	premiere of *Chicago*
12 Oct	premiere of *42nd Street*
30 Oct	premiere of *Oxygen*
23–26 Oct	800 hostages at Moscow Theater (Nord Ost): 120 dead
Nov	premiere of *Terrorism* (Moscow Arts Theater)
Dec	suicide bombers in Moscow-backed Chechen government in Grozny

2003

08 Feb	revival of *Nord-Ost*
28 Feb	newspaper *Novye Izvestiya* suspended
Mar	Chechen referendum
24 Mar	TaTu at Jay Leno's
31 Mar	release of Baltser's *Don't Even Think*
May	suicide bombers attack Chechen government in Grozny; Kadyrov escapes narrowly
10 May	*Nord-Ost* closed
27 May	300th Anniversary of St. Petersburg
June	suicide bomber on bus near Mozdok
	TV6 successor, TVS, axed
16 June	death of Novaya Opera conductor Yevgeni Kolobov
28 June	release of Buslov's *Bimmer*
06 July	suicide bomb at rock festival in Tushchino, Moscow
Sept	suicide bomb at military hospital in Mozdok, Ossetia

06 Sep	*The Return* wins the Golden Lion in Venice
Oct	border dispute with Ukraine (agreement in December)
25 Oct	arrest of Yukos manager Mikhail Khodorkovsky (fraud, tax evasion)
27 Oct	death of filmmaker Elem Klimov
08 Nov	premiere of *Twelve Chairs*
10 Nov	*Lines of Fate* starts on RTR
25 Nov	release of *Anti-Killer 2*
07 Dec	Duma elections: CP 12.5%; Edinaya Rossiya 37.5%; LDPR 11.5%; Rodina 9%
09 Dec	suicide bomb near National Hotel, Moscow

2004

22 Jan	KinoPark multiplex opened
06 Feb	terrorist attack in the Moscow metro station Avtozavodskaya
14 Feb	collapse of roof in Transvaal leisure center, Moscow
24 Feb	Putin dismisses Prime Minister Kasianov and cabinet
09 Mar	new cabinet under Prime Minister Mikhail Fradkov; reorganization of ministerial apparatus
14 Mar	fire in the Manège exhibition hall
14 Mar	presidential elections: Putin gains 57% of the votes

Introduction

Although the term *popular culture* is appropriate for contemporary Russian culture, it was, in a sense, contradictory to the entire Soviet ethos. The Soviet regime wanted to educate its people in a particular ideological context, namely that of communism. It wanted to create a sophisticated, high culture, raising the general levels of education of the working class rather than pander to an audience. The term *mass culture* remained synonymous with *commercial* and *bourgeois* throughout the Soviet period. A parallel can be drawn, however, between mass culture in the capitalist world, serving commercial aims, and mass culture in the USSR, serving a political aim (Macdonald 1998). In this introduction I recapitulate Soviet cultural history in the light of mass appeal and popular taste before exploring concepts of popular culture.

After the Revolution

The October Revolution of 1917 was supported by a great number of artists, who put their art at the service of the Revolutionary cause. The Revolution had an enormous impact on cultural life in general, and on theater and cinema in particular, as a potential tool for agitation among the masses and the propagation of socialist ideas. The theater director Vsevolod Meyerhold (1874–1940), who had staged rather grandiose productions at the Imperial Alexandrinsky Theater in St. Petersburg before the Revolution, instantly declared that he would dedicate his art to socialism. Along with the young directors Sergei Eisenstein, Nikolai Yevreinov, and Nikolai Okhlopkov, Meyerhold favored spectacles that would both stun and actively involve the audience. A striking example of this was Yevreinov's *Storming of the Winter Palace* (Vziatie zimnego dvortsa), performed on 7 November 1920 for 100,000 spectators with 8,000 participants directed over a field phone. A celebration of the Revolution, the spectacle underlined the theatricalization of life (it was based on the real events of the Bolshevik seizure of the tsar's residence) and the politicization of art while involving the masses.

Artists continued to theatricalize political themes in the years immediately after the Revolution. The poet and playwright Vladimir Mayakovsky not only wrote plays that advertised the advantages of the new Bolshevik regime and mocked the remnants of the bourgeois lifestyle but also wrote slogans for posters that supported the Revolution. The artist and designer Alexander Rodchenko designed political posters and worked as a photographer. The artist Varvara Stepanova designed proletarian fashion. Sergei Eisenstein made his acclaimed film, *The Battleship Potyomkin* (Bronenosets Potemkin, 1925), at the state's command.

Avant-garde artists may have actively supported the Revolution in the 1920s, but connection to the masses was not that straightforward. Crowds may have attended the first of the mass spectacles in 1920, but they did not wear Stepanova's proletarian collection, nor did they crowd Meyerhold's experimental theater where the actors moved with machine-like movement to demonstrate their subordination to a larger mechanism (and the director's will); and they certainly did not pack the cinemas to see *The Battleship Potyomkin*. It may have been "the best film of all times," according to a critics' poll in 1958, but it was no hit in the USSR. In fact, it was a flop, reaching only 70,000 viewers in the first two weeks of a mere four-week run. Meanwhile, Soviet audiences flocked to the cinema to see American films starring Mary Pickford and Douglas Fairbanks (*Robin Hood* was *Potyomkin*'s stiffest competitor). In the late 1920s, the melodrama, best represented by Abram Room's *Bed and Sofa* (Tret'ia Meshchanskaia, 1927), could easily attract more than a million viewers within six months. Konstantin Eggert's melodrama *The Bear's Wedding* (Medvezh'ia svad'ba, 1926), Boris Barnet's comedy *The Cigarette Girl from Mosselprom* (Papirosnitsa ot Mossel'prom, 1924), and Ivan Perestiani's adventure *Little Red Devils* (Krasnye

d'iavoliata, 1923) emerged as the most profitable, if internationally least acclaimed, films. The experiment in art that was conducted by the avant-garde failed with the masses, who wanted to see emotionally engaging films, watch theater where they could suffer with the protagonists, and wear fashionable, not artistic and experimental, clothes. Consequently, the avant-garde fell out of favor with the Communist leadership, which was concerned with the use of art to reach the masses. For this purpose the concept of Socialist Realism, stipulating a portrayal of the Soviet Union in its development toward the ideal of communism, was adopted in 1934 as the only mode of artistic expression.

Lenin may have supported a certain diversity of artistic forms, those that appealed to the masses as well as those that engaged in experimentation and sought new forms of expression. Yet after Lenin's death in 1924, and certainly by the late 1920s and early 1930s, artistic movements were streamlined. Single unions were created, such as the Soviet Unions of Composers, of Artists, of Cinematographers, of Theater Workers, of Writers, and so on, in order to ensure that all artists would express themselves in a way that was understood by the masses and—needless to say—that was ideologically correct. This new art was to advertise the utopia of communism: the bright future toward which the country was rapidly progressing, even though it was in reality struggling with economic mismanagement, famines, war, and the purges.

In cinema, a directive was issued to educate and enlighten the masses through film. Foreign film imports were stopped, and the audience was fed a solid Soviet diet. In 1935 Boris Shumiatsky, the new head of the Soviet film industry, launched an appeal for a "cinema for the millions"; he implemented a rigid campaign against formalism in cinema, practically annihilating the great experiments in Soviet cinema of the 1920s. The entertainment value of a film presented suitable packaging whereby the ideological message would reach the masses. The blockbuster became a tool for ideology. At the same time, popular elements (comic or melodramatic genres, the promotion of stars, the inclusion of mass and folk songs) were incorporated into official Stalinist culture. The popular films of the 1930s all relied on a simple narrative and conventional style, with a linear plot, reducing complex issues to a level that could be understood by the masses. The hero Chapayev can explain his complex military strategy with the help of potatoes. Folksy tunes and triumphant marches such as "Black Raven" ("Chernyi voron," in the Vasiliev brothers' [Georgi and Sergei] *Chapayev*, 1934) and "Song of the Motherland" ("Pesnia o rodine," in Grigori Alexandrov's *Circus*, 1936) assisted the plot and even became hits in their own right. The Stalinist musical comedies were blockbusters, loved by the audiences for their glorified and glossy demonstration of life through the beautiful, feminine characters played by Marina Ladynina and Liubov Orlova; they were loved for showing the victory of those Soviet ideals that the population was forced to believe in and for the predictability of their plots.

In theater, the experiments of Meyerhold and other avant-garde directors were stopped, and Konstantin Stanislavsky's psychological realism was elevated to the "method." For the next fifty years, the actor's training would rely on this "method," which drew exclusively on emotional experience for a psychologically convincing character portrayal, allowing the spectator to experience the same emotions as the character but never inviting him to think or interact with the stage world behind the so-called fourth wall.

Stalin simplified the cultural discourse to make it accessible to the masses and used those tools that promised mass appeal as packaging for simple tales. Socialist Realism—the projection of the bright future of the USSR into a simple, linear plot and a realistic form—was the only artistic form of expression tolerated by the Soviet regime. Consumerism was a marginal feature of everyday life; excess and luxury were part of a special elitist culture to which only the privileged had access.

Toward the end of Stalin's life, cultural activity in the USSR was almost dead: the purges had exterminated a number of great experimenters; World War II had taken the lives of many artists; the campaign in 1949 against "cosmopolitans" (a euphemism for Jews) had taken its toll. Culture, high and low, was struggling to find means of expression; appealing to the masses was a secondary consideration after the main one: ideological and political correctness. At this point in history it had also become obvious that Socialist Realism, which excludes the notion of conflict (other than between the evil aggressor and the Soviet hero), precluded the notion of tension, thus limiting the emotional or intellectual challenge of its artistic product. Here the relaxation that was brought on with Nikita Khrushchev's Thaw took effect.

After World War II

The Thaw had begun with Khrushchev's "Secret Speech" at the Twentieth Party Congress in 1956, in which he disclosed the crimes of the Stalin era. A period of liberalization, both in political and cultural terms, began. The Thaw had a number of positive effects on cultural life. Works that were critical of Soviet society, such as Alexander Solzhenitsyn's *Day in the Life of Ivan Denisovich* (Odin den' Ivana Denisovicha, 1962) about life in a prison camp, were published. New theaters opened, including the Sovremennik and Taganka. In cinema a move occurred away from the glorification of collective Soviet heroism toward an individual heroism. Modern art was publicly displayed in major exhibitions, such as the Picasso exhibition in 1956 or the scandalous Manège exhibition of 1962, when Khrushchev labeled the abstract paintings in the exhibition as "sh**" and their painters "sodomites." Artistic cafés opened in Moscow in 1961. Moreover, there was the celebration of the International Youth Festival in Moscow in 1957. The Thaw also had a reverse side, however, that reflected the struggle within the party between hardliners and reformers. The reformist uprising in Hungary was crushed in 1956. In 1958, Boris Pasternak was forced to reject the Nobel Prize for Literature, which he had been awarded for his novel *Doctor Zhivago*, published in Italy. The poet Joseph Brodsky was arrested in 1964 for "parasitism" (*tuneyadstvo*, not having a job). These examples underscore the process of hard-line Communists gaining the upper hand. The tension between the two factions in the Central Committee of the Communist Party climaxed with the removal of Khrushchev from office in October 1964.

The Thaw, to a certain extent, exposed the low quality of Stalinist culture: the cheap gloss of the Stalinist musicals, the false tone of Socialist Realist literature, the stale nature of theatrical performance. In the postwar period the taste for Western culture grew rapidly among those who had been brought up during the war but had never fought in it: often children of single mothers whose fathers had died in the war. This generation was tired of the official version of war, the glorification of life in the collective farm (*kolkhoz*), and industrial progress. Instead, they preferred a pseudo-Western lifestyle. The satirical magazine *Krokodil* (Crocodile) defined them as "stilyagi"; they were mocked as uneducated dandies, concerned with appearance rather than intellectual achievement. In this sense they were the extreme opposite of what the Soviet Union wanted its youth to be and therefore the first sign of a rebellion against the officially prescribed cultural diet.

Detective and spy stories thrived in the postwar period: on the one hand, they provided the background for a conflict between an enemy and a Soviet hero; on the other hand, they were a pale reflection of the American spy thrillers à la Alfred Hitchcock. Yulian Semyonov emerged as one of the most popular writers of the period, creating the hero-figure Stirlitz, a Soviet spy in Nazi Germany. His works were later serialized for television and have become part of Russian popular culture in the form of anecdotes.

Mass song, which proliferated in the 1930s owing to the advent of sound film, was confronted by the bard movement, which distributed its recordings by the modest means of illegal tape recordings (*magnitizdat*). Magnitizdat implied the creation of an altogether more individualized product that was spread through a personal and private distribution system. In 1956 Radio Moscow replaced the film music "Song of the Motherland" (from *Circus*) with "Suburban Moscow Evenings"

("Podmoskovnye vechera"). Estrada, or pop music, emulated Western styles, setting trivial lyrics to fine tunes. Jazz music was prohibited for public performance: it involved an element of improvisation, and this unpredictable quality made the censors always nervous. Illegal copies of jazz music were circulated in the 1960s, however, including American jazz music by Glenn Miller, Bing Crosby, and Louis Armstrong. The musical comedy copied the behavior and looks of Western musical stars rather than dwelling on propaganda plots (for example, Eldar Riazanov's *Carnival Night* [Karnaval'naia noch'], 1956), and American films were back in the cinemas, turning *Tarzan* into the most popular film of the postwar years.

Film demonumentalized the past: heroes became simple human beings rather than superhuman characters. Cinema thus began to deconstruct its grand narratives of the 1930s: the emphasis shifted in historical films from collective heroism to the deeds of the individual. This is evident in the treatment of World War II in Mikhail Kalatozov's *The Cranes Are Flying* (Letiat zhuravli, 1957), Pavel Chukhrai's *The Forty-First* (Sorok pervyi, 1956) and *Ballad of a Soldier* (Ballada o soldate, 1959), and Alexander Stolper's *Living and Dead* (Zhivye i mertvye, 1964), all of which enjoyed great popularity both at home and abroad. They attracted between 25 and 30 million viewers each. Kalatozov's *The Cranes Are Flying* received the Palme d'Or in Cannes in 1958; Chukhrai's *The Forty-First* and his *Ballad of a Soldier* were shown at the Cannes Film Festival in 1957 and 1960 respectively. *Cranes* was only tenth in the box-office charts at the time of its release, however, thus not the most popular film of its year. The international success of these films can be attributed to the common experience of World War II and shared conventions of the portrayal of the war hero in Russian and European culture, which made them international mainstream rather than national blockbusters.

The Thaw bore upon the theater in a variety of ways: first, a new generation of playwrights emerged with Leonid Zorin, Viktor Rozov, Alexander Shtein, and others. Second, young and promising directors were appointed to head prestigious theaters. Most significant for the future were the appointments of Georgi Tovstonogov to the Bolshoi Drama Theater (BDT) in Leningrad; Anatoli Efros to the Lenin Komsomol Theater, Moscow; and Yuri Liubimov to the Taganka Theater of Drama and Comedy, Moscow. Third, new theaters were founded, such as the Sovremennik (Contemporary) in Moscow under Oleg Yefremov.

The plays of Viktor Rozov provided the impulse for young directors to explore further the psychological realism of Stanislavsky. Rozov's plays focused on "young boys," children on the way to adulthood, and therefore appealed to a theater that wanted to create a hero with whom both actor and audience could easily identify psychologically. His plays became the main source for the repertoire of Anatoli Efros and Oleg Yefremov. In Rozov's *In Search of Joy* (V poiskakh radosti, 1957), the hero demolishes a piece of furniture, symbol of the petty bourgeoisie, with his father's saber; the gesture accompanying this act became symbolic for the break with tradition. The Sovremennik started as a studio of the Moscow Arts Theater (Moskovskii khudozhestvennyi akademicheskii teatr, MkhAT) School under Yefremov, opening in 1957 with Rozov's *Alive Forever* (Vechno zhivye). Yefremov had begun acting at a time when monumental realism was receding. He did not aim at outward verisimilitude and consciously combined a stylized, abstract set with the everyday realism of "kitchen sink drama," emerging on the British stage at about the same time.

In 1956, Georgi Tovstonogov (1913–1989) was appointed chief artistic director of the BDT in Leningrad. Tovstonogov merged the approaches of Stanislavsky and Meyerhold, stylization with authenticity and figurativeness with psychological analysis. Tovstonogov's repertoire included contemporary plays, classics, and prose adaptations. A remarkable production was the adaptation of Lev Tolstoy's *Strider: The Story of a Horse* (Kholstomer, 1975). Sackcloth was draped around the stage, and the costumes were made from the same material. The actors playing horses wore leather straps around their heads and bodies as a harness, imprisoning the body. Tovstonogov made ample use of cinematic devices, such as a disembodied voice reading texts or assuming a narrator function. Tovstonogov interpreted the condition of the horse as a tragic metaphor for human life, creating at the same time an allegory for the deformation of nature by claiming it as human property. His concern rested with the universal rather than with explicit social criticism. Tovstonogov never was a controversial figure.

The opposite is true for the enfant terrible of Soviet theater, Yuri Liubimov (b. 1917). Liubimov had noticed the dangerous uniformity in Soviet theater and abhorred the use of makeup, costumes, and decorative props. With his acting class, he staged in 1963 Bertolt Brecht's *The Good Person of Szechwan*, in which he mastered the concept of Brecht's epic theater. *The Good Person* was set on a bare stage; posters decorated the sides; panels indicated locations; songs were used for comment, and a musical rhythm set the pace of the production; choreographed movement replaced verbal action. These elements, drawn from Brecht and Meyerhold, characterized Liubimov's style of the 1960s. The message of the production—the individual's solidarity with the people—enhanced the strong sociopolitical stance of the theater. The range of theatrical devices was fully explored in the initial years but especially vividly in *Ten Days that Shook the World* (Desiat' dnei, kotorye potriasli mir, 1965), based on John Reed's account of the Revolution. Liubimov drew heavily on the devices of circus, shadow play, folk theater, agitational theater, and documentary theater to create a revolutionary spectacle. The integration of the audience into the festive revolutionary atmosphere served to deprive history of its magnificence and private life of its seclusion. Like many other directors of his time, Liubimov staged prose adaptations and poetic montages to establish a repertoire in the absence of genuinely good drama. Liubimov's theater therefore is an "author's theater" (*avtorskii teatr):* the director composes the text and offers his personal interpretation in the production. The Sovremennik and the Taganka as well as the BDT in Leningrad were the most popular theaters in the two cities: tickets were almost impossible to obtain.

After the Thaw

The period that followed under Leonid Brezhnev's leadership is commonly called the period of "stagnation," as it consolidated Communist rule through pragmatic policies rather than opening an ideological debate about the adaptation of communism to contemporary society. The period is characterized by a much more aggressive policy, manifested in internal politics in the arrest of Andrei Siniavsky and Yuli Daniel in 1966 for publishing abroad under the pseudonyms of Abram Terts and Nikolai Arzhak and in foreign politics in the intervention in Czechoslovakia in 1968. This increased suppression of opposition led to the emergence of a dissident movement that began formally with a letter protesting against Soviet foreign policy in 1967, signed by a number of members of the Soviet Writers' Union.

In the late 1970s, the stagnation led to a dearth of activity in Soviet cultural life. Many artists and intellectuals had emigrated in the first half of the 1970s, when the wave of emigration to Israel had ripped a large hole in intelligentsia circles. In 1972 the Leningrad poet Joseph Brodsky had been expelled and in 1974 Solzhenitsyn deported from the USSR. In 1970 the liberal editor in chief of the leading literary journal *Novy Mir*, Alexander Tvardovsky, had been removed from office. All these acts of repression were now showing their effects on cultural life while, in terms of cultural politics, the stifling atmosphere continued. In 1974 the open-air exhibition of modern art in the Moscow suburb Beliayevo was torn down by bulldozers (the so-called Bulldozer Exhibition). In 1975, when Andrei Sakharov was awarded the Nobel Prize for Peace, he was not permitted to leave for the ceremony in Stockholm; in 1980 he was exiled to Gorky (now Nizhny Novgorod) and later placed under house arrest. In 1978 the dissident Anatoli Shcharansky was arrested; the writer Vasili Aksyonov was exiled in 1981. In 1979, Soviet troops invaded Afghanistan, causing an of-

ficial boycott of the 1980 Olympic Games in Moscow by the Americans and several other Western states. Many writers could not publish their works and instead resorted to the so-called *samizdat* (self-publishing typescripts with carbon paper—in the absence of photocopiers). A last attempt at opposition was manifested through the underground publication of the almanac *Metropol*, uniting works that were not accepted for publication in the Soviet Union. The doom and gloom of the late 1970s was offset, however, by activities in the artistic underground, including studio and amateur theater and "private" art exhibitions (the so-called apartment exhibitions [*kvartirnye vystavki*]). The songs of the bard Vladimir Vysotsky voiced opposition to the system by addressing taboo issues such as alcoholism and drugs. Filmmakers attempted to provide relief through blockbusters that distracted with exotic settings and exhilarating plots.

Whereas the 1960s had been governed by clampdown, censorship, and bans, the 1970s saw deportations, exile, and house arrest. The dissidents' fight within the country had given way to the elimination of the opposition through the state. Many dissonant voices withdrew into the rural idyll, writing prose that was set in the villages and the countryside, inspired by folk traditions and rituals, with characters speaking the coarse language of rural Russia. This retreat, which may seem regressive and conservative, was in fact a form of opposition to the dominant cultural discourse.

At the same time, the Brezhnev years were a period of relative material growth and economic stability. Products were in supply, jobs available, pensions paid, accommodation improving, transport systems expanding. A "second economy" (black market and underground culture) flourished to satisfy the demand for "deficit" products. Lavish state rituals, monumental parades, and holiday celebrations went hand in hand with the cult of the leader, Brezhnev. They covered up the increasing dissatisfaction with the system that reduced the individual to a marionette. On an international level, Soviet music was represented by the folk ensembles of Igor Moiseyev, Pavel Virsky (Ukraine), and Boris Alexandrov (Soviet Army Ensemble). The other showcases of Soviet culture were the Bolshoi and Kirov (Mariinsky) Ballets, the internationally acclaimed and politically controversial filmmaker Andrei Tarkovsky, and the ideologically sound circus stunts of Oleg Popov with the Moscow State Circus. At home, Tarkovsky was by no means the most popular filmmaker; the people's favorites were the comedy filmmakers Eldar Riazanov, Leonid Gaidai, and Georgi Daneliya, whereas the folk ensembles attracted great numbers—of tourists.

As the number of television sets in households was increasing, the pop stars Mark Bernes and Iosif Kobzon appeared on television with their patriotic and elegiac songs, accompanied by Soviet bands. Another popular singer was Zhanna Bichevskaya, who presented a mix of folk and country music based on northern Russian folk songs. In those years the pop singers Alexandra Pakhmutova, Alla Pugacheva, and Valeri Leontiev made their debuts. The cabaret actor Arkadi Raikin, whose mockery of the system was combined with a high level of compassion for human flaws, moved from Leningrad to Moscow in 1981 and frequently appeared on television. His "heir," Mikhail Zhvanetsky, enjoys popularity to the present day.

The level of reading was unusually high in the Soviet Union. This fact was deployed to advocate the standards of Soviet readers in contrast with the capitalist (supposedly "uneducated") West. The science fiction literature of the Strugatsky brothers (Arkadi and Boris), the spy thrillers of Yulian Semyonov, and the historical novels of Valentin Pikul were at the top in the lists of best-selling (that is, "most wanted") books. Soviet fiction of the period was characterized by the absence of violence and sex but also void of descriptions of fashion and appearance that are so characteristic of Western "trash" literature.

Censorship interfered heavily with the creation of new repertoires in the late 1960s when, during the Twenty-Third Party Congress in 1966, several critical and controversial productions were banned, such as Alexander Tvardovsky's *Tyorkin in the Other World* (Terkin v tom svete) and Eduard Radzinsky's *A Film Is Being Shot* (Snimaetsia kino). Efros was dismissed for "ideological shortcomings" in 1967. Cultural policy continued along a reactionary line in the 1970s. The Twenty-Fifth Party Congress of 1976 promoted the "production theme" in drama, compelling playwrights to show the hero at work. Since such plays were not very attractive for the audience, the theaters instead adapted prose works. Young directors started to work under the auspices of the established theaters, however, which opened so-called small stages in the late 1970s for experimental work, allowing also for a more intimate contact with the audience.

Censorship also interfered in the making of films. Andrei Konchalovsky's *Asya's Happiness* (Asino schast'e, also known as "Istoriia Asi Kliachinoi, kotoraia liubila da i ne vyshla zamuzh . . . ," 1966, released 1988) was shelved for portraying the life of a single mother, living in a collective farm (*kolkhoz*), who prefers to raise her child alone rather than marry the child's alcoholic father. Kira Muratova's *Short Encounters* (Korotkie vstrechi, 1967, released 1987) was shelved—along with the sequel *Long Farewells* (Dolgie provody, 1971, released 1987)—for the portrayal of the unsettled lifestyle of a geologist, played by Vladimir Vysotsky. Alexander Askoldov's *The Commissar* (Komissar, 1967) was banned for positively showing the life of the Jewish population in Berdichev and for portraying the life of a Bolshevik commissar who has a child out of wedlock. Konchalovsky emigrated, Muratova did not make her next film until the 1980s, and Askoldov never made another film.

During the stifled cultural atmosphere of the Brezhnev years, the state tried to promote "high" culture in order to demonstrate the educated status of the Soviet people while driving those areas of culture that were wanted by the masses (rock, jazz, detective and crime fiction) into the underground. The divide between high and low culture is more complex in Soviet culture than in Western cultures: any experiment is dissident, and therefore experimental art (art-house film, abstract art, jazz music) was part of underground culture. The art conceived for the few was wanted by the masses as a "forbidden fruit." Because forbidden, underground culture appealed by definition to a much broader range of people than the intelligentsia—that spectrum of Soviet society that saw itself in dissent with the political system and at the same time defined itself as its chief perpetrator and advocate of moral values. The official and politically correct culture was, as it were, for the masses. Popular culture, on the other hand, was what the masses were craving: dissident and Western culture. At the same time popular culture also encompassed official culture,

which was made widely available by the system of distribution. Consequently, mass culture contained elements of the official (which was kitsch because it was official) and of the underground culture (which was exotic because forbidden). Thus, the bard Vladimir Vysotsky is part of dissident popular culture, as is the Taganka Theater. The comedies of Leonid Gaidai and the television spy thriller *Seventeen Moments of Spring* (17 mgnovenii vesny), on the other hand, are popular culture. It is worth noting that critical attention and international recognition have often focused on dissident popular culture. This, however, should not imply that the Taganka Theater or Vysotsky are "high" culture. Rather, they are part of a popular culture that—at the time—included both high and low forms.

After Brezhnev

When Gorbachev took up office in 1985 he replaced, within a year, most of the hardliners in key positions in the cultural sector. Vasili Zakharov was appointed minister of culture, succeeding Peter Demichev. Boris Yeltsin took over the Moscow City Committee from Viktor Grishin. At the Central Committee level, Yegor Ligachev became responsible for ideology in the Secretariat, succeeding Mikhail Zimianin, and the reformer Alexander Yakovlev was put in charge of the Department of Agitprop. Gorbachev invited the so-called creative intelligentsia to a meeting on 3 December 1986, during which he encouraged a process of liberalization in the arts.

His encouragement very quickly translated into action. The reform of artistic unions was the first step in this direction: the filmmaker Elem Klimov took over the Filmmakers' Union, setting up a commission to release the films shelved by the censors; in the theater Mark Zakharov took the lead in arguing for the responsibility of theater repertoires to be removed from the city authorities and handed over to the Theater Union, while encouraging experiment in the theaters. The Union of Writers established a committee that rehabilitated writers and released documents from the state archive, including the archive of the KGB (Komitet gosudarstvennoi bezopasnosti); the editors of literary journals were encouraged to publish formerly banned texts. In this sense, *glasnost* lifted the lid from the barrel of forbidden, banned, and suppressed art. This sudden release swept to the surface a whole new culture. The thirst for the censored, forbidden culture was, for a while, greater than that for the "popular," the taste of which would come with the onset of more commercial terms of cultural production after 1991.

Cultural taste in the Gorbachev period (1985–1991) has to be seen in the light of the previous withdrawal. The popularity of certain novels, songs, films, television, or radio programs was directly related to the taboo themes they touched upon and the new areas they opened up for investigation. Popularity in the Gorbachev era therefore depended not so much on taste as on the wish to taste the forbidden fruit. Indeed, in the Soviet cultural context, the demand for classical Western literature should be seen not just as a sign of the high level of education but as an indication of the possibility to access any cultural products from the West. The popularity of released art-house movies, of historical novels about the blank pages of Soviet history, and of the lyrics rather than the tunes of rock music has to be read in the context of an "artificial" popular taste in the late 1980s.

The New Russia

This book covers the media, music, performing and visual arts, sports, religious tradition, and consumer culture in the New Russia. Each chapter begins with the cultural history of the Soviet era to provide a context for developments in the 1980s and 1990s, before exploring each phenomenon in more depth. Broadly speaking, the discussions follow three stages: first, the Gorbachev era (1985–1991); second, Yeltsin's reign (1991–1999), marked by the coup of 1993, the presidential elections of 1996, and the economic crisis of 1998; and third, Putin's first term as president (1999–2004). Rather than applying theoretical frameworks, the discussion of popular culture in the New Russia offers a survey of the developments of popular culture in the present while attempting to trace its history that may serve to explain some reasons for the shape popular culture has taken in the New Russia.

Although Western theories of culture tended to perceive "popular" or "mass" culture as a manifestation of capitalism, demonstrating the grip of capitalist economies on culture and thus securing control over society, its taste, and consumer behavior (a position held by the so-called Frankfurt School), the development of Soviet and Russian culture does not lend itself to be positioned within such traditional Western cultural theories. The Soviet Union tended to "level" cultural production in an attempt to make it a vessel for ideology that would be widely accessible to the masses. Where Lenin had tried to raise the level of culturedness (*kulturnost*) of the masses, Stalin had emphasized the necessity to reach the masses by resorting to more conventional forms such as realism. The Soviet Union had neither a proper cultural industry nor a consumer market, however. In ideological terms it ensured the accessibility of its cultural production, but in commercial terms it could not satisfy the demand for those cultural products that the people wanted. Even the "popular" spy thrillers of Yulian Semyonov and the historical novels of Valentin Pikul had such low print runs that they were hardly sufficient to cater for the readership. Thus, the centralized Soviet propaganda machine manipulated the taste of the masses to ensure that the levels would not drop down to a "mass" (speak "trash") culture.

During the Gorbachev era, culture was once again designated to play an ideological role, namely to ensure the trust of the people in the reforms. As Richard Stites has argued, "The new popular culture—much of it legalised 'old' culture—contained strong currents of iconoclasm, demythologizing, and open irreverence" (Stites 1999). Only the late *perestroika* years saw another, genuinely "trash" culture emerge, which glorified not the Soviet forbidden fruit but that of Western commercial culture that had previously been inaccessible.

The Soviet system entertained two power centers: the party represented official ideology, whereas the dissident intelligentsia opposed the party line. Between those two poles there existed a "middle" class that was disinterested in ideology and politics and preoccupied instead with everyday life. This large group of people sustained the "second economy" (or "shadow economy") that—on black markets and in the underground—provided goods and objects for consumption: foreign books, American jeans, and Western fashion.

Throughout the Soviet era, the state and the dissidents had shared a common ground in their rejection of commerce. Market forces were categorically rejected by the dissident intelligentsia, who perceived commercialization as a threat. This attitude was shared by the state, which also perceived the flourishing shadow economy, which satisfied consumer demands, as a threat to the state's more and more dysfunctional economy. When commercial forces, now supported by the state, took grip of the economy in 1991, the state no longer needed the intelligentsia to preach spirituality over materialism. Once consumerism invaded Soviet society, the intelligentsia lost its role as opponent to the official view and eventually also as a key player in the balance of power. Its opposition (or pseudo-opposition) was no longer needed. Therefore the intelligentsia has been marginalized in the New Russia, which is well echoed in the poor performance of the parties that it supports (SPS [Union of Right Forces] and Yabloko).

When the Soviet system collapsed in 1991, a shift from the ideological to the commercial culture took place. Globalization fully hit the New Russia and exposed it to all the trash and commercial culture that people had known only through negative propaganda. As Robert Edelman aptly commented in his article on sports in the New Russia, "It turns out that post-Soviet popular culture is less distinctive than Soviet popular culture was" (Edelman 1999). Culture (at least official, highbrow culture) had always been focused on the text, associating the writer with a prophet who provides moral guidance and reveals the absolute truth in his text. Now, visual culture gained ground, reflected in changes of urban planning and in the appearance of advertising posters in the cityscape.

Whereas previously the leveling of culture had taken place within the Soviet Union, the new consumer culture leveled Russian culture with Western culture. The Soviet Union had upheld a concept of "socialism in one country" and set standards within that culture, excluding—at least officially—any influence of Western cultures. After the fall of the iron curtain, Russia was flooded with Western consumer products and lifestyle. The country swung toward an extreme form of capitalism, turning almost any manifestation of culture into a commercial enterprise. Therefore many institutions, such as the Bolshoi and Mariinsky Theaters, the Hermitage Museum, and the Tretiakov Gallery, took a long while to recover and to convince the state of the need for subsidies, as well as securing grants from both Russian and international organizations and businesses.

Therefore, the post-Soviet phenomenon of postmodernism (with its manifestations of sots-art and conceptualism) may be seen through Western eyes as high art, whereas in fact the attempt to domesticate and trivialize Soviet culture and ideology (especially of the Stalin era) brings the apparently highbrow Soviet culture closer to the masses by parodying it, thus turning it into a commercially desirable product. Examples of such transgressions from high to low culture are the "postmodernist" bestsellers of Viktor Pelevin, the satirical glosses in the lyrics of the rock band Leningrad, or the New Russian versions of the cherished Russian lacquer boxes portraying tennis courts and Mercedes cars.

The divide between high and low, popular and art-house, intellectual and consumer, is often blurred in the New Russia. Thus, for example, haute couture or glossy journals appeal to many, although they are affordable only for a few. The attraction for the consumer lies in the novelty and accessibility of these products, not in their affordability: they are signs, but not goods for mass consumption. Russian cinema and theater try to attract audiences with star actors appearing in commercial projects, but many people cannot afford the tickets for such commercial enterprises and therefore prefer the "old," State-subsidized theaters that are more affordable. In other words, the commercialization of Russian culture is shaping two groups of consumers: those who can afford the products allegedly made to cater for the masses; and those who cannot afford them and therefore stick with the old, verified, and trusted Soviet forms of entertainment and consumption, now available cheaply and readily. An exception is television, where trash culture, be it American serials or home-grown crime thrillers, captures mass audiences, rich and poor, as well as the book market, which has made most books available in paperback editions that are quite affordable for the majority of people.

References

Edelman, Robert. 1999. "There Are No Rules on Planet Russia: Post-Soviet Spectator Sport." In *Consuming Russia. Popular Culture, Sex and Society since Gorbachev*, ed. Adele Barker, 219. Durham, NC: Duke University Press.

Macdonald, Dwight. 1998. "A Theory of Mass Culture." In *Cultural Theory and Popular Culture*, 2nd ed., ed. John Storey, 23–24. London: Prentice Hall.

Stites, Richard. 1992. *Russian Popular Culture*. Cambridge: Cambridge University Press, 178.

1
The Media

The Broadcasting Media

Television

The Russian media have made headlines in recent years because of the involvement of the oligarchs, Boris Berezovsky and Vladimir Gusinsky, in politics. Then their exiles and arrests were a news item: Berezovsky sought political asylum in the United Kingdom, and Gusinsky, an Israeli citizen, took up residence in Spain but was repeatedly arrested and threatened with extradition. Then the headlines were preoccupied with the NTV (Nezavisimoe televidenie, Independent Television) takeover through GazProm and the dismissal of Yevgeni Kiselyov. Finally, the feature film *The Tycoon* (Oligarkh, 2002), by Pavel Lungin, based on Yuli Dubov's novel *The Great Solder* (Bol'shaia paika, 2001), made the international film festival circuit. The international interest in Russia's media management has reached almost the same level as that in the media empire of Silvio Berlusconi, Rupert Murdoch, or Ludwig Kirch. This chapter looks at the rapid development from state control to an extremely commercial media market within a decade.

Businessman Boris Berezovsky during the tenth anniversary of the newspaper *Kommersant*, the flagship of his publishing empire. (Photo by Dmitry Azarov/Kommersant)

Soviet Television: From Its Origins to Perestroika   If, in the 1920s, Lenin had hailed cinema as the "most important of all arts," this was because it could reach a large number of people at once. The medium also overcame the problem of illiteracy, which still dogged the new socialist empire in those days. For the modern era, the medium that can reach out to millions simultaneously and span its network across the eleven time zones of the Soviet territory is television.

Television is more than that, however: it is a powerful tool for the manipulation of public opinion. In the Soviet era the primary aim of television was the education of the people and their socialization. Television was supposed to act as a model for imitation: hence no crime, violence, or sex was shown on Soviet television. The news served not to inform people but to reassure them that everything was on the right track: therefore news about murders, disasters, and accidents would be missing from the standard repertoire or mentioned in passing with a minimum of information. Political news prevailed, and this tended to be of an authentic and documentary nature: speeches were transmitted in full or reprinted verbatim in the print media. As the Soviet socialist society was based on equality, there were no stars or celebrities. Naturally, people cherished "their" heroes and admired "their" stars, but these images were neither created by nor promoted in the media. Thus, the hugely popular bard Vladimir Vysotsky would never appear on television shows, whereas the officially supported stars of the Soviet estrada, such as Arkadi Raikin, Alla Pugacheva, and Iosif Kobzon, had conquered the new medium in the 1970s with a number of musical shows and programs. Similarly, game shows re- frained from offering prizes to individual competitors; instead there were shows that helped develop job-related skills. Horoscopes and clairvoyance were completely absent from Soviet television (and the print media as well), because the country collectively believed in a bright future, a communist future, and there was no need to predict that.

In the USSR, television spread widely, as it was one means of communication whereby the political center (Moscow) could reach the entire country effectively and immediately. If, in the infant days of television, there were 400 television sets (1940), this figure grew rapidly to 10,000 in 1950, and five million by 1960. At this point the television era had just started: the five million owners of sets in 1960 represented only 5 percent of the population; by 1986 almost the entire population (93 percent) had access to television. The television tower in Ostankino, 533 meters high and 65 meters in diameter, marked the new television era. Its adjacent television center was expanded to accommodate more offices in 1970. Television coverage expanded also: television could reach 86 percent of the country's population in 1980 and almost 99 percent in 1996, reflecting the growing realization of television's power and the state's concern with making this medium as widely available as possible. Having said that, the state also wished to remain in control: in 1996 there were still 30 percent of households that could receive only the two national channels (First Channel and Second Channel). From the mid-1990s onward, cable and satellite television became available and more and more affordable.

The USSR had two nationwide channels: the First Channel, established in 1960, and the Second Channel, which opened in 1982 to transmit largely second-rate material left over from the First Channel. Apart from that there were a number of regional and local stations. Nevertheless, 80 percent of the Soviet population watched the evening news program at 9 PM, *Vremia* (Time). Several other news programs were also very popular, such as *Segodnia v mire* (Today in the World), an analytical program offering an international panorama. In Moscow a third channel started local transmission in 1965, focusing on education; in 1967 the fourth evening channel began to cover sports and local events; and the fifth was the Leningrad channel. Despite the range of channels, the news programs all originated from the same news agencies: TASS (Telegraph Agency of the Soviet Union) for national news (since 1992, ITAR-TASS, Information Telegraph Agency of Russia) and APN (Agence Press Novosti, now RIA Novosti/RIA Vesti, Russian International Agency Novosti) for international news and longer features. Both agencies were controlled by the state; the first independent news agency, Interfax, was formed in 1989. Soviet television showed 29 percent films, 20 percent news, 9 percent history, 12 percent economy, 15 percent culture, 4 percent sports, 8 percent children's programs, and 3 percent science and travel. These figures reflect the relative absence of entertainment in the viewers' diet.

When Mikhail Gorbachev came to power in 1985, he realized the importance of the media. He was himself very keen to be portrayed on television; unlike his successor Boris Yeltsin, Gorbachev felt at ease in front of the camera and made ample use of his telegenic appearance. Gorbachev began his reform course with public opinion: he wanted the people to express their needs, their wishes, their problems; he en-couraged criticism, which he perceived as a tool for eradicating the corruption and mismanagement inherent in the Soviet bureaucracy. Since ideology and propaganda were key instruments in this fight for an open and outspoken public opinion, Gorbachev began his reform by placing the reformers Alexander Yakovlev and Yegor Ligachev into key positions in the Communist Party's think tank, the Central Committee. Yakovlev, who advocated the power of television, was put in charge of propaganda (and thereby mass media), and Ligachev took charge of ideology. By 1988 Yakovlev and Ligachev would adopt different viewpoints on the issue of how critical the media ought to be. In this rift, Ligachev professed a more conservative view, wanting to limit the breadth of the debate.

Gorbachev himself brought a number of innovations to television: he encouraged live broadcasts; he called for openness (glasnost) in the treatment of news; he stressed the importance of timeliness (*operativnost*), of breaking the news as and when it happens; and he advocated pluralism of opinions, shattering the Soviet practice of offering only one line: the Communist Party's line. One striking example of innovative television was the creation of a *telemost*, a space bridge, which was used frequently during the late 1980s and enjoyed tremendous popularity. The first space bridge took place in February 1986 between studios in Leningrad and Seattle; it was followed in 1986 by a bridge between Moscow and Kabul, paying tribute to the Soviet forces in Afghanistan. The direct link to a studio abroad created a window on the West formally; the content of programs would be adopted from the West only too soon.

Gorbachev's emphasis on television and

the leader's frequent appearance on the blue screen provoked not only favorable comments from his compatriots. The coverage of Raisa Gorbacheva, for example, was in harmony with Western style, but it did not go down well with audiences at home: people were queuing for food while the first lady was representing the USSR abroad.

Notwithstanding the innovations Gorbachev's leadership brought to the variety of programs and the methods of presenting the news, central television was still obliged to cover all appearances of members of the Politburo and the Central Committee, to read all their names in full in every news item, and to transmit the leadership's—often long—speeches. Gorbachev encouraged criticism, yet this criticism seemed never ending. Furthermore, there were no quick solutions that Gorbachev could offer. Ultimately, he used television to destroy the old order, without encouraging the medium to engage actively in building public opinion. The public, which once suffered from "disinformation," was now being overfed with information, unable to comprehend fully the sophisticated language, the new style of reporting, the struggle that went on behind the screens for real power. This use of the media for political aims rather than as a stronghold of standards and values, combined with the transition from state-finance to independent television, made television wide open for corruption. The new generation of managers and reporters who arrived on the screens during Yeltsin's presidency offered different views, operated with changed ethics, and—to varying degrees—vied for power.

Maximum Exposure: News on Television   Soviet television programming had contained some entertainment; however, the game show had the aim to instill the desire for self-improvement into the candidates, urging them to compete in skills. The television serial was an immensely popular genre, with the spy and detective thriller at the top of the league table during the Soviet years. The serial *TASS Is Authorised to Report* (TASS upolnomochen soobshchit', 1984) and *Seventeen Moments of Spring* (17 mgnovenii vesny, 1973), both written by the best-selling writer Yulian Semyonov, were watched by millions and have become part of urban folklore with anecdotes about Stirlitz, the Soviet spy in Hitler's administration. *The Eternal Call* (Vechnyi zov), a best-selling novel by Anatoli Ivanov that traces the fate of several Siberian families during the Soviet era, was also serialized. Stanislav Govorukhin's *The Meeting Place Cannot Be Changed* (Mesto vstrechi izmenit' nel'zia, 1979), starring the bard and actor Vladimir Vysotsky, has become a classic.

With the advent of Gorbachev's reforms, however, the main interest of people, educated or not, lay with politics and history. For the first time in years they were allowed access to the previously blank pages of Soviet history: they could read previously censored works of literature, watch films that had been shelved, discover hitherto hidden historical facts in documentaries and historical novels. They were able to hear things about their country that they were aware of but that had never been pronounced in the open. The interest of viewers was first and foremost in the analytical programs about the past and in innovative, live (rather than prerecorded) coverage of current affairs.

Therefore, most important and most popular were the news programs. The news program *Vremia* took the lead. It had been shown since January 1968 in the 9 PM slot and was traditionally preceded by a trailer showing a view of the Kremlin tower and its clock, accompanied by a triumphant, marchlike tune. Gorbachev's new head of *Vremia*, Eduard Sagalayev, replaced this logo in May 1986 with a more global symbol: a red star rising from behind a globe. One of his successors reverted from the new tune by the modern composer Alfred Schnittke, widely known in the West, back to the old music. *Vremia* mainly covered news from the USSR, with just under a fifth of its stories reaching beyond the country's borders. *Vremia* was invariably presented by two newsreaders, one male and one female, seated at a table and facing their large microphones. There were no teleprompters, so the news was read from a script. The old-fashioned *Vremia* was replaced temporarily by *TSN*, or *Tele Sluzhba Novosti* (Tele Service News), but returned with the old name in 1994. *TSN* had started as an alternative news program on 1 January 1990, where the texts were read from a teleprompter by the anchors Tatiana Mitkova and Dmitri Kiselyov, who would move to the New Russian channel RTR (Rossiiskoe Televidenie i Radio, Russian Television and Radio) in 1991.

One of the first and most exciting innovations was the program *Vzgliad* (Viewpoint), shown initially on Fridays as a late evening weekend show, starting from October 1987. In light of the fact that the jamming of foreign radio stations would end by the autumn of 1989, the new homemade programs had to be competitive and offer a different quality of journalism in a different kind of news. Fresh faces were needed, so the program hired its presenters from the

Eduard Sagalayev, president of the National Association of Television and Radio Broadcasters, 2001. (Photo by Valery Melnikov/Kommersant)

foreign section of Radio Moscow, since they were most versed in a Western-style approach to news. Alexander Liubimov, Vlad Listiev, Vladimir Mukusev, and Sergei Lomakin formed the *Vzgliad* team under Anatoli Lysenko. Four young men in sweatshirts would lead the country's most challenging information program. Listiev was popular on television because of his game show *Pole chudes* (Miracle Field), modeled on *Wheel of Fortune*. *Vzgliad* covered a number of sensitive themes, ranging from Afghan students complaining about the new Soviet-supported regime (January 1989), to a show in which the director of the Lenkom Theater, Mark Zakharov, suggested that Lenin's body, embalmed in the mausoleum, should be finally laid to rest (March 1989). The latter programs led to the forced "retirement' of television chief Alexander Aksyonov. It became clear that glasnost had its limits: Lenin's tomb was a sacred cow for the Soviet regime. In October 1989 *Vzgliad* had to refrain from live broadcasting, using instead a taped interview with the dissident and nuclear physicist Andrei Sakharov, who had been released from exile in Gorky (Nizhny Novgorod) only 18 months earlier. *Vzgliad* achieved ratings of up to 70 percent, even though being repeatedly threatened with closure. In December 1990 the *Vzgliad* team was not allowed to cover Foreign Minister Eduard Shevardnadze's resignation but instead was forced to focus on the new vice president, Gennadi Yanayev. On 9 January 1991 the program was closed by the television chief's deputy, Petr Reshetov, who would himself be sacked only days later over the coverage of the events in Vilnius (see "Event 3" below). The team of *Vzgliad* continued the production of their program, transmitting it via regional stations. Their production company VID (Vzgliad i drugie, Viewpoint and others) continues to the present day to make and sell political and analytical programs.

The second successful program was *Dvenadtsatyi etazh* (Twelfth Floor), named after the location of the youth department in Gosteleradio and launched in 1986 by Eduard Sagalayev. Sagalayev exploited his Uzbek origin and his role as an outsider in Moscow. *Dvenadtsatyi etazh* was a youth program, inviting young people to comment on a number of themes. It went on air for the first time in January 1986 as a supplement to *Mir i yunost* (World and Youth). *Dvenadtsatyi etazh* distinguished itself by a lively, natural atmosphere, where satellite links were set up to remote areas of the Soviet Union, to interview young people in their own environment rather than in a hostile studio. It transpired that the young generation lacked a sense of meaning in life: they complained about the boring textbooks at school, the absence of interesting leisure-time provisions, and the obstructions of the *komsomol* youth organization when they tried to set up events that were interesting to them. In the studio were ministers or their deputies, answering questions and promising solutions. *Dvenadtsatyi etazh* told the country and its leadership about the needs of ordinary people, teenagers, youngsters; it made the politicians aware of a general lack of inspiration—a vital ingredient if the population was to be mobilized to support the reform course. And this was clearly on Gorbachev's agenda: the need to have the support of the people for his reforms, to involve the people in the process of change were things that Khrushchev had failed to do in the attempted reforms of his Thaw (1956–1964). *Dvenadtsatyi etazh* raised expectations and showed no results; or else it exposed the fact that such results were not delivered. The Kremlin worried about the young generation in particular, perceiving the danger of youth opting out of a Soviet future. The blame for this lack of motivation to participate in the construction of the country's new future was laid at the feet of bourgeois propaganda and Western influences, such as rock music. *Dvenadtsatyi etazh* was condemned by the press and was suspended in the autumn of 1987 on Ligachev's order. It was back in May 1988 and later replaced by *Do i posle polunochi* (Before and after Midnight), a program with music and news, created and hosted by Vladimir Molchanov.

Vladimir Pozner presenting *Drugie vremena*, September 2001. (Photo by Vasily Shaposhnikov/ Kommersant)

Prozhektor perestroiki (Spotlight on Pere-stroika) started in August 1987 as an evening program hosted by Alexander Tikhomirov; it exposed corruption all across the country, causing ministers to make local visits and sort things out, prompted by the events covered in the program. Tikhomirov was fired in January 1990. Like *Vzgliad* and *Dvenadtsatyi etazh*, the program had come under attack for controversial coverage.

Journalists became stars as they explored and exposed the wounds of socialism, leaving the healing process to politicians, who were more than often unprepared for such a task. Suddenly the socialist system, taken as perfect by the ruling elite, opened up a minefield of problems. Investigative journalists rose to the status of public heroes: Bella Kurkova,

Alexander Nevzorov, and Vladimir Pozner were three such figures. Bella Kurkova ran the Leningrad program *Piatoye koleso* (Fifth Wheel), an investigative news program. Kurkova was elected to parliament, using her position of parliamentary immunity to save her program from closure in 1990 and 1991 when other challenging programs were closed; indeed, she even offered airtime to the *Vzgliad* team in 1991. Alexander Nevzorov's *600 sekund* (600 Seconds) covered local news in Leningrad, touching on sensitive topics similar to those brought up in *Vzgliad:* drugs, rock music, violence. Nevzorov's rather unrefined manners on his program, the blunt and obtrusive questioning, betrayed the fact that he trained not as a journalist but as a circus artist. His unusual style and his overtly nationalist views made him a popular, but also despised, figure, which was revealed in the attempt on his life in December 1990. When he supported Gorbachev's attempts to stop Lithuanian independence, the ratings for his program slumped. The two programs *Nashi* (Ours) on the Lithuanian independence movement (1991) and on Chechnya (1995) defended strongly the action of the Soviet/Russian troops without attempting a more objective portrayal of the events. Vladimir Pozner had been in charge of American and British affairs on radio since 1961. In 1986 he presented the first space bridges between Leningrad and Seattle and between Leningrad and Boston. He joined central television as a political observer and left the Soviet Union in April 1991, the year of clampdown on new programs that would end with a political coup and the dissolution of the Soviet Union. He moved to the United States, where he hosted a show with Phil Donahue (*Pozner and Donahue*), and returned to Russia in 1997. In these three presenters we can observe different attitudes to political events: Kurkova's investigative journalism that survived the impasse of 1990 and 1991 thanks to her political involvement; Nevzorov's nationalist views that lost popularity with audiences and television directors; and Pozner's approach to open the viewer's field of vision to life in the West, which became controversial and led to his emigration.

The years 1990 and 1991 in this sense mark a watershed: the limits of glasnost had been tested, television offered no remedies, and Ligachev put an end to the exposure of the system's "wounds." Three events of the Gorbachev period (1985–1991) may serve here as case studies of changes in the news coverage.

Event 1: April/May 1986: Chernobyl

The events of Chernobyl and their treatment in the Soviet media are regarded as a watershed in Soviet news coverage. The reports started off in Soviet style, playing down the events; they ended in a full investigation. After Chernobyl, the media were quicker to respond and more eager to discover the truth of a story, and they applied a more investigative style of reporting. The way in which information was reported (not only to the media) during the incident in Chernobyl gave Gorbachev a lever to force the media to adopt a different approach and change strategy. The media were quick to respond to this challenge. By exposing the rotten state of the Soviet system, they contributed to a much more rapid disclosure of the need for reform than Gorbachev had envisaged. This eventually led to Gorbachev's defeat and prepared the ground for the spectacular role the media would play during Yeltsin's years. Gorbachev wanted to expose the faults of the Soviet bureaucracy and put them right, without realizing that he was opening a Pandora's box. The flow of criticism was never ending, and problems could not be solved with the needed expediency in a system that was partly still in the grip of the old, Communist guard.

The explosion at the fourth reactor of the Chernobyl nuclear power station in the early hours of 26 April 1986 was first noted in a news report on 28 April from Sweden, where high radioactivity had been measured and traced back to the Ukraine. The largest nuclear accident of the twentieth century had to be reported by Western media two days after the event to make the Soviet Union respond at all. The Soviet news program *Vremia* reported that an accident had occurred at Chernobyl and that things were under control, probably unable to ignore the accident altogether, as it had been picked up by the Western media. No measures were taken to evacuate children or stop the May Day parades out in the open air, or to warn the population in any other way, thus exposing them unnecessarily to radiation in order to avoid panic. The USSR released sparse reports on the incident, mentioning it briefly and low down on the news agenda, whereas the West exaggerated the incident by claiming that there was a danger of meltdown. Clearly, the USSR underplayed grossly, but the Western media also overreacted. Local people were not informed either. The official version was formulated after a visit of Politburo members to the site, in which Gorbachev had not taken part. Gorbachev addressed the people only on 14 May.

With hindsight it is most likely not only that the Soviet information system proved inadequate to provide a low level of information on disasters and accidents to its people but that the information flow within the structures of power also was at fault. According to the eminent Russian journalist Vladimir Pozner, the Ukraine tried to conceal from Moscow the scale of the accident, so that it was not until the official delegation from Moscow visited the plant at the beginning of May that the full scale of the accident became apparent. Others have argued that Moscow deliberately tried to play down the incident, wanting to avoid panic and trying to delay the evacuation of children until the start of the summer vacation later in May. No matter which version comes closest to the truth, after Chernobyl the Soviet media responded promptly and swiftly to calamities. They had learned a lesson and would often give a clearer picture of events than the official versions (for example, in the coverage on Chechnya).

Event 2: May 1990: May Day Parade

Gorbachev expected gratitude from the people for the reforms he initiated. Instead, he suffered huge public humiliation. During the traditional May Day Parade in 1990, Gorbachev and the party leadership watched the parade from the balcony of the Lenin Mausoleum on Red Square. The official part of the parade was usually followed by a demonstration organized by the Moscow City Council, calling on trade union associations and workers' unions. In 1990, however, the mayor, Gavriil Popov, had been denied the right to organize this part of the parade because of fears that he might use the demonstration to air views about those people disadvantaged by reforms, for whom he tried to construct safety nets. The nonofficial parade appeared with posters challenging Gorbachev to resign. According to (unwritten) television law, the cameras had to stay with the parade until the leaders left the tribune. Although Gorbachev had been advised to leave the tribune after the official part of the demonstration, he stayed on and witnessed the protest against his own person. Television had to show the protestors, thus contributing to the public humiliation of the country's leader. The transmission was duly cut off as soon as Gorbachev left the tribune. The television coverage of this minor incident shows that television was still forced to adhere to unwritten conventions of the coverage of the leadership and high-ranking officials. It also reflects the population's dissatisfaction with the politics of their president.

Event 3: January 1991: Vilnius   The events in Vilnius in January 1991 are highly significant and cannot be underestimated. The Baltic republics Lithuania, Latvia, and Estonia vehemently opposed Soviet control and demanded independence. In a historic sense, they had been the last "additions" to the Soviet Empire and had been effectively annexed in 1939 by the Molotov-Ribbentrop Pact. In Lithuania the independence movement had begun in 1988 with Sajudis (Lithuanian Popular Front), and independence had been declared on 11 March 1990. On 7 January 1991, the minister of defense deployed troops in the Baltic Republics in order to ensure that the draft into the Soviet army would continue; this was a clear signal that independence would not be acknowledged. On 13 January these Soviet troops stormed the television tower in Vilnius, killing unarmed protesters in the process. After the incident, no high-ranking Soviet official took respon-

Television presenter Tatiana Mitkova in her Ostankino office, 2003. (Photo by Vasily Shaposhnikov/Kommersant)

sibility: Defense minister Dmitri Yazov and KGB head Vladimir Kriuchkov claimed they knew nothing, and Gorbachev insisted he had not ordered the storming. With hindsight, again this must be seen as an attempt to undermine Gorbachev's policies and to enforce the Soviet Union's unity, particularly in the light of Yazov's and Kriuchkov's roles later in August 1991. The official media reports on this event supported the Soviet intervention. Television had become investigative, however, and reporters had got into the habit of asking questions rather than just executing orders. TSN anchor Tatiana Mitkova refused to read the text produced by the head of news, Petr Reshetov, handing it to the head of television, who dismissed Reshetov. By January 1991 the media were living up to the role required by Gorbachev: to report as objectively and independently as possible, with utmost "openness" and "timeliness," even if this meant discrediting the Kremlin leadership. The price they paid was that the anchors were subsequently fired and TSN censored. The team moved to the newly founded channel RTR.

The topics of social problems, historical analysis, and current affairs had soon become largely exhausted. But more than that: exposure alone could not resolve the problems, and although many programs were closed, others simply became repetitive. When the demand for such programs had been saturated, the viewers' attention did not shift toward television serials or foreign films, which became available on Soviet television. The viewers were glued to the political show. For the first time, they felt actively involved in politics rather than ruled by unbending bureaucrats. In the late 1980s the transmission of political meetings gripped large parts of the population, to the extent that productivity fell during sessions of the Party Congress or the Congress of People's Deputies. The congress's live transmissions, for eight hours every day, captivated television audiences all over the country in the summer of 1989 (25 May–9 June) when for the first time elected deputies could speak up in front of the congress, in front of an audience of millions. They turned politics into a show and found a receptive audience. Elections to the congress had taken place on 26 March 1989. Many journalists and members of the cultural elite had been elected to the congress, which thus consisted not only of bureaucrats but also of people who had spoken up in favor of reform. The coverage of the congress meant that the people's deputies could be heard: they could voice their opinions and address the cameras, thus legitimizing their views by expressing them to the leadership and the public simultaneously.

The Political Show: Gorbachev versus Yeltsin   Even though public debate was at the forefront of the media's attention and had become a routine, both in terms of transmissions of debates and analytical political programmes, elections had never been covered before (other than reporting results), since Soviet elections represented a ritual rather than a real vote. The first election to the Congress of People's Deputies on 26 March 1989 involved no political parties, as the Communist Party remained the only admitted party to the elections. It was an opportunity for the people to elect deputies they trusted, and deputies were often from the artistic intelligentsia: they were actors, directors, filmmakers, and journalists rather than party bureaucrats. The congress to be elected would, how-

ever, have a pseudodemocratic status and elect the president, Mikhail Gorbachev, in March 1990. Despite the absence of party competition, the head of television, Alexander Aksyonov, was dismissed over the coverage of the elections. He had shown too much of Boris Yeltsin, who had been excluded from the Politburo and sacked as Moscow party boss in November 1987 after his severe criticism of Gorbachev and Ligachev. Again, it was clear that glasnost had its limits: a candidate for people's deputy who had fallen from grace was not an appropriate subject for television coverage. The portrayal of Yeltsin on television was further restricted during the run-up to the elections for the Russian Soviet Federated Socialist Republic (RSFSR) Congress of People's Deputies. It was in the light of these restrictions that the acquisition of a television channel became of prime importance to the Yeltsin camp, leading to a phased access to channel 2 for the new, pro-Yeltsin channel RTR in the autumn of 1990. Radio Russia was set up in December 1990 by the same structures (VGTRK, the All-Russian Television and Radio Broadcasting Company, Vserossiiskaia gosudarstvennaia televizionnaia i radioveshchatel'naia kompaniia). Effectively, the First Channel was the Soviet, pro-Gorbachev channel; the Second Channel was the Russian Federation's pro-Yeltsin channel. On 13 May 1991, a month before Yeltsin's election as president of the RSFSR on 12 June 1991, RTR began broadcasting with an airtime allocation of six hours a day in three segments, with their flagship *Vesti*, the evening news program. The Soviet Union now had two channels, with different political allegiances; one Soviet, the other owned by the RSFSR (Russian) government. This prepared the ground for the "battle" to be fought over coverage during the August coup of 1991.

In the prelude to the coup, the press had established its power to force and push for decisions. The media had conquered a position whereby they could influence the ruler, and therefore the ownership of the media became a crucial issue in the future. The press, which had supported Yeltsin in 1990 when showing information on Vilnius and crushing of demonstrations in Tiflis, both disadvantageous to Gorbachev, also sided with Yeltsin during the coup.

The Putsch (Coup): 19–21 August 1991

On 19 August 1991, President Gorbachev was on holiday in the Crimean resort of Foros. In Moscow, Prime Minister Vladimir Pavlov, Defense Minister Dmitri Yazov, Minister of the Interior Boris Pugo, KGB head Vladimir Kriuchkov, and Vice President Gennadi Yanayev formed a State Emergency Committee, the GKChP (Gosudarstvennyi komitet po chrezvychainomu polozheniiu). They declared that Gorbachev was in poor health and incapable of running the country's affairs. Politically, they wanted to preserve the Soviet Union and stop the break-up that was being negotiated between Gorbachev and other heads of Soviet republics. The sudden turn that the coup took on the third day depended to a large extent on the media coverage, however.

The State Emergency Committee had realized the crucial role of the media and had blacked out RTR on the morning of 19 August while the First Channel transmitted *Swan Lake*, interrupted by communiqués of the coup leaders. The head of state television (Central Television, the First Channel), Leonid Kravchenko, had been ordered to the television center in the early hours

of the morning to ensure the transmission of statements from the State Emergency Committee. Statements by the committee were brought into the station in Yanayev's handwriting, highlighting the rushed nature of the coup. With RTR switched off, the oppositional Leningrad television not available in Moscow, and no foreign source available (Cable News Network [CNN] was not yet broadcast in Russia), the committee seemed in charge of the flow of information. Eleven newspapers were outlawed, but—in an extraordinary display of courage and ingenuity—their editors joined forces to publish, and print outside Moscow, the *Obshchaya gazeta* (Common Gazette).

Although the State Emergency Committee had apparently taken control of the television center, it had underestimated the investigative spirit aroused in journalists under Gorbachev's reforms. The correspondent Sergei Medvedev asked for permission to go to the "Bely dom," the Russian "White House" and seat of parliament (symbol of the opposition to the coup plotters, of Yeltsin's resistance as he stood on a tank there, surrounded by the rallying crowds), and to do coverage on location. He filmed the crowds, making them look larger than in reality. He showed Yeltsin from a low camera angle, making him tower up on a tank. Medvedev did everything possible to cover the events but to make the resistance look powerful. Back in the television center, the head of news, Olvar Kakuchaya, managed to slot Medvedev's report into the news program *Vremia* that evening, thus making the public aware of the opposition to the coup and demonstrating that it was far from a smooth and well-planned operation as the State Emergency Committee would have liked to perceive it. The illegitimacy of their actions was further under-lined in a press conference, where Yanay-ev's shaking hands were deliberately not edited out, hinting at his uncertainty: he was not in control of the situation. Televi-sion manipulated the coverage of the State Emergency Committee—despite censor-ship and control—in such a way that made the illegitimacy of the coup obvious and ul-timately forced the coup leaders to surren-der. The role of television's coverage of Yeltsin leading the crowds against the State Emergency Committee contributed to the coup's failure. It was the media's decisive point of view that had mattered. In a sense this helps explain the overvalued role of television in subsequent elections, espe-cially presidential ones, and the attempt of leading politicians to control the media by purchasing shares in channels. The ap-pointment of the editor of the liberal paper *Moscow News* (published in several lan-guages), Yegor Yakovlev, and of the pioneer of challenging current affairs programs, Eduard Sagalayev, to the two controlling positions at the First Channel was a logical step that coincided with the transfer of the ownership of central television from the Soviet authorities to the Russian Federa-tion (RSFSR).

The Second Coup: President versus Parliament in October 1993   Although the August 1991 coup posed a genuine threat to the process of liberalization in-duced by Gorbachev, the October coup was a muscle test between President Yeltsin and the elected Russian parliament. Yeltsin had exercised the right to overrule and disband parliament, whereas the par-liamentary opposition wanted to see the role of the president reduced along the lines of the French representative model. A referendum on 25 April 1993 had given sup-port to the president, empowering him to rule over parliament, overrule decisions, and dissolve parliament.

On 21 September 1993, Yeltsin dis-banded parliament by decree and ordered new elections. The parliament in its turn, led by Vice President Alexander Rutskoy and the speaker of parliament Ruslan Khasbulatov, ordered the removal of the president. The White House was cordoned off, and the parliamentarians inside were given a deadline: to surrender by 4 Octo-ber. On 2 October a demonstration took place outside the White House, assaulting police forces and breaking the cordon. The mob moved on to the television center Os-tankino, throwing Molotov cocktails into the building, killing 143 people and leaving 735 wounded. On 3 October Yeltsin or-dered the tanks to fire, charring the facade of the White House. Rutskoy and Khasbula-tov surrendered. Another attempt to topple the president had failed because of the in-ability of the coup leaders to control and manipulate the media.

After the break-up of the USSR, the First (formerly Soviet) Channel served the presi-dent; the second channel (RTR) was loyal to parliament, in theory at least. RTR was forced by the Russian parliament to in-crease its coverage of parliamentary dis-cussion and transmit Parliamentary Hour five times a week; however, when re-quested to move it to a prime time slot, the Yeltsin loyalist and head of the station Oleg Poptsov resisted. On the evening of 2 Octo-ber, as the mob attacked Ostankino, the head of central television, Viacheslav Bra-gin, took the decision to close down trans-mission. This meant that millions of televi-sion screens all over the country went dark, suggesting to the nation that the

Svetlana Sorokina presenting the program *Glaz naroda*, September 2001. (Photo by Vasily Shaposhnikov/Kommersant)

country was without leadership. In order to remedy this potentially dangerous situation, RTR managed to secure access to the frequency of central television and broadcast on the first channel nationwide. It placed the anchor Svetlana Sorokina, a face familiar to the population from *Vesti*, in the news studio. If RTR managed to use its emergency studios, it leaves the question why central television did not resort to its emergency studios. The conduct of RTR in this situation was just one more indication of the responsiveness of newer television channels in comparison with the once favored central television. Yeltsin reintroduced censorship in the aftermath of this coup. Several papers left blank spaces for suppressed articles. Yeltsin indicated his willingness to manipulate the press, as would later become evident in the manipu-

lation of television both for the coverage of Chechnya on NTV and of the elections.

The First Electoral Campaign: Parliament (Duma) 1993

After the attempted coup had been averted, the president called for new elections to parliament. These elections in December 1993 were the first multiparty elections. For the first time the media, above all television, played a crucial role in party broadcasting. In the aftermath it would transpire that the ownership of television stations and control of airtime were of prime importance. This would lead to a battle over control of the television networks that would dominate the second term of Yeltsin's rule (1996–2000). Thirteen parties were admitted to the elections, which also comprised a vote on the new constitution that made parliament less powerful. Free airtime was allocated to each party, and unlimited additional time could be purchased for party broadcasts. The Communist Party and Grigori Yavlinsky's liberal and democratic Yabloko (means "apple" but is formed from the names of Yavlinsky, Boldyrev, Lukin, and company), however, bought no airtime at all. None of the political parties had any experience of political party broadcasts; neither did the Russian viewers and voters know what they were looking for: a political program, a charismatic leader, or a good political advertisement.

The party that supported Yeltsin, Russia's Choice (Vybor Rossii), simply modeled its campaign on product advertisements in the style of "buy this." The media were used to build candidates, often little known outside Moscow. The candidate of the Liberal Democrats (LDP), Vladimir Zhirinovsky, was "made" by the media. He had the ability to address viewers in normal language, which they felt spoke to them directly, avoiding the official jargon that had infected so many ex-Soviet politicians. He vowed to get rid of advertising that inundated television and the market with American products and promised a return to the Russian style, using in his campaign the chocolate bar Snickers as the symbol for American influence. The Communist Party's candidate Gennadi Ziuganov also led a campaign against American influence. In a country inexperienced in pluralistic political broadcasting, the creation of a media image was more important than the political agenda offered by the parties. For a population that for more than seventy years had voted only in order to approve of the system, the new real and meaningful elections took them to another extreme. People were called to the ballot box more than six times in five years in a variety of elections, from Soviet to Russian, parliamentary to presidential—not to mention census and referenda.

"Vote or You'll Lose": The Presidential Elections of 1996 The presidential elections of 1996 represented the first elections with competing candidates for the presidency. Gorbachev had been elected president of the Soviet Union by the Soviet Congress of People's Deputies, and the RSFSR's Congress had voted for Yeltsin as president of the RSFSR in June 1991. In the 1996 elections, Boris Yeltsin's strongest opponent was the Communist Gennadi Ziuganov. The forecasts were all in favor of Ziuganov, as a majority of the population was dissatisfied with the economic chaos that had gripped the country with the liberalization of prices (they had previously been fixed by the state) in 1992. Especially the older generation, largely on disgracefully low pensions, wished for a return to a stable economic system, and the Communist system had offered that for more than seventy years. To make sure they knew what they were voting for by supporting Ziuganov, Nikita Mikhalkov's Oscar-winning film *Burnt by the Sun* (*Utomlennye solntsem*, 1994), exposing the horrors of Stalin's regime, was broadcast on the eve of the election. The media were thus far from objective, both in the active involvement in the electoral campaign and in programming.

If Gorbachev loved to give television interviews and felt at ease in front of the camera, then Yeltsin did not: he was not telegenic. He apparently considered radio a far more effective medium. But above all, he preferred contact with the people without mediation. With presidential elections coming up in 1996, the support of the media was crucial. RTR was state owned, and the state was a major shareholder in ORT (Obshestvennoe rossiiskoe televidenie, Public Russian Television) (now part-privatized); the other major shareholder in the channel, the media mogul Boris Berezovsky, supported Yeltsin, so that the support of the two major channels was certain. The chief of the new and highly popular news channel NTV, Igor Malashenko, was invited to act as Yeltsin's election adviser, thus securing the support also of the third major channel. Malashenko hoped to acquire for NTV full airtime, which was subsequently granted in autumn 1996. Malashenko was ready to sacrifice NTV's objectivity, fearing the return of the Communists. Although journalistically and morally his actions deserve condemnation, he acted in political and economic self-interest. NTV used his role as a trusted and politically independent commentator, acquired as a result of the coverage of Chechnya, to manipulate the voters.

Malashenko's campaign group successfully built up Yeltsin's media image. With the help of Yeltsin's daughter Tatiana Diachenko, the campaign team mounted for Yeltsin a tour of the country that allowed him to feature prominently on the news, thus enhancing his television presence. In order to improve his appearance in front of the camera, NTV's major shareholder, Vladimir Gusinsky, purchased a teleprompter for Yeltsin. The coverage of the electoral campaign showed Yeltsin dancing and singing with the people, in direct contact with the population, which was what he was best at (certainly better than at talking to the camera). Since it was crucial to get over 50 percent of the population to vote, Sergei Lisovsky led a campaign especially directed at young voters with the slogan "Vote or you'll lose." Moreover, to avoid a majority for Ziuganov in the first round, a strong third candidate was brought into the arena in order to split voters between Yeltsin and Ziuganov. For this purpose, ORT built the image of General Alexander Lebed and raised his popularity by 10 percent. After the first round Lebed appealed to his voters to support Yeltsin.

Between the first round (16 June) and the second round (3 July), Yeltsin did not appear on television; by now he had serious health problems leading to a multiple bypass operation later that year. In the weeks between the two rounds of voting another scandal blew up, which almost destroyed the campaign team's efforts. Presidential security boss and former KGB officer Alexander Korzhakov ordered the arrest of two aides in Yeltsin's team as they removed half a million dollars (as payment for the electoral campaign) from the White House on 20 June. Korzhakov tried to implicate the Yeltsin team (and the privatization minister Anatoli Chubais) in improper use of campaign money. The spilling of the information could have seriously endangered Yeltsin's campaign, and it is possible the incident was set up to discredit him. Korzhakov was dismissed. On 3 July, Yeltsin was elected president of the Russian Federation, and the media had played a decisive and crucial role in building up his image as a people's president and running his campaign. It had also become clear that the relationship between political power and the media was riddled with corruption.

Not between Snickers and Tampax: The Presidential Elections of 2000   If the presidential elections of 1996 had captured the television viewers' attention by the scandals that surrounded the media coverage, then Putin's campaign happened before he even announced his candidature. Putin had no direct involvement with the media, nor did he have a campaign team. His campaign was therefore, as it were, conducted behind the screen rather than on the screen, clearly indicated in a statement made on a television. He asserted that he was not going to conduct an electoral campaign through the media, advertising himself between Snickers and Tampax, the products that dominated Russian advertising at the time.

Vladimir Putin had been designated prime minister in August 1999. In the five months before Yeltsin's resignation on New Year's Eve of the new millennium, when Putin became acting president until his proper election in March 2000, the state-owned media (ORT, RTR) covered Putin's travels across the country in his capacity as prime minister. As he promised to raise pensions, fight terrorism, bring back some sectors of the economy into the state's hands, and put an end to the Chechen conflict, he created his image as a strong leader. The bombing of two apartment blocks in Moscow in September 1999 justified strong measures against Chechnya and effectively triggered the second Chechen war. The media speculated for a while whether these bombings had been genuine acts of terror or mere pretexts for the commencement of a second campaign. Chechnya propelled Putin into the limelight as a tough leader. Later, when elected president, Putin would often avoid that kind of media attention, for example when delaying his comments on such calamities as the accident of the *Kursk* submarine, the terrorist attack in the Pushkin Square subway, or the arrest of NTV's boss Gusinsky.

The media's attention in those months

ORT journalist Sergei Dorenko conducted a number of current affairs programs during November and December 1999 that discredited Yuri Luzhkov. (Photo by Pavel Smertin/ Kommersant)

was focused on the electoral campaign for the parliamentary elections in December 1999, which proved decisive in the preparation of Putin's victory. The party supported by Putin, Unity (Edinstvo), was headed by Igor Shoigu; the apparently strongest political bloc was Fatherland—All Russia (Otechestvo—vsia Rossiya, OVR), headed by former prime minister Yevgeni Primakov, and the Communist Party of Gennadi Ziuganov. Apart from Primakov and Ziuganov, the other major player for the presidential campaign was the Moscow mayor, Yuri Luzhkov. As the state-controlled media (ORT, RTR) followed Putin on his journeys, they not only supported the prime minister's party Unity, but they also discredited Primakov and his party OVR as well as the potentially strong presidential candidate, Yuri Luzhkov. The alliance between Luzhkov and Primakov under OVR formed in the summer of 1999 had led Yeltsin to realize the urgent need to find a successor who would protect the "family," the people working around Yeltsin. ORT journalist Sergei Dorenko conducted a number of current affairs programs during November and December 1999 that discredited Yuri Luzhkov. Only the Moscow-owned TV-Center and the independent channel NTV resisted the state channels, offering airtime to Primakov. After the defeat of OVR in the elections, where the Communists came in first and the pro-Putin Unity took second place, NTV changed its portrayal of Putin to a more favorable view. It is worth noting, however, that reprimands followed: NTV was subjected to tax inspection raids, and TV Center was asked in February 2000 to bid for the renewal of its license (which was subsequently granted). Vladimir Putin was elected president on 26 March 2000 with a majority of 53 percent of the votes in the first round.

Television Conflicts   The Afghan war coverage under Gorbachev departed from the old-style view of the campaign as social reform toward a conflict that involved fighting; at the same time it was also a war where the military lost control of media coverage. In the Chechen conflict the journalists developed their investigation styles and showed reports that contradicted— openly and visually—the official version offered by the Russian government spokesmen, not unlike the coverage of the events in Vilnius.

Particularly blunt and challenging were the reports shown on NTV by its reporter Yelena Masiuk, who had covered Chechnya since September 1994. When from December 1994 to January 1995 (the beginning of the first Chechen war) the official reports spoke of the peaceful capture of Grozny, NTV showed pictures of bombs and tanks in Grozny, which contradicted the official version. As a result, the channel was threatened with having its licence revoked. Masiuk was then subjected to criticism from LDP leader Zhirinovsky, accusing her of taking bribes from the Chechens. Masiuk sued Zhirinovsky and won the case in 1996. Later, during her coverage of the war, Masiuk was seized by Chechen rebels and held hostage from May until August 1997, until she was released for a ransom of allegedly ten million dollars.

The Chechen war coverage was probably the largest thorn in the flesh of the Russian government with regard to television. The military apparently feared and hated the journalists. In one incident, Sergei Govorukhin, the son of the well-known filmmaker and one time politician Stanislav Govorukhin, was making a documentary about the war when he was injured in Chechnya. The injury to his leg urgently needed medical attention, but he could only be flown out of the war zone by a Russian military helicopter. As he had no military papers, he was left waiting for transportation, having received emergency treatment only. Subsequently he lost his leg.

The case of Andrei Babitsky caused more of an international scandal, since he worked for Radio Liberty (funded by the U.S. Congress), thus ensuring media coverage of his case outside Russia. Babitsky was reporting from Chechnya, not following the official line of war coverage, when

Radio Liberty journalist Andrei Babitsky shortly after his release from captivity in Chechnya, 2000. (Photo by Alexey Myakishev/Kommersant)

he suddenly and mysteriously disappeared in January 2000. With a massive delay, official Russian sources announced that he had been arrested for not carrying the relevant documents and would be released. Instead, he was exchanged for two Russian prisoners of war and handed over to Chechen captivity in February 2000. Three weeks later he turned up in Makhachkala, the capital of Daghestan, charged with possession of false documents. Until his trial in the autumn of that year, Babitsky's documents were withheld. When they were reissued and he was free to travel, Babitsky moved to Radio Liberty's headquarters in Prague. It has been suggested that the arrest was set up by the Russian authorities (and that the Chechen rebels who held Babitsky were pro-Moscow) in order to constitute an example for the journalistic community.

According to the Kremlin spokesman on Chechnya, Sergei Yastrzhembsky, the media coverage of the second Chechen war should signal support for the state, and thus for Russia's campaign. Accreditation rules for the press in the war zone restricted the movement of journalists. Journalists had to be accompanied by Russian soldiers or escorts and were not allowed to interview Chechen leaders. Many of the above journalists were in breach of this rule, unwilling to show loyalty to the state. This was particularly blatant in the coverage of the apartment bock bombings: a very blunt program of *Kukly* (Puppets) alleged the truck bombs had been planted by the FSB (Federalnaia sluzhba bezopasnosti, or Federal Security Agency). This and other anti-Russian comments were taken as treason and journalists turned to enemies, as the cases of Babitsky and Govorukhin show. Similarly, Anna Politkovskaya, journalist for *Obshchaya gazeta*, was detained and harassed for her coverage of the conflict.

These cases reveal the dangers to the Russian journalist when investigating in matters that were sensitive for the state and in contradicting the official view. Several journalists investigating corruption had already paid their price for coming too close to the structures of power in their investigations of corruption. The investigative journalist Dmitri Kholodov of *Komsomolskaya pravda* was killed by a bomb delivered to his office in the autumn of 1994. ORT head Vlad Listiev was shot on 1 March 1995, at a time when ORT was being privatized and he opposed the commercialization of the station.

Once again, the media assumed real power: they were able to sway public opinion, increasing Yeltsin's popularity over Ziuganov in the run-up to the 1996 presidential elections, or to stimulate public hostility to the second Chechen war. In the 1990s the media were a much stronger influence on public opinion than they had ever been before. Now "independent," they could seriously damage or help the president, manipulate elections, and, of course, divert attention through entertainment.

Program Variety   The new channels had to compete with regard to the entertainment sector and, later, over television serial production and purchase. Therefore, after its launch in 1991, RTR immediately established its reputation by creating a host of new programs.

In the early 1990s national channels were competing with regional and local stations, which screen pirated American movies. This practice was stopped when Russia signed the copyright act in 1994, although piracy continued to pose a problem until the late 1990s (in particular video piracy, but also compact discs [CDs] and computer software). Moreover, it was cheaper and easier for channels to purchase television programs and screen them, rather than produce their own, especially as the appetite for foreign products was much greater than for the New Russian products during the years that followed the collapse of the Soviet Union.

RTR focused on new entertainment, whereas NTV in the first instance boasted its own film production arm, NTV Profit (now NTV Film), which invested in and produced New Russian cinema. NTV scheduled a good deal of such New Russian films on its channel. ORT stuck largely with the Soviet diet, screening films of the Soviet era, which suddenly gained immense popularity, because they reminded the often older generation (who watched television during the daytime) of the stable, golden, Soviet times and distracted from the chaos of rising prices and disappearing Soviet products that reigned in Russia in the first half of the 1990s. One such program on ORT was the new year edition of *Old Songs about the Main Things* (Starye pesni o glavnom), produced by Konstantin Ernst and Leonid Parfyonov and broadcast between 1997 and 1999, presenting old pop songs performed by contemporary estrada singers. TV6 was not a strong news channel, but it proved to be most inventive in entertainment programs and talk shows, generating thereby a new wave of programs from its competitors.

The satellite or cable channels MTV (Music Television), TNT, and CTC (Set' Tele-

Konstantin Ernst, head of First Channel television (formerly ORT) in his office, July 2002. (Photo by Dmitry Azarov/Kommersant)

vizionnykh Stantsii, Network of Television Stations) became more widely accessible and rather popular in the large cities, especially Moscow. Most significant was the establishment of a television award, TEFI, by the Russian Television Academy in 1994 to select and honor the best presenters, programs, and directors working on television.

Current Affairs, Political Satire, and Crime. Competition for viewers in the post-Soviet television landscape was huge. The First Channel had always focused on news broadcasts and political programs, and so did RTR and NTV when they followed suit. In terms of the news presentations, RTR had taken the lead over ORT in the early 1990s, because RTR's *Vesti* were infinitely more investigative than the First Channel's news programs. After 1994, NTV attracted a vast majority of news viewers from RTR and ORT. Both NTV's evening news *Segodnia* and analytical programs such as *Itogi* (Conclusions) had clearly taken the lead among the public. NTV remained at the top of the league table for news until its management changed in April 2001, when viewers returned to *Vremia*, and ORT resumed its leading position in news coverage.

Apart from the news, current affairs programs were highly relevant to establish a channel's credibility. RTR ran a program, *Sovershenno sekretno* (Top Secret), hosted by Artyom Borovik, that replicated the investigative journalism he had demonstrated in his weekly paper of the same title. The most popular current affairs program was NTV's *Itogi*, hosted by Yevgeni Kiselyov until he left NTV in 2000. The history program *Namedni* (Lately) by Leonid Parfyonov is another one of NTV's assets. Parfyonov here plays games with history, reassembling historical documents in high-quality technology. The program often contains reports from the well-known investigative reporter Andrei Loshak. Along the lines of Kiselyov's *Itogi*, other channels too presented their analytical programs on the week's events, using presenters such as Sergei Dorenko or Alexander Liubimov. NTV's *Strana i mir* (The Country and the World, NTV) covers the day's main events and is presented by Julia Bordovskikh and Anton Khrenov. Vladimir Pozner hosts *Vremena* (Times, ORT); *Vesti nedeli* (News of the Week, RTR) is presented by Yevgeni Revenko; *Vremechko* (A Bit of Time) is authored by Andrei Maximov, formerly director and journalist of the tabloid *Komsomolskaya pravda*; and the program *Zerkalo* (Mirror, RTR) has been hosted since 1996 by Nikolai Svanidze, the former director of RTR, who engages in rather dull discussions with politicians.

A significant innovation in television programs began with *Itogo* (Total) by Viktor Shenderovich, which was a trademark of NTV—a sharp political magazine, summing up the events of the week, parodying the title of the conclusions (*itogi*) drawn in Yevgeni Kiselyov's program. Another highly popular and successful program was the equivalent of *Spitting Image*, called *Kukly* (Puppets), shown on NTV and created by Viktor Shenderovich. The puppets have pet names, such as Borka (Yeltsin), Yegorka (Yegor Gaidar, the engineer of eco-

nomic "shock therapy"), Ziuga (Ziuganov), Michel Stavropolsky (Mikhail Gorbachev, who originally came from Stavropol); Tolik Voucher (Anatoli Chubais, the privatization minister), and Zhirik (Zhirinovsky). With biting satire, the programme commented on the events of the week, often exposing political leaders in quite a provocative way (for example, Yeltsin surviving on a state pension, exposing the ridiculously low level of pensions). A program after the blowing up of two apartment blocks in Moscow in 1999 alleged that this was arranged by the Russians to instigate the continuation of warfare in Chechnya. *Kukly* was controversial and removed from the schedule several times.

Programs about cultural life were largely relegated to the channel Kultura after its inception, but other channels offered coverage of cultural events as well. The cinema programs *Moye kino* (My Cinema, TV6), hosted by scriptwriter Viktor Merezhko, and Peter Shepotinnik's *Kineskop* (Cinescope, TV6), which started in 1994 and was one of the first newly commissioned programmes of the channel, covered the film scene both in Russia and abroad. *Teatralnyi ponedelnik* (Theatrical Monday, TV6) reported on theater events.

Programs about street crime rose in popularity along with the current affairs programs that exposed organized crime. *Dorozhnyi patrul* (Street Watch, TV6) was an innovative program that provided a short daily update on the criminal chronicle; it was created by Kirill Legat. Legat later produced *Telespetsnaz* (Tele-Special-Force, TV6), a program that explained the difficult and dangerous work of the police and special forces to ensure people's safety; it was hosted by Andrei Khoroshev, who outraged the Russian film market in the mid-1990s

Puppet of Boris Yeltsin, 2002. With biting satire the television program *Kukly* commented on the events of the week, often exposing political leaders in quite a provocative way. (Photo by Ivan Shapovalov/Kommersant)

with his films made under the pseudonym Andrei I.

The Game Show. The game show came as a novelty to Russia in the sense that it now offered prizes. Often programs were modeled on Western programs, and especially in the new millennium the trend to purchase licences has increased. One of the first game shows, modeled on *Wheel of Fortune*, was Vlad Listiev's *Pole chudes* (Miracle Field), now presented by the public's favorite host, Leonid Yakubovich. Game shows enjoy huge popularity with the viewers: *Slaboe zveno* (The Weakest Link), hosted by Maria Kiselyova, runs on ORT, and *Kto khochet stat millionerom?* (Who Wants to Be a Millionaire?) is hosted

by the popular presenter—and brilliant impersonator of politicians—Maxim Galkin on ORT. Dmitri Dibrov is best known for his NTV quiz show *O shchastlivchik* (O, Happy Man). *Svoya igra* (Your Game, NTV) is a version of *Jeopardy*, presented by Peter Kuleshov.

Other game shows are more theme focused, such as *Agenstvo odinokikh serdets* (Agency of Lonely Hearts, RTR), presented by the popular singer Alika Smekhova and the entertainer Valeri Zakutsky. ORT's Sunday morning program, *Poka vse doma* (While Everybody's Still at Home), is presented by Timur Kiziakov, who pays a "surprise" visit to the apartment of a famous person and his or her family. NTV's *Kvar-*

tirny vopros (Apartment Question) is almost modeled on *Changing Rooms*. ORT's *Dog Show* revolves around dogs and their respective owners. One of the most popular evening programs is *Poslednii geroi* (The Last Hero), a show that is set on a remote island, where sixteen people of show business are divided into two teams and have to complete a number of tasks while struggling with the adverse conditions on the island. The show used to be presented by the "last hero," Sergei Bodrov Jr., who tragically died in a glacier slide in September 2002. ORT's *Fabrika zvezd* (Star Factory) is a project where real stars and the audience vote for the best amateur performer, somewhat like RTL's *Deutschland sucht den Superstar* (Germany Seeks the Superstar) or *Fame Academy* on the British Broadcasting Corporation (BBC). It is extremely popular and has had several editions since its start in December 2002.

MTV runs a number of quite popular game shows, such as the *Totalnoye Shou* (Total Show), an interactive program where the audience votes on the best music clip. *Rokirovka* (Castling) is a competitive game of sportsmen who change disciplines, so that a boxer has to play tennis, a footballer has to wrestle, and so on. *Hand-Made* shows stars making things with their own hands, engaging in jewelry making, handicrafts, knitting, and sewing.

Reality TV made a short appearance on the Russian television space: *Big Brother*, called *Za steklom* (Behind the Glass), was shown on TV6 before the station was closed in 2002.

The Tok-shou. Most of the new shows were talk shows (*tok-shou* in Russian), exposing famous guests to questions about their private life or inviting ordinary people into the studio to publicly discuss their personal problems. Television filled the gap by creating shows that brought private life into the public domain. It was not as if Russians did not know of the problems of their friends and family, since privacy was not one of the privileges of the Soviet population, who shared apartments among three generations or inhabited communal apartments. The novelty and attraction of these programs, however, was to present a personal point of view in public and be heard and seen by millions.

Lev Novozhenov, an elderly gentleman, is the host of NTV's show *Vremechko* (Little Time), which is based on the concept of the little man, symbolized in Nikolai Gogol's famous character, Akaki Akakievich, whose overcoat is stolen in the eponymous story. *Vremechko* alludes in its title to the major news program *Vremia*, but it is concerned with news of the little man, the ordinary citizen, who is more important than war and politics for Novozhenov. He interviews people who are extraordinary, abnormal, unusual and highlights the absurdity of everyday life by stressing the psychopathology of society at large.

The humorous show *Gorodok* (Little Town, RTR), which exposes people and events to laughter, was produced and hosted by Ilia Oleinikov and Yuri Stoyanov, who received four TEFI awards. *Sam sebe rezhisser* (Directing Myself, RTR) began as a show with amateur video clips and gradually developed into a weekly program on the lines of *Candid Camera;* its host is Alexei Lysenkov. *Znak kachestva* (Proof of Quality, TV6) was a show where people from the street could demonstrate their talents, starting in 1996 and hosted by Oleg Komarov.

The program *Anshlag* (Sold Out, RTR), hosted by Regina Dubovitskaya, brings fa-

Julia Menshova with her father, the filmmaker and Oscar winner Vladimir Menshov, attend the "Moskovskaya Premiera" (Moscow Premiere) awards in 2002. The ceremony took place in the Baltschug Kempinsky hotel, Moscow. (Photo by Alexey Kudenko/Kommersant)

mous people in front of the camera. *Skandaly nedeli* (Scandals of the Week, TV6), hosted by Petr Tolstoi since 1996, reflects television's growing interest in the more mundane aspects of life. Dmitri Dibrov is a popular presenter who created his image as a "dandy" with his smart suits and colorful ties. The trained journalist and director of night programming on ORT hosts, above all, the programs *Nochnaya smena* (Night Shift). With wit, charm, and inventiveness, he hosts the show *Antropologiya* (Anthropology), where he interviews famous cultural figures. Although noncommercial and independent of ratings, the channel Kultura has also started a number of challenging talk shows. *Shkola zlosloviya* (The School of Scandal)—in a reference to Richard Sheridan's play—is hosted by the

writer Tatiana Tolstaya and the scriptwriter Dunia Smirnova, who expose artists to their "evil tongues." The quibbling and quizzing Andrei Maximov presents the program *Nochnoi polet* (Night Flight) on Kultura, subjecting artists to harsh and challenging questions. The writer and critic Viktor Yerofeyev presents the literature program *Apocryph*.

Yelena Yakovleva's *Chto khochet zhenshchina* (What a Woman Wants, RTR) is one of the numerous women's shows that have appeared on television. Julia Menshova, daughter of the Oscar-winning director Vladimir Menshov, has hosted *Ya sama* (I Myself, TV6) since 1995. It is a talk show for women, who place the men in the studio on the bench for the accused, as they indict the men's sins with examples from their private lives. More new programs have been launched. In *Zhenskii vzgliad* (Women's View, TV6), Oxana Pushkina interviews famous women or the wives of celebrities. A relatively young and very popular program is Svetlana Sorokina's *Osnovnoi instinkt* (Basic Instinct, ORT, since 2003), which returns to the blue screen the television anchor of the Gorbachev years.

MTV boasts of some of the most popular presenters among their staff. Tutta Larsen hosts *Razum i chuvstvo* (Sense and Sensibility). Larsen, who also works on Radio Maximum, is one of the most outrageously dressed presenters of television. With a nose ring, tattoos, and bleached hair, she dresses extravagantly and combines styles that do not go together. On the show, young people discuss problems with viewer participation. She also has her own show, *Tants-pol* (Dance Floor), for new dance music. Another star presenter on MTV is Viacheslav Petkun with his show *Cherno-beloye* (Black and White) on aspects of show business.

Children's Television. The channels TVTs (Television Center, TV Tsentr) and Kultura schedule a number of educational programs, some of which tend to suggest a moral warning: they show, for example, documentaries on children in a youth prison, or the life of poor and underprivileged children, as a warning. Generally, children's programs were largely based on the very ample and beautiful production of Russian animators. Soviet and Russian animation still proves extremely popular with Russian children and provides the basic television diet, alongside the Disney cartoons that have flooded the market. *Sesame Street* (Ulitsa Sezam) was adapted to the Russian context before it was broadcast: Russian characters were added, Vlas and Enik replaced Bert and Ernie, and the action took place in a Russian courtyard. *Spokoinoi nochi, malyshi* (Good Night, Kids) is a good-night program for the preschool age presented by Anna Mikhalkova, later by Oxana Fedorova. The Yeralash films, produced by the Gorky studios, are short educational spots produced with a great deal of appeal for children.

Miscellaneous. After its initial role as a platform for political debate and main critic of the system, television has conducted investigative journalism on independent channels, although it has not developed a coherent model of programming. Television criticizes politics and entertains the viewer but offers no forum for the formation of public opinion. Instead, it resorts to entertainment programs, which draw on the amateur music clubs of the past. Or on humorous programs in which, à la Arkadi Raikin, the little man is not confronted with the obstacles posed by the system, but in which he is the odd man out, thus justifying the individual's rather passive role in the political process. Television reiterates the common concepts of individual versus state, the little man lost in a larger system, who searches for and finds a sense of community with his brothers-in-arms—the other television spectators. The popularity of wildlife programs, such as *V mire zhivotnykh* (In the Animal World), *Dialogi s zhivotnymi* (Dialogues with Animals), and *Planeta zemlia* (Planet Earth), fits into this overall picture as much as *Vremechko:* they explore the behavior of animals and humans in unusual circumstances and analyze the divergence from normative behavior as an absurdity that matches the absurdity of life. Such divergence from the norm is also manifest in the behavior of criminals and offers an additional reason for the popularity of the crime story in contemporary Russia. It is this feature that made *Vremechko* so phenomenally successful, with its exposure of psychopathology as the norm. In this sense, television entertainment and news offer a substitute for reality, where the substitute is more recognizable than the real world. Reality is repeated until it can be understood and consumed in private among friends, requiring no active response. The political show that happened on the blue screen in the late 1990s has turned television into a device that replays reality and offers a variety of distractions from it to cradle the spectator in the illusion of something happening out there that does not affect his life, his television programs. When seen in this light, the closing of television channels and changes in management were initially perceived as a real threat, more important than the party programs broadcast in the electoral campaigns.

Television Serials   The role of television serials underwent a complete transformation in Russia during the 1990s. Initially the public was yearning for Western serials: the American serials *Santa Barbara*, *The X Files*, *Dynasty*, and *Dallas* were acquired and shown. Then soap operas of Mexican provenance kept mass audiences glued to the television screen: melodrama replaced the family dynasty-drama and the detective series. Audiences eagerly devoured *Just Maria* (Prosto Maria), *Wild Rose* (Dikaia Roza), and the 1979 *The Rich Also Cry* (Bogatye tozhe plachut), watched by 43 percent of the population in Moscow during 1991. True, it was cheaper to buy than to produce, but at the same time the audience demand was higher for foreign or Soviet products, not New Russian films. In the mid-1990s, Russian television began to invest in home-grown television serial production. RTR led in this area with the serial *Maroseika 12*, set in the tax police department Cobra, and *Turetsky's March* (Marsh Turetskogo), based on a novel by the detective writer Friedrich Neznansky, starring Alexander Domogarov as chief investigator Turetsky. The production of crime serials is expensive but popular, and they can be released on video and repeated on various channels. Nevertheless, *Petersburg Secrets* (Peterburgskie tainy, 1994–1995) could hardly compete with *Dynasty*.

Toward the end of the 1990s, domestic production of serials really took off. On the one hand, television could offer more money to filmmakers than they could find in the free market for feature films. On the other hand, after the financial crisis of August 1998 it was cheaper to produce than to buy. The result was a flood of television serials that conquered Russian audiences and reached top ratings on television, pushing to the side the former leaders, old Soviet films and contemporary American cinema.

Streets of Broken Lights (Ulitsy razbitykh fonarei, 1997–1999) was the first, tremendously successful serial. It generated numerous sequels and was released on video under the title *Cops* (Menty). It is a crime series showing street crime in Petersburg. It engages in a realistic depiction of the police work, showing the dilapidated living conditions of a society where old structures have collapsed. The series, parts of which have been directed by the established filmmaker Alexander Rogozhkin, has drawn on star actors but has also turned other new actors into popular heroes.

Detective Dubrovsky's Dossier (Dos'e detektiva Dubrovskogo, 1999) is a detective series starring the well-known actor Nikolai Karachentsov, who is famous for his production of and role in the first Russian rock opera, *Juno and Avos. Hunting Cinderella* (Okhota na zolushku, 1999) stars the redhead Amalia Mordvinova, who suffers from memory loss after an accident and is used by criminal structures to carry out a series of special assignments. *Criminal Petersburg* (Banditskii Peterburg, 2000) was produced by NTV. It is a family saga about a Mafioso family in Petersburg, where "Antibiotik" is a Russian version of Mario Puzo's *Godfather. The Truckers* (Dal'noboishchiki) is a road-movie cum crime series. The most popular crime series is *The Crushing Force* (Uboinaia sila, 2000) made by ORT, which follows the Petersburg investigator Plakhov as he exposes a large-scale political scandal. *Kamenskaya* (1999–2000) was a serial dealing with large-scale crime, based on the detective novels of Alexandra Marinina, in which Yelena Yakovleva played the main part. The complex structure of Marinina's detective novels reflects the interwoven lines of fate in the investigation of organized crime. *Bourgeois's Birthday* (Den' rozhdeniia Burzhuia, 1999) revolves around a family engaged in the business world of the New Russia and deals with their personal and professional worries. *The Diary of a Killer* (Dnevnik ubiitsy, 2003), directed by the young and fashionable director Kirill Serebrennikov, mixes a melodramatic plot in the present with an investigation of a mystery crime resolved through the consultation of archival documents by a librarian. In 2003, two serials kept people in front of the blue screen. The first, *The Brigade* (Brigada, RTR), is based on a novel by Alexander Belov about four lads from Moscow who try to make money in the early 1990s and end in the criminal world. The second, *Ice Age* (Lednikovyi period, ORT), is set in the Moscow of the 1990s in the special section of the police force, which faces the task of investigating moles in police apparatus.

The production of serials concentrated on detective and crime plots rather than sitcoms. It appears that Russian audiences are grappling with the rise in crime rates more than with the comic genre. Moreover, they see in the criminal investigation an attempt to analyze the changes in Russia that still confront them. Neither the sitcom *Funny Business, Family Business* (Smeshnye dela, semeinye dela) nor the high school drama *Simple Truths* (Prostye istiny, 1999–2000) has proved attractive.

The Television Channels   Between 1991 and 2001, the media developed very quickly as a result of the investments of tycoons, called "oligarchs" in Russia. They invested in the media, encouraging them to offer a challenging assessment of politics. As the media had demonstrated their power under Gorbachev and during the two attempted coups, they had the potential to become a powerful instrument for whoever owned or controlled them. This had been shown during the presidential campaign of 1996: the media could be used to build a president or to discredit government policies. A game between the state and the media followed.

The structural organization of media ownership is so complex that it obscures the issue of who really controls the media. In 1985, when Gorbachev came to power, there was one national channel and several regional ones, all owned and controlled by the party. Under Yeltsin the channels proliferated and privatization set in, creating a number of independent media (1990–1993); this led to a situation where the private shareholders invested more into the media than the state, even into those stations in which the state owned a majority of shares. From 1996 to 1999, a status quo reigned over the media market, which was shaken up in the aftermath of the 1999 parliamentary elections and under Putin. By the summer of 2003, the six main nationwide channels were once again controlled by the state, directly or indirectly. A number of cable and digital channels existed alongside, but since they are not accessible to wide parts of the population they are not discussed here.

Privatization and Freedom of the Press: 1991–1995 The former First Channel (Central Television) had belonged to the Soviet state. After the August Coup (1991), ownership was transferred from the Soviet Union to the Russian Federation (RSFSR). With increasing costs and decreasing economic stability, however, the state could not maintain the budget for the television channel. The channel was served by production units while relying for up to 80 percent on the state budget with no right to generate advertising income. Those advertisements that were shown on the First Channel provided income to the numerous individual production units but not to the central management. The independent production companies kept the advertising revenue to themselves rather than sharing it; also, much more income was received for advertising than they declared. Largely in order to remedy this situation and to allow ORT to generate an income through advertising, Yeltsin ordered

the privatization of the First Channel in 1995, when the company could not even pay its electricity bills. He decreed the formation of ORT (Obshestvennoe rossiiskoe televidenie, Public Russian Television), which took effect as of April 1995. ORT now receives 30–50 percent of its revenue from advertising.

Out of the need to have a channel to oppose Gorbachev, the RSFSR launched RTR (Russian Television) on 13 May 1991, a month before Yeltsin's election as RSFSR president. Oleg Poptsov was appointed RTR's general director, supported by a team of investigative reporters. The news program *Vesti* became the flagship of the new channel; it was anchored by presenters such as Oleg Dobrodeyev, Yevgeni Kiselyov, Tatiana Mitkova, and Svetlana Sorokina. RTR inspired more confidence in its news coverage because of the role it, and Poptsov in particular, had played during the two coups. The first direct sponsorship between political power and the media came to an end before the presidential electoral campaign: in February 1996, Oleg Poptsov was removed from office by Yeltsin's decree. Yeltsin would place his stake for support on another, temporary director and on the two media moguls, Vladimir Gusinsky and Boris Berezovsky.

In August 1991 the company Moscow Independent Broadcasting Corporation (MNVK, Moskovskaia nezavisimaia veshchatel'naia korporatsiia), largely owned by the Moscow government, was founded to provide a local channel that would support Moscow's mayor Luzhkov, running for election against Gavriil Popov. After Gorbachev and Yeltsin on the federal level, another politician (Luzhkov) had acquired his own media organ on a local level. Luzhkov's "empire" grew to include the

Moscow-loyal city periodical *Metro*, *Ob-shchaya gazeta*, TV6, *Versiya*, *Moskovskii komsomolets*, and TVTs.

In this media landscape where each of the major players in politics effectively owned a television station, the channel NTV meant a significant change: it was the first independent channel, established by the media holding Most, owned by the media mogul Vladimir Gusinsky. It began transmission in 1993 on the frequency of the fourth channel. It first transmitted part of the day, then all day starting in November 1996 (as a token for the channel's support in the electoral campaign of 1996). NTV took pride both in its web design and the design of its logo: a green ball above the slogan "news is our profession," but it gained real fame for its news programs particularly. Yevgeni Kiselyov presented his weekly critical political magazine *Itogi* on Sunday evenings. The news program *Segodnia* (Today) rose to become the most popular news program. NTV also showed contemporary foreign cinema and New Russian films, often created by its own film production unit, NTV Profit. It also covered international sports events.

By 1996, the crucial year of Yeltsin's re-election, those media formerly owned by the state had been partly privatized, whereas the state offered no major investment. Thus, although the private sector may only have been holding a majority of shares, the shareholders were in control because of the financial power they had over the media corporations. The state, and the president in particular with his power consolidated after the attempted coup of 1993, had maneuvered itself into a position whereby the state depended on television, owning shares in television without holding real (financial) control. It

was this situation of dependence on media tycoons on the one hand, and the involvement of these tycoons in politics on the other hand, that created a dangerous tension between political power and political control. The privatization of the media in a "smash and grab" style to oligarchs would take its toll.

Stalemate: 1995–1999   The elections of 1996 had tied together inseparably political power and the media. This status quo, of a general support of all major channels for the president, would last through several prime ministers and the economic crisis of 1998. The media world was divided only in the run-up to the parliamentary elections of 1999, which would prove a decisive factor in determining the relationship of the new power (Putin) with the media.

The latter half of the 1990s saw the proliferation of cable and satellite television and the foundation of two new television stations. The channel Kultura started transmission in November 1997 as a noncommercial station that reports on culture only; it is part of VGTRK and thus belongs to the Russian state. TVTs (TV Center), which has transmitted on the third frequency since June 1997, belongs to the Moscow government; it is effectively Luzhkov's channel. In February 2000 the former RTR boss, Oleg Poptsov, was appointed as the channel's new director. It is the only Russian channel with rights for Formula One. The MTV musical channel started in 1998, bringing musical television to the Russian viewers through the presenter, the so-called video jockey (VJ) Tutta Larsen, with her bleached hair and nose ring mirroring her U.S. equivalents.

During those stalemate years it was mainly NTV's coverage that was often controversial. Especially the reports from Chechnya have exposed the channel to frequent threats of license withdrawal, which has become one way of controlling the media in the absence of direct censorship. Its journalists were exposed to public and political threats. A criminal case was staged against Yelena Masiuk (July 1995) for interviewing the Chechen rebel leader Shamil Basayev (she was accused of harboring a criminal). The head of the program *Kukly* (Puppets), Viktor Shenderovich, was charged with slander, and the program was pulled from the schedule numerous times for its all too critical comments on politicians under the guise of satire.

Deprivatization after 2000 After the television stations had played their role during the parliamentary elections in 1999, they had to pay the price for meddling in politics. ORT and RTR had supported Putin and discredited Luzhkov; NTV and TV Center had offered airtime to the politicians of parties that were competitors of the Putin-supported bloc Unity. ORT's journalist Sergei Dorenko, who had contributed in his interviews and shows to a discreditation of Luzhkov, was plagued by a scandal. His current affairs program *Versii* (Versions) was banned after a critical report on the *Kursk* submarine incident, which implied that a Soviet missile had misfired. Dorenko also spoke out against the forced handover of Berezovsky's shares. Dorenko was arrested for hooliganism and sentenced to a term in prison in November 2001, with the verdict overturned and changed to a fine in December 2002. Another investigative journalist had been removed from television.

During the presidential elections, therefore, Berezovsky's media arms had tried to

Businessman Vladimir Gusinsky, founder of Most Bank and later Media Most (including NTV), in 1997. (Photo by Pavel Kassin/ Kommersant)

implicate Luzhkov in corruption and make allegations about Primakov's ill health, effectively backing Putin. Gusinsky's media, on the other hand, were trying to support Luzhkov and Primakov. After the victory of the Unity block over Luzhkov's and Primakov's OVR in December 1999, Gusinsky had, in fact, already lost the game for power.

But more important was the massive campaign against the media tycoons. Berezovsky, who had been accused of embezzlement with regard to Aeroflot shares, had already moved to London to avoid charges. He was urged to sell his shares. After making a gesture and handing his shares to the artistic intelligentsia, he sold to the busi-

Yevgeni Kiselyov in the studio presenting *Itogi*, 3 April 2001 during the conflict with GazProm Media. (Photo by Alexey Kudenko/Kommersant)

nessman Roman Abramovich, owner of the rights to trade under Slavneft the resources of the Chukotka region, of which he was elected governor. RTR was taken over by Oleg Dobrodeyev on 31 January 2000. *Vesti* soon recovered its place as a leading news program, supporting the military action in Chechnya. The situation at NTV was more critical. In September 2000, Gazprom Media (a subsidiary of the state-run gas monopoly company Gazprom) filed a suit against Media Most (parent company of NTV) to call in the debt (a loan of two million dollars granted for the launch of the Bonum 2 satellite). In April 2001, Gazprom (a shareholder in NTV) prematurely recalled loans from Gusinsky and assumed control over NTV. Gazprom's head, Albert Kokh, appointed a new general director, the American Boris Jordan, and removed from office the popular journalist Yevgeni Kiselyov. The old NTV team of Kiselyov's *Itogi* and Shenderovich's *Kukly* moved to TV6. The news anchor Tatiana Mitkova resigned also but was reappointed head of news under the new management.

TV6 (or rather its parent company MNVK) was subsequently sued for bankruptcy by LukOil Garant (the pension fund), part of the private, but Kremlin-close, LukOil, which demanded the liquidation of the station on the grounds that it made no profit and its assets did not offset the debts. In January 2002 the channel was closed, but in May 2002 the Kiselyov team formed the station TVS (Television Spectrum). TVS was closed in June 2003 for alleged nonpayment of bills for cable use, which were charged at an excessive rate. A new sports channel started to broadcast

Viktor Shenderovich, anchor of the *Itogo* political satire program (left) and Svetlana Sorokina, anchor of the *Glaz naroda* program on NTV (right) during the press conference after the meeting of a group of NTV journalists with Russian president Vladimir Putin concerning the situation of Media Most Holding, at Ekho Moskvy radio station. (Photo by Valery Melnikov/Kommersant)

immediately. The last independent channel had folded, and the media industry was deprivatized.

It appears that under Putin the state took control of the media by strictly financial manipulation. This process shows how the political power structures, backed by the (state-owned) oil and gas industry, have resumed control over the media rather than continuing on the basis of a mutually beneficial relationship, which was entertained in the second part of Yeltsin's rule.

Media Control   If the scandal surrounding Berezovsky's surrender of shares was watched anxiously by the media, the scandal surrounding NTV's takeover by the state-controlled GazProm came under fire from the public, which staged demonstrations in the streets and supported the NTV management under Kiselyov. These protests were to no avail, however. After April 2001, TVS was the last remaining independent channel, a channel in which the state, partly state-owned companies, or the city did not hold a majority of shares. Its closure in 2003 bears witness to the continuous attempts of the state structures to remove inquisitive journalists from the mass media without applying censorship or force but simply by economic and financial manipulation. The new form of entertainment involves the public's watching how their television is deprivatized. The NTV takeover occurred live on-air, making the mass media themselves news item number one.

The Internet revolution has not passed Russia by. All the above-mentioned television channels operate elaborate Web sites, which also provide news, sometimes supplying video clips. There are also special news sites, such as strana.ru and lenta.ru, which offer news on line. *Pravda*, too, has had an online service since 1999. These new media offer up-to-date information, but it is early days to speak of political trends or investigative journalism in these media.

Soviet television was used for social control and engineering rather than communication. Under Gorbachev the media addressed the viewer not as an object into which an ideological message would be injected but as an individual with his own views. This individual remained, however, the plaything of politics rather than taking on an active role. Television had the chance to form public opinion. Instead, it taught its viewers to criticize and later it exercised only that function: to criticize and expose the failures of the system, the state, the government. Television's role was not a constructive one and failed to involve the formation of a new value system at a time when the old one had collapsed. Its "harbinger," the intelligentsia, had lost its influence. Instead, television indoctrinates the viewer not to trust politics. And not to trust reality, but only television's version of it.

Taking Stock   In 2004 the Russian mass media are, broadly speaking, owned and ruled by several large conglomerates. GazPromMedia (former MostMedia) controls the television stations NTV and TNT; Radio Echo Moscow; the publications *Sem dnei*, *Segodnia* (discontinued), *Itogi*, and *Karavan;* and the film production company NTV Profit (now NTV Film). ProfMedia (InterRos) holds shares in the papers *Izvestiya*, *Komsomolskaya pravda*, and *Ekspert* and in radio Europe Plus. Its subsidiary, Independent Media, holds shares in many journal publications. Berezovsky indirectly holds (or held) stakes in ORT and TV6; the papers *Kommersant*, *Nezavisimaya gazeta*, and *Novye Izvestiya;* and the journal *Ogonyok*. The state controls VGTRK (Channel Kultura and RTR), the news agencies ITAR-TASS and RIA Vesti, and the paper *Rossiiskaya gazeta* as well as a majority of shares in ORT. The Moscow government controls TVTs and the paper *Vecherniaya Moskva*. Other major publishing houses are holding companies in their own right, such as the edition *SPEED-Info*, *Moskovskii komsomolets*, and *Argumenty i fakty*, with their own subsidiaries.

Radio

Soviet Radio   Although the electrification of the country had been on Lenin's agenda in the 1920s, by the late 1970s only half of the Soviet population was in possession of a radio receiver; receivers with a shortwave facility (international range) were especially rare. This is low not only by comparison with Europe and the United States, but also stunning in view of the fact that cable radio provided access without an aerial for most households.

As a visible sign of the "radiofication," a radio tower was built in the south of Moscow on Shabolovka, with an extraordinary constructivist design of interconnected metal grids that spiral into the sky (design Vladimir Shukhov, 1919). The Soviet Union possessed five stations covering different areas of broadcasting: political programs and news, international news, education, music, and information for expatriates. The jamming of foreign stations, such as Voice of America (VoA), the BBC, and Deutsche Welle, had begun in 1948, and although it contravened the UN resolution of 1950 and was stopped in other Eastern Bloc countries, it continued in the Soviet Union well into the Gorbachev era. Jamming of VoA and the BBC stopped in 1987; for Radio Liberty this was even later. The impact of Gorbachev's reforms on the radio was slower, in a sense, than on television, which was clearly privileged by the leader. In the light of the most interesting music's being distributed by *magnitizdat* (the circulation of music on tapes), however, and in a media market that pirated any tune before its official release, the status of radio has clearly been deflated.

During the Soviet period, two national radio stations fed into the cable network, and in 1964 they were joined by Radio Mayak (Lighthouse), which played light music and broadcast news on a 24-hour basis. Although uninterrupted broadcasting was clearly a novelty for Soviet listeners, the frequency of Mayak overlapped with foreign stations, so that it also fulfilled the function of blocking international news. The year 1964, the last year of Khrushchev's Thaw, also saw the launch of Radio Yunost (Youth). These two stations, which were founded during the Thaw, played an important role during perestroika: the lively and popular music made Mayak a suitable competitor for foreign radio stations once the jamming had stopped, and Yunost fed into the television revolution. It was from this station that Eduard Sagalayev (head of Yunost from 1980 to 1984) recruited the four journalists who started the television revolution with programs such as *Vzgliad* (Viewpoint) and *Dvenadtsatyi etazh* (Twelfth Floor).

Russian Radio   At the end of the 1980s, when the law did not yet allow for independent television to be launched, the radio stations seized on the liberalization that had allowed access to foreign broadcasting stations. Several new stations were formed, the first of which was a Russian-French joint venture: Radio Europa Plus was the first commercial musical radio station; it started broadcasting in April 1990. It began with evening broadcasts from 7 PM to 1 AM and expanded to full-day coverage. Europa Plus plays music, which is interrupted for news and horoscopes. Nowadays there are more than 1,400 radio stations, of which only 300 are state owned. Most stations are regional or local, but more and more radio stations become available online. Many commercial stations have emphasized music rather than information in order to save money on journalists. So far, advertising has generated less income for Russian radio than for its European or U.S. counterparts.

The state-owned Radio Rossii (Radio Russia) followed suit, starting on 10 December 1990. It was initiated by the reform-supportive journalists on the *Vzgliad* team and recruited its staff, just like the legendary television program, from Radio Yunost. The programs cover news (on the hour), literary themes, problems of Russian language, and theater events. Radio Rossii offers a relatively high level of programming, especially on current affairs. It counts among its staff Russia's top political commentator, Alexander Bovin, a journalist of the Soviet school, who hosts *The World in a Week* (Mir za nedeliu). The 30-minute program started in 2001; in it Bovin combines analytical skills with a tolerant attitude to the events he explores. Andrei Dementiev runs a program called *Twists of the Times* (Virazhi vremeni), where he talks with prominent figures of Russian culture or their heirs. Natalia Bekhtina leads the program *In the First Person* (Ot pervogo litsa), in which she interviews politicians and other people who make a contribution to society, such as doctors, teachers, lawyers, artists, and economists. Radio Rossii also broadcasts literary and educational programs. Overall, its programs are of a high intellectual standard.

Radio Ekho Moskvy (Echo Moscow) went on air on 22 August 1990. It was gradually acquired by the MediaMost holding, which meant that its journalistic positions reflected a liberal democratic position and engaged critically with current affairs. Under the leadership of Alexei Venediktov, Ekho broadcasts news, sports, reviews of the press, and programs on the economy. It has been available online since 1997. Ekho is probably the most liberal radio station, a reputation it created for itself in the early 1990s with its reports on the events in Vilnius and on the August coup, which presented alternative views to the official versions. Ekho excels with its news and political talk shows, which are mixed with music. It makes extensive use of an interactive link with its listeners, who can phone in to live programs. Ekho is aimed, like Radio Russia, at the more mature (age 35–50), educated, intellectual listener. Therefore, such recognized writers as Julia Latynina and Sergei Parkhomenko are for the audience apt and recognized commentators.

The local station Radio Govorit Moskva (Moscow Speaking) was founded in August 1997 as a cable network, offering local news, coverage of themes pertinent to Moscow life, and music. There are also horoscopes, ratings of all sorts (the best, the highest, and the biggest), programs on health, sports news, and press reviews. Other local stations can be found in most major cities of the Russian Federation, such as Peterburg Radio in St. Petersburg.

The old Soviet stations continue to broadcast. Yunost has adapted to the new interests of the younger generation and now employs a range of DJs (disc jockeys; *di-dzheis*) who present musical programs. It also runs regular programs on fashion, cars, Russian language and its pronunciation, computers, and—with the Ministry of Defense—"military correspondence" as well as a program on the history of Russian rock music. Mayak is owned by VGTRK. Its programs range from analytical to musical and include surveys of the press, programs on the history of rock music, and financial-economic programs. On Mayak, the popular crime fiction writer Daria Dontsova presents a program on literature, and the musical program with Artur Makariev enjoys popularity thanks to his vast music collection from the 1940s to the 1990s.

Some radio stations address specific target groups: Avtoradio (Autoradio) is for drivers, with updates on the traffic situation in the capital. Now transmitting for ten years, the station is one of the most popular for the increasing number of drivers trying to navigate through Moscow. Sport FM is for sports fans; Nadezhda is a station that deals specifically with women's issues; and there are several radio stations that serve the orthodox church.

Music Radio   The interest in Western pop music was massive once the recordings (vinyls, tapes, and later CDs) of Western bands became available in the Soviet Union. Most radio stations played Western rock and pop, and new channels were established to cater especially for the younger audience who wanted to listen only to Western music. Such stations mushroomed in the mid-1990s, when around 25 new private stations were launched. Among the most popular musical stations are Serebrianyi dozhd (Silver Rain, 1995), which is also available online, offering music and news but also programs on sport, fashion, stolen cars, and specials with famous guests; Radio Chanson, a music channel that plays mainly retro music; Radio Maximum, which broadcasts music and shows; Otkrytoye Radio (Open Radio); Radio Dinamit (Dynamite); and Radio Nostalgie.

Russkoye Radio (Russian Radio) was established in August 1995 to counterbalance the inundation of Russian radio with foreign music. Its remit, or charter, is to play only Russian music. With its slogan "Russian Radio—all will be well," it is rather apolitical, although the emphasis on domestic tunes reveals a certain national pride.

It is curious that the two leading radio stations for surveys in 2003 should be the two Russian channels, the state-owned Radio Rossii and the musical channel Russkoye Radio, which plays only Russian music. Clearly this trend reflects a reaction against the Americanization of Russian culture, also aired in the electoral campaigns of the popular politicians Zhirinovsky and Ziuganov, who held majorities in the parliament (Duma) elected in 1995 and 1999. Radio Rossii and Russkoye Radio are closely followed by Radio Mayak and Europa Plus. Foreign radio stations, including Radio Liberty, rank very low on the list of the most-listened-to stations. It is clear that they cater for an educated minority and the former dissident intelligentsia.

Although the number of radio stations has clearly multiplied in the New Russia, the radio is a far less important medium than television. Most stations focus on music and news, but other reporting is mostly left to television, and print media rank last. In terms of ownership, the control of radio stations is an important issue, but not such a decisive one as with television. GazProm controls Sport FM, Ekho, and Troika; the Russian Media Group controls Russkoye Radio and Dinamit; ProfMedia oversees Avtoradio. Russkoye Radio has recently launched a project with the television channel ORT to boost its commercial viability: together they ran the competition, the Golden Gramophone (Zolotoi gramofon), for the best popular song and edited a CD collection of the competitors for the award.

Internet

The Internet is growing in importance in the New Russia. Access to the World Wide Web is significantly lower in Russia than in any other European country or the United States, however: by 2002 merely 6 percent of the population had access to the Internet. The issue has been dealt with on a parliamentary level, and the state duma adopted a project called "electronic Russia" in July 2001 that is designed to raise the level of Internet access.

Since the mid-1990s, the Internet has been available in Russia, but access is restricted because of the low number of personal computers. At the same time the availability of the Web for design initiatives was open to anyone, since the software was available cheaply and widely, nonlicensed. The first Russian sites on the World Wide Web were an evening news edition (ok.ru), followed by zhurnal.ru, which was launched in 1996. Soon thereafter came Russian search engines, such as Rambler (rambler.ru), which began with ratings, followed by Internet service providers, such as cityline and relkom. Anton Nosik, a consultant at MediaMost, developed Rambler but later also advised on such online newspapers as gazeta.ru, lenta.ru, and vesti.ru.

Surprisingly maybe for the foreign observer, but explicable in the light of the eagerness of Russians to read, text libraries proved a very important and popular aspect of the Russian net. Such sites as lib.ru, rema.ru, and litera.ru were set up from 1994 onward by Maxim Moshkov and provided access to literature. Authors would even send their new works to Moshkov for online publication.

Some other popular, quirky sites on the Russian virtual space were the flash animation cartoons of the Petersburg designer Oleg Kuvayev on the site mult.ru, where he created the Masiania cartoons. Masiania, dressed in her short skirt and T-shirt in the colors of the Russian flag, with her squeaky voice and complete lack of manners, became a superstar of animation. Another strange site was kogot.ru (*kogot* is a claw), which released compromising material. In 1998 it published a list of the telephone numbers of the political elite; later a recorded telephone conversation between Boris Berezovsky and Tatiana Diachenko (Yeltsin's daughter and aide) appeared here, but those were isolated incidents.

The need for Internet service providers (ISPs) soon acquired the potential of commercial business and attracted foreign investment. The U.S.-owned Golden Telecom acquired glasnet, one of oldest ISPs in Russia, and turned it into "rol" (russia-on-line, as equivalent to "aol" for America-on-line); they also purchased Agama and the search engine aport.ru. In terms of providers for search facilities and mail, mail.ru is a major player, whereas Rambler remains the most frequently used search engine, rating device, and dictionary; it also owns 70 percent of lenta.ru. The group ru-net owns the online bookshop ozon.ru, the search engine and mail provider Yandex (yandex.ru), and the popular sites of narod.ru. The absence of an extensive credit card system puts limits onto e-trade, however.

Many media are available online, especially radio stations and print media. Television channels largely offer program information online, with the exception of RTR and NTV, who also run news information online. Newspapers almost all have Internet versions, and the literary journals are grouped in a site called Reading Room (Chitalnyi zal). A number of newspapers exist only online, such as lenta.ru, gazeta.ru, strana.ru, and utro.ru. They were under huge demand in the weeks after the fire at the Ostankino television tower in September 2000, when aerial television transmission was interrupted for about a month in the aftermath of the disaster. According to Rambler, *Komsomolskaya pravda*, *Izvestiya*, and *Nezavisimaya gazeta* are among the top 100 Russian sites and thus the most popular newspapers accessed online. The site smi.ru reports news on the Russian media, and strana.ru specializes on Russian news. The encyclopedias of Cyril and Methodius, available on compact disc–read-only memory (CD-ROM) and online at km.ru, are frequently consulted.

It is astonishing to find some of the top web design studios in Russia. Artemy Lebedev's studio is one example of highly sophisticated, interactive, and innovative use of the Internet with sites such as www. metro.ru that recreates the Moscow underground network on the web and provides a whole host of archival information and related documents.

The Print Media

Newspapers

Soviet papers: Pravda and Company

Under the Soviet system the print media were rigidly controlled. They were owned by either state, party, or a trade union organization, and the chief editors were responsible for the ideological content of their papers while also working under the supervision of a censor, usually one of the in-house editors. The Soviet system was hypersensitive to any inappropriate allusion, any hinted criticism that might occur in print. One example of the pettiness of the control system is the incident over Boris Pasternak's obituary. Although Pasternak was awarded the Nobel Prize for Literature in 1958 for *Doctor Zhivago*, which had been published in Italy and rejected for publication in the Soviet Union, he was forced to decline the award. He had become persona non grata. When he died a few years later, *Literaturnaya gazeta* (Literary Gazette) carried an obituary. This was placed—not on the front page, but a few pages into the paper—next to an article entitled "A Great Poet," which was not concerned with Pasternak at all. The layout might have suggested, however, that the "great poet" of the article's headline re-

ferred to Pasternak. The editor in charge was fired immediately. Subsequently, journalists and section editors knew what was acceptable and exercised self-censorship, keeping within the permissible to avoid trouble.

Newspapers were a very important medium for the delivery of official speeches. Soviet newspapers tended to print verbatim the full speeches of the party leaders, adding little comment; their tone was a mixture of official jargon and Soviet "news-speak." The most important newspaper in the country was *Pravda* (Truth), established in 1912 to voice Lenin's cause. The official organ of the Communist Party, it had by far the highest print run of all newspapers, reaching ten million by the time Gorbachev came to office. *Pravda* was followed in importance by *Izvestiya* (News), the organ of the Supreme Soviet of the Council of Ministers (the highest body of the state apparatus), founded in 1917. *Izvestiya* had a print run of about seven million at the beginning of the Gorbachev era. During perestroika, *Komsomolskaya pravda* (Komsomol's Truth), the organ of the youth organization (komsomol), and the trade unions' paper *Trud* (Work) became increasingly popular and reached print runs of 13 and 16 million respectively, thus towering even above *Pravda*. The coverage in these papers was more or less the same, but what is interesting to note here is the readership's trend away from the official organs of state and party to those media published by other organizations, albeit also state or party controlled. These national papers were complemented by a host of local papers. For Moscow, these were *Vecherniaya Moskva* (Evening Moscow), *Moskovskaya pravda* (Moscow Truth), and *Moskovskii komsomolets*

(Moscow's Komsomol). In addition to the daily papers a few weeklies appeared, such as the paper *Sovetskaya Rossiya* (Soviet Russia), founded in 1956 with a remit to de-Stalinize the media sphere. The weekly papers *Argumenty i fakty* (Arguments and Facts), which started in 1978, and the foreign-language paper *Moskovskiye novosti* (Moscow News), which launched a Russian edition in 1980, were the youngest papers and therefore predestined to take on an innovative and challenging role in the new Gorbachev era.

Alongside the largely daily newspapers, the Soviet media market also produced specialized papers. So, for example, *Literaturnaya gazeta* is the organ of the Writers' Union and covers literary matters. It traces its origins back to the great Russian poet of the nineteenth century, Alexander Pushkin, a detail in which the paper takes pride and which it uses to legitimize itself (the profile of Pushkin appears on the front page as a logo). The weekly *Sovetskaya kultura* (Soviet Culture) dealt with cultural matters. The satirical weekly (or thrice-monthly) paper *Krokodil* (Crocodile) was very popular, but under the guise of satire it promulgated the official view through exposure of ideologically flawed social trends.

Gorbachev and the Newspapers

When Gorbachev became general secretary, the media landscape looked rather dull. There were several rather thin (four–six page) newspapers, some unexciting literary magazines, and a few political journals. There were no glossy magazines, leisure and entertainment magazines, youth magazines, or fashion journals. The production of papers reached more than 215 million printed items per year, however. Unfortunately, most papers were printed on low-quality paper using out-of-date printing presses. Nevertheless—despite the restrictions due to lack of printing equipment, state-owned printing presses, and paper that resembled more a slice of a tree than a sheet of paper—by 1988 newspaper production had increased by 23 million. The principles of openness (*glasnost*) and timeliness (*operativnost*) advocated by Gorbachev were also working for the print media. Nevertheless, photocopiers remained guarded and locked behind steel doors for the time being.

Although the newspapers continued to publish and distribute official speeches, the weeklies *Argumenty i fakty* (AiF) and *Moscow News* carried longer, more inquisitive articles. The journal *Ogonyok* started to investigate, expose, and criticize just as much as its colleagues on television were doing. *Ogonyok*'s editor in chief, Vitali Korotich, became, like his counterpart at *Moscow News*, Yegor Yakovlev, an emblematic figure of liberal journalism. The paper covered previously taboo subjects, such as Stalinist repression, economic mismanagement, corruption, alcoholism, drugs, prostitution, and the Afghan war. All these weekly editions were later graced with the gratitude of the readers and remain to date among the most popular print media in Russia. The daily paper *Komsomolskaya pravda* began its course of investigative journalism, for which it would gain fame and readers (but also pay a price—the murder of Dmitri Kholodov in 1994 being one example), in the mid-1990s. The daily *Pravda* took a rather conservative view of the proposed reforms, but *Izvestiya* adopted a more liberal stance and supported the reforms. Again, both editions have paid their price: *Pravda* is reduced to a very low print run and mainly reaches its audience through its online news site, whereas *Izvestiya* is still relatively popular in the twenty-first century.

Access to foreign print media (along with the end of the jamming of foreign radio stations and the gradual availability of foreign television) also contributed to a more informed picture, which the media were able to present in the Gorbachev period. The print runs rose steadily as interest in politics and history grew, but no new titles appeared until the new Press Law in 1990. The media contributed to glasnost, with critical voices offset by more conservative ones, echoing the debate that went on within the country and within the Soviet leadership. On 13 March 1987, *Sovetskaya Rossiya* published a letter by Leningrad lecturer Nina Andreyeva, in which she criticized the media's obsession with exposure and attack. The paper deployed the ancient device of using a letter to the editor to disguise the paper's (and supposedly the party's) view on a certain matter and launch a vitriolic attack on glasnost and the revisionist view of Soviet history, echoing and reinforcing the hard-line position of Yegor Ligachev. This practice was common in the 1960s and 1970s when criticism of controversial plays, theater productions, or films would not take the form of an editorial but would frequently be attributed to letters from readers. The voice of the people, as it were, was used to condemn or criticize, replacing the censor's intervention. The device also served as make-believe that the people had power over ideological issues.

In the late 1980s, the landscape of the press changed: a different style of journalism emerged, dwelling on the exposure of historical facts and documents, offering coverage of controversial events, and featuring rock musicians and stars of the new youth culture. This extended not only to the Russian media but also to *samizdat* papers, tackling issues of ecology, human rights, and so on, that were circulated openly. In terms of the political spectrum, papers veered between the old Communist views (*Pravda*, *Sovetskaya Rossiya*), the more democratic positions (*Komsomolskaya pravda*, *Izvestiya*, *Moskovskii komsomolets*), and the new political forces (*Nezavisimaya gazeta*, *Kommersant*). The foreign press featured a range of material on the Soviet Union and its culture, making the first Soviet "sex" star, Natalia Negoda, a cover girl for *Playboy* in 1989. Negoda had played the main part in Vasili Pichul's film *Little Vera* (Malen'kaia Vera, 1988), which exposed the dullness and lack of meaning in the life of the younger Soviet generation, showing them at a forbidden rock concert, in illegal possession of hard currency, and—the greatest taboo of all—in bed. Beauty competitions, fashion journals, and the much-sought-after editions of Burda's sewing patterns were waiting just around the corner.

In 1989 the journalist Artyom Borovik and the writer Yulian Semyonov, author of the Stirlitz spy thrillers, started the paper *Sovershenno sekretno* (Top Secret), in which they published archival material designed to disclose matters that were previously hidden or obscured. The figure of Semyonov, not only a best-selling author but also one with well-known insider information from the KGB, infused the enterprise with a sense of trustworthiness. On 40 pages the monthly paper covered secrets of the economy, the special services, business, sport, history, and the stage as well as lines of investigation. Apart from *Sover-*

shenno sekretno, the company formed by Borovik later launched a monthly journal, *Litsa* (Faces), in 1996 and a weekly paper, *Versiya* (Version), in 1998. The latter stressed the "male" sides of business and pleasure.

The new Press Law of 1990 required the print media to register while also allowing for financial restructuring; it established the rights and responsibilities of journalists as well as those of the readers to refute inaccurate reports. Censorship ceased, although there have been incidents of articles being blanked out after Yeltsin reintroduced censorship after the October coup in 1993.

The ownership of newspapers had passed to the Russian government after the August coup of 1991. Increases in the cost of paper, growing inflation, the drop in subscriptions, and the reliance on state subsidy, however, led the print media to the brink of bankruptcy. Although the subscription rates for 1992 had been raised, the increase in postage, paper price, and printing was much higher than anticipated. In this new economic system the media still relied on the state for support while failing to take the opportunity to raise prices or resort to advertising. At the same time the papers insisted on their wish to be independent. The government satisfied the demand for support and offered loans in February 1992, issuing a decree that forced paper factories to sell paper at fixed rates to newspapers. In the course of this crisis, *Pravda* ceased to appear for three weeks, resuming publication three times a week rather than daily. The completely outmoded polygraphic conditions represented a massive problem. Most journals wanting to use color were printed abroad, at great cost, to achieve the desired quality. In 1997,

Distribution of the nationalist paper *Zavtra* (Tomorrow) in Moscow in 2004. (Steve Raymer/Corbis)

56 percent of journals and almost 20 percent of papers were still printed abroad, especially in Finland. While this remains true for many glossy journals, numerous publications are now printed in Moscow presses. Neither the Russian state nor the media moguls have invested in substantially improving the printing conditions in Russia.

The 1990s saw a proliferation of new titles, including papers of marginal social and political groups, such as the paper of the homeless in Petersburg, *Na Dne* (Lower Depths), the writer Eduard Limonov's paper *Limonovka*, and the ultranationalist paper *Den* (The Day), edited by writer Alexander Prokhanov and later published under the title *Zavtra* (Tomorrow).

The list could continue with ecological, agrarian, or religious publications. Women's magazines such as *Natalie* and *Moskvichka* (The Muscovite) addressed the changed role of women; children's and teenage journals proliferated, catering for a new generation of teenagers. Although the number of newspapers increased, the number of journals doubled, and the print runs slumped.

Newspapers in the New Russia   In 1993, in the aftermath of the paper, price, and subsidy crisis of the national press, the first new independent papers appeared on the market. Gusinsky's Most Group launched the liberal *Segodnia* (Today), anticipating the name of NTV's evening news program. *Nezavisimaya gazeta* (Independent Gazette) started as an independent, 12-page newspaper, later with various supplements. The media tycoons ventured into the world of the printed press before expanding their empires into television and radio, although the print market ranked last in surveys about sources of information (after television and radio).

Nezavisimaya gazeta was founded on 21 December 1990 under the editor Vitali Tretiakov. The paper was genuinely independent, appearing three times a week, and later daily. It was a prestigious paper, read by the intelligentsia, and many journalists who had to work elsewhere for a living considered it an honor to publish in *Nezavisimaya*. In 1992, during the paper crisis, Tretiakov refused to seek state support, as most other papers did. In the aftermath of that crisis, a team of journalists under Dmitri Ostalsky split off and founded the paper *Segodnia* in 1993. In May 1995 *Nezavisimaya* was effectively bankrupt; resources and donations had been used up and faded in a growing capitalist market,

and the paper ceased to appear. It resumed only after a deal with Berezovsky had been struck, in the autumn of 1995. In its second life, the paper expanded with a number of special and regional supplements (for example, Ex Libris), and established the Anti-Booker Prize. *Nezavisimaya* remains an important, if no longer independent, newspaper.

In Putin's Russia the most popular paper is *Moskovskii komsomolets*, an eight-page tabloid offering sensational stories about corruption and scandalous exposure, with sexually appealing images, slang language, and cartoon-like stories in abundance. Its print run is more than two million, whereas all other dailies run below half a million. The paper *Trud*, with its six pages of coverage of current affairs, and the six-page *Moskovskaya pravda*, covering society life as well as current affairs, have print runs of a quarter to half a million, just like the Moscow evening paper *Vecherniaya Moskva*. Several new titles have gained huge popularity with the readers: the Russian Federation's official organ, *Rossiiskaya gazeta* (Russian Gazette), with eight pages of coverage on politics, events, and the law was founded in 1990. The 24-page *Kommersant* of the publishing group Kommersant, covering politics, economics, culture, and sports, was the first paper to have leads for each article. *Novye Izvestiya* (New Izvestiya), with eight pages of news about current affairs, split off from the liberal *Izvestiya*. LukOil, which held 20 percent of the shares in *Izvestiya*, had never meddled in editorial politics. In April 1997 *Izvestiya*'s editor Igor Golembiovsky was forced to change his editorial politics vis-à-vis the prime minister Viktor Chernomyrdin. When the editor refused to do so, LukOil gained 41 percent of the shares

Moscow Mayor Yuri Luzhkov attended the "Slava" award ceremony. The second ceremony of the national sports award took place in the Moscow International Music House in May 2004. (Photo by DmitryAzarov/Kommersant)

and pushed Golembiovsky out. Vladimir Potanin's Oneksimbank later bought the controlling stake in the newspaper. Golembiovsky set up a new paper, *Novye Izvestiya*, financed by Berezovsky and published in color. The paper was discontinued for three months in 2003 before it was revived under a new editor, Valeri Yakov. After the campaign against the media tycoons, or oligarchs, Boris Berezovsky and Vladimir Gusinsky, the future of *Nezavisimaya gazeta* became uncertain and its readership declined; *Segodnia* was closed in April 2001. At the same time, Oleg Poptsov, who had organized the television channel RTR, having been dismissed from his post there, set up the publishing outfit Pushkin Square (Pushkinskaya Ploshchad), which published a number of dailies

and weeklies, most prominently the daily newspaper *Versty* (Versts).

The weeklies *Argumenty i fakty* (26 pages) and *Sovershenno sekretno* have maintained print runs of more than two million. The tabloids *Spid-Info* (AIDS-Info, or SPEED-Info) and *Megapolis Ekspress*, which represent a new type of newspaper with gossip columns about stars and fashion, belong to the yellow press. Like any other European megalopolis, Moscow also has a paper called *Metro*, distributed free of charge on the subway. A new feature on the print market is the advertising papers for secondhand purchases, apartment exchange, and other services, such as *Vse dlia vas* (Everything for You), launched in 1991 in Moscow and then in other cities, and *Iz ruk v ruki* (From Hand to Hand, 1992). *Tsentr Plius* (Center Plus, 1992) and *Extra M* are free papers with print runs of more than three million copies, as is the weekly *Metro*, which was acquired in 2003 by Boris Jordan's media empire.

Regional papers remain popular and are mostly acquired by subscription at the local level. The central papers are purchased, both in the cities and the regions, and the subscription has dropped rapidly as increased postal charges have devolved onto the subscriber. In the light of this development, many central papers have expanded and launched regional editions of their papers or regional supplements to the central editions.

The print media in Russia today offer a great number of products that are wanted by the readers, and these tend to be tabloids, glossy magazines, and celebrity gossip around television programs. In this sense, the Russian media market has responded to customer demand and adjusted prices and print runs to the new market.

What is lacking are newspapers of the size, complexity, and acumen of the *Guardian* or the *Times*, the *Herald Tribune* or the *New York Times*. *Kommersant* had that potential, but its print run has dropped sharply.

The once-so-popular Russian edition of *Moscow News* was taken over by the Yukos-supported fund Open Russia, and the new owners brought in Yevgeni Kiselyov as editor in chief in September 2003. Apart from the foreign-language editions of *Moscow News*, a number of foreign papers are published in Moscow and Petersburg, including the English-language editions of the *Moscow Times* and the *Petersburg Times*. The latter two were begun by Derk Sauer, a Dutch entrepreneur and head of Independent Media, who later ventured further into the Russian market with Russian editions of *Cosmopolitan*, *Playboy*, *OM*, *Marie Claire*, and *Harper's Bazaar*. The 21-year-old Shakhri Amirkhanova was appointed as editor in chief of *Harper's Bazaar*. Andrew Paulson joined forces with Boris Jordan, a U.S.-born financial consultant of Russian extraction, who is also associated with GazProm Media. They publish the entertainment guide *Afisha* (Billboard) and the free paper *Bolshoi gorod* (Big City). Another partnership exists between *Vedomosti* (Information), launched in 1999 by Independent Media in collaboration with the *Wall Street Journal* and the *Financial Times*, as well as the *Izvestiya* supplement *Finansovye izvestiya* (Financial News), with *Financial Times*. In 2004 the UK-based entertainment guide *Time Out* launched Russian editions in St. Petersburg and Moscow.

The leaders among newspapers are the weekly *AiF*, the tabloid *Komsomolskaya pravda*, the daily quality paper *Izvestiya*, the tabloid *SPEED Info*, and the daily *Trud*, now with a weekend edition to boost sales. This is well reflected in their annual advertising turnover: for 1997 this was 10 million dollars for *Komsomolskaya pravda*, 9 million for *AiF*, and 600,000 dollars for *Trud*.

Journals

Next to the papers stood the journals, and we need here to distinguish between the journal as we understand it in the West (a "glossy" journal) and the literary journals ("thick" journals), which publish contemporary literature.

From Soviet to Russian Although there were a few journals on the Soviet market dealing with women's issues (*Rabotnitsa* [The Woman Worker] and *Krestianka* [The Peasant Woman]), they typified women according to their social status as worker or farmer. There was also a very popular health journal, *Zdorovie* (Health), since the 1950s. The analytical journal *Ogonyok* (Little Flame) had been going since the last century. It carried larger features on culture, sport, and social and political comments. None of these journals contained "glossy" pictures (color photos on good-quality paper), horoscopes, fashion or beauty advice; they featured hardly any advertising as we understand it today; instead, they would print "product guides" explaining the use of new goods or the content and value of new food products. There were also a number of highly specialized journals, such as the film magazine *Sovetskii Ekran* (Soviet Screen), the theater journal *Teatralnaya zhizn* (Theater Life), the musical journal *Muzykalnaya zhizn* (Musical Life), the ballet journal *Sovetskii balet* (Soviet Ballet), and *Sovetskii tsirk* (Soviet Circus). Quite a few of these were also published—on better-quality paper—in foreign

Printed Press: Central Publications

Paper	Est.	Print Run[a]	Proprietor/Shareholder[b]
Dailies			
Pravda (3/7 days)	1912	100,300	ANO Pravda, CPRF
Izvestiya	1917	234,000	OAO Izvestiya
Moskovskaya pravda	1918	244,000	ZAO Mosk.Pravda
Moskovskii komsomolets	1919	2,225,458	Editorial Staff Mosk.Koms.
Trud	1921	612,850	ANO Trud
Vecherniaya Moskva	1923	300,000	ZAO Vech.Moskva
Komsomolskaya pravda	1925	754,800	ZAO Koms.Pravda
Rossiiskaya gazeta	1990	309,550	Russian Federation Government
Kommersant daily	1990	105,278	Kommersant
Nezavisimaya gazeta	1990	48,147	ZAO Nez.Gaz
Segodnia	1993–2001	57,000	OOO Segodnia
Novye Izvestiya	1997	42,169	ZAO Novye Izv.
Vremia MN	1998	54,000	Media Finance
Versty (3/7 days)	1998	60,000	OAO Pushkin Square
Vedomosti	1999	47,000	Independent Media
Gazeta	2001–4	61,300	Charity Fund
Vremia Novostei	2000	51,000	Vremia
Stolichnaya	2003–4	65,000	OOO Stolichnaya
Weeklies			
Literaturnaya gazeta	1830	83,000	OAO Lit.Gaz
Moskovskiye novosti	1930	63,700	Mosk.Novosti
Literaturnaya Rossiya	1958	24,000	ANO Lit.Ross
Argumenty i fakty	1978	2,964,000	Collective of Journalists
Sobesednik	1984	252,000	Collective of Journalists
Rossiiskiye vesti	1990	50,000	Culture Fond., Film Union, V. Kucher, Dept. of RF President
Megapolis Ekspress	1990	700,000	ZAO Megapolis
Vechernii klub	1991	30,000	OOO Vech.Klub
Zavtra	1991	100,000	A. Khudorozhkov
Obshchaya gazeta	1991	203,442	Yegor Yakovlev
SPEED-Info (bi-monthly)	1989/92	2,863,000	OOO Speed
Novaya gazeta (twice weekly)	1993	138,280	ANO Novaya Gaz.
Versiya: Sovershenno. sekretno	1998	97,550	ZAO MAPT -Media
Iz ruk v ruki	1998	85,000	Pronto
Konservator	2002-3	54,800	Leibman Media Group
Metro	2001	1,000,000	AO Metro, Moscow Gov.
Metro St. Petersburg	1999	400,000	Tri Korony

Journal	Est.	Print Run[a]	Proprietor/Investor[b]
Weeklies			
Ogonyok	1899	50,000	OOO OVA- Press
Sovershenno sekretno	1989	301,800	ZAO Sovershenno sekretno
Vlast – Kommersant	1993	56,532	Kommersant
Novoye Vremya	1993	25,000	OOO Editorial Staff
Dengi – Kommersant	1994	81,102	Kommersant
TV Park	1994	389,000	ZAO Media Park
Ekspert	1995	78,500	ZAO Expert (ProfMedia)
Itogi	1996	85,000	7 Dnei
Sem dnei	1996	895,000	7 Dnei
Profil	1996	75,000	Publ. Rodionova
Otdokhni	1998	580,000	Burda
Zhurnal	2001	71,200	OOO Ostrov
Russkii Fokus	2001	31,900	Infomaker
Monthlies			
Rabotnitsa	1914	160,000	Editorial staff
Krestianka	1922	81,190	ZAO Krestianka
Zdoroviye	1955	195,000	ZAO Zdorovie
Andrei	1991	50,000	Andrei (Veitsler)
Moscow Times	1992	35,000	Independent Media
Domovoi	1993	104,500	ZAO 108
Cosmopolitan	1994	420,000	Independent Media
Ptiuch	1994–2000	110,000	ZAO Gertruda
Krasota (6/12)	1995	30,000	Mikhailova
Elle	1995	180,000	Hachette
Playboy	1995	105,000	Burda
OM	1995	70,000	Independent Media
Harper's Bazaar	1996	65,000	Independent Media
Medved	1996	74,500	OOO Medved
Persona (9/12)	1996	10,000	Novy Arbat
Litsa	1996	50,000	ZAO/Borovik
St. Petersburg Times	1996	20,000	Independent Media
Marie Claire	1997	90,000	Independent Media
Ona/She	1997	150,000	Aprel
Men's Health	1997	135,000	Independent Media
Karavan (istorii)	1998	319,000	7 Dnei
Vogue	1998	150,000	Conde Nast
L'Officiel	1999	50,000	Glossy
Oops!	2001	250,000	Burda

Notes: [a]Print run as of 2003. [b]AO = Aktsionernoe obshchestvo (shareholding company); ANO = Avtonomnaia nekommercheskaia organizatsiia (autonomous, noncommercial organization); CPRF = Communist Party of the Russian Federation; OOO = Obshchestvo s ogranichennoi otvetstvennost'iu (company with limited liability); ZAO/OAO (zakrytoe/otkrytoe aktsionernoe obshchestvo) = closed or open shareholding company.

languages for libraries and subscribers abroad while also serving as publicity material. In a sense, all these journals testified to the high level of education and the sophisticated cultural tastes of the Soviet citizen. None of the popular culture that just entertained the Soviet people formed part of the official cultural discourse.

Numerous new journals have emerged on the map in post-Soviet Russia. The current affairs journal *Ogonyok* (62 pages) changed its image in 1995 for a style more like *Time* magazine or *Newsweek*, offering less text and more images and covering lighter topics. Although the journal lost its heavy liberal political and moral angle, it remains a popular edition alongside the new journals *Vlast* (Control), *Expert, Itogi* (Conclusions), which has 64 pages and was initially launched with *Newsweek* (until 2001), as well as *Profil* (Profile, 104 pages). The best-sellers among weekly journals are, however, the television programs with some society gossip offered by *Sem dnei* (Seven Days) and *TV Park*, as well as the leisure magazine *Otdokhni* (Relax), published by the German publishing house Burda; the women's journal *Liza;* the society journal *Gala;* and *Avtomir* (Car World). All others journals remain under 100,000— a huge drop when compared to *Ogonyok*'s print run for 1989 of more than three million. The interest in politics has evidently shrunk, whereas the hunger for leisure and entertainment has increased, filling a gap in the cultural sector but also signaling a certain level of political lethargy.

Glossy Magazines   This tendency goes hand in hand with the rise of the "glossy" (*gliantsevye*) journals, both of general interest and for men or women. Again, the rise in these publications can partly be ex-plained by a complete absence of men's and women's magazines in the Soviet period. The first journal of this category to be launched was the men's magazine *Andrei* in 1991—a timid equivalent of *Playboy*. The Russian edition of *Playboy* itself hit the market in 1995, together with a variety of other journals owned by the global media corporations, such as *Cosmopolitan, Elle, Harper's Bazaar, Marie Claire, L'Officiel,* and—last but not least—*Vogue,* all of which entered the Russian market between 1995 and 2000. These women's magazines clearly aim at the upper middle classes, with features on fashion, lifestyle, culture, and beauty rather than the more traditional family, children, kitchen themes. They mirror a world that is utopian for the average citizen.

They were complemented by a range of home-grown journals, such as the youth magazine *Ptiuch*, which folded in 2000 after the offices were raided by the police. The men's journal *Medved* (Bear), edited by Igor Maltsev and based on a concept by the TV presenter Vlad Listiev, covers men's issues and hunting. It includes no pornography, but restores the macho image suppressed in Soviet times, returning to pre-Revolutionary images of men (hunting). *OM* (edited by Igor Grigoriev), *Men's Health*, and *MaKhaOn* are men's journals that stress male potency and do not always refrain from nude images. They build the image of the superman and reassure men of their (sexual) power. The women's magazines *Krasota* (Beauty), *Rabotnitsa* (Working Woman), and *Krestianka* (The Peasant Woman) cover fashion and cooking. *Liza* is more for the domestic woman, offering advice on manners, holiday resorts, and plants and is part of a range of publications by Burda, all aimed at domes-

Vlad Listiev, the first director of ORT television, with the prizes for the game show *Pole chudes*, which he presented in the early 1990s. (Photo by Kommersant Archive)

tic issues and youngsters: *Otdokhni* (Relax); *Moi rebyonok* (My Child); *Burda DIY*, *Cool Girl*, and *Oops!*

The general interest journals are *Domovoi* (House Spirit) and *Karavan istorii* (Caravan of History). Alongside these general interest journals is a host of specialist journals on computer issues, motorist interests, and others. These glossy magazines are quite expensive for the ordinary Russian, who is used to paying kopecks for printed matter, be it a newspaper, a journal, or a book. But all of the above-mentioned journals achieve print runs of 100,000 and more and are thus clearly in great demand.

Entertainment guides might seem to be not even worth mentioning, were it not for the fact that they too were a "deficit" (a product in high demand and low supply) of the Soviet media market. In the Soviet times there was one entertainment guide, the newspaper *Dosug v Moskve* (Leisure in

Moscow), which had such a low print run that it was sold out by 8 AM on Saturdays. In the mid-1990s when the media market expanded, there was a variety of attempts to launch a journal-size entertainment guide, until eventually in 1998 the journal *Afisha* (Billboard) was launched. It has risen to an extremely comprehensive, reliable, and valued guide to Moscow's day- and nightlife. *Afisha* also publishes book editions of its information on restaurants, films, and Moscow life as well as city guides. At two dollars it is more expensive than the old *Dosug*—but, unlike it, is available for several hours, and even days, after its publication.

The cultural sector is well served with a number of low-print-run editions, such as the weekly papers *Kultura* (Culture, the former *Sovetskaya Kultura*) and *Ekran i stsena* (Screen and Stage). The monthly film journal *Premiere* was launched in 1997 and edited by the film critic Alexander Kulish, until it was placed under new management in February 2004, restricting its scope to international releases covered largely by translated articles from the U.S. edition of the journal. There is also a Russian-grown counterpart, publishing Russian critics, called *KinoPark*. The journal *Teatr* (Theater) folded in 1994 and was relaunched in 2000 with substantial support from the state; during the interim the matters were covered by *Moskovskii nabliudatel* (Moscow Observer), which had started in 1991 and folded in 1998. *Teatralnaya zhizn* (Theatrical Life), a bimonthly, covered the theater experiments under Gorbachev extremely well, with four editions per year run by a "youth" editorial board composed of students from the Theater Institute. By 1992, *Teatralnaya zhizn* was forced to reduce the number of issues to 12 per year, and since 1996 the journal has often published editions sponsored (bought) by a theater or an actor for promotion purposes. The *Petersburg Theater Journal* (Peterburgskii teatralnyi zhurnal) has been running since 1992. The journal is unique in offering reviews not only on theater life in St. Petersburg but also on provincial theaters. The journal *Sovremennaya dramaturgiya* (Contemporary Drama) was complemented by *Dramaturg* (1993–1997), which also published plays and drama criticism, and *Kinostsenarii* (Film Scripts) carries film scripts and film criticism. Many new plays are now available online.

The post-Soviet journals thus cover a breadth of issues, and although a few editions are part of international publishing networks, there are still a few indigenous Russian editions, in particular the specialized cultural journals, many of which are supported by the Ministry of Culture. The print media landscape overall has changed, though, in the last decade. If in 1990 there were 43 publications with an average print run of 2.5 million, then in 2000 we had 333 publications with an average print run of 117,000. This shows on the one hand the democratization of the print media, which are able to offer a broader variety of editions and titles to the consumer. On the other hand, the overall figure of readers is clearly down by more than half and represents a lower per-head consumption of print media than in the United States or Western Europe.

The "Thick" Journals   The literary journals gave even more evidence of the highbrow tastes of the Soviet readership. The so-called thick journals such as *Novyi Mir* (New World), *Druzhba narodov* (Na-

tions' Friendship), *Znamia* (Banner), *Yunost* (Youth), *Oktiabr* (October), *Moskva* (Moscow), *Molodaya gvardiya* (Young Guard), and *Nash sovremennik* (Our Contemporary) as well as *Neva* and *Avrora* (Aurora) in Leningrad and other regional journals published new writing. These journals were always in demand, from libraries as well as from individuals. The "thick" journals were the main, and first, outlet for contemporary prose and poetry. Plays were published more rarely, a fact that was remedied in 1982 with the new journal *Sovremennaya dramaturgiya*. During the 1960s the editors of the literary journals fought many battles with the party's censors over permission to publish pieces by Mikhail Bulgakov, Solzhenitsyn, or some other dissident writer. Sometimes they could slip a work past the censors; sometimes they could obtain permission from the top leadership (Khrushchev personally allowed the publication of Solzhenitsyn's novel about the senselessness and brutality of life in the prison camp, *A Day in the Life of Ivan Denisovich*, in 1962). On other occasions they would be stopped in their efforts. Some journals tried harder than others; some preferred to stick with the official line. During these years *Novyi Mir* had gained a reputation as a probing and very liberal journal, especially under its editor Alexander Tvardovsky. Alongside the literary journals were journals of literary criticism, philosophy, film criticism, art history, and theater. When Gorbachev called for openness and the Filmmakers' Union began to unshelve banned films, signaling a change in the censorship of art, the editors of literary journals rushed to their desks and authors hurried to their secret drawers to pull out those texts they had been unable to publish earlier. In this

Russian journalist Anna Politkovskaya of the paper *Novaya Gazeta* takes part in the round-table conference summoned to discuss terrorism-related issues. The conference was held in the Central Journalist House, 15 February 2005. (Photo by Dmitry Saltykovsky/ Kommersant)

cessors as editors in chief are tellingly not writers, but literary critics: Sergei Chuprinin and Andrei Vasilevsky. It is no longer significant for a journal to have a prominent person at the wheel to steer the journal through political tempests; it is more important to have a professional with a good grasp of the literary developments and trends. The literary journals' print runs are down substantially from the heyday of the 1980s, however, when they printed previously banned and forbidden texts and had print runs of more than a million. In 2003, they reached 10,000 at most. The "thick" literary journal is faltering in a market where new works are published in book format and publishing houses decide on the publication of already established authors. The literary journals have, however, the important task of discovering new talents.

way, most literary journals supported the cause of glasnost, except for the more conservative *Moskva*, *Nash sovremennik*, and *Molodaya gvardiya*, which veered in a more nationalist direction.

The literary journals have declined hugely both in status and in print run. The major journals that remain on the market are *Znamia* and *Novyi mir*, both competing in a sense over the publication of the Booker Prize winner-to-be. If in the glasnost period these journals were both run by eminent writers, Grigori Baklanov and Sergei Zalygin respectively, then their suc-

A to Z

Abramovich, Roman: b. 1966. Since 2000, governor of the Chukotka Autonomous Region. Since 1992 in the oil business; has made joint deals with Berezovsky since 1995. Since 1996 on the board of directors of Sibneft and holds right for the exploitation of oil and gas resources of Slavneft. He owns shares in ORT. According to Forbes, one of the richest people in the world. He purchased London's Chelsea Football Club in July 2003.

***Argumenty i fakty* (AiF, Arguments and Facts):** Weekly paper that started in 1978 and was very popular under Gorbachev. Commercially successful, it reaches print runs of more than two million. With its subsidiary publications, one of the largest Russian publishing companies. Supplements: AiF Health, Culture, Regions, and others. [www.aif.ru]

Berezovsky, Boris: b. 1946. Founded the automobile company LogoVaz in 1989. Later formed an alliance of automobile producers (Avtomobil'nyi Vserossiiskii Al'ans, All-Russian Automobile Alliance, AVVA). Participated in the launch of ORT in 1995, acquiring a substantial amount of shares in the holding company. In 1996 joined the presidential security council. In 1999 launched Our Radio (Nashe Radio) and in 1999 invested in TV6. Owns shares in the journal *Matador*, the papers *Kommersant* and *Nezavisimaya gazeta*, and the journal *Ogonyok*. Lives in London, having sold his ORT shares to Abramovich. Associated with Rupert Murdoch.

Dorenko, Sergei: b. 1959. Since 1985 with Gosteleradio. From 1990 to 1993 television presenter with the First Channel, then *Vesti* on RTR. Famed for coverage of events in Lithuania. In 1995 had his program *Versii* (Versions) on ORT, which was closed. 1998–1999, producer on ORT, then TV6. November 1999 deputy director of ORT. April 2001 accusation of grievous bodily harm caused to a civil servant following an accident with his motorcycle. Used by Berezovsky to denounce politicians as and when needed to manipulate public opinion. Conviction of four years in prison in November 2001, reduced by appeals court to a fine in 2002.

***Dvenatdsatyi etazh* (Twelfth Floor):** television youth program conceived by Eduard Sagalayev in the youth editor's office on the twelfth floor of the television building;

live coverage with links to remote locations and guests in the studio; exposure of the dullness of life for the young generation, of bureaucratic mismanagement in the provinces.

Echo Moscow (Ekho Moskvy): radio station set up on 22 August 1990; gradually acquired by Media Most (shareholder since 1994, owner since 1998). News, sports, reviews of the press, and programs on the economy. Liberal democratic orientation, often critical reports on political affairs. Director: Alexei Venediktov. [www.echo.ru]

Europa Plus: first commercial musical radio station, founded in April 1990 as a joint venture with France. The station plays largely music, with news. Owned by Oneksimbank and Hachette Media France. [www.europaplus.ru]

Gusinsky, Vladimir: b. 1952; graduated in 1973 from the Institute of Oil Production and in 1981 from the Theater Institute (GITIS). In 1988 set up a financial consulting agency. In 1991 founded Most Bank. In 1992 formed the Most Group and in 1997 established Media Most, which included NTV Holding and the program *Itogi*, Radio Echo Moscow, TNT television, and the publishing group Seven Days (Sem' dnei), which publishes the journal *Itogi*. In 1999 and 2000, Vneshekonombank and GazProm demanded repayments for loans to launch the satellite Bonum 2. In order to repay the debt, Gusinsky tried to sell Most Bank, but the deal was stopped by the state. In June 2000 he was arrested for embezzlement and imprisoned for four days in the Butyrka prison in Moscow, where common criminals are held. He sold shares to GazProm and left for Spain. Further claims by GazProm and other banks led to brief arrests of Gusinsky in Spain and Greece, but each time the case was dropped. In May 2004 the European court decided in favour of Gusinsky and ordered the Russian state to pay him a compensation of 88 million euros for losses to his business.

Itogi **(Conclusions):** weekly magazine with 64 pages, initially launched with *Newsweek* and copublished with it until 2001. [www.itogi.ru] Also the title of NTV's flagship political program, hosted by Yevgeni Kiselyov until 2001.

Izvestiya **(News):** daily newspaper founded in 1917, organ of the Supreme Soviet of the Council of Ministers (the highest body of the state apparatus). Remained one of the most popular papers in the 1990s. Owned by Oneksimbank (Mikhail Potanin). Split in 1997 into *Izvestiya* and *Novye Izvestiya* after a shareholder attempted to force a change in editorial policy. Chief editor: Mikhail Kozhanin. [www.izvestia.ru]

Kiselyov, Yevgeni: b. 1956. Joined television in 1987, leading the news program *Vremia*. From 1990 to 1991 with *Tele Sluzhba Novosti*, then anchored *Vesti* on RTR. In September 1991 returned to ORT with Oleg Dobrodeyev; launched the program *Itogi* in 1992. In 1994 moved to NTV. Created the show *Geroi dnia* (Man of the Day). Director of NTV since 1993 and general director after Dobrodeyev left in February 2000. After the hand-over of shares to GazProm in 2001, Kiselyov joined TV6. After the dissolution of TV6 in 2002, he established TV Spectrum, which was taken off the air in June 2003. Since September 2003, chief editor of *Moskovskiye novosti.*

Kommersant: daily paper of the publishing group Kommersant, launched in 1990 under Berezovsky. Comprehensive, analytical journalism distinguishes the paper, which is one of the most important dailies in Russia. [www.kommersant.ru]

Komsomolskaya pravda **(Komsomol's Truth):** daily newspaper, organ of the youth organization (*komsomol*). Characterized by investigative journalism in the mid-1990s. One of the most popular newspapers in the 1990s. [www.kp.ru]

Listiev, Vlad: b. 1956–murdered 1 March 1995. Presenter of the *Vzgliad* program, television presenter. Head of ORT in 1995. Shows included *Field of Miracles*, *Rush Hour*. Listiev had demanded a moratorium on advertising during the privatization of the First Channel/Ostankino into ORT.

Mayak (Lighthouse): radio station established in 1964 as a 24-hour station. Light music and news, increasing its program variety. Mayak is owned by VGTRK. [www.radiomayak.ru]

Mitkova, Tatiana: b. 1957; television anchor. Worked on central television in the international news section. From 1990 to 1991 presenter of the news program *Tele Sluzhba Novosti*. In 1991 made a program on the church's involvement with the KGB. In January 1991 refused to read the official version of the events in Vilnius. Since 1995 at NTV, where she stayed after the management change in April 2001.

Moskovskiye novosti **(Moscow News):** weekly newspaper established in 1930 by Anna Louise Strong as an English-language paper; closed in 1949 when Strong was expelled from the USSR; relaunched in 1956. Spanish, French, and Arabic editions since the 1960s; Russian edition since 1980. Under chief editor Yegor Yakovlev, a flagship of perestroika and liberal journalism. [www.mn.ru]; English version [www.moscownews.ru]

Moskovskii komsomolets (Moscow's Komsomol): daily newspaper, dating back to the Revolution; an eight-page tabloid offering sensational stories about corruption and scandalous exposure. Print run more than two million.[www.mk.ru]

News Agencies: ITAR-TASS is one of the largest news agencies in the world. [www.tass.ru] Interfax was founded in 1989 as a nonstate news agency, distributing information by fax. RIA Vesti succeeded APN in 1992 and is also state owned. [www.apn.ru]

Nezavisimaya gazeta (Independent Gazette): daily newspaper launched by Vitali Tretiakov in 1990 as independent newspaper. Some journalists left in 1993 after the paper crisis and the refusal to demand state subsidies. Bought by Berezovsky in 1995; since then several supplements, and it awards the Anti-Booker Prize. [www.ng.ru]

Novyi mir (New World): liberal literary journal that was famous in the 1960s for bold editorial decisions under Alexander Tvardovsky. During perestroika, chief editor Sergei Zalygin; in the late 1990s, succeeded by Andrei Vasilevsky. Publication of previously forbidden novels in the late 1980s. [http://magazines.russ.ru/novy_mir/]

NTV: television station that began broadcasting on 10 October 1993. First used airtime on the Petersburg channel. In December 1993 allocated the frequency of the fourth channel, on which it transmitted in the evenings beginning in January 1994 and for the full day from November 1996 on. In January 1998 its frequency could reach all over Russia. GazProm acquired shares through a loan granted for equipment purchase. In 1999–2000, banks and Gazprom demanded repayment of loan granted for expansion of the network and satellite launches. A deal whereby Gazprom would suspend its repayment demands in return for shares fell through. In order to repay the debt, Gusinsky tried to sell Most Bank but was stopped. In May 2000, tax police stormed the offices of NTV and Media Most to search the premises for evidence of tax evasion. A month later, Gusinsky was arrested for embezzlement and imprisoned for four days. He agreed to sell shares to GazProm that would give the company a controlling majority; in exchange GazProm would guarantee Gusinsky free travel and drop charges. Gusinsky left for Spain but was sued there briefly as well. In September 2000 Gazprom filed a suit against Media Most demanding repayment of 473 million dollars, and other banks followed suit with their claims. In April 2001, Gazprom repeated its claims for more shares after prematurely recalling loans from Gusinsky and assumed control over NTV. When Gazprom's representative, Boris Jordan, was appointed new general director of the channel, the old NTV team (Kiselyov and Shenderovich) resigned and moved to TV6. The news anchor Tatiana Mitkova resigned also but was reappointed head of news under the new management. In January 2003 Jordan was replaced by Alexander Dybal of the new holding company GazProm Media. [www.ntv.ru]

Ostankino/ORT: Central Television (First Channel). Main news program *Vremia* since January 1968 on 9 PM slot. Headed by Alexander Aksyonov (January 1986–May 89); Mikhail Nenashev (until autumn 1990); Leonid Kravchenko (until August 1991). From August 1991 to October 1992, headed by Yegor Yakovlev with Eduard Sagalayev and Oleg Dobrodeyev (head of news). Yakovlev was sacked by Yeltsin because of a documentary about the Ossetian-Ingush conflict that exposed the Russian army as siding with the orthodox Ossetians. Viacheslav Bragin held the post until December 1993, when he was dismissed following coverage of the October coup. On 1 April 1995 formation of ORT (Obshestvennoe rossiiskoe televidenie, Public Russian Television), with general director Vlad Listiev (presenter of *Vzgliad* and game shows). Listiev was murdered in March 1995; though the case has never been resolved, it appears that his refusal to allow advertising may have played a role. In September 1995 the channel formed the holding company ORT Reklama, collaborating with Sergei Lisovsky's Premier SV, which sold advertising time on ORT's behalf until 1999. Since September 1999, television presenter Konstantin Ernst has been general director of the channel. ORT was owned by the state (majority of 51 percent of shares), a consortium of banks associated with Berezovsky (38 percent), and LogoVaz (9 percent, plus an additional 3 percent acquired from GazProm in 1996). ORT came under fire in 2000 in connection with the campaign against oligarchs. In a loan repayment claim, Berezovsky was forced to surrender his shares; he sold to Roman Abramovich. [www.1tv.ru]

***Piatoye koleso* (Fifth Wheel):** current affairs program during perestroika on Leningrad channel run by Bella Kurkova. Kurkova was elected to parliament and was chairman of Petersburg Television and Radio Company.

Pozner, Vladimir: b. 1934, president of the Russian Academy of Television. Since 1961 with APN and radio editor for US/UK; until 1985 daily on the radio news. In 1986 space bridges with Leningrad, Seattle, and Boston; political observer for central television. Left the Soviet Union in April 1991 for the United States, where he hosted a program with Phil Donahue (*Pozner and Donahue*) and later *Final Edition*. Returned to Moscow in February 1997. Presents shows on television, such as *Chelovek v maske* (Person in the Mask), and works for the radio.

***Pravda* (Truth):** daily newspaper established in 1912, official organ of the Communist Party. Lost popularity in the 1990s. Launched as online paper in 1999. [www.pravda.ru]

***Prozhektor perestroiki* (Spotlight on Perestroika):** television program that ran from August 1987 to January 1990, presented by Alexander Tikhomirov.

Radio Russia (Radio Rossiia): radio station started on 10 December 1990; owned by the state. Variety of current affairs and entertainment programs with some music. [www.radiorus.ru]

RTR (Russian Television): launched on 13 May 1991 under Oleg Poptsov as RTR's general director. After the coup, Poptsov declined the offer to switch to the First Channel and to take over the Fourth Channel. In 1993 Poptsov surrendered the

Fourth Channel to Ostankino (Central Television) for Russian Universities; six hours were allocated to NTV, which later took over the entire airtime on the channel. On 14 February 1996, Oleg Poptsov was removed from office by Yeltsin's decree. Eduard Sagalayev followed for a year, resigning in February 1997, as his attempt to move the channel onto a commercial footing failed and his policy of purchasing rather than producing contradicted the spirit of the channel. He was succeeded by Nikolai Svanidze, who resigned in May 1998. RTR's general director is Alexander Akopov. [www.rutv.ru]

Russian Radio (Russkoye Radio): radio station established in August 1995 with a remit to play only Russian music. It is one of the most popular in Russia. [www.rus radio.ru]

Sagalayev, Eduard: b. 1946, Uzbekistan. From 1980 to 1984 head of youth section (radio station Radio Yunost). From 1984 to 1988, producer of *Vzgliad* and *Dvenadtsatyi etazh*. From 1988 to 1990, news editor on central television. From 1991 to 1992, at VGTRK, then 1992 to 1996 at Moscow Independent Broadcasting Corporation (MNVK), launching channel TV6. In 1996 and 1997, head of RTR. In 1997 returned to TV6. In 1999 sold his shares in TV6. Head of National Association of Television and Radio. Head of the National Association of Radio and Television Broadcasters (NAT). [www.nat.ru]

Segodnia (Today): daily newspaper 1993–2001. Anticipating the title of NTV's news flagship, the paper was launched by Gusinsky's Most Group and founded by staff from the *Nezavisimaya gazeta* (Dmitri Os-

talsky). From 1996 on, Yevgeni Serov has been chief editor. [www.segodnya.ru]

600 sekund (600 seconds): Leningrad program about crime in the city transmitted from December 1987 to November 1991. It was conceived and presented by Alexander Nevzorov (b. 1958, circus artist). Nevzorov also presented *Dikoye pole* (Wild Field). *600 sekund* was removed from the air in 1993 when Nevzorov became a Duma deputy and sided with the coup leaders in Moscow. Nevzorov also directed the film *Purgatory* (Chistilishche) about the Chechen war in 1998.

Sorokina, Svetlana: b. 1957. Television presenter. She began on the program *600 sekund*, which she presented from 1987 to 1990; then moved to the news program *Vesti* on RTR, which she anchored from 1991 to 1997. Then she moved to NTV to host the show *Geroi dnia* (1997–2000) and *Glaz naroda* (2000–2001). Recently returned to ORT to present *Osnovnoi instinkt*. Known as the "face" of RTR.

Sovershenno sekretno (Top secret): monthly paper launched in 1989 by the journalist Artyom Borovik and the writer Yulian Semyonov. Publishes archival material that discloses secrets. Also a holding company, which has owned *Litsa* (Faces) since 1996 and the weekly paper, *Versiya* (Version), since 1998. [www.sovsek retno.ru]

Trud (Work): daily newspaper established in the early 1920s, organ of the trade unions. *Trud* is one of the top newspapers in the news in Russia, with a large print run, reliable and sound information, and a positive balance sheet. [www.TRUD.ru]

TV Tsentr (TV Center): television station; since June 1997 transmits on the third frequency previously used by MTK/2x2 channels (founded in 1989 as first commercial channels). Registered on 31 December 1996 and belongs to the Moscow government (Luzhkov). Headed by Vladimir Yevtushenkov until June 1999; since February 2000 by Oleg Poptsov. Available on the Internet since October 1998. [www.tvc.ru]

TV6/TVS: television station. Formation in August 1991 of Moscow Independent Broadcasting Corporation (MNVK, Moskovskaia nezavisimaia veshchatel'naia korporatsiia), owned by the Moscow government, LukOil, LogoVaz, and several banks. Concept developed by Eduard Sagalayev with CNN boss Ted Turner. On 12 November 1992, license granted for the sixth channel; transmission started 1 January 1993 under director Alexander Ponomarev. In April 1994 the channel expanded coverage for all of Russia. In October 1999 Sagalayev sold his shares (37.5 percent) to Berezovsky. After the change in management at NTV in April 2001, Kiselyov and his team joined TV6. In 2001, TV6 was sued for bankruptcy by LukOil (15 percent shares), demanding the station's liquidation because it made no profit and its assets did not offset the debts. On 14 January 2002, the channel was closed. In May 2002, Kiselyov formed the independent station TVS (Television Spectrum). TVS was closed in June 2003 for nonpayment of bills for cable use, which were charged at an excessive rate. A new sports channel took over the frequency.

VGTRK: All-Russian Television and Radio Broadcasting Company; owns a variety of television and radio stations, including RTR and Radio Russia. General director Alexander Akopov, succeeded by Oleg Dobrodeyev. VGTRK owns the channel Kultura (registered in August 1993), which has transmitted on the fifth channel since 1 November 1997; headed by Mikhail Shvydkoy (until he was appointed minister of culture in April 2001), then Alexander Ponomarev. [www.vgtrk.com]

Vzgliad (Viewpoint): weekly current affairs program on the First Channel from October 1987 to January 1991. First program to touch upon sensitive themes and offer live coverage.

Yunost' (Youth): radio station founded 1964. Musical programs presented by DJs and a variety of fashion, automobile, language, and entertainment programs. One of the most liberal radio stations in the Gorbachev era, and from here a number of journalists were recruited for television. [www.unost.da.ru]

Bibliography

Belin, Laura. "Politics and the Mass Media under Putin." In *Russian Politics under Putin*, ed. Cameron Ross, 133–152. Manchester: Manchester University Press, 2004.

Bonnell, Victoria, and Gregory Freidin. "Televorot: The Role of Television Coverage in Russia's August 1991 Coup." In *Soviet Hieroglyphics: Visual Culture in Late Twentieth-Century Russia*, ed. by Nancy Condee, 22–51. Bloomington and Indianapolis: Indiana University Press and British Film Institute, 1995.

Dunn, John. "A Pot of Boiling Milk." *Rusistika* 8 (1993): 46–51.

———. "The Rise, Fall and Rise? of Soviet Television." *Rusistika* 4 (1991): 10–15.

Gudkov, Lev, and Boris Dubin. "Fernsehen in Russland am Ende der 1990er Jahre. Das Medium als Kommunikationsverfahren." In *Kommerz, Kunst, Unterhaltung: Die neue Popularkultur in Zentral- und Osteuropa*, ed. by Ivo Bock, Wolfgang Schlott, and Hartmute Trepper, 207–219. Bremen: Edition Temmen, 2002.

Mass Culture and Perestroika in the Soviet Union. Special issue, *Journal of Communication* 41, no 2 (Spring 1991).

McNair, Brian. *Glasnost, Perestroika and the Soviet Media*. London: Routledge, 1991.

Mickiewicz, Ellen. *Changing Channels: Television and the Struggle for Power in Russia*. (New York and Oxford: Oxford University Press, 1997.) Rev. ed. Durham NC: Duke University Press, 1999.

———. "Piracy, Policy, and Russia's Emerging Media Market." *Harvard International Journal of Press/Politics* 6, no. 2 (2001): 30–51.

———. *Split Signals: Television and Politics in the Soviet Union*. New York: Oxford University Press, 1988.

Murray, John. *The Russian Press from Brezhnev to Yeltsin: Behind the Paper Curtain*. Brookfield, VT: Edward Elgar, 1994.

Zassoursky, Ivan. *Media and Power in Post-Soviet Russia*. Armonk, NY: M. E. Sharpe, 2004.

Zasurskii, Ya., Vartanova, E., Zasurskii, I., Raskin, A., and Rikhter, A., comps. *Sredstva massovoi informatsii postsovetskoi Rossii*. Moscow: Aspekt, 2002.

2

Visual Culture

The Cinema

Feature Films

On 6 September 2003, the director Andrei Zviagintsev's *The Return* (Vozvrashchenie, 2003) received the Golden Lion for the best debut at the Venice International Film Festival. A few minutes later, Zviagintsev was called onto the stage again, and this time it was to receive the Golden Lion for the best film. The closing ceremony of the festival showered Russia with more awards: Alexei Gherman Jr. received the award for "promising debut" in the New Territories section for his film *The Last Train* (Poslednii poezd), and Murad Ibragimbekov was given an award for best short film for his film *Oil* (Neft'). Three Russian films shown in the festival received a total of four awards. There could be no better confirmation of the fact that Russian art-house cinema was again competitive on the international market and had overcome the crisis of the 1990s.

A few months after the Venice success, the largest multiplex with nine screens opened in Moscow. Meanwhile, the commercially released *Antikiller 2* (released 25 November 2003) and *Bimmer* (Bumer, released 28 June 2003) had grossed $2.7 and $1.6 million respectively. In 2003 the state had supported 60 features, 400 documentaries, and 30 animated films and was able to offer even more support for animation with its increased budget for 2004. The Russian box office figures were rising steeply, from $112 million in 2002 to $200 million in 2003. When in July 2004, Russia's First Channel ORT launched the blockbuster *Night Watch* (Nochnoi dozor), based on the fantasy thriller by Sergei Lukianenko, the film grossed $8.4 million in the first two weeks after its release. How did Russian cinema, which had hit an all-time low and produced just 20 features in 1996, none of which made a profit or a significant impact on international markets, get to this point?

The Film Industry: Production and Distribution Most discussions of Soviet and Russian cinema begin with Lenin's acknowledgment that cinema was "the most important of all arts." For almost seventy

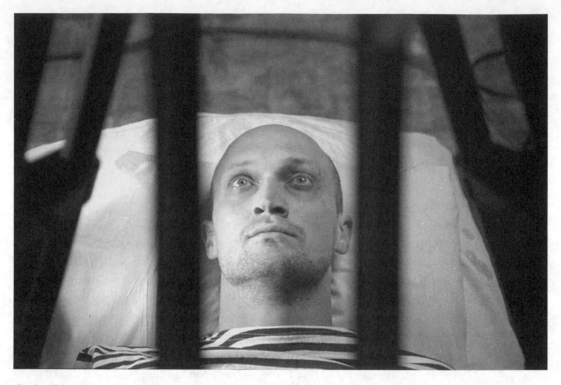

Gosha Kutsenko as Lis in Yegor Konchalovsky's film *Antikiller* (2002). (Photo Courtesy of Iskusstvo Kino)

years, cinema was controlled by the state and used by the Communist Party for propaganda purposes in its role as a medium that could convey an ideological message in the form of entertainment. Despite this, or because of this, the history of the Soviet film industry and the history of popular cinema remain usually beyond the scope of scholarship and the film historian's investigation. This chapter therefore first addresses the issues of the film "industry" and popular films before exploring the collapse of Russia's film industry in the mid-1990s and its recent revival.

The Soviet film industry had always relied on the state to finance and distribute its films. State-run film studios, such as Mosfilm, Lenfilm, and the Gorky Film Studios would employ screenwriters and directors, actors, and technical personnel; provide all the facilities for shooting and editing; produce the film; and take charge of the distribution to state-owned cinemas. Audience considerations were not crucial for the funding of a film, although until 1983 state investments in the film sector as a whole were not only recouped through ticket sales but returns would exceed expenditure: the state made a profit. Many of the films made in the 1960s and 1970s attracted more than 50 million spectators, and "auteur" or art-house films could be made without market pressures.

The climax of popularity for cinema as an art form lies between 1965 and 1980, when attendance at cinemas peaked, with an annual average of 20 visits per capita. The increase in television sets per household, rising steadily after 1970, explains the subsequent decrease in the attendance at

The Return

The Return tells the story of a father who returns after twelve years of absence to his wife and his two boys, Ivan (aged twelve) and Andrei (aged fifteen). He takes the boys fishing, but along the way he has to complete an urgent job and retrieve a coffer from an island. The father is strict with the children, and when the boys come back late, he hits the older brother. The younger boy threatens the father with a knife, but—frightened by his own aggression—runs away and climbs onto a makeshift observation tower (although he is afraid of heights), threatening to jump if the father comes any closer. The father follows him, but falls off the tower when a wooden plank becomes undone. The children pull the body to the boat and return to the mainland; as they disembark, the boat drifts back onto the open sea and sinks. The boys return home.

The Return follows the cinematic traditions of the 1960s manifest in the films of Andrei Tarkovsky and Michelangelo Antonioni, with all the corresponding religious symbolism. *The Return* is divided into sections, covering the seven days of the working week, or the seven days of God's creation of the world. This double significance immediately establishes the two main levels on which the film can be read: the everyday and the religious. On the everyday level the film explores the relationship between father and son(s), a theme dominating several new Russian films (such as the debut film by Alexei Popogrebsky and Boris Khlebnikov, *Koktebel,* 2003). If the film is read as a family drama, then the father is an unjust and cruel man who shows hardly any love for his children. He reprimands the children, never praising them or encouraging them. In this respect, Ivan's rejection of the father as a figure of authority and the ensuing disrespect are a most natural response, much more so than Andrei's unfounded and unlimited admiration for the father and his agreement with anything the father suggests. In modern terminology, Andrei is a creep, Ivan a rebellious "difficult" child. On the religious level this father makes his first appearance as a risen Christ figure straight from Andrea Mantegna's *Lamentation over Dead Christ.* The boys rush into the attic, where they search for a picture of their father, which they find in an old edition of the Bible, richly illustrated with etchings. Then they go to the dinner table, replicating da Vinci's *Last Supper,* where the father shares wine and bread (here the chicken) with his disciples, or his family. Visually, Zviagintsev creates a stunning sequence of images from art history to nature shots and cinematic quotations, which impressed spectators and jurors at Venice.

---

theaters and cinemas in the 1980s and 1990s to around eight visits per capita by 1990.

Alongside the "natural" loss of interest in cinema, which had been predictable since the late 1980s, the system of film production and distribution collapsed with the demise of the Soviet Union's nationalized industry. The large film studios gradually broke up into small, independent production companies. Goskino, the state Department for Cinematography, continued to subsidize national film production. Despite the crisis in production and distribution, and against all indicators speaking of a substantial drop in the number of spectators in cinemas, the number of new films remained stable at approximately 150 per year before rising abruptly to 300 titles in 1990; these were largely funded by private investors seeking to launder money. Film production was thus an entirely artificial branch of industry: more films were produced than were in demand, and the films made were not the sort of films that would draw audiences. The ensuing crisis in the film industry became evident in 1995, when the number of new films plummeted to a new low in the history of Russian and Soviet cinema, matched only by the lows reached during the civil war and under Stalin.

The sharp drop in film production by 1996 reflects a crisis in the role and the function of cinema in a changing society. Although more than 300 films were produced in 1991, Russian films almost vanished from the repertoire of cinemas owing to problems with finance and distribution. The themes of films made after 1991 show a concern with the loss of values in a society that had become more and more consumer oriented and materialist. The Soviet state had built huge movie theaters. These needed to be refurbished, modernized, adapted, and fitted with Dolby systems. The old theaters attracted fewer and fewer people: between 1994 and 1996, the number of spectators in Moscow dropped from 3.8 million to 1.2 million, and screenings dropped by half. Most cinemas were closed, and only six venues operated on a reasonably profitable basis. The first Dolby system was installed in the Kodak KinoMir (Kodak Cinema World), which opened in 1996 in a prestigious, trendy location for an "evening out." The American Center in the Radisson Slavianskaya Hotel has a stage and a screen, showing films largely in their original language. The Pushkin Cinema (formerly Rossiya) has the largest screen in Eastern Europe (20 by 10 meters) and has 2,500 seats. The Cinema Center

(KinoTsentr) and the Udarnik Theater refurbished first the technical equipment and then the auditorium. Finally, the House of Cinema served as a venue for premieres for members of the Filmmakers' Union. Moreover, television deflected audiences away from cinema and theater. Most films could be seen on television, and the old Soviet blockbusters proved especially popular: more than half of the feature films shown on television in the mid-1990s were Soviet films. Finally, the video market made any film available for the price of a cinema ticket or less—ticket prices ranged between two and ten dollars, whereas a video film cost six dollars in 1996, and about half of all households in Moscow are equipped with a video recorder. Videopiracy became a huge problem for the film industry, since most films were copied illegally, depriving the film industry of a return on production costs.

Goskino has maintained its existence with the remit to support the national film industry, officially sustained by the new law on cinema in 1996. With its annual budget of $10–15 million, it finances around a dozen films fully and some others partly. The average cost of production is $700,000–$1 million. At the end of the 1990s, the average return on a film was $80,000 from theatrical release, $200,000 from video release, and $30–50,000 from television rights. Under such conditions, no film could repay.

Production companies and distribution agencies have established themselves in the last decade. The major studios today are Mosfilm (headed by Vladimir Dostal, later by the filmmaker Karen Shakhnazarov), Lenfilm (Viktor Sergeyev), and Gorky Film Studios (Sergei Livnev, later Vladimir Grammatikov, who was replaced by Stanislav Yershov in 2002). Although the studios have been partly or fully privatized since the collapse of the Soviet Union and of national film production, many new production and distribution companies have appeared. The network of cinemas was refurbished and expanded in the latter part of the 1990s and is partly owned by distribution companies (for example, Karo). Sergei Selianov's Petersburg-based company CTB produces a mix of art-house and commercial cinema. Sergei Chliants's Moscow-based company Pygmalion promotes young directors' work. CineMax was founded by Roman Borisevich in 2000 and specializes on debut films (*Koktebel*, 2003). The studio Slovo, headed by Yelena Yatsuro and Sergei Melkumov, specializes in art-house films. Vladimir Dostal's Dom Film produces large commercial projects and television serials. Sergei Gribkov's Top Line produces young filmmakers, including Ruslan Baltser's highly popular films *Don't Even Think* (Dazhe ne dumai, 2003; sequel in 2004). Mikhalkov's TriTe, managed by Leonid Vereshchagin, prioritizes the production of Mikhalkov's projects. Television channels actively produce television serials and feature films: ORT's film production arm is headed by Konstantin Ernst and Anatoli Maximov (*Night Watch*, 2004); RTR's film production is run by Valeri Todorovsky, and Igor Tolstunov is the head of production at NTV/STS (Set' televisionnykh stantsii, Network of Television Stations). *The Return* was made by a private television station REN-TV and produced by Dmitri Lesnovsky.

In the early 1990s, festivals were the only real outlet for art-house films. The most important festival with a competition program was the Moscow International Film Festival, held biannually until it moved to an annual schedule in 1999. The Kinotavr Sochi Open Russian Film Festival (president Oleg Yankovsky, producer Mark Rudinstein, held in June) is the most important festival for Russian film; without it, some Russian filmmakers would never have been able to screen their films in the mid-1990s. The festival is still an important forum for Russian film in 2004. The Vyborg festival Window on Europe is a relatively new showcase for new Russian cinema, held in August. The Kinoshok festival in Anapa complemented the range of festivals, covering Commonwealth of Independent States (CIS) films also. The Russian Filmmakers' Association awards each year its Oscars, the "Nika" award (established in 1990).

From 1996 onward, production picked up, with television investing both in serials and film production. By 2003 the number of cinemas had risen again to a normal level, with the first multiplexes opening in Moscow in 2000 and 2001, and the first IMAX in 2003. The multiplexes opened on the sites of old cinemas: MDM (Moskovskii dvorets molodezhi, Moscow Youth Culture Palace) in the Youth Palace on Frunze Street; Piat Zvezd (Five Stars) in an old cinema on Bakhrushchin Street; the Rolan (named in honor of Rolan Bykov) on Chistoprudnyi Boulevard, with two screens with a 200- and an 80-seat capacity; the Strela (Arrow); 35 millimeters on Pokrovka Street; and the Khudozhestvennyi (Artistic). A similar practice of refurbishing was adopted in other major cities; St. Petersburg's Kristall Palace and Neva have been upgraded, and the Dom Kino shows a repertoire of recent Russian films as well as European art-house. The Karo distribution chain opened its cinemas in the Ramstore malls, and the Formula Kino chain followed suit with multiplexes in shopping malls. In 2004 the first vertically integrated production-distribution-exhibition complex, KinoPark, opened the largest multiplex on Kaluzhskaya Street in Moscow, with nine screens. The project was backed by Vladimir Potanin's ProfMedia's subsidiary InterRos and Mikhalkov's TriTe.

Soviet Blockbusters?   Soviet film history has largely been written around those films that represented innovation and experiment, rather than mass appeal. Sergei Eisenstein's *The Battleship Potyomkin* (1925) may have been "the best film of all times," but it was no hit in the USSR. The commercial concept of the "blockbuster," moreover, has, at first sight, limited value in the context of the Soviet film industry, where profit appeared to be irrelevant. Yet the Soviet film industry acknowledged both the cost of a film and the level of its likely popularity, even if profit was not the ultimate goal. After all, ticket sales in the Soviet Union were not related to the sale of popcorn and Coca-Cola, which constitutes a major income for U.S. cinema chains. So what were the "popular" films seen by the masses?

In the 1930s the climate of film production changed drastically, when the party issued a directive to educate and enlighten the masses, a task best carried out by Soviet film directors. Therefore, although foreign film imports were much higher than Soviet films produced in the mid-1920s, the production of Soviet films rose steadily after 1928 and outstripped foreign imports. Boris Shumiatsky, the new head of the Soviet film industry, launched an appeal for a "cinema for millions." He implemented a rigid campaign that put a halt to the great experiments that had characterized Soviet cinema of the 1920s. Preoccupied with a mass audience, Shumiatsky exercised control through mass distribution, saturating the distribution sector with Soviet films while withholding foreign films.

The entertainment value of a film presented suitable packaging whereby the ideological message would reach the masses. Popular elements, from the comic to the melodramatic genre, along with the promotion of stars and the inclusion of mass and folk songs, were purposefully incorporated into official Stalinist culture. The popular films of the 1930s all relied on a simple narrative and conventional style, with a linear plot, reducing complex issues to a level that could be understood by the masses. The Stalinist musical comedies were loved by the audiences for their glorified and glossy demonstration of life through the beautiful, feminine characters played by Marina Ladynina and Liubov Orlova; they were loved for showing the victory of those Soviet ideals that the population was forced to believe in. They invariably presented a love triangle, in which the loving couple was ultimately reunited and supported by the collective after having made a contribution to society, whereas the villain either became socialized or was expelled from the community. The musical was intended to reach a maximum audience by means of memorable tunes and mass songs. Most of the scores for Grigori Alexandrov's musicals were composed by Isaak Dunaevsky, the lyrics written by Vasili Lebedev-Kumach (*Veselye rebiata* [Jolly Fellows], 1934; *Circus*, 1936; *Volga-Volga*, 1938). These sought to transfer the Hollywood musical to Soviet film, dwelling on the superior quality of the domestic product. Thus, several films contain parodic allusions to foreign lands no longer accessible to the masses: in the Soviet Union, Marion Dixon was freed from the capitalist exploitation of Kneischitz by the blue-eyed, blond Soviet engineer Martynov; her son Jimmy was liberated from racial discrimination in the United States by the great Soviet collective as embodied in the ethnically mixed circus audience. Soviet film asserted that it could do without American stars such as Charlie Chaplin, Harold Lloyd, and Buster Keaton, as the introductory frames to *Jolly Fellows* claimed, trumpeting the Soviet Union's own stars instead, even if Chaplinesque features can be found in the portrayal of numerous Soviet characters.

After the turmoil of World War II had left both production and distribution at a low ebb, audience numbers rose only slowly in the early 1950s. With the onset of the Thaw, cinema turned to the comic genre, which moved individual (personal) happiness into the foreground. This change was marked by Eldar Riazanov's *Carnival Night* (Karnaval'naia noch', 1956), which took first place in the charts for 1956 with almost 50 million viewers and paved the way for the glorious return of the most successful genre of Soviet cinema, the comedy. *Carnival Night* was a musical comedy, with the debut performance of Liudmila Gurchenko in the role of Lena Krylova. The love intrigue between Krylova and Koltsov would have a happy end, but before that, she had to fulfill her duty to the community. *Carnival Night* parodied the pettiness of the bureaucrats: Krylova's attempts to freshen up the stuffy program of a New Year party were stifled by a bureaucrat, who was portrayed as the "enemy" in an exaggerated manner and subjected to parody. *Carnival Night* is a New Year classic of Soviet cinema, because of

the songs (the most popular being Anatoli Lepin's "Song about Five Minutes"), its carnivalesque atmosphere, and its parody of Soviet bureaucracy and officialdom.

The most popular comedies of the 1960s and 1970s were directed by Leonid Gaidai and reached audiences of around seventy million spectators at a time when the art form of cinema peaked in popularity (the 1970s) before being superseded by the new medium of television. Gaidai's comedies were popular, because they replaced the coherent linear plots of earlier Soviet films with an episodic and fragmented world that corresponded more to reality than the varnished fairy tales of Stalin's cinema. In a way, Gaidai laughed at the cracks that appeared on the varnished surface. Comedies clearly dominated the box office in the 1960s and 1970s. Vladimir Menshov's *Moscow Does Not Believe in Tears* (Moskva slezam ne verit, 1980) was one of the last Soviet blockbusters, with eighty-five million viewers. Its plot stretches over 20 years, from the 1950s to the 1970s. In good socialist style the heroine, Katia, is rewarded with personal happiness only after she has made her contribution to social progress. The film's popularity is largely due to the "feel-good factor," which effectively shows that man can master his fate even in the most adverse circumstances.

The blockbusters of perestroika still attracted significant numbers of viewers, but not the levels of the 1970s and 1980s. Although many of the perestroika films are aesthetically and thematically worthy, they often owe their popularity also to political circumstances: they were beacons of reform. Vasili Pichul's *Little Vera* (Malen'kaia Vera, 1988) attracted 55 million people with a story about the hopelessness and dullness of everyday life. Other perestroika blockbusters dealt with previously forbidden topics, such as Tengiz Abuladze's *Repentance* (Pokaianie/Monanieba, 1986), which addressed the Stalin purges. Perestroika also saw the rise of a new generation of filmmakers, who produced their first "hits" by touching upon previous taboo themes: the Stalin period, rock music, crime, prostitution, and drug dealing. Although comedy and adventure had dominated Soviet popular cinema, the initial years of perestroika saw the interest shift toward formerly forbidden themes and social taboos, such as drug dealing, prostitution, and alcoholism.

Russian Cinema in the 1990s: Reality as Chernukha

Soviet cinema produced entertaining comedies, or monumental, historical movies, but alongside existed a movement that made art-house films for the (dissident) intelligentsia. All film production, entertainment and art-house, was seen primarily as a means to raise the spirit of the people and to set moral standards, or at least show the possibility of improvement. Filmmakers such as Tarkovsky, Muratova, Gherman and Alexander Sokurov, Klimov and Larisa Shepitko had assumed the roles of prophets, setting moral standards for a country where the state was busy showing reality in positive and bright colors.

After the collapse of the Communist ideology, filmmakers rejected these demands to varnish reality (state command) or act as prophets (intelligentsia expectations) and started portraying reality as they saw it, without the ideological constraints hitherto imposed. And what they saw, in the late 1980s and early 1990s, was a bleak picture: beggars on the streets, impoverished pensioners, economic chaos, street crime, Mafia shootings, pornographic magazines and videos, decaying houses and apartments, and the emergence of a new class, the New Russians, who adapted quickly and learned how to make money in a society that was being reconstructed. The literature and film, visual art and music, that are set in this bleak reality and use it as their only space are commonly called *chernukha* (literally: that which is made black).

The mainstream of Russian cinema of the early 1990s (1990–1996) largely indulged in this bleakness, or blackness, and offered neither alternative nor perspective. Filmmakers rejected their remit to act as prophets, to guide morally and aesthetically. The audience rejected in its turn films that offered no positive outlook or spiritual guidance in the chaos and turned instead to Latin American soap operas screened daily on Russian television. The issue of the function of cinema in the New Russia dominated the debates of the early 1990s. Could cinema offer what reality could not provide: an aim, a goal for people to live up to at a time when politics and ideology failed to provide directions?

Audiences mattered little to many younger Russian filmmakers, who discharged their creative energy into making movies for festivals. After all, this was the only opportunity to get an award and repay at least partly the production cost, although many investors, including Goskino, invested without the need to repay, making filmmakers even more independent of audience taste. Although Soviet films were clearly made for Soviet audiences (the need to reach the masses accounts for the popularity to the present day of the Soviet blockbusters, from the musical comedies of the 1930s to social drama of the Brezhnev period such as *Moscow Does Not Believe in*

Tears), many contemporary films failed to capture the imagination of the people. Few Russian films of the 1990s were popular with audiences. Few films offered a happy ending. Dmitri Astrakhan's *Everything Will Be OK* (Vsc budet khorosho, 1995) was one of the first, and few, exceptions. And although Russian critics were complaining about the lack of positive heroes and a bright future in their national cinema, they immediately rose to criticize Astrakhan's optimism. Similarly, Rogozhkin's *Peculiarities of the National Hunt* (Osobennosti natsional'noi okhoty, 1995) was one of the most popular films with audiences at the time of its release, even though critics had a hard time defending its artistic merit and imposing an interpretation that justified the film's success.

In the 1990s a number of directors gained widespread popularity. These were Alexander Rogozhkin, Alexei Balabanov, Sergei Bodrov Sr., and Pavel Chukhrai. Rogozhkin specializes in eccentric comedies, and Balabanov and Bodrov are concerned with contemporary social issues. Chukhrai is a gifted director of films set in the postwar period. The work of these directors in different genres and on different themes prepared the ground for a number of new directors emerging in the new millennium: Yegor Konchalovsky and Petr Buslov undeniably follow the path of the hero who stands above good and evil, as featured in Balabanov's *Brother*. Ruslan Baltser, with his *Don't Even Think* (Dazhe ne dumai), maybe follows the path of the eccentric comedy of Rogozhkin. These directors make popular and commercial films, and they will be explored in further detail here. Directors such as Sokurov and Muratova make very distinct art-house films that may be shown on festivals and released in Euro-

pean distribution for art-house cinemas but that rarely have a mass appeal.

The collapse of an ideological, social, political, and economic system left both critics and filmmakers wondering about the function of cinema. At the same time, audiences turned away from cinema as a forum for debate and demanded entertainment. It was not until 1997 that cinema reemerged as an industry and art form. If the early 1990s were dominated by gloomy chernukha films, then the mid-1990s saw a reaction against that with the comedies of Dmitri Astrakhan and Alexander Rogozhkin. With the outbreak of the Chechen war, many filmmakers turned to the theme of war in general. Moreover, filmmakers showed an interest in debating Russia's national identity; to this end many turned the pages of Russian history and explored different period of the country's past. These themes serve as headings for the following discussion, in which plot synopses of the most important films are provided in text boxes.

Comedy: From Astrakhan to Rogozhkin   Dmitri Astrakhan was one of the first directors to cater deliberately for what he perceived to be an audience taste. He made comedies and films with "happy endings" rather than the artistically innovative and thematically engaging films that dominated in the mid-1990s. Astrakhan's early films were family melodramas with a happy ending, but it was with his film *Everything Will Be OK* that he landed a "hit," relatively speaking. It is a modern Cinderella tale: local beauty Olga is engaged to local boy Kolia when Smirnov, who had emigrated to the United States a long time before, pays a visit to his hometown. With him arrives his son Petia, a young mathematical genius

Alexei Buldakov as General Ivolgin in Alexander Rogozhkin's *Peculiarities of National Fishing* (1998). (Photo by Anton Verbin, courtesy of Miroslava Segida)

who has already won the Nobel Prize. And Petia falls in love with Olga, who realizes that she really does not love Kolia after all. Astrakhan's film leaves everybody happy at the end; social differences and problems with alcohol are overcome. The bleakness usually found in the portrayal of social reality has finally given way to a positive view, to a world in which events are hilariously construed. Astrakhan continued in this vein, but his later films were less popular than *Everything Will Be OK*.

Alexander Rogozhkin had made some films engaging with history in the late 1980s and early 1990s and was considered an art-house director. His films about the oddities of the Russian national character—*Peculiarities of the National Hunt in Autumn* (Osobennosti natsional'noi okhoty v osennii period, 1995), *Operation "Happy New Year"* (Operatsiia "S novym godom,"

1996), *Peculiarities of National Fishing* (Osobennosti natsional'noi rybalki, 1998), and *Peculiarities of the National Hunt in Winter* (Osobennosti natsional'noi okhoty v zimnii period, 2000)—became national hits, however, and found numerous imitators (*Peculiarities of National Politics*, *Peculiarities of the National Bath-house*). The films all have a fragmented structure, in which episodes are not held together by a stringent narrative. They rely on physical rather than verbal humour and are centered around one central comic presence (Alexei Buldakov, the ultimate parody of a Russian military man with his cigar smoking and vodka drinking and his indulgence in the Russian folk traditions, from the sauna to fishing to bear hunting).

Rogozhkin selects representatives of the New Russian society, which is no longer classless: apart from the military, there is

Peculiarities of the National Hunt: Plot

In *Peculiarities of the National Hunt,* the Finn Raimo (Ville Haapassalo), who is researching the traditions of the Russian hunt from the time of the tsars to the present day, joins the group of "hunters." The excessive drinking bouts the Russians associate with hunting are, however, not what the Finn expects. He initially refuses to drink, and he dreams all the time of the imperial hunting party of the late nineteenth century, stylishly hunting down a fox with their dogs, elegantly riding horses, and, of course, conversing in French, while he, the non-Russian speaker, is marginalized in the group. Russian reality and the foreigner's imagination do not match. Neither do the stereotypes of society. The military and the police hardly reinforce order: military aircraft are used to transport vodka and animals and the police vans and staff to organize a trip to the prostitutes. Moreover, the breakdown of social order in contemporary Russia is treated with self-irony. No animal is killed on this Russian hunt: the cow—illegally transported on a bomber plane to another forest area—is not dropped from the plane according to plan since the bribery of the pilots is discovered; the cow later survives when shot at accidentally by the hunters; the baby bear gets drunk on vodka; and the fish that Raimo catches is thrown back into the water. The hunt consists of baths in the steam-house (*banya*), peasant-girl prostitutes, and vodka.

the New Russian, the state official, and the policeman. Beneath their social image, however, these characters hide their true faces—the love of animals, the love of humans, and the love of nature—that contradict the external, social image. Under the influence of vodka, they show their real faces: the good and honest demeanor of a Russian folk hero, who kills no animal, who helps his fellow human beings, who contemplates nature, and who loves water. Therefore, the general, "Mikhailych" Ivolgin (Alexei Buldakov), deploys his skills to organize a party or a hunt; the state official, Lev Soloveichik (Semen Strugachev), is a poor and pitiable creature when it comes to practical things; the policeman, Semenov (Sergei Gusinsky), is always helpful; the businessman, Sergei Olegovich (Sergei Russkin), has domestic problems, and the forester, Kuzmich (Viktor Bychkov), meditates instead of clearing forests and hunting animals. Rogozhkin removes all negative attributes of these social "types" and replaces them with positive qualities.

Drinking may have no purpose, but it is a habit that makes social and national differences disappear, lifts temporal boundaries in bringing together past and present, and annihilates the borders between animals and humans. The world returns to its purest form, without any boundaries or limits. As the eminent Russian critic and writer Tatiana Moskvina commented: "The film is as good for the soul as 250 grams of vodka in good company." What matters in the hunt is the process and the time spent in good company, not the result.

Peculiarities of National Fishing is a continuation of *Peculiarities of the National Hunt.* Again, alcohol is responsible for the group of fishermen's accidentally mooring on the Finnish coast when they get lost on the Baltic sea because Kuzmich is drunk. When Kuzmich realizes that they are outside Russia, he swiftly hurries everybody back onto the boat, leaving the vodka behind. Once they discover the absence of vodka at Kuzmich's, they set off to bribe the captain of a military vessel. With a submarine they enter Finnish waters and retrieve the vodka. Indeed, *Peculiarities of National Fishing* is a hunt for vodka.

Peculiarities of the National Hunt in Winter continues the adventures of the hunters, who are joined by two inspection teams from the ministry: Yuri Kurtsov and Igor Rechnikov want to have fun for a few days, whereas the second team of inspectors, Olga Masliuk and Oleg Piatakov, want to put an end to the hunt and protect the environment. On this hunt, too, no animal is harmed: Olga knocks out the "guy" who looked into the toilet—and when realizing it was a baby bear, worries about the animal; the boar tramples over the Jeep, but the passengers escape unscathed; the horn used to attract the deer is echoed by a train; and even the fish is set free, as it cannot be pulled out of the ice hole. Instead, a series of minor mishaps brings the rather diverse characters together: after a long walk they have to be defrosted in a large wooden barrel; and Soloveichik flies away on a chair attached to some red balloons in an attempt to catch birds on the trees— only to be rescued by an army helicopter.

Each film of the *Peculiarities* cycle consists of a series of events connected to one particular situation: the hunt organized for a foreigner, fishing staged for a guest, and another hunt performed for the inspectors. Each film includes a series of mishaps that all end well, that happen because of the complexities of Russian reality, and that end well because of the intervention of the Russian military and police forces. Rogozhkin combines the anecdotal style de-

ployed in earlier films with alcoholism. His films have no ending but appear to be a series of gags. Under the influence of alcohol, things make sense: there may be no meaning, but there is a game to engage in, a game of which the rules are known. Rogozhkin combines Soviet heroism with Russian character: the general is head of the military (a monumental figure), but he is always drunk (the Russian folk hero).

As Rogozhkin turned to more serious themes in films such as *Cuckoo* (Kukushka, 2002), other comedies appeared: Roman Kachanov made a parody of the life of soldiers with the film *DMB* (Demobilized, 2000). Kachanov portrays the army service of the young recruit with the nickname "Pulia" ("bullet") as a respite from his creditors and as an experience that offers a series of jokes and gags, not unlike Rogozhkin's *Peculiarities*. Kachanov's clever use of a number of popular bands for the sound track heightened the mass appeal of the movie and led to the release of a separate CD. Ruslan Baltser produced a comedy based on the adventures of three young men: *Don't Even Think* (2003) and the sequel *Don't Even Think—The Independence Game* (Dazhe ne dumai II: Ten' nezavisimosti, 2004). Baltser's films are adventure comedies, following three young men in their pursuit of success and happiness, using not always legal methods. Indeed, in the first sequel they are caught stealing. Baltser deploys animation within the film, parodying the action of the heroes in the style of *Run, Lola, Run* (Tom Tykwer; Lola rennt, 1998). Both Baltser and Kachanov follow the episodic structure and refrain from a coherent narrative, presenting instead a series of gags or adventures. These comedies, along with some crime thrillers, were most popular in Rus-

Zhilin (Sergei Bodrov) and Kostylin (Oleg Menshikov) in Sergei Bodrov's *The Prisoner of the Mountains*, nominated for an Academy Award in 1996. (Photo courtesy of Birgit Beumers)

sia in the years of their release, each grossing more than one million dollars at the box office.

Lost Values and the Chechen War: Bodrov and Rogozhkin

As the Soviet Union collapsed, so did the ideals of a fatherland. This is a prominent theme in films about regional wars, such as Sergei Bodrov Sr.'s *Prisoner of the Mountains* (Kavkazskii plennik, 1996), one of the most popular films of the time, nominated for an Oscar in 1997.

Bodrov shows the traditions of the Caucasian people firsthand, as the viewer travels with the camera around the mountain village. Abdul's daughter Dina provides the main link between the Muslim world and that of the prisoners. She looks after not only her father but also the prisoners.

Zhilin attempts to accept the Muslim civilization with tolerance. When Dina releases Zhilin, knowing that Abdul would kill him, Zhilin even refuses to run away, aware that Dina would not be forgiven in the village if it became known that she had helped his escape. By contrast with Kostylin, Zhilin does not kill, nor does he endanger Dina's life. Kostylin is unscrupulous in his attempts to escape from captivity; however, he takes responsibility for his actions and for the young recruit Zhilin.

Bodrov does not discriminate against any culture. The personal history of the two captives is told with the same compassion as the history of Abdul's family. The Muslims are both victims and aggressors, and so are the Russians. Whereas Kostylin is active and fights, Zhilin surrenders. And he survives the war. At the end of the film,

Prisoner of the Mountains: Plot

The film tells the story of two Russian soldiers held prisoner in the Caucasus to be exchanged for a Caucasian hostage held by the Russian army. Bodrov passes no moral judgment but rather exposes the creative power of memory. *Prisoner of the Mountains* is based on Tolstoy's story of the same title. It offers a perspective on the war in terms of individual human loss, rather than the clash of ideas or ideals. Vania Zhilin is a young recruit posted to the Caucasus, whose detachment comes under attack. Together with Sasha Kostylin he becomes a prisoner of Abdul, who wants to exchange them for his son, who is held captive by the Russian military. The exchange fails, but Abdul tries to get Zhilin's mother involved. The prison-

ers eventually manage to run away, but they are caught after Kostylin kills a shepherd to steal his rifle and a shot misfires. Kostylin admits the murder and is executed, and Zhilin is taken back to Abdul. In the meantime, Zhilin's mother has almost arranged an exchange of prisoners, when Abdul's son uses an opportune moment to run away and is shot. Abdul grieves over the loss when Dina, his daughter, who has grown very fond of the kind recruit Zhilin, asks her father not to kill the captive, whom she had just been trying to let escape. Abdul takes Zhilin into the mountains and pretends to shoot him. As Abdul returns to his Muslim village, and Zhilin returns to freedom, Russian helicopters arrive to destroy the village in an act of revenge.

Zhilin reports on the events that have followed his captivity: he can no longer see in dreams the people he once loved; the human dimension of the war, the human loss is far more important than anything else. Bodrov places the personal above the political. The film investigates the response of men who are reduced to objects of the state and deprived of political ideals. When man is reduced to an object, he is either subdued, and nonaggressive, or crippled by the system, forced to produce masks in order to hide the real self and act aggressively. Ideas may be the cause of the conflict, but the lives of individuals are more important in a society that has lost its values and in a country that has lost its ideals.

If Bodrov shows the cultural conflict between the indigenous population and the Russian soldiers, Rogozhkin shows the absurdity that underlies any war. Rogozhkin's recent feature films deal with the wars of

Chechnya (*Checkpoint*) and the Russo-Finnish war during World War II (*Cuckoo*). *Checkpoint* (Blokpost, 1998) is an antiwar film set in the Caucasus. The lack of a general sense of the soldiers' mission and their part in the overall strategy of the operation is reflected in the film's composition, focused on detail and episodic in structure.

The film is structured along the lines of notes taken during the war, with a chronicler-narrator telling the events as they happen. A detachment of Russian soldiers had raided a house in a local village where a boy was holding on to a mine that he set off as they entered. The men managed to escape before the house exploded, but they were—mistakenly—thought to have caused the explosion and attacked by a howling and screaming crowd of local women, one of whom starts shooting. A soldier shoots her in the leg in an act of defense. The detachment is taken to task for the incident, however, and "exiled" to a remote checkpoint on a road that leads only to a Muslim cemetery. Under pressure from the local community to turn over the culprit, the military authority surrenders "Rat" (Krysa): they sacrifice one of their own men to maintain the status quo. Rat's body is returned to the checkpoint, wrapped in a sheepskin.

Rogozhkin shows the everyday life and trivial events of the war without glorifying the war or creating heroes. There is no sense of purpose in what they are doing, yet they put on a brave face and play their roles in this absurd war. Their life seems like routine, but "mishaps" have drastic consequences in the real world. The soldiers have no identity: they have nicknames only, and identification badges are all they have to take pride in. They are oddballs in a remote location, because of the role they are forced to play in an absurd war against the Muslim community, with whom the soldiers make deals but to whom the authorities bow in fear of escalation.

Cuckoo is set during the last days of World War II in a remote location in northern Russia. Two soldiers arrive at the hut of the Saami woman Anni, who lives on her own since her husband has been drafted into the war. The isolation, and the inability of the three people to understand each other (Anni speaks Saami, Veiko speaks Finnish, and Ivan Russian) and the potential danger from the outside (war) turns men into cranks. Ivan's response to the question about his name is "p'shol-ty" (*poshel ty:* f*** off), so this is what Veiko and Anni call him: Psholty. Anni resuscitates the injured Russian soldier, Ivan, and brings back to life the Finnish soldier, Veiko, whom Ivan has shot in a rage. Anni calls him back from the dead in a pagan ritual she has learned from her grandmother:

she calls the dying Veiko with howling and screaming, until he turns round on the mountainous road into the kingdom of the dead. Anni represents the force of those people who live in a close bond with nature, whereas the actions of Veiko and Ivan are futile. People are playthings of politics and ideas, even if Ivan pretends he is still at war. *Cuckoo* was commercially successful, with extensive runs in major cinemas, the achievement of numerous national film awards, and an international release in several countries.

A number of other films of the Putin era were concerned with the theme of conflict and war. Nikolai Lebedev's *The Star* (Zvezda, 2002) was the first Russian film about World War II that showed the brutality of the war and used special effects in order to shift a war film into the genre conventions of an action movie. Valeri Ogorodnikov's *Red Sky* (Krasnoe nebo, 2004) is set in the Urals in 1943. The evacuated citizens of Moscow and Petersburg arrive, among them the young and attractive woman Lida, who stirs up the men in the small town. She flirts with the men, but the personal romantic drama acquires a different perspective when the young men are drafted to the front. Alexei Gherman Jr.'s *Last Train* (Poslednii poezd, 2003) looks at the fate of two men who have failed to make the right choice (or a choice) at the right time rather than at a specific event of the war. They are the victims of circumstances, of politics, of regimes—which they have or have not elected. Gherman's concern is with people in particular circumstances that are not their choice and how they cope with these unwanted situations. A German military doctor, a man who vowed to help man rather than kill him, and a postman are Gherman's main characters. Doctor Fischbach had seen the horrors of World War I; now he has been sent to a military hospital at the front line. Although soldiers are being evacuated from there when he arrives, he decides to stay and help the injured. Yet the commanding officer, out of a sense of duty, sends him into the forest as the enemy advances. Fischbach is doomed to die: through the bullets of the advancing Russian army or through adverse weather conditions.

The narrative of this film is presented through the eyes of Fischbach, accompanied by the postman Kreutzer; together they err in the fields in the search for salvation. It is a challenging move to have the German soldiers and the Russian partisans played by Russian actors, with most of the dialogue in German and rendered through Russian subtitles. Kreutzer and Fischbach are human beings in the first instance: these men die without having entered the books of history for cruelty or heroic deeds. They die, nameless and forgotten, without family and relatives. It is from the horror of their absurd and vain attempts at humanitarian aid (medical or communicative) that they resign to their fates—and die: their acts are meaningless in a world of cruelty.

If it is surprising that a young director like Gherman could make such a fine and subtle film about the war, the fact that Dmitri Meskhiev turned to the war theme after having made successful television serials set in contemporary Moscow is even more surprising. For his film *Ours* (also known as *Friendlies* or *Friendly Troops; Svoi,* 2004), Meskhiev won the main prize (Saint Georgi) of the Moscow International Film festival in July 2004. His film is set in 1941 when Soviet prisoners of war escape from captivity. The preoccupation of a number of young filmmakers with the theme of World War II is a reflection of the concern with the ongoing wars, nationally and internationally.

Stalinism Revisited: From Abuladze to Mikhalkov Gorbachev's politics of glasnost and perestroika had an enormous impact on the production and release of films dealing with aspects of Soviet history. The 1930s in particular became the subject of many works in film, theater, and literature. Although Khrushchev in his Secret Speech (1956) had addressed the terror and the injustice of the Stalin regime, open discussion of the Soviet past did not extend to areas of cultural life. The Thaw in the arts (1956–1964) primarily allowed the discussion of problems of contemporary life, whereas any reassessment of the past remained the privilege of the party officials and those in charge of rehabilitation. Glasnost and perestroika of the late 1980s opened the closed chapters of Soviet history for reinterpretation and thus led to the publication of literature dealing with Soviet history of the Stalin era. For the first time, the Stalinist era was explicitly dealt with in many films, plays, and novels; the newly available accessibility of archival material and documents relating to the period furthered this interest.

In the late 1980s, the concern with the 1930s was reflected in an attempt to restore in the people's memory those pages of Soviet history that had been blotted out. This was expressed through an appeal to remember the Stalinist era both for the horror of the purges and for the human sacrifice afforded in the fight against fascism during World War II. In the 1990s, the interest in the Stalinist period coincided with the active rewriting of the history of a

Burnt by the Sun: Plot

Burnt by the Sun is set on a Sunday in June 1936 when secret service (NKVD, Narodnyi komitet vnutrennykh del, People's Committee for Internal Affairs) officer Mitia (Oleg Menshikov) accepts and carries out a special assignment: the arrest of Red Army Commander Kotov (Mikhalkov) at his family's dacha near Moscow. Meanwhile, Kotov enjoys domestic life with his wife, Marusia (Ingeborga Dapkunaite), and daughter, Nadia (Nadia Mikhalkova). Mitia, a friend of the family and Marusia's first love, arrives and spends the day with the family, taking Kotov with him back to Moscow in the evening. Upon his return to Moscow, Mitia succeeds in his second suicide attempt (having tried to shoot himself the day before): he cuts his wrists in the bath.

state that had at that point collapsed: documents had been released, and history had been discussed openly, explicitly, and subjectively. Now it was time to consider the lessons to be drawn from the 1930s; to look for parallels in the quest of both decades, the 1930s and the 1990s; to define a new nationhood. Issues of individual choice and responsibility with regard to history and politics are also treated differently in films of the postperestroika and the post-Soviet periods.

Tengiz Abuladze's *Repentance* (1984, released 1986) became a cult film of the 1980s. It was the first film to address the purges of the 1930s, even if it did so in a highly allegorical form. The film's poetic language and its complexity can partly be explained by the use of Aesopian language typical of authors treating "forbidden" themes in the Brezhnev era and by the school of Georgian filmmakers traditionally using a more symbolic film language. The film offers an utterly pessimistic perspective on the relationship between history and the individual and on the lack of a future for either victims or oppressors. Keti is decorating cakes at the beginning and the end of the film. Her childhood memories and her present occupation are the only realities the film offers. Her resistance to terror (her exhumation of the dictator Aravidze's body, the consequent trial, and her forgiveness) only happens in her imagination; in reality she lacks the courage she wishes she might have. *Repentance* paralyzes its characters in their imagination, and many other films of the 1990s dealing with Stalinist terror interpret the potential for activity in the 1930s as an illusion. Keti's reality is ruled by forgiveness, not repentance. This Christian message informs the reply of the old woman asking for the way: any road will lead to the church; any path will eventually lead to God, and He will pass the ultimate judgement. Keti is a victim of a collective history in which individual action led to destruction. Keti's freedom and her potential for activity are crippled by the force of history. The only morality that remains intact lies in the church. Such escapism, or withdrawal to religion instead of political activity, would be rejected by filmmakers in the 1990s: in Mikhalkov's *Burnt by the Sun*, the road that in *Repentance* led to the church would lead to Moscow, representing both Mitia's and Kotov's death.

Kotov (Nikita Mikhalkov), Nadia (Nadia Mikhalkova), and Marusia (Ingeborga Dapkunaite) in Nikita Mikhalkov's Academy Award winning *Burnt by the Sun* (1994). (Photo Courtesy of Pathe Cinema)

Even though the filmmakers of the 1990s remained interested in the Stalin era, the emphasis shifted to issues of culture rather than those of responsibility and memory that had predominated in Abuladze's film. Often, films concerned themselves with parodic references to Stalinist culture, turning history into a plaything, an artifact, a construct that had little to do with the characters in the film. Filmmakers of the 1990s denied politics the right to play a serious part in their films. Examples of this may be found in Ivan Dykhovichny's *Moscow Parade* (Prorva, 1992) and Sergei Livnev's *Hammer and Sickle* (Serp i molot, 1993). Both films were important preludes to the last film to deal with Stalinism, Nikita Mikhalkov's *Burnt by the Sun* (1994), which was awarded an Oscar for best foreign film in 1995.

Moscow Parade exposed the immoral sexuality that underlay Stalinist culture. The film comments on the nature of high Stalinist culture: the disciplined parades, monumental buildings, and muscle-controlled bodies are contrasted with the decadent lifestyle of the heroine Anna (played by the German musical-star Ute Lemper). Decadence reigns behind the neat and tidy facades and parades of Stalinist culture. The film is concerned with decadence and culture, with the breakdown of morality in a world where only appearances matter, and with the sexual perversity of all aspects of life, almost in analogy with the political perversion. *Hammer and Sickle* parodies and mocks the myth making of Socialist Realism while it constructs a new myth of the Stalinist past. The film is about a state command in

1936 that the country should have more soldiers. Stalin's aide masterminds an experiment whereby the female tractor driver Yevdokiya Kuznetsova becomes the male construction worker Yevdokim Kuznetsov. Evdokim becomes a successful model worker in the metro construction brigade, is awarded a medal, and marries Liza Voronina, a model kolkhoz worker. They literally become models for Vera Mukhina's statue of the Worker and the Collective Farmer and a model Soviet family: they adopt a girl, Dolores, who has been orphaned during the Spanish civil war. When Yevdokim realizes his true feelings for another woman, who nursed him during the operation, he meets Stalin and challenges the leader's control of his life: he attacks Stalin and is shot. Paralyzed and unable to speak, Yevdokim is turned into a hero once more: he has supposedly saved Stalin's life and is exhibited as a museum piece. His wife controls his mind (she writes his book *Hammer and Sickle*), and she is also the master of his body, which she uses to satisfy her lust.

Hammer and Sickle challenged the assumption that the individual carries any responsibility for history: history is an artificial construct. Liza and Yevdokim are artifacts, creations of a system: the model worker and peasant. Ideally, all human beings will end like Yevdokim, in a museum, displayed to foreign visitors and pioneers as objects who will not change. Kuznetsov in the museum resembles Lenin in the mausoleum as he is comfortably cushioned on a bed decorated with a hammer and sickle, reduced to total passivity and functioning as a mouthpiece for the state view. Livnev created a myth: he resisted the movement of eradicating the Soviet past and instead erected again the monument of the Worker and the Peasant, while mocking totalitarian values. Livnev's film belongs totally with the postmodernist movement. It was a popular and much talked-about film at its time, when films could not get a commercial release because of the collapse of the distribution system.

***Mikhalkov:* Burnt by the Sun**   The film's title draws on the 1930s tango "Utomlennoye solntse" ("The Weary Sun"), changing the grammatical correlation to "Utomlennye solntsem"—"those worn out by the sun." The title creates an assonance between *Burnt by the Sun* and another grand narrative of U.S. history, *Gone with the Wind* (in Russian, "Unesennye vetrom"), attempting to appeal to a wide audience.

Burnt by the Sun operates within a closed circular structure in terms of space and time: the story begins at 6 AM and ends in the early hours of the following morning; it begins and ends in Mitia's flat in the house of the government, the House on the Embankment. The film contrasts urban and peasant life: the life of Marusia's family with an intellectual background, the *dachniki*, with that of Mitia, the representative of the new order, who comes from the city.

The happy past is remembered in the form of a fairy tale narrated by Mitia; as he tells this story, a fireball emerges on the river, enters the house, and makes the glass on a photograph burst. The fireball eventually burns one tree in the wood, representing the destruction of Mitia's life for the first time. The second fireball effect accompanies Mitia's physical destruction: his suicide. The effect is symbolic and not integrated into the overall realism of the film. It obtrudes as artificial, although it is reported in the newspaper article that Filipp reads at the beginning of the film. It is also unreal in that nobody notices the fireball, nor the effect it has on the picture (showing Kotov and Stalin).

The film distinguishes and intertwines the political and personal: Mitia is politically successful, but his personal life has failed. Kotov has personal happiness and political power, which he loses. Mitia commits suicide when he realizes the potential permanence of personal happiness as opposed to the transience of political success when looking at the crushed face of Kotov. *Burnt by the Sun* underlines the personal aspect of history rather than the potential civil courage to sacrifice one's personal life for a political cause.

Mitia is usually interpreted by Russian critics as lacking strength and courage: he argues that he was forced to join the secret service and there was no choice. Kotov has courage and power, enjoying "paternal" protection from Stalin. Once he realizes that a change has taken place and Stalin is now a protector and father-figure for Mitia, Kotov cries like a child disappointed by his parent, deprived of paternal love. The phrase he used to reproach Mitia—there is always a choice—is tragically proven wrong: there is no choice for Kotov. The film raises the question of where the borderline lies between victim and oppressor, between the victim Kotov and the victim Mitia. Although one might argue at first sight that there is a crude line between the "goodies" and the "baddies," between Kotov's Soviet heroism and Mitia's Western decadence (his French past), the film is much more complex than that. The fireball indicates that Mitia had died a long time ago, when he lost his love, Marusia. Indeed, he tried to kill himself minutes before accepting the mission to arrest Kotov. He knows that, without love, he is spiritually dead.

Burnt by the Sun was premiered in the competition program of the International Film Festival in Cannes in May 1994, where it was awarded the Grand Prix of the jury, the second most important award after the Palme d'Or, which went to Quentin Tarantino's *Pulp Fiction*. Moreover, *Burnt by the Sun* won the Grand Prix jointly with the Chinese film *Living* (Huozhe, 1994), by Bin Wang and Xleochun Zhang. Mikhalkov was appalled at getting only the second prize and at having to share it when his ambition had been to be the first Russian since Mikhail Kalatozov in 1958 to take the Palm. Winning the Oscar a year later was no bad achievement either, however. The first scandal had begun: the Russian press reported the failure of the film to win the main award and, instead of praising how well a Russian film had done—at long last—at an international festival, they shouted "defeat."

Russia's Past Revisited   In the late 1990s the creation of historical films was popular, but historical sets and costumes were also costly. Once the film industry had begun its ascent into the new millennium, however, a number of films have dealt with Russia's history and have been set predominantly in the nineteenth or early twentieth century. *The Romanovs* (Romanovy—ventsenosnaia sem'ia, 2000) was a lavish film made by Gleb Panfilov that looked into the murder of the Romanov family in 1917. *The Captain's Daughter* (Russkii bunt, 2000) was an adaptation of Pushkin's story. This interest in historical drama peaked in the production of a television serial of Fyodor Dostoevsky's *Idiot*, which was so successful that it even spurred on book sales. The return to the past here was motivated either by an interest in the literary heritage or in that moment of Russian history when the imperial era came to an end.

The postwar Soviet years were another historical period that interested filmmakers. Pavel Chukhrai made his debut film with *The Thief* (Vor, 1997), which deals in a masterful way with the theme of fatherlessness that has been so important for Soviet culture (the loss of fathers—men—during World War II as well as the betrayal by Stalin, who had elevated himself to the "father" of the nation). In *The Thief*, Chukhrai follows the path of a young boy, Sania, whose father died in the war. After the war his mother lives with a thief, who tries to inspire in the boy "masculine" behavior but deprives Sania of his mother's love and protection and betrays the boy when he leaves him in an orphanage after his mother's death. This child, unloved, is seen at the end of the film as a military commander in a belligerent region: the fatherless and unloved children of the postwar era are doomed. Chukhrai's second film, *A Driver for Vera* (Voditel' dlia Very, 2004), is set in 1962 and captures with immense precision the Khrushchev Thaw, when politically things seemed to loosen up but when effectively there was no scope for real reform. Vadim Abdrashitov also explored the past in his film *Magnetic Storms* (Magnitnye buri, 2003), set in the early perestroika period when the first deals were struck over factory management and ownership, leaving the workers literally in a gray zone.

Most significant in the revision of the past, however, was Mikhalkov's *The Barber of Siberia* (Sibirskii tsiriul'nik, 1998 [1999]). If in *Burnt by the Sun* Mikhalkov had explored the impossibility for the individual to change the course of events during Stalin's terror, and remembered the

Tsar Alexander (Nikita Mikhalkov) and his son in Nikita Mikhalkov's *The Barber of Siberia* (1998). (Photo by Igor Gnevashev)

lifestyle lost with nostalgia, then here Mikhalkov returns to the nineteenth century with a restorative nostalgia for an absolute monarchy. He wishes to return to a past that he sees in a distorted manner.

Mikhalkov was a megastar in the emerging new Russian film world. Winning an Oscar at the time when Russian cinema was in the worst crisis ever enhanced his already high reputation in the professional and political world. This granted him the opportunity to realize a long-term project with an enormous budget for any film industry—the immense sum of $45 million. *The Barber of Siberia* was to be Russia's first blockbuster. If *Burnt by the Sun* was subjected to a stunning marketing campaign in Russia, with the distillery Kristall launching the vodka brand KomDiv (Divi-

The Barber of Siberia Plot

The Barber of Siberia tells the story of Jane Callaghan (Julia Ormond), an American woman who travels to Russia in 1885 in order to help the Irish American inventor Douglas McCracken (Richard Harris) to secure funding for his machine, the "barber," which is designed to cut down the Siberian forests. McCracken, under pressure from his creditors, has hired Jane to charm General Radlov (Alexei Petrenko), the head of the Military Academy, in order to gain through him the support of Grand Duke Alexei. Jane achieves this task by pretending to be McCracken's daughter and flirting with the vain general, who proposes to her. In her business-oriented approach to life, Jane offers her ability to charm for hire ever since she was abused as a child by her stepfather and forced to fend for herself. Then she meets the cadet Andrei Tolstoy (Oleg Menshikov), who falls in love with her. The cadet Tolstoy has very high moral values: he defends his feelings for Jane in a duel, he humiliates himself when he proposes to Jane in front of the general, and he is prepared to abandon his career for Jane. She, however, continues her intrigues in order to fulfill her contract and get McCracken's papers signed by the grand duke. Unwilling to sacrifice her scheme for the sake of love, she spends a day with the general at a Shrovetide fair and encourages him to drink, seeking to compromise him. When Tolstoy sees Jane flirt with the general in the theater just after she has spent the night with the cadet, he attacks his rival with a violin bow during a performance of The Marriage of Figaro in which Tolstoy plays Figaro. The production by the Military Academy takes place in the presence of the grand duke, and Radlov swiftly accuses Tolstoy of an attempt upon the grand duke's life. Thus Radlov secures promotion for himself by "preventing a terrorist act," and Tolstoy is found guilty and sent to a prison camp in Siberia, without ever attempting to defend his actions. Ten years later, Jane has married McCracken so that her son (Tolstoy's child) will have a father. On the occasion of the launch of McCracken's invention, Jane travels to Siberia. As the machine begins the massive destruction of the Siberian taiga, Jane finds the house where Tolstoy now lives with his wife, Dunia (formerly a maid in the Tolstoys' Moscow house), and their children. Jane leaves Russia.

The love story of Jane and Andrei Tolstoy is embedded in an English narration by Jane, who, in 1905, writes a letter to her son Andrew (the English version of his father's name, Andrei), a recruit at a U.S. military base. Time and again, we see her writing the letter while her voice reads parts of it, and we see Andrew at the U.S. base, as stubborn as his father and upholding values and principles that he defends with his life: he stands up for Mozart by refusing to repeat a phrase denigrating the composer. Rather than obeying Commander O'Leary's order to denounce Mozart's talent, he wears a gas mask for more than twenty-four hours. Andrew's endurance wins out, and the explanation for his stubbornness comes from Jane, who shows the commander a portrait of Andrew's father, the former Russian cadet Tolstoy.

sional Commander) with Mikhalkov's profile as Kotov on the bottle label, then the publicity campaign around The Barber was even more carefully coordinated. Banners and posters were positioned all over central Moscow, a new brand of vodka, Russian Standard, was launched as well as a new perfume range, Cadet No. 1 and Cadet No. 3. A shawl by Hermès, designed especially for the premiere, was offered to select guests. Mikhalkov appeared for more than a week on almost all television shows, and several channels screened retrospectives of his films. The premiere brought the invited guests to the Kremlin Palace of Congresses, specially fitted with a Dolby stereo system and a new projection screen for this purpose.

The Barber of Siberia represented Mikhalkov's attempt to make a blockbuster and to offer moral guidance to an audience at a time when the mainstream of Russian filmmakers portrayed the bleakness, the abyss, and the degeneration surrounding them. *The Barber of Siberia* shaped the values of the future by telling a story about Russia's past, which elevated the traditions of the East above those of the West. The film used a historical setting for this romantic plot with a positive hero to transport the moral values of the past into the present. In terms of box office, it was one of the most successful films in Russia in the 1990s, although its distribution in the West did not bring the desired success.

The Barber explores the qualities of the Russian character and juxtaposes them to the traits of Western characters. The way Tolstoy behaves toward Jane parallels the stubborn insistence upon principle displayed by the recruit Andrew, and both men's obsessive behavior is classified as typically Russian in the film. Jane is still unable fully to understand Russia, implying that Russia "cannot be grasped by reason alone." The Western characters acknowledge success only in business or the achievement of goals, whereas most of the Russian characters surrender to a fatalistic vision of their life, accepting suffering and solitude.

The film dwells on the absence of a father figure: Jane comes from a broken family; after her father's death she was abused by her stepfather. Tolstoy's family is broken too: his mother lives with an uncle. Both army captains (Captain Mokin and Commander O'Leary) act like father figures to their cadets. Life in the military with its discipline is idealized. In the absence of intact family life and father figures, the military community replaces the family, and the tsar replaces the father who is also represented on a lower level by the military commanders. In Mikhalkov's vision the whole of Russian society is transformed into one large family with a patriarch at its head. And Tsar Alexander III is played by Mikhalkov himself.

As a political manifesto the film contained a strangely nationalistic statement for the future of Russia, envisaging the resurrection of order and discipline that would reinstate a value system and thus benefit the Russian population. In this sense Mikhalkov preempted the stability brought about by Putin's rule after the chaos of the Yeltsin era.

Alexei Balabanov's Brothers *and Bodrov's* Sisters

Although Rogozhkin was concerned with comedy, Bodrov with society and war, and Mikhalkov with the past and Russia's national identity, all these directors belonged to the mainstream of Russian culture and cinema. Alexei Balabanov chose to take another path: he went against the current and deliberately created a hero who lacked moral values. He thus prepared the ground for a new generation of filmmakers to emerge with films where psychology can no longer explain the motivation for characters' actions, as indeed is manifest in contemporary cinema in Gus van Sant's 2003 Cannes Festival winner, *Elephant*.

Sergei Bodrov Jr. as Danila Bagrov in Alexei Balabanov's *Brother* (1997), the first Russian "blockbuster," albeit in video releases only. (Photo courtesy of Sergei Selianov, CTB)

Balabanov veered for a long time between "auteur" cinema and blockbusters. *Of Freaks and Men* (Pro urodov i liudei, 1998) investigated the amoral attitudes in Russian society at the beginning of the twentieth century and exposed the photo-camera as an instrument of commercial exploitation (the production of sadomasochistic and pornographic images and films). At the same time Balabanov wrote and directed the blockbusters *Brother* (Brat, 1997), *Brother 2* (Brat 2, 2000), and *War* (Voina, 2002). Sergei Bodrov Jr., who became a cult figure through the role of Danila Bagrov (*Brother*), was supported by CTB in his directorial debut, *Sisters* (Sestry, 2001), where he explored the relationship of two half sisters trying to survive in the criminal world of the younger sister's father.

The resurgence of the Russian blockbuster came only in 1997 with Balabanov's *Brother* and the sequel *Brother*, which playfully engaged with the action movie genre. *Brother* is an example of a filmmaker's moving away from his "auteur" status toward the mass audience.

Brother defines a new type of hero, who upholds no moral standards at all. On the one hand, Danila possesses skill, strength, and courage. He knows how to use guns, he is physically fit to fight, and his actions display a sense of military logistics. He helps the poor (he defends an old man—Hoffman, the German—on the street against a racketeer, helps the conductor collect a fine from two Caucasians—"black arses"—traveling on a tram without a ticket, and shoots at his girlfriend Sveta's violent hus-

Brother: Plot

Danila Bagrov returns to his provincial hometown from service in the army. When he gets into trouble with the police, his mother sends him to visit his elder brother, Viktor, in Petersburg. Viktor is a killer, who engages Danila to shoot the "Chechen." Carrying out the assignment, Danila realizes that his brother has betrayed him, whereas an unknown woman tram driver, Sveta, helps him. They subsequently have an affair, but Sveta stays with her husband, who beats her. Danila shoots the "Chechen" and bails out his brother when the latter is in trouble. Danila is a professional killer, but he is also a knight who helps the poor, suppressed, and underprivileged (the German Hoffman, Sveta, the drug-addict Kat, the fare collector in the tram, and his own brother). Having conquered the criminal world of Petersburg, he leaves for Moscow.

band). Yet he is ruthless to his enemies and is a man of action. In the tradition of the romantic hero, he is a knight who keeps his word. In the criminal world he is a killer. He combines within himself the contradictions at the heart of the Russian idea: the right to judge and the compassion to redeem. Balabanov debunks the socialist myth, which sees the hero as part of a historical process: Danila has no role in society at large. A true killer, he is a loner, an individual, acting without a reason. Moreover, Balabanov rejects the chernukha model, which perceives man as a victim of circumstance and therefore essentially nonheroic. The new hero makes no choices but lives on the spur of the moment.

The title of the film parodied the concept of a "brotherhood of people" (the collective spirit of the Soviet people). Real "brotherhood" is further mocked when Viktor, the elder brother who replaces the absent father, is protected by Danila: Danila saves him from the Mafia bosses who have hired him as a killer after he successfully carried out the killing that Viktor was paid for. Danila reverses the relationship of authority and respect for his elder brother and sends him back home to look after his mother.

Danila sets no model to follow. He offers neither a lead to the future, nor does he have a past. If he does have a history, it is the fictional biography of Bodrov's previous hero, the soldier of the Chechen war, Vania Zhilin. At the beginning of the film, Danila Bagrov has just returned home from service in the army, claiming that he has merely worked as a scribe in some office. It soon becomes clear that this is a myth: he has a very good knowledge of firearms, and his maneuvers are much too carefully planned. It is much more likely that Danila has served in the Caucasus or Chechnya. Bagrov is a young man hardened to the realities of life by his experience of war. Indeed, Danila's personality and background are like a blank page, onto which any story could be written. This is reflected in the technique of blackouts after each episode, which fragment the film and almost allow it to be reassembled in any order. Danila is deprived of any psychological depth, and the choice of a nonprofessional actor reflects Balabanov's need for a facade rather than a character.

Danila accidentally walks into the location of a clip for the rock group Nautilus Pompilius's latest album "Wings" (Kryl'ia), and later he literally marches into lead singer Butusov's flat: he seeks to identify with the group but fails to realize that these are different worlds. In both cases, he crashes back into reality: at the police station, bruised and beaten; and into a murder scene. Nautilus's music functions as a leitmotif for Danila's journey to St. Petersburg. The band is originally from Sverdlovsk but moved to St. Petersburg in the 1990s; Danila, too, comes from provincial Russia and arrives in St. Petersburg. where he finally acquires a compact disc of "Wings." Danila plays Nautilus most of the time on his personal CD player. He lives in the world of the music and only partly perceives the reality that surrounds him. The songs endow the film with a dreamlike quality. Bagrov's movements are paced by the rhythm of the music and thus appear as though they were performed under a spell or under the influence of drugs, but not by an individual who reflects upon the surrounding reality. Nautilus's songs are about another reality, about daydreams, and about the crippling effect of this reality; the wings that enable man to fly have been lost and all that remains are scars. The songs accompany Danila's arrival, his "new life," the lead-up to the shootings at the market and in Viktor's flat. They are all from the albums "Atlantida" and "Yablokitai," which, in fact, Danila fails to acquire in the music shop. In other words, the film's spectators hear the music Danila wishes to hear on his CD player but has actually not yet managed to acquire. The hero lives in the sound track of another world, in which he is immortal: the CD player saves his life when it deflects a bullet.

Balabanov refrained from moralizing and preaching, a function that Soviet directors had taken on for such a long time; he no longer provided ideals to be followed and no longer set moral standards. He did not condemn or reject the amoral conduct of his protagonists but portrayed a new type. Balabanov's approach to the protagonist as a hero who sets no standards opposed the mainstream of Russian cinema (such as the elevation of the cadet Tolstoy to hero status) and inspired other filmmakers, including Sergei Bodrov in his debut as filmmaker.

The Last Hero: Sergei Bodrov Jr.

Sergei Bodrov Jr., son of the film director Sergei Bodrov, made his debut as an actor in 1996, playing the soldier Vania Zhilin in his father's film *The Prisoner of the Mountains*. The casting of the nonprofessional Bodrov alongside Russia's top film star, Oleg Menshikov, seemed risky at first, but Bodrov and Menshikov complemented each other perfectly in their approaches. The professional Menshikov played his character through several layers of masks, whereas Bodrov created his role through his absolutely natural conduct in front of the camera. Jointly they received a major Russian acting award for their performance in this film. Bodrov's Zhilin is an honest and quiet Russian soldier, who accepts the conditions of his captivity in a Muslim village in the Caucasus. He makes friends with his captors and never risks their lives: he is not a man of action. Following the success of *The Prisoner of the Mountains*, Bodrov became the presenter of the talk-show *Vzgliad* on Russia's First Television Channel.

After his success as Zhilin, Alexei Balabanov invited Bodrov to play the main part in *Brother* and the later sequel *Brother 2*. Here Bodrov created the new Russian hero: his character, Danila Bagrov, returns from the Chechen war and travels to Petersburg, where he acts like a professional killer in order to rescue his elder brother from the grip of the Chechen Mafia. In true heroic fashion, Danila kills the baddies and helps the goodies. He displays the features of a knight who helps the poor, while killing his brother's "enemies" cold-bloodedly. This combination of the assertive killer with the humble romantic knight characterized the hero figure that the young generation of the new Russia adopted. Bagrov-Bodrov established justice by turning into a killer: he followed the right aim by doubtful means, but means that required taking things into his own hands rather than relying on the state. In *Brother 2* Danila travelled to Chicago to get the brother of a fellow soldier out of the thralls of the American sports Mafia. Bodrov's characters almost always support Russian ideals, echoing his repeatedly stated love for Russia.

Bodrov featured in many international projects, such as Regis Wargnier's *East-West* (1999), in which he played the part of a young swimmer who is refused travel outside Stalin's Soviet Union. Encouraged by the love of his neighbor's French wife (Sandrine Bonnaire), he manages to swim to a vessel in the Black Sea outside Soviet waters.

Bodrov built his image of the good and simple guy through natural and leisurely conduct: he never seemed to play-act but just existed in front of the camera. It was his professionalism of seeming "unprofessional" and natural in front of the camera that made his acting so unique. Similarly, in his talk shows on Russian television he always presented himself as if he were "just

himself," creating the impression of a seemingly unprepared, unplanned discussion. At the peak of his career he gave up television to devote himself to film, making his debut as a filmmaker with *Sisters* (2001)—a risky move at a time when most actors turned to television as a better source of income. *Sisters* tells the story of two girls, Sveta (Oxana Akinshina) and her younger half sister Dina. Sveta dreams of becoming a sniper, whereas her younger half sister is a spoiled little girl who plays the violin and is the pride of her gangster-daddy. Suddenly Sveta has to protect herself and her sister from some gangsters who come after Dina's father. Bodrov himself appears in one scene as a kind-hearted gangster, offering Sveta protection. With *Sisters*, which won awards for the best debut film in 2001, Bodrov paved the path for Akinshina's career: she next starred in Lucas Moodyson's *Lilya 4ever*.

Bodrov appeared in Balabanov's *War* (2002), where he played the injured Captain Medvedev. Together with an English couple (Ian McKellen and Ingeborga Dapkunaite), he is held hostage by Chechen partisans. Their ultimate escape is possible thanks to Medvedev, who calls the army to evacuate them once they have freed themselves. Bodrov again plays a lovable soldier, who remains in good spirits in a dire situation and who never loses faith in Russia.

On 20 September 2002, a glacier slid down into the Karmadon Gorge in the North Caucasus. It buried the inhabitants of the mountain settlement and the film crew of Sergei Bodrov Jr. under a thick layer of ice and mud. Bodrov was shooting his second feature film, *The Messenger* (Sviaznoi). The loss of Russia's "Last Hero" (the title of a television program he hosted) has left a gap that will not be easy to fill.

Thrillers, Killers, and Antikillers

The film *Bimmer* by Petr Buslov follows the experiments in genre made by Bodrov and Balabanov. Buslov made a gangster movie, where the title role is attributed to a car, a BMW 750 (*bumer* in Russian slang). Four men—Tomcat (Kot), Rama, Killa, and Burnt (Oshparenny)—have to flee Moscow because they are wanted by the Mafia. These petty gangsters are used to operating within the Mafia circles of the capital, but out in the countryside they lack survival skills and are rendered almost helpless. The film follows their escape in the style of a road movie, where the foreign car is unsuited for the Russian roads but superior in technology. On a number of occasions the car saves them; on others it fails them, just like a human being. Although the automobile displays features of human emotions (compassionately winking or groaning), the four men behave like wild animals, indeed like the hunted wolves described in Vysotsky's legendary ballad of the "Wolf Hunt." As in Balabanov's films, there is no moral message in Buslov's debut. The viewer merely follows the gangsters and their adventures while adopting a position of ironic superiority, often knowing better how to prevent trouble than the gangsters. The music to the film was composed by Sergei Shnurov of the band Leningrad, which added to the popularity that the film enjoyed at the box office.

Yegor Konchalovsky's *Antikiller* and the sequel *Antikiller 2* were also a considerable success at the Russian box office (*Antikiller 2* grossed $2.7 million), although they have not been distributed abroad. *Antikiller* is based on the very popular novel by Danil Koretsky and set in the criminal world. The former police lieutenant Korenev (nickname "Lis," or Fox), played by the very popular actor Gosha Kutsenko, has been set up and arrested for abuse of power. Having served his sentence, he is released from prison and now tries to figure out the new constellation of power in the criminal world in order to set the gangs up against each other. The criminal boss Shaman (Alexander Baluyev) has ordered the murder of Fox's friend and former colleague. Shaman is a new player in the criminal world, not following the codes of the old Mafia bosses Father (Mikhail Ulianov), King (Alexander Beliavsky), and Cross (Sergei Shakurov). Into this Mafia war of old and new clans erupts the violence of the gang of Ambal (Viktor Sukhorukov), a brutal gangster whose level of pain has been reduced significantly since an operation when parts of his brain were removed. Ambal has no values, no understanding of the order of the criminal "authorities" and knows only the force of his pistol. In many ways, Konchalovsky's film is a continuation of the amoral killer of *Brother*, although offering a broader insight into the criminal world. In the sequel *Antikiller 2*, Korenev has returned to the police force and is married to Liuba. The unit of his colleague has caught the Chechen commander Aduyev. By this arrest they bring about danger for the city. Aduyev's son Uzhak seeks revenge and prepares a terrorist attack. Liuba, who has saved Aduyev Senior's life, falls into captivity. Both films contain a number of special effects, are professionally made, and offer a high standard of acting. Konchalovsky's visual handling of the detective stories raises the suspense level and creates visually tantalizing sequences, which explain the films' success.

As film production is increasing, Russian films are becoming box office hits, outstripping new U.S. releases on the national

Konstantin Khabensky as Anton Gorodetsky in *Night Watch*, the Russian mega blockbuster of 2004, directed by Timur Bekmambetov. (Photo courtesy of First Channel Press Service)

market. This is achieved once again, as in Soviet times, by films that are shown, but not widely distributed, in the West. Timur Bekmambetov's *Night Watch* (Nochnoi dozor, 2004) contains numerous special effects, but most important it is based on Lukianenko's gripping fantasy (sci-fi) thriller and performed by fine actors. The film addresses the issue of good and evil, the worlds of light and darkness. The literary source actually consists of a trilogy, where *Night Watch* is followed by *Day Watch* and *Twilight Watch*. Into the struggle before good and evil, which is explained in a historical prologue, come fortune-tellers, magicians, and vampires as representatives of the good and evil forces. The plot revolves around Anton Gorodetsky (Konstantin Khabensky) who ten years earlier had wanted to get rid of his wife's lover (and her unborn child). To this end he had turned to a sorceress, but she was prevented from casting the spell by the forces of "light." Now Gorodetsky fights on the side of "light" and helps protect Moscow and its inhabitants from disaster, catastrophe, and evil. *Night Watch* contains all the ingredients of an American action movie (for example, *Terminator*) while expanding the fantasy component to the level where it almost becomes parodic. Moreover, the difference between the worlds of good and evil, light and dark, is never drawn in black and white colors but uses the gray shades rather than falling back on absolutes and stereotypes. The film is set to become Russia's biggest box office hit in decades.

Animation

In the early years of the Soviet period, many animators put their art at the service of the state: cartoons and animation were frequently used for political propaganda. During the 1930s and 1940s, animation was increasingly considered as a tool for ideo-

logical instruction of the younger generation and targeted at children. Many scripts
for animation were written on the basis of
Soviet children's literature and Russian
fairy tales. It is interesting to note here the
contribution of many "banned" writers to
the genre of animation scripts, especially
the satirist Nikolai Erdman, who, after his
arrest in the 1930s, subsequently refrained
from play writing but produced more than
fifty scenarios before his death in 1970.

Classic Animation   In the 1960s, a new
generation of animators emerged: Roman
Kachanov invented the Soviet equivalents
of Mickey Mouse: Cheburashka and Gena
the Crocodile. From the late 1960s onward,
animation moved into more sophisticated
territory: some animators created films for
the sake of artistic expression and poetic
reflection while addressing themselves to
an adult audience. Ivan Ivanov-Vano, Lev
Atamanov and Leonid Amalrik, the Brumberg sisters (Valentina and Zinaida), Ivan
Ufimtsev, Fyodor Khitruk, and Vladimir
Suteyev became famous for films of Soviet
and popular fairy tales. Their works were
based on Eduard Uspensky, Nikolai Nosov,
Vladimir Suteyev, and Boris Zakhoder as
well as the classic Kornei Chukovsky.

In the last decades of the USSR, some
well-known animators, such as Yuri Norstein and Andrei Khrzhanovsky, emerged
onto the international stage. They collaborated with contemporary writers, such as
Liudmila Petrushevskaya in the case of
Norstein's world-famous *Tale of Tales*
(Skazka skazok, 1979). With the artist
Francesca Yarbusova, Norstein created
some of the finest drawn animation, moving his cell objects on several layers of
glass in order to create a three-dimensional
effect. Norstein's films are poetic and not

made for mass consumption, unlike some
of the cheaper animation for children. He
made a trailer for the children's program
Good Night, Kids, which was removed almost before he completed it. His work on
Gogol's *Overcoat* (Shinel') has been ongoing for more than ten years, and only
twenty minutes of the film are complete.

Andrei Khrzhanovsky has a long history
as a filmmaker and a reputation for literary
and historical themes. Thus, he made animated films about Alexander Pushkin and
Federico Fellini. He has also made children's animation, such as *The Lion with
the Gray Beard* (Lev s sedoi borodoi,
1994). He heads the studio Shar, which as-
sists young animators in their work. Irina
Yevteyeva, too, makes hand-drawn animation. She has made films on the poet
Vladimir Mayakovsky and the German romantic writer Ernst Theodor Amadeus
Hoffmann, combining animation with documentary footage, and thereby taking animation into a new dimension. Her film *Petersburg* (2003), made to mark the 300th
anniversary of the city, drew on a variety of
highly sophisticated literary associations
while creating an artistically innovative
view of the city's cultural history. *The
Clown* is a film she made with Slava Polunin. Sergei Ovcharov initially came from
filmmaking before creating a series of animated myths, from antiquity to Russian
folk traditions. In *Pharaoh*, Ovcharov uses
Egyptian drawings in which the characters
are animated. The result of their actions is
often funny, bringing out the erotic elements underlying mythology. In *Sochinushki*, based on Russian folklore, Ovcharov animated scenes from Russian
lubok (woodcut) and folk drawings, parodying the old rituals of peasant life.

The animator Alexander Petrov has made

several films in his studio in Yaroslavl, including *The Cow* (Korova, 1989), which told the story of a cow and her calf, which was taken away for slaughtering. Suffering from grief, the cow throws herself under a train. The film sets out Petrov's main concern: the relationship between man and nature. His film *Rusalka* (1998) explored the theme of a Russian fairy tale and was nominated for an Oscar, the highest possible recognition for a film. Petrov's animation is painted on glass, and it was his skill at this that won him an invitation to work abroad. In the late 1990s, as funding became a massive problem for animators who could not work in advertising to finance their work, he was invited to make a film in Canada. He made a hand-painted animation for the new IMAX format: *The Old Man and the Sea* won the Oscar in 2000. The film again explores the relationship of man and nature, this time creating most subtle and nuanced images of the sea and its life.

The studio Pilot was founded in 1988 and is financed through commercial activity. Its director, Alexander Tatarsky, is the creator of the *Pilot Brothers* series, made in the 1990s; this was followed by the series of *Fund of Legal Reforms*. This series of films is largely based on a play with the current social and political situation, providing a satirical gloss on contemporary life and politics. The Pilot brothers are two simply drawn characters, whose main characteristic is their rolling eyes. The art director at the studio is Mikhail Aldashin, whose *Bukashka* won the "Nika" award for best Russian animation in 2003.

Garri Bardin founded his own studio, Staier, after the collapse of state subsidies for animation. After his successes at international festivals with films such as *Brake* in the 1980s, he made a New Year's film,

Choocha (Chucha). *Choocha* is nonverbal, based only on the tunes of Glenn Miller. Using puppet animation, Bardin showed a little boy in the midst of a party. The adults dance and the boy sees only legs: the camera follows the child's perspective. Utterly bored and neglected, he ties the adults' legs together under the table and leaves. He ventures into the attic and creates his own "nanny" (a scarecrow, in Russian *chuchelo*), which he calls Choocha. He uses cushions, pots and pans, braces, and other clutter stored in the attic. Choocha becomes alive and dances around the room. Choocha climbs onto the roof, and together they play with the bats and the icicles. Then the boy goes to bed, with Choocha. When the adults enter the room, they too turn into little children. Bardin's film is a parable for the adults' lack of understanding vis-à-vis children.

Russia's animators are mostly known through festivals, rather than to mass audiences. Sergei Ainutdinov works in Ekaterinburg. His animation is drawn and two-dimensional. In his films he parodies the erotic subconscious of the frustrated office worker; he explores the dementia of people living in the modern world. His films are funny, cheeky, and point at the absurdity of human life. Natalia Dabizha has been in animation since the 1970s. In the 1990s she joined Christmas Films in the UK and made *The Tree with the Golden Apples*. Konstantin Bronzit from St. Petersburg creates drawn animation, and his French coproduction, *The House at the End of the World* (La Maison au bout du Monde, 1999), was shown internationally. It is a simple story of people living in a house on the top of a hill, and the difficulties associated with this life, which are overcome with a sense of lightness and ease.

Neznaika and Masiania   The most popular children's cartoon of the 1990s was the sequel to a 1970s film, *Neznaika in Sun City* (Neznaika v solnechnom gorode, 1976–1977), based on a popular children's story by Nikolai Nosov. The film had originally been created as a puppet animation by Petr Murashov and others, making the central character a gentle boy with red hair. The post-Soviet sequel, *Neznaika on the Moon* (Neznaika na lune, 1997–1999) was created as drawn animation by A. Liutkevich and Yuri Butyrin and became a bestseller among videos. With the voice of Kristina Orbakaite and music by Valeri Meladze, the project was ostensibly commercial. This film explores the adventure of the child, Neznaika, who learns though his mistakes. Ultimately Neznaika's right and good acts are triumphant.

The hero of animation, however, has not been created manually: *Masiania*, the first flash animation, which uses flash graphics to create animation rather than the traditional techniques of filmed drawings online, later appeared on television and on video releases. Masiania was launched in October 2001 by the St. Petersburg graphic designer Oleg Kuvayev on the site mult.ru (*mult* is a short word for *multik*, or *multiplikatsionnyi fil'm*, a cartoon). By 2002, Masiania had become a megastar and was invited onto NTV's most prestigious news program, *Namedni*. After the return to the

Web artist Oleg Kuvayev (left), with the Masiania puppet (right), attends the press conference of the companies "Masiania" (right) and NTV television, agreeing to the televised broadcasting of the flash animation cartoons. (Photo by Vasily Shaposhnikov/Kommersant)

Internet and numerous illegal sites using and re-using the material of mult.ru, the site moved temporarily to hrundel.ru and disappeared from cyberspace, before returning to the old site mult.ru in early 2004. The new site also hosts projects by younger animators, such as the series of clips by Masha Yakunina about Jerzy and Petruccio, the clips about Mel by Masha Stepanova, and the episodes of the rabbit Bo and his cranky human friends.

Masiania is a character made up from a few strokes of a pen: two lines form arms and legs, a circle for her body and an oval shape for her face. She is dressed in a red top and a blue short skirt. She swears and smokes and is promiscuous. She is hardly well educated, but rather the "underground" outsider teenager of today. She is not feminine at all, and were it not for a "nude" scene and reference to her menstruation, it would be difficult to pinpoint her gender. She is shameless and egocentric, and combined with her outright egoism this strangely makes her rather charming. She is surrounded in the fifty or so episodes by her boyfriend, Hrundel, by Lokhmaty, and Liaska, her Moscow friend. The verbal puns in the clips make the dialogue hard to render in another language.

Masiania and her boyfriend, Hrundel, pose in the Worker and Farmer statue's pose that is the emblem of Mosfilm, crossed by beams of light that symbolize Lenfilm, to mark the opening logo of Masfilm. Masiania's stories appeared in ten episodes on the Internet. In the first part she was sketched as a character: she tries to sing, watches telly, puffs cigarettes. She uses swearwords, annoys people on a train, tells a joke that only amuses herself, and makes fun of her friends. In these early sketches Masiania always appeared alone.

She came across as an immature and egocentric person, who failed to see the borderline between play and seriousness—a sign of her childishness. She is also sexless, as she does not define herself as a girl until the second part, in the mult "Birthday," when the character proper is born.

Masiania develops in the following episodes, indeed almost grows up and undergoes a process of maturation. She continues to use vulgar language and contemporary street jargon. It becomes clear, however, that her abusive language and her egoism cover a very lonely and delicate soul. She is alone on her birthday; she tries to hitchhike and ends up in the same location as before, catching a cold; she is scared walking through the city on her own at night, then boosts her confidence by screaming at a beggar and being ready to scare others. She gains confidence through her apparently aggressive behavior and her inventiveness. Yet in reality she is never superior: she falls down the stairs on her roller skates just like Lokhmaty; she is knocked off the boat just as Hrundel fell off a bridge. She is occasionally very depressed ("Depresniak") and goes to the seaside to sing a song and find her happiness again while her friends worry about her. She buys a rat after an argument with Hrundel so that she won't be alone, and although she commands the rat around she is genuinely sad when it dies.

Masiania is not a model teenager, though: she drinks, she and her friends use drugs, she is promiscuous, and she smokes like a chimney. She has compassion for the poor: she cares for the orphan boy in the basement of a house, although he has stolen her purse, and gathers the crowds who wish the boy a merry Christmas ("Skazka," 2003), or she is concerned for the poor and talented musician Okolo-bakha ("Near-Bach"). Not all her acts are driven by compassion, however. She also seeks attention. Her multiple appearances on stage, trying to become a singer, end without success. She is beaten over the head when dancing on stage during a rock concert ("Spleen"); she is disappointed when she realizes that sex appeal matters more than talent ("Pops"); she is sad when a producer tells her that her figure is not good enough for a pop star ("Show-business").

Her boyfriend, Hrundel, first appears as a friend who makes advances: he tries to talk her into staying overnight; then he asks her out for a drink and she ends up with a hangover; then they are in bed together and she—with an air of embarrassment—asks him to use condoms. They support each other: she gets him out of a bad trip; he stops her from laughing hysterically. She bails Hrundel out of debt by selling her car. When Masiania is ashamed of dressing up as a dog for a pharmacy ad in the street, Hrundel confesses to doing the same job. Both Masiania and Hrundel have a streak of selfishness when they try to make money: Hrundel by selling the musician's violin ("Okolobakha"), Masiania by reselling ice cream ("Ice Cream"). By the last part of the series, Masiania and Hrundel live together. Masiania no longer needs to prove she is part of the male world, nor to be embarrassed or prove that she is as good as or better than men. In that sense, she has matured. In another sense, she is still up to naughty tricks and games: resting in a coffin to be carried home; not being able to get out of bed and work; being so drunk that she puts Lokhmaty on a train to Moscow instead of a German visitor. Nevertheless, Masiania is a figure who ap-peals because of her charm with which she combines those features criticized by society in the lifestyle of the young generation.

Visual Arts and Crafts

Visual culture is more prominent in the New Russia than it was in the Soviet era, which had relied on the power of the word. As cinema struggled to find its feet in a market swamped with foreign films, advertisements, and television serials, the visual arts were fast to use new opportunities and present their installations, paintings, and posters in galleries and museums. Performance art gained ground in the Moscow galleries, where Marat Guelman became a key organizer in events of "nonofficial" culture on the 1990s, and in Petersburg activities centered around Timur Novikov's Neoclassical Academy. Art movements that had previously been banned to an underground existence suddenly had the opportunity not only of exhibiting in private galleries but also of selling their paintings. The auction of contemporary painting held by Sotheby's in Moscow on 7 July 1988 not only attracted the attention of art dealers from all over the world to contemporary Russian art but also surprised everybody with the high prices Russian art was able to fetch.

Conceptualism and sots-art parodied Soviet culture, but they also fed into consumer culture through their appropriation of traditional, popular art forms. Thus, the design of popular crafts adopted the satirical and parodic treatment characteristic of sots-art, for example, in the distortion of the *matrioshka* to a *patrioshka* that represents political leaders, reducing Russian and Soviet history to a series of toys. The New Russia thus acquired a number of visual arts forms that fall neatly between national heritage (high culture) and consumerism, between avant-garde experiments and kitsch. Objects of Russian crafts are handmade and designed, but they are also made for (mass) consumption: porcelain, wooden objects and toys, jewelry.

Urban planning responded quickly to the opportunity of using design to appeal to a new clientele, from the design of shopping venues to the construction of new apartment complexes. Moreover, the New Russia has developed a unique relationship to its past in the creation of monuments, not as national heritage but as pieces created seemingly for the consumer's pleasure and entertainment. Architecture is of crucial importance in particular in Moscow, where Luzhkov's rule as mayor has led to a recreation of the city's identity by destroying the Soviet past and rebuilding it in pseudo-Stalinist style but in better quality.

Art Movements

In the 1970s, many artists departed from the prescribed mode of Socialist Realism, moving either into a deliberately abstract and rational art or into parodying Socialist Realism (according to which the artists should portray Soviet life in a positive light). As artists tried to exhibit their work, they were stopped by the authorities. The most famous intervention is the so-called bulldozer exhibition in the park Bitsa in Moscow in 1973, when bulldozers were brought in to disperse the crowds and destroy the paintings. Subsequently many artists emigrated.

Conceptualism flourished during 1970s both in visual arts and poetry. Conceptualism based itself on exploring concepts and illustrating them, in an attempt to discover the original meaning behind words that

had been tainted. Its main exponent is Ilia Kabakov (b. 1933), who has had major international exhibitions since glasnost. He created canvases with questions and answers, focusing on the word as object. Or he would place objects of everyday life into the frame to move them out of context, make them strange, and create new meaning (for example, *The Fly* or *The Grater*). In *List of People Who Have the Right to Receive* ... (1982) he painted on canvas a list of names of people. In the heading "List of People Who Have the Right to Receive ... ," the object is left blank, with a small pocket for a piece of paper to be inserted so that the object may be changed while the list of people remains unchanged. He deconstructed the orders of Soviet authorities, allowing people to receive apartments or food product by a special order. The group of the recipients of such benefits remains the same, only the favors or privileges change. Kabakov thus mocked the system and undermined its claims of democratic treatment of the people by underscoring that the group of the privileged never changes. Dmitri Prigov (b. 1940) revised the concept of poetic creation by rejecting poetry collection in favor of collating poetry on index cards, allowing reshuffling. He also created installations and paintings, such as a *Graph of History*, where the vertical axis represented months and the horizontal axis listed the years in a graph to record party congresses. The graph, completely useless and dysfunctional, parodied the USSR's obsession with and falsification of statistics but also presented a curve of cardiac activity or temperature, making the Soviet Union appear like a sick patient.

Although conceptualism presented riddles to the viewer for him or her to deci-

Artist Ilya Kabakov in one of the ten rooms of his art installation "The Man Who Flew into Space" at a SoHo art gallery in New York in August 1988. The work is based on the Moscow flat in which the Russian artist grew up; seen in the center is the contraption that catapults the fictitious character into space. (AP Photo/Marty Lederhandler)

pher, sots-art simply parodied Socialist Realism. Sots-art artists elevated the individual over the collective and mocked Soviet practices, such as the creation of monuments or the obsession with banners, flags, and slogans. Boris Orlov (b. 1941) created sculptures that mocked the Soviet obsession with banners, badges, and flags. His *Bouquet in Triumphant Style* (1988) was made of badges (*znachki*) and banners. *General* (1988) consisted of a bust created from orders and flags, but without a face: Orlov pointed at the annihilation of individuality, the emptiness of the hero whose form is created with symbols of the Soviet age. The artists Vitali Komar and Alexander Melamid (b. 1943 and 1945) emigrated to

the United States in 1978 and are the most well-known representatives of sots-art. They painted themselves in Socialist Realist manner, appearing in a painting of pioneers. They are adults, not young boys (as pioneers would be), and mock the political drive to create collective heroes while they individualize the Socialist Realist composition by placing themselves (in other pictures their relatives) into the image to protest against the anonymity of the collective system (*Double Self-portrait as Pioneers*, 1982–1983). In *Skyscraper* (1986–1987), Stalin's bust serves as a plinth for the skyscraper composed of cubes. Each cube contains a part of the human body (legs and lap that sit on Stalin's head, bust, head) in a different style—abstract, expressionist, and realist, providing as it were a journey through forbidden art forms of the Soviet years. Grisha Bruskin (b. 1945) is a key artist of sots-art, whose *Fundamental Lexicon* (1986) created a sensation when it fetched £220,000 at the 1988 Sotheby's auction in Moscow. The painting consists of a grid of cells, each containing a white figure holding an object or symbols of Soviet everyday life, thus showing the annihilation of man in a society where only signs and symbols count.

Alexander Kosolapov (b. 1943) also emigrated to the United States in 1975, where he created a series of posters mocking U.S. and Soviet political symbols. *Times Square* (1982) showed a Coca-Cola advertisement, with Lenin on a red backdrop and the simple slogan, "Coca-Cola. It's the real thing. Lenin," mocking the Soviet obsession with the word of Lenin and reducing his function from a political theorist to an advertising star. *Two Flags* (1989) showed the American and Soviet flags, where the stars were covered by the emblem of hammer and sickle, and the Soviet flag decorated with a Lenin order with Mickey Mouse. Leonid Sokov (b. 1941) also emigrated to the United States in 1980s. He used the Russian popular art of woodcutting, combining it with lubok (satirical and naive prints from woodcuts) to parody the political and sexual alliances of Stalin: *Stalin and Marilyn* (1985) and *Stalin and Hitler* (1983), the latter as a seesaw toy with both figures hacking wood in the style of Bogorodsk toys (see the section "Matrioshkas and Patrioshkas").

Although conceptualism remained largely part of high culture and was consumed by intellectual circles, the sots-art movement greatly influenced popular culture, from literature to crafts, where traditional craft objects were used to mock Soviet history. A further phenomenon of visual culture that transgressed strict definitions, however, by venturing into poetry, music, and film of the Leningrad movement was the Mitki, who appeared in the early 1990s. The group used the lubok, the simplified portrayal typical for woodcuts, together with the *chastushka* (ditty) that provided sarcastic and deadpan commentaries on the drawings. The Mitki were a group of people who were always in good spirits and who saw each other as brothers (*bratishki*), a community of friendly individuals formed largely after the collapse of the "underground" movement in the late Soviet era. The group was formed by Oleg Grigoriev and Alexander Florensky, and other artists joined later, including Dmitri Shagin, Olga Florenskaya, and Vladimir Shinkarev. The Mitki wear striped sailors' shirts, padded jackets (vatniki), and boots, and they love vodka.

In 1992, the Mitki created a calendar with their drawings and ditties. The banal situation of a husband and wife arguing was depicted by two simple and plain figures, with her pushing him back and kicking him (hitting him) in the face. The ditty was written on the sides of the drawing in large capitals: "H was chasing W / Grabbed her by the B / W got sore with her H / Kicked him in his F." Another image for May illustrated the Victory Day (9 May) with a prisoner who is the proud builder of communism, holding a shovel and a crowbar. "With shining bald heads / in zebra-striped clothes/ we are building communism / with shovels and crows." Another illustration parodied the widespread alcohol problem, showing two men with bottles and glasses, who are so drunk that they can't even pick up the food on the table. "Bottle after bottle we're swilling / In an endless swizzle-dazzle / Our trembling forks unwilling / to pick the grub we'd love to gobble."

In 1995 they released a music album with Boris Grebenshchikov, entitled "Mitkovskaya tishina," with old bard songs and Soviet criminal songs (*blatnye pesni*) performed by the Mitki but also by the rock stars Viacheslav Butusov and Chizh. They have released two further albums after the success of the first and also made the animation *MitkiMayer* (1992).

Crafts

Matrioshkas and Patrioshkas   The matrioshka is probably Russia's single best-known art object (apart from the icon, which is an artwork and object of religious veneration). The matrioshka is a wooden nesting doll, first made in 1890 in Abramtsevo, an estate outside Moscow famous for its crafts, and subsidized by the arts patron Savva Mamontov. Even before that, there seem to have been matrioshkas made by a Russian monk in Japan. The nesting doll was modeled on the wooden Easter eggs made in Russia; the shape of the doll was new, and its appearance as the mother of numerous "children" (little dolls) gave it the Latin name *mater* (mother), from which the diminutive matrioshka derived.

The matrioshkas were made in Sergiyev Posad (during the Soviet time Zagorsk), a village near the Monastery of the Holy Trinity (Troitsa lavra), which was known for its crafts. The dolls consisted largely of faces, not unlike icon painting, and little attention was paid to details of clothes. Matrioshkas could contain between two and 24 pieces inside. The other famous manufacture of

matrioshkas emerged in Semyonovo. The Semyonovo dolls were more decorative in style, and much more attention was paid to the peasant dress (skirt, apron, headscarf), with rich ornaments on the wooden surface of the doll. The matrioshkas of Polkhov Maidan (a village near Arzamas) were also brightly painted and decorated with large ornaments, but their base was never left untreated and instead was also covered in a base paint. The peasant style and floral ornaments are characteristic of the Maidan dolls.

During the Soviet period everything was production driven, and little attention was paid to manual work. Therefore matrioshka production became industrialized in the Soviet period and transferred to toy factories, although the distinctive design of Sergiyev Posad, Maidan, and Semyonovo was maintained. It was not until the 1990s that matrioshkas were again made, often drawing on fairy tale themes, or indeed on politicians: the patrioshka (now derived from the Latin *pater* for the male figures they represented) set of Gorbachev and his predecessors as leaders of communism (Gorbachev, Brezhnev, Khrushchev, Stalin, Lenin, Marx) and the set of the coup leaders of 1991 were curious objects of political satire.

Traditional wooden toys were also made in Beresta, which continued the tradition of carving birds from a single piece of wood, and Bogorodsk with its manufacture of the little seesaw toys with Russian bears.

Lacquer Boxes   Lacquer boxes have a long-standing tradition in Russian history. They are made from papier mâché to form a firm base for the boxes (a technique used for the Braunschweig tobacco boxes). The

Matrioshkas (Russian dolls) representing Russian president Vladimir Putin in front of the Savior clock tower above the fortifications facing Red Square. (Michel Setboun/Corbis)

boxes are then treated and painted with gouache or tempera, before being varnished. The motifs most often are derived from fairy tales. In the Soviet period they often reflected Soviet themes of work and industry, and in the New Russia they often represent motifs of the new Russian world.

The style of the lacquer box is determined by the school. There are four main "schools" where the technique is applied: Palekh, Mstera, Kholui, and Fedoskino. Fedoskino is in the Moscow region, and lacquer box painting started there in the late eighteenth century and competed with miniature boxes from Persia and Japan. Fedoskino characteristically drew on peasant and rural themes and the use of gray, green, and brown shades as well as mother of pearl. Whereas Fedoskino started out as lacquer art, the other three schools all developed from icon painting and turned to

lacquer art after the Revolution, when icon painting was no longer a state priority. Palekh, in the Ivanov region, had been a center of icon painting and moved into miniature painting in tempera in the 1920s. Palekh motifs represent fine figures on a black background. Often the theme of the central part of the box is developed on the sides. Palekh prefers Russian fairy tales as themes for illustrations. Kholui, in the Vladimir region, shifted to lacquer in the 1930s. Kholui uses bright colors for its scenes set on a colorful backdrop. Mstera is also in the Vladimir region and turned to lacquer in the 1920s. Mstera drew both on fairy tales and themes of everyday life, historical and architectural monuments and used the colors blue and yellow predominantly. Mstera's backdrops are always of a fairy tale–like beauty and set in rich ornamentation. Of the four, Palekh is considered the most prestigious, because it is the oldest center. Lacquer boxes as well as brooches made a very valuable present in Soviet Russia.

Other wooden products of less value are the wooden objects made in Khokhloma, near Nizhny Novgorod. These are wooden jars, bowls, spoons, tables, vases, and other utensils painted in black with red and golden ornaments.

Porcelain and Glass   Gzhel is the most famous and most widespread porcelain manufacturer, making blue-on-white porcelain. Gzhel is located about sixty kilometers from Moscow. Until the seventeenth century, the city produced majolica and ceramics, largely using white enamel as a base. Only in the nineteenth century did Gzhel begin to make semifayence and later porcelain. In the 1970s, the six work-

shops produced new molds for the products, which are all hand painted in cobalt blue. The range consists of vases, statuettes, figurines, plates, and cups, and Gzhel is a most traditional Russian style of everyday tableware.

The Lomonosov Porcelain Factory (LFZ) in St. Petersburg is one of the oldest porcelain manufacturers in the country. LFZ was founded in 1744, after D. Vinogradov had brought the technique for making porcelain to Russia. The factory belonged to the emperor's family, the Romanovs, for more than 150 years and supplied largely for the emperor and the aristocracy. LFZ created not only plates and cups but also figurines and vases. In the nineteenth century, designers from the French Sèvres workshops were invited to develop the designs of LFZ. After the Revolution, the factory produced for a time optical glass and military sup-

A woman paints porcelain dishes at the Lomonosov Porcelain Factory in St. Petersburg, Russia. (Steve Raymer/Corbis)

plies. In 1925 it was renamed the Lomonosov Factory and continued to produce china. By the 1960s, LFZ had launched a fine range of bone china, fully reviving its porcelain manufacture. LFZ produces sets of china in different shapes, of which the most popular is the design called cobalt net (*kobal'tovaia setka*). The bone china sets come in white with gold or with fine flower designs in delicate forms and colors. The porcelain range includes different designs in the house-style blue, such as Blue Bird, Singing Garden, Bells (onion domes and bells in blue and gold), the dark blue with gold inlay Winter Evening, and Snowflake, a blue net with fine ornaments. The colored range includes Russian lubok, with traditional red-blue themes.

Dulevo china is a more sturdy porcelain for everyday use. In the 1830s, the Gzhel entrepreneur Terenti Kuznetsov bought the Dulevo factory, neighboring onto the Smirnov textile factory in Likino. By the 1930s a technical college was added, and Dulevo produced a good amount of china, largely with bright colors. Dulevo was represented at the Paris and New York exhibitions of 1937 and 1939. After the war, the villages became a major industrial complex when the automobile plant ZIL (Zavod im. Likhacheva, Likhachev Factory) opened a branch in Likino.

Gus-Khrustalnyi was the first crystal manufacturer, founded in 1756 by the Maltsev family near Orel (between Moscow and the Urals). To the present day Gus Crystal, a coarsely cut glass, trades on the Russian market alongside glass from Bohemia.

Jewelry There are two major forms of traditional Russian jewelry. The first is Finift, a fine miniature painting on enamel and framed in silver, made in Rostov-on-Don. Finift produces boxes, jewelry, pendants, bracelets, rings, earrings, and other fine objects. The white enamel base is decorated with a miniature design or painting. The technique of painting on porcelain is used on a white enamel plate that is then embedded in the silver fitting. The second well-known type of jewelry is the black silver from the northern town of Veliky Ustiug. The silver and gold inlays are placed into blackened silver (chern') to make jewelry and small objects, such as napkin rings, goblets, or spoons.

The firm Jenavi was founded in St. Petersburg in the 1990s, taking up production at the former Etalon factory (label Jenavi Etalon). They have created an affordable range of modern silver jewelry that uses Svarowski crystal to very great effect.

Another industry is the production of shawls. There is, on the one hand, the feather-light and very warm Orenburg shawl, knitted or woven from goat's hair. The more common type is the Pavlovo Posad woollen shawl with large, colorful flowers printed on them and fringes. Vologda linen and lace are also famous.

The World of the New Russians The World of the New Russians (Mir novykh russkikh) is a shop that opened initially in Okhotny Riad shopping mall, and later on Arbat Street in the mid-1990s. The shop, founded by Grigori Baltser, specializes in producing objects that parody the tastelessness of New Russians while catering for them. They sell designer objects that use the traditional Russian crafts of Khokhloma wooden painting, lacquer art, and Gzhel to make objects that in form belong to the old Russia but portray the antics of the "new Russians," the rich and bored businesspeople. The shop offers, for example, lacquer boxes depicting not fairy tales but the New Russians playing tennis or driving a Western car. A Gzhel figurine represents a diver, a skier, or a water-cyclist; a hunter or a man in love; a troika, consisting not of three horses but of three businessmen. The Khokhloma range includes a jar for savings, parodying the assonance of *banka* (jar) and bank. The wooden range also includes symbols of the sporting interests of the New Russian, where the brand is most important: a weight from Kettler, a set of skis from Fischer, a rugby ball, bowling balls and pins, as well as a baseball bat. The New Russian housewife may be attracted to the Gzhel jars for *khren* (horseradish; also the slang word for sod), the porcelain bottle for Evian, the Khokhloma wooden spoons for caviar, the wooden plate with Versace inscription, or the wooden decorated chopsticks. The New Russian may also desire the Gzhel condom plate or the little jar for Viagra.

The World of the New Russians is a shop that parodies and mocks the lack of taste of the New Russians, even though the price range makes the products affordable only to them. Russia's crafts—porcelain, jewelry, wooden objects, or shawls—are popular both among foreign visitors and Russians.

Architecture

Urban Design

If we remember Eisenstein's film *October*, commemorating the October Revolution of 1917, one of the most striking scenes in the film is the toppling of the monument to the tsar, the careful removal of head and body parts in the process of the monument being dismantled.

The Fall of Monuments   Monuments, their creation, but also their location, indicate popular sympathies. As the Soviet era wanted to erect monuments to its heroes, many monuments to thinkers, writers, and emperors created in the nineteenth and earlier centuries were removed, or else the Soviet regime created its own monuments to revered writers and politicians. During the Soviet era, monuments to poets, writers, and politicians were erected. The monuments to the great Russian writers of the nineteenth century such as Pushkin, Gogol, and Dostoevsky dominated the landscape. The first monument to Pushkin, erected in 1880 by Alexander Opekushin, was moved to the other side of Pushkin Square (on Tverskaya Street) in 1937 in the process of widening the street to forty meters. Pushkin Square was, and still is, a popular meeting place, both for amorous couples and for dissidents. There are few monuments to Dostoevsky in St. Petersburg; indeed, the first monument to the writer was positioned near Kuznechny Lane (where the writer lived) outside a pub in the late 1990s, representing the writer in a seated position. Gogol's monument created by Nikolai Andreyev in 1909 was removed from the Gogol (Prechistenka) Boulevard because he looked too meek and worried: the sculptor had depicted the writer just after the burning of his novel *Dead Souls*. During the Soviet era, the monument was moved into the courtyard of the Literary Institute on Tverskoi Boulevard and another one commissioned for the exposed space on the boulevard. This second monument was created in 1952 by Nikolai Tomsky and shows Gogol in a majestic mood.

Moreover, statues were created to honor the great achievements of Soviet politicians, and streets, metro stations, even entire cities were renamed to mark the Communist heroes. Between the Revolution of 1917 and the mid-1920s, Ekaterinburg became Sverdlovsk, Petersburg became Leningrad, and Lenin's birthplace Simbirsk turned into Ulianovsk in 1924 (Ulianov was Lenin's real name). Volgograd became Stalingrad in 1925 in honor of Stalin, who had been stationed there during the civil war; in 1961, after Stalin's cult was exposed, it reverted to Volgograd. The capital of the Kyrgyz Republic (now Kyrgyzstan), Bishkek, was named Frunze, in honor of the revolutionary Mikhail Frunze who came from there. Nizhny Novgorod was named Gorky after the revolutionary writer Maxim Gorky (whose real name was Alexei Peshkov). Tver was named after Mikhail Kalinin (USSR head of state [chairman of the Council of Ministers] from 1938 to 1946) in 1931. Those Moscow metro stations completed in the 1940s and 1950s were named after politicians: Frunzenskaya, Kalininskaya, Sverdlov Square (Yakov Sverdlov was the first head of the RSFSR). Street names were also "adapted": Tverskaya Street became Gorky Street in 1932; Hunter's Row (Okhotny Riad) became Marx Avenue; Vozdvizhenka Street became Kalinin Avenue; Bolshaya and Malaya Dmitrovka turned into Pushkin and Chekhov Street; Miasnitskaya Street became Kirov Street. All these street and location names that were derived from revolutionaries and communist leaders changed back to their original names after the collapse of the USSR.

Monuments were erected to Communist leaders, too. Felix Dzerzhinsky had a monument outside the Lubianka (headquarters of the KGB), erected by the monumentalist Yevgeni Vuchetich in 1926. There were numerous monuments to Lenin, at least one in the central square of every Soviet city (indeed, in most cities the main artery was called Lenin Street or Lenin Avenue). These monuments were "shoved around" according to political correctness and opportunism. When Stalin was disclosed as a tyrant during the Khrushchev Thaw, his body was removed from the mausoleum and buried in the Kremlin wall. Lenin's body was embalmed and is still on display in the Lenin Mausoleum. The Soviet regime also paid tribute to the classical writers: a monument to Alexander Ostrovsky was designed by Nikolai Andreyev in 1929 and positioned outside the Maly Theater, where Ostrovsky worked. A monument to the composer Pyotr Tchaikovsky, designed by Vera Mukhina (author of the famous "Worker and Farmworker"), was completed in 1954 and placed outside the Conservatory.

When the USSR collapsed, numerous statues of Communist heroes fell: Stalin, Dzerzhinsky, Sverdlov, and others were literally dumped in the garden of "fallen statues" behind the former Central Artists' House, now the branch of the Tretiakov Gallery on Krymsky Val. Later, the fallen monuments were neatly arranged for visitors to the garden. The relationship to monuments reflects, on the one hand, people's attitudes to the past, their political and cultural heritage. It also continues to echo popular taste: the heroes of the people are commemorated in monuments (for example, Vladimir Vysotsky), whereas the city administration and the politicians have their own agenda in creating an urban space that, in their minds, will please the people.

Luzhkov's Moscow   In the post-Soviet state, monuments therefore continued to play an important role. The monuments to political leaders were removed and ceased to form part of everyday life. Nevertheless, the portrait of the president would still hang in official premises. A more flippant attitude to politics emerged, however, in the creation of cardboard figures of Yeltsin and Gorbachev, which were used for tourists to pose for a photo with them. Similarly, they, together with other political figures of the past and present, were immortalized in sets of matrioshka dolls. Official art took a different turn, at least in Moscow. The chief designers of Luzhkov's Moscow were the architect Mikhail Posokhin and the designer Zurab Tsereteli.

The Moscow architecture of the 1990s has been termed "Luzhkov style" and is characterized by monumentalism combined with a frilly, yet majestic, decorum and ornamentation. Examples of this architectural style abound, but the most striking ones shall be explored here. The Moscow zoo, founded in 1864 and in a desolate condition in the late Soviet period, but even more so with the onset of capitalism in the 1990s, was revamped completely. This concerned the appearance of the zoo rather than the range of animals it could maintain. Tsereteli was invited to design the main entrance, consisting of an artificial set of rocks, inviting the visitor into a cavelike structure decorated with bronze figures of animals. Water, an essential ingredient in all Tsereteli's work, was bursting from folds in the rock to offer a sense of fresh air in the summer.

The monument to Peter the Great was a more controversial project than the zoo. Tsereteli's monument to the founder of St. Petersburg seemed misplaced in Moscow in any case. Moreover, the massive bronze sculpture represented Peter as a shipbuilder and traveler, positioned against a

Entrance to the Moscow Zoo, designed by Zurab Tsereteli. (Photo by Birgit Beumers)

sail and a mast, so that the statue had to float. It was eventually anchored on the Moscow River opposite the Cathedral of Christ the Savior, another monument of Luzhkov's Moscow. The Cathedral of Christ the Savior had been built by Konstantin Ton and completed in the 1880s. In 1931 it was destroyed on Stalin's order to create on its territory the Palace of Soviets, the tallest building in Moscow, which would tower over the new Soviet land. The project turned out to be too heavy for the boggy patch of land, however, and the area lay barren until the 1960s when Brezhnev, in the hype of physical culture programs, decided to build an open-air swimming pool, the Bassein Moskva. Luzhkov decided to resurrect the cathedral, and Posokhin implemented the project of revival.

A view of the sculpture of Peter the Great by Zurab Tsereteli on the Moscow River. (Photo by Pavel Kassin/Kommersant)

Another controversial project was the construction of the Manège Square. The Manège, the building of the former Riding School, had been revamped as an exhibition space in the Soviet period. The square outside the Manège, between the Hotels Moskva and National and the Kremlin wall, was a traffic knot, however. Luzhkov decided to build a shopping mall here, following the location of the old nineteenth-century trade rows. The project was built by Mosproekt-2 under Mikhail Posokhin. The mall was built underground, with five levels of subterranean galleries much along the lines of the project Les Halles in Paris. Instead of an open central court, however, Luzhkov's central area would be covered by a cupola representing the globe. Out-

side, the transition from the mall to Alexander Garden was designed by Tsereteli: he placed Disney-like fairy tale figures—frogs, bears, and goldfish—in fountains and artificial ponds and rivulets, evoking childhood memories at best. The fountains are encircled by white marble railings. The engineer Nodar Kancheli projected a glass chapel on Manège Square, which has so far not been implemented.

Other projects of Luzhkov's Moscow are the reconstruction of Gostinyi Dvor (an old shopping center), which was redesigned as a shopping mall and exhibition space. The "city" outside the Krasnopresnenskaya Embankment with the International Trade Center is still under construction. The city is linked to Kutuzov Avenue by the Bagrationov Bridge, a modern bridge-shopping center. The opera singer Galina Vishnevskaya's Center on Ostozhenka was also created by Posokhin, in neoclassical style with a richly decorated facade. The war memorial on Poklonnaya Gora is also designed by Tsereteli, and this monument borders on kitsch with its colored fountains.

For the 850th anniversary of Moscow (1998) and the 200th anniversary of Pushkin's birth (1999), a number of projects were rushed to completion. These included the erection of monuments to Pushkin and his wife on the Arbat; the restoration of Pushkin's wedding church; the completion of Christ the Savior and of the Manège complex.

The "Moscow style" or "Luzhkov style" also characterizes the remainder of Moscow's cityscape. The style bears witness to a restorative nostalgia: it reworks elements of Stalin's monumentalism and neoclassicism while also reviving the splendor of nineteenth-century grand style. A "modern" feature of the style is the creation of pyramid-shaped empty glass cupolas on buildings, first implemented in the building of Toko Bank on the Krasnopresnenskaya Embankment. The empty glass pyramids represent the void—the absence of a meaning in this architectural style, as well as the emptiness of the form, replicating merely the aspirations of Stalinist utopias by building higher and higher, as in the case of the Stalin Teeth, the seven highrises built in the 1950s, including the Ministry of Foreign Affairs on Smolenskaya and the Moscow State University on Sparrow Hills as well as two apartment blocks on Taganskaya and Barrikadnaya and the Hotel Ukraine. Most of Moscow's architectural projects are designed by Moscow Planning Bureaus (Mosproekt) in close collaboration with Luzhkov's city planners.

Petersburg and Its 300th Anniversary

Petersburg has not undergone such radical change as Moscow, but it too was restored for its 300th anniversary in 2003. Petersburg's architectural history does not allow much room for large-scale change and demolition, since most of the city center consists of listed buildings constructed by Italian architects in the eighteenth and nineteenth centuries. On 27 May 1703 (the official date of the foundation of the city), building of the Peter and Paul Fortress commenced under Domenico Trezzini. After a building boom in the early eighteenth century, more attention was paid to public spaces between the baroque buildings of Trezzini and Bartolomo Rastrelli and the classical designs of Giacomo Quarenghi. Carlo Rossi's ensemble of the Alexandrinsky Theater, the library, and the street behind the theater leading to Fontanka canal is, in its completeness, a unique architectural composition. In the nineteenth cen-

tury, monumental projects, such as the Kazan Cathedral, the Exchange, and St. Isaak's Cathedral, were inserted into the cityscape. Partly because of its history and partly because of the marshland, the center of Petersburg has no high-rises. Stalinist architecture is limited to the outskirts and suburbs and especially prominent on Moskovskii Prospekt. Many of these historic monuments have been restored, including St. Isaak's Cathedral and the Savior's Cathedral, which was built in Russian style in the 1880s to commemorate the assassination of Alexander II.

Consumer City

An old Soviet saying explains: there is never anything in the shops, but everything is on the table. Most Soviet shops had very few desirable products on offer. Instead, there were a lot of unwanted or unattractive goods. Thus, for example, there were Soviet-made technical appliances on sale, but people knew they would neither last long nor function properly; instead, they wished to purchase Western-made appliances. Soviet foodstuff was hard to come by. Most people ordered their food products through work if a special supply service was available. Furthermore, there were hardly any self-service stores, or supermarkets as we know them. Instead, people had to queue, have meat or cheese weighed, be told a price, and then pay before returning to receive the goods. If goods were on display, the customer had to add up the prices and pay at the till and then present the receipt in order to receive the goods. Many goods were purchased through the workplace in the Soviet days and not accessible to the consumer in the shop.

Until 1991, however, all prices were fixed by the state. Many goods were only available on ration cards in the later perestroika years, such as sugar, vodka, and other consumer goods. When the Soviet Union collapsed, the price-fixing ended in order to allow a transition to a market economy. From January 1992 on, almost all products disappeared from the shelves—people had bought and stored whatever they could, expecting prices to soar. And they did. Inflation made the dollar go from 80 rubles in 1991 to a value of 1,000 rubles within two years.

Consumer Temples: Markets and Malls   The state shops offered little to satisfy customer needs in the Soviet era. In order to purchase meat, dairy products, or fruit and vegetables, the better-off Russians and foreigners went to private markets, where kolkhoz farmers offered their produce: fresh, but at a price. These markets continue to exist in the present, and fresh and domestic produce is best purchased there. The main markets in Moscow are the Danilovskii market near Tulskaya, the market on Tsevtnoi Boulevard, and the Novye Cheremushki market, or Kuznechnyi Lane market in St. Petersburg. Many markets appear along end-of-the-line metro stops, where traders offer goods, especially during the evening rush hour. Alongside such food markets there also emerged markets where people offered clothes, secondhand or cheap Asian imports. Such *veshchevoi* (things) markets are mostly organized in the open air. The Rizhskii and Tishinskii markets were such trade points, and both were demolished in the mid-1990s when Moscow's cityscape was tidied up before the 850th anniversary of the city, to make way for more expensive shopping malls that replaced the old cheap trade stalls. Tishinskii and Rizhskii

made room for roofed trade centers. On the Olympic arena (Prospekt Mira), book trade takes place on weekdays, whereas in Petersburg this is at weekends in the DK Krupskaya. The shabby street markets have, however, given way to more elegant shopping centers.

A few of these markets have survived, however. One is Apraxin Dvor on Sadovaya Street in Petersburg, in existence since the eighteenth century, with lines of old buildings accommodating less smart shops while vendors also trade in front of the buildings and on the street. In Moscow, the most extraordinary market has been the Gorbushka, organized in the park surrounding the Gorbunov Culture Club in the west of Moscow and trading on Saturdays and Sundays with video and audio material. The Gorbushka was threatened several times with closure, partly because of the pirated videos that could be purchased there. In 2002 it moved into the abandoned factory halls of the electronics company Rubin on the other side of the metro line, where the video trade continues, as well as the sale of digital video discs (DVDs), CDs, computers, and accessories. There is also a computer market at Mitino. The park of Izmailovo is known for its weekend trade with souvenirs and crafts (Vernissage), cheap paintings, and antiquarian objects of little value. The Bird Market (*ptichii rynok*) works also at weekends and offers animals of all names and descriptions for sale.

Indeed, the conversion of old markets and trade rows into shopping centers is not unique to the twentieth century, nor to Moscow. The street market in Paris was converted into the shopping center Les Halles in the 1970s; Covent Garden was largely converted into a center for elegant

Underground mall "Okhotny Riad" (Hunter's Row) on Manège Square with the Hotel Moskva before its demolition in 2004. (Photo by Birgit Beumers)

boutiques and shops at around the same time. In Moscow, too, Hunters Row (Okhotny Riad), the old trade rows near the river Neglinka, was demolished at the turn of the nineteenth century, when the river Neglinka was channeled into a tunnel and hidden from the surface. Around the same period the Manège was built to mark the fifth anniversary of the victory over Napoleon and used for the tsar's inspection of troops. In 1883 the Historical Museum was added to the ensemble on the Manège Square, in 1892 the Duma was built, and in 1903 the Hotel National flanked the northern side of the square. Plans for the reconstruction of the trading rows were never implemented. The Revolution interfered, and in 1932 the Hotel Moscow was built in the center of the square. Only in the post-Soviet period has Moscow's mayor Luzhkov turned his attention again to the area and decided to build an underground shopping mall. In 1994, Zurab Tsereteli began the creation of the fountains and surface water channels of the river Neglinka and designed the clock of the world in the shape of a glass cupola for the underground shopping center. The cupola turns once a day and indicates the time in different zones of the world. The Okhotny Riad Mall (torgovyi kompleks) opened in 1997 and consists of four levels of subterranean shopping, largely exclusive shops and designer boutiques. In 2003 the reconstruction of the Hotel Moskva began, reshaping partly the facade; in March 2004 the Manège Exhibition Hall burned down after an alleged electrical failure, leaving only the facade intact and destroying the unique roof construction, which represented the largest roof that required no support columns.

Interior of the GUM department store, Moscow, during the Soviet era. (Peter Turnley/Corbis)

Similar projects were implemented in the reconstruction of the Petrovsky Passage (1993) between Petrovka and Neglinnaya Street, which consists of luxurious and expensive boutiques. It was originally built in 1906 by S. Kalugin, with the engineer Vladimir Shukhov, who also designed the glass roof over GUM (Gosudarstvennyi universal'nyi magazin, the state department store), containing two lines with three levels. It accommodates exclusive shops and designer boutiques of Givenchy, Ricci, Kelian, Kenzo, Bally, the Belgian chocolate creators Godiva, and the perfume store Rivoli. The Smolenskii Passage was built as a shopping mall on Smolensk Square, at the end of the Arbat Street, with a Kalinka Stockman department store as part of the mall. The former House of the Actor was reconstructed after a fire to accommodate business offices and a shopping mall on underground and ground level, the Gallery Actor (Aktyor), with luxury boutiques. The Atrium (2002) is a new shopping mall in front of Kursk Railway station, initially planned as a multiplex cinema by Sergei Lisovsky. It now contains the multiplex Formula Kino and a range of expensive shops, from the Parisian Agatha bijouterie to a two-story Arbat Prestige.

In Petersburg, the Passage, first opened in 1848 as a gallery for fashion and perfume stores under a glass roof, was also reconstructed as a shopping mall. In Moscow, new, smaller malls emerged in the center, such as the French Passage near the GUM department store, Baza 14 in Stoleshnikov Lane, the Berlin House on Petrovka, and Nautilus on Nikolskaya Street. Malls are no longer restricted to the center, or to exclusive and expensive stores, as more and more trade centers are springing up in more remote quarters of Moscow, especially with the emergence of Ramstore on the Russian market. Ramstore opened its first branch on Yartsev Street, which has since been followed by four more Ramstores (Sheremetyevskoye in 1999, Kashirskoye in 2000, Beliayevo in 2002, and Vernadskii Avenue and Sevastopolskii Road in 2004).

Moscow has 2.5 million square meters of retail space. Most of this is located on the outskirts, not in the city center. Indeed, retail space on the central streets (Tverskaya, Nikitskaya, Kuznetskii Most, and Piatnitskaya) is expensive at a rental price from $1,000–5,000 per square meter and a sale price of $3,000–20,000. Therefore, most investors in shopping centers locate their centers on the outskirts and convenient road junctures: the Swedish home furniture store IKEA and the German-based do-it-yourself store OBI are located on the northern and southern intersections of a main carriageway with the Moscow Orbital (MKAD, Moskovskaya kol'tsevaya avtomobil'naya doroga). At the same time, smaller malls and retail centers replace the street stalls near metro stations and are clearly aimed at a less well-off consumer who uses the metro (rather than a car). The gallery Aeroport near the metro stop of the same name is such an example, where the old infrastructure of street traders has been replaced by a shopping pavilion. Many metro stations are surrounded by makeshift huts with twenty-four-hour shops. Retail parks are still under discussion, and the problem that remains is matching shops with the target customer.

The old, exclusive department stores continue to exist. GUM was built where originally there were trade rows. At the end of the nineteenth century a large shop was created, arranged in three rows, with electrical supply and glass roof. The architect was Alexander Pomerantsev. The rows create a space for three lines of streets with separate shops on three levels, located between Ilyinka Street, Red Square, and Nikolskaya Street. GUM, restored in 1997, accommodates shops of Max Mara, Rinaldi, Joseph, Benetton, and Sisley. Gostinyi Dvor in Moscow, located behind GUM, was originally designed between 1791 and 1830 by the Italian architect Quarenghi, who duplicated the design for the Petersburg Gostinyi Dvor. The design was intended for a flat square space, whereas the plot in Moscow was on a slope and nonrectangular. The building was implemented by the architect of the Bolshoi Theater, Osip Bove, and acquired rounded corners, leaving the inside courtyard intended for deliveries fully intact. The complex was divided up between a number of organizations in the Soviet era and completely reconstructed in the 1990s as a shopping mall and exhibition area. A similar structure of management applies to the shopping arcade Gostinyi Dvor in Petersburg, built on two levels and in the shape of a square stretching almost a mile on each side. Gostinyi Dvor, originally built to Rastrelli's plans by the architect Vallin de la Mothe (1764–85) consists of a regular, classical arcade that occupies an area of almost a square mile. It has been restored and sublet to exclusive shops in the front on Nevsky, but some cheaper parts remain in the sidelines. Another well-known department store in central Petersburg is the DLT (Dom Leningradskoi torgovli, House of Leningrad Trade), also with an art-nouveau interior.

The Moscow Central Department Store (TsUM) was originally the shop Muir and

Merrilees, founded by the Scotsmen Andrew Muir and Archibald Merrilees, who transferred their business from St. Petersburg to Moscow in the 1880s. The store, built by the architect Roman Klein on Petrovka Street, contained elements of European gothic style and was completed in glass and concrete (1908–1910). At the beginning of the twentieth century, this was the largest store in Moscow, with elevators and electric lighting. The store was nationalized after the Revolution and renamed TsUM. A new corpus was added at the northern side in 1974. In the late 1990s the store was more democratic in its layout and more affordable than GUM, but refurbishment has begun and brought more expensive retailers onto the premises. The top floor is sublet to a megastore of the musical and audio chain Soyuz. Other department stores in Moscow include the Moskva (Leninskii Prospekt) and the Moskovskii.

Western companies and especially designers have opened boutiques in Moscow. Such boutiques include Dolce and Gabbana, Chanel, Yamamoto, Donna Karan, Versace, Krizia, and Escada. There are also exclusive fashion shops, such as Nostalgie, Podium, and Bosco di Ciliegi with a few designer labels only. Fashion shops are clustered on Tverskaya, Kutuzovskii Avenue, Kuznetskii Most, and in the Okhotny Riad Mall, which are the epicenters of fashion in Moscow. There are also shops that sell the previous season's designer clothes (*stokovye magaziny*), as well as a host of secondhand stores. A number of cosmetics and perfume shops have opened: Arbat Prestige, Articoli, L'Etoile, Rivoli. Japanese cosmetics such as Kanebo and Shiseido but also the perfumes Matsushima, Kusado, and Annayake, which are very popular among trendy Muscovites, can be found

in Arbor. There are also a number of Yves Rocher shops as well as a shop of the Russian cosmetics firm Linda on Kuznetskii Most. Many Soviet perfume brands such as Krasnaya Moskva (Red Moscow) and Persidskaya Siren (Persian Lilac) produced by Novaya Zaria and Svoboda have been discontinued.

The Perlov House on Miasnitskaya Street was used by a tea merchant to sell his imports from China. The house, built by Roman Klein between 1890 and 1893, has a facade richly decorated in the Chinese style; the building is undergoing restoration. The Yeliseyev Shop (former Kozitskii House) was established in the 1790 building, with a newly designed interior created in 1898 by G. Baranovsky. This store was the most prestigious food store in Moscow and still retains its glamorous interior, although the space is now used as a supermarket. Tverskaya No. 10 is occupied by the Filippov Bakery, now accommodating also a Coffee Bean. The baker Ivan Filippov was well-known in the nineteenth century and supplied to the tsar and the Moscow governor. There is a famous episode that relates how a cockroach ended up in a bread-roll that was served to the governor. When summoned, Filippov—trying to save his head—claimed this was a raisin, took the cockroach, and swallowed it. The next day rolls with raisins were launched as an innovation in his bakery.

As far as food stores were concerned, the most lavish store was Yeliseyev's, which also had a branch in Petersburg. The stores were decorated with a lavish interior, with carved wooden counters and stained glass and crystal chandeliers; they maintain this design to the present day. The largest children's store in Moscow remains Detskii Mir (Children's World), lo-

The interior of the famous Yeliseyev food store on Tverskaya Street before restoration in 2002. (Photo by Andrey Stempkovsky/Kommersant)

cated opposite the Lubianka (former KGB, therefore nicknamed Adult World), which sells everything for children, from toys to clothes, furniture to games, on five floors.

Furniture was standardized in the Soviet Union. After the collapse of the Soviet Union, when people began to build their own dachas and to refurbish their apartments, which had been privatized and therefore were worthy of investment, there were no furniture supplies. When IKEA opened a store in 2000 in the north of Moscow, people came in such crowds that the store ran out of pencils and shopping bags on the opening day—every customer wanted to take these items away with them. There were a number of items that sold out on that first day; another store in the south of Moscow opened in 2001.

The lingerie chain Wild Orchid (Dikaya orchideya) started in 1993 and spread from Moscow across Russia. The chain sells elite labels of lingerie and added swimming suits to its range in the late 1990s. Since 1999, collections have been shown in fashion weeks. There are seventeen shops in Moscow alone.

The jewelry business picked up in Russia in the mid-1990s. Although there are Western jewelry designers with branches in Russia, the majority of jewelry is produced in Russia, both silver and gold. It is usually fashion jewelry that is imported, although the company Etalon-Jenavi, founded as a family business in St. Petersburg in 1991 and located in the old Etalon factory, makes affordable jewelry from crystal and surgical silver. The Petersburg-based firm RosSilver also creates silver jewelry, using a technology that makes large silver pieces of light weight. A chain of jewelry shops is Center-Jeweler (Tsentr-Yuvelir, Samotsvety), which sells gold jewelry, and there are also designers, such as Andrei Ananov in Petersburg (Nevsky 36). His business was set up in 1989 and has since received numerous awards. Ananov creates exclusive and expensive jewelry, inspired by Carl Fabergé. The house Petr Privalov in Moscow, managed by Marina Korotayeva, is a design company specializing in decorative art objects. Both Ananov and Privalov have created awards for festivals (such as prizes for the Kinotavr film festivals).

Bookshops converted swiftly in the latter half of the 1990s to self-service stores rather than the old-fashioned layout whereby customers would have to ask the salesperson for a book for inspection. The largest stores are Biblio Globus on Lubianka, Dom Knigi on the New Arbat, Moskva on Tverskaya Street, and Progress for dictionaries. There are also a number of specialized bookstores and outlets in publishing houses. In Petersburg, the Dom Knigi occupied the house of the Singer sewing-machine makers (built in 1902) until 2003, when the former owners reclaimed the property, and the bookshop moved to a different address on Nevsky Prospekt. The video and entertainment chain stores Titanik and Soyuz can be found in most major cities.

The old *apteka*, the chemist's shop or pharmacy, has also been largely replaced by modern drugstores, with chains such as 36–6 and Chudo Doktor (Miracle Doctor) dominating the market for pharmaceuticals. Most of these drugstores sell not only medicines but also cosmetics and homeopathic remedies.

The face of major cities has changed not only because of the appearance of malls and the revamping of department stores but also because of the trade points in the underground passages, which offer a cheap range of products, from videos to mobile phones, fashion to shoes, batteries to foodstuffs.

Churches and Icons

Churches Under Soviet rule, a great number of churches were destroyed or else turned into museums, cinemas, and warehouses. Only a few churches remained open during the Soviet regime, and this only after concessions were made by Stalin during World War II, when the church greatly assisted the regime in its fight against fascism. Famous museums were housed in the Kazan and St. Isaak's Cathedrals in Petersburg and St. Basil's in Moscow.

Moscow's main church is the Cathedral Church of the Epiphany (Bogoyavlenie) in Yelokhov (Yelokhovskii sobor). It was built in 1835–1848 by Evgraf Tiurin, and it is the main Orthodox church and burial place of many patriarchs and metropolitans, including Alexei I (1378). The Cathedral of Christ the Savior (Khram Khrista Spasitelia) was founded on 10 September 1839 to mark the victory over Napoleon. On 5 December 1931, it was blown up upon Stalin's order to make room for the never-built Palace of Soviets. It was reconstructed between 1994 and 1999. The Kremlin cathedrals belong to the oldest parts of Moscow architecture. The Assumption Cathedral (Uspenskii sobor) was built in 1475–1479; the Cathedral of the Annunciation (Blagoveshchenskii sobor) in 1484–1489; the Archangel Cathedral (Arkhangelskii sobor) in 1505–1508. The Cathedral of St. Basil's (Sobor Vasiliya Blazhennogo) was built between 1555 and

Zurab Tsereteli (left), sculptor and artist, president of the Russian Fine Arts Academy, attends the opening ceremony of the pedestrian bridge across the Moscow River linking Christ the Savior Cathedral and Yakimanka Street, March 2004. (Photo by Alexander Miridonov/Kommersant)

1561. All these churches served as museums during the Soviet period.

The oldest monasteries in Russia are the *laura* (lavra, a monastery of highest rank that is directly subordinated to the Holy Synod). The Peshcherskaya Lavra in Kiev (1598) is the oldest, along with the Trinity St. Sergius Lavra-Monastery near Moscow (1744) and the Alexandro-Nevsky Lavra-Monastery (1797) in Petersburg, as well as the Pochayevo-Uspenskaya Lavra-Monastery (1833). Monasteries are numerous in Moscow and elsewhere. The Danilov Monastery is one of the oldest, founded in the thirteenth century; the Vysoko Petrovskii, Sretenskii, and Rozhdestvenskii monasteries were all built in the fourteenth century. The Andronnikov Monastery, be-

gun in the fourteenth century, contains numerous icons by the famous icon painter and saint, Andrei Rublyov. The New Maiden's Convent (Novodevich'e monastyr') was founded in the sixteenth century. Its cemetery is the burial place for many artists, writers, and intellectuals. Many churches were closed in the 1920s. The Church of the Resurrection in Briusov Lane (Moscow), headed by Pitirim Metropolitan of Volokolamsk and Yurevsk, one of the few churches that remained open during the Soviet period, has traditionally attracted the artistic world. Other central churches include the Ascension Church in Kolomenskoye, the Church of the Assumption near Taganka Square, the Church of the Birth of the Blessed Virgin in Putinki on

Malaya Dmitrovka, and St. Nicholas Church on the Ordynka Street. Today, most churches are active and restored to their former glory. The main Church of the Old-Believers (*staroobryadtsy*) is Pokorovskii Cathedral in Rogozhin Cemetery in the southeast of Moscow.

Churches were traditionally built in the shape of a ship, the ark, with the altar always pointing toward the east. Many churches in the countryside are located on elevations to make them visible to a wide community. Indeed, many people continue to make the sign of the cross when they pass a church. The church consists of an entrance hall, the main area, and the altar. The iconostasis separates the secular from the heavenly space, so that people face the icons, which represent God. The royal gates (*tsarskie vrata*) of the iconostasis open up onto the space behind the altar, which is reserved for priests. The gates open at certain times during mass to allow a glimpse of the other world. Women are not allowed in the altar. The icons in the iconostasis are arranged in a certain order: on the side there are the archangels Gabriel and Michael. On the lower row the local saints are positioned, further up the evangelists; and on the top level, Christ, Mary, and John the Baptist. If there are more rows, then the upper levels would be filled with prophets and figures of the Old Testament.

The rules of visiting churches stipulate that women should not wear trousers or short skirts, and they should cover their head with a scarf. No sports or leisurely dress is allowed, nor are short sleeves. People cross themselves three times upon entering the church. An Orthodox believer crosses himself with three fingers (thumb, index, and middle finger) for the Father,

the Son, and the Holy Spirit, with the remaining fingers representing the world and heaven folded on the palm. The fingers touch forehead, chest, right and left shoulders. Russian churches are usually full of candles that, it is believed, through light help to transmit prayers. There are morning, day, and evening services in churches, and the liturgy with communion is usually in the evening.

The Orthodox church knows seven sacraments. Baptism (*kreshchenie*) and chrismation (*miropomazanaie*) are administered together, on the 8th or 40th day after the birth of a child. Children are christened by triple immersion, after which they are handed to the godparent. Communion (*prichashchenie*), and confession (*pokaianie* or *ispoved'*) can be administered from the age of seven on. Marriage (*brak*) consists of exchanging rings and a blessing (*obruchenie* and *venchanie*). The bridegroom and bride hold candles and wear crowns during the ceremony; they drink wine from a common cup and walk around the church three times, before receiving icons of Christ and the Blessed Virgin from the priest. A civil ceremony at the registry office (ZAGS, otdel zapisi aktov grazhdanskogo sostoianiia) must precede the church service. No marriages are concluded between Christmas and Epiphany (7–19 January), during Shrovetide, during the week before Easter, and on 11 and 27 September. The unction, or anointing of the sick (*eleosviashchenie*), is administered by seven priests in church or at home for the very sick. The seventh sacrament is priesthood.

Icons   Icons play a very important role in Orthodox faith and in everyday culture. The icons of the Mother of God are often endowed with special power and significance and are believed to have miraculous powers. Icons are created from templates, not from the real world or a living model; there are pocket-size icons, icons for display at home of a large book size, and icons for display in an altar, which have the size of a painting. They are not decorative, as was advocated by Charlemagne (whose position led to the breakaway of the Catholic from the Orthodox church), but they have equal status to the Bible, with the only difference being the means of expression, word and image. Icons facilitate addressing God through line and color. Therefore, although an icon may have certain divine powers, its copies can also assist in a similar way. Icons were painted in monasteries, and their masters are not usually named artists. The golden background represents the heavenly light, which penetrates the figure represented and therefore precludes any shadow. There is no perspective, since it was deemed that man's vision is imperfect and icons are narrative in character, opening a window into the sacred world. Believers cross twice before an icon, bow and cross again; they may kiss the hand or feet of the icon but never the icon's face. The Russian Orthodox church reveres several icons of the Mother of God, which have a distinct role and history, especially as helpers in defending Russia against invaders of another faith.

The most common representation is that of the Virgin Mary holding the infant. Such representation is found on the icons of Vladimir, Tikhvin, Kazan, and Feodorov, whereas the Ivesk icon shows the Madonna cradling the infant. The Vladimir Icon is believed to have been painted by the evangelist Luke and shows the Mother of God holding the Child. In 1131, it was given to the Kievan grand prince Yuri Dol-

goruky, who placed it in a Kievan monastery. When Yuri's son Andrei went to Vladimir, he took the icon for protection. On the way Andrei had an apparition at Bogoliubovo. The Vladimir icon survived several wars and fires, and three times helped Moscow to be freed from the Tatar yoke. First, when Tamerlane had a vision of the Mother of God in a circle of fiery swords, he turned back (8 September). Second, the icon assisted the defense of Moscow against the Tatars in 1480 under Ivan III (6 July). And finally, in 1521 it helped Moscow to be liberated from the Tatars (3 June). It is before this icon that Russian tsars and soldiers took the oath to the fatherland. It is kept in the Tretiakov Gallery.

The Tikhvin Icon shows Mary holding her Child and is also thought to have been painted by Luke. In 1383 it was brought from Constantinople to Russia and appeared on Lake Ladoga, and later in Tikhvin near Veliki Novgorod. In 1560 a monastery was founded, and the icon helped to defend the country against the Swedes in the seventeenth century. It is supposed to have healing powers. During World War II, it was seized and eventually taken to the United States via Riga by the Orthodox bishop Janis Garklavs in 1949. It was returned to the Tikhvin Monastery on 9 July 2004.

The Kazan Icon portrays the Mother of God holding the Child, but not cradling it. The icon was discovered in Kazan in 1579 after a girl had had a dream about an icon that had been hidden away from the Tatars. The icon supported and inspired Moscow when it was under threat from the Poles in 1648. The icon protects the country and was kept in the Cathedral of the Epiphany until it was taken to Rome in the twentieth century. The icon has been returned to Russia by the Vatican in an attempt to

Russian president Vladimir Putin bows before the Tikhvin icon of the Virgin, 2004. (Rodionov Vladimir/ITAR-TASS/Corbis)

smooth the relationship between the Catholic and the Orthodox churches in August 2004.

The Feodorov Icon is celebrated on 27 March (and 29 August). It is believed that the icon was painted by the evangelist Luke. It shows the Mother of God holding the Infant. It was found near the monastery of Fyodor Stratilat (hence the name) and brought to Kostroma after a Tatar attack, where it defended the town by blinding the attacking Tatars with its light and forcing them to retreat. The mother of the first Romanov tsar presented her son to the icon; the Feodorov icon has been the symbol of the Romanov dynasty. People pray to it when they need to relieve themselves of a burden or before giving birth.

The Iversk Icon shows the Mother of God cradling the child. The icon belonged to a widow; when warriors slashed it, blood ran across the face. The widow floated the icon in the sea to remove it from the invaders, but it hovered over the waves. The widow's son founded a monastery where the icon appeared. A copy of the Iversk icon is in the bell-tower of the Iversk Gates in Moscow. The icon is believed to perform extraordinary acts in the week before Easter. The icon was kept in Iveria (old name of Georgia) in the monastery on Mount Athon (in Abkhazia).

Other icons show the Madonna preaching, as a companion, or guiding. The Bogoliubov Icon shows the Virgin Mary in the unusual position of a preacher and without the infant Christ. It was painted in 1157. Prince Andrei Yurievich, the founder of Russia, was traveling to Vladimir; on the way the prince had a vision, which made him build a monastery at that place, called Bogoliubovo. He had an icon painted with the image of Our Lady as she appeared to him in his dream. The icon has the power to heal and to fight epidemics, such as plague and cholera. The Pochayev Icon shows Mary with the Child, but at the bottom of this icon there is a rock with a footprint. In 1340 Mary appeared on a hill and left a footprint, where a spring surged up. In 1597 the icon was given to the landowner, whose blind brother gained his ability to see. The icon helped to defend the Uspensko-Pochayev Monastery (lavra) against the Turks in 1675. The icon is part of the iconostasis presented to the monastery by the tsar, and it is lowered especially for veneration. The Smolensk Icon is an *odigitreia* (companion), showing the Madonna and Child. It is believed to have been painted by Luke. The icon accompanied Anna, the daughter of the Byzantine emperor, when she went to marry a Chernigorsk prince in 1046. Her son Vladimir (Monomakh) took the icon to Smolensk, where it helped to defend the town against the Tatars in 1238. In the fifteenth century the icon was briefly brought to Moscow to protect the city but returned to Smolensk. In 1524 the tsar, grateful for the victory over the Lithuanians at Smolensk, founded the Novodevichye (New Maiden's) Monastery in Moscow. Before the battle of Borodino, the icon was also brought to Moscow but returned to Smolensk, where it remained until 1941.

The Kursk Icon of Mother of God is celebrated on 21 September and 5 August. The Mother of God is represented in the rare form "of the banner" (*znameni*). She does not hold the child, but the child is in her womb as she stretches her arms (making a sign, hence "banner"). The Kursk icon is also called the icon "of the root," as it was found by the root of a tree on 8 September 1295 (old style) after the destruction of Kursk by the Tatars. It was cut in half and pieced together, and many times survived destruction. In the 1920s it was taken out of Russia and is now kept in the United States.

A to Z

Astrakhan, Dmitri: b. 1957. Graduated from the Leningrad State Institute for Theater, Music and Cinema in 1982. Artistic Director of the Sverdlovsk Theater of the Young Spectator from 1981 to 987. From 1987 to 1990 staged plays at theaters in Leningrad and abroad. His films, *You Are My Only One* (Ty u menia odna, 1994) and *Everything Will Be OK* (Vse budet khorosho, 1995), were the most popular films with the Russian audiences in their years of release. Astrakhan makes commercial, rather than art-house film, and works for television.

Balabanov, Aleksei: b. 1959. Graduated from the Foreign Languages Institute in Gorky (now Nizhny Novgorod) and served in the Soviet Army. Graduated from the Higher Courses for Scriptwriters and Directors in Moscow. Since 1990 he has lived in St. Petersburg, where he founded, with Sergei Selianov, the studio CTB. [www.ctb. ru] His first films, *Happy Days* (Schastlivye dni, 1991) and *The Castle* (Zamok,

1994), were based on Samuel Beckett and Franz Kafka and belong clearly to the art-house films. He then made blockbusters with the film *Brother* (Brat, 1997) and the sequel *Brother 2* (Brat 2, 2000) [http://brat2.film.ru], starring Sergei Bodrov Jr. as the killer and savior of the poor and humiliated, Danila Bagrov. His film *Of Freaks and Men* (Pro urodov i liudei, 1998) explored the exploits of the camera for pornographic purposes at the beginning of the twentieth century. His film *War* (Voina, 2002) juxtaposed the attitude of a Russian soldier and a British man held hostage by Chechen rebels toward issues of morality, of right and wrong, of means and ends.

Bardin, Garri: b. 1941. Graduated as an actor from the Moscow Art Theater School in 1968. Bardin came to animation by writing for the Obraztsov Puppet Theater. Since 1975 animator, now a leader of Russian animation. *The Flying Ship* (Letuchii korabl', 1979), based on a Russian fairy tale; *Brake!* (Brek, 985), a plasticine animation parodying moves of boxers; *The Banquet* (Banket, 1986), puppet animation, satirizing dinner parties; *The Gray Wolf and Red Riding-Hood* (Seryi volk end krasnaia shapochka, 1990). Since 1991 has run his own studio, Staier. Here he made *Choocha* (Chucha, 1998) and the sequel *Choocha 2* (Chucha 2, 2001), which tell the story of a little boy who models his own nanny. [www.animator.ru/db/]

Bodrov, Sergei, Jr.: (1971–2002). Born in Moscow and son of the film director Sergei Bodrov. Bodrov studied history at Moscow State University, graduating in 1993. Despite his fast-moving career in television and film, he completed his Master's degree in history in 1998. A nonprofessional, he starred in *Prisoner of the Mountains* (Kavkazskii plennik, 1996), Balabanov's film *Brother* (Brat, 1997), and the sequel *Brother 2* (Brat 2, 2000). He made his first feature film, *Sisters* (Sestry, 2001), and prepared a new film, called *The Messenger* (Sviaznoi), which he began to shoot in September 2002. He and his film crew died on 20 September 2002, when a glacier slid into a valley in the Caucasus mountains on the third day of shooting. [http://s-bodrov.narod.ru]

Bodrov, Sergei, Sr.: b. 1948. Graduated from the Script Department at VGIK (Vserossiiskii gosudarstvennyi institut kinematografii, All-Russian State Institute for Cinematography) in 1974. Special correspondent for the satirical weekly *Crocodile* from 1975 to 1980. Scriptwriter for more than 20 films. Author of stories and satirical sketches. Since 1984 has worked both in Russia and abroad. Lives partly in Los Angeles, partly in Moscow. His experience as a scriptwriter in the United States has taught him the principles of successful storytelling, as demonstrated in his *Prisoner of the Mountains* (Kavkazskii plennik, 1996), which fared well abroad and in Russia. Bodrov's film *The Kiss of a Bear* (2002) is set in a circus. His films include: *Freedom Is Paradise* (SER: Svoboda—eto rai, 1989); *The Swindler* (Katala, 1989); *White King, Red Queen* (Belyi korol', krasnaia koroleva, 1992); *I Wanted to See Angels* (Ia khotela uvidet' angelov, 1992).

Cathedral of Christ the Savior (Khram Khrista Spasitelia): The foundation to the cathedral was laid on 10 September 1839 to mark the victory over Napoleon. It was designed by Konstantin Ton. On 5 December 1931 the cathedral was blown up upon Stalin's order to make room for the Palace of Soviets, which was never built, as the ground turned out to be too boggy for the ambitious projects of Stalin's architects. The area lay idle until Khrushchev decided to build there an open-air swimming pool. The pool attracted many swimmers but also numerous angry voices as the steam from the heated pool affected adversely the storage areas of the nearby Pushkin Museum. The pool was closed in the early 1990s, and between 1994 and 1999 the cathedral was reconstructed under the supervision of Moscow's mayor, Yuri Luzhkov. It is the main landmark of Moscow's cityscape and also Moscow's main church, although the older generation continues to frequent the former central church, the Yelokhov cathedral.

Fedoskino: center of lacquer box manufacture in the Moscow region. Fedoskino boxes are decorated with themes from paintings, reproduced in subdued colors and often using mother-of-pearl for inlays. [http://fedoskino.nm.ru]

Gostinyi Dvor: (Petersburg) Department store and shopping mall, built in the late eighteenth century and projected by the architect Quarenghi on two levels in a square with an inner courtyard for deliveries. Restored in the 1990s. (Moscow) Duplicate of the Petersburg Gostinyi Dvor, projected by Quarenghi but implemented by Osip Bove, to fit into the sloped and rectangular plot behind Ilyinka Street. [www.bgd.ru]

GUM (Gosudarstvennyi universalnyi magazin, or State Department Store): main department store, built 1889–1893 to replace nineteenth-century trade rows. It is located between Ilyinka Street, Red Square, and Nikolskaya Street. Designed by Osip Bove

(architect of the Bolshoi Theater) and Alexander Pomerantsev, the building was made of granite, marble, and sandstone. There is an upper GUM, described above, and a "middle" complex, designed by architect Roman Klein. The main complex consists of three lines or rows reaching over three levels. The rows stretch more than 250 meters in length and are covered by a metal and glass roof by the engineer V. Shukhov. The building implemented a modern idea combined with Russian design. The store was closed during the civil war and from 1937 to 1952. GUM was restored in 1997. [www.gum.ru]

Gzhel: village and craft center in the Moscow region. Gzhel is famous for its blue on white handmade ceramics. Gzhel is similar to the Dutch Delft chinaware in color, although the design draws on typically Russian themes. Gzhel deploys a technique of white enamel on the ceramics (made from plaster molds), which are then decorated with blue motifs. [www.gzhel.ru]

Lomonosov Porcelain Factory (LFZ, Lomonosovskii farfornyi zavod): oldest porcelain manufacture in Russia, established in Petersburg in the mid-eighteenth century to supply porcelain for the tsar and create china in the style of Sèvres. Renamed to LFZ after the Revolution, when production was concentrated on optical glass. In the 1960s, again production of porcelain and bone china. LFZ is famous for its use of cobalt and gold designs, such as the Cobalt Net for the sets of tea and coffee china. [www.lomonosov.ru]

Manège (Moscow): Built between 1817 and 1825 by architect Osip Bove to mark the fifth anniversary of the victory over

Napoleon. The hall was used for the tsar's inspection of troops, concerts, riding, and cycling. Under Stalin it served as a garage and was divided into two levels. The extraordinary architectural feature was a roof that stretched more than 45 meters without support columns, created by the engineers I. Betancourt and L. Carbonier. The Manège served as an exhibition hall for contemporary art and other exhibits. In March 2004 a fire destroyed the building, leaving only the facade intact.

Masiania: b. 2001, St. Petersburg. Flash animation figure. Masiania was created in October 2001 by the Petersburg designer Oleg Kuvayev on the site www.mult.ru. She quickly became the most popular figure of Russian cyberspace, and the cartoons were later shown on television.

matrioshka: nesting dolls made from wood and painted. Matrioshkas were first made in Abramtsevo (an estate outside Moscow) in the late nineteenth century. The main centers for manufacturing matrioshkas were in Sergiyev Posad (Zagorsk, in Soviet times), a school that focused on the doll's face. The dolls made in Semyonovo and Maidan were more decorative, and emphasis was placed on the dress and headscarf, with bright colorful flowers. During the Soviet period, most matrioshkas were machine made. In post-Soviet Russia, hand-painted matrioshkas can be found in art and souvenir shops and markets. A popular variety is sets of matrioshkas with different themes, from fairy tales to faces of politicians.

Mikhalkov, Nikita: b. 1945, son of the poet and children's writer Sergei Mikhalkov, who wrote the text for the Soviet national anthem. The most well-known director of contemporary Russian cinema, who won an Oscar award for *Burnt by the Sun*. He has his own studio, TriTe, and excellent connections with the French film industry (Michel Seydoux). His *Barber of Siberia* (Sibirskii tsiriul'nik, 1999) had a budget of $45 million and was the most expensive film ever made in Russia. His films include *A Slave of Love* (Raba liubvi, 1976); *Unfinished Piece for a Mechanical Piano* (Neokonchennaia p'esa dlia mekhanicheskogo pianino, 1977); *Oblomov* (1979); *Dark Eyes* (Oci chernye, 1987); *Urga* (1991); *Burnt by the Sun* (Utomlennye solntsem, 1994).

Mstera: village in the Vladimir region and second-best-known center for lacquer box production. Mstera boxes produce themes of fairy tales and history on a richly decorated background.

Norstein, Yuri: b. 1941. Internationally known animator who has worked in animation since 1961. Norstein invented a unique technique of multilayered cell animation. Numerous awards at international festivals. *The Fox and the Hare* (Lisa i zaiats, 1974), *The Heron and the Crane* (Tsaplia i zhuravl', 1975), *The Hedgehog in the Fog* (Ezhik v tumane, 1976), and *Tale of Tales* (Skazka skazok, 1979) won him fame, the last film being named the best animated film of all times. Since the 1980s Norstein has been working on *The Overcoat*, based on Gogol's story. The film is still in production; 20 or so minutes of it are complete. [www.animator.ru/db/]

Okhotny Riad (Hunters Row): The old trade rows in Moscow near the river Neglinka were demolished at the turn of the century. The Neglinka was channeled into a tunnel.

In 1930 the square was flattened. Plans for the reconstruction of the trading rows in a better construction were never implemented. In 1994, Zurab Tsereteli created surface water channels of the Neglinka, and the Okhotny Riad Mall opened in 1997. It consists of four levels of subterranean shopping areas, built by Mosproekt 2 (M. Posokhin, D. Dukaev, O. Steller, V. Orlov). [www.or-tk.ru]

Ovcharov, Sergei: b. 1955. Graduated from the Moscow Institute of Culture and in 1979 from the Higher Courses for Directors and Scriptwriters. Ovcharov began to make films with a strong folk character, such as *A Fantastic Story* (1983); *Lefty* (Levsha, 1986); *It* (Ono, 1989); *Drum Rolls* (Barabaniada, 1993). Then he made animated films, based on antique and traditional folk art. He animated paintings and drawings representing such myths and legends and animated them with a touch of humor: *The Pharaoh* (Faraon, 1999), *Myths. Heracles' Feats* (Mify. Podvigi Gerakla, 2000), and *Sochinushki* (2000) were the first films in this project. [www.animator.ru/db/]

Palekh: village in the Ivanovo region that is famous for its lacquer boxes. A former center of icon painting, the Palekh masters used their skills on lacquer boxes after the Revolution. Palekh designs are always on a black background, the scenes from Russian fairy tales finely drawn and often continued on the side of the box. Palekh is one of the oldest centers of painting, and its boxes are most valuable. [www.palekh.net and www.remesla.ru]

Petrov, Alexander: b. 1957. Animator from Yaroslavl. Since 1983 works as animator and director. *The Cow* (Korova, 1989) gained him an Oscar nomination for a story about a cow whose calf is taken away to be slaughtered, upon which the mother cow commits suicide out of despair. *Rusalka* (The Mermaid, 1996) is based on a Russian fairy tale; it won Petrov another Oscar nomination. In 1999 he completed the first-ever drawn animation for IMAX format, working in Canada. *The Old Man and the Sea*, based on Hemingway's story, explores visually with extremely fine drawings on large format the relationship between man and nature. The film finally won Petrov the Oscar in 2000. [www.animator.ru/db/]

Rogozhkin, Alexander: b. 1949. Prolific and successful scriptwriter, director. His early films include *The Chekist* (1991) and *Life with an Idiot* (Zhizn' s idiotom, 1993), which explore the absurd conditions of human life in Russia, present and past. His major breakthrough came with the film *Peculiarities of the National Hunt* (Osobennosti natsional'noi okhoty, 1995), which is a parody of the Russian hunt transformed into a series of drinking bouts. Rogozhkin made several sequels to the film.

sots–art: An art movement that emerged in the underground in the 1960s. It derived its name in an analogy with "pop-art." If pop-art parodied popular, consumer culture, then sots-art parodied the Socialist Realist canon prescribed by the Communist Party in the 1930s for all forms of artistic expression: Any work of art should show the development of the Soviet people towards a bright future. This concept was mocked, first unofficially by underground dissident artists, and after glasnost openly, both in visual arts and in literature.

Tsereteli, Zurab (real name Tsulukidze):
b. 1934. Artist from Georgia. Studied in
Tblisi from 1952 to 1959. Created monumental and decorative works, such as panels and mosaics, as well as sculptures,
which usually connect the work with the
architectural ensemble. Uses bright colors,
stark forms, and a variety of materials.
Southern style particularly suited for his
work in Georgian spas. In the 1970s decorated the railway station in Tbilisi, a children's complex in Adler/Sochi, the spa
complex in the Black Sea resort Pitsunda,
as well as the Soviet Embassy in Brazil. In
the 1990s became a favored designer for
the new Moscow urban planning under the
Mayor Yuri Luzhkov.

Bibliography

Beardow, Frank. *Little Vera.* Kinofile Film
Companion 8. London: I. B. Tauris, 2003.
Beumers, Birgit. *Burnt by the Sun.* Kinofile
Film Companion 3. London: I. B. Tauris,
2000.
———. "Cinemarket, or the Russian Film
Industry." In "Mission Possible," *Europe-
Asia Studies* 51, no. 5 (1999): 871–896.
———. *Mikhalkov.* KinoPeople. London: I. B.
Tauris, 2005.
———. "Mikhalkov: The Barber of Siberia." In
European Cinema, ed. by Sarah Street and
Jill Forbes, 195–206. London: Palgrave, 2000.
Beumers, Birgit, ed. *Russia on Reels. The
Russian Idea in Post-Soviet Cinema.*
London: I. B. Tauris, 1999.
———. "Soviet and Russian Blockbusters."
Slavic Review 62, no. 3 (Fall 2003): 441–454.
*BFI Companion to Eastern European and
Russian Cinema.* London: British Film
Institute, 2000.

Boym, Svetlana. *Common Places. Mythologies
of Everyday Life in Russia.* Cambridge:
Harvard University Press, 1994.
Brashinsky, M., and A. Horton. *Russian Critics
on the Cinema of Glasnost'.* Cambridge:
Cambridge University Press, 1994.
Condee, Nancy, ed. *Soviet Hieroglyphics:
Visual Culture in Late Twentieth-Century
Russia.* Bloomington, Indiana, and London:
Indiana University Press British Film
Institute, 1995.
Freidin, Gregory, ed. *Russian Culture in
Transition.* Stanford Slavic Studies 7.
Stanford: Department of Slavic Languages
and Literatures, Stanford University, 1993.
Gillespie, David. *Russian Cinema.* Harlow:
Longman, 2003.
Horton, A., and M. Brashinsky. *The Zero Hour:
Glasnost and Soviet Cinema in Transition.*
Princeton: Princeton University Press, 1992.
Kelly, Catriona, and David Shepherd, eds.
Russian Cultural Studies: An Introduction.
New York and Oxford: Oxford University
Press, 1998.
Larsen, Susan. "In Search of an Audience: The
New Russian Cinema of Reconciliation." In
*Consuming Russia. Popular Culture, Sex
and Society since Gorbachev,* ed. by Adele
Barker, 192–216. Durham, NC: Duke
University Press, 1999.
Lawton, Anna. *Kinoglasnost: Soviet Cinema in
Our Time.* Cambridge: Cambridge University
Press, 1992.
Shalin, Dmitri, ed. *Russian Culture at the
Crossroads: Paradoxes of Postcommunist
Consciousness.* Boulder, CO: Westview
Press, 1996.
Shlapentokh, Dmitry, and Vladimir
Shlapentokh. *Soviet Cinematography
1918–1991: Ideological Conflict and Social
Reality.* New York: Aldine de Gruyter, 1993.
Youngblood, Denise, and Josephine Woll.
Repentance. Kinofile Film Companion 4.
London: I. B. Tauris, 2001.

3

Performing Arts

The Theater

Russian theater is traditionally known for its "high" standard. Ballet and opera are first and foremost known in the West, especially the Bolshoi Theater and the Mariinsky Opera and Ballet Theater (still largely touring under its old name, the Kirov Theater). Thanks to such internationally known stars as Valeri Gergiev, conductor of the Mariinsky, or the ballerina Maya Plisetskaya, the international reputation of these art forms has remained at a very high level since the collapse of the USSR. The USSR pitched culture very high to raise the level of educatedness of the masses and create a genuinely "cultured" population. Forms of popular entertainment, such as boulevard theaters, musicals, street theater, practically did not exist in the Soviet era and were therefore underdeveloped after the collapse of the socialist system when compared with similar art forms in the West. In the performing arts, this higher pitch still applies to the present day and explains a relative delay of genuinely commercial art forms to conquer the Russian market. As a result, the musical established its popularity only in the late 1990s. In the circus, artists joined international troupes in the early 1990s when the circuses were struggling for survival, making a strong impact on the international stage but leaving Russian circus somewhere behind. As far as theater is concerned, popular entertainment remains the stepchild of Russian theater and a minor part of the theater landscape. Even ratings in *Afisha*, the Moscow entertainment guide, rank productions at established theaters in the top ten, whereas independent projects are rarely featured, and hardly ever does *Afisha* include commercial projects that draw on star actors and are hastily put together to draw large audiences with low-quality performance. Therefore, some of the drama productions discussed here would not be considered "popular" forms of entertainment in the West, but they remain popular in the former Soviet Union, where taste remains conservative in an entertainment sector that puts high prices on the new forms of entertainment.

Drama Theater

Soviet Theater   The conventions of Russian theater of the twentieth century were dominated by the so-called method (or system) of Konstantin Stanislavsky (1863–1938), the founder of the Moscow Arts Theater. Stanislavsky worked on the basis of psychological realism, aiming for the stage world to create a perfect illusion of reality, in which the actors would live through the emotions of their characters and evoke a response in the audience, clearly separated from the stage world. His concept of emotional experience (*perezhivanie*) was opposed by the concept of theater as demonstration (*predstavlenie*), especially prominent during the avant-garde movement of the 1920s. Vsevolod Meyerhold (1874–1940) had perceived theater as a magnifying glass that could enhance certain fragments or episodes from reality and highlight critically those aspects of society that needed improvement. Meyerhold fragmented the narrative of plays in order to challenge the audience intellectually. The sets and costumes for Meyerhold's productions were often created by the leading constructivist artists of the time and shaped like mechanical compositions. Meyerhold used placards for locations, citations from documentary sources, and cinematic features such as screens, slogans, and projections to draw parallels with real life. His actors were trained in "biomechanics" (the science of rational movement), so that movements on stage would be choreographed rather than motivated by psychological identification and bring man closer to a perfect, machine-like state. Between these two directors, traditionally perceived as polar opposites, stood the approach of Yevgeni Vakhtangov (1883–1922), one of Stanislavsky's pupils. He sought an imaginative interpretation of the text and emphasized the grotesque features of reality, drawing on the Italian commedia dell'arte. His "fantastic realism" is embedded in his 1922 production of *Princess Turandot*, which has been preserved to date in the Vakhtangov Theater's repertoire. Meyerhold and his theater were suppressed during the 1930s, whereas Stanislavsky and Vakhtangov were the dominant figures who influenced Soviet theater, not only in terms of teaching (the theater schools of the Moscow Arts Theater and the Shchukin School) but also by the theaters they founded, the Moscow Arts Theater and the Vakhtangov Theater. The only other, older, theater that had a school attached was the Malyi Theater, founded in the nineteenth century and named after its leading playwright, Alexander Ostrovsky.

Experiments in theater came to an abrupt halt in the 1930s when Socialist Realism became the only acceptable form of artistic expression. Artists had to express themselves in a realistic way and show Soviet society as an ideal, socialist land. Drama, built upon conflict, had to show progress from good to better but form itself without a conflict to trigger this betterment. Consequently, the level in dramatic writing dropped sharply, and numerous directors left the USSR or fell silent. Some, including Meyerhold, were arrested as "enemies of the people" and executed. The obsession with realism crippled the performing arts. It leveled artistic creation and was applied to drama and puppet theaters as well as the circus. The second important aspect was that theater was seen as a tool for education and thus for political propaganda. Even during the periods of the so-called liberalization in the arts under

Khrushchev (1956–1964) and Gorbachev (1985–1991), the theater served largely as a tool for propaganda. It exposed moral errors, criticized human conduct in order to improve the behavior of man in a socialist society, or highlighted areas of social reality that were subjected to review, such as the sacrifice of the individual during the war, Stalin's crimes, or youth problems.

The cultural policies of the Thaw affected the theater in terms of its management and organization. In 1953, the Ministry of Culture took over repertoire control but delegated responsibility for municipal theaters to the Moscow City Council. In the following years, a number of reputable theaters in Moscow and Leningrad were handed over to young, active, and engaged theater directors. Maria Knebel, a pupil of the great actor Michael Chekhov, became director of the Central Children's Theater, where she helped Oleg Yefremov and Anatoli Efros make their stage debuts as actor and director. Georgi Tovstonogov became head of the Bolshoi Drama Theater (BDT) in Leningrad. Anatoli Efros was given the Theater of the Lenin Komsomol, and Yuri Liubimov was appointed artistic director at the Taganka Theater. Oleg Yefremov, together with a group of young Moscow Arts School graduates, founded the Sovremennik (Contemporary) Theater. These new appointments had a huge impact on Soviet theater until the Gorbachev era, when the performing arts were revived by placing theaters under new management.

The Sovremennik Theater was extremely popular among younger audiences in the postwar Soviet Union. In creating the repertoire of the new theater, Oleg Yefremov (1927–2000) mainly chose texts with young protagonists and by young playwrights, so that both actor and audience could identify with the characters. Yefremov rejected makeup, costume, or elaborate sets and relied instead on the actor to bring his personality into the role. The actors shared experiences with the audience, with whom they formed psychological bonds.

In Leningrad, the postwar theater scene was dominated by Georgi Tovstonogov (1913–1989), who headed the Bolshoi Drama Theater from 1957 until his death. Not unlike Yefremov, he mixed authentic performance techniques with stylization of the set. Tovstonogov favored nondramatic literature and treated the text as a musical score while also deploying cinematic devices, such as cuts and voice-overs. In 1975 Tovstonogov staged, with his assistant Mark Rozovsky, Tolstoy's *Strider—The Story of a Horse* (Kholstomer), reading the condition of the exploited horse as a tragic metaphor for human life, refraining from explicit social criticism. This production became the flagship for the BDT.

Anatoli Efros (1925–1987) played a crucial role in investigating the theme of children on their way to adulthood, as he centered his repertoire on contemporary drama. For Efros, the actors' movements made inner psychological changes visible. This is best captured in the movement of cutting into the air with a saber—a gesture that expressed the hero's wish to demolish a piece of furniture, symbol of a bourgeois lifestyle (Viktor Rozov, *In Search of Joy* [V poiskakh radosti], 1957). Toward the end of the 1960s, Efros's interpretations of two of Anton Chekhov's classics proved so controversial that Efros was dismissed from the Theater of the Lenin Komsomol. *The Seagull* (Theater of the Lenin Komsomol, 1966) was condemned for its unorthodox interpretation of Chekhov in terms of "lack of communication" (reserved for the theater of the absurd, which was taboo in the Soviet Union). The characters were deprived of a meaning in life (unthinkable under socialism), and relationships were dominated by the impossibility of communication. Efros thus challenged the assumption of Socialist Realism that man by definition has a meaning in life. Similarly, in *Three Sisters* (Malaya Bronnaya Theater, 1967), bitterness and disappointment pervaded the characters, who experienced existential despair. The set repeated in the Russian "style moderne" the ornamentation of the Moscow Arts Theater, thus making an ironic reference to the outmoded Arts Theater productions of Chekhov.

The last of the four most popular postwar directors is Yuri Liubimov (b. 1917), who was also its enfant terrible. After an immensely successful student production of the German dramatist Bertolt Brecht's *The Good Person of Szechwan* (1964), Liubimov was put in charge of the Taganka Theater of Drama and Comedy. Although combining devices from Brecht's epic theater (placard and song) with Meyerhold's stylization and Vakhtangov's fantastic realism into a mélange, Liubimov perceived society as a generator of social and political change. He created his own "scenarios" from poetry, prose, drama, and factual documents and imposed his personal interpretation on the production. Liubimov always stressed the theatricality of his productions, making the spectator aware that he is in the theater and demanding that the actor should not pretend to play a part but should react both to the role and to the audience. The range of theatrical devices available to Liubimov was fully displayed in *Ten Days that Shook the World* (1965), a spectacle

Yuri Liubimov rehearsing *The Good Person of Szechwan*. (Photo by Birgit Beumers)

loosely based on John Reed's account of the October Revolution, in which Liubimov deployed mime and shadow-play, musical interludes and circus numbers to create a genuine theatrical festivity. A "light curtain" (light projected from the stage floor to the balcony) distanced stage events and marked scene changes as cuts do between cinema scenes. Brecht's alienation devices, such as songs to comment on the action, projections of Lenin, placards to indicate the place of action, abounded. The audience was part of the festive revolutionary atmosphere and even participated in the spectacle by casting their vote at the end. History was brought down to the level of everyday life and made tangible to the ordinary citizen. Later, during the period of stagnation, Liubimov's productions focused on the individual as tragically alone in a hostile and evil society and on the isolated individual and his conscience. The Taganka theater was one of the most popular theaters in Moscow, attracting the dissident intelligentsia, often people who had served prison sentences on political grounds. The tickets were an object of trade on the black markets, but also for theater staff, who were entitled to free tickets, which they traded for special services (medical treatment and other "favors"). Many Taganka actors were active in literature, film, or music as well as the theater, but the Taganka's star was the bard and actor Vladimir Vysotsky (1938–1980), who was best known as a guitar poet and whose songs were illegally circulated on tapes (*magnitizdat*) throughout the USSR.

During the late 1960s and 1970s, theatrical life stagnated: no new theaters emerged on the theatrical map of the major cities. Censorship interfered heavily with the creation of repertoires, especially in the late 1960s, when during the 23rd Party Congress (1966), several controversial productions were banned and the editor of the journal *Teatr* was relieved from his duties after he had published a series of positive reviews on controversial productions. Young directors had almost no opportunity to work in the established theater. In order to remedy this situation, some large theaters opened "small stages" (former rehearsal rooms) in the late 1970s for experimental work.

The productions of the "great four"—Efros, Yefremov, Tovstonogov, and Liubimov—dominated Soviet theater after the Thaw, and their theaters belonged to the most popular theaters in the Soviet Union. People would queue for hours to obtain tickets to see one of the "scandalous" productions of the Taganka Theater, the new style of the Sovremennik, the contemporary interpretations of the classics by Tovstonogov, or the fine psychological analysis of Efros. The popularity of largely conventional dramatic theaters must be seen in the context of the Soviet attempt to level the arts, to make them accessible to the masses while maintaining high artistic standards. This attempt to water down the divide between high and low culture destroyed the concept of theater as entertainment, stifled the work of puppet theaters, and institutionalized the circus. It removed musicals from the real stage to the silver screen, where the musical comedies of the 1930s and the vital role of popular music in Soviet blockbusters of the 1960s manifest this tendency. The stepchild of the performing arts, the estrada—the "small" stage for popular entertainment—had no claim on "high" culture but at least allowed popular music to flourish in the stagnation period.

Theater and Glasnost   In the transition toward a new cultural system, the theater was confronted with the need to emerge from the high culture to which it had pertained under the Soviet system and find its path toward a culture that saw the function of theater as entertainment, based on commercial principles. This transition was far from straightforward, since the process was initiated from above and aimed at using theater once more as a propaganda tool, only this time to announce the new artistic (and political) freedom.

When Gorbachev came to power, the control exercised by the state and party apparatus over cultural production was undermined. In 1986, the All-Russian Theater Society (VTO, Vserossiiskoe teatral'noe obshchestvo) was disbanded on the initiative of the Moscow Arts Theater's director, Oleg Yefremov, and reconstituted as the Theater Workers' Union (STD, Soiuz teatral'nykh deiatelei). For the first time leading actors—rather than functionaries—stood at the head of the unions: the Leningrad actor Kirill Lavrov took over the Soviet Theater Union, and the Russian branch was headed by the actor Mikhail Ulianov. The Theater Union removed the power of control over the theaters from the city council by assuming the authority to block any unfounded bureaucratic decision interfering with the artistic process of any theater. Only propaganda of violence and pornography remained prohibited, in line with the Soviet constitution.

From January 1987 on, 83 Soviet theaters took part in an administrative experiment: the testing ground for a new law on theater organization. In this experiment the theaters were still financed by the municipal authorities, but the subsidy was fixed and enabled the theaters to run their own budgets. Moreover, the power of control would rest in the hands of an elected artistic council, composed of actors and theater staff. The statutes of the experiment granted the theaters financial and artistic independence and the right to make direct temporary contracts with actors and playwrights, but still perceived ideological instruction as the key function of theater.

The first unexpected side effect of this experiment was that differences of opinion among the members of artistic councils led to the splitting of entire companies. In 1987, the Moscow Arts Theater split when its artistic director, Oleg Yefremov, pleaded to reduce the size of the enormous troupe (catering for three stages simultaneously)

in order to allow for a more creative and less managerial approach to the performing arts. His proposal was sharply rejected by those actors who had not played a role in years and were at risk of losing their jobs. The opposition was led by the actress Tatiana Doronina: she and about half of the actors left Yefremov's group, dividing the staff, the repertoire, and the two buildings between the two new companies. There are now two Moscow Arts Theaters: the Chekhov Moscow Arts Theater resides in the theater's original building in Kamergerskii Lane and the Gorky Moscow Arts Theater in the new building on Tverskoi Boulevard. The building on Petrovsky Lane (formerly Moskvin Street) underwent restoration and—even while the building work was still going on—reopened as the Theater of Nations, to offer a base for tours by companies from within the former empire. A similar situation arose at the Taganka Theater, where differences of opinion over the introduction of a contract system led to a dividing of the theater in 1991 into the Fellowship of Taganka Actors, headed by Nikolai Gubenko, and Liubimov's Taganka Theater.

The main targets of the experiment were the studio theaters. A small number of studio theaters had existed since the 1960s and 1970s, notably the Moscow State University Theater Nash Dom (Our House), Mark Rozovsky's U Nikitskikh Vorot (At the Nikitsky Gates), and Valeri Beliakovich's Na Iugo-Zapade (South-West). Now these and other collectives were able to obtain official status (independent of whether the actors were professional or amateur) and claim a subsidy from the city; consequently, their number grew rapidly. With the beginning of the experiment in 1987, only three studios stayed solely on state

Artistic director of the Chekhov MKhAT Oleg Tabakov (left) and artistic director of the Lenkom theatre Mark Zakharov (right) at a reception on the occasion of the premiere of *Uncle Vanya*. (Photo by Valery Levitin/Kommersant)

subsidy: Anatoli Vasiliev's School of Dramatic Art, Oleg Tabakov's Studio Theater, and Svetlana Vragova's Theater on Spartakov Square (now Theater Moderne). The studios enjoyed enormous popularity during the initial years of glasnost and perestroika, outdoing in spectator numbers the established theaters and partaking more than the established theaters in international tours in the late 1980s and early 1990s.

The number of theaters and studios grew rapidly in the years of perestroika, reaching 250 in Moscow. This rise occurred mainly in the years immediately following the introduction of the experiment of 1987 and stagnated during the 1990s. During the early 1990s, the first private enterprises also emerged, which represented a large proportion of theaters. With an ever-growing number of theaters, the early 1990s witnessed a sharp drop in the number of spectators generally but especially with regard to the established theaters. Even though the number of theaters (and therefore the total of performances) rose steadily, a constantly decreasing number of spectators were distributed over more venues than ever before. The experiment was gradually transformed into a new law on theater organization. The new statutes were finalized in the Council of Ministers' resolution of May 1991, which allowed the theaters to find private sponsors and open foreign currency accounts and enabled them to rent out premises while retaining the rent. Most theaters in central Moscow started to rent out a part of their premises to business, especially clubs and restaurants. Although this is often at the expense of the small experimental stages, it enables theaters to remain largely independent of box office. The theaters control the repertoire, appointments and dismissals, and ticket prices. The actor receives a fixed salary and special remuneration for his roles; he has to compensate the theater if he disrupts the repertoire by long absences (shooting films or failing to appear for a rehearsal or a show, especially because of the frequent insobriety).

Theaters gained financial independence and ideological freedom. Some of the studio theaters and independent groups in particular have contributed to the maintenance of the high level of tradition and innovation in Russian theater. Although the transition to a different economic system was difficult for the theaters in the initial years, the introduction of new legislation has made it possible for the theaters to exist with or without sponsors. The state has recognized its responsibility to subsidize the arts in a market economy. Commercial and independent theaters have benefited from the changes, as have some selected theaters in the capitals and provinces that are under an extremely competent management. Again and again such competent managers have clashed with the old-guard artistic directors, however: the director-

manager Maria Reviakina had successfully transformed the Novosibirsk Globe Theater before being appointed to the Moscow Arts Theater; she left her post after two years owing to disagreements with the Arts Theater's artistic director, Oleg Tabakov. Boris Mezdrich revived the Omsk Drama Theater; after conflicts in artistic affairs with the artistic director, Vladimir Petrov, the latter resigned, and Mezdrich was removed from his post by the local authorities. The conflict also occurs in the other direction: a commercially oriented director may clash with an old-guard director-manager, as in the case of the Malaya Bronnaya Theater, whose Ilia Kogan dismissed both Sergei Zhenovach and Andrei Zhitinkin; or Boris Erman at the Sovremennik, clashing frequently with young staff directors. The artistic leadership of the Lenkom and Satirikon Theaters in Moscow has demonstrated its competence in securing sponsorship and municipal support. There is also some danger inherent in any involvement with property in the center of Moscow, now valued very highly. Anatoli Vasiliev was threatened with having his premises on Sretenka Street removed after continuous delays with the formal exploitation of the new building. Oleg Lerner, who managed the financing of the new building that accommodates, among other investors, the Meyerhold Center and who set up a similar arrangement for the new Cultural Center of the STD, was shot in 2003.

The Studio Boom (1986–1993) The impact of the studios is vital as a backdrop for the new theater scene. Many directors of the 1990s benefited from the experience of the studio movement. Amateur theater studios that had existed long before 1987 emerged from their underground existence. They were often associated with technical institutes and performed in houses of culture (DK), or they were groups of people who met during their leisure time. The importance of the space, the premises, the "house" explains both the commitment that various troupes displayed in furbishing their new homes and the fact that so many theaters named themselves after their new address.

As "alternative" theaters, the studios had been attractive to audiences; once they were official and had become part of the mainstream, they had become above ground. Many people had seen underground performances. Now some lost interest in these theaters and instead experienced the intimacy of the studio space in established theaters, where increasingly the small stages were opened for public performances. As a result, most studios disappeared in the early 1990s, and only "the fittest" survived—those that had funding or an artistic program that pulled in audiences.

The collectives of the late 1980s certainly performed with great enthusiasm and brought to the Soviet Union a whole range of plays from the theater of the Absurd (Eugene Ionesco, Harold Pinter, Samuel Beckett), especially suited for small spaces. These plays were extremely popular during glasnost, the sensation being that is was possible to see, hear, and experience what had been censored and driven into the underground before. Overall, one was left with a feeling of excitement for glasnost, not knowing how long this new openness would last, and with a sense that these productions were remarkable for *what* they expressed rather than *how* they said it. Their invitations to inter-

national festivals in Munich, Paris, and other European cities largely reflected the desire of international festivals to support Gorbachev's political course rather than the artistic program of a particular director. There is one production from those years that left a deep impression solely for its artistic merit: Anatoli Vasiliev's *Cerceau* (1986), which toured Europe between 1987 and 1991. It was, however, not part of the mainstream popular theater but paved the way for a new theory of performance to be developed in Vasiliev's later work, thus reviving the concern with theater theory severed in the early twentieth century.

The studios of the "boom" fall into three groups: first, the studios that had existed on an amateur basis before; second, the studios that were founded as professional theaters (Vragova, Vasiliev, Tabakov); and third, those established by student collectives immediately after the experiment started, more or less jumping at the possibility of obtaining official status.

Leningrad's Mimes   The studio boom in Leningrad happened not only on a smaller scale than in Moscow, but also a year later. By the end of 1989 there were 166 studios in Leningrad, including a number of children's and musical theaters as well as a large number of shows and variety performances in restaurants. The Leningrad studios were therefore immediately hit by the economic crisis of 1991 when prices were freed. Moreover, audience numbers dropped owing to a lack of interest in the theater in the early 1990s.

The groups of mimes and clowns of plastic theater were particularly well represented in Leningrad. The group Litsedei (Actors/Hypocrites) was founded by Viacheslav Polunin and engaged in clownish

Case 1: The Theater South-West

The Theater South-West (Na Yugo-zapade) started in 1974 as an informal theater group with meetings in a library. In 1977 the district committee allowed the group to use a basement in a housing block in the southwest of Moscow. In 1980 the theater's director, Valeri Beliakovich, completed his professional training. By 1987 the ensemble already had 24 titles in its repertoire and had given more than 2,000 performances. In 1988 the studio adopted independent financial management and in 1991 gained the status of the Moscow theater in the southwest. The theater, with an audience capacity of 110, derived its name, as so many studios, from its location in the outskirts of Moscow.

In the beginning, the theater appealed mainly through its thematic concerns with political issues, such as the themes of lies and truth, or the relationship between the individual and the system. Beliakovich himself directs all the productions at his theater, where he has worked since the late 1970s with his collective of actors, from which some genuine talents have emerged, such as Viktor Avilov or Sergei Beliakovich. Valeri Beliakovich's style is very theatrical, using all the devices the theater has to offer, from music and lighting down to fog machines and other special effects. The productions are all very lively, and the music often serves to generate the rhythm of the production and accelerate the pace. Indeed, most critical reviews of the theater's productions concern the themes of the repertoire and the liveliness of performance. Yet although the productions are well paced and well acted, the pattern underlying each production—rhythm provided through music, expressive gestures, energetic acting—is repetitive and remains essentially unchanged. The space of the studio is very limited; it is decorated with a minimum of objects for each production.

Beliakovich's standardized grid of theatrical devices that he imposes onto any play appeared innovative in the 1980s, but it came across as stale and artificial in the 1990s. The expansion of the repertoire went at the expense of content. The theater remains popular with those who seek—and find—there the lost community spirit of the 1980s. The studio offers a sense of belonging to the generation of people brought up in the late 1960s and associated with the underground movements. This desire to share the common past with a collective of "confederates" or "accomplices" (*edinomyshlennik,* somebody who holds the same views) reflects a wish to return to the golden past. Indeed, the root of the term *edinomyshlennik* itself reflects the unity of opinion usually emphasized in Communist Party conferences (and opposed by Gorbachev's pluralism) when votes were always "unanimous" (*edinoglasno*). Such a longing for the (Soviet) past and the unity that bonded those opposing the system can also be observed in the cinema, where statistics have proven the greater popularity of films of the Soviet period (especially the 1960s) over contemporary films. A similar phenomenon can also be noted in connection with the studio of Mark Rozovsky.

mime shows that revived circus traditions as well as elements of street theater performance. Viktor Kramer, director of Polunin's shows, started up his own mime theater Farces in Leningrad. With the group, Kramer produced *Six Persons in Search of Wind* (Shest' personazhei v poiskakh vetra, 1996), a pure mime performance, before venturing into spoken theater with a show based on Ivan Turgenev's *A Conversation on the Highway* (1997) and with a production of Shakespeare's *Hamlet* (1998).

Case 2: The Theater At the Nikitsky Gates

The theater At the Nikitsky Gates (U Nikitskikh vorot) was formed under Mark Rozovsky, officially opening on 27 March (International Day of Theater) 1983 with a performance of *Doctor Chekhov* at the House of Medics on Herzen Street. When the studio gained official status in 1987, it had given some 500 performances of its seven productions in repertoire. The theater played under the auspices of the House of Culture for Medical Workers, like many underground and amateur studios that had formed under the wings of technical institutes, and attracted physicists, medics, and mathematicians to the stage. In fact, they were lucky, since they did not have to equip the stage themselves, as so many other studios did in the years of their underground existence.

Rozovsky had studied journalism at Moscow State University (having been rejected at the Theater Institute on grounds of his "appearance"—a euphemism for his Jewishness). In 1958 he founded the student theater of Moscow University, Our House (Nash dom), which he headed until it was closed by the authorities in 1969. Then he worked in a number of provincial theaters before becoming an assistant director to Georgi Tovstonogov at the Bolshoi Drama Theater in Leningrad, where he prepared and rehearsed Tovstonogov's legendary production *Strider: The Story of a Horse* (1975), based on Lev Tolstoi's story. Upon Rozovsky's return to Moscow he started, with amateur actors, the theater studio At the Nikitsky Gates in the House of Medical Workers. Here, they would continue to perform until they moved into their new theater on the corner of Herzen Street and Nikitsky Boulevard, a small, narrow venue seating approximately 80 spectators.

The borderline between theater and boulevard entertainment in Nikitsky Gates was blurred right from the outset. The dilettantism and amateur quality of the productions overall (not individual performances) may have been acceptable in a studio, but not in a theater. Rozovsky's own reading of the Russian classics, his collages of works, his productions in homage to Meyerhold or Vysotsky became the trademark of his theater. Rozovsky turned the theater into a place where the classics were made accessible by reducing them to the essential, by enacting text to a narrator's account, by setting them to music. This made the classics widely accessible (as though this had not been the case in the Soviet Union) and reduced them to mass culture, "domesticated" them through a performance in a theater that occupied a former communal flat. Rozovsky's preoccupation with song and music has triggered the creation of a series of musical recollections, such as *Songs of Our Courtyard* (Pesni nashego dvora, 1996) and *Songs of Our Communal Flat* (Pesni nashei kommunalki, 1999), that feed again the hunger of older generations for the golden Soviet times and their culture.

Kramer clearly has a great comic talent and a very creative mind, as he has been invited to direct opera productions both at the Bolshoi Theater (Ruslan and Liudmila, 2003) and the Mariinsky Theater (Tsar Demian, 2002; Boris Godunov, 2002). The Comic Trust is run by Vadim Fisson and is a poetic clowns' theater. *The White Story* (Belaia istoriia, 2002) is based on Dead Can Dance music and tells of the fairy tale themes of a white kingdom.

The mime group Derevo of Anton Adasinsky is very well known abroad but had no premises in Leningrad and therefore toured most of the time. Established in April 1988, they stayed in Leningrad for

Case 3: The Tabakerka (Tabakov Theater)

The Theater of Oleg Tabakov was formed in 1974 and emerged as an official, state-subsidized theater studio in 1987. It has resided in a basement in Chaplygin Street since 1977, and although the building has been refurbished, the size of the auditorium remains limited to some 120 seats. The theater, nicknamed the Tabakerka (snuff-box), is one of the most popular addresses in Moscow. This is largely due to the acting ensemble rather than the directors who have worked here or the kind of plays that form the repertoire.

Tabakov's theater started out with a group of student actors, and the ensemble has since recruited new actors and actresses from Tabakov's courses at the Moscow Arts Theater School, which he heads. In the perestroika years, the Tabakerka made its reputation with lively performances of hitherto forbidden plays, such as Barrie Keefe's youth drama *Gotcha* (Prichuchil), directed by Konstantin Raikin in 1984, or Mikhail Bulgakov's *The Crazy Jourdain* (Poloumnyi Zhurden, staged 1985), starring the comic actor Avangard Leontiev. Tabakov was quick to include works that had been released from the censor's shelves only during the glasnost period into his repertoire, such as Vasili Aksyonov's *Surplused Barrelware* (Zatovarennaia bochkotara, staged 1989) or Aleksandr Galich's scandalous *Seaman's Silence* (Matrosskaia Tishina, 1990), banned in an infamous affair in 1956 as the opening show for the new Sovremennik Theater, in which Tabakov had himself participated. The affair is rendered with great poignancy in Aleksandr Galich's novel *The Dress Rehearsal.* Tabakov also included in his repertoire such plays as Neil Simon's *Biloxi Blues* (staged 1987) or Jean-Paul Sartre's *Huis Clos* (staged 1992), but most important from the 1990s onward was his attempt to draw the best actors to his theater while never forgetting the need to give young directors a chance. In this way, some of his own actors (Alexander Marin, Vladimir Mashkov) began as directors in the Tabakerka, and other now well-known directors also worked in the theater: Andrei Zhitinkin, Valeri Fokin, and Adolf Shapiro were all invited to the stage exactly at those points in their career when they were in difficulty: Fokin was waiting for the completion of his theater center; Zhitinkin was seeking a permanent appointment; Shapiro had been dismissed from his theater in Riga. The actors are the real trump card of the theater, and after Tabakov took on the artistic leadership of the Moscow Art Theater in 2000, many of them performed both at the Tabakerka and the Arts Theater. Yevgeni Mironov is a brilliant stage actor and has starred in a number of Russian films; he has played the impostor Dmitri in Declan Donnellan's *Boris Godunov* (2000) and the title role in Peter Stein's *Hamlet* (1998). Evdokiya Germanova stars frequently in films. Vladimir Mashkov is a film star and considered to be Russia's sex symbol. Sergei Bezrukov has made a reputation for himself with a couple of stunning roles, including Felix Krull. He frequently appears in rather trashy films and also in boulevard theater shows. Alexander Marin has taken on the full-time task of staff director. Andrei Smoliakov is one of Tabakov's star actors both on stage and in film. Maria Zudina is a well-known actress and Tabakov's wife.

the first season, and since 1989 have mostly played abroad, facilitated by the fact that theirs is a nonverbal art. They use principles of immersion and meditation and are strongly influenced by Kazuo Ono and Tazumi Hijikata and the *buto*, which envisages the revelation of the soul through a meditative approach to theater. Adasinsky himself first trained in engineering, abandoned his studies to travel to Asia, returned and started a course in photography, gave that up to work with the clown and mime Viacheslav (Slava) Polunin, and made clips for the rock group Avia. With Polunin he founded Litsedei but left to set up his own group in 1990, working mainly with producers in Prague, and later Italy and Germany. The group's theater uses a meditative approach to mime, claiming to return to the roots. It appeals largely to a nontheatrical audience of the young generation. Its work lacks connections between episodes, which gives the work a certain incoherence, even though it often has a therapeutic (or the opposite) effect on the spectator. The group is clearly surrounded by a myth, rather than reputation, and remains popular among the young generation. Its performances during Russian theater festivals in recent years have always been sold out.

Andrei Moguchy started off with street theater in the early 1990s. His Formal Theater's performance of *Treplyov: People, Lions and Eagles . . .* (Treplev: liudi, l'vi i kuropaty, 1992) was based on Chekhov's *Seagull* and took Nina's monologue into the streets and courtyards of Leningrad. His later productions brought the theater to the conventional theater stage while consistently breaking the boundaries between stage and auditorium: in *The Bald Singer* (1990) he teased the audience verbally and

psychologically, locking them into the same room as the characters; in *Orlando Furioso* (1993) he opened the fire wall at the back of the stage for a bonfire; in *Hamlet Machine* (1996) he played physical tricks on the spectators, (mis)leading them through some performance spaces before allowing the audience to take a seat in a conventional performance space for the second part of the production. Although Moguchy's early works were clearly experimental, his *School for Fools* (Shkola dlia durakov, 1998) toured internationally and won major awards. In 2001 he collaborated with Yevgeni Grishkovets on an original performance, before venturing into a new area. In 2004 he staged the circus performance *Krakatuk*, based on E. T. A. Hoffmann's *Nutcracker*, involving acrobatic acts, video projection, and computer graphics in a stunning show where acrobatic acts were thematically united through a story.

At the end of the studio boom, the Leningrad studio movement had allowed some young directors to be discovered: the Formal Theater under Andrei Moguchy and the Farces under Viktor Kramer had both been internationally recognized. But most important was the impact the studio boom has had on the clowns and mimes, which is discussed in more detail in the section "The Circus."

A Catapult for Commercialization: Mirzoyev and Viktiuk

In 1988 the Theater Union channeled funding into the Creative Workshops (VOTM). In effect this was a generous, but utopian, "grand plan" for the construction of a mechanism that would allow young artists to emerge and integrate into existing structures in the world of theater. Like many grand plans of the Soviet system, it did not work; but it

Theater director Roman Viktiuk, the "enfant terrible" of Russian theater of the 1990s. (Photo by Pavel Smertin/Kommersant)

achieved something else, namely to create a basis, if only temporarily, for some directors to find their feet and work with an ensemble before the groups disbanded. Although some directors found their way into established theaters, others did not.

The first groups formed under the VOTM were numerous. They included Domino of Vladimir Mirzoyev, who emigrated to Canada in 1989 and left the group to Klim (Vladimir Klimenko); Even-Odd (Chet-Nechet) of Alexander Ponomaryov, who now successfully directs at the Central Children's Theater; and the group of Yuri Yeryomin, who later took over the artistic leadership of the Pushkin Theater for a period. Others were the group of Roman Viktiuk, who would soon thereafter set up his own Fora Theater; the Workshop of Mikhail Mokeyev, who staged both at the

Moscow Arts Theater and internationally in later years; and the group of Vladimir Kosmachevsky, who later emigrated. Finally, there was the group of Sasha Tikhy, following in the footsteps of the Almanakh group of the conceptualist poets Dmitri Prigov and Lev Rubinstein, that dissolved into the RussianImpostureMasterclass under the former designer Jacques (Vadim Zhakevich) and created highly abstract and conceptualized live installations in the late 1990s (such as Gogol's *Overcoat # 2434.5*, shown in 1999 and based on the calculation that all the numerals in Gogol's short story added up produce the sum of 2434.5). Both Mirzoyev and Viktiuk have thus used the VOTM as a base.

Vladimir Mirzoyev is probably the most successful of the former VOTM directors in the commercial and established structures of Moscow's theatrical life. His time with the VOTM was cut short by his emigration to Canada, however, where he continued to work in the theater before returning to Moscow in the late 1990s. He has since directed productions in established and commercial theaters with huge success. In the workshops, he began in November 1988 with a production of Roberto Atayad's *Madame Margarita*, in which the audience is mocked by a fascist sex-maniac teacher. The teacher takes the audience for her class and locks them in the room, so that there is no escape. The tone of the performance, combined with the provocation of the entrapped audience, caused a stir in theatrical circles. In August Strindberg's *Miss Julie*, staged in the same season, Mirzoyev incorporated a scene from Chekhov's *Uncle Vania*. He presented the dialogue between Yelena Andreyevna and Sonia as a meeting between two lesbians in order to implicate a parallel to Julie preferring Cristina's company. Mirzoyev clearly revealed his taste for the provocative and sensational in the sexual references he chose to highlight in the texts.

After his return from Canada, Mirzoyev staged Gogol's *The Marriage* (1994) at the Stanislavsky Theater, working with the designer he knew from VOTM, Pavel Kaplevich, now also a producer of commercial projects. This was followed by Gogol's comedy *The Government Inspector* (Revizor, 1996). Mirzoyev's productions invariably star Maxim Sukhanov, then a rising star of the Moscow stage: tall, chubby, and bald, he has an unusual physiognomy with gentle and muscular features at the same time. Mirzoyev worked at established theaters in the following years, creating a series of interpretations of the classics in a modern and very bold spirit, such as Jean-

Baptiste Molière's *Amphitryon* (1998), where people fool each other with masks, and the Shakespearean comedies *The Taming of the Shrew* (1999) and *Twelfth Night* (1999), which are read as comedies of masking and playing roles. He took over the artistic management of the Stanislavsky Theater after a series of hapless attempts to appoint a new artistic management to that theater. Mirzoyev is best at directing comedy, when he visually underlines the comic situation and makes great use of extravagant costumes. He mostly relies on the star appearance of Maxim Sukhanov, sometimes also the film star Sergei Makovetsky, both displaying in their acting a certain degree of sexual ambivalence. Mirzoyev's productions attract young and old, intellectual and middle-class audiences alike, as he offers a highly professional approach to theater and a bold interpretation of the text, verging on the sensational.

The Theater of Roman Viktiuk was one of the first successful commercial (as opposed to subsidized) theaters in Moscow. Viktiuk was the first artist to out himself as a homosexual, taking part in rallies and conferences organized by the gay community. At the same time as working in experimental, unofficial studio theaters, he continued directing by invitation at a number of prime addresses in theatrical Moscow (and not only Moscow), such as the Vakhtangov and Mossovet Theaters. His numerous engagements were, and still are, one of the myths surrounding Viktiuk: he often works on six to eight productions simultaneously, with the consequence that some productions are simply bad, and the overall profile is uneven. Viktiuk had worked as a director in the provinces until, in the mid 1970s, he took over the Theater of Moscow State University, where he directed Liudmila Petrushevskaya's *Music Lessons* (Uroki muzyki, 1980). Already in this much acclaimed, but banned production, he demonstrated his interest in theatricality and the inversion of reality. It was not until the onset of reforms in the arts that Viktiuk could develop his own style to the full, mixing elements of dance, music hall, and cabaret. His is a magic theater, a place that leads performer and spectator into dream-like states where the borderline between dream and reality is effaced.

In pursuit of the theme of role-play and disguise in the world of theater explored in *The Maids*, Viktiuk staged David Huang's play *M Butterfly* (1991), in which the protagonist Song Liling was played by the countertenor Erik Kurmangaliev (also known as Erik Salim-Meruet). Song Liling is an actress of the Chinese opera with whom Réné Gallimard (Sergei Makovetsky) falls in love. He forgets, however—as we do in the performance—that female roles in the Chinese opera were always played by men. The change of sex is manifest in the kimono dress of Song Liling and Kurmangaliev's soprano voice. Gallimard, a young diplomat and admirer of Puccini, is supposed to supply the embassy with information from Song Liling, who, instead, uses Gallimard for her own espionage. After the cultural revolution, Gallimard finds himself back in Paris and under arrest. Viktiuk provided a subtle analysis of the impact of role-play and disguise on Gallimard by expressing emotions, dreams, and fears through choreographed movement and images.

During the 1990s, Viktiuk chose texts for his productions that enabled him to identify social constraints as a cause for role-play and to investigate the crippling effects of role-play. Although the underlying principle is almost always one of suppressed sexuality, this does not necessarily reflect in the images that dominate the production. An example of this is Vladimir Nabokov's *Lolita* (1992), where Viktiuk dwelled *not* on the pedophiliac tendency of the main character, Humbert Humbert, but on his dual personality: a man tries to kill his double. Lolita (played by the ballet star Natalia Makarova) functions merely as a litmus test for Humbert's personality. The choice of Marquis de Sade's diaries for a production entitled *Boudoir Philosophy* (Filosofiia v buduare, 1996) proved Viktiuk's recognition of aesthetics and ethics as separate entities. Along with de Sade, Viktiuk advertised the joy of pain and poeticized the sodomic setting in the Charenton clinic where de Sade forced a young girl to reject the values of her bourgeois upbringing in exchange for "sadistic" pleasures. The polished surface of Viktiuk's artistic reality was exhausted, and cracks began to appear in the mask he had created. In *Boudoir Philosophy* the costumes reveal the actors' naked torsos, with some decorated in the relevant places with slack or erect penises or tiny conical caps with tassels to emphasise their sexual role. Microphones ensure the full translation of the actors' heavy breathing. Viktiuk sacrificed form for content, polishing sound, movement, and music to a perfect surface beneath which a perverse enjoyment of suffering reigned. At the same time, he defended the values of education, family, and love in an overtly didactic manifesto. The production caused outrage among theater critics, which indicates that the promulgation of sadism is not tolerated; in this production Viktiuk overestimated the tolerance level of Moscow audiences.

Most theatrical devices and themes chosen by Viktiuk are not new but were simply

Case Study: The Maids

Viktiuk's most renowned production, Jean Genet's *The Maids* (Les Bonnes, 1988; revived 1992), was created by the set designer Vladimir Boer, the costume designer Alla Kozhenkova, and the circus choreographer Valentin Gneushev (see the section "The Circus in Moscow and Leningrad"). Both the director, Viktiuk, and the author of the play, Jean Genet, share their perception of society in that they both take the perspective of a social outcast because of their homosexuality. Provoked by Genet's remark that men should play in *The Maids,* Viktiuk cast men for all the parts: Konstantin Raikin, the artistic director and actor of the Satirikon Theater, and Alexander Korzhenkov played the maids Solange and Claire. The controversy over the casting added to the popularity of the production, which was revived in a new version with a different cast in 1992.

The setting was reminiscent of a dance class with art nouveau mirrors and railings limiting the stage. This set symbolized the closed world of the two maids, from which there is no escape. The railings could also be used as exercise bars of a rehearsal room. The actors appeared in trousers before putting on skirts: a red one for Claire, a black one for Solange, and a white one for Madame. This transformation took place in front of the audience so that the spectator would be perfectly aware of the disguise. At the same time, Genet's voice proclaimed: "I wanted men to play the maids . . . ." Viktiuk dwelt in his production on the aspect of role-play contained in the text: Solange plays Claire, and Claire plays Madame in their rehearsal to poison the real Madame so that they would be free; the passion for the ideal of freedom leads to a potential, and real, crime. In the course of their role-play, Claire (that is, Solange) kills Madame (that is, Claire) because

they failed to kill the real Madame; therefore they have to realize their liberation in another reality, where Solange kills Claire. The fact that Viktiuk had men play women added yet another dimension to the role-play. One reality is distorted by the creation of other realities, so that eventually any reality becomes deceptive: when Solange poisons Madame, she poisons the person she imagines Claire to be. Role-play is shown to be a dangerous game, since it simulates false worlds; it creates imaginary realities, dream worlds, that are more real and more vivid than reality. This deception and distortion are illustrated through choreographic scores performed to the lulling songs of Dalida. Only at the point of the murder does Viktiuk set a musical counterpoint with the "Dies irae" from Giuseppe Verdi's *Requiem.* At the end, Viktiuk gradually leads his actors out of their parts, bringing them back to reality in a music-hall dance finale that emphasizes the show element. He thereby also introduces a positive element into the world of evil shown in the play and reestablishes a balance between good and evil, illusion and reality.

Viktiuk adheres to the decadent movement of the late nineteenth century, to the spirit of the fin de siècle, where the artist distinguishes between art and life as separate realities. The artist withdraws from a reality in which he is unable to live, creating for himself a different (sexual) identity, a mirror image that contains those features that the real person dare not reveal, not unlike Oscar Wilde's *Portrait of Dorian Gray.* Beneath the polished surfaces of the ballet-class railings and the mirrors lurk amoral behavior and perversity: a world deprived of life and stylized to a mere artistic reflection lacks a moral value system.

prohibited in the Soviet Union for a variety of reasons. Viktiuk released formerly suppressed potentials: aestheticism where the party had required a clear political and moral content; themes of homosexuality and transvestism where there had been a taboo on pornography and sexuality. Viktiuk's theater was extremely popular for breaching the taboos of conventional Soviet theater in the 1990s. His many other productions, however, deploy the same devices and apply the same kind of interpretation to a number of different texts. Viktiuk has abandoned entirely the established theaters and works in commercial structures only, and critics and spectators have gone quiet over his name and have lost interest in an ever-repeating approach to theater.

The Popularity of Soviet Directors   A few theater directors who had begun in the Soviet period remain popular to the present day, both with young and older audiences. The two most important names that have come across from the Soviet period are Mark Zakharov and Lev Dodin. Mark Zakharov (b.1933), artistic director of the Theater of the Lenin Komsomol (Lenkom) in Moscow since 1973, has created a wide-ranging repertoire and built up an ensemble with many actors known for their work in the cinema. He was the first to stage a rock-opera, *Perchance* (*Iunona i Avos'*, 1981) by the poet Andrei Voznesensky and composer Alexei Rybnikov, which attracted large crowds to the theater. Zakharov was highly regarded for his political engagement in the early perestroika period when he was one of the first directors to catch the spirit of reform, challenging in his articles the interference of bureaucrats. In his productions he tackled historical issues with a hitherto unknown openness, as in Mikhail Shatrov's

The Dictatorship of Conscience (Diktatura sovesti, 1985), which became a hallmark of perestroika because of its mention of such suppressed political figures as Bukharin and Trotsky, who had been banned from Soviet history books. Zakharov's troupe boasts some of the most popular film actors, including Inna Churikova, Alexander Abdulov, and Oleg Yankovsky as well as the television serial stars of the late 1990s, Nikolai Karachentsov and Dmitri Pevtsov.

Lev Dodin (b. 1944) graduated from the Leningrad Theater Institute in 1965 and in 1982 was appointed chief artistic director at the Maly Drama Theater (now Theater of Europe) in Leningrad/Petersburg, where he has created a fine repertoire, initially adapting prose for the stage. His adaptations of the trilogy based on Fyodor Abramov's village prose *The House* (Dom) and *Brothers and Sisters* (Brat'ia i sestry, 1980–1985) caused a stir at the time because of the outspoken treatment of human suffering during Stalin's purges of the 1930s, when those who allegedly resisted the forced collectivization of farms were arrested and often executed. The production won him international acclaim. He not only returned a part of the Soviet past but also researched with ethnographical precision the local folklore of the northern regions of Russia. His 1987 production of Alexander Galin's *Stars in the Morning Sky* (Zvezdy na utrennem nebe) underscored the theater's role as an advocate of glasnost in choosing a play about Moscow prostitutes, evacuated from the city to clean it up for the 1980 Olympics. His production of Dostoevsky's *The Devils* (Besy, 1991) was based on études with students, but it brought onto the stage one of Dostoevsky's novels that had been banned during the Soviet era. Some of Dodin's produc-

Artistic director of the St. Petersburg Maly Drama theater Lev Dodin. (Photo by Sergey Semyenov/Kommersant)

tions of the late 1980s resembled in style those of Liubimov; especially the Abramov trilogy drew heavily on the very plain and yet poetic set that had originally been designed for a production by Liubimov (also based on village prose and set in northern Russia) that had been banned in 1968. In the 1990s, Dodin took on a new group of actors from the Petersburg Theater Institute. In *Claustrophobia* (Klaustrofobiia, 1994), based on études and improvisations of contemporary prose, he demonstrated a visual and choreographic interpretation that functions not as illustration of the text. *The Cherry Orchard* (Vishnevyi sad, 1995) showed his skillful psychological exploration, but his directorial work was limited to individual scenes and episodes of the play rather than the overall composition. Chekhov's *Platonov* (*Play without a Title;* P'esa bez nazvaniia, 1998) and Platonov's *Chevengur* (1999) revealed Dodin's preoccupation with mechanical stage con-

structions rather than poetic images. The omnipresence of water in these works protruded, and it seems that the director wanted to submerge the individual, both the actor and the character. Dodin's theater has enjoyed a general popularity among theater audiences in Russia as well as on the international festival circuit, where Dodin seemed to be the only theater that could represent Russia.

The popularity of Dodin and Zakharov runs well into the post-Soviet period, and their work belongs to a different class of society already: their shows remain popular not just among the intelligentsia but also with middle-class and foreign audiences in the post-Soviet period. By contrast, theaters such as the Taganka, the Sovremennik, and the Moscow Arts Theater have to succumb to more commercial approaches in order to attract audiences.

Several other directors deserve a brief mention here, although they do not make "popular" theater or cater for the "masses." They have made an important contribution in one way or another, however, to the development of theater and acting in the period of transition. Petr Fomenko (b. 1932) moved from Moscow to Leningrad after the banning of several productions in 1968. He returned to Moscow in the 1980s to teach at the State Institute for Theater Arts (GITIS/RATI). His work as a pedagogue is as outstanding as are his productions in the professional theater. He has set up a workshop (Masterskaya Petra Fomenko), where his former students produce excellent work in a realistic vein. Fomenko's work with his former students, now of three generations, is remarkable, and the small auditorium of the theater can never accommodate the number of those wishing to see the productions. Fomenko's productions show his masterful accomplishment of a fine psychological analysis of the play in the best traditions of the Moscow Arts Theater. In this sense his work may not be "popular," but his actors have made a huge contribution to art-house and popular cinema, starring in numerous films: the twin sisters Polina and Xenia Kutepova, Sergei Taramayev, and Kirill Pirogov, to name but a few.

Valeri Fokin worked for many years at the Sovremennik Theater (1971–1985), where he directed numerous contemporary plays. In 1986 he became artistic director of the Yermolova Theater, where the production of a political play, Valentin Ovechkin's *Speak!* (Govori, 1986), underscored his commitment to Gorbachev's reforms. In 1991 he created the Meyerhold Center, which initially functioned as a production company for experimental theater, such as Kafka's *Metamorphosis* (Prevrashchenie, 1995) and *A Room in a Hotel in the City of N* (Numer v gostinitse goroda N, 1994, based on Gogol's *Dead Souls*), set in the space of a small hotel room. Now, with the new premises on Novoslobodskaya Street, it serves as a creative theater center that organizes productions, lectures, and workshops. Fokin's center is, like Anatoli Vasiliev's School of Dramatic Art, hardly a popular theater, but these two centers show the most experimental work and are the only institutions engaged in theater theory and research. The school occupies uniquely designed premises on Sretenka Street and belongs to the group of Theater of Europe. The school is not a popular theater, but an experimental one that works on Russian and world classics and develops new acting methods.

Finally, the Satirikon Theater under Konstantin Raikin deserves a mention as one of the most popular theaters. It is run, however, by a director neither of the old nor the new generation, but by the actor Konstantin Raikin, son of the famous estrada artist Arkadi Raikin. The theater, far from offering light estrada-type entertainment, comprises a number of reputable artists in its ensemble and offers a repertoire of classical theater, directed by some of the star directors of contemporary theater, including such names as Roman Viktiuk, Valeri Fokin, the Georgian director Robert Sturua, and the Petersburg director Yuri Butusov.

Stars of the New Russian Stage   After the crisis in audience numbers had ended and people returned to the theaters in the second half of the 1990s, the studios lost their role as the most popular venues. The interest in seeing what was only just accepted into official culture that had given the studios a hype in the late 1980s was now over, and there was no interest of the masses in the former "underground" aesthetics and themes. Instead, the crowds wanted to see stars and often made their choices of shows based on the appearance of their "idols," whose status was enforced by their appearance in film and in the late 1990s increasingly in television serials. They included Mikhail Trukhin and Konstantin Khabensky from the Lensovet Theater in Petersburg, both appearing in *Cops* (*Menty*), or Nikolai Karachentsov from *Detective Dubrovsky's Dossier.* Alongside, a new generation of directors entered the theaters and created a reputation as professional, efficient directors. They had a vision that they could implement on stage in a specified time frame, something that the older generation of directors had clearly great difficulty doing after years of work without pressure to premiere a new production in the old repertoire theater system.

In dramatic theaters, a number of young directors, such as Leonid Trushkin and Boris Milgram, ventured into commercial theater production. Commercial enterprises produced on the one hand shows with a star cast that would draw an older generation audience, who wanted to look at their "heroes" of the Soviet stage: Inna Churikova, Valentin Gaft, Valeri Garkalin, Tatiana Vasilieva, Liubov Polishchuk, Liudmila Gurchenko. Or else they appealed to a younger generation through younger stars, such as Chulpan Khamatova, Gosha Kutsenko, and Nikolai Fomenko. The Moscow Arts Theater even resorted to hiring the Petersburg television star Konstantin Khabensky to boost audience numbers.

In the process of a preoccupation with star names on the playbill, the name of the director has somewhat been relegated to second rank. A remarkable exception is Kirill Serebrennikov, who came from Rostov-on-Don and made his debut in film and television serials (*Rostov-Papa*, 2000, and *Diary of a Murder*, 2002), before he ventured into the Moscow stage world. In 2001 he directed the first play of the playwright Vasili Sigarev, *Plasticine* (Plastilin). Sigarev has since proven a shooting star not only in Russian theater but also internationally, with plays in a number of European theaters. Serebrennikov, who prefers contemporary plays (Mark Ravenhill's *Explicit Polaroids* [2002], Sigarev's *Plasticine*, the Presniakov brothers' (Oleg and Vladimir) *Terrorism* in 2002), refrains from illustrating the text with its more than often vulgar language. Instead, he creates a series of situations that underscore the origin for this vulgar discourse and finds it in the harsh and bleak circumstances of social reality, in Russia or elsewhere. For

Plasticine, a play by the Presniakov Brothers, directed by Kirill Serebrennikov in Moscow in 2001. (Photo by V. Bazhenov, courtesy of Centre for Drama and Directing)

Serebrennikov, the social and political circumstances directly contribute to man's
degradation, reflected in his vulgar language. His discovery of a key to these new
dramatists has been instrumental in ensuring the international success of Sigarev and
the Presniakov brothers.

Nina Chusova, a master of the comic, had
staged a number of small stage productions
before being invited by Pavel Kaplevich to
independent projects, such as *The Rubber
Prince* (2003) and *IMAGO* (Maxim Kurochkin's version of *Pygmalion*, 2002). At the
Sovremennik Theater, she staged Biljana
Srbljanovic's *A Belgrade Family* (performance title *Mumdadsondog* [Mamapapa-
synsobaka], 2003), starring the film actress
Chulpan Khamatova. The show explores
the life of an ordinary family and the education of their children while making clownish gags about the children's disobedience.
Her interpretation of Ostrovsky's *Storm*
(Groza, 2004) with Chulpan Khamatova as
Katerina and television star Yelena Yakovleva as Kabanova draws audiences and is
visually effective with a clever set and inventive costume design. The comic interpretation of the play, however, is based on
the assumption that Katerina is mad from
the start, leaving the actress hardly any
scope for character development during
the three-hour performance.

Yevgeni Grishkovets is a star of a different kind. Originally working in an amateur
theater in Kemerovo (Siberia), he made his
stage debut with a composition of his own,
which he performed solo: *How I Ate a Dog*
(Kak ia s"el sobaku, 1999). In this show
Grishkovets remembered, not with nostalgia but with an air of mockery and parody,
his Soviet childhood and how useless and
vain these recollections now sounded in
the New Russia of the late 1990s. This was

Scene from Biljana Srbljanovic's *A Belgrade
Family*, directed by Nina Chusova at the
Sovremennik Theatre in Moscow in 2003.
(Photo by Irina Kaledina)

followed by *Simultaneously* (Odnovremenno, 1999), based on similar principles.
Then he embarked on plays for more actors: one of these was *Winter* (Zima, 2000),
about two men, maybe soldiers, trying to
pass their time in the trench. *Winter* has
been successfully staged by a number of
theaters, including the Voronezh Chamber
Theater, where director Mikhail Bychkov
organized a season of new drama in 2002–
2003. *The Town* (Gorod, 2001) became a hit
when staged by two of Moscow's leading
studio theaters (Tabakov Studio and School
of Contemporary Play), with the television
star and presenter Julia Menshova playing
the lead in the latter. Grishkovets worked
with verbatim techniques in order to create
a text that brought back to the Russian audiences their memories of a Soviet childhood. He struck a chord with the middle-
aged generation, whereas his ironic
distance from the Soviet past allowed the
younger generation to recognize their child-

Evgeni Grishkovets in his most famous theater performance, *How I Ate a Dog* (1999). (Photo by Irina Kaledina)

hood experiences in Grishkovets's texts. Grishkovets experiments in ways of creating his texts: *The Siege* (Osada, 2003) was based on Joint Stock work with actors of the Moscow Arts Theater and explored the theme of war, now and in the past. Grishkovets has performed abroad and has reached a high level of popularity and prestige in Russian culture.

One of the most cherished stars of audiences of all ages and classes is Oleg Menshikov, who graduated in 1982 from the Malyi's Theater School in Moscow. He worked in a number of repertoire theaters in Moscow before beginning to work freelance in the early 1990s. He made a reputation in the theater for his roles as the dictator Caligula (1991) in a production directed by Petr Fomenko. *N* (1993) was produced by the theatrical agency BOGIS with the actors Oleg Menshikov and Alexander Feklis-

tov. It was based on the diaries of the early-twentieth-century ballet dancer Vaclav Nijinski and was staged in the Musical School on Prechistenka Street, which later became a popular theatrical venue. The windows on either side of the stage were instrumental for Nijinski's final jump—out of the window. Nijinski's mental world, his split character come to life on stage—a puppet represents the other half of his dual personality. The spectator was taken into the mental world of the character as though there was none besides this. Menshikov played the poet Sergei Esenin in the London production of *When She Danced . . .* (1992), where he performed alongside Vanessa Redgrave. In 1998 he made his directorial debut with a production of Alexander Griboyedov's *Woe from Wit*, in which he also played Chatsky. This was followed in 2000 by a production of a specially commissioned play, written by the winner of the Anti-Booker Prize for drama, Maxim Kurochkin, entitled *Kitchen*. The play explored contemporary relationships through the Nibelungen myth. Despite the use of classical texts as literary references, Menshikov's theater is popular and appeals to the masses.

Vladimir Mashkov is one of the most popular film actors in Russia. He works at Tabakov's studio theater, where he has also directed a number of performances. Oleg Antonov's play *A Fatal Number* (Smertel'nyi nomer, 1994) features a clown who falls off the rope and breaks into pieces: these become four different clowns, who all show their "special numbers" in the course of the play, ranging from illusions and clown numbers to song and dance. Eventually they realize that they cannot make a living with the bits and pieces their abilities represent, and they need to unite

Oleg Menshikov in *N*, a performance created by the independent agency BOGIS in 1993, based on Vaclav Njinski. Here he dances with a puppet (representing Nijinski). (Photo courtesy of BOGIS)

their forces again to resurrect the "great clown." The theme of collective spirit is emphasized after the collapse of social structures in the play, and the performance reflects on the medium of circus, which is brought into the context of the theater. The theater spectator travels into the illusion of being at the circus, and the theater once again has recourse to the circus art to revive its appeal to the masses. Brecht's *Threepenny Opera*, directed by Mashkov in the autumn of 1996, stirred the theater world more because of ticket prices than because of any artistic achievements: tickets were selling from $75 up. The production parodied the Mafia style and underground behavior. Using the latest technology (laser projection) and a constructivist set, Mashkov created a typical postmodernist show.

New Drama   In 2002 the Golden Mask, the main organizer of theater festivals in Russia, started up a new festival, the New Drama. This move reflected the rise of a new generation of dramatists and the introduction of a new wave of drama into the Russian theater landscape. Nikolai Koliada (b. 1957) is one of the most popular playwrights, with his plays running at prestigious theaters in Moscow as well as abroad. He trained as an actor at Sverdlovsk (now Ekaterinburg) Drama Theater, which he quit when defending an elderly actress who was sacked for alcohol abuse; he later graduated from the Moscow Literature Institute. Koliada is interested in exotic themes, eccentric characters, and marginal social groups, such as prostitutes, homosexuals, transvestites, and alcoholics, and focuses on the guises people adopt to live with a reality they do not really want to accept and who withdraw into an imaginary world.

Reality and the imaginary merge, the past fuses with the present. In *Oginski's Polonaise* (Polonez Oginskogo, 1994) the memory of the past forms the backdrop for the events. Tania, an ambassador's daughter, defects to the United States when her parents die in a car crash. She returns to Moscow after the collapse of the Soviet Union to find the old family apartment converted into a communal flat. Dima, her nanny's son, whom she used to be fond of as a child, now lives there together with the former servants of the diplomats' household. Dima earns a living by playing one of Michal Oginski's (Polish composer, 1765–1833) polonaises, entitled "Farewell to the Fatherland," in an underground passage. Tania is unable to confront reality: she fails to accept the *byt* (circumstances of everyday life) of contemporary Russia. She even refuses to use the metro to visit her parents' grave. Instead, she withdraws into an imagined and idealized world, one that corresponds neither to the reality of her life in the United States, where she earned a living as a prostitute, nor to her life in Moscow. Koliada drew her detachment from reality very vividly: she fails to communicate with the other characters, and she never considers Dima's feelings, but speaks only of her love for him. She is self-centred and has withdrawn into a world of her own.

Koliada teaches at the Theater Institute of Ekaterinburg, preparing new playwrights for their careers. As editor of the literary journal *Ural*, he has the opportunity of publishing first plays and regional prose works. He also directs at the Drama Theater and has recently established his own theater,

Koliada Teatr. In this way, Koliada has taught and brought to publication the first plays of Oleg Bogayev and Vasili Sigarev, who both found their way into prestigious Moscow theaters. Sigarev's *Black Milk* (written in 2002) was staged at the Gogol Theater and *Plasticine* (written in 2000) at the Center for Drama and Playwriting in a production by Kirill Serebrennikov. Bogayev's *Russian National Post* was staged by Kama Ginkas with the people's darling actor (and head of the Moscow Arts Theater) Oleg Tabakov in the lead.

Ivan Vyrypayev created a hit in Moscow in October 2002 with *Oxygen* (Kislorod). It is a performance à la Grishkovets, where the playwright also acts as a performer. Grishkovets draws on a common past experience, whereas Vyrypayev is of a younger generation and makes fun of his own life and the present, using contemporary material. He structured his performance in ten episodes, as if they were ten commandments. Yet his performance rejects any moral implications of the testament and instead subjects all his action only to the need for oxygen.

Originally from Ekaterinburg, the Presniakov brothers first conquered the Moscow theater with a production of *Terrorism* (2002) at the Moscow Arts Theater by Kirill Serebrennikov. This play is fragmented and consists of scenes from everyday life that all revolve around the threat of terrorist attacks: there is a bomb scare at an airport, a suicide attack, a woman who plots a murder. The fragments are disconnected, the characters have nothing in common; unity is achieved thematically by the threat of a terrorist attack that permeates every aspect of our lives, infiltrating into the domestic and political spheres. *Terrorism* has since been staged at the

Ivan Vyrypayev created a hit in Moscow in October 2002 with his play *Oxygen* (Kislorod), in which he also performs. (Photo courtesy of Golden Mask Festival)

Royal Court Theater, London, to great acclaim; the Royal Court commissioned a play, *Playing the Victim* (Izobrazhaia zhertvy), from the Presniakov brothers.

As mentioned earlier, Vasili Sigarev made his debut on the Moscow stages in a production of *Plasticine* directed by Kirill Serebrennikov, who specializes in modern drama. This time, however, the show premiered in a small theater center that is devoted to experiment. Yet most of these experiments have the potential for commercial success, had it not been for the small size of the stage and the auditorium limited to some 80 seats in the rented space of the Vysotsky Museum. Sigarev's play evolves in a provincial town, where a teenage boy dies. His friends from school try to cope with the loss, but his friend Maxim is deeply upset and begins to see everyday life as hell, both repulsive and enjoyable. He plays tricks in an attempt to show his contempt for the false orderliness of school life, he tries to behave like an adult and learns about the horrible sides of life (crime, sexual abuse, drugs), and he experiences the seeds of love. Yet his process of maturing is hampered by the environment, which ultimately destroys his still unprotected and unformed personality.

Both the Presniakov brothers and Sigarev share a portrayal of the world as a grim and hostile environment, ridden with crime and abuse, which is reflected in their use of vulgar language, slang, and nonnormative words. Both, however, leave occasional room for laughter that arises from the clumsiness of the characters, which is funny despite of or because of the tragic situation. Maxim Kurochkin is a historian

Stage director Kirill Serebrennikov. (Photo by Victor Bazhenov/Kommersant)

by training. His plays are dominated by the theme of war, which haunts civilization from the past to the future. Kurochkin uses language skillfully, with local dialects underscoring historic or regional authenticity. In 1995 he made his debut with *The Destroyer of the Class Medea* (Istrebitel' klassa "Medeia"), where a war is ongoing between an internationally united male force being attacked and undermined by their female counterparts. In *Steel Will* (Stal'ova volia, 1999), the Polish gentry fight with the help of the computer station Steel Will.

New Russian drama has made an impact on British theater with the Charles Wintour Award for the most promising playwright 2002 to Sigarev's *Plasticine* and the nomination of the Presniakov brothers' *Terrorism* for the 2003 TMA (Theatrical Management Association) award for best new play. Both have had their plays produced at the

Royal Court, followed by national tours. Translations of new Russian plays are becoming available in English and other European languages, thus finding their way into European and world theater.

Puppet Theater

Puppet theater in Russia has a long-standing tradition and is an important part of contemporary popular and children's culture. Because of the size of the audience for puppet theater, it is not for the masses strictly speaking, but it reflects genuine popular forms in the historical sense and appeals to a wide audience in Russia today.

From Petrushka to the State Puppet Theater

Puppet theater worldwide has a long-standing tradition as a form of popular entertainment. The tradition of puppet theater in European culture reaches back well into the medieval period. Indeed, the stock character Pulcinella appeared for the first time in fifteenth-century Italy. In medieval times, puppet performances were most commonly put on in a cardboard box that formed a little theater; the puppet was held on the hand (glove-puppet or finger-puppet) and moved by the so-called *burattini* (puppeteer). The marionette, held and moved by strings from above, appeared only in the seventeenth century and was brought to Russia under the Empress Anna Ivanovna (1730–1740), who also imported the commedia dell'arte with its masks to the Russian court. Marionettes were thus part of court culture, whereas handheld and glove or finger puppets were part of folk traditions and had their place among the people. A third type of puppet came from Asian culture, where puppets formed part of rituals of worship; these were stick or rod puppets (*trostevye kukly*) that can be moved by three or more actors, depending on the difficulty of the movement, and are between 40–120 centimeters tall.

In popular and street theater, the puppet arrived in Russia only in the nineteenth century. The most popular was the glove puppet (*kukla na perchatkakh*), which was also called Petrushka, after the stock character of Russian puppet theater. Moreover, stick-puppets were used to enact the nativity plays and Christmas cribs in their Russian equivalent: the *vertep*.

The main male stock character of puppet theater varied from country to country: he was called Pulcinella in Italy, Polichinelle in France, Kasperle in Germany, and Punch in England. The Russian Punch figure was called Petrushka: a trickster and a rebel hero, he dished out beatings with his club (the *dubinka*) to those who cheated him or who were treating others unjustly; as such, he exerted moral justice. Yet Petrushka was also socially inept: he would beat his wife or fiancée, he could not ride the horse he bought, and he argued with the devil. Petrushka was a character who was laughed at and whose texts were satirical of social stereotypes. Petrushka greeted the audience with his squeaky voice, before carrying on with his text; sometimes he would have responses from the musician, normally an accordion player, who repeated his phrases so that they could be better understood. Petrushka was not beautiful or of noble birth; he had a hunchback and a long nose, as well as other physical abnormalities. He sported a red peasant shirt and a cap of some sort and was usually accompanied by his dog, Barbos. The plot of the performances repeated certain key scenes, although not always following the same pattern, yet at the end Petrushka would inevitably be dragged off by Barbos.

In the nineteenth century, the performances of Russian puppet theater toured the amusement parks and fairgrounds and dominated the street life in provincial towns. The shows were cheap and accessible to the lower, subordinate (serf) classes, and they also attracted children. Such popular entertainment in the form of street theater came to an end after the Revolution and the civil war. The Bolsheviks attempted to raise the level of culture and educate the people and therefore suppressed all form of popular, mass culture. Puppet performances became part of high culture, and therefore both the creation of puppets and the performances had to be sophisticated. Before the Revolution, however, Julia Slonimskaya and Pavel Sazonov formed the first puppet theater, creating at the same time artistically sophisticated and elegant puppets—as opposed to the robust, wood-carved Petrushka. Moreover, during the early years of the Soviet state many avant-garde artists, filmmakers, and actors were interested in puppets for use on stage and in film. The puppet could be a symbol for the human condition: a fragile being, subjected to the rule of fate. By the 1930s, a state-run union (the State Department of Music Hall, Variety Theaters, and Circus; GOMETs) not only controlled all circus, variety, and music hall performances, but the puppet theaters were forced out of the streets into established theater venues. Puppet theater became a means of entertaining children only, and puppets were no longer part of touring funfairs (now replaced by leisure parks) or used by wandering troupes in the streets (but instead in stationary theaters). Puppetry acquired an agitational function, and puppet theater was largely perceived to target children as its primary audience.

One of the most significant figures for contemporary puppet theater was Sergei Obraztsov (1901–1992). He organized the State Puppet Theater in 1931, opening with A. Globa's *Jim and Dollar*, a play that told the story of a little Afro-American boy who found refuge in the USSR. This was followed by a series of other shows of a propagandist nature that portrayed life in the Soviet Union as positive. He also devised a number of folk and fairy tale shows, such as *To the Pike's Command* (Po shchuchemu veleniiu, 1936) and *Aladdin's Magic Lamp* (1940). Obraztsov's performances with glove-puppets and finger-puppets or objects, such as a bear, the puppet Tyapa, or balls, became his trademark in the 1940s and 1950s. *The (Un)Usual Concert* (1946) opened the path for the satirical and parodic use of puppets. The theater's repertoire also included the Russian classics, such as Chekhov's *Kashtanka*, a tale about a homeless dog; Hans Christian Andersen's and Russian fairy tales; and the works of Soviet children's authors, such as Kornei Chukovsky, Agniya Barto, Sergei Mikhalkov, and Sofia Prokofieva. The theater also adapted the heroes of Soviet children's animated cartoons for the stage and created puppets for Cheburashka and Moidodyr. The theater had occupied a building on Mayakovsky Square since 1936, but in 1970 it moved into new premises on the Ring Road. Obraztsov's Puppet Theater is famous for the clock that decorates the facade of the new building, which was created by Dmitri Shakhovsky and Pavel Shimes: each hour is decorated by a little house with a door that opens for an animal from a fairy tale to appear to the tune of a Russian folk song. Under Obraztsov, the puppet theater focused on the literary sophistication of the plays. The puppets played their roles as if

Sergei Obraztsov, director of Moscow Puppet Theater, with one of his puppets. (Yevgeny Khaldei/Corbis)

to express emotion, in line with the realism that dominated dramatic theaters at the time. Puppets no longer caricatured and satirized and moved away from the poetic and grotesque potential inherent in a puppet. The crisis for puppet theater effectively began in the 1950s, when puppets became like humans in their movement and their emotions. The puppet theater mainly used stick-puppets or glove-puppets, not marionettes. Once institutionalized, the puppet theater lost its spontaneity, its potential for carnivalization and festivity. Its audiences were no longer the masses, but people of all ages and backgrounds.

During the Soviet era a number of puppet theaters were set up in other Russian cities, including the Leningrad Demmeni Puppet Theater and the Fairy Tale Theater and theaters in the provincial towns of Yaroslavl, Nizhny Novgorod (Gorky),

Samara, Rybinsk, Arkhangelsk, Ivanovo, and Rostov. Moreover, the national and ethnic traditions of some regions and republics made them very strong puppet theater performers. Georgia in particular was famous for its marionette theater. The Khakassian town of Abakan formed a well-known puppet theater after World War II. Finally, puppet theater became part of the state's training programs when a puppet department was created at the Leningrad Institute for Music, Film and Theater (LGITMIK) in 1959, and Obraztsov became a professor at the Moscow Institute for Theater Arts (GITIS/RATI) in 1973. The puppetry section at RATI has been vacant since his death in 1992.

Puppet Theater of the New Russia
During the Gorbachev era, experiments began that were designed to integrate the puppeteers into the performance and attribute specific roles to them. Moreover, human actors played puppets that were moved by puppeteers, so that variety was introduced into the relationship between the puppeteers and the puppet. Puppets also appeared as characters in traditional drama theaters, as for example at the Theater of the Young Spectator. In Kama Ginkas's version of Pushkin's *Golden Cockerel* (Zolotoi petushok), a puppet of the cockerel is made up in front of the audience and becomes an object for the actors' play. The theater director Igor Larin made use of porcelain dolls for the characters of Chekhov's *The Cherry Orchard* in a production in Magnitogorsk, in which only Lopakhin is a real character. After purchasing the estate, Lopakhin (played by Larin) accidentally smashes the glass display with the puppets. It is as though his act, which contributes to the demise of the Russian

gentry, was not deliberate; in any case the gentry is immobile and immortal: they are dolls that serve as a mere decoration.

Only in the 1990s did the New Russia begin to return the puppets and dolls to the people. In 2000 an exhibition of dolls and puppets made by stars from film, theater, and television was organized by the Museum of Architecture in Moscow, showing the approach of artists and designers to the object. Puppet theater has gradually freed itself from the constraints of realism, from the aversion against marionettes, and from the need to cater for children only. "Nothing and nobody can replace man on earth; without him, the gods, clowns and puppets have nothing to do," as the critic Irina Uvarova commented on the state of post-Soviet puppet theater. Puppets have begun to appear in conventional theater. Moreover, the puppeteer has acquired a new role: he may be a visible character, who moves within the set and is clearly the manipulator of the puppet's movements. A new range of approaches to the puppet theater has been explored, such as the integration of shadow theater, the use of the human body as a puppet, and the use of ordinary toys. Texts are often specially composed for the puppet theater rather than adapted for it.

The puppet theaters of the regions, such as Ekaterinburg, Abakan, and Arkhangelsk, have developed a sound repertoire, including children's and adult shows. They draw on local traditions in the specific use and creation of their puppets. The Puppet Theater of Ekaterinburg, which employs the best-known puppet makers in Russia, is headed by Alexander Borok. The theater dresses the actors in costumes and places them onto the stage, from where they move the puppets in the set. His *Pictures*

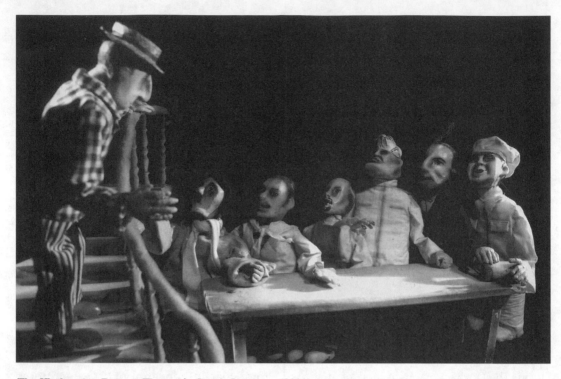

The Khakassian Puppet Theater's *Jacob Jacobson* (2002) was nominated for the Golden Mask national theater award. (Courtesy of Golden Mask Festival)

of an Exhibition (Kartinki s vystavki, 1996) was a contemporary version of Modest Mussorgsky's piece in a new musical version by the theater's house composer, Sergei Sidelnikov. He also wrote the score for *The Nightingale* (Solovei, 2000), a children's fairy tale.

The Khakassian Puppet Theater Fairy Tale from Abakan uses traditional wooden carved dolls for their performances, usually based on biblical themes: *Judas Iscariot* (1998) and *Jacob Jacobson* (2002) were both nominated for the national theater award, the Golden Mask. The theater's director, Yevgeni Ibragimov (b. 1967), graduated from LGITMiK and has headed the theater since 1998. The Arkhangelsk Puppet Theater is directed by Dmitri Lokhov (b. 1950), also a graduate of LGITMiK, and draws on ethnographic traditions for the creation of its puppets. As the chair in puppetry at the Moscow Theater Institute remains vacant, it is the Petersburg Theater Academy (formerly LGITMiK, now the St. Petersburg Academy of Theater Arts SPATI) that produces a new generation of puppeteers.

Although traditional puppet theaters continue to exist, the most innovative and popular puppet theaters of the New Russia are the theater Potudan in Petersburg; the Theater Ten' (Shadow) in Moscow; and—although this is not Russian by origin—the puppet theater of the Georgian artist Rezo Gabriadze.

Theater Potudan, St. Petersburg

This theater, formed in 2000, was named after its first production, *Potudan*, based on Andrei Platonov's eponymous story. Potudan consists of a group of graduates of SPATI who had studied under Grigori Kozlov. Kozlov himself trained in that department but has since moved to drama theaters and currently holds the post of artistic director of the Theater of the Young Spectator in St. Petersburg. *Potudan* was presented in 2002 at the Baltic House Theater, in a coproduction with the film studio Darfilm under Valeri Ogorodnikov. Potudan's director is Ruslan Kudashov (b. 1972), who graduated from SPATI in 1999. The production is not just an adaptation of Platonov's story, but it is the deliberate choice of a specific text whose fragile characters are suited for representation through puppetry. The sand and snow form elements of the story and the production, very reminiscent of the use of sand in Gabriadze's *Song on the Volga*, culminating in the final image of the war as a river that sweeps away the sand. The story deals with the universal theme of love in a world that makes man a fragile object and tosses him about.

In May 2002, Potudan presented its second show, *Nevsky Prospekt*, based on Gogol's famous story about the phantasmagoric aspect of life in nineteenth-century Petersburg. *Nevsky Prospekt* made use of different kinds of marionettes—dolls, cardboard figures, body parts, and wooden puppets—to recreate the eccentricity of Gogol's world. The parade of types and social classes on Nevsky Prospekt (Petersburg's main artery), with which Gogol begins his story, presents a variety of marionettes: the foreigners are cardboard figures, whereas wooden dolls are used for the bureaucrats. Each class is represented by a corresponding kind of puppet that immediately characterizes it. The protagonists, Piskarev and Pirogov, ap-

pear first as shadows, whose stories mirror each other. The backdrop for the performance is a reproduction of an etching by Vasili Sadovnikov, showing the city of St. Petersburg. The choice of puppets for this show is deliberate: only puppets make it possible to differentiate between flat and three-dimensional figures, to label women as "dolls" and men as shadows, and to represent instead as full-blown "characters" the main actors of Gogol's world: noses, lips, and moustaches, which make up the phantasmagoric city. Another ingenious move was the representation of Piskarev's suicide, when a hand in a glove cuts the strings of the marionette, terminating the puppet's life. The entire performance takes place behind a glass pane; at the end, water pours down the pane as if it were raining, washing away the image of the city and making room for a new one.

Potudan is popular not among children, but adults. The director makes every attempt to move puppet theater away from the dead end in which it found itself after the Soviet era, trying to compete with dramatic theater instead of finding, and redefining, its own poetic texts and images.

Shadow Theater (Teatr Ten'), Moscow

The Shadow Theater, which essentially renames itself for each new production or project, was founded in 1989 by Maya Krasnopolskaya and Ilia Eppelbaum. Since 1991, it has been a municipal theater and occupies an apartment in a house on Novoslobodskaya Street.

In 1996 the Shadow Theater presented the project *The Russian Tour of the Grand Royal Lilikan Theater of Drama, Opera and Ballet* (Gastroli lilikanskogo bol'shogo korolevskogo teatra dramy, opery i baleta v Rossii; *Lilikan* is a mixture between

At the Lilikan theater the directors Ilia Eppelbaum and Maya Krasnopolskaya place puppets into a miniature replica of the Bolshoi Theater. (Courtesy of Ten Theater)

liliput and *velikan*, the lilliput and the giant), which is continued in the project of the *Lilikan Museum* (2002–2003) and in *Ruslan and Ludmila: A New Year's Performance* (2003–2004). In the Lilikan Theater, the directors create not so much a performance as the conditions for it: they place miniature puppets into a dolls' house (a replica of the Bolshoi Theater) and invite the spectators to observe the movements through the windows of the theater. A maximum of five spectators can therefore watch each performance. *Ruslan and Ludmila: A New Year's Performance* parodies conventional forms that cripple performances of the classics. On the Bolshoi's stage, a Christmas performance takes place. The clash between a *yolka* (Christmas tree, also the word for the visit of Santa Claus to deliver the presents)—in itself a popular form of performance, usually with Father Christmas (Ded Moroz) and his assistant Snowflake (*snegurochka*) delivering the presents to a group of children—and the most conventional, lavish interior of the Bolshoi Theater prepares the ground for parody. The action of Pushkin's classic romantic tale now becomes the story of a Christmas tree flying into space; the design deliberately and clumsily repeats the setting of Viktor Vasnetsov's fairy tale theme painting, which every child knows from school visits to the Tretiakov Gallery.

As Theater Shadow-Opera (Ten' opery), Krasnopolskaya and Eppelbaum presented *Swan Lake. An Opera* (Lebedinoe ozero. Opera, 1998). The directors parodied Tchaikovsky's *Swan Lake*, claiming it was intended and conceived as an opera and not a ballet. The actors here play puppets that are moved by other actors. Effective use is also made of shadow theater.

As the Theater of the Father's Shadow (Teatr Ten' ottsa), the directors presented a show based on *Hamlet* (2001), where normal toys were used instead of puppets in a journey through a variety of theatrical genres, from opera and operetta to tragic and comic drama. The performers introduce the children to the theater: they explain to them the seating, the interval, the program; and they show them how the actors dress up in a costume and how they use masks. Therefore, the actors stand on stage and play, as it were, with the toys, explaining their function in each episode. The bear plays the classical characters from Pushkin, Mikhail Glinka, Molière, and Chekhov: Eugene Onegin, Ivan Susanin, Don Juan, and Konstantin Treplyov; a simple ball is Leporello and Lensky (ingeniously Lensky's death in the duel is represented by the ball being deflated). A little excavator plays the statue of the commander, whom Don Juan challenges in an attempt to win Dona Anna.

The Shadow Theater is not only one of the most innovative and experimental puppet theaters in Russia but also a most popular theater. Largely owing to the small number of places available, it is difficult to get a ticket; the company also tours extensively.

Rezo Gabriadze   Gabriadze is probably the best-known puppeteer of the former Soviet Russia but also a poet and painter. He makes poetic use of the puppet, which he employs not to tell a story and illustrate the character's emotions but to create images and metaphors for universal themes and eternal values, in particular the theme of love: its birth, pain, and death.

In *Alfred and Violetta* (1986/7) he explored the birth of love. Alfred, an astrophysicist, falls in love with Violetta on the eve of his departure to Venice on a research trip. His father opposes the son's love for a girl who is not of his standing. Violetta is ill. They travel to Venice, where she will die. Alfred names a star after her, while she names a falling autumn leaf after him. The permanence of the star immortalizes their love, whereas the transience of the leaf implies the cyclical and regenerative force of nature.

Autumn of Our Spring (Osen' nashei vesny, 1989) creates a powerful image for the pain that love can inflict. The pterodactyl Boria loves the woman Ninel, who is married and pregnant. She chases him away when he sings for her, so that she may not be seen to be in love with a bird and then attract the rage of her husband, who would shoot Boria. Yet Boria sings and dies for Ninel. But Boria's romance is only an episode in his adventurous life. He lives with an elderly couple, Domna and Varlam. Varlam dies in World War I, and Boria takes it upon himself to look after Domna, who works hard and is always short of money. The mischievous and flirtatious bird flirts with the statue that guards the local bank and steals a large sum of money. He tries to use this to support Domna, who is suspicious of the large sums he offers. When he feels that money is not what helps and interests Domna, he loses sight of the important things in life and leads a debauched life. He is arrested and serves a sentence in prison, and Domna dies. After his release

Rezo Gabriadze's puppets Domna and Boria from *Autumn of Our Spring*. (Photo from production press kit)

he too dies and joins Domna and Varlam for a happy reunion in the other world. With the simple wooden bird that only rolls its eyes and opens its beak, Gabriadze created a puppet that conquered the hearts of many audiences.

The Song about the Volga (also known as *The Battle of Stalingrad* [Pesnia o Volge], 1996) deals with the theme of love and death. It was inspired by reports that Gabriadze read about the corpses of horses that filled the battlefields after Stalingrad. The action takes place during the war, outside Stalingrad. The performance is set to Dmitri Shostakovich's Seventh Symphony. *The Song about the Volga* treats the love of two horses for each other as a symbol for human love. Alyosha and Natasha fall in love—like humans—and they die like hu-

mans. Alyosha dies in battle, but his love is so strong that he rises and follows Natasha. Only when he finds her killed in battle does he die too. Gabriadze enhances the transience of life, human or animal, through the interchange of elements such as sand and sugar, which run through one's fingers faster than we can think, thus implying that life slips away without us noticing it, whereas love has the power of making Alyosha immortal, until the object of his love dies.

Gabriadze not only tours internationally with his puppet theater, but his performances in Russia are immensely popular with the people, whether educated or not. They genuinely appeal to all classes and ages.

Puppet theaters in contemporary Russia have—after almost 70 years of a pseudo-competition with drama theaters and an existence in an alien cultural sector (established rather than wandering)—finally managed to come to grips with this predicament. Young directors are emerging, notably from the St. Petersburg puppetry department, who return to the traditional forms of puppets and use them to create poetic images. The return of the original Petrushka figures is unlikely to happen, however: the time for puppet theater may indeed have faded away in other European cultures in a natural way. Gabriadze has been at a number of international festivals, including London's BITE (Barbican International Theatre Events), and the Shadow Theater has visited Europe.

Estrada and Popular Entertainment

The term *estrada* applies mainly to Eastern European cultures. It was used in the former socialist countries to describe the concerts and shows that, in the commercialized world, would fall under the category "show-business." Indeed, the term has become less used since the collapse of socialist systems and has given way to the term *show.*

The word *estrada* comes from the Italian and means "raised floor," a raised stage. Estrada combines the performance of music, dance, circus, song, speech, and puppetry, including transformations and acrobatic acts. It seeks direct contact with audiences and appeals to the masses, although it is usually a "small form," in that it is shown on a stage from which the audience is directly addressed and spoken to. The estrada show presents short, attractive, and eccentric numbers and sketches. In its origins estrada is part of urban folklore, drawing on traditions of the *balagan* (fairground booth), the frivolous and circus-like entertainment of pre-Revolutionary times. In pre-Revolutionary Russia, estrada shows were performed in the open air, in cabarets and *variétés* (variety performances). This bourgeois culture was not supported by the new regime, however, which transformed estrada into state-managed "miniature theaters."

Staged Estrada

Most of the shows are difficult to detach from the Soviet context, and many estrada artists never reached recognition beyond the boundaries of the USSR. Whereas the early estrada shows were presented by a *conférencier* (master of ceremonies) and consisted of a variety of numbers, in the 1960s solo shows became the rule. In the 1960s the KVN clubs (Klub veselykh i nakhodlivykh [Club of the Cheerful and Inventive]), which organized competitions

Arkadi Raikin, estrada artist and founder of the Satirikon Theater in Moscow. (Photo by Irina Kaledina)

between student groups, appeared on television and subsequently a number of KVNs sprang up across the country. In 1972 the KVNs were stopped by censorship and revived in 1986 in a commercialized form.

The greatest star of Soviet estrada was Arkadi Raikin (1911–1987). Having founded the Leningrad Theater of Miniature just before World War II, Raikin created the so-called *feuilleton*, where the performer delivers a monologue with comments on a particular event. In the course of his numbers, Raikin used puppets and deployed all the other components of estrada art, from parody to dance, mime, and song. Many of the phrases he created were appropriated and entered common Russian usage, such as the word *avoska* which appeared in Raikin's repertoire in the 1940s to describe a string shopping bag. The word derived from the term *avos* (off chance; perhaps); the avoska is the bag for the products found "perhaps" by the little man who carries this shopping bag on the "off chance" of finding some products in the shops, alluding to the chronic shortage of goods in the USSR. Later he created the stock character Lyzin, a lazy alcoholic, who is ruled by envy. Lyzin thinks he can boss everybody around, so that the character turns into a frightening image of the power image and jealous Soviet *nachalnik* (line manager). Raikin always sought direct contact with his audience, performing his monologues as if he were thinking aloud. Later he would also change costume and character during the show, stepping from one image into another. Raikin's performances always defended the "little man," the vulnerable average Soviet citizen. Raikin's contribution to the Soviet estrada was enormous, but more important has been his influence on everyday speech, which has adopted many of his stock phrases.

Another famous estrada artist was Mikhail Zhvanetsky, an admirer of Raikin's from Odessa, who joined the Leningrad Theater of Miniature in the early 1960s and wrote some of the texts for Raikin's performances, such as *Traffic Light* (Svetofor, 1967). In the 1970s Zhvanetsky began to perform his own texts, working both in Moscow and Odessa as well as touring the country with his shows. Zhvanetsky's great skill lay in the texts, where he forced the truth about Soviet everyday life into a formula that sounded convincing and easy, making people laugh at the absurdity of Soviet reality and thus making their struggle seem normal. Some of Zhvanetsky's phrases also entered the spoken language: "the country of ever green tomatoes" (strana vechno zelenykh pomidorov) re-

Mikhail Zhvanetsky performs during the concert dedicated to the anniversary of the great artist Arkadi Raikin (October 2001). (Photo by Alexey Kudenko/Kommersant)

ferred to the lack of vegetables on Soviet markets; if vegetables did appear, they were either not ripe or foul. He coined the phrase "solve problems as they enter the shop" (perezhivat' nepriiatnosti po mere ikh postupleniia), meaning people should deal with problems one after the other and not worry about everything at once. At the same time Zhvanetsky mocked the lack of a regular food supply in Soviet shops, where abundance was never a real issue. Another phrase was the "continuous improvement that leads to a deterioration" (nepreryvnoe uluchshenie privodiashchee k ukhudshcheniiu), mocking the Soviet-speak of the press that always praised the country, whereas in reality things were getting worse and worse.

Although Raikin and Zhvanetsky were the leaders of Soviet estrada and made an immense impact not only on Russian language but also on the tradition of mocking Soviet reality, other estrada artists gained great popularity with their shows. The comedian Gennadi Khazanov first created the character of the streetwise simpleton, a student of the culinary institute. He later included musical sections in his shows, presenting parodies on Alla Pugacheva and other singers. Khazanov's texts tended to target politics rather than everyday life (as

Gennadi Khazanov, artistic director of the Moscow Estrada Theater. (Photo by Irina Kaledina)

Raikin and Zhvanetsky had done), and in 1984 he was banned from the stage. In 1987 he came back with spectacular and theatricalized shows and made his debut on the dramatic stage and in film. Mikhail Zadornov is primarily a writer of satirical monologues but also a performer. He boldly parodied political leaders and gave stunning impersonations of Gorbachev while also targeting celebrities in his satirical sketches. Such mockery of politicians had become acceptable by the perestroika period. Yefim Shifrin (b. 1956) gained fame with his numbers where his character, an infantile little man who evokes laughter and compassion, holds telephone conversations with the imaginary girl Lucie (Liusia).

Estrada is and was an important part of television programming. Indeed, the television show *Old Songs about the Main Thing* (1996–1998), conceived by Leonid Parfyonov and Konstantin Ernst, was staged in the best estrada traditions. The artist Yevgeni Petrosian (b. 1945) hosts the show *Smekhopanorama* (Laughterpanorama) on television, where he presents old estrada clips, tapping once more into the retro mode and dwelling on the popular estrada shows of the 1960s and 1970s.

Boulevard Theater   In the 1990s a number of commercial enterprises sprang up, offering theater for entertainment, or rather drawing on star names to attract audiences. Trushkin and his Chekhov theater drew on much-loved actors, and Viktiuk used both star names and sexual ambiguity to attract audiences. These stars of Soviet stage and screen included artists of high culture, including such figures as Oleg Tabakov, now artistic director of the Moscow Arts Theater. In commercial theaters the stakes are set on actors rather than directors, largely of the older generation, to appeal to the audience. Many repertoire theaters invite directors or actors of reputation to create attractions in their repertoire: *Hamlet* stars Valeri Garkalin at the Stanislavsky Theater; Petr Mamonov features in two shows at the Stanislavsky Theater. The Moscow Arts Theater has realized also a lack of star names and recruits largely from the Tabakov Studio for its productions. Film actors are invited to appear on the theatrical stage to attract numbers: Alexei Buldakov, the general of Alexander Rogozhkin's film cycle *National Peculiarities . . .* (1996–), the *Antikiller* star Gosha Kutsenko, or Marat Basharov are invited to commercial projects. The Pushkin Theater has recruited the actors Andrei Panin and Nikolai Fomenko, who are famous for their film and television work.

Although theaters put their stakes on star names, actors leave the theater because of the working conditions (low pay, rehearsals). The Lensovet actors Mikhail Trukhin and Konstantin Khabensky have quit the theater because they could not coordinate acting on stage with the filming schedule for the television series *Criminal Petersburg*. Mark Zakharov at the Lenkom Theater has a privileged theater that is home to a number of film stars: Dmitri Pevtsov, Alexander Abdulov, Oleg Yankovsky, Nikolai Karachentsov, Alexander Lazarev, Inna Churikova. He apparently has managed to work out a repertoire and rehearsal schedule that allows them to appear on the silver and blue screens, which in turn makes them even more sought-after stars when they do appear on stage. The Sovremennik theater can boast of the star actors Marina Neyolova, Avangard Leontiev, Igor Kvasha, Sergei Gazarov, Sergei

Garmash, and Olga Drozdova, all admired by a more middle-aged to older generation; Chulpan Khamatova pulls in younger audiences. A number of theaters that provide pure entertainment have recently appeared on the Moscow map, most notably Quartett I (Kvartet I), a group of four actors with amateurish and clownish performances, and L'A Teatr, with a similar agenda.

Boulevard theaters chose a variety of plays, but more recently a trend has manifested itself here: Agatha Christie's *The Mousetrap* (starring Alexei Buldakov) stands next to comedies, such as *Silvia* (starring Chulpan Khamatova, Yevgeniya Simonova, Georgi Taratorkin) and Pinter's *Lover* (with the same Yevgeniya Simonova and Sergei Makovetsky). Aldo Nikolai is a popular playwright in boulevard productions: *The Temptation* features Sergei Bezrukov, Boris Shcherbakov, and Liubov Polishchuk. Most recently Roman Kozak has directed a commercial production of Yosef Bar-Yosef's *Gold* with the ever-popular Tatiana Vasilieva, Vladimir Garkalin, and Alexander Feklistov.

Although there are a number of private theater companies and a number of boulevard theaters, the interest in this form of culture has been unable to sustain lasting support from the masses, for which it seems to have been intended. Russian audiences, treated as "educated" classes despite their background in the unifying and leveling approach of the Soviet state, have maintained rather high theatrical standards and a refined taste. Popular theater in Russia is not synonymous with popular theater in the UK or the United States, and there is no Broadway or West End in Moscow or St. Petersburg. Instead, there are stars of the older generation and idols of the younger generation whom the respective fans flock to admire.

Anecdotes and Jokes

The Soviet Union was famous for its numerous anecdotes and jokes. In anecdotes, Soviet life seemed much more believable and realistic than the absurd reality of Soviet life. The joke is part of oral culture and takes its root in some social or political event. In a sense, jokes are safety valves, but in the Soviet period they were more than that: by describing accurately the realities of Soviet life, they highlighted the absurdity (the anecdotal character) of reality. In the anecdote, Russians turned their own history into a spectacle and the present life into a performance. The anecdote helped understand everyday life and politics as a routine, a ritual, rather than real life, which could be shaped. Man always features as an object, a plaything, or victim, never as an agent, in these jokes.

In the 1970s and 1980s in particular, the anecdotes on Russian life and politics rewrote the entire Soviet history. When the satirical weekly *Krokodil* began to print anecdotes in the 1990s in order to boost its popularity, jokes were commercially used and lost their function in oral culture. The Internet nowadays is a great source of Russian anecdotes while offering a way of people telling anecdotes to each other.

The first major group of anecdotes is concerned with Russian history. Here, jokes about Soviet history and its leaders are most common. Many jokes parody the banality of "Soviet-speak," the official Soviet discourse. They confront high-brow words and the emptiness of the real world. Other jokes rewrite Soviet history, telling the listener what really happened that led to such ridiculous, devastating, and embarrassing results. The Radio Yerevan jokes (Armenian Radio) exposed the utter nonsense of politics by asking questions and providing the logical answer.

Lenin and the Revolution

Vladimir Ilyich Lenin was the founder of the Soviet state and the leading revolutionary. The alleged support of the people for the Communist movement is exposed as exaggeration, however: only Lenin (real name Ulianov) supported the Communist cause. The Revolution, set off by a gunshot from the battleship *Aurora*, is described as more devastating than a nuclear bomb, and Lenin's name has penetrated the most trivial aspect of life. The slogan "Lenin is with us" (Lenin s nami) gave rise to a whole host of anecdotes when people imagined situations in which the leader would be with them at all times, even in bed when making love.

> Lenin said: "There are only three genuine communists in the Party: Ulianov, Lenin and I."

> —What is more terrifying than the nuclear bomb?
> —A salvo from the *Aurora*: one blank shot and 70 years devastation.

> Special products: Draft Beer Lenin, Sausages Member of the CPSU, perfume Lenin's Spirit, face powder Ilyich's Ashes, and the new model: triple bed Lenin is with us.

Stalin

Stalin was a much-feared leader. During the purges of the 1930s, many Bolshevik leaders who had worked with Lenin were annihilated (arrested, exiled, executed).

—*Why are you running, rabbit?*
—*They are shooting camels.*
—*But you are a rabbit!*
—*Once they've shot you, you try and prove that you're not a camel.*

Gorbachev meets Stalin.
Stalin: "Comrade Gorbachev, I heard you have difficulties. I advise you: first, arrest all the members of the Central Committee. Second, destroy the church of St. Basil's.
—*Comrade Stalin, but why the church?*
—*I am glad we have no difference in opinion about the first point.*

Khrushchev and the Thaw   There are many anecdotes about Nikita Khrushchev and his uneducated, peasant background, his campaign to grow sweet corn (*kukuruza*). A rich target for mockery during his term of government was the minister of culture, Ekaterina Furtseva, a textile worker by profession, who had little knowledge of the world of culture.

An exhibition of Picasso opens. The ticket controller asks:
—*Your ticket.*
—*But I am Picasso!*
—*Prove it.*
Picasso paints the dove of peace and is admitted. Behind him comes Furtseva, also without a ticket. The controller asks:
—*We admitted Picasso and we'll let you pass if you can prove that you are the minister of culture of the USSR.*
—*Who is Picasso?*
—*Please go through, Comrade Furtseva.*

Brezhnev   Leonid Ilyich Brezhnev ruled the country for almost 20 years. During his term of office the members of the Polit-

buro and the Central Committee grew older and older without retiring. The senility and physical disability of the party bosses were mocked in numerous jokes.

Brezhnev meets the old lady of the Russian Revolution.
—*Hello, Leonid Ilyich. You probably don't remember me. I am Nadezhda Konstantinovna Krupskaya.**
— *Of course, of course.*
—*And do you remember my husband Vladimir Ilyich?*
— *Of course, Vladimir Ilyich Krupsky, a very good man indeed.*

Brezhnev asks from the other world:
— *Who is ruling after me?*
—*Gorbachev*
—*Do the people support him?*
—*No, he walks on his own.*

The Politburo decided to improve working conditions and replace the chairs and tables in the conference room. A worker: "In my youth I was in a brothel, but they changed the whores, not the beds."

Gorbachev   The Gorbachev era lent itself to mockery and parody. Mikhail Sergeyevich Gorbachev did things differently from the previous leaders. Yet in the eyes of the people he did not push the changes far enough, and an especially sore issue was that of the privatization of the land. The indecision of the reform course was parodied.

The chairman announces:
— *Comrades! Deputies! Those in support of socialism, please sit on the left; those for capitalism sit on the right.*

---

*Krupskaya was the wife of Vladimir Ilyich Lenin.

One deputy hovers around.
—And you, Comrade?
—I am for socialism, but want to live like in capitalism.
*—But Comrade, then your place is in the presidium.**

—Mikhail Sergeyevich, the German aviator Rust has crossed the border illegally and landed on Red Square.
—And what do you want me to do—go and greet him?

Indeed, the landing on Red Square in May 1988 of a Cessna aircraft piloted by Mathias Rust led the president of the Moscow International Film Festival in July 1988 to greet his international guests in the Hotel Rossiya, adjacent to Red Square, with an apology for the detour to Sheremetievo II (the international airport), rather than landing on Sheremetyevo III, as Red Square was jokingly referred to for awhile after the event.

The Mausoleum Moscow is the only place in the world where the central square is occupied by a dead man: the leader of the Communist movement, Lenin, lies in a mausoleum on Red Square. It is also an indication of the treatment of the leader as if he were a saint. In the 1980s, after almost 20 years of Brezhnev's rule, three leaders succeeded each other within three years, all requiring a burial space (Brezhnev, Andropov, and Chernenko).

A man comes to Chernenko's funeral.
— Your ticket?
—I have a subscription to these shows.

Lenin and Stalin lie in the mausoleum. Noise on the street. Lenin to Stalin: "Iosif Vissarionovich, go and have a look what's going on." Stalin goes out and comes back: "Again that Khrushchev with his camp bed."

A Georgian comes to Moscow and goes to Red Square. He asks the guards:
— My dears, I would like to see Lenin.
—The Mausoleum is closed.
The Georgian stacks some banknotes on the bayonets of the guards and, opening the gates, they ask: "Will you go inside or shall we bring him out?"

A man from the provinces comes to Moscow. All his friends ask him to bring back presents for them. When he asks where to shop, they tell him to go wherever he sees the longest queue. Upon his return, he has no presents. His friends ask what happened, and he explains:
— As you told me, I went to the place with the longest queue. And I waited and waited, and when my turn came, the salesman was lying there, dead.

Soviet Politics Soviet politics were presented in anecdotes as a series of haphazard events, almost accidents, rather than an implementation of a planned and clearly thought-through policy.

The Soviet troops moved into Czechoslovakia. Friendship knows no borders.

—Why did they send our troops to Afghanistan.
— They began with A.

A soldier on duty falls asleep over the control panel of some strategic missiles. When the commanding officer enters he jumps up, stands to order, and reports:

— Comrade Lieutenant, nothing to report.
—Nothing to report . . . And where is Belgium, hell? Two missiles!!!

The Press   The press and the media were known not for supplying information but for "disinforming" people, covering up disasters, and avoiding the important issues. The media were perceived as telling lies. The only reliable (but forbidden and jammed) media were foreign radio stations.

—What is the difference between Russian and Soviet fairy tales?
—Old Russian fairy tales begin with the words: "Behind the sea and the hills, behind the forests and rivers . . . ." Soviet fairy tales begin with the words: "TASS* reports."

— What is the difference between Pravda *(Truth) and* Izvestiya *(News)?*
—There's no news in Pravda *and no truth in* Izvestiya.

Gorbachev went out onto the balcony to have a cigarette. His wife, Raisa Maximovna, calls from the inside:
— Misha, are you again smoking in secret?
—Yes, but how do you know?
— They've just said so on the BBC.

Education   Sex was a taboo subject in Soviet culture. In the style of George Mikes saying that "The English have no sex; they have a hot water bottle," the Russians had no sex, but they had the Communist Party. There was certainly no sex education. Instead, the constraints on living space re-

duced sex to a sport of finding a quiet corner for lovemaking. Therefore, all talk about sex was reduced to the private sphere.

In the sixth form a new subject was introduced: sexology. The teacher: "The love between man and man or between woman and woman is a sexual perversion, which we will not study. About the love between man and woman you know enough without me. The fourth and fifth kinds of love are the love of the Party for the people and the love of the people for the Party. This is what we shall study during the course of the year."

Strategic Control   The state and party controlled everything. Spying and control were abundant in every sphere of life. At the same time chaos reigned everywhere. The "happy coincidences" that saved dissidents from raids and spies from being caught are described in numerous memoirs of the Soviet era. While the country was ruled by chaos, the citizens learned to live by the rules of the unpredictable. Obtaining "deficit" products of low supply and high demand was a skill that demanded much more expertise than spying. Obtaining toilet paper in Moscow led some foreigners to theft: they pinched it from embassies and large Western-style hotels to which they had access thanks to their foreign passports. Others knew that toilet paper would be on sale toward the end of the quarter, when certain shops had to fulfill their plans and release the goods they had stacked away to sell on the side.

Ivanov, a lonely old man complains to his friend:
—I am sick, I can't dig up the garden any more, nor can I chop wood.

---

*TASS was the Soviet news agency.

—OK, I shall help you, said the friend and rang the KGB: it seems that Ivanov has hidden foreign currency in his garden and some microfilms in the logs.

The next day they meet again:

—Thank you, my friend, They thoroughly dug up the garden and hacked all the firewood.

A foreign spy is sent to a large Soviet company. Soon he reports:

— The secrecy is such that you can't figure out anything. They say one thing, think another, and do something totally different.

A provincial man comes to Moscow and catches a cab. He tells the driver to take him to the department store Principle. The driver frowns, trying to remember, but in the end says:

—Sorry, but there is no such store.

— But how is that? My friend tells me that there is nothing at all in Moscow, but in "principle" you can buy everything.

Emigration   In the postwar Soviet era many people wished to emigrate, and many defected during trips to the West. A number of anecdotes tell about the desperate attempts of people to leave the country, and they all stress that really nobody wanted to stay.

Kosygin*: I ordered the borders to be opened.

Brezhnev: Have you gone mad. There will be only two people left.

Kosygin: Who is the second?

---

*Kosygin was a minister of Brezhnev's government.

Leningrad airport. An aircraft bound for Tallinn (Estonia) takes off. A young man enters the cockpit and pulls out a pistol:

— Change direction.

—I can't.

— Turn to London, or I'll shoot you.

—I can't. But talk to the girl with the bomb in the first row; she ordered us to fly to Stockholm.

A metro train is hijacked. The hijackers demand that the driver take them to Copenhagen. The driver explains: "But guys, this is the metro." The hijackers insist. The driver explains: "Even worse, guys, this is the circle line." The hijackers insist, further threatening the driver. Eventually the driver sighs, switches on the speakers, and announces: "Mind the closing doors. Next stop: Copenhagen."

Radio Yerevan   The questions asked by Armenian Radio were naive, whereas the answers provided a gloss on the absurdity of Soviet politics. The following three questions address the succession of leaders in the 1980s. Konstantin Chernenko was very old and sick when elected general secretary. He succeeded Yuri Andropov and preceded Mikhail Gorbachev. The Ruriks were the dynasty that laid the foundation of the Russian Empire.

Armenian Radio:

— Why does Chernenko appear before several microphones?

— He holds on to one microphone, another supplies oxygen, and into the third they whisper his prompts.

Armenian Radio:

— How will Russian history be written under Andropov?

— From Rurik to Yurik.

Armenian Radio:
—What was the funeral of Andropov?
— A dress rehearsal for Chernenko's
    funeral.

There were also jokes about "nationalities," about the Jews, Ukrainians, and Caucasians, mocking their national characteristics in the same way that any nation has its target group for mockery. As the thick and dumb people for the British are the Irish, and for the Germans they are the East-Friesians, so for the Russians the "idiot" was embodied by the *chukcha*, the indigenous peoples of the Chukotka. At the same time the Russians would make themselves out as the "holy fools" among the world nations, not so rich in material terms but rich in their soul.

Chukcha   The jokes about the chukcha expose these people as stupid and naive, a quality attributed to them for their remote life in the tundra, which leaves them unaccustomed to modern urban civilization.

A Russian, a Frenchman, and a chukcha undergo a hunger experiment in individual cells that are equipped with telephones so they can call an end to their hunger term. The Frenchman calls after three days and asks for food. The Russian calls after four days. A week passes by, two weeks. They look in on the chukcha as he sits in front of the telephone and taps the phone with his fingers, exclaiming: "telephone, telephone, chukcha wants eat."

Chukcha goes along the platform and knocks his head against each car.
—Why are you doing that?

—It says on my ticket the car is soft*. So I am checking.

Chukcha travels on the train. He goes to the restaurant car and, when returning, can't find his compartment.
The conductor asks: "Can you remember the car?"
— No, but I can remember that there were lots of birch trees outside the window.

Chukcha brings his novel to the editor of a journal. The editor reads it and says:
—You see, it is a little weak. You should read some of the classics. Have you read Turgenev? Tolstoy? Dostoevsky?
—However, not. Chukcha is no reader, chukcha is a writer.

Chukcha bought a car. He drives along the road and hits a tree. He gets out of the car, climbs under the hood, and picks up a headlight: "Such big eyes and can't see a thing . . ."

Russians and Other Nationalities   In their anecdotes, Russians always perceive their inferiority and naïveté vis-à-vis the West, thus debunking Russia's ambition to demonstrate its uniqueness and superiority in all areas. The Russian tends to react in a nonstandard way, concerned with his belly rather than his reputation and with good company rather than money. The Russian is educated in the party spirit and therefore responds accordingly, even in extreme situations.

Men of different nationalities when they catch their wife with a lover:

---

* A soft car is a wagon-lit (*miagki vagon*).

The Englishman (coldly): Lady, may I ask you kindly to leave my house.

The Frenchman: Oh, pardon, Monsieur. It seems I have come at an inconvenient moment.

The Russian: You whore! You are lying around, and they're selling herring round the corner.

A Russian, an American, and an English man in the desert. They are losing their strength, and the Russian suggests that they drink some vodka before they die. From the empty bottle emerges the genie of the bottle.

— You have two wishes each.

The American asks for a million dollars and to return home. He disappears. The Englishman asks for a million pounds and to return home. He disappears. The Russian waves his arms in despair.

— We started off so well . . . a case of vodka and the guy's back.

Two men and a woman on a desert island. If they are English, they'll fight a duel for the only woman around. If they are French, they set up a menage-à-trois. If they are Americans, they fight over the woman. If they are Russians, they set up a kolkhoz: one man is the chairman, the other the party secretary, and the people (the woman) are sent into the fields.

What is sex?

French sex is when a Frenchman locks himself up in a room with a French woman and does with her what he wants.

Italian sex is when a Frenchman locks himself up in a room with a French woman and does with her what he wants while the Italian watches through the keyhole.

American sex is when two Americans write a novel about how a Frenchman locks himself up in a room with a French woman and does with her what he wants while being watched by an Italian through the keyhole.

Russian sex is when the party office discusses a young Communist who has read the novel of two American writers about a Frenchman who locks himself up in a room with a French woman and does with her what he wants while being watched by an Italian through the keyhole.

Film and Everyday Language

Blockbusters have had a huge impact on language. A number of phrases have entered everyday speech in a variety of situations. Most of these phrases come from the few genuine blockbusters of the 1960s and 1970s, the comedies of Eldar Riazanov and Leonid Gaidai. However, quotations from *Chapayev* are almost more frequent in everyday speech than the jokes about him. The remark "Yes, a merry discussion this!" (Da, veselyi razgovor!), refers to a situation that is taking a bad turn. "Quiet, people, Chapayev will think" (tikho, grazhdane, Chapaev dumat' budet) is an ironic comment asking for silence while mocking Chapayev's talent as a "thinker" (which he was not). The phrase "are you mocking Chapayev?" (ty chto, nad Chapaevym izdevatsia?) is used, however, to eliminate any doubt about the person in question: Chapayev may not be a thinker, but his support for the cause (the Revolution) is beyond doubt.

Other phrases have taken their place in everyday speech without people necessarily being aware of their origin. Somebody who frequently says "I think" may be commented upon with the word "Try to think less" (A ty men'she dumai), a citation from Riazanov's *Welcome!* The phrase "he has

Quotations from Films

As one of my late friends said, "I knew too much" (Kak govoril odin moi znakomyi pokoinik: "ia slishkom mnogo znal"): An ironic comment on somebody who can't be silent or keep a secret. (*Diamond Arm*)

On the whole, they're all dead (V obshchem, vse umerli): Ironic remark at the end of a discussion, indicating that everything has been said. (*Formula of Love*)

They're all running, and so am I (Vse pobezhali—i ia pobezhal): I'll do as everybody else does. (*Gentlemen of Success*)

I am running, flying, rushing (Begu, lechu, mchus!): Ironic statement to say "I am on my way" when the speaker is not really rushing. (*Hello, I Am Your Aunt!*)

How about ironing your shoelaces? (A shnurki tebe ne pogladit'?): You're asking a bit much. (*Moscow Does Not Believe in Tears*)

All clear; the wedding is called off (Vse iasno; Svad'by ne budet): You understand, without further explanation, that something is canceled. (*Swineherd and Shepherd*)

Who can't? (A kto ne mozhet?): Ironic response when people must do something to get out of danger. (*Volga-Volga*)

The East is a delicate matter (Vostok—delo tonkoe.): A remark about a tricky issue. (*White Sun of the Desert*)

Any questions? No questions (Voprosy est? Voprosov net.): This is not subject to discussion. (*White Sun of the Desert*)

five minutes to go before his doctorate" (on bez piati minut kandidat nauk), from the film *When September Comes*, is used to say that somebody is about to defend his dissertation but also to describe a very clever person. Similarly, the phrases "Anyone here, hey!" (Liudi, au!) from *Carnival Night*, asking where people are, or the phrase "Go to the sauna" (Idi v baniu) from *Irony of Fate*, telling a person to clear off ("bugger off"), or the phrase "in the case of a fire" (na vsiakii pozharnyi sluchai) from *Diamond Arm*, saying that something is done "just in case," have all become part of everyday language without referring to specific contexts of the films. There are also phrases that refer more specifically to the films' contexts.

The Heroes Stirlitz and Chapayev

Jokes about cult figures as well as references in everyday speech that cite the lines of Soviet blockbusters penetrated and still penetrate contemporary speech. The figure of Stirlitz, the resident Soviet spy in Hitler's think tank in Berlin during World War II, was the main character of the spy thriller *Seventeen Moments of Spring*, first broadcast in 1972 and repeated annually, usually around Victory Day. The film used the device of opening "files" on the main characters to explain their role in the complicated structure of Hitler's Schutzstaffel (SS); each file was usually preceded by the words "information for consideration" (Informatsiia k razmyshleniiu), a phrase that is still a classic quotation in contemporary speech when ironically giving additional but meaningless information. The series makes Stirlitz out as a brilliant spy, yet most of the time he gains his knowledge by doing nothing. Action is presented through the narrative voiceover, making the role of the spy look ridiculous for the modern spectator accustomed to the hyperactive James Bond.

The other cult figure of Soviet cinema is the character of Chapayev, the hero of the 1934 film. Chapayev is an uneducated peasant who plays his dutiful role in the Revolution and civil war. Rather than underline his revolutionary heroism, as the film does, the jokes parody Chapayev's idiocy. In this way, both the Stirlitz and Chapayev jokes undermine the intelligence of the hero, revolutionary and spy.

The Soviet spy Stirlitz and the Revolutionary hero Chapayev feature in anecdotes as simpleton. Much of the humor is drawn from the flat, deadpan portrayal of Stirlitz in his heroic actions during World War II. The film comments—often unnecessarily—on things that are obvious from the actions.

Stirlitz goes into Muller's office and sees him lying on the floor. "Poisoned, poor chap," thought Stirlitz, touching the handle of the axe sticking out of Muller's back.

Stirlitz goes into the SS headquarters and finds a sign on his door: "Residence of the Soviet Intelligence." "Glasnost (openness)," thinks Stirlitz.

Stirlitz catches a mouse and injects petrol into its vein. The mouse runs for two meters and then drops dead. "Ran out of petrol," thought Stirlitz.

Stirlitz approaches Berlin. The city is veiled in smoke from the fires. "Again forgot to switch off the iron," thought Stirlitz with slight irritation.

Chapayev is a revolutionary hero, but an uneducated man, a man of the people. The film was designed to show how, through revolutionary activity, Chapayev became a more educated man.

Chapayev goes to matriculate in the military academy.
— Have you given (passed)* everything?
—Not everything, Petka. I have given blood, I have given urine, but not maths.

Chapayev fails his matriculation exams.
—What went wrong, then, Vasili Ivanovich?
—Maths.
— What happened?
—You see, Petka, they asked: how much is 0.5 plus 0.5, and I felt that it is a litre, but how to express that mathematically— I don't know!

New Russians   As with all other nations, there is a whole range of Russian jokes about lovers and mistresses, about the army, and about hunting and fishing. The most recent target of Russian anecdotes are the New Russians (*novye russkie*): the uneducated but rich, illiterate but powerful, inarticulate but good-natured Russians who made a lot of money illegally and live in great wealth while the rest of the country is struggling for survival.

The jokes about the New Russians crystallized the characteristics of this group as a new social "class" and not only mocked, but defined it. The New Russian is portrayed as benevolent but thick. The jokes then create an image of a powerful group in society that makes them appear inferior to the intelligentsia.

A New Russian stops his Mercedes 600 at a red light. With screeching brakes a Zaporozhets† approaches and rear-ends it. The

---

*The word for "give blood" and "pass an exam" uses the same verb, *sdavat.*

†an old Soviet car

New Russian gets out of his Mercedes and approaches the Zaporozhets. Behind the wheel is a meek little man, looking in great fear at the New Russian.
—"Don't be afraid," says the New Russian, "just tell me one thing: how do you stop at the light when I am not there?"

A journalist comes to a New Russian and notices four mobile phones on the table.
—"What is this for?"
— International calls.
—And this?
—Intercity calls.
— And this?
—Local calls.
—And this one?
—Well, you can ask questions, internal calls!

New Russian to his wife:
—Our tamagotchi [virtual reality pet] is pregnant. Look.
He gets out a gadget and presses a button. The line appears: "I am pregnant."
—You idiot, this is your pager.

A New Russian is racing around Moscow in his Mercedes and hits a number of pedestrians. The police stop him. What are you hitting people for? And what do you think I should do? Why else do I have a sight* on the bonnet?

A New Russian at a funeral:
— How did Kolya die?
—He wanted to send a letter bomb, and then he thought that would take too long and tried to fax it.

---

* *pritsel*, referring to the Mercedes star.

The Circus

A History of the Circus

Today, as in the past, people across the world still flock to see the Moscow State Circus. The Russian circus today is only a pale reflection of its former, Soviet self, however. Most artists train in Russia, begin their career there, and then move on to international companies in order to earn a decent living. Contemporary circus takes place less in Russia, as many artists perform with international circuses. Today, some of the finest international artists come from Russia but perform with Circus Roncalli, at the Berlin Wintergarten, with the Canadian touring circus Cirque du Soleil, or other prestigious circuses.

The Circus Is Leaving   Circus has always been a form of popular entertainment, and this is also what it was in pre-Revolutionary Russia. Like most popular art forms, however, it was usurped by the state to be elevated onto a higher level in order to promulgate the new, high-pitched cultural values of the new Soviet state. Therefore, it suffered a fate similar to that of the puppet theater during the Soviet period, when it was nationalized and largely turned into a stationary establishment.

Circus originally involved the performance of trained horses; it was an equestrian theater of the style nowadays run by the French director Bartabas and his ensemble Zingaro, emphasizing a style that is still vibrant in contemporary France and represents a popular form of entertainment. Only later did the circus appropriate the so-called intermedia: sketches and divertissements originating often from the street and puppet theater, or the balagan, and involving amusement park artistes and clowns who would participate in the circus performance and bring with them carnival elements. In many ways, the circus was part of street entertainment, offering its performance only temporarily to a particular region, and often associated with amusement parks, thus being part of the *narodnoe gulianie*, the "people's walks" around such street carnivals and amusement parks.

In the twentieth century the circus became stationary, and performances were theatricalized and sanitized. Popular culture became part of high culture, although in reality many avant-garde artists were using elements of low culture in their works. The highly renowned theater director Vsevolod Meyerhold had used circus artistes in *Mystery Bouffe;* the famous dramatist Nikolai Erdman had written satires and sketches for the music hall and circus. Yet Soviet propaganda wanted a high level of culture and education and raised levels of popular mass culture in the 1930s rather than using its appeal to reach the masses. In the Soviet view, the art of the circus was coarse and needed to become sophisticated. Therefore, in the first instance people from the "high" culture of the ballet were entrusted with circuses. Alexander Gorsky (1871–1924), a ballet master of none other than the Bolshoi Theater, was drawn in to polish the circus performance. He used monumental sets and classical music in his productions, with greetings and overtures at the beginning to welcome the audience. His shows were constructed like a chess game between Russian and European literary and dramatic characters, thus appealing to an educated, sophisticated audience. Kasian Goleizovsky (1892–1960) deployed more eccentric devices in his shows, which in-

cluded acrobats, stylized sports, and political caricature. His spectacular shows resembled more the Harlequinade of the nineteenth century, with jugglers, equestrian numbers, and clowns. Among the clowns, the famous Vitali Lazarenko (1890–1939) was outstanding. Lazarenko was a satiric clown from the balagan tradition, who performed virtuoso jumps, such as a salto over three elephants that was recorded on film in 1914 by the cameraman of Pathé Films. Lazarenko took part in Meyerhold's *Mystery Bouffe* (1921), thus demonstrating the influence of circus performers on avant-garde art. Indeed, in the 1920s many circus numbers were scripted by Vladimir Mass and Nikolai Erdman, recognized writers and playwrights who founded the Theater of Satire in 1924.

After the nationalization of the circuses (1919), the first and second state circus were created in Moscow, and later other Soviet towns followed suit. By the 1930s there were 23 stationary circuses. This coincided with the formation of a Central Administration of State Circuses (TsUGTs) to ensure that there would be a smooth change of artistes in circuses all across Russia; in 1931 this became GOMETs. In the late 1920s and 1930s the attempts to theatricalize the circus performance were particularly evident. The potential to use circus for agitation and propaganda was recognized, but circus should be pitched higher to raise the level of educatedness of the masses. The circus began to integrate physical culture (sports and acrobatic perfection) into the performance. Attempts were made to create a thematically or stylistically unified performance to achieve a sense of linearity and narrative. Particularly important in this respect was the figure of Boris Shakhet (1899–1950), who had begun his work with the Blue Blouses in the 1920s before turning to the circus. Circus directors became director-choreographers, and they often had theatrical rather than acrobatic training. The circus was supposed to offer relaxation and fill the worker with new energy, to advertise and incite physical culture, and to serve the purpose of propaganda.

While the Soviet circus was trying to unify its artistic presentation the popularity of foreign numbers rose, and many of them were copied into the Russian repertoire. During and after World War II, the circus suffered from a lack of sufficiently trained acrobats, an issue addressed by the formation of a circus section in the Theater Institutes. After the war the circus numbers fell, and so did spectator numbers. The unsatisfactory preparation of artists was to blame for the former; it transpired (although not to policymakers) that without family traditions and artistic families the circus cannot survive, not even if the state runs its finances and offers the training. In the 1970s the Moscow Institute for Theater Arts (GITIS) set up a course for circus directors, which was led by Mark Mestechkin (1900–1981), who had worked in the estrada and in acrobatics. In 1948 he headed the union of circuses, and after 1954 he was artistic director of the circus on Tsvetnoi Boulevard, where he appeared as a clown. In 1966 he chose students for the GITIS course, where he was professor from 1977 on.

The Circus in Moscow and Leningrad

Before the collapse of the Soviet Union, Moscow had two stationary circuses, Leningrad one. In Moscow the circus had always been part of the space in the city center. The seventeenth-century *sko-morokhi* had performed in central Moscow; amusement parks took place in central parks (Devichye Pole [Maiden Field]; Novinskii Boulevard; Sokolniki; Maryina Roshcha); touring circuses took residence in Neskuchny and Hermitage Gardens. The first stationary circus (Novosiltsev) opened in 1853 on Petrovka Street (the location of the present Central Department Store, TsUM). In 1869, Karl Ginne's circus opened on Vozdvizhenka Street, opposite the Kremlin. More honor came to the circus when in May 1883, on the occasion of the coronation of Alexander III, a celebration was held on Khodynskoye Field, where Albert Salamonsky (1839–1913) appeared with his horses. In 1880, Salamonsky opened an equestrian circus in a brick building on Tsvetnoi Boulevard, to which a stable was added. The shows of Salamonsky's circus included themes of the Nibelungen myth, the Ukrainian historical figure Mazepa, and Cinderella. In 1886 the Nikitins acquired the premises of the present cinema Mir, just down the road from Salamonsky, and started a rivalry between the two circuses. The Nikitins were three brothers—Dmitri (1835–1918), Akim (1843–1917), and Petr (1846–1921)—who had started off as buskers and acrobats. They went on to establish the first stationary circuses in a number of Russian cities. Salamonsky eventually closed his establishment. In 1911 the Nikitins' circus moved into a new building, with a moving arena and a pool on the site of today's Satire Theater on Mayakovsky Square. After the Nikitin Brothers' deaths, the circus was taken on by the juggler Nikolai Nikitin (1887–1963). In 1919, both the Nikitin and Salamonsky circuses were nationalized. In 1944 the circus on Tsvetnoi Boulevard (formerly Salamonsky) reopened. From 1983 to 1997 it was di-

A circus number in the Nikulin circus on Tsvetnoi Boulevard. (Photo by Roman Mukhametzhanov/Kommersant)

rected by the clown Yuri Nikulin, and since his death by Mikhail Nikulin. It was closed from 1985 to 1989 for refurbishment. It is a modern and experimental circus, which is reflected in the creation of a studio by the choreographer Valentin Gneushev.

The circus on Vernadskii Prospekt was built in 1971 to house a larger number of spectators (3,350 seats). It is equipped with hydraulic devices to lower the arena for a three-meter-deep pool or to elevate it to create an ice rink. The show *Lights of the New Circus* (1971) opened the new building. The circus was directed by Yevgeni Milayev (1910–1983), a tightrope acrobat and "white" clown; and since 1984 by Leonid Gostiuk.

Another important artistic dynasty of the nationalized Soviet circus was the Durovs. Vladimir Durov (1863–1934) worked with Salamonsky in Moscow as a clown, satirist,

and trainer of animals. His wife, Anna, also trained animals; their daughter, Anna, recreated the Durov Circus of Animals in 1943. Their granddaughter, Natalia (b. 1934), worked in the state circus and trained sea lions, before forming in 1978 Granddad Durov's Theater of Beasts, of which she has been general director since 1992.

In Leningrad, Yevgeni Kuznetsov made an important contribution to the strengthening of the technical side of the circus during the 1930s and 1940s. He choreographed the shows and used effective lighting, making them look like music hall performances with a corps-de-ballet to unite the show. Georgi Venetsianov (1886–1965), who had headed the music hall and the estrada theater, brought even more choreography to the Leningrad circus, changing the genre and the tone of individual numbers set to the tunes of Isaak Dunayevsky and other film music. Venetsianov created thematic-oriented spectacles, but most important, he advanced the technology in creating a circus on water and on ice (*Holiday on Water* [Prazdnik na vode], 1952; *Carnival on Ice*, 1952). *Circus of Bears* transformed the entire arena into a parody of the circus itself, with bears playing the parts of jugglers, acrobats, and clowns.

After the collapse of the USSR, Ros-tsirk (Ros-gos-tsirk after 1995) took over the management of circuses. The collapse of the Soviet Union meant the loss of the republics' stationary circuses as well as republican national groups. That, together with the growing emigration of circus artistes in an economically unstable period of transition, in which foreign tours were the only financial salvation, left the circus struggling for survival. By the end of the 1990s, the Great Moscow Circus (Vernadskii Prospekt), the Leningrad/St. Petersburg circus on Fontanka canal, and Nikulin's circus on Tsvetnoi Boulevard had survived as well as a number of regional circuses. In 1997, the year of Moscow's 850th anniversary, the Great Moscow Circus staged the show *My Dear Muscovites* (Dorogie moi moskvichi), paying homage to the city with popular tunes of the 1960s and 1970s, from the estrada and the bards, and remembering the capital's history in a nostalgic review.

If we take circus performances to mean a large body of people attending, then Polunin's clown shows are the only circus performances outside the circus of Nikulin and the Petersburg circus on Fontanka. The Great Moscow Circus on Vernadskii Prospekt caters largely for visitors; Muscovites take their children to Nikulin's circus. It is only thanks to the clowns, Nikulin

and Polunin, that the circus has survived. The maintenance of circuses, the repertoire problems aside, leaves the circus management with the gigantic task of feeding and maintaining the animals, not to mention the salary of artistes. It would seem that the departure of so many talented circus artistes abroad has left a gap in the world of the Russian circus that will be difficult to patch up.

Choreographed Acrobatics and Clowns

The Choreography of the Act   In the 1980s more attempts were made to create a thematically unified show, often by defining the genre of the numbers and dramatizing them. Numbers were held together by costumes and music as well as the performance of tricks in a given situation. Thus, for example, Dana Kaseyeva performed her hula hoops number in a dance, with only one hoop.

The contribution of Valentin Gneushev is most important for the development of the circus on the threshold of a new era. Gneushev (b. 1951) graduated from the State Institute of Circus and Variety Theater (GUTsEI) as a clown, having been taught by Roman Viktiuk. He then graduated from the State Institute of Theater in 1986 as director of circus performance and worked in the theater and the circus. From 1996 to 1998 he was director of the circus on Tsvetnoi Boulevard, where he created the *Funfair of Miracles* (Yarmarka chudes, 1996), a circus show focused on the visitor of a sheikh, who is shown old Russian-style circus and street theater, beginning with Petrushka. A master of choreography, for the circus or the theater, Gneushev was the first choreographer to incorporate ele-

Valentin Gneushev, choreographer and artistic director of the circus on Tsvetnoi Boulevard, and the clown Yuri Nikulin. (Photo by Roman Mukhametzhanov/Kommersant)

ments of break dancing into his work, and subsequently into circus performance. In "Red Harlequin" (modeled on Pablo Picasso's "Harlequin" painting), the juggler Vladimir Tsarkov (b. 1963) performed his tricks in Harlequin costume to the rhythm and movement of break dance. Similarly, Gneushev assisted the Odintsov equilibrists by creating for them the choreography of a working brigade, dressing them in working overalls and helmets for their number "The Builders." He devised a rhythmical pattern for the movements of Yelena Panova, when she had to gain height on the trapeze for her numbers. For the tiger trainer Nikolai Pavlenko, Gneushev invented the image of the conductor-trainer, dressing Pavlenko in a tailcoat with a conductor's stick (the rod he used on the tigers); Pavlenko was subsequently labeled

the "Karajan of the circus" (in analogy to the great twentieth-century conductor Herbert von Karajan).

In the early 1990s many internationally renowned artists had their numbers choreographed by Valentin Gneushev. This is true for the aerial artist Alexander Streltsov, who initially trained in Moscow and received the Future award at the Cirque de Demain festival in Paris in 1991, when aged only 12. The Zemtsovs, a group of Russian pole acrobats, received the Golden Prize of the Cirque de Demain in 1993. The monocycle number by Diana Alechenko and Yuri Chavro, choreographed also by Gneushev, received the Golden Prize of the Cirque de Demain in 1996, and in the same year the Popovs' trampoline number took the Silver Prize. In 1994, the Silver Prize of the Cirque de Demain went to Yelena Larkina for her hula hoop number, choreographed by Gneushev. The hand-balancing act of Yelena Borodina, performed on a white cube under the title "Silencio," received the Silver Prize of the Cirque de Demain in 2001. Borodina has since performed at the Wintergarten in Berlin, a stationary variety theater, and with the Circus Roncalli.

Although Moscow circus numbers were refined in their choreographic presentation and "aestheticized" by Gneushev, in Leningrad circus matters took a different turn. In the studio boom of the late 1980s, the Leningrad studios concentrated on the development of the art of mime (rather than exclusively dramatic performance). In their midst emerged the group of the Farces, initially a nonverbal theater directed by Viktor Kramer; Derevo, the group of Anton Adasinsky, who was inspired to a nonverbal, theatrical performance by traditions of *buto* theater in studio conditions; and the experimental mime theater of Alexander Pliush, staging classical dramatic texts through expressive movements. If Petersburg had many studios working with mime, then Moscow could only boast of BlackSkyWhite (ChernoNeboBeloye) run by Dmitri Ariupin and his wife, the mime Marcella Soltan, who has won prizes at theater and mime festivals. Her solo shows are thematically unified. *Imitator Dei* (Kosvennoe dokazatel'stvo zhizni na zemle), *Bertrand's Toys* (Igrushki Bertranda), and *Here Was the USSR* (Zdes' byl SSSR) are all set in a small space so as to ensure the visibility of Marcella's mimicry and facial expression. The intimacy of the experience of the show is essential. Ariupin creates powerful associative images about the past, childhood, the relationship between man and the world. These are, however, not circus, but mime theater performances.

Clowns   Clowns have always played an integral part in the circus, and also in the Soviet circus, although clown numbers too were threatened by the stifling cultural process in the immediate postwar years. The clown Carandache (Mikhail Rumiantsev, 1901–1983), who took his name from the pencil makers Caran D'Ache, played a caricaturist in the mask of Chaplin. He was a small man with inadequate behavior, who invariably appeared with his Scottish terrier Kliaksa (the blob) and provided a unifying element in the circus shows. Yuri Kuklachev (b. 1949) is a folk clown (also known as Vasilyok), a man from the people, a jolly guy and simpleton. In 1985 he was awarded the Silver Clown at the Monte Carlo International Circus Festival. He later worked with cats, and since 1990 he has run his own theater with trained cats in a former cinema in Moscow. It is the only cats' theater in the world, known as Teatr Koshek. Boris Viatkin (1913–1994) was a clown from Novosibirsk, who worked in Leningrad in the postwar years. There he coined his character: a mask of Chaplin, which he wore as he walked the tightrope. He sported a leisure suit and was accompanied by his dog, Maniuna. Probably the best-known Soviet Russian clown in the west is Oleg Popov (b. 1930), who plays an Ivan the Fool–type character. He is known as "the sunny clown," with straight red hair, a red nose, striped trousers, and a black jacket with a red bow tie. He became the Soviet Union's clown-laureate in the 1970s and is the winner of numerous international awards, including the Golden Clown of the Monte Carlo International Circus Festival in 1981. Popov is a "red clown," a phlegmatic character, a simpleton—as opposed to the "white clown," who is a comic figure, often an acrobat or animal trainer, in short trousers with a jacket and a white face, modeled on Pierrot. The pair of the red and the white clown often appeared as a duo, such as Yuri Nikulin (1921–1997) and Mikhail Shuidin (1922–1983), with their buffoon numbers creating a unique rendering of the classical duo. Other such duos were the buffoons Mik and Mak (Nikolai Kormiltsev and Andrei Sharnin): Mik was the white, elegant, and supple clown, opposed to the red clown with his stroppy and stubborn character. In one of their numbers, they presented a parody of Anna Karenina and her suicide and mocked other classical literary and circus themes in their numbers. Dolly and Domino (Lada and Alexander Sarnatsky) played a pair of everyday characters: he a bit retarded, she elegant and dominant, with her huge bust made by melons.

Andrei Jigalov is a major international circus clown. He trained in Moscow and received his first major international award with the clown Alexeyenko in 1992: the Golden Prize of the Cirque de Demain. His trademark is a jacket that sits far too tightly over a pair of trousers that are sloppy and far too large. He performs for Roncalli with Peter Shub, the American clown with the trademark trench coat, photo camera, and hat, creating the image of the eternal tourist. In 2003, Jigalov, with his partners Konstantin and Csaba in a new clown number, received the Silver Clown at the International Monte Carlo Circus Festival. Also recognized in Monte Carlo in 2002 was the clown duo Emelin and Zagorsky, specializing in parody. None of them, however, can match the poetic style and idiosyncrasy of Slava Polunin.

The Litsedei Polunin The group Litsedei (Hypocrites, Actors) was formed by Slava Polunin in 1979. Polunin (b. 1950) graduated from LGITMiK and formed Litsedei as the first mime group in Leningrad, where they worked until 1992. He staged the show *Asisyai*, which created Polunin's prototype, a clown with red fluffy slippers and yellow rompers. Litsedei took part in the Caravan of Peace organized by Polunin in 1989: it was a huge international operation, a festival of street theaters that traveled across the Soviet Union and Eastern and Western Europe. After the caravan, Polunin wanted to run a series of festivals and formed the Academy of Fools in Leningrad (1992–1993), which soon ran out of funding. Four of the Litsedei split off from the original group, calling themselves Litsedei Minus Four. They presented their first show, *Bezsolnitsa* (a mix of the words

The clown Slava Polunin in his red and yellow costume of Asisyai, the character he invented for the Asisyai show. (Photo by Irina Kaledina)

insomnia and *lack of sun*), in 1993. Without support from the state for experimentation, Polunin left the country and spent two years in the United States, then two years in France; since 1997 he has been based in London. He has undertaken a number of international tours with *Snow Show*, which premiered in St. Petersburg in 1993 and follows on from *Asisyai*. *Snow Show* has had runs in Edinburgh and London and has toured world wide.

In *Snow Show*, Polunin-Asisyai (the clown in the yellow suit with red fluffy slippers) enters with a rope, possibly a dog's leash. But there is no dog; instead, a second clown follows, this one dressed in green. The yellow clown contemplates suicide and is deterred when his partner tries to use the other end of the rope for the same purpose. The show is set on a snowy, white stage, emphasising solitude in the Arctic, where man faces the adverse elements and is eventually swept away by a blizzard. Polunin dances with an empty overcoat: there is no other human soul. He leads a tragic, lonely existence. From his suitcase he takes a yellow balloon, which tragically pops after he has managed to hold a conversation with it by means of a whistle, to which the balloon seemingly responds. Through his cheerful comportment and his invitation to the audience to play, he underlines the (Beckettian) absurdity of life as a condition for the clown's existence. The "other" clowns, in green jumpsuits with large, flapping ears, live in a clan and wreak havoc, both on stage and in the auditorium. A telephone conversation, cited from the earlier show *Asisyai*, is inserted into the second part of the show: Polunin speaks as it were with his alter ego, thus strengthening again the sense of the clown's loneliness. Before the interval

the audience is wrapped in the web of the padding pulled from the sheets that form the stage wall; these represent either snow (white) or the night (dark blue). Polunin creates a powerful image of a lonely man, who never surrenders to his loneliness. Polunin was awarded the prize Triumph (established by the tycoon Boris Berezovsky) in 1999 and subsequently returned to Russia with *Asisyai* in 2002–2003 and with *Snow Show* in 2003. Polunin's interest in the borderline between life and play/game and his perception of the clown's existence as a permanent condition of carnival make him one of the most outstanding clowns of his age.

Polunin's shows attract crowds. He has participated in the work of the Cirque du Soleil, whose popularity in Russia surmounts that of Polunin. Their shows too have a unifying theme and develop a universal, mythical or legendary, story. In the first show they explored the opposition between circus people and ordinary human beings. Later they dwelt on Chinese legends or fantastic spirits or on historical figures to inspire their performances and set the style and rhythm for each show. Choreography, music, numbers, and special effects create a total performance, indeed much as in Polunin's shows (only with fewer artistes). Cirque du Soleil was founded by Guy Laliberté in 1984 in Quebec and has since conquered the world with four or five shows running simultaneously in international tours while two are stationary in the United States. Many circus artistes of the former Eastern Europe, including Russia and Ukraine, are part of one of the collectives of Cirque du Soleil.

The International Arena   The Cirque du Soleil has incorporated a number of

Russian acrobats into its shows. Serious collaboration began in the show *Alegria* (1994), when the famous clown Slava Polunin devised a number that he would later develop into his own, full-blown show, the *Snow Show*. Its was performed by the clown Yuri Medvedev, with Sergei Chachalev. The two clowns entered onto the stage, observing a puffing miniature train on the stage that was gradually covered in snow (paper flakes). Medvedev would sit on a suitcase, which he carried, opening it to retrieve some bright yellow balloons with red ribbons, reminders of Polunin's original Asisyai costume. The clown is lonely in the snow, in an act performed to the "Nocturne" that highlights man's solitude. In *O* (1998), Valeri Keft and Leonid Leikin, former Litsedei actors, took on the clown numbers. In *La Nouba* (1998), the clown Sergei Chachalev appeared in a solo sketch.

In terms of acrobatics, the Soleil draws regularly on Russian acrobats. Igor Arefiev performed on the high wire in *La Nouba*, before offering an aerial pas de deux with Colette Morrow (UK) in *Dralion* (1999). The Ukrainian-born gymnast and graduate of Kiev's circus school, Viktor Kee, performs a juggling act combined with body contortion in the same show. He has also appeared in other shows in Paris and Las Vegas. In *Saltimbanco* (1992), Maria Markova presented a juggling act. In the most recent show, *Varekai* (2002), Anton Chelnokov presented the "Flight of Icarus," an aerial act, in which he—failing to fly—falls into the net—a forest—where he meets a beautiful spirit. This is Olga Pikhienko with her hand-balancing act, whom he joins for an aerial contortion act. The number, directed by Chelnokov's father, Nikolai, has won great acclaim. Both artists have re-

ceived awards: Olga Pikhienko received the Future award of the Cirque de Demain in 1992 for an "Adagio" in an earlier Cirque du Soleil performance; Anton Chelnokov won the same award for aerial net in 2001.

The recognition of circus artistes is measured in international terms by the awards of the Cirque de Demain festival in Paris and the Monte Carlo International Circus Festival. Russia itself organized a few national and international circus festivals also in the 1990s, notably the All-Russian Circus Festival, which took place in Yaroslavl in 1997 and in Saratov in 1999. Moscow held a World Circus Festival in 1996, on Red Square, in which, for the most part, artistes from the former Soviet countries and China participated.

It is in the world of acrobatics that Russia takes the lead both nationally and internationally, however. In 1992 the trapeze artist Yelena Fomina won the Silver Prize at the Cirque de Demain. Fomina today teaches trapeze at the Montreal Circus School. In 1994 Vitali Jouravel won the Golden Prize at the Cirque de Demain for his gymnastic performance on fixed bars; he has since worked with Circus Althoff. The Kurbanovs won in the same year the Future award for their motorcycle number of "Icarian acrobatics." In 2003 they performed their new number of motorcycle acrobatics in rocker-style choreography in Monte Carlo. Sergei Tayekin and Olga Budziovich were awarded a Golden Prize at the Cirque de Demain in 1995 for their gymnastics. They went on to the circus Roncalli. The Kuznetsovs are gymnasts who work on Russian bars; they received the Golden Prize at the Cirque de Demain in 1996. In the same year, Oleg Izosimov won recognition in Monte Carlo for his ballet-styled act of hand-balancing, which he has since shown both at the Wintergarten and Roncalli. Natalia Jigalova received a Silver Prize at the Cirque de Demain in 1996 for her work on the trapeze, followed by her colleague Yelena Popova, who received an award in the same discipline in 2001. Two of the most prestigious awards, the Golden Clowns of Monte Carlo, have gone to teeterboard artists: to the Chernievsky troupe in 2000, and to the Puzanovi group in 2003. The Puzanovis developed their number in the style of Russian folklore. Another Golden Award at the Cirque de Demain 2003 went to the Rokashkovs. Sergei and Natalia Rokashkov perform aerial gymnastics on a fixed bar to Latin American music, in a number choreographed by Alexander Grimailo. They work with Roncalli. Most internationally recognized artistes thus move to European circus ensembles at the first opportunity.

A to Z

Chapayev, Vasili Ivanovich: 1887–1919; came from a peasant family. He fought during World War I and joined the revolutionaries. He was a hero of the civil war. He is portrayed and immortalized in the 1923 novel by Dmitri Furmanov (1891–1926) that served as the basis for a film made in 1934 by the Vasiliev brothers. Furmanov had studied philosophy and joined the Revolutionary movement in 1917; he was commander of Chapayev's division in Kazakhstan. This encounter and the battles provided the backdrop for the events covered in the novel and the film. Chapayev's heroism and his fervent support of the Revolution are combined with his lack of education. Through the Revolutionary cause

and the admiration for the figure of the commander Furmanov, Chapayev's wish to become more educated was awakened. He thus served as a model for Communist culture, which aimed to raise the level of literacy and education among peasants.

Cirque du Soleil: founded in 1984 in Gaspé, Quebec, by Guy Laliberté. Creative directors are Guy Caron and Gilles Ste.-Croix. Shows have included *We Reinvent the Circus*, 1987; *Nouvelle Experience*, 1990; *Fascination*, 1992; *Saltimbanco*, 1992; *Mystere*, 1994, at a stationary theater in Las Vegas; *Alegria*, 1994; *Quidam*, 1996; *O*, 1998, at a permanent base in Las Vegas; *La Nouba*, 1998, at a theater in Orlando; *Dralion*, 1999; *Varekai*, 2002; *Zumanity*, 2003, at a theater in Las Vegas. Cirque du Soleil's shows are thematically arranged and lavishly designed, with a precise choreography to lend coherence to the show and emphasize each number. The Cirque works with international artists. [www.cirquedusoleil.com]

Derevo: mime group founded by Anton Adasinsky, who left Litsedei with Tania Khabarova, Lena Yarovaya, and Alexei Merkushev in April 1988 (Leningrad). Since 1989, mostly abroad, practically based in Germany. Their shows have included *Red Zone* (1988); *The Rider* (1992); *Once* (1997); *Islands in the Stream* (2003). [www.derevo.org]

Dodin, Lev: b. 1944; graduated from the Leningrad Theater Institute in 1965. Worked at the Leningrad Young Spectator's Theater. Chief artistic director to the Malyi Drama Theater (now Theater of Europe) in Leningrad (now St. Petersburg) since 1982. Repertoire includes numerous prose adaptations, including the world-famous trilogy based on Fyodor Abramov's village prose (*The House*, 1980, and *Brothers and Sisters*, 1985). Other adaptations have included William Golding's *The Lord of the Flies* (1986), Yuri Trifonov's *The Old Man* (1988), Sergei Kaledin's prose (*Gaudeamus*, 1990), and Dostoevsky's *The Devils* (1991). His 1987 production of Alexander Galin's *Stars in the Morning Sky*, a play about Moscow prostitutes during the 1980 Olympics, made a furor on the waves of glasnost. Productions of the 1990s included *Claustrophobia* (1994), based on the contemporary prose of Vladimir Sorokin and Liudmila Ulitskaya; Chekhov's *The Cherry Orchard* (1995), *Ivanov* (*Play without a Title*, 1998), and *Uncle Vania* (2003); and Andrei Platonov's *Chevengur* (1999). [www.mdt-dodin.ru]

Fomenko, Petr: b. 1932, worked in Moscow until 1974, when he moved to Leningrad, where from 1977 to 1981 he headed the Theater of Comedy. In 1984 he returned to Moscow; Fomenko teaches at GITIS/RATI and set up his own theater, the Workshop Petr Fomenko, with graduates from his courses. His own directing style is a visually expressive, but psychologically fine reading of the text. [www.teatr.ru]

Grishkovets, Yevgeni: b. 1967 and lived in Kemerovo, Siberia, where he founded the Lozha Theater. In the late 1990s presented solo performances of his own texts, *How I Ate a Dog* (Kak ia s"el sobaku) and *Simultaneously* (Odnovremenno). Later wrote plays: *Winter* (Zima), *The Town* (Gorod), and—in joint stock method with the Arts Theater—*The Siege* (Osada, 2003). [www.odnovremenno.ru] and [www.grishkovets.com]

Khazanov, Gennadi: b. 1945. Comedian of the estrada, whose career started as conférencier for Leonid Utesov's jazz band in the 1960s. Because of his political text, he was banned from the stage in 1984. In 1987 his show was directed by Viktiuk. In the 1990s he appeared on the stage of drama theaters and in films. Since 1997 he has been artistic director of the Moscow Estrada Theater.

Koliada, Nikolai: b. 1957. Major playwright of the 1990s, actor at the Drama Theater in Ekaterinburg. Later began to direct on his own and founded his own theater. Editor of the journal *Ural*, where he published a number of new writers and playwrights. Teaches at Ekaterinburg's Theater Institute; some of the most talented writers emerged from his classes; he often publishes their works at his own expense. His own plays—*The Catapult* (Rogatka), *Oginski's Polonaise* (Polonez Oginskogo), *We Go and Go* (My edem, edem, edem)—play at Moscow's largest theaters and many of them have been translated into several languages. [http://kolyada.ur.ru]

Kozak, Roman: b. 1957; graduated from Moscow Arts Theater School. Kozak worked in the studio movement, where he became famous for a production of Ludmila Petrushevskaya's *Cinzano*, written in 1973 but previously banned from the stage for its treatment of alcoholism. He is married to the choreographer Alla Sigalova. He was associated with Moscow Arts Theater until he took over the Pushkin Theater in 2000.

Kurochkin, Maxim: b. 1970. Playwright, who graduated from the History Department of Kiev University. *The Destroyer of the Class Medea* (Istrebitel' klassa

"Medeia", 1995) and *Steel Will* (Stal'ova volia, 1999) demonstrate his technique of blending a historical plot with a contemporary setting into a science-fiction-type drama. *The Kitchen* (Kukhnia, 2000) was commissioned and directed by Oleg Menshikov. [www.newdrama.ru/authors/]

Litsedei: (Actors, or Hypocrites). Litsedei was founded by Viacheslav Polunin. They performed clown and mime shows and took part in street theater festivals. The group split several times. Litsedei Minus Four—Leonid Leikin, Anvar Libabov, Vasili Soboliev, Valeri Keft, and Anna Orlova—presented *Bezsolnitsa* (1993).

Makovetsky, Sergei: b. 1958. Graduated from the Shchukin Theater School in 1980. Actor of the Vakhtangov Theater and, since 1989, of the Theater of Roman Viktiuk; performed in *Masterclass* (1989), *M Butterfly* (1990), *Lolita* (1993*), The Catapult* (1993). Honored Artist of the Russian Federation, 1992; NIKA Award of the Russian Film Academy in the category best actor for *Makarov*, 1994.

Mashkov, Vladimir: b. 1963, actor at the Tabakov Theater. Mashkov has played in numerous films and been cast for international projects as well. Since the mid-1990s has directed (*A Fatal Number*, 1994, Bertolt Brecht's *Threepenny Opera*, 1996, and Ray Cooney's *Out of Order* [stage title *No. 13*], Moscow Arts Theater, 2001). He has also embarked on work as a film director (*Papa*, 2004). Mashkov is a sex symbol and a Russian megastar on stage and screen.

Menshikov, Oleg: b. 1960. One of the top film and theater actors in Russia. Menshikov graduated in 1982 from the Shchep-

kin Theater School. His parts as Caligula (1991), and the dancer Nijinski (1993) created his reputation. He played the poet Sergei Esenin in the London production of *When She Danced . . .* (1992, with Vanessa Redgrave). In 1998 established his own theater company, Tovarishchestvo 814, where he directs and acts. Work as director has included *Woe from Wit* (1999), *Kitchen* (2000), *The Gamblers* (2002).

Mirzoyev, Vladimir: b. 1957, graduated from the circus department at GITIS in 1981. From 1987 to 1989 worked in the VOTM. From 1989 to 1993 lived and worked in Canada. In 1993 returned to Russia. Has worked at the Stanislavsky Theater and other established theaters in Moscow and usually casts the actor Maxim Sukhanov in his productions, which enjoy huge popularity. Productions have included *The Marriage* (1994); *Khlestakov* (1996); *Amphytrion* (1998); *Two Women* (*A Month in the Country*) (1998); *The Taming of the Shrew* (1999); *Twelfth Night* (1999); *Pinter's Collection* (2000); *Cyrano de Bergerac* (2000).

Moscow Arts Theater (MkhAT): founded in 1898 by Konstantin Stanislavsky and Vladimir Nemirovich-Danchenko, this theater is one of the oldest and most prestigious theaters in Moscow. After 1970 it was under the leadership of Oleg Yefremov. After his death in 2000 it was taken over by Oleg Tabakov. [www.mxat.ru]

New Russian (novyi russkii): The term used for a new "class" of Russian society that emerged after the collapse of the Soviet Union. In the 1990s many opportunities opened up that allowed people to make a lot of money; not all these opportunities were legal. At the same time, business opportunities were followed up by people of the younger generation with a great deal of initiative, leaving the intelligentsia in the role of the poor beggar at the mercy of those who had managed to do better than they. Writers, academics, artists, and other groups who belonged to the intelligentsia that had always formed the "think tank" for the state, whether as dissident voices or as supportive of Gorbachev's reforms, had suddenly lost their influence, status, and income. The intelligentsia, educated and cultured, mocked the habits of the new rich class in numerous jokes. The shop The World of New Russians also exposes mockingly the attitude of the older generation toward the class that now influences Russia's economy and politics. The New Russian is allegedly uneducated and rude, but rich. [www.newrussian.net]

Obraztsov, Sergei: (1901–1992). Trained as a painter and designer, then went to the Moscow Arts Theater studio, later at the MkhAT 2 studio. After 1920, worked with puppets on the estrada. He organized the State Puppet Theater in 1931, on Mayakovsky Square. In 1970 the theater moved into new premises on the Ring Road. After 1973 was professor at GITIS. Headed the puppet theater and set the dominant tone for theories on puppet theater for most of the Soviet period. Different approaches to puppet theater not until after his death. Famous for his puppet Tiapa. The repertoire included classical texts rendered suitable for children, Soviet children's literature, and figures of animation for the stage. [www.puppet.ru]

Polunin, Slava: b. 1950. Clown, based in Leningrad/St. Petersburg; later in London.

Polunin created a Mime Parade (1982) and in 1987 founded the Listedei Litsei (Lyceum of Hypocrites); in 1988 organized the Congress of Fools; in 1989 launched the Caravan of Peace, touring most of the world over the following year. In 1992 set up the Academy of Fools, before leaving Russia in 1993. His shows *Asisyai* and *SnowShow* have toured the entire world. He has worked with Cirque du Soleil; in 2001 he organized the street theater program for the Theater Olympics in Moscow. [www.slavasnowshow.com]

Popov, Oleg: b. 1930. A "sunny clown," with straight red hair, a red nose, striped trousers, and a black jacket with a red bow tie. Golden Clown award of the Monte Carlo International Circus Festival in 1981.

Potudan Theater: Puppet theater formed in 2000 by graduates of the Petersburg Theater Institute (SPATI) from Grigori Kozlov's course. Headed by Ruslan Kudashov (b. 1972), a graduate of SPATI. Named after *Potudan*, a show based on Andrei Platonov's story. *Nevsky Prospekt* opened 2002. Innovative use of puppets while following the poetic tradition of puppet theater. [www.potudan.ru]

Presniakov, Oleg and Vladimir: b. 1969 and 1974 in Sverdlovsk. They created their own theater at the Ural State University where they were students of philology. Their play *Terrorism* has been translated into several languages. *Playing the Victim* opened at the Royal Court London in 2003. [www.newdrama.ru/authors/]

Raikin, Arkadi: (1911–1987). Raikin studied at the Leningrad Theater Institute. In 1939, created the Leningrad Theater of

Miniature. His contribution to the development of estrada as a cabaret and entertainment genre cannot be underestimated. Raikin gave a great number of performances in Leningrad and all across Russia, and in 1987 he moved to his own theater, the Satirikon in Moscow. His son, Konstantin Raikin, an actor and director of dramatic theater, took on the artistic management of the Satirikon and made it one of the finest drama theaters in Moscow.

Serebrennikov, Kirill: b. 1969 in Rostov-on-Don, where he studied theater. After making a little-known film, he moved to Moscow in the late 1990s. He made the television serials *Rostov-Papa* and *Diary of a Murder*. His Moscow stage debut was with Vasili Sigarev's *Plasticine* in a small experimental theater. Specializes in contemporary plays, including Ravenhill's *Explicit Polaroids*, Sigarev's *Plasticine*, the Presniakov brothers' *Terrorism*. Has also staged commercial productions at established theaters, including Lermontov's *Demon* with Oleg Menshikov (2003) and Tennessee Williams's *Sweet Bird of Youth* with Marina Neyolova (2002) at the Sovremennik.

Sigarev, Vasili: b. 1977 in Nizhny Tagil, Urals. Studied under Nikolai Koliada. *Plasticine* (Plastilin) was read at the Liubimovka festival in Moscow and staged in 2001 by Kirill Serebrennikov. *Black Milk* followed in 2002. His plays have been translated into several languages. [http://sigarev.narod.ru]

Stirlitz: The best-known figure of Russian cinematic history. He is the protagonist of the television serial *Seventeen Moments of Spring*, based on Yulian Semyonov's spy novel and filmed by Tatiana Lioznova in 1972. The part of Stirlitz was played by Viacheslav Tikhonov. The twelve series are repeated frequently on Russian television and remain popular. The series deals with the role of a Soviet resident spy in Hitler's SS headquarters during World War II. Stirlitz tries to understand the moves of the Germans and communicate the information to Moscow, awaiting instructions from there how to proceed. He also has to travel to Switzerland on a special mission. The film presents a Soviet spy who works with his mind rather than his muscles, unlike James Bond.

Tabakov, Oleg: b. 1935; graduated from the Moscow Arts Theater School; acted at the Sovremennik under Oleg Yefremov; left the Sovremennik in 1983 to join Yefremov at the Moscow Arts Theater. Since 1987, dean of the Moscow Arts Theater School; since 2000, artistic director of the Arts Theater.

Tabakov Theater (Tabakerka): founded in 1974 with student actors. Since 1987 the studio operates as theater on Chaplygin Street. The repertoire of the Tabakov Theater has included Gorky's *The Last Ones* (Poslednie, 1995) and *The Lower Depths* (Na dne, 2000), both directed by Adolf Shapiro; Oleg Antonov's *The Fatal Number* (Smertelnyi nomer, 1994), directed by Vladimir Mashkov (1994); *Anecdotes* (based on Dostoevsky and Alexander Vampilov, 1995), starring Vladimir Mashkov; Nabokov's *Camera Obscura* (1997); *A Room of Laughter* (Komnata smekha), by the Anti–Booker Prize winner Oleg Bogayev, directed by Kama Ginkas (1998). [http://tabakov.theatre.ru]

Ten' (Teatr Ten'): The Shadow Theater, located in Moscow on Novoslobodskaya

Street, was founded in 1989 by Maya Krasnopolskaya and Ilia Eppelbaum. The repertoire includes puppet shows for children; shadow theater; puppet/shadow theater for adults with parodies of classical forms. A unique feature of the theater is its Lilikan Theater (1996), a miniature replica of the Bolshoi Theater, in which parodic performances are enacted with puppets.

Viktiuk, Roman: b. 1936; graduated from GITIS in 1956. Between 1965 and 1968 in Lvov, from 1968 to 1970 in Kaliningrad; from 1971 to 1977 director of the Russian Drama Theater, Vilnius. From 1977 to 1979 at the Moscow State University Theater, where he staged *Music Lessons*, by Petrushevskaya, 1980. Then productions at various Moscow theaters, including *Anna Karenina* (Vakhtangov Theater 1983) and *Colombine's Apartment* by Petrushevskaya (Sovremennik, 1986). His production of *The Petty Demon* by Sologub, at the Sovremennik Theater in 1988, stirred a controversy over his art because of its open homoeroticism, tending more and more toward an open homosexuality. With *The Maids* by Genet, at the Satirikon Theater, in 1988 and revived in 1992, he outed himself. Later productions commercially exploited the hitherto taboo theme of homosexuality: *Masterclass*, by David Pownell, Vakhtangov Theater, 1990; *Lolita* by Nabokov, 1992, and *Two for the Seesaw*, by William Gibson, 1992, both at the Fora Theater. Then he founded his own theater, Viktiuk Theater, for the shows *The Catapult* and *Oginski's Polonaise* by Koliada (1993–1994); *Salome* by Oscar Wilde, 1998; *Spring Awakening* by Franz Wedekind, 1999. *Boudoir Philosophy*, based on the Marquis de Sade, was shown at the Satirikon Theater in 1996.

Zadornov, Mikhail: b. 1948 in Riga. Estrada artist who moved to Moscow in 1968 after having worked at the KVN in Riga. In 1974 graduated from the Aviation Institute. Zadornov writes satirical monologues and intermedia: *Who's Louder* (Kto gromche, 1975) for the duo Alexander Livshits and Alexander Levenbuk. Zadornov is famous for his impersonations of Gorbachev and other celebrities.

Zakharov, Mark: b. 1933; artistic director of the Theater of the Lenin Komsomol, Moscow, since 1973. Developed a contemporary repertoire, including plays by Grigori Gorin, Mikhail Shatrov, Liudmila Petrushevskaya. The ensemble includes stars of film and television: Inna Churikova, Alexander Abdulov, Oleg Yankovsky, Dmitri Pevtsov. In 1981 staged the now legendary rock opera *Perchance* (Junona and Avos) with a libretto by the poet Andrei Voznesensky and the music composed by Rybnikov.

Zhitinkin, Andrei: b. 1960; graduated in 1982 as actor, in 1988 as director from the Shchukin School. From 1988 to 1991 at the Yermolova Theater; since 1991 at the Mossovet Theater, where he created furor with a production by the gay playwright Mikhail Volokhov, *Igra v zhmuriki* (Mossovet 1993). Other productions at the Mossovet included *The Promise* by Alexei Arbuzov, 1995; *He Came* by J. B. Priestley, 1996; *The Merchant of Venice* by William Shakespeare, 1999. Also challenging were his productions at the Tabakov Theater: *The Crank* by Alexander Minchin, 1995, and *The Adventures of Felix Krull* by Thomas Mann, 1998. From 2001 to 2003, art director at the Malaya Bronnaya Theater, where he staged *Nijinski* by Glenn Blumstein, 1999, and *Portrait of Dorian Gray* by Wilde, 2001, before being sacked by the conservative director Ilia Kogan for his overtly homosexual productions.

Zhvanetsky, Mikhail: b. 1934 in Odessa. Started his career with Roman Kartsev in the local Odessa theater club. In 1963 moved to the Leningrad Theater of Miniature to work for Arkadi Raikin. As dramaturge, he wrote the show *Traffic Light* (*Svetofor,* 1967), before beginning to perform his own texts: *Plus Minus* (1970). In 1969 left the theater and created a Theater of Miniature in Odessa at the local Philharmonic Orchestra, which he ran from 1970 to 1979. Shows included *How to Get to Deribasov Street* (Kak proiti na Derbasovskuiu) and *Been and Gone* (Vstretilis' i razbezhalis'). In 1973, staged the show *Red Arrow* (Krasnaia strela) at the Moscow Music Hall. Performed at the Hermitage Theater Moscow (then Miniature Theater): *When We Relaxed* (Kogda my otdykhali, 1979), *Bravo, Satire* (Bravo satira, 1984), and the political cabaret *Bird Flight* (Ptichii polet). In 1988 he opened his own Miniature Theater of Zhvanetsky.

Bibliography

Beumers, Birgit. "Commercial Enterprise on the Stage: Changes in Russian Theatre Management between 1986 and 1996." *Europe-Asia Studies* 48, no. 8 (1996): 1403–1416.

———. *Yury Lyubimov at the Taganka Theatre 1964–1994.* Amsterdam: Harwood, 1997.

Costanzo, Susan. "A Theatre of Their Own: The Cultural Spaces of Moscow and Leningrad Amateur Studios 1957–1986." *Canadian Slavonic Papers* 36, no. 3–4 (1994): 333–347.

Freedman, John. *Moscow Performances. The New Russian Theatre 1991–1996.* Amsterdam: Harwood, 1997.

———. *Moscow Performances. The 1996–1997 Season.* Amsterdam: Harwood, 1998.

Kelly, Catriona. *Petrushka: The Russian Carnival Puppet Theatre.* Cambridge: Cambridge University Press, 1990.

Kelly, Catriona, and David Shepherd, eds. *Russian Cultural Studies: An Introduction.* Oxford: Oxford University Press, 1998.

Kennedy, Dennis, ed. *Oxford Encyclopedia of Theatre and Performance.* Oxford and New York: Oxford University Press, 2003.

Krylova, Anna. "Saying 'Lenin' and Meaning 'Party': Subversion and Laughter in Soviet and Post-Soviet Society." In *Consuming Russia. Popular Culture, Sex and Society since Gorbachev,* ed. by Adele Barker, 243–265. Durham, NC: Duke University Press, 1999.

Leach, Robert, and Viktor Borovsky, eds. *A History of Russian Theatre.* Cambridge: Cambridge University Press, 1999.

Markova, Elena. *Off Nevsky Prospekt: St Petersburg's Theatre Studios in the 1980s and 1990s.* Amsterdam: Harwood, 1998.

Shevtsova, Maria. *Dodin and the Maly Drama Theatre.* London and New York: Routledge, 2004.

Smeliansky, Anatoly. *The Russian Theatre after Stalin.* Cambridge: Cambridge University Press, 1999.

4
Music and Word

The phenomenal success of the Russian duo t.A.T.u, which topped the British charts in the summer of 2002 with their album *200kmh in the Wrong Lane*, placed Russian pop music on a firm footing internationally for the first time. Although there had been occasional releases in the West and tours of Russian pop and rock bands in Europe and the United States, to actually reach a place in the charts was unheard of. Even Alsou, the discovery of 1999 who lives and studies in London, had not reached that level of success in the West.

Before dealing with the manifestations of contemporary pop music in Russia, this chapter explores its homegrown origins, which lay on the one hand in the official Soviet pop culture of the 1960s and 1970s (estrada) and on the other hand in the underground bard and rock movement that surfaced eventually in the late 1980s during Gorbachev's perestroika.

Jazz and Rock

The Beginnings of Jazz and Rock Music
After the Revolution, popular musical expression was controlled so as to remain accessible to the masses and ideologically acceptable. The "mass song" was developed, and marches and secular anthems remained prominent. Folk songs were also popular, but more in their kitschy and arranged orchestrated versions for public performance than as a continuation of ancient rituals (fake lore). Western popular music, on the other hand, became suspect: jazz and the fox-trot were labeled decadent, and jazz in particular was controversial because it was perceived as dangerously democratic and uncontrollable, since it relied on improvisation. Furthermore, it was an art of the black people. This made it especially difficult to deal with from an official point of view: produced by the oppressed of the capitalist world, jazz was supposedly silenced. In 1928, the fox-trot and tango were declared harmful, largely because of their sexually arousing movements; the fox-trot in particular was associated

with homosexuality, drugs, and eroticism (according to Maxim Gorky). The vitriolic campaign against Western music was scaled down somewhat in the 1930s, when a sanitized form of jazz and tango created by Soviet composers gained popularity. Only such sanitized forms were popular in the West, and free from censorship.

Jazz Music   Leonid Utesov (1895–1982) and Alexander Tsfasman (1906–1971) were the two most famous jazzmen of the 1930s and 1940s, who produced an equivalent of big band swing for dancing. Both provided entertainment at the front during the war. Utesov also wrote the music for a number of films made during the 1930s, including the musical *Jolly Fellows*. He became one of the most popular composers in the USSR. Oskar Strok (1893–1975) was perhaps lesser known, but he was the Soviet king of the tango.

At the end of the war, jazz again came into the firing line of ideology when the secretary for ideology, Andrei Zhdanov, attacked jazz music as hysterical and cacophonous. He ordered the arrest of jazz musicians, such as Eddie Rosner and Leonid Piatigorsky, and also the "arrest" of saxophones. This ban was lifted only in the mid 1950s under Khrushchev, but even then jazz remained an alien musical style, until the performance of foreign jazz and rock at the Sixth International Youth Festival in Moscow in 1957.

During the 1950s another phenomenon occurred in Soviet culture: the appearance of *stilyagi* (style hunters), people who imitated Western dress and style. On the one hand they represented the dandy, concerned only with the consumer culture of the West; at the same time, the stilyagi offered a revolt against the stifled dress

habits in the Soviet Union. The state answered this trend with a campaign against Western influences, exposing the antics of the stilyagi to satire: they had "cocktail hours," loved jazz music, wore colorful ties and tight suits, representing all the worst features of Western consumerism. Music—both jazz and rock—was seen as a bad influence on young people. The *chuvikha* (youth slang: girl, "bird"; sometimes there is also a masculine form, *chuvak*) was the female version of the stilyaga, a woman sporting short hair and skirts and blouses instead of the traditional long hair and pinafore dress. The *shtatniki* (*shtaty* mean the United States) donned Italo-American-style suits and the *beatniki* appeared in jeans and sneakers. Glenn Miller's "Chattanooga Choo Choo" became the anthem of the jazz movement. In 1955 the jazz opera *Porgy and Bess* was shown in Moscow. In 1962 Benny Goodman toured the USSR. On the home front, improvised jazz concerts took place on Mayakovsky Square in the late 1950s, and the first history of jazz was published in 1960, indicating the increasingly official acceptance of the music. Dixieland bands performed in restaurants, even if there was no dance floor and the repertoire was tightly controlled by the state. Jazz cafes were organized to get a grip on Soviet youth and control those that had gone out of control. By 1966 the state record firm Melodiya was releasing jazz and pop records, giving further proof of a relaxation.

Although jazz had been more or less accepted by the mid-1960s when Brezhnev came to power, the real thing for the new generation was by then pop and rock. Jazz remained of interest to the cultural elite and the intellectuals, but not the masses. Jazz remained an important factor in the development of rock music in the USSR but also as a movement that broke the wall keeping musical influences from the West from having an impact on popular Soviet culture. Voice of America's broadcasts of Western jazz and pop music were crucial, however.

Soviet jazz musicians and groups were more or less respectable. Important jazz musicians were Igor Brill (b.1944), a pianist who participated in a number of jazz groups in the 1960s, including a band with the jazz musician Yuri Saulsky (b.1928). In the 1990s Brill still had his own band and played occasional concerts, spending the rest of his time as teacher at the Gnesin Institute for Music. The Ganelin Trio (1971–1986), composed of Viacheslav Ganelin, Vladimir Chekasin, and Vladimir Tarasov, was one of the most respected jazz bands in the 1970s, playing avant-garde jazz that fused different styles and offered a theatrical performance. Finally, Sergei Kuryokhin's (1954–1996) band Popular Mechanics, founded in 1985, became famous for its mixture of jazz, rock, and other musical forms in the 1980s, with saxophone player Anatoli Vapirov. The band and Kuryokhin performed abroad and were featured in the BBC series *Comrades* (1986).

Jazz and Rock "on the Bones"   From the mid-1960s onward, the thorn in the flesh of the authorities was called rock and roll. Rock music reached the USSR via jazz bands and in some ways was more acceptable than jazz, as it seemed to appeal to the lower, proletarian classes as well as to a different, younger, generation. In a sense, jazz had paved the way for rock music.

In 1961 a decree on parasitism had been passed, however, obliging every Soviet citizen to have a workplace. This created, in the long term, the phenomenon of the "generation of janitors and night watchmen," those who sought a fake employment that left them free time to do what they wanted to do: paint, compose, sing. In 1962, Khrushchev's attacks on modern art, especially the young, abstract art movement, had further undermined a potential for the development of a culture that would interest the young generation. Another complication in the spread of rock music was the absence of a homegrown production facility for electric guitars, which were made only in Poland and East Germany.

The impact of Western rock music on the Soviet scene cannot be underestimated. The Sixth International Youth Festival (1957) had brought musical groups from the entire world to Moscow. Moreover, the invention of the vinyl that could be printed onto any piece of plastic led to the appearance of pirated recordings of Western rock, which were available from the 1950s on in the form of *roentgen-izdat* ("music on the ribs" or "music on the bones"): records printed on X-ray plates. Later this activity was linked to crime (the state was not making a profit from this "business") and made illegal. In the 1960s, some X-ray record makers were even arrested.

Although Elvis Presley had a relatively small impact, Joan Baez, Bob Dylan, and the East German bard (*Liedermacher*) Wolf Biermann were popular, underscoring the strong tradition of the word in Soviet culture. The public recital of poetry for large audiences had a long-standing tradition, going back to Vladimir Mayakovsky in the 1920s and ending with the mass performances of Yevgeni Evtushenko and Andrei Voznesensky in the 1960s and 1970s. Therefore, the recital of poetry to a melodic accompaniment from piano or guitar was only a small step away from this tradition. Here the so-called bard movement sprang up, with the poet composing and performing his song (the *avtorskaya pesnia*, the author's song).

The Bard Movement

The main exponents of the bard movement have been Bulat Okudzhava, Alexander Galich, and Vladimir Vysotsky, although other names may be associated with the movement as well, especially Yuri Vizbor (1934–1984). The bard song remains important both for the development of Russian rock in its emphasis on the lyrics rather than the tune and for contemporary Russian culture. Bard songs continue to be performed and remain very popular in the performance of other singers, such as Yelena Kamburova (b.1940), who has appeared on the Moscow stages since the 1960s. Although the bard songs were initially performed only for a small circle of friends, the appearance of reel-to-reel tape recorders, which replaced the X-ray plate vinyls, allowed the recording of the performances and their copying and distribution in what came to be known as *magnitizdat* (publishing on magnetic tape, a word formed in allusion to *samizdat* and *tamizdat*, the—illegal—publication of books as carbon copy or abroad). Indeed, by 1960 there were more than 100,000 tape recorders available, and production was increased further.

Many of these bard songs were critical of the heroic manner with which Soviet historiography dealt with the victory in World War II, ignoring the sacrifice of the individual to achieve that victory. Others dealt with the horror of the Stalin era (still much of a taboo despite the 20th Party Congress and Khrushchev's Secret Speech on Stalin's

Vladimir Vysotsky, actor and bard, reciting Boris Pasternak's poem "Hamlet" to the guitar at the beginning of *Hamlet*, directed at the Taganka Theater by Yuri Liubimov in 1971. (Photo by Valeri Plotnikov)

crimes) or touched upon the lonely and isolated individual, estranged from the state and society.

The first songs were performed in the late 1950s and 1960s by Bulat Okudzhava, dealing with themes of love and the horror of war. Okudzhava avoided direct reference to Stalin but created allegorical references to Stalin as a "black tomcat" ("The Black Cat" [Chernyi kot]). Galich's songs dealt with the gulag and the suffering of the people more poignantly and directly, turning the statue of Stalin into a vampire ("Night Watch" [Nochnoi dozor]). Yet even the bard movement, requiring no official acknowledgment or support from party or state (since performances were private and so was distribution), aroused the wrath of the state, which tightened up cultural politics in preparation for the 50th anniversary

Galich, "Night Watch" (Nochnoi dozor) *excerpt*

The bronze statues go back where they came
    from,
But the alabaster ones lie hidden away.
Maybe they're crippled for the time being,
But even their dust retains its shape,
These alabaster ones just need some human
    flesh,

And once more they'll acquire their greatness!
And the drums will beat!
The drums will beat,
Beat, beat, beat!

—translation by G. S. Smith

of the Revolution in 1967. In 1968 the media launched a massive attack on Vysotsky, who was later also accused of profiteering; in 1971 Galich was expelled from the Writers' Union, and he emigrated in 1974. Okudzhava was suspended from the Writers' Union in 1972. Of the three, Vysotsky was best positioned in the Taganka Theater (where he was employed as an actor) to perform his songs and to record them in France.

The bard movement was really begun by Bulat Okudzhava, who began to recite his poems in a modest, nondeclamatory way and to accompany himself on the guitar. Galich and Vysotsky joined this tradition later, engaging more in Muscovite jargon and the underground and back streets; Okudzhava remained largely within a classical, nineteenth-century tradition.

Bulat Okudzhava was born in Moscow. His father was executed during the purges of the 1930s; his mother was arrested and released only in 1955. He volunteered for the army and served at the front and thus drew on his first-hand experience of the war in his lyrics. He was a novelist, member of the Writers' Union, and poet-bard. Okudzhava began performing in the mid-1950s, and the songs were distributed through tape distribution (magnitizdat) and not offi-

cially released on record until the 1980s. He used a simple vocabulary and plaintive melodies, focusing on traditional themes: women, love, war, and the city of Moscow.

His treatment of these themes was always unconventional. When dealing with the war in such songs as "Paper Soldier" (Bumazhnyi soldat, 1959) or "A Song about Soldiers' Boots" (Pesnia o soldatskikh sapogakh, 1956–1958), Okudzhava never glorified the war but emphasized instead the loss of individual life. This was very much against the official war ethos in the Soviet Union, which celebrated Victory Day with parades and reminded the nation of the hard fight the country had put up against fascism. The emphasis on individual lives, on the other hand, was very much in line with the ethos of the Thaw. During the 1950s, artists had begun to stress the individual's heroism rather than the collective feat, so that in this sense Okudzhava tapped into the cultural context of his time. "Paper Soldier" illustrated the fragility of life and the heroism of the individual displayed during a war in which so many perished.

His Moscow songs were hymns to the old city, singling out the different transport systems (the metro and the trolleybus), as well as his native Arbat district (now a pedestrian zone) in such songs as "Song

Okudzhava, "Paper Soldier" (Bumazhnyi soldat)

But once there was a soldier boy,
And he was bold and handsome,
But he was just a children's toy,
He was a paper soldier.

He wanted to remake the world,
So everyone would be happy,
But he was hanging on a string,
He was a paper soldier.

For you he would be glad to die
In fire and smoke twice over,
But all you did was play with him
He was a paper soldier.

And you would never share with him
Your most important secrets,
And why was that? It was because
He was a paper soldier.

And he would keep cursing his fate,
No quiet life he wanted,
And he kept asking: Fire, fire!
Forgetting he was paper.

Fire? I don't mind. Go on! You'll go?
And one day he went marching.
And then he died for nothing, for
He was a paper soldier.

—*translation by G. S. Smith*

about the Arbat" (Pesnia ob Arbate, 1959), "The Last Trolleybus" (Poslednii trolleibus, 1957), and "The Moscow Ant" (Moskovskii muravei, 1956–1958). His "Moscow Metro" (Moskovskoe metro, 1956–1964) ironically echoed with its refrain "Stand on the right, pass on the left!" the command given by the escalator guards on the Moscow metro during peak hours while commenting, by extension, on the attempt of the Soviet system to regulate absolutely everything. In his love songs, he always glorified women, elevating them to the level of an adored icon. One of his best-known songs is "The Blue Balloon" (Pesnia o golubom sharike, 1957), which touched upon folk traditions in its simplicity and brought out the lyrical tone characteristic of Okudzhava's treatment of the theme of women.

Okudzhava's songs never contained a positive, socialist hero. They were sung in a melancholic voice to a guitar accompani-ment. His songs are an integral part of ur-ban popular song culture and feature in nu-merous references to urban culture on the television and cinema screen as well as in the theater. His songs are frequently per-formed by stars of popular music.

Vladimir Vysotsky was an actor by train-ing and joined the company of the Taganka Theater, where he created his reputation as a stage actor. In 1966 he married the French actress Marina Vlady (Poliakova), which al-lowed him to travel abroad and enabled him to record several albums in France. Vysotsky grew up in the back streets of cen-tral Moscow, which exerted a long-lasting effect on his later career: he would always remain loyal to colloquial language, under-ground jargon, and alcohol. While training as an actor, Vysotsky began to write poems, which he sang to his own guitar accompani-ment. He was one of the bards or "guitar poets," to use the phrase coined by G. S.

Smith in *Songs to Seven Strings*, and his hoarse voice became his trademark. Vysotsky's songs dealt with themes incompatible with socialism: alcoholism, Stalinism, street life, prostitution, crime, and quite simply everyday Soviet life. He addressed the people and their problems and therefore received popular veneration. He was never officially recognized as a poet during his lifetime, however.

Vysotsky started performing his songs around 1960, initially to friends, and only later to a large audience. He dealt with different themes: "street" or "crime" songs stylized his own experience of life in the Moscow streets. He explicitly referred to those aspects of Soviet life that were taboo subjects: eroticism and promiscuity in "The Lady Nark" (Ninka, or "Navodchitsa"), prostitution and theft in "Sad Romance" (Grustnyi romans), or alcoholism in "Militia Report" (Militseiskii protokol). He used colloquial language, right down to the vulgar slang of Moscow's streets, and parodied fairy tales and folk legends.

A number of Vysotsky's poems concerned everyday Soviet life. He mocked lifestyles, past and present: "Dialogue in Front of the TV" (Dialog u televizora) was an understanding, yet parodic report of an everyday conversation of a couple in front of the television set, which he sang parodying the speakers' voices. In "Tender Truth" (Nezhnaia Pravda) he attacked the pseudo-objectivity of the Soviet press, echoing the unjust and uninformed campaign a Soviet paper (*Sovetskaya Rossiya*) had launched against him in 1968. He investigated the problems of everyday life: the delays and cancellations of internal flights, the formalities and surveillance associated with travel abroad, overcrowded transport, discussions with the telephone operator.

There were also several songs about sport, which offered an ironic perspective on the Soviet obsession with fitness and physical exercises, such as "a.m. P.T." (Utrenniaia gimnastika) with its mockery of the daily morning exercises on radio, or "The Sentimental Boxer" (O sentimental'nom boksere), where the movements of the boxer carry political undertones.

Songs about the war formed an important part of Vysotsky's work: although he had no first-hand experience of war, his songs revealed a deep understanding of individual suffering. He expressed an unorthodox attitude to the war by rejecting the heroic tone prevailing in descriptions of the great patriotic war (World War II) in favor of an emphasis on the individual and human sacrifice. In "Seriozha Fomin" he challenged the heroic principles of the Soviet Union when he reported that Fomin had been made a Hero of the Soviet Union although he avoided the draft and never fought during the war, whereas the little man goes without any reward. In "He Didn't Come Back" (On ne vernulsia iz boia) he mourned the death of a friend during battle, underlining the feeling of personal loss. In "In No-Man's Land" (Na neitral'noi polose) he described the attempt of a Soviet and a Turkish frontier guard to pick flowers for their beloved ones on neutral land and asked why borders exist at all. Vysotsky's songs about war were descriptive and mournful, sad but without explicit reproach. His stance, nevertheless, was essentially a pacifist one.

A major theme throughout Vysotsky's career was the role of the poet in society: his delicate and fragile position, his loneliness, and his responsibility were reflected best in his most famous song, "Wolf Hunt" (Okhota na volkov). Here he identified

Vysotsky, "Wolf Hunt" (Okhota na volkov)

I'm straining my utmost, every sinew,
But yet again, today like yesterday,
They've surrounded me, surrounded me,
And they're merrily herding me in to do my
   tricks.

The shotguns are busy from behind the spruce
   trees,
The hunters are hiding in their shadow,
And the wolves go head over heels in the snow,
Turned into living targets.

The wolf hunt is on, the hunt is on!
For gray prowlers, old ones, and cubs;
The beaters shout, the dogs howl themselves
   sick,
There's blood on the snow and the red spots of
   flags.

Our legs and jaws are swift.
Why, pack leader, answer us,

Do we turn toward the shots as if doped,
And never try to go beyond the prohibitions?

The wolf cannot and must not do otherwise . . .
And now my time's coming to its end!
The man I'm destined for
Has smiled and lifted his gun . . .

The wolf hunt is on, the hunt is on! etc.
But I've transgressed my obedience and gone
Beyond the flags the thirst for life was stronger!
   And behind me I heard with joy
The amazed cries of the people.

I'm straining my utmost, every sinew,
But today's not the same as yesterday!
They've surrounded me, surrounded me,
But the hunters have been left empty-handed!

—translation by G. S. Smith

with a wolf, doomed to be hunted by the huntsmen (the Soviet system), but finally breaking with all conventions and escaping. This song reflected a poem by Sergei Yesenin in which the latter also identified with a hunted wolf—who is killed. Its only hope is that somebody will write a song about him; Vysotsky fulfilled that request; and he replaced Yesenin as Russia's most genuinely popular poet.

Alexander Galich was an accomplished playwright before he began writing poems, which he sang to the guitar. With a large amount of political bitterness, Galich satirized the system, its victors as much as its victims. In "Episodes from the Life of Klim Petrovich Kolomiitsev," both the worker Klim and the party official are ridiculed:

Klim for reading the wrong speech, the party official for not realizing the mistake. Galich investigated the grind of everyday Soviet reality, such as sexual exploitation for social advancement ("Tonechka") or adultery and subsequent denunciation ("The Red Triangle").

Galich regarded himself as belonging to the "generation of the doomed"—survivors of the purges and of campaigns against "cosmopolitanism," who preferred, however, to immerse the memory of those days in oblivion. He acknowledged a collective guilt, which to him lay in silence about the past. "Petersburg Romance" and "Goldminers' Waltz" were full of self-reproach for his own lack of outspokenness at the right time. His song "When I Return" reflected both the desire and hope to return and the need for the Russian soil, culture, and audience. His language combined refinement with street jargon, as his style combined high culture with prison manners.

If Galich has always been better known as playwright than as bard, and known among the intellectual circles, then Vysotsky and Okudzhava were both popular heroes for their civic courage in singing about themes that were not part of the official discourse and, in Vysotsky's case, for mocking, parodying, and ridiculing Soviet life.

Rock Underground

Although the bards were a significant influence on the importance of the lyrics, the main source of inspiration for the rock movement of the 1960s was the Beatles. Their popularity from 1964 onward was unbroken, despite the press attacks on the group, despite derision in the satirical magazine *Krokodil*, and despite accusations that the band played into hands of capitalism. In the early 1960s, rock musicals were banned, and the first rock groups were arrested. The authorities then co-opted the bands, however, in order to keep tabs on them and ensure proper monitoring. Clubs with dance facilities and vocal instrumental ensembles (VIAs) were permitted in the mid 1960s and placed under official control. The most important of these clubs were the Vremena Goda (Seasons) in Gorky Park and the Molodezhnoye (Youth) Café.

Illegal Rock: The Beginnings of Soviet Rock (1970s)

In 1963 Alexander Gradsky, at the age of 14, performed some Presley tunes in a school concert. He formed the band Tarakany (Cockroaches), which imitated Beatles songs. Then Gradsky played with Mikhail Turkov, the grandson of Nobel Prize winner Mikhail Sholokhov, for Slaviane (The Slavs, 1965–1966), which was the first proper Soviet rock band. Here, and with his subsequent band, the Skify (Scythians, 1966), Gradsky sang in English. Subsequently he set up the band Skomorokhy (1966–1976), which sang in Russian. Gradsky's classical bel canto tenor is an excellent voice for the rock band but also for solo performances, which he still gives to audiences of the New Russia.

In 1969 a rock festival was organized in Yerevan; it was held annually until 1972, when the organizer was arrested for embezzlement. There were few international concerts in the 1960s and 1970s that would have enabled Soviet rock fans to see live performances: in 1967 the Rolling Stones visited Warsaw. In 1968 the planned Donovan tour was canceled because of the Soviet invasion in Prague. Between 1968 and 1970, a campaign against hippies led to arrests and the shaven heads of Soviet hippies. In 1975, Cliff Richard was the first Western pop star to visit the USSR, followed by Elton John in 1979. The latter performed the Beatles hit "Back in the USSR" at the last concert, despite official prohibition.

An important development in the acceptance of rock music was the creation of several rock musicals, with an orthodox socialist plot but rock music. In 1975 the rock opera *Orpheus and Eurydice* by Alexander Zhurbin (b. 1945) was directed by Mark Rozovsky in Leningrad. A guitar ensemble accompanied the performance that featured Orpheus as a rock star. The sound track of *Jesus Christ Superstar* was popular and performed publicly in 1973 by the band Arsenal at the Central Writers' House (TsDL) in Moscow. Arsenal had emerged from an official Soviet jazz group under the

Alexander Gradsky performs during his concert at the Central Concert Hall Rossiya, 2001. (Photo by: Alexey Kudenko/Kommersant)

saxophonist Alexei Kozlov (b. 1935). The band had performed jazz and rock music in the Molodezhnoye Café before Kozlov joined a band with Yuri Saulsky. The group continues to play to the present day, but now at the Moscow Philharmonic with a classical repertoire, providing another example of the gradual acceptance of jazz music into official culture. The composer Alexei Rybnikov (b. 1945) created the rock opera *The Death and Radiance of Joaquin Murietta*, based on Pablo Neruda's play, staged at the Moscow Theater of the Lenin Komsomol in the 1970s. His rock opera *Perchance*, based on the long poem by Andrei Voznesensky, created the megahit "I Will Never Forget You" (Ia tebia nikogda ne zabudu).

At the same time the disco wave of the 1970s hit the Soviet scene, and—strangely enough—it appealed to Soviet officials. Especially the image of John Travolta in *Saturday Night Fever*, with short hair and a tidy suit, was found attractive. The tunes of the Swedish band ABBA were popular and officially accepted. In 1978 a British company was hired to equip a number of discos in the USSR in an attempt to make the disco an attractive venue for the young generation. The Metelitsa (Blizzard) disco on Kalinin Avenue (now New Arbat) became a prototype of disco with strobe lights and mirrored walls. In 1978 the West German band Boney M was invited, although their song "Ra-Ra-Rasputin"—rhymed with love machine—was banned from the concert on 19 September. In 1977 the Soviet label Melodiya (after a deal with EMI records) released Paul McCartney's album with the Wings, "Band on the Run." The Bee Gees,

Rolling Stones, and sporadic Beatles songs were finally released on vinyl.

The 1970s saw a number of important rock groups being formed, most of which fed directly or indirectly into the rock scene of the 1990s. These were unofficial groups and they remained underground, with their members performing fake jobs as janitors and night watchmen in order not to attract the attention of the authorities as "parasites." Many Soviet rock groups imitated the Western style rather than creating and developing their own. Only in the mid-1980s did the rock groups begin to develop their own style and become more popular and more widely circulated on tapes than foreign rock bands. They now addressed issues of Soviet reality and Soviet life that mattered to their audiences.

The first major rock band was Andrei Makarevich and Mashina Vremeni (Time Machine), formed in 1968. This—unofficial—band mocked official stars, making *styob*, the satirical and parodic reference to the official canon, one of the key characteristics of rock music. Makarevich exploited similar themes to those of the bard songs but used rock language instead of a plain melody. With his stilted manner and nasal voice, he tackled issues of time and existence, remaining apolitical. Makarevich expressed an underlying indifference toward the system. The song "Battle with Fools" labeled all Soviet people fools. "Masks" asserted that the only way to be yourself was to wear a mask. In 1979 the band was taken under the wings of the state concert agency and allowed to give official concerts. It took part in the Tblisi rock festival in 1980 and won the main prize. Time Machine was the voice of youth.

In 1972 the art-rock group Vysokosnoye Leto (Leap Year Summer) formed under Alexander Sitkovetsky. Stas Namin, the grandson of a high-ranking Soviet party official, played in school and university bands in the late 1960s and 1970s before setting up the band Tsvety (Flowers), performing romantic and lyrical songs on the album *Flowers Have Eyes* (Est' glaza u tsvetov), launched by Melodiya. The band was dissolved by decree in 1975 as a hippie band, but by that time Namin had managed (as the first rocker) to join the Union of Composers. In 1978 Namin revived his group for concerts but became actively engaged in the "rock for peace" movement and later created a center for the promotion of Soviet rock that produced the band Gorky Park (1988) as a flagship for Russian rock music for the United States. Gorky Park was designed to sell Soviet rock abroad, with the symbol of a hammer and sickle and using for its name the title of Martin Cruz Smith's thriller. The metal rock group produced clips on television and gave concerts in 1988–1999 before moving to the United States. Their second album, *Moscow Calling* (1993), was not a hit, and the members of the group moved back to Russia as the group gradually fell apart.

The most significant formation of the 1970s was the band Aquarium by Boris Grebenshchikov (BG), formed in 1972. The Leningrader Grebenshchikov had indulged in Beatles songs in the 1960s and performed them in English. In forming the band Aquarium, he combined rock, theater, and Eastern philosophy. The band was named Aquarium—by analogy with the feeling of a fish in an aquarium—to convey their isolation in society. The group included Seva Gakkel, Andrei (Diushka) Romanov, and Mikhail Vasiliev (Fainstein). The instruments were unusual for a rock band, sometimes including a violin and a

Front man Boris Grebenshchikov of the Aquarium rock band is interviewed at the press conference launching the band's first DVD, *25 Years of Aquarium*, at the President Hotel, Moscow, in 2001. (Photo by Sergey Ponomarev/Kommersant)

cello. In the late 1970s the influence of Bob Dylan made itself felt, and around 1980 the band had a brief punk phase with dissonant sound. During one rock festival in Tblisi, Grebenshchikov rolled on the floor clutching his guitar while the cellist was standing above him. This was interpreted as a sexual act, and the officials left. After the Tblisi concert, BG was expelled from the Komsomol and lost his job. All the other band members began working in pro forma jobs (night watchmen) but spent their time making music. The band continually sought new ideas and experimented. They attracted several leading sax players for their albums and recorded three albums (1981–1984) with the pianist Sergei

Kuryokhin, who provided an ironic counterpoint that disappeared when he left the band.

Although at first Aquarium's lyrics reflected the typical stagnation attitude of indifference and lack of belief in any system, later lyrics were inspired by ideas taken from J. R. R. Tolkien's *Lord of the Rings*, populating the songs with gnomes and knowledge of the center of the earth. Grebenshchikov hovered between orthodox and pagan imagery, divided between anguish and hope for Russia and its potential. His moods changed from despondency to lamentation, anger to darkness. In the 1990s he increasingly turned to Eastern philosophy. Aquarium's most political song

Aquarium and Boris Grebenshchikov, "The Generation of Janitors"

The generation of janitors and night watchmen
has lost each other:
in the endless space of the earth
everybody has gone home.
In our time every third person is a hero:
they don't write articles,
they don't send telegrams.

They stand like flights of steps
when the burning oil
lashes down from one floor to the next.
And from somewhere they hear singing
Yet who am I to tell them that this is a mirage?

We were silent like fish
while everything you could think of
was up for sale
including our children.
And the poisoned rain
was pouring down into the rotting gulf
And we still watch the screen
And we still wait for the news.

And our fathers never lie to us—
they don't know how to lie,
like a wolf does not know how to eat meat,
like birds do not know how to fly . . .

Tell me what I have done to you,
why there is that pain,
which has no explanation;
it runs apparently in the blood.
But I kindled the fire myself, which is burning
   me from inside,
I digressed from the law,
but did not reach love.

But pray for us,
pray for us, if you can.
We have no hope
but this is our way.
And the voices sound nearer and louder
And may I be cursed, if this is a mirage.

—translation by Birgit Beumers

was the 1988 title "Train on Fire" (Poezd v ogne) with a video clip where the band members were dressed as revolutionary soldiers, led by the Gorbachev-type figure Colonel Vasin. Soviet history was reversed, the Revolution turned back, but at the same time the entire planet was turned upside down. Politics never remained on the level of simple satire but were always embedded in larger existential or spiritual patterns. An anthem of their generation was the song "Generation of Janitors" (Pokolenie dvornikov), which bemoaned the fate of those who once abandoned their social status for independence from a system that began to put up everything for sale, ideals and property. Indeed, the role of the rock musician as a prophet and an idol of a different alternative lifestyle had become outdated: "the generation of janitors and night watchmen have lost each other in endless space." Ultimately, they have "no hope, but this is our way." Grebenshchikov accurately described the predicament of his own role as musician and poet, whose voice became redundant in the new consumer-oriented Russia.

Musically Grebenshchikov combined Western and Soviet traditions and styles. The influence of the Beatles and Bob Dylan was clear in the 1970s songs. In 1988, BG was offered a contract by the Columbia Broadcasting System (CBS) for recording *Radio Silence*, but he returned disappointed with the album. He has written music for the films of Sergei Soloviev that have enhanced his popularity and that of the films, especially *ASSA*. Since 1998 BG gives concerts only solo or with specially assembled musicians (pick-up groups), and Aquarium has been disbanded. Grebenshchikov, although a phenomenally talented composer who has made a massive impact on Soviet and Russian rock music, has ultimately surrendered to the impossibility of matching the former unofficial underground status of his band, his status, and his lyrics with the world of commercial rock music in the New Russia. Indeed, in the 1980s when his band was officially acknowledged, he was one of the few people to be anxious about the implications of this change.

From Clampdown to Freedom (1980s)

Although many rock groups were recognized officially in rock concerts in the early 1980s, the years between the death of the head of ideology, Mikhail Suslov, in 1982 and the arrival of Mikhail Gorbachev in 1985 were three terrible years for underground culture. After Suslov's death, Konstantin Chernenko was put in charge of ideology. He attacked the lax ideological supervision and was very critical of disco sound. By 1984 he had ordered the compilation of a list of unacceptable bands. Between 1982 and 1984, numerous raids were carried out to confiscate illegal tapes and equipment. Furthermore, the political climate—under the impact of the Soviet invasion in Afghanistan and the subsequent anti-Western campaigns—had a detrimental effect on the rock scene, which became increasingly demoralized. After 1985, when Gorbachev came to power and reformed the Central Committee posts of ideology

and propaganda, the state interfered very little in musical culture. Indeed, in 1987 the Union of Composers admitted both the composer Rodion Shchedrin and the jazz musician Yuri Saulsky. Despite the initial clampdowns, the 1980s saw a proliferation of rock bands, some temporary features of the scene, others lasting well into the era of the New Russia. By the Gorbachev era, rock music had become acceptable, although it was still despised by the intellectuals and some of the party elite for the vulgarity they perceived as inherent in any form of mass culture. Soviet rock music tackled existential issues and explored the meaning of life for a generation of people who had felt indifferent to the state and society, who had marginalized themselves from that society and established for themselves an alternative (underground) lifestyle. Once this alternative style became accepted and merged into the mainstream, the special role played by many of these groups in the 1980s vanished, and those who failed to redefine themselves and find their own style disintegrated.

The influence of the bard tradition continued in the 1980s, with the popularity of Vysotsky increasing after his death. The emergence of a new bard, however, stressed once again the predominance of the word for the rock movement. The biggest rock star of the 1980s generation never performed with a band, only with his acoustic guitar; he never gave concerts beyond the scope of a theater, avoiding large arenas that were popular among the bands. Yet his voice and his songs remain treasured to the present day. Alexander Bashlachev (1960–1988) was the first rocker with authentic poetry. He led rock out of the antisocial satire mode and the styob attitude that were predominant in groups

Bashlachev, "Time for Little Bells" (Vremia kolokolchikov)

For a long time we had sultriness and frost.
All were removed and set free.
We gobbled the snow and the birch
and grew as tall as the bells.

When lamenting we did not spare salt.
When having a feast we did not spare
    gingerbread.
The bell-ringers with black blisters
pulled the nerve of the brass dynamics.

But with every day times change.
The cupolas lose their gold.
The bell-ringers loiter about the world,
The bells are broken and smashed.

What are we beating around the bush for now
like underground men in our own field.
If nobody cast us a bell
that means the time is for little bells.

The heart is ringing under the shirt.
Ravens scatter in haste, in all directions.
Hey, bring the shaft-horses out with their traces
and all their four hooves.

But how many years have the horses not been
    shod
wheels have not been oiled,
there are no lashes, the saddles are broken
and all knots undone.

But in the rain all roads are rainbows.
We are in no mood for laughter.

But if there is a little bell under the arc,
that's it. Get ready and let's go!

We whip them, whistle and urge them on,
struck to the bones, to the marrow.
Hey, brothers, can you sense with your livers
the threatening laughter of little Russian bells?

For centuries we chew the curses and the
    prayers
For centuries we live with our eyes gouged out
We sleep and drink—day by day, litre by litre
We sing no more—we are unable to . . .

We waited. We wait. Everybody was filthy.
Therefore we all looked alike.
But under the rain it turned out we were all
    different.
The majority—honest and good.

May the Big Bell be broken to pieces.
We have come with our black guitars.
Big Beat, Blues and Rock 'n' Roll
Have enchanted us with their rhythmical spell.

In our hearts—sparks of electricity
Hats in the snow. And turn up the volume!
Rock 'n' Roll is the pagan religion—
I love the time of the little bells!

—*translation by Birgit Beumers*

such as Mashina Vremeni. His song "Time of the Little Bells" (Vremia kolokolchikov) became the anthem of the rock movement. Bashlachev wrote his songs easily, drawing on pagan Russian imagery and on Russian folk rhythms (such as the pace of the troika), creating a network of emblems and symbols while taking the listener on a journey through history: not official history but that of the Russian people. His images of Russia and its people reflected a profound understanding of the spiritual strength, the vastness of space that knows no measure. In this song he advocated the need for a bell (a voice, a spokesperson), which is not available. Therefore he called for the polyphony of several bells (voices). Politically, he asserted the strength of the people as opposed to a single-person leadership while also alluding to the return to nature (*kolokolchik* is also a bluebell). Bashlachev combined poetry and rock music in a unique way. He left his hometown of Cherepovets in 1984 and performed his songs and ballads in the bard tradition, telling stories of Russia and its roots, parodying Russia's decline, and uncovering the dark pages of Stalinism and fascism. Bashlachev's song "Vaniusha" was about the resurrection of the Russian soul and typified the always optimistic and hopeful endings of his songs. He performed and traveled a great deal and married a Leningrad girl to get permission to live in Leningrad (*propiska*). He committed suicide in 1988.

Rock and Film   The cinema of the late 1980s had a huge impact on spreading rock music, offering the musicians an opportunity both for background music as well as for roles in the films. Many films featured performances of rock bands, creating, as it were, free music clips for the bands. The filmmaker Sergei Soloviev (b. 1944) made a number of films, including adaptations of classical literature and films dealing with youth problems. Particularly significant was the film *ASSA* (1988), starring figures of the Leningrad underground movement, including Sergei Bugayev, Timur Novikov, Irena Kuksenaite, Viktor Tsoy, Boris Grebenshchikov, and Zhanna Aguzarova. In *ASSA*, rock music stands in the center, offering a different, alternative lifestyle rather than being the source of destruction

and unrest, as in Iuris Podnieks's documentary *Is It Easy to Be Young?* (Legko li byt' molodym?, 1986), about the demolition of a train after a rock concert in Oger, Latvia, in July 1985. The documentary had for the first time shown a rock concert in the Soviet Union. It had explored the problems of the young generation, who were fans of the forbidden fruit of rock music, who lacked confidence, who rejected materialism, who felt they were not needed, who had no place in the society that surrounded them and could not identify with its values, who used drugs and alcohol to escape from a reality to which they had no relation, and who sought their place in life. The film did nothing outstanding by today's or Western standards, but for the Soviet Union of 1986 this was an outrageously open statement about a young generation that felt superfluous to society. The lyrics of rock music commented on the false ideals suggested by official culture and supported an escape into a dream world. The band leaders soon became role models, ideals, heroes.

The Russian rock scene had many such "heroes" to offer, and *ASSA* was not the first film to star rock musicians, but the first to show them in a positive light and as a positive influence: Valeri Ogorodnikov's *Burglar* (Vzlomshchik, 1986) had underscored the negative influence of a rock musician, inciting his younger brother to steal a synthesizer for him. Both in *Little Vera* (Malen'kaia Vera, 1988) and *Is It Easy to Be Young?* the rock concerts were crushed by the police. In this sense, *ASSA* represented a strong change in the perception of underground culture in general and rock music in particular. Bananan (played by the Leningrad artist Sergei Bugayev, known as Afrika) is a nonviolent and innately good character, who stands apart

Zhanna Aguzarova, the stunning performer who has always sought new ways to outrage and shock her audiences. (Photo by Irina Kaledina)

from the others because of his behavior and his appearance (he has one earring). He is juxtaposed to the "Soviet" official Krymov, played by the documentary film-maker Stanislav Govorukhin—a representative of the establishment—who holds power over his mistress Alika (Tatiana Drubich). He may possess the power to have Bananan killed, but Alika becomes aware of the plot and kills Krymov. Bananan is a romantic hero, who triumphs—even if in death. In the finale a concert by Viktor Tsoy takes place against all the rules and regulations, and the song "I Want Change" (Ia khochu peremen) expresses dissatisfaction with a world where happiness is possible only through escapism into a dream world.

As the Soviet Union collapsed, Sergei Soloviev set up a course at the Moscow Film Institute VGIK (Vserossiiskii gosudarstvennyi institut kinematografii, All-Russian State Institute for Cinematography) consisting of a group of students who came from Kazakhstan, including Rashid Nugmanov, Darejan Omirbaev, and Serik Aprymov, who would become the leading talents of Kazakh cinema in the 1990s. *ASSA* marked a watershed in the representation of rock music and also greatly influenced the first and most important film of the 1980s by one of Soloviev's Kazakh students: Rashid Nugmanov's *The Needle* (Igla, 1988).

Nugmanov's *Needle* was the first film to openly address the issue of drugs. As in *ASSA*, the hero—Moro—is played by a rock star: Viktor Tsoy. Moro returns to his hometown Alma-Ata to collect debts from Spartak (Alexander Bashirov), visits his former girlfriend Dina, and finds she is on drugs. He tries to get her clean, taking her to a deserted *aul* (village) by the dried-up Aral Sea. When Moro discloses the dealer's identity (the freaky doctor is played by another rock star, Petr Mamonov) and prepares to leave with Dina, he is stabbed by the dealer on a wintry road. Heroes never die, however: Moro lives on, walking down the snow-covered road with his blood leaving red dots on the white surface to the tune "Blood Type" (Gruppa krovi). The positive moral values are perpetuated as he continues to live, but only in a world of dream and escape, whereas the drug dealer triumphs in reality. Nugmanov had no illusions about reality but instilled such illusions in his viewers. In this sense he followed his teacher's solution offered in *ASSA*, where rock music offers salvation from a reality that has no room for honesty and change.

Nugmanov's film revealed not only the meaninglessness of life (drug addiction, debt collection, drug dealing) but also the

Kino and Viktor Tsoy, "Blood Type" (Gruppa krovi)

A warm place, but the streets await the stamp
   of our feet
the stardust on our boots
The soft chair, the chequered plaid, the
   cigarette put out too late.
A sunny day in blinding dreams.

   The blood group on the sleeve
   My ordinal number on the sleeve
   Wish me luck in the fight
   Wish me
   Not to remain in the grass
   Not to remain in the grass
   Wish me luck
   Wish me luck

I have money to pay but I do not want to win at
   any price

I don't want to put my foot on anyone's chest
I would like to stay with you
Simply stay with you
But a star high up in the sky guides me onto
   my way.

   The blood group on the sleeve
   My ordinal number on the sleeve
   Wish me luck in the fight
   Wish me
   Not to remain in the grass
   Not to remain in the grass
   Wish me luck
   Wish me luck

—translation by Birgit Beumers

barrenness of the land, symbolizing the absence of a future. If there is a future, it lies on the snow-covered road that leads to the land of illusions and dreams. *The Needle* also raised the issue of country and city: life in the city is corrupt and flawed. It is in the desert by the Aral Sea that Dina comes clean and finds her way back to Moro. Urban civilization may mean progress, but purity lies in a return to one's roots. Soloviev inspired his pupils to address the problems of the young generation and, in putting their faith in rock stars, to express dissent with the system.

Moscow Rock The 12th International Youth Festival was held in Moscow in 1985 and had an effect similar to that of the youth festival of 1957: many Western rock stars, including Udo Lindenberg and Bob Dylan, visited the USSR and influenced the domestic rock scene. In 1986 Melodiya finally released the first Beatles album in the USSR. In October 1986 the band UB40 gave a concert in Moscow, and numerous visits by Western pop and rock stars followed during the glasnost years. Moreover, domestic rock music was also recognized and officially distributed, and in 1987 Melodiya released the first Aquarium album. The West's interest in Russian rock was equally great, however, and thus Artemy Troitsky's book on the rock movement in the USSR was first published in English in 1987, and the American producer Joanna Stingray released the first major collection of Soviet rock (the album *Red Waves*) in 1986.

The rock scene in Moscow developed during the late 1980s and fed into the formation of the musical taste of the audiences for both pop and rock music. Although Moscow was the center for music production and business, the Leningrad rock scene brought forth the more experimental and innovative groups, maybe less popular with large audiences but appreciated by music lovers. The rock scene in Moscow gradually gathered around various clubs and concert halls, but mainly the Gorbunov House of Culture (DK Gorbunova) in the northwest of Moscow. Most famous rock groups gave concerts there and do so to the present day. Moreover, a market developed around the concert hall for the trade of musical releases. Many of these were pirated copies, and there is a historical reason for such widespread piracy. The official prohibition of rock and jazz music in the 1960s and 1970s had led to a homegrown, illegal production of records ("on the bones") and tapes (magnitizdat). Most of these tapes were not only traded for money but also exchanged for other recordings in the 1960s and 1970s, and this pattern laid the foundation for the production and distribution of rock albums in the same way. In any case, only the state, which had initially forbidden their official release, was losing money in this operation. Rock bands would record their albums and release them on tape, often supplying insufficient copies to satisfy demand, and pirates copied the tapes and later the CDs to satisfy the demand and sell their releases at lower prices. This business spread substantially in the mid-1990s, when the park around the Gorbunov House transformed into a video and audio market. Films suffered the same fate of being copied illegally and sold at a lower price on the Gorbushka. The concept of pirated products preventing the producer (and the band) from recouping the money invested in the release was alien for the ex-Soviet "consumer," who was used to dealing only with the state as producer, supplier, and distributor. And there was no harm perceived in deceiving the state, hence the blooming "shadow economy" in the Soviet era, where a minimal segment of the production sector was private, yet produced more steadily than the state-run enterprises (for example, vegetable produce from private gardens). The clampdown on videopiracy began when the American Motion Picture Association complained to the World Trade Organization, as it was losing large sums of money through the illegal distribution of U.S. films. Piracy of computer programs continues, as does piracy of music. The Gorbushka moved from the open-air park to the former television factory Rubin in 2002 and now sells largely licensed VHSs and DVDs. The range of CDs available at the Gorbushka is huge, but the percentage of pirated disks is probably still more than half of the products on offer at the market.

Initially, a number of bands populated the Moscow rock scene. The group Cruise was one of the first hard rock bands, formed in 1979 under a VIA. Voskresenie (Sunday), set up in 1979 with ex-members of Mashina Vremeni, performed many bard songs, exploiting the theme of the lyrical hero who, despite a hard life, has not been broken by the system. Both bands disintegrated in the 1980s when their "underground" themes were no longer in demand and became part of official discourse.

The art-rock group Avtograf (Autograph) was formed in 1979 with members from the band Vysokosnoye Leto (see above) with Alexander Sitkovetsky and the sax player Sergei Mazayev. It won second place at the Tbilisi rock festival in 1980. The band was very popular in the 1980s and became especially well known as the first Russian band to participate in the concert Live Aid for Africa in July 1985, with two songs broadcast live to the concert arena. They also took part in the benefit concert for the victims of Chernobyl on 30 May 1986 in the Olympic Stadium Moscow, run under the title "Account 904" and organized by Alla Pugacheva and the rock critic Artemy Troitsky. Avtograf turned to pop rock in the late 1980s and produced an album in the United States (*Stone Border*, [Kamennyi krai], 1990). Soon after it dispersed in the United States, but most of its members returned to Russia later. The role of rock bands in the peace movement of the 1980s was a very important one, and it fed into the official political agenda of the new Soviet leadership that sought nuclear disarmament.

A massive impact, however, was made by the new groups formed in the mid-1980s. The group Bravo, established in 1983, is one such example. Bravo's leader, Yevgeni Khavtun, was looking for a lead singer when he was contacted by a woman called Ivana Anders from Moscow, who had an extravagant performance style. Ivana claimed to reside in a large apartment of her diplomat parents in central Moscow while they were working abroad. A year later Ivana was the star singer of the group, but she was arrested for falsifying documents and imprisoned for eight months with a period of "exile" in her Siberian hometown near Novosibirsk. In order not to be labeled a "provincial" girl and to avoid problems with a Moscow residence permit (*propiska*), Zhanna Aguzarova had "borrowed" the passport of a friend, Ivan Anders, after having failed to enter the Moscow Theater Institute (which would have given her the right to reside in Moscow), since she was deemed too capricious, with likely bouts of laziness and excesses of stardom. Aguza-

rova impressed with her colored hair, her miniskirts and trouser suits, and a variety of costumes and makeups she created for herself. Bravo's music was easy-going and stylish, and the rest of the band was well dressed, so that it was quite distinct from the other underground rock bands. The song "Yellow Shoes" (1984) was a megahit, as were other tunes from the first Bravo album. As an innovative and stunning performer, Zhanna was always seeking new ways to outrage and shock her audiences. She left the band in 1989 for a solo career, and Bravo hired Irina Yepifanova as their lead singer. Aguzarova spent several years in the United States with the band Nighty Nighties and upon her return to Russia in 1996 turned toward techno music. She performs regularly and remains one of the top singers of the new Russian pop and rock scene.

Heavy metal music was represented by the band Ariya (Aria, 1984), organized on the basis of the VIA Singing Hearts (Poiushchie serdtsa) under Viktor Bekstein. Its album *Megalo-Mania* (Maniia velichiia) sounded pretty much like the tunes of the Iron Maidens. The band underwent several substantial changes and crises in the late 1980s, turning to simplified and American-style tunes. They continued to perform in the 1990s with successful concert tours and new albums, and their popularity rose substantially with their image-maker and sponsor, Harley Davidson. The hit "Carefree Angel" (Bespechnyi angel) served as a promotion tune for the motorcycle design.

The band Crematorium (1983) was organized by the Moscow students Armen Grigorian and Viktor Troyegubov. At first they played tunes with existential themes, and the song "Koma" made them widely known, with the clip "Waste Wind" (Musornyi veter) shown on the television youth programme *Vzgliad*. They have since released a range of albums and remain one of the most popular rock bands in the New Russia, with regular concert tours. Va Banque (1986) was founded by Alexander Skliar in Moscow, playing hard orthodox rock and punk. Skliar's hoarse voice lent itself to that type of music. The band toured in the late 1980s, both within Russia and beyond, and recorded an album in English. They experimented with the creative process, recording the album *na kukhne* literally "in the kitchen," with an accidental accordionist picked up in an underground passage participating in the improvised play. The hit "Black Flag" (Chernoe znamia) bemoans the deception of the Russian simple man by the authorities in a parable where bandits, stealing the black flag, betray the people while they are being watched by a commissar and a general. The song effectively deploys an accordion to underscore the gypsy and folk tunes that form the basic melody for the song. Thus the text strips the situation of the Russian people by parodically using a Russian folk tune, as if the predicament of the people were normal. A further example of the parodic use of conventions is the association of spring not with bright colors and romantic feelings but with the drunken housekeeper sweeping the courtyard ("Spring" [Vesna]). Demonstrating once again the close relationship between text and music in Russian rock music, they released an album in 1999, entitled *Lower Tundra* (Nizhniaia tundra), inspired by the fashionable and popular postmodernist writer Viktor Pelevin.

The group Mongol Shuudan may not be one of the most popular rock groups in Russia but has reached a wide international audience with their participation in Sergei Bodrov's film *I Wanted to See Angels* (Ia khotela uvidet' angelov, Russia/United States, 1992). The band was formed around Valeri Skoroded and Igor Toropov in 1988. Mongol Shuudan plays anarchic rock and thus occupies a rare niche in the Moscow rock scene. Moreover, they combine rock compositions with folk intonation and quotations from Cossack songs or ditties from the period of the civil war. Their hero is Batka Makhno, a rock hero and Cossack chief, whose story is told to racy rock melodies with jazz saxophone interludes, parodying the heroic narrative.

A phenomenon exclusive to the Moscow scene is the appearance of performers. Petr Mamonov is the best example of such a performer. A Moscow street urchin, he was brought up in the same area as Vladimir Vysotsky, on Karetnyi Riad. Without completing his education, he tried a number of jobs and careers, but failed. In 1982 he began to write songs and perform them in a sexy and obscene, aggressive manner. In these songs Mamonov recounts his own life. In 1983 he formed the band Zvuki Mu (Sounds of Mu, where Mu stands for the first two letters of "music" or as the "mooing" of cows), sponsored and organized by the bored son of the general secretary's official English interpreters, Sasha Lipnitsky. In 1988 Mamonov debuted as an actor in Nugmanov's cult film *The Needle*, and his acting continued in a number of top films of the 1990s. His musical illiteracy makes the songs sound unlike the typical tunes of the rock scene, which led Brian Eno to choose this group for a recording in 1987. The songs witness the hero's lack of involvement with reality (for example, "Soviet Press"). In the 1990s Mamonov released further albums as Mamonov and Alexei, having abandoned Zvuki Mu. At the

Actor and rock musician Petr Mamonov performs in the stage play *Pushkin of Chocolate*, staged in the Stanislavsky theater, 2001. (Photo by Dmitry Lekay/Kommersant)

same time he began to perform on the stage of the Stanislavsky Theater, where the productions *Bald Brunet* (Lysyi briunet), based on a play by Dana Gink (published in English), and *Nobody Writes to the Lieutenant* (Polkovniku nikto ne pishet) allowed his stage talent to develop to the full. His eccentric antics provide the driving force for the productions, which are essentially shows of Mamonov, only with an underlying dramatic text. This dramatic foundation was abandoned in the show *Is There Life on Mars?* (Est' li zhizn na Marse?) and subsequent shows of Mamonov staged at the Stanislavsky Theater, which draw a full house.

Another performer is Igor (Garik) Suka-chev. He initially formed the band Brigada S (1986) and established his bandit-like conduct as the group's leader. In the mid-1990s Sukhachev formed the group Botsman i Brodyaga (Boatswain and Vagrant, 1995–1996) for a project with Alexander Skliar, in order to create an album of the favorite songs of Soviet times, including songs composed by Vysotsky and Utesov. At around the same time he disbanded Brigada S and created the band Neprikasa-yemye (Untouchables). More important is Sukachev's input into the cultural scene with his films *Midlife Crisis* (Krizis sred-nego vozrasta, 1997) and the autobiographical account of his childhood, *The Holiday* (Prazdnik, 2001).

Rock band Agatha Christie performs on the stage of Luzhniki Sports Complex. The 2003 concert marked the band's fifteenth anniversary. (Photo by Ilya Pitalev/Kommersant)

Numerous bands arrived on the Moscow (and Petersburg) stage from the provinces in the late 1980s and 1990s. The Urals proved a genuine cradle of rock music: Alexander Bashlachev came from there, and the city of Sverdlovsk represented a vibrant center. Indeed, the composer Alexander Pantykin played an important role in this development, not only as leader and founder of the band Urfin Dzhuis (Urphin Juice), which earned him the title Granddad of Ural rock (dedushka Uralskogo roka), but also subsequently as a composer and producer of rock music. Pantykin as-sisted in the discovery and promotion of young regional talents with his recording studio and the record label Tutti Records. Thus, Pantykin helped the group Nautilus Pompilius to record their first album long before they moved to Petersburg.

The band Agata Kristi (Agatha Christie, 1985) emerged from the Urals with an album *Second Front* (Vtoroi front, 1988) that mixed postpunk with elements of chamber music. The group, like so many of the 1980s, represented the indifference and nonconformism of their generation. In the 1990s they moved to Moscow, where they were produced by Sergei Lisovsky's company, and released the album *Opium* (1992). Further albums that followed indicate the band's move toward more psychedelic pop. Of the album *Main Kaif* (parodying Hitler's *Mein Kampf* with the substitution of *kaif*, meaning pleasure) in 2000, only the song "Secret" made it onto radio. Although Agata Kristi remain popular, they produce sombre and heavy music where the sound drowns the melodies.

The group ChaiF (1984) also stems from Sverdlovsk. The title of the band combines the word *chai* (tea) and kaif (pleasure, high). It was established by Vladimir Shakhrin and Vladimir Begunov, who initially composed songs for themselves before they gave stage performances with drum and trumpet accompaniment to their guitars. Gradually, the group expanded and presented a tour of a dynamic rock show. By 1992 they had reached national fame with their Beatles-style songs that invited the audience to join into the refrain and that abstained from the parodic and satirical tones of many other rock bands. ChaiF's "Don't Hurry" (Ne speshi) reminds people to enjoy life, and the hit "17" is a romantic song where the singer reminds his wife of the days when they were young (when she was 17) and promises to do the same things he used to do for her when they were first in love: buy flowers and write songs. Thanks to their melodic tunes and the universal and general themes tackled in the songs, ChaiF enjoys wide popularity among all ages.

Sektor Gaza was formed in Voronezh in 1987 by Yuri Klinsky. It followed the punk style of the Sex Pistols but created more melodic songs that were "punk for the people." Their use of slang and vulgar language (especially in the album *Gas Attack* [Gazo-

vaia ataka]) made their songs rare on radio, from which they were censored. The group disbanded in 2000 when Klinsky died of cardiac arrest.

Leningrad Rock   In Leningrad the rock club on 13 Rubinstein Street, formed in 1981, became the chief venue for new rock bands to appear. Indeed, in many ways the "northern capital" overtook Moscow in the number and proliferation of rock bands, and festivals were held largely in the Caucasian capitals Yerevan and Tbilisi in the 1970s and 1980s, and later in the Baltic republics, thus away from the tight control exercised in Moscow. The Leningrad café Saigon (on the corner of Nevsky Prospekt and Liteinyi Avenue) served as a major meeting place and later as the main music store. In the late 1990s the shop was closed, and the building converted into the Radisson SAS Hotel.

The group Zoopark (Zoo, 1981), formed by Mikhail "Maik" Naumenko (1955–1991), became an immediate success at the rock club. Naumenko was the ideal rock star hero, following the street aesthetics of Vladimir Vysotsky and creating the image of the gentle rebel. He broached formerly taboo themes in his songs, such as the issue of sex, best illustrated in his song "Sweet N" (Sladkaia N), which openly addressed a debauched lifestyle that included prostitution and alcoholism. Naumenko and Zoopark gave numerous concerts in Leningrad and beyond the city, but sadly the group dissolved with the untimely death of Naumenko.

Another tragic rock hero was Viktor Tsoy (1961–1990). He played in various bands while a student at a design and craft school (having been thrown out of the Art Academy after an "ideological" conflict),

Zoopark and Mikhail Naumenko, "Sweet N" (Sladkaia N)

I woke up in the morning, in my clothes,
in an armchair in my closet within my own four
   walls.
I waited till dawn for you to come,
and wonder Sweet N where you spent the
   night.

I washed and brushed my teeth,
thought about it, but decided not to shave.
I stepped outside and followed my nose,
it was light outside and the day had begun.

And on the bridge I met a man
who told me that he knew me.
He had a rouble, and I had four,
and therefore we bought two bottles of wine.

And he took me to the strangest place,
Where people were dancing so the house was
   rocking
Where people were drinking cocktails and
   played dice
And nobody thought about what would happen
   after.

It was a typical attic scene
from two speakers wafted Bach.
Everyone thought of his own affairs
one about six billion*, the other about six
   roubles.

*world population

And someone as always was babbling about
   flying saucers
and someone as always was preaching about
   Zen,
but I sat like a statue and wondered stupidly
where you spent the night, Sweet N.

Not sharing the general high spirits
I forgot myself and sipped rum in the armchair
People came and went
And again couriers were sent shopping

The ladies were particularly polite,
and one tried to capture me
I was silent in the corner and wondered myself
where you spent the night, Sweet N.?

I was angry at myself, angry at the evening
and could only find my boot with difficulty.
And although I was asked to stay
I decided to leave although I could have stayed.

And when I came home, you were asleep
But I did not wake you up to have an argument
   with you.
I thought to myself: "Is it really that important
   with whom and where
you spent the night, my Sweet N?"

—*translation by Birgit Beumers*

before forming a duo in 1982 with Alexei Rybin. Their songs echoed the thirst for love of a generation that felt unwanted, and the attempts to make sarcastic comments led only to tender and understanding notes. In 1984 Rybin and Tsoy were joined by Yuri Kasparian, Alexander Titov, and Yuri Gurianov to form Kino. Their 1984 album *Captain of the Kamchatka* (Nachal'nik Kamchatki) became an instant success. Tsoy's technique of evenly pronouncing the words meant that every word was clear, but it also struck the audience as a laconic statement. The notes of loneliness and despair still underlay the songs' melodies. Kino continued its massive suc-

The rock star and actor Viktor Tsoy, whose premature death in 1990 turned him into a genuine rock legend in Russia and abroad. (Henry Diltz/Corbis)

cess, and Tsoy appeared in the films *ASSA* and *The Needle*. The song "Blood Group" accompanied the final scene of *The Needle* when the knightlike Moro wandered off into the other world, having failed to realize his noble aims in this world. The tune "I Want Change" ended Soloviev's film *ASSA* (1988), where the alternative hippie lifestyle represented in the film by the character of Bananan finally triumphs—albeit after Bananan's destruction by the current, prevailing system—in a semi-forbidden concert. Tsoy died in a car accident while on holiday in the Latvian Baltic Sea resort Jurmala. His premature death turned him into a genuine rock legend in Russia and abroad.

The group Auktsyon (1983) emerged from a series of attempts by Leonid Fyodorov to form a band at the Polytechnic Institute in Leningrad. Eventually he teamed up with the poet and DJ Oleg Garkusha and formed Auktsion (Auction), a band that played postpunk and new wave music. Later they became influenced by the ethnic music of southern Europe and Central Asia. The group's name was once misspelled as Auktsyon and thus they arrived at their current name. They played, like so many bands, in the Leningrad rock club, with visually striking performances of the absurd texts of Garkusha. Their costumes were designed by the hip Leningrad designer Kirill Miller ("Killer Miller"). Their albums, released from 1987 onward, sold well. In the early 1990s they worked with the émigré poet Alexei Khvostenko for their albums *Kettle of Wine* (Chainik vina, 1992) and *Lodger of Heights* (Zhilets vershin, 1995), with the latter drawing on the experimental poetry of the 1920s writer Velimir Khlebnikov. Again, a rock band drew on "high" Russian culture and the literary traditions of the early twentieth century for its lyrics. In the latter half of the 1990s, the band became less active, and Fyodorov produced the band Leningrad.

In Leningrad in 1983, Sviatoslav Zaderny formed the band Alisa that, until 1985, lacked a successful lead singer; Zaderny found such a singer in Konstantin Kinchev from Moscow. The band immediately landed a hit with "My Generation" (Moe pokolenie), which became a youth anthem. The song bemoaned the reduction of an entire generation to silent witnesses of their time, who feared the light and lived withdrawn in the underground. Such a gloomy view of life in Russia is typical of Kinchev. Alisa alluded to the world of Lewis Car-

Alisa and Konstantin Kinchev, "My Generation" (Moe pokolenie)

2013 moons
are given to the absurd game.
The light of passing stars
is still light.
It's so difficult to believe in your path
from this wall to that wall.
Answer!
Did you hear me or not?

Unfortunately I am weak
as the witness to the events on the Bald Hill.
I can foresee,
but cannot foretell.
But if you suddenly see
my eyes in your window
then know
that I have come to disturb your sleep.

  This is my generation standing silent in the
  corners
    my generation dares not sing,
    my generation feels the pain
    but again puts itself under the lash.
    My generation looks down,
    my generation fears the day,
    my generation cherishes the night,
    and devours itself in the mornings.

A blue-green day
rose, once the thunderstorm was over.
What an amazing event,

but we miss it.
It's so difficult for you to make up your mind,
  you are used
to weighing up the pros and cons.
Understand
I give you a chance.

It is my job to be alive,
it's a cheek, but it runs in the blood.
I know how to read in the clouds the names
of those who know how to fly.
If ever
you feel the pulse of great love
know
I have come to help you get up!

  This is my generation standing silent in the
  corners
    my generation dares not sing,
    my generation feels the pain
    but again puts itself under the lash.
    My generation looks down,
    my generation fears the day,
    my generation cherishes the night,
    and devours itself in the mornings.

Hey, generation, answer.
Can you hear me? Can you hear me?
I am here.

—*translation by Birgit Beumers*

roll's *Alice in Wonderland* and parodied Western rock music with inclusions of Russian folk elements. Kinchev offered a powerful requiem to Alexander Bashlachev with the album *The End* (Shabash). Alisa continued to release albums during the 1990s and remained very popular. Their musical styles moved from hard rock to disco and techno sounds, and thematically the lyrics revealed an increasing preoccupation with spiritual elements, not unlike the development of Grebenshchikov. Around the same time as Alisa, Mike Borzykin formed his group Televizor (1984), beginning like so many groups in the Leningrad rock club. Borzykin had the

Televizor, "Get out of Control" (Vyiti)

We were watched from the days of kinder-
  garten
Sweet aunties and kind uncles found our soft
  spots
And hit us there as if we were their livestock.
So we grew up as an obedient herd
We sing what they want, we live like they want
We look up to them with the eyes of slaves
We watch them beating us up . . .

> Get out of control
> Get out—and sing what you feel
> Not what is allowed—
> We have a right to yell!
> Get out of control
> Get out of these walls!
> Get out—we were born to be free
> Get out and fly!

We have become sly, have learnt how to hide,
and new aunties, new uncles
look into our eyes and pat our heads
asking us to disappear into the lower depths.
But we stand, we are sick of falling down,
tell us: what for?
Who are we? Who provokes our bad dreams?
Here we are, not easy to get on with.
Hide the birches—there are not enough for
  everybody.
Today ten, tomorrow twenty.
That's the way it was, that's the way it will be.

—translation by Birgit Beumers

reputation of being a difficult child, which lent itself to the formation of the image of an egocentric and lonely rocker. He continually broke rules and taboos, and an underlying pessimism resounded from his songs and themes of teenage frustration dominated his early work. In 1986 two songs were forbidden for concert performance (but played nevertheless). "Get out of Control" (Vyiti) dealt with the supervision of every aspect of daily life by the Soviet system and supported the need to break free to "get out of these walls." Of course, any censorship intervention in the mid-1980s raised the profile of a group, and performance despite the prohibition made Televizor the leading band in the mid-1980s. In another song they condemned the Stalinist generation and the system that still overshadowed the present, creating—following the model of Bashlachev—a parallel between fascism and Stalinism in the song "Your Father Is a Fascist" (Tvoi papa fashist). The band was barred from performing in Moscow until the summer of 1988, very late into the Gorbachev period.

The Leningrad scene fed on its own amateur rock bands, but a number of bands from the provinces also moved to that city rather than to Moscow. Yuri Shevchuk was born and raised in Ufa (Bashkortostan) and formed a band there in the early 1980s, with whom he participated in a number of festivals. In 1987 he moved to Leningrad after the authorities in Ufa forbade further performances of his group. He instantly formed a new group around him, called DDT, and also found a musical style leaning toward hard rock, but using both violinists and saxophonists. Shevchuk's lyrics were imbued with social concerns. "I Got This Role" (Ia poluchil etu rol') became the

Yuri Shevchuk, leader of the DDT rock group at a jubilee concert of his group at the Olympic Sport Complex, 2000. (Photo by Dmitry Lebedev/Kommersant)

new anthem of the rock movement. Shevchuk followed in many ways the traditions of Vysotsky: a concern for social ills, the hoarse and emotionally charged voice, and a love for Russia and her past informed his songs. The album *Actress Spring* (Aktrisa vesna, 1992) revealed a mixture of Russian folk and rock styles. As the 1990s moved on, and the need for a voice of opposition gave way to a voice that entertained, Shevchuk became less angry and challenging and more disillusioned with the role of a rock poet in the New Russia. Although DDT continues as a band, he has, in many ways, suffered a fate of marginalization from the mainstream similar to that of Grebenshchikov.

The other "migrant" group was the band Nautilus Pompilius, formed in 1978 by Via-cheslav Butusov and Dmitri Umetsky in Sverdlovsk, who made their first album in 1982 with Alexander Pantykin. The lyrics written for the group by Ilia Kormiltsev represented a poetic world that was most suitable for Butusov's fragile melodies. After some years of performing, Butusov dissolved the group and moved to Petersburg, where he reinvented Nautilus in 1990. The following albums had a huge success in Russia and beyond, developing a style of guitar-based rock compositions for lyrics that dealt with the fragility of human life and that did not necessarily possess any political or social resonance. By 1997 the band had disintegrated, however, and although the albums *Yablokitai*, recorded in London with electric music by Bill Nelson, and *Atlantida* still carried the name of the

Viacheslav Butusov with his new band Ju-Piter performing on the stage of the B-2 Club in Moscow in 2004. (Photo by Alexey Kudenko/Kommersant)

band, they were recorded by Butusov with free-lance musicians. A genuine experimenter, Butusov continues to compose music and has collaborated with the band DeadUshki (literally "dead ears," or phonetically "dedushki," grandfathers, formed in 1998), which creates electronic music. Butusov features prominently in Alexei Balabanov's blockbuster *Brother*, where the opening of the film captures the hero stumbling onto the set where the clip "Wings" (Kryl'ia) is being shot. He gets beaten up and continues his search for the latest album of "Nau" throughout the film, at one point accidentally walking into a party at Butusov's flat. The song explores the fragility of the human soul but uses the image of wings that allow man to fly and that have been removed from man's back,

leaving a scar. The crippled individual, unable to "fly," is condemned to a profane existence, so unlike Viktor Tsoy's lines that allow man to step with ease into the skies, guided by the "star high up in the sky" and still carrying "stardust on our boots." Butusov's lyrical heroes are condemned to a sullen existence in the New Russia.

Pop Culture

Rock Meets Pop

The rock movement of the 1980s continued well into the 1990s. Some bands lost their voice of opposition, unable to find a role in a society that no longer relied on the underground to spell out truths. Others established themselves with a particular musical

Nautilus Pompilius, "Wings" (Kryl'ia)

You are taking off your evening dress, standing
with your face to the wall.
I can see the fresh scars on your spine which
is as soft as velvet.
I want to cry with pain, or forget myself in a
dream.
Where are your wings which I liked so much?

Where are your wings which I liked so much?
Where are your wings which I liked so much?

Some time ago we used to have time, now we
have things to do:
To prove that the strong gobble up the weak, to
prove that soot is white.
We have all lost something in this senseless
war,
By the way—Where are your wings which I
liked so much?

Where are your wings which I liked so much?
Where are your wings which I liked so much?

I don't ask how much money you have, or how
many men,
I see that you are afraid of open windows and
upper floors,
And if tomorrow there is a fire and the whole
building is in flames,
We will die without those wings which I liked
so much.

Where are your wings which I liked so much?
Where are your wings which I liked so much?

—translation by Birgit Beumers

style, from punk to hard rock, techno, and jazz. At the same time, rock music had now become official and moved into the public arena, thereby mixing with popular music.

Boys and Girls (1990s) A new phenomenon occurred of managers and producers launching and promoting rock bands. The composer Igor Matvienko launched a project with the vocalist Nikolai Rastorguyev and formed the group Liube (1989) after a successful concert in Izmailovo. He promoted the band through an album and a film (*Liube Zone*, [Zona Liube, 1994]). At concerts the group presented itself in black T-shirts and checked trousers, playing a heavy and loud pop and folk mix. The image of the band, and indeed their name, drew on the youth gang "liubery," named after the Moscow work-

ing-class suburb Liubertsy. The "liubery" manifested a harsh opposition to Western influence (unattainable to them financially), not unlike the skinheads. Liube hits included the song "Makhno" (1988), which drew on Cossack-style tunes. For the hit "Atas," they created a stage image in military uniforms of the 1940s for a lyrical and humorous song that contributed to their image as a neofascist band.

Another novelty for the 1990s was the emergence of girls' bands. Although the rock scene had been largely male dominated, with women taking their place on the lighter estrada stage, several girl bands were formed. The first and most successful was the band Kolibri from Leningrad/St. Petersburg, organized as a musical and aesthetic project by Natalia Pivovarova in 1988. Together with Yelena Yudanova and

Inna Volkova, Pivovarova formed a trio that performed hits of the 1950s, accompanied by the sax player from DDT, Mikhail Chernov. In 1990 the trio was joined by Irina Sharovatova and called itself Kolibri. The song "Yellow Autumn Leaf" (Zheltyi list osennii) became an instant hit, establishing the style of the band with a decadent, sentimental note, without however abandoning the satirical and parodic touches (styob) so typical of the Soviet rock movement. The lyrics were concerned with love and female secrets. In 1999 Pivovarova left the band for a solo career, indeed taking a short stint at directing a play. The group Litsei (Lyceum, 1992) also started off with three girls, one of them the daughter of Andrei Makarevich, Anastasia. Dressed in jeans and sneakers, they offered a repertoire of harmonized and melodious songs, composed and produced by Makarevich. The most successful girls' band was Strelki (Arrows, 1998), which was formed, like Liube, by a producer and composer who selected the girls with a specific project in mind. Their songs "Ma Mummy" (Mamochka mamulia) and "You Ditched Me" (Ty brosil menia) became hits among a largely teenage audience. The trio ViaGra was formed originally in Kiev in 2001, when the group had a clip shown on Biz TV. Under a powerful Moscow producer, they soon signed a contract with Sony and received the Ovation award. The trio, with changing singers, but always consisting of a blonde, a redhead, and a brunet, draw heavily on their sex appeal, sporting short skirts and using the nurse-look to enhance their erotic appearance.

After the success of the girl band, the boy band followed suit. A-Studio, a band from Almaty (hence A-studio), had worked as an orchestra for the Kazakh singer Rosa Rymbaeva since 1981 before venturing on their own pop and jazz tunes with Eastern influences in 1987. In 1989, "Julia" became a hit, followed by successful albums in the early 1990s. The band dissolved in 2000. A greater resonance was achieved by the project of Bari Alibasov with the group NaNa (1994). They were the first boy group to perform in the Hard Rock Café in New York, building their performances on choreographed dance acts. Alibasov formed the group by competition and casting, recruiting Vladimir Levkin, Vladimir Asimov, Vladimir Politov, and Viacheslav Zherebkin for the band while he managed the group. The emphasis was less on song than on stage performance, as the group was modeled on the Beatles with a neat appearance and a groomed hairstyle. An element of eroticism had become an integral part of show business, and NaNa was soon accused of promoting itself as a gay band.

Ivanushki International (1995) was another youth project launched by Igor Matvienko (who had also launched Liube). He recruited the dancer and singer Andrei Grigoriev-Apollonov from Sochi and matched him with a singer and actor from Moscow, Igor Sorin, to form a group. In 1996 they launched their debut album of techno dance music and in order to achieve maximum publicity resorted to free concerts in Moscow schools. Their video clips were successfully shown on the major music channels, and Ivanushki became very popular among a teenage audience.

Although in Moscow music became more and more a business and bands were assembled to meet the needs of a producer, the Petersburg scene relied on organic formations. The band Tequilajazzz (1991) brought together Yevgeni Fyodorov, Konstantin Fyodorov, and Alexei Voronov. They played heavy guitar music largely for

The pop group Ivanushki International performs during the celebration of the group's fifth birthday at the Olympic Sports Center in 2001. (Photo by Sergey Mikheev/Kommersant)

club performances, becoming gradually more melodic and more appealing. They have composed music for the theater and have recorded two albums with Kolibri. The band Chizh and Co. (1993) under Sergei Chigrakov (Chizh) is characterized by his falsetto voice and guitar play. Chizh recorded his first album with support from Petersburg musicians. His songs are autobiographical and deal with contemporary life. Chizh is extremely prolific. His 1997 album *Bombers* (Bombardirovshchiki), with the song "Tanks Thundered in the Fields"

(Na pole tanki grokhotali), was the bestselling album of the year. The song mockingly tells the story of a war and makes pointed references to the ongoing Chechen war. Korol i Shut (King and Jester, 1989) represented punk music in its early days and launched its first album only in 1996, presenting frightening stories in their lyrics set to dynamic rock music. Their songs have caught on with audiences and are frequently played on radio. Ruki Vverkh (Hands Up, 1997) is a dance band originally from Saratov, formed by the duo Sergei

Zhukov and Andrei Potekhin. The song "Little Boy" (Malysh) included the voice of a little boy and turned into a major hit. Another discovery from the provinces was the band Mumii Troll (Mummy Troll) formed in Vladivostok in 1979 by Igor Lagutenko. After work placements in China and London, Lagutenko recorded his debut album in London in 1996 and gained attention with his rhythmic and melodic provocative punk. His songs became hits and were played on the radio in the late 1990s. Lagutenko started to promote young talent, among others Zemfira. His band was nominated to represent Russia in the Eurovision Song Contest 2001 with "Lay Alpine Blues" and took twelfth place. He has recently written the music for Leonid Rybakov's debut film, *Book Stealers* (Pokhititeli knig, 2004).

The American-based band Bering Strait was formed in the mid-1990s by a group of teenagers from Obninsk, Siberia, who traveled to Nashville, Tennessee, and began performing a Russian-inspired form of country music. Natasha Borzilova and Lydia Salnikova play the guitar and keyboard and perform the vocals in the band, and Ilia Toshinsky, Alexander Ostrovsky, Alexander Arzamastsev, and Sergei Olkhovsky provide the musical accompaniment. Bering Strait is popular in the United States, where the band has released its records with Universal, although it remains obscure in Russia.

Pop and Scandal   After boy bands and girl bands, the turn came for scandals to create publicity for groups. Zapreshchennye barabanshchiki (The Forbidden Drummers) were the discovery of 1999 with the song "A Killed Negro" (Ubili negra). The band from Rostov indeed initially consisted of drummers who were joined by an orchestra and arrived in Moscow in 1997. They play rock with interesting rhythm changes, introducing a samba rhythm for "A Killed Negro," telling the story of a Negro who is not playing basketball and not dancing hip hop, using clichés of the Negro to establish that he is dead while the refrains express outrage that he has been murdered. He is then revived by a healer and returns as a zombie. The text is mocked by its pronunciation with a seemingly foreign accent. This creates a slow and monotonous recital of the words that lends them a deadpan tone while telling the story of the killed Negro with a mockingly low-key refrain "oi oi oi."

Even more outrageous are the texts of the Petersburg folk-punk band Leningrad founded in 1997 by Sergei Shnurov (Shnur) with some members of Tequilajazzz. The band's lyrics are full of extremely vulgar language, parodying the establishment while offering melodic rock tunes for the musical ear. The song "Sluts" (Bliadi) is a good example of the vulgar texts produced by the group. The song tells the story of a man who is looking for a warm place for his penis ("tolko khui rabotaet / khochetsia emu tepla / khot odna by mne dala"), appealing to the sluts to help out this "uncle" (diadia). Another song, Paedos (Pidarasy), deals with the dull life in town, leaving sexual aberration as the only way out for the lyrical hero. Leningrad's texts may be spoofs of contemporary pop groups or established rock bands. Thus, they have recorded parodies of Zemfira and even of the Kino hit "Blood Type." Because of their obscene language they have been banned by Moscow's mayor from playing concerts in the city, although they have appeared in several rock clubs (B2 and Jao Ja). The vulgarity of their texts, combined with a dead-pan, folksy rendering, makes their songs not unlike those of the London-based Tiger Lillies.

The preoccupation with sexuality, straight and otherwise, is one of the key factors in the contemporary Russian rock scene to model the image of a group and promote it in the mass media. The homosexual theme was alluded to by NaNa, although they did not deliberately stage homoerotic performances. Gosti iz Budushchego (Guests from the Future, 1998), organized by the composer Yuri Usachev with his singing partner Eva Polsna (who is half Polish), were initially concerned with their pop and rave songs, arranged for them by the top Russian DJ, Groove. "Run from Me" (Begi ot menia, 1999) became a hit, however, largely because of the clip where Eva features along with another girl. Moreover she slurs the line "you turned out not to be my fate, but" (ty moei sudboyu ne stal . . . a) so that the verb indicates that she is speaking of another woman, not a man (*stal* is the masculine form, *stala* the feminine form of the verb, which in the past tense in Russian gives a clue to the gender of the speaker). The second hit, "Hatred" (Neliubov'), featured in the clip Yuri Usachev with another man, alluding to homosexual love. The sadomasochistic rhythm, combined with groaning, did the rest to create two songs that, through their clips and performance, promoted lesbianism and male homosexuality for the first time deliberately.

This trend would be trumped, however, by the most popular pop band in Russian history, the duo t.A.T.u, playing in a Europop rock style. They deliberately alluded to their lesbian relationship, but moreover this was a relationship of teenagers (and

minors), not adults. The duo was formed in 1999 by the producer Ivan Shapovalov. He cast Lena Katina (b. 1984) and Julia Volkova (b. 1985) for the band, dressing them in school uniforms (white blouses, ties, and checked miniskirts) and taught them some lesbian antics. With that they became the most popular band in Russia; with 1.5 million albums sold, they conquered the international charts and toured Europe and the United States, finally representing Russia at the Eurovision Song Contest in 2003 with "Don't Trust, Don't Be Afraid" (Ne ver, ne boisia), gaining third place.

The band's name derived from *Ta liubit tu* (this girl loves that girl). They advertised their young, forbidden love in the clips to their songs and their interviews. They first launched their single "I've Gone Mad" (Ia soshla s uma, 2000; English version "All the Things She Said'), which reached number one on Russian radio, backed by a video clip on MTV and a mini album. This was followed by "Not Gonna Get Us" (Nas ne dogoniat, 2001), which led to a contract with Universal. By 2002 they had an album in English, *200kmh in the Wrong Lane*, and reached the top of the charts in Europe. All this was achieved by a careful marketing campaign that styled the girls as lesbians (which they were, in fact, not), and by their maintaining this facade in interviews. Once their image collapsed as both started dating boys, their career came to an end.

t.A.T.u's songs describe the anxiety of the girls that they might be discovered doing wrong. The song "Malchik Gay" deals with the frustrations of a girl in love with a gay boy. In their hit "All the Things She Said" (Ia soshla s uma) they mention forbidden love; they emphasize that the girls are "mixed up and cornered" but that they want each other so much. In "I've Gone Mad" the girls

The girl band t.A.T.u takes part in the "Stopudovyi" Hit (Hundred-Pound Hit) Awards ceremony held by Hit-FM radio in the Kremlin Palace, 2001. (Photo by Alexey Kudenko/Kommersant)

present themselves as considered to be mad by others and in need of a cure. The clips illustrated the girls' feelings for each other, and their entrapment in a society from which they sought to escape.

> And I'm all mixed up, feeling cornered and
>   rushed
> They say it's my fault but I want her so much
> Wanna fly her away where the sun and rain
> Come in over my face, wash away all the
>   shame
> When they stop and stare—don't worry me
> 'Cause I'm feeling for her what she's feeling
>   for me

> I can try to pretend, I can try to forget
> But it's driving me mad, going out of my head

While they seemed naive and in love in television interviews, they clearly knew very well the roles they had to play and broke free from the expectations at every opportunity. For example, after being criticized for kissing on one television show in the United States during their tour in February 2003, they were allowed to kiss during another but chose not to do so. On the *Tonight Show* with Jay Leno on 24 February 2003, they benefited from the fact that the studio staff did not know Russian to express their opposition to the war in Iraq, when they quite outrageously sported T-shirts with the phrase "KHUI VOINE" (f*** the war). On the next evening, on *Jimmy Kimmel Live*, they wore T-shirts with the word *censored*. t.A.T.u may have been the most important pop duo to bring Russian pop music to the attention of the West, but their image was a very fine construct that ultimately broke apart.

If the image of the t.A.T.u girls had been entirely artificially created, then Alsou is a genuinely talented singer, who used publicity to market her talent rather than create it. Born in Tatarstan, Alsou (Alsu Safina) is the daughter of LukOil's vice president. She moved to Moscow in 1991 and attended a musical school, but in 1993 her family sent her to a London school specializing in design. In 1999 Alsou, aged 15, sang her tune "Winter Dream" (Zimnii son) in a clip directed by the gifted and popular film- and clip-maker Yuri Grymov, who created a clip where she featured as a Lolita-type character alongside the star actor Sergei Makovetsky (who looks not unlike Jeremy Irons, who had just starred in Adrian Lyne's remake of *Lolita*) and Yelena Yakovleva. Alsou signed a contract with Universal, and in 2000 she was the youngest-ever singer to represent Russia at the Eurovision Song contest, taking second place in the competition with her song, "Solo." In 2000 Alsou launched her first English album and subsequently received the European Music Award. She returned to Moscow in 2003 to study at the Theater Institute.

Zemfira (Ramazanova) was discovered in 1998 at a rock festival in Moscow and was helped in her career by Ilia Lagutenko of Mumii Troll for her first album. *SPID* (Aids) became an instant hit and was played frequently on radio. Zemfira's individual man-

Alsou, the talented singer who represented Russia in the 2000 Eurovision Song Contest. (Photo by Irina Kaledina)

ner of singing made her one of the most popular performers in Russian pop and allowed her to form a group around her for her next albums. Also known for their voices rather than their media image are the Nochnye Snaipery (Night Snipers, 1997), a duo of Diana Arbenina from Magadan and Svetlana Urganova from Petersburg, who perform their songs to electronic music arranged with help from ex-Nautilus musicians. Another successful voice is that of Julia Chicherina from Ekaterinburg, who launched her career in 1997 with the single "40,000 km" that became a radio hit. She moved to Moscow, where "Tu-la-la" became popular on radio and allowed her to launch a number of albums.

The rock singer Zemfira performs at the Maxidrom rock festival in the Olympic Sports Complex in 2002. (Photo by Alexey Kudenko/Kommersant)

The most innovative new talent is that of Natasha Ionova, but she has conquered the charts not with her voice, but by the creation of her puppet personality. The 17-year-old Natasha, who performs as the band Gliukoza (original spelling ГЛЮК':)ZA where *gliuk* means a *high* and the complete word *glucose*), appeared on the stage in 2003. Gliukoza loaded her first composition onto the Internet as mp3 files and then gained popularity with her cartoon figure. She wears a mask of this character for her clips and performances, portraying a girl with blond hair (like her) through her mask.

The Russian rock scene clearly moved into the public domain and turned into a fully fledged business in the 1990s. Although talents still emerge onto the public arena, many pop groups are created and produced, manipulated by producers and mass media to bring in a commercial profit.

Estrada and Pop Music

The record company Melodiya was founded in 1964 to control the releases of Soviet music; the majority of its sales were pop music, not recordings of classical music. And this music was pop music of the estrada genre.

If rock music had a massive impact on popular music in the 1990s from the underground, then estrada was the official popular entertainment. It was popular despite its official status, whereas underground was popular because of its unofficial nature. Estrada draws on jazz music and performance, merged with some disco element. Performances on the estrada stage are usually in the form of a concert version with an audience to watch a spectacle rather than dance. Estrada is mass entertainment of a stage concert, requiring preparation and choreography, design and movement as well as costumes; it is a theatricalized performance.

In the 1960s famous estrada singers included Mark Bernes (1911–1969), who performed both on stage and in film; the native Polish singer Edita Piekha (b. 1937); Sofia Rotaru (b. 1947), whose success came in 1968 with a song about soldiers who did not return; the bass baritone Lev Leshchenko (b. 1942); Iosif Kobzon (b. 1937), who since 1959 has performed as a singer. Many of the estrada songs came from the pen of Alexandra Pakhmutova (b. 1929, Sverdlovsk), a composer who graduated from the Moscow Conservatory in 1956 and has written more than 300 songs. Pakhmutova followed the tradition of the 1930s ballads and the bard song, and the jumps in octaves are a characteristic feature of her compositions. Her most famous song is "Tenderness" (Nezhnost', 1966), which is extremely popular to the present day. The composers played an increasingly significant role in creating the right tunes but also collaborating with appropriate interpreters. Igor Krutoy (b. 1954) is a composer who founded in 1988 the ARS center, which among other things produced television shows on music. Raimond Pauls (b. 1936, Riga) had worked with a jazz sextet and conducted the Riga Estrada Orchestra before beginning to write his own music. He worked closely with such poets as Andrei Voznesensky, Robert Rozhdestvensky, and Ilia Reznik for the lyrics.

The 1960s and 1970s also saw a revival of the folk song, much in the style of country folk song in the performance of Zhanna Bichevskaya (b. 1944), who collects and performs folk songs and accompanies herself on the guitar, dressed in plain and simple black dresses to avoid the theatrical effects achieved on the estrada stage. Nadezhda Babkina (b. 1950) is a singer with an alto voice who not only performs folk songs but also heads the folk section at the Gnesin Institute and has founded a center for folk music.

An extremely popular singer of the 1970s was the opera baritone Muslim Magomayev (b. 1942, Baku), who is little known in the West. Magomayev had studied music at Baku Conservatory and spent a short term at La Scala in Milan before becoming a solo singer of the Azerbaijan National Opera and Ballet Theater (1963–1969, 1978–1987). In between he performed on the estrada, lending his lyrical intonation and his velvety, romantic voice to the songs of Ario Babadzhanyan (1921–1983). His "Beauty Queen" (Koroleva krasoty) was a megahit of the 1970s and is still frequently played at concerts and on radio. Magomayev later returned to the classical opera stage but even then continued to use his direct contact with the audience in order to popularize opera music.

The major discovery of the 1970s, however, was Alla Pugacheva. Her song "Harlequin" (1975) not only won the main prize at a prestigious festival in Bulgaria but also established her fame as the leading Russian pop diva, a reputation that survives into the present day. Although scorned by the intelligentsia, which hated anything popular and therefore profane, she became the pop queen, with all the stormy affairs and eccentricities of a star. Pugacheva staged her songs as theatrical performances, where the singer adopts a role and changes this role from show to show, but also from song

Alla Pugacheva, the Soviet pop legend, performing her hit "Harlequin" in the costume designed for her theatrical performance of this 1970s hit. (Photo by Irina Kaledina)

to song, varying her intonation, changing costumes, and altering the pitch of her voice to match the mood of the song. Most of Pugacheva's songs of the 1970s and 1980s were composed by the team of Raimond Pauls and Ilia Reznik, who wrote the hit "Yellow Leaves" (Zheltye list'ia, 1978). Although the heyday of her career was clearly in the late 1970s, Pugacheva continues to make the headlines, whether it is with her marriage to the much younger pop star Filipp Kirkorov, or the launch of a shoe and fashion label, or the participation in 1997 in the Eurovision Song Contest with "Primadonna," where she came in only fifteenth.

Pop Ladies   Pugacheva created a precedent for women to cast themselves in different roles and theatricalize song performance almost to the level of Western show business. Her model was followed, directly and indirectly, by many people in the 1980s. The soprano Larisa Dolina (b. 1955) made her appearance on stage with exotic stage numbers for her light dance tunes. Irina Allegrova cast her image as a femme fatale with her smoky voice while still performing as lead singer in bands. The songs written by Igor Nikolayev launched her solo career in the early 1990s, and later she also worked with composer Igor Krutoy, who created dramatic ballads for her. The Latvian Laima Vaikule (b. 1954) was discovered by Raimond Pauls when she performed in Riga's restaurants and clubs in the 1980s. She cast herself in various roles, creating a choreographic score for her performances. Her tall figure, short blond hair, and cabaret and variety style made her demeanor similar to that of Liza Minelli. She became popular with a song written for her by Ilia Reznik, "Night Bonfire" (Nochnoi koster, 1986), which featured on radio.

Natalia Vetlitskaya made her debut in 1984 with the group Mirage but gained popularity through her affair with the pop singer Dmitri Malikov (b.1970), whom she married in 1989. The blond sex symbol performed rhythmic tunes with a mischievous voice. The song "Playboy" (1994), written by composer Oleg Molchanov and presented with a video clip, was a hit that marked her comeback after divorcing Malikov. After marrying a businessman, she has disappeared from bohemian circles but not from the stage. Irina Saltykova also began in the group Mirage, before marrying pop star Viktor Saltykov, whom she divorced in 1995, going on then to launch a solo career. Saltykova gained popularity with songs by Oleg Molchanov, especially "Gray Eyes" (Serye glaza) with a rather erotic video clip, and "Doll's House" (Kukolnyi dom), both drawing on techno and disco rhythms. In 2000, she starred in the blockbuster *Brother 2* as herself, a star singer who has a brief affair with Danila Bagrov (played by Sergei Bodrov Jr.). Saltykova's erotic poses and gestures, sometimes bordering on vulgarity, make her a frequent object of scandals reported in the tabloid press and also qualify her as the "face" that advertises Life Style condoms. Alyona Sviridova not only sings but also composes her own songs. She promoted herself with video clips made by the filmmaker Ivan Dykhovichny and later by Fyodor Bondarchuk ("Poor Lamb" [Bednaia ovechka]). In 1999 she featured on the cover of the Russian edition of *Playboy*. Although all these pop singers are perhaps talented and have appealing voices, most created their stage image not through performance but through media scandals. This demonstrates how fast Russian pop culture has assimilated the working mechanisms of Western show business, where the media can build or destroy the image of a star. The fact that so many new bands and voices are not discoveries, but the creations of producers, ties in with this development.

Gentlemen of the Estrada   If the women build their images on erotic attraction, the male pop stars tend to draw on a more classical image. Oleg Gazmanov's education in the navy shows in the creation of song cycles in different styles, from Cossack to navy and officers' songs. His songs moved from rock and folk intonations to a disco sound, and then to romances. For a while he performed some songs with his son, Rodion, underscoring his image as a family man. Valeri Meladze also appears as a well-groomed singer, mainly performing compositions by his brother. Although the stage image of the tenor Valeri Leontiev carries some degree of sexual ambivalence, with his songs from the pen of Pauls, he established himself as a talented singer with slightly effeminate manners and appearance. Later he worked with the composer Lora Kvint (b. 1953), who also wrote the rock opera *Giordano* (1988), in which Leontiev sang the main part.

The Pugacheva clan includes, in the wider sense, two further male singers: her husband and her ex-son-in-law. Pugacheva's husband, Filipp Kirkorov, is a star in his own right, but the relationship feeds the media with stories because Kirkorov is almost 20 years younger than Alla. Born in Bulgaria into the family of a famous singer, Kirkorov studied music at the Gnesin Institute in Moscow and began performing at the Leningrad Music Hall and in Alla Pugacheva's Theater, before embarking on a solo career. In 1994 he married Alla Pugacheva, a union that has shed no negative light on his career; in a sense, Kirkorov revived attention toward Pugacheva's waning star and thus perpetuated her name. Kirkorov has given concerts in large international venues (Madison Square Garden, Friedrichstadtpalast Berlin) and is produced by Russia's most powerful music producer, Sergei Lisovsky. His outfits come from the designer Valentin Yudashkin. Kirkorov has quickly become a cult figure, and his appearances in films and on stage (in the musical *Chicago*) are a guarantee for box office success. Born in Sverdlovsk,

Russian pop diva Alla Pugacheva (right) and her husband Filipp Kirkorov (left) arrive at the Kremlin Congress Palace to attend the Eighth Golden Gramophone Awards ceremony, 2003. (Photo by Alexey Kudenko/Kommersant)

Vladimir Presniakov could hardly have missed the rock movement that was so strongly represented in the town. After a stint in a hard rock group, his voice broke, and he turned to modern jazz and break dancing. With his falsetto voice, he soon launched a solo career. Presniakov's liaison with Pugacheva's daughter, the actress and occasional singer Kristina Orbakaite, with whom he has a son, provided mundane stuff for the tabloids.

The New Russian Estrada   If in Soviet times the estrada had provided light entertainment for the masses through theatricalized performances of songs and concerts, then in post-Soviet Russia the theatrical element decreased and the image making was left to producers and the media rather than talent. Gradually, the role of the producer increased in importance, and music became a business rather than a form of keeping people entertained in an ideologically suitable manner. The rise of the mass media, especially television, facilitated the creation of images through music clips. Although these were expensive to place on the national channels, with the appearance of musical channels, clips became the most important way of promoting a new star. Some clip makers reached designer status: Yuri Grymov and Fyodor Bondarchuk are the top directors and image makers. In 1995, Muz TV began to transmit in 21 cities, charging a flat fee for every song played. In September 1998, MTV followed suit, creating a competing outlet for new musical clips.

Moreover, the pop scene was subjected to fast changes in taste. In the early 1990s audiences were eager to go to Russian rock concerts, especially those groups that had previously remained in the underground. As the underground rock surfaced and became mainstream, many of the bands lost their remit and failed to keep the audience's attention. New rock groups satisfied new demands. By the mid-1990s, a generation of teenagers had grown up, born around 1980, that had seen very little of the old Soviet system. These teenagers of the mid-1990s had entered school during the Gorbachev years, had benefited from reforms in society, and had been exposed to Western influences. At the same time, this generation had also seen their parents work hard and struggle to survive during the economic chaos of the Yeltsin years. These teenagers were no longer interested in the stories of underground rock bands and dissident voices, but in disco rhythms that allowed them to escape from the chaos that surrounded them and that many could not understand. They followed fashion trends rather than idols, and the arrows signaling what is "in" and what is "out" changed very fast in the latter half of the 1990s and in the new millennium.

The television programs *Golden Gramophone* (Zolotoi grammofon) and *Star Factory* (Fabrika Zvezd) keep teenagers and younger children glued to the television set. *Golden Gramophone* is a competition of the best songs of the season, and it is produced in collaboration with Russkoye Radio, the radio station that has made it its policy to broadcast predominantly Russian music in order to promote it over and above Western tunes. *Star Factory* is a talent show, where—in the manner of the German talent show *Deutschland sucht den Superstar* (which even produced a singer who represented the country at the Eurovision Song Contest)—amateurs are allowed to present their songs. By contrast with the German variant, though, here they perform with the star they try to imitate.

A uniquely Russian, and apparently temporary, phenomenon was the popularity of old Soviet music in the latter half of the 1990s. Culturally, there is a logical explanation for this "nostalgia for the golden Soviet times." The nostalgia was motivated not so much by politics as by the fact that many television viewers were pensioners, who were very badly off in the Yeltsin era, much worse than they had ever been in Soviet times. Moreover, with the massive influx and overpowering force of Western products and culture, many people, old and young, who could not afford the Western luxuries rejected Western culture not for ideological, but for economic reasons, and reverted to the good old Russian product. This phenomenon also applied to musical taste, and in 1995 ORT television producer Konstantin Ernst launched the New Year's Eve show *Old Songs about the Main Thing* (Starye pesni o glavnom). The show was so successful that he produced two further shows in subsequent years. The shows presented old estrada songs, re-recorded and sung in a contemporary vein by the stars of the 1990s. The first program was set on a collective farm in southern Russia in the 1930s and consisted of musical hits of that period. The second part moved to a more urban setting in northern Russia and presented hits of the 1950s. The final part moved on to the 1970s, and, through the time machine of *Ivan Vasilievich Changes Profession* (Ivan Vasil'evich meniaet professii, a film based on the play by Mikhail Bulgakov) took the viewer from ancient history to the present in a costumed journey through the Mosfilm studios. Top estrada and pop stars participated in the shows.

Solo, with Support   Most new solo singers of recent years are women. It would appear that men still tend to perform in bands and groups, whereas women move on in solo careers. Even the popular singer Leonid Agutin now performs with his wife, Angelica Varum, as a duo. Agutin studied jazz and launched a hit with "Barefoot Boy" (Bosonogii mal'chik, 1992). His Latin American and samba rhythms made his music smooth and suitable for dancing. His song "Hop Hei, La-la-lei" was a second major hit and also revealed the decreasing impor-

tance of the lyrics for modern pop music. In 1997 he performed the song "Queen" (Koroleva) with Angelica Varum, whom he married in 1998. Varum, the daughter of the composer Yuri Varum, had created her stage image as a fragile childlike fairy tale creature, singing about childhood themes. Her "Midnight Cowboy" (Polunochnoi kovboi 1991) revealed an infantile demeanor and childlike images. Agutin and Varum have also produced a joint album *Business Romance* (Sluzhebnyi roman).

With the increasing need for a financially strong producer, corporate and private sponsorship has become vital for the Russian pop star scene. Moreover, singers rely on good composers and songwriters to create hits for them. Natasha Koroleva was

Leonid Agutin with his wife Angelica Varum, performing together. (Photo by Irina Kaledina)

discovered by the composer Igor Nikolayev at a competition in Eupatoria (Crimea) and later married him. Koroleva initially performed children's songs and romantic love songs but moved to pop music in the late 1990s. Her stage image uses her sex appeal, marketed when she posed for *Playboy* in 1997. Alena Apina from Saratov arrived in Moscow in 1988 and married the manager Alexander Iratov. She embarked on a solo career, having performed with a band in her home town. "Dance till Morning" (Tantsevat' do utra, 1992) was a hit that brought out her coquettish manners. Later in her career she adopted a more dramatic style, and her performances became less mischievous and had less fervor. With songs composed by Oleg Molchanov, she tries to move to energetic pop music and performs with the young singer Murat Nasyrov. Tatiana Bulanova played dance pop music with the group Letnii Sad (Summer Garden) and developed her reputation as a singer with a weeping voice. She married the musician Nikolai Tagrin and launched a solo career. Her songs drew on Slavic folk and rock traditions and were rendered in a tearful and emotional manner. In the mid-1990s she changed her style, moving to the composer Oleg Molchanov for her songs, which allow her to display her erotic appearance in magnificent outfits. Linda is sponsored by her father. Her exotic appearance and unusual performance are manifest in the clips by Fyodor Bondarchuk: in the clip for "Underwater Dance" (Tanets pod vodoi), she is a girl with many plaits in her hair. On Linda's albums *Songs of the Tibetian Lamas* (Pesni tibetskikh lam) and *Crow* (Vorona), the backing vocals are by Olga Dzusova, one of the finest singers in Russia. Dzusova's extraordinary voice has sounded as lead of the hard rock band SS20, in her own album *Parisian Tango*, and in the eerie and parodic interpretations of Soviet songs in the film *Moscow* (directed by Alexander Zeldovich, 2000). Katia Lel is a self-made star, who came to Moscow in 1996 and collected money from friends and sponsors to make her first song recordings and clips. She has gained wide popularity through her producer Max Fadeyev, whom she personally thanks on the cover of her album *Djaga-Djaga*.

Over the last decade Russia has created its own musical stars, whose music is more popular in the new millennium than foreign imported recordings. Although some of the rock bands still rely on parodic and provocative texts to entertain and amuse their audiences, pop stars rely on catchy tunes and appealing rhythms to reach large audiences, both in concerts and record releases. In this sense, the Russian rock and pop scene has gained full independence and stands commercially on a sound footing.

Youth Culture and Language

The language spoken, taught, and written in the Soviet Union was an "official" language, adapted by the chief ideologues for the purpose of unifying speech habits. The richness of nineteenth-century vocabulary, documented in classical Russian literature and in the four volumes of Vladimir Dal's dictionary, as well as the old spelling was standardized after the Revolution, allegedly to combat the widespread illiteracy. The simplification of the Russian language went much further during the twentieth century, however, requiring the knowledge of a relatively small number of words in order to read the daily newspapers. Likewise, the range of words was reduced, as is evident in the editions of Russian dictionaries published in the Soviet era. Russian was also "purified" from any swear words and indeed any sexual terminology. This led to the publication in the late Soviet period of a number of émigré editions, such as Alex Flegon's famous *Beyond the Russian Dictionary* (Za predelami russkogo slovaria), listing all those words excised from the Russian dictionary with citations of their use by writers, literati, and essayists.

At the same time, another fascinating phenomenon occurred when many intellectuals, writers, and dissidents returned from the labor camps in the 1950s and 1960s. Having been exposed to criminal jargon in the camps, they began to use the behavior, gesture, and jargon of the common criminals, both in assimilation of the behavior they had been exposed to and in rejection of the current Soviet etiquette. The use of *blatnoi zhargon* (prison slang) infested intellectual discourse and the lifestyle of those rejecting ideological values per se. This is exemplified in Venedikt Yerofeyev's *Moscow to the End of the Line* (Moskva-Petushki), written in the 1970s and circulated in samizdat, in which the author-narrator's drunkenness is a way of perceiving the reality that surrounds him. Likewise, the singer and poet Vladimir Vysotsky used street and criminal jargon in his songs, even if he was never exposed to prison. Thus, intellectuals and dissidents often colored their works with the use of nonstandard language.

In the perestroika period, in particular, English words were borrowed and became an integral part of the Russian language. The *Perestroika Dictionary* (Slovar' perestroiki) mainly lists terms from the business and market economy that found their way into the Russian language in the Gorbachev era. This impact of foreign terms went hand in hand with the introduction of the hitherto unknown principles and structures that went with them, however. Therefore these words did not stand out in the everyday discourse.

In the 1990s a new generation of people grew up who had not been exposed to the indoctrination of the party at home, in schools, and in the streets. Instead, they were exposed to a world of extreme capitalism, in which their parents were mostly struggling. These children had no responsibilities toward the state; were often neglected by their parents, who were busy with often two or three jobs to survive; and were largely left to their own devices, or at best under a babushka's (grandmother's) care. The youth jargon that developed is probably the most significant change in the Russian language since 1917.

Although youth groups had used selected foreign words to communicate and develop their own "code" in an attempt not to be understood by adults, as had been the origin of argot (talk among criminals so that they could not be understood), these "codes" expanded rapidly in the 1990s. They incorporated both the once unofficial criminal jargon as well as foreign terms. Thus, for example, a new concept that arrived with the market economy and business was public relation, in short PR. In the Russian language this became *piar* with the verb *piarit* and the noun *piar-shchik*, the adjective *piarovskii*. *Ofis* has entered the language to designate an office space, often occupied by many people, as opposed to the Russian word *kabinet*, usually reserved for one person. Other examples are *reiting*, *marketing*, *realtor*, and *notariius*.

The youth slang that developed in the language in the 1990s remains, not reserved to certain youth groups but spread across the population in general. After all, the babushki are exposed to new words used by the grandchildren they care for, and many middle-aged people have teenage children who bring into usage new terms.

Youth Jargon and Slang

One term that describes a whole set of values embraced by the 1990s generation is *styob*, derived from the verb *stebat* (synonym of *stegat:* to whip, to lash). Styob describes the exposure to mockery that leads to an irreversible and permanent profanation. The critic Viktor Matizen has devoted a short essay to the roots of this phenomenon (*Iskusstvo kino* 9, 1993), tracing those roots to the absurdist pieces of Daniil Kharms, who wrote a parody of Pushkin in anecdotes in an attempt to counter the latter's canonization by the state. In the 1960s the anecdotes on Chapayev also showed irreverence toward the man who was, in official discourse, described as a Soviet hero. In the 1970s the term was used in the underground rock movement. Styob is close to postmodernism in its parody of elements of socialist culture, and this has a parallel appearance in "high" culture. Styob in popular culture is a remake, where the author plays a game with the public and creates a new myth based on the sacred status of past culture. Thus, for example, the anecdotes about Stirlitz in the 1990s bear witness to the mockery of Soviet intelligence, in the same way as the recourse to criminal jargon and vulgar language parodies the Soviet state's concern with propriety and standards.

Another term that incorporates an entire lifestyle of the young generation is the word *tusovka. Tusovka* became a trendy word in the early 1990s and was used by Artyom Troitsky as the title for his English-language book on new Soviet rock culture. The word *tusovka* is derived from the French term *se tasser*, and *tusovat* means primarily "to shuffle cards." *Tusovatsya* describes the activity of just being with friends, with a group not necessarily of the same composition, thus exposing the *tusovshchik* not to the experience of allegiance to a group or gang but making it possible to move around different groups. The term *tusovka* defines all groups with flexible membership, however, and this creates its own kind of secluded circle. People who are out to *tusovatsya* want to have fun, without any obligations and allegiances. The tusovka of the 1960s underground generation (*shestidesyatniki*) used a different vocabulary than the young generation of today. Other words that entered the Russian language from the 1970s and 1980s underground are *kaif*, describing pleasure or a "high" under the influence of drugs; *vrubatsya* (and the noun *vrub*), meaning "to suss out, switch on," literally to cut one's way into; *fenka*, the "main thing," originally used to describe beads worn by hippies; and *fishka*, also used for "the main thing." The term *lokh* is used for a loser, a simpleton.

Russian Teen Language

Trendy words used by the young generation that have become part of everyday speech include adjectives that describe excitement and acceptance—*prikolno* (*prikolot:* to pierce); *klyovo* (*klyover* is *gluck*, high); *kruto* (steep, aggressive, powerful); *obaldenno* (*obaldet:* be stunned)—all more or less meaning good, cool, super, or brilliant. For indifference, young people use words such as *do banki* (up to the can); *do bara-*

banu (up to the drum); *do lampady/lampochki* (up to the icon/lamp); *pofigu* (figuratively: nothing; *pofigu:* does not matter); *pofigu* forms the nouns *pofigism* (indifferent attitude) and *fignya* (nothing, nonsense). The ultimate state of such indifference and inactivity is *khalyava:* to get something for nothing, free of charge, without working for it. For acceptance (okay), they use the words *normalyok* (normal); *nishtyak* (nothing); *prosto taid* (simply Tide); *vse khokei* (all hockey). These are playful adaptations of the words *normal* and *okay* and draw upon the Tide detergent advertising spot. Parents are often irreverently, often out of embarrassment, referred to as *predki* (ancestors); *nachaltsvo* (superiors); *startsy* (elders); *kosti* (bones).

Youth jargon also replaces words of standard usage with words that are more visual in the description of a particular state: *oblom* means a failure or an interruption of a pleasurable experience and is derived from the term *to break off*; *prikid* is a euphemism for dress, outfit, or garment, where *prikidyvat* means "to throw on." Trendy details are not accessories, but *pribambasy* (trendy details). Leisure is not *otdykh*, but *ottyag*, from the word *ottyagivatsya:* to stretch out. Understanding is not signaled by the word *ponimat* but by the verb *prosekat*, literally "to cut through." Other words originate from a more commercial understanding of everyday reality: *bazarit* means "to talk your way out," "to beat around the bush," and refers to the term *bazar* (market). The verb *kolbasitsya* means "to have fun" and stems from *kolbasa* (sausage).

Slang   A number of words that have been principally used by teenagers have found their way also into everyday speech. The main area of slang that has entered everyday speech, however, largely through the crime serials on television, is the criminal jargon as well as the language in which criminals (and not only criminals) speak about money, cars, alcohol, and sex. Slang words often replace proper words in everyday speech, not only of teenagers.

Swearing

Russian swearwords were never part of dictionaries, and they were considered rather more vulgar than in other European cultures. When translated into English in standard dictionaries, however, they are mostly rendered more harmless than the literal meaning would suggest, thus allowing for a leveling and an adaptation to suggest these are comparatives and not superlatives. The most commonly used phrases are *idi na khui/idi v zhopu* (go to . . .), which, along with *yob (eb) tvoyu mat* (f*** your mother), is rendered as "go to hell." Derivatives of these swearwords are *yolki-palki*, *yolki-motalki*, and *yomoye*, which are almost commonplace, especially bearing in mind the name of the restaurant chain Yolki-Palki in Moscow. The adjectives *yobnutyi* and *yobanyi* (f***ing) are also widespread. The verb and noun *mudit* and *mudak* mean "bulls***," and *mudak* is also a term used for a strange man or a weirdo. A perfectly acceptable term is *blin* (pancake), a milder version of "s***" (used when something has gone wrong), and this remains commonly used by all classes and ages.

Musicals

'The musical has no tradition in the Soviet Union" was the apologetic assertion made

Slang

Drink

To drink: *bukhat* (to thump, bang), *grokhnut* (crash), *nazhirat'sia* (fill up), *drinchit* (English: to drink), *gazanut* (step on it, accelerate), *zapayat* (to solder), *dubasit* (to bang on); also: *ostakanitsya* (get a glass), *ografinitsya* (get a jug), *oflakonitsya* (get a perfume bottle).

Alcoholic: *alik, bukharik/bukhach, drinkach.*

Sex

To have sex (vulgar terms): *trakhat/trakhatsya* (shake), *ebat/ebatsya* (f***), *zavintit* (screw).

Prostitute: *zhaba* (toad), *blyad, blyakha* (whore), *shliukha* (tart), *shmara* (thing).

Male homosexual: *pedik, pider, gomik, goluboi* (blue), *teply brat* (warm brother).

Arse: *zhopa.*

Penis: *khui* (tool, prick), *palka* (stick), *bolt* (bolt), *khuyovy* (adjective) (rotten, lousy), *khuinya* (noun) (bulls***, nonsense).

Vagina: *pizda* (c***), *pizdets* (idiot).

Crime

Policeman: *ment.*

Thug: *shpana* (young), *ambal* (strong).

To kill: *(za)mochit* (to wet, soak), *zagasit* (extinguish), *grokhnut* (to crash, bang), *zavalit* (overthrow), *zakolbasit* (butcher).

To beat (up): *gasit* (extinguish), *kantovat* (frame), *kolot* (pierce), *mochit* (soak), *grokhnut* (crash), *smazat mozgi* (smear the brain).

Boss (head of organized crime): *avtoritet* (authority), *pakhan* (*pakhat:* to plow).

Member of a criminal group: *bratan, bratello, bratok* (brother).

Criminal group: *bratva* (brotherhood).

Money

Money: *babki.*

Roubles: *derevyannye* (wooden).

Dollars: *baksy* (bucks), *zelyonye* (greens).

Limon (lemon): a million.

Shtuka (thing): a thousand (rubles, dollars).

Fistashki (pistachios)]: a large sum of money.

Beznal for *beznalichnye* (per invoice) and *nal* for *nalichnye* (cash).

Cars

Bus: *bukhanka.*

Car: tachka, kareta; *tachka* is also a motorbike.

BMW: *akula* (shark), *bavarets* (Bavarian), *bumer/bimer* (bimmer); *be-em-vushka.*

Mercedes: *mers.*

VW: *zhuchok* (beetle); *bozhya korovka* (ladybug).

by most reviewers of the few musicals staged in Moscow in the late 1990s. These reviewers ignored the musical film comedies of the 1930s as well as two productions of the immediate pre- and postperestroika years. The first was the rock-opera *Perchance* (Iunona i Avos), composed by Alexei Rybnikov to the lyrics of Andrei Voznesensky and staged at the Moscow Lenkom Theater in 1981 by Mark Zakharov and the actor Nikolai Karachentsov, who also played the main part. The musical dealt with the trans-Pacific expedition of the Russian Count Rezanov to California in the early nineteenth century. It was a mixture of adventure drama and melodrama, thus combining the two most popular genres of film, theater and literature. Rezanov is a romantic dreamer, who is obsessed with the desire to travel to California. Imploring the icon of Our Lady, he falls in love with her image. His dream comes true, and he travels to California; there he meets Conchita, the daughter of the local governor, who is engaged to Federico. Rezanov, who sees in Conchita the face of Our Lady, strives to gain her love, which Conchita reciprocates. Eventually Rezanov has to leave for Siberia, where he dies. Conchita remains faithful to him and enters a convent. The melodrama has love triumph over death in the final song "Hallelujah of Love," which can compete in its melodic appeal with the songs of Western musicals. Second was the rock-musical *Jesus Christ Superstar*, which opened at the Mossovet Theater in 1990 in a production directed by Pavel Khomsky and Sergei Prokhanov. Both *Perchance* and *Jesus Christ Superstar* are, however, repertoire productions in established dramatic theaters rather than productions for a stationary stage; they are performed several times a month in repertoire.

The first professionally produced musical, Janusz Stoklosa's *Metro*, opened in October 1999 at the Moscow Operetta Theater. It was managed by the team of Katherina von Gecmen-Waldeck and Alexander Vainshtok with the operetta's head, Vladimir Tartakovsky. This musical is no import from Broadway or the West End (which would have incurred high license fees), but was originally staged in Poland in 1991. The Moscow production was cre-

ated by the Polish director and the choreographer of the original show, Janusz Sosnowski and Janusz Josefowicz. *Metro* did not make stars, as *Perchance* and *Jesus Christ Superstar* had made stars of Nikolai Karachentsov and Oleg Kazancheyev respectively; instead, it included stars in its cast list for guest appearances. Within the first 15 months, the show, which runs for eight to ten days en bloc every month, was seen by more than 150,000 people. It appealed to the public because of its special laser effects, because of the choreography and the professional performances of the young actors, and because of the story line, dealing with the young generation's aspirations for the theater, which are frustrated but ultimately lead to a successful underground production. Today's young generation is presented with the possibility of realizing a dream, and the musical therefore appealed first and foremost to the young audience.

Several other musicals followed on a semistationary basis. In November 1999 the rock legend Stas Namin (Tsvety) staged the musical *Hair* at the Estrada Theater. Namin had directed rock musicals before, even if largely as concert versions in his theater in Gorky Park. The Moscow Operetta's success with *Metro* was followed by *Notre Dame de Paris*, which premiered on 21 May 2002, created by the same production team that had worked on *Metro*. This time, though, the theater set its stakes higher and engaged the leader of the group Tantsy, Viachaslav Petkun, for the main part of Quasimodo. The musical *Chicago* opened at the Estrada Theater in Moscow on 4 October 2002 with Filipp Kirkorov in the main part; the competition for star names on the playbills was getting stronger in a growing musical market. Kirkorov subsequently also dubbed the film musical *Chicago* (Russian release 2003). In March 2002, the joint Slovak-Russian production of *Dracula* (composed by Karel Svoboda, directed by Josef Bernadik) opened with a joint cast at the DK on Lenin Prospekt. *42nd Street* premiered on 12 October 2002 at the DK Molodezhi as a joint American-Russian venture, directed by Mark Bramble and choreographed by Randy Skinner, repeating their 2001 Broadway version with a mixed troupe. *The Witches of Eastwick* has been playing at the Theater of the Film Actor since 2002. Thus, although American and European musicals were adapted for the Russian stage, there was no originality in the productions, which were imitations of Western musicals.

Nord-Ost: *The First Russian Musical*

Nord-Ost declared itself the "first Russian musical" that would play on a daily basis rather than in a repertoire theater. The casting drew on a pool of young, talented entertainment actors rather than stars so as to allow for a long-term run of the musical: Yekaterina Guseva and Andrei Bogdanov came to fame through their roles in *Nord-Ost*. In the advertising campaign, *Nord-Ost* placed itself in the context of other great world musicals, although this may simply have been part of the publicity exercise relating to Cameron Mackintosh Ltd., one of the largest musical production companies, with whom the producers Georgi Vasiliev and Alexander Tsekalo initially had a deal on *Les Miserables* for the Russian stage before the default of August 1998 made this project impossible.

Nord-Ost launched a massive publicity campaign in the style of Western musicals. A Web site was created primarily for marketing purposes. It was the first show with

A scene from the musical *Nord-Ost*, the first Russian musical to open in Moscow at the Dubrovka Theatre in 2001. (Photo by Irina Kaledina)

an elaborate ticket booking system via the Internet, thus clearly appealing to an audience that was more middle class and was in possession of or had access to a computer. The site carried information on the music, the performance archive, program information, cast and production team, press releases and reviews of the show (only positive ones), and "surprises," which included downloadable desktop pictures and mobile phone tunes. The design itself was not stunning but rather of an informational nature. The lax maintenance of the site after the initial launch was striking; most news items were announced in the chat-room and on unofficial sites rather than the official section. *Nord-Ost* led a publicity campaign comparable to Western standards: there were banners in the metro, advertisements on radio and clips on television, posters in the streets, and information on the back of metro tickets all through the summer before the show opened. The slogan for the production not only stuck in everybody's mind but actually began to get on one's nerves: "Every evening exactly at 21:45 a full-size bomber plane lands on the stage."

The production was staged in the House of Culture of Moscow's Ball-Bearing Factory on Dubrovka; it cost four million dollars and opened on 19 October 2001 in the refurbished and specially equipped DK, renamed Dubrovka Theater Center, seating 1,150 spectators for a price of 300–900 rubles (US$10–30) per ticket. Clearly, the equivalent of US$30 for a ticket can hardly be called mass appeal (average monthly wages in 2001 ranged from around US$500 in the cultural sector to less than US$100 for pensions), but *Nord-Ost* attracted 350,000 spectators in the first year of its run (in other words, a full house every night).

The special effects of Broadway musicals, the imported technology for light and sound, and the professional casting process were to make this show a success story à la Broadway. The live orchestra, elaborate sets and costumes, and the special effects were designed to outdo Western musicals. But all this would be achieved on the basis of a Russian, or rather Soviet, text that had even been awarded the State (Stalin) Prize in 1946: Veniamin Kaverin's (1902–1989) epic *Two Captains* (Dva kapitana). The novel stretches over thirty years, from 1913 to 1943, thus encompassing the most crucial and formative years of the Soviet state, from the Revolution to the civil war, through the Stalin era to World War II. Moreover, the text was of a suitable genre, combining two love triangles in an essen-

tially melodramatic plot and drawing clear distinctions between good and bad characters. The authors placed their stakes on the Russian reader of Kaverin: on the generation of parents, who had read Kaverin in their childhood; on the 32 million people who had seen the 1955 film by Vladimir Vengerov, which dwells on the protagonists' heroism and focuses on the dilemma between political and private as well as the theme of war heroism, both characteristic features for the cinema of the Thaw; and on the millions of television spectators who had watched the six-part television series made by Yevgeni Karelov in 1976. Now, so the producers assumed, the generation of grandparents born in the 1950s and parents born in the 1970s had passed the story of *Two Captains* on to their children and grandchildren (even if those read *Harry Potter*). The show was intended to appeal to a family audience, thus to an older audience than *Metro*. At the same time, the ambition of the project was to create a piece of indigenous Russian culture by recycling the plot of a 1940s epic and drawing on the traditions of the Stalinist musical. *Nord-Ost* explores features of Soviet life, such as communal living, bureaucracy, and technological progress, parodying them slightly, but taking pride in them as experiences that have unified the people, who bore hardship with humour. The music is full of references and allusions to the musical traditions of the 1920s and 1930s. The melodramatic plot is also in line with the traditions of the 1930s musical, when melodramas were perceived to appeal to the masses, offering a plot in which personal happiness is the reward for courage and heroism in political and public life. In this sense, the story of *Two Captains* literally lent itself to be worked into a musical.

Nord-Ost: Plot

Nord-Ost begins with the reported failure in 1913 of the expedition of Captain Tatarinov on the *Santa Maria.* In Arkhangelsk in 1916, the dumb Sania Grigoriev witnesses the murder of a postman who carries a letter in which Tatarinov implicates his brother Nikolai Antonovich in the failure of the expedition. Shortly after, Sania's father is arrested for the murder. Tatarinov's widow, Maria Vasilievna, leaves for Moscow with her mother, Nina Kapitonovna, and her daughter, Katia. The Tatarinovs' family friend Korablev looks after Sania and teaches him to speak and helps Sania find a place in a boarding school during the civil war. When the headmaster, Nikolai Antonovich, discovers that Korablev has proposed to Maria Vasilievna, Korablev and Sania are thrown out. Katia Tatarinova and Sania have fallen in love, but Sania's schoolmate Romashov also loves Katia and vies for her love. After Maria Vasilievna has married Nikolai, she learns about Captain Tatarinov's accusations in the letter that Sania keeps in the bag he took from the murdered postman, and she commits suicide. Sania leaves Moscow to find the *Santa Maria.* By 1938 Sania has become a pilot, still dreaming of discovering the *Santa Maria.* He has the support of the Soviet hero pilot Valeri Chkalov to fly to the Arctic, but his permission is withheld at the Main Directorate of Northern Waterways, GlavSevMorPut, where Romashov has intervened. Romashov courts Katia, but she remains loyal to Sania. During the war Katia lives through the Leningrad blockade. Romashov finds her and lies to her that Sania is dead; when he finds that this is of no avail, he tells Sania—in an attempt to destroy the love of Katia and Sania—that Katia has died during the blockade. In 1943 Grigoriev makes an emergency landing in the Arctic, and finds Tatarinov's diary kept by the indigenous people of the Nenetsk region in northern Russia. Katia finds him there, and he gives her the diary. At the end of the story, the high moral code of right and wrong upheld by the two captains of sea and air is triumphant, and their love wins.

The libretto was written by Alexei Ivashchenko and Georgi Vasiliev, also known as the duo Ivasi, who had gained fame with their song collections in the late 1990s. Ivasi was also known for their television shows on music as well as the edition of "Songs of Our Century" (Pesni nashego veka). Familiar with the songs of the past, Ivasi drew heavily on the music of the 1920s and 1930s, and its compositions were riddled with references and allusions to Soviet music from the operetta and musical composers of the Stalin era, Isaak Dunayevsky and Yuri Miliutin, clearly aiming to strike a familiar vein with the audiences. The tunes paced the movements. Although the melodies sounded familiar, however, there were no hits: none of the melodies stick in the mind.

The set consisted of five multifunctional walkways that ran from the back of the stage to the front; they could be raised and lowered, forming bridges and platforms, ramps and ceilings. The backdrops occasionally bordered on kitsch, showing a starry sky or a sunset to enhance the lyrical atmosphere. The choreography complied with the high standard normally expected of Western musicals while drawing on a variety of indigenous and foreign dance styles to set a rhythm. The pilots performed a tap dance; the secretaries moved their legs to a cancan; the skiers clicked their heels in a *chechetka* (a dance where the heels set the rhythm); the Nenetsk people showed a traditional dance; the skaters danced a tango. Solos and duets rendered some scenes more romantic and dramatic. There are elephantine tunes for scenes at the school; accordion music and a polonaise for the New Year; and the chattering of people's teeth in the cold weather rendered through the repetition of the first syllable. Objects, such as the kitchen utensils in the communal flat, the secretaries' office equipment, and the skis and skates, turn into instruments that are used to beat the rhythm.

Nord-Ost eclipsed historical themes and moved personal lives into the foreground. Nikolai Antonovich betrayed Tatarinov when failing to equip his expedition; Romashov is a compulsive liar. Neither of these villains wins: Nikolai Antonovich is crippled, relying on Romashov's help. At the same time, the bureaucratic system is blamed for obstructing achievements: GlavSevMorPut is parodied, but the bureaucracy prevents not the achievement of political feats but of personal desires. The scenes at GlavSevMorPut are carefully set against the lyric theme of the musical; through this contrast the bureaucracy is caricatured and satirized. The monotony of the secretaries' movement is juxtaposed to the open space of the world represented on a huge map at the back. The five secretaries, with huge bows in their hair, wish to look attractive while they inefficiently use their office tools (abacus, hammer, typewriter) to tap an elephantine rhythm, thus parodying their own monotonous inefficiency.

The slogan for the revived production was "the history of the country, a love story" (istoriia strany—istoriia liubvi).

Nord-Ost stressed the personal motives above the political agendas and dwelt on the possibility of love as long as man adheres to a firm moral code of right and wrong. Just as with Broadway musicals, the special effects of the Russian or Soviet musical lay in a glorification of its national achievements rather than a critique of society. The essential ingredients of Socialist Realism were reinforced as attributes of the national heritage. The spectator was invited to take pride in the Soviet past, in his personal memories rather than the official historical discourse.

Nord-Ost was an exploration of the Soviet past in personal, not political, terms. It stressed the continuity between past and present. Parallels may be drawn between the early years of the Soviet period and the years of the collapse of socialism: inflation, chaos, the ability to speak up, access to formerly closed territories. Putin's Russia of the present reinstates the lost connection with the Soviet past as an experience that people have lived through and that they remember with nostalgia. *Nord-Ost* legitimized Russia's history by presenting a unified discourse on the level not of political but popular history (personal theme, melodramatic genre, mass scenes). Russian history is uninterrupted, rather than halted for 74 years, thus returning to the nation the sense of belonging and continuity. This is why *Nord-Ost* was a symbol of Russia—not the New Russia, but a country with tradition rather than one where traditions were severed. It offered an innovative view on Russia and its history, reiterating Soviet history through the popular lens.

Nord-Ost was the first *Russian* musical, popular with audiences and critics alike. It became a status symbol for Russia's pride in its own history and culture. Suddenly, with the terrorist attack of 23–26 October 2002, in which Chechen terrorists held the troupe and the audience hostage, it became a symbol of Russia's weakness and failure. It is no coincidence that no memorial has been erected to those who died as a consequence of the gas introduced during the liberation of the hostages on 26 October 2002. These people died in an act that shames Russia to the extent that nobody wishes to remember it. Similarly, the absence from the Web site of any information about the events of 23–26 October was striking: the list of victims appeared on another site (www.vazhno.ru). The lack of concern for the victims is further manifested in the absence of a memorial plaque in the theater; in the omission of any mention of the victims in the new program booklet (printed for the revival on 8 February 2003); and in the failure to commemorate the victims during the last performance on 10 May 2003. *Nord-Ost* wanted to remain a show, and as such detached itself from the terrorist attack. The government, too, strove to forget the events of October 2002 by assisting the revival of the musical in order to brush over allegations of mishandling the storming of the theater. Russia's pride had turned into Russia's shame; the revival of the show could not renew its entertainment value.

Soviet Musicals—The Revival?

Twelve Chairs (Dvenadtsat' stul'ev), based on Ilia Ilf and Yevgeni Petrov's satire written in 1928, was Tsekalo's next project, which opened in Moscow in November 2003. This time a different team of composers and directors was employed: the director, Tigran Keosayan, had previously worked on film, in particular children's film; the music was composed by Igor Zubkov, song writer and composer for a number of pop groups. The publicity campaign declared all across the city: "The Ice Is Moving" (Led tronulsia). The show was staged on the rented stage of the Moscow Youth Culture Palace (MDM), located in the southern parts of the city center.

The staging of *Twelve Chairs* is in many ways reminiscent of *Nord-Ost*. The production opens with a curtain carrying advertisements of the 1920s. The musical overture represents a medley. The set is constructivist in style, echoing the 1920s with references to Tatlin's Tower; it consists of three revolving semicircles that interconnect and revolve to form bridges, piers, and platforms. The set is much less complex and much more mobile than that of *Nord-Ost*.

The first act presents the story's characters as types: the businessmen are evil, the doctor wears a pince-nez à la Chekhov, the priest is sly and corrupt like Eisenstein's priest in *The Battleship Potyomkin*. The secret service agents (OGPU) appear stereotyped in black leather jackets, performing a tap dance, and shooting their pistols to pace the rhythm. "The ice moves" when Bender (sporting a green jacket and white trousers) becomes Ippolit's partner: they move on to find the diamonds, and the construction begins to move. There are numerous scenes in this act that offer scope for collective dances: the pioneers' orchestra is dressed in blue and red kerchiefs; the children perform a dance in which they kick each other; Madam Gritsatsuyeva and Bender's wedding is performed at a long table with food and drink, to a cabaret show with tap dance. The train and its passengers are hailed by a melody from the 1962 film *I Walk across Moscow*. The glorification of Moscow, both musically and vi-

Scene from the musical *Twelve Chairs*, which opened in Moscow in 2003. Ostap Bender (left) is seen trying to inspect one of the chairs for the hidden treasure. (Photo by Irina Kaledina)

sually—in the use of an orange backdrop for the sunrise and the city waking, or the use of kitchen tools to characterize the hostel—is reminiscent of *Nord-Ost*, as are the red stars of the Kremlin appearing from on high.

In the second act the visit to the editorial office of the newspaper resembles to some extent the treatment of bureaucracy in *Nord-Ost* in the visit to the Sea Committee. The editorial secretaries too perform synchronized movements to the rhythm of typewriters. The engineer Shchukin is portrayed as a bard with his guitar, reminiscent more of a dissident singer than of an engineer. The boat trip also reminds one of the port scenes in *Nord-Ost:* the sailors are

efficient, dressed in immaculate white suits. Bender's design for the theater, which is rejected by the troupe but liked by Gorky, is in fact a replica of Kazimir Malevich's suprematist masterpiece of the 1910s (banned in the Soviet Union), *Black Square.* The spa of Piatigorsk is crowded with patients and nurses to make it recognizable as such. The finale brings all the characters together to confirm the legendary and heroic status of Ostap Bender, the real hero of the musical. Bender's performance is weaker than that of Ippolit, however, so that there is somewhat of an imbalance in the production.

Musicals based on Soviet literature may have been appealing to the new audience

Twelve Chairs: Plot

Twelve Chairs is set in the early years of the Soviet period, in the 1920s. Ippolit Vorobianinov visits his dying aunt, Klavdiya Petukhova, who tells him (and the priest Vostrikov) that she has stitched the family fortune, in the form of diamonds, into one of the twelve chairs in her old family house's dining-room. After Petukhova's death, Ippolit begins to search for the diamonds. In the first instance he is followed by the priest, who has learned about the inheritance during the confession, thus underscoring the greed of the clergy. Ippolit meets Ostap Bender, a young man of 28, who is staying in the old family house, now an almshouse. Bender becomes Ippolit's ally in the search for the diamonds, for a share of 50 percent. Similarly, the chairs have been dispersed, like the wealth and the families themselves, and their large apartments have been turned into communal flats. The search for the chairs begins.

Two chairs turn out to be close by: one has been sold to a trader and purchased by the priest. Ippolit discovers it and has a fight with the priest, in the course of which Bender rips the chair open: it is empty. The second chair now belongs to Madam Gritsatsuyeva: Bender proposes and marries her, only to leave his newly wed wife and take the—empty—chair with him. The remaining ten chairs are for auction in Moscow. Ippolit has a romantic outing with Liza, however, during which he squanders the money needed for the auction, and the chairs are sold: four to the Colombine Theater, three to a newspaper, one to the engineer Shchukin, one to Ellochka, and one to the October Railway station. Ellochka's chair proves empty. While Ippolit poses as a medium and provides a recipe for success to the editorial staff of the newspaper, Bender searches for the chairs, with no result. The engineer has locked himself out of his flat: his chair too proves empty. The theater is about to go on tour, and Bender poses as an artist to join the group. He is found out and gets kicked off the boat. Having rejoined the theater in the spa Piatigorsk, he finds the chairs—all empty. He poses as a professional chess player to cheat some people in order to get the fare to return to Moscow. Here, at the railway station, must be the last chair. Ippolit and Bender decide to wait until the morning to retrieve the diamonds. During the night Ippolit kills Bender, only to find that the railway club where they stay has been built from the money for the diamonds. Bender becomes a myth.

of musicals that acquired the taste for the new genre in the late 1990s, but they cannot sustain a long-term interest. Neither thematically nor musically have the two Soviet musicals been able to compete with their rivals from Europe and the United States. It remains to be seen whether a musical tradition that would draw on nineteenth-century literature or on contemporary themes could attract a more sustained interest from the public.

A to Z

Agutin, Leonid: b. 1968. Agutin studied jazz at musical school and a cultural institute. At a festival in Yalta he won an award for the hit "Barefoot Boy" (Bosonogii mal'chik, 1992). He composes his own songs and also writes for Filipp Kirkorov. In 1997, performed "Queen" (Koroleva) with the daughter of the composer Yuri Varum, Angelica (b. 1969, Lviv), whom he married in 1998. Varum and Agutin frequently perform their songs together.

Aguzarova, Zhanna: b. in 1967 in Novosibirsk. Came to Moscow in 1983 and worked with the group Bravo under the false name of Ivana Anders. Arrested for fake documents in 1984 and sentenced to eight months in prison. Returned to Moscow in 1985 and played as Bravo lead singer until 1989. Embarked on a solo career and performed from 1991 to 1996 in the United States with the band Nighty Nighties. In 1996, returned to Russia and adopted a techno style. Since 1999, with a new manager and performs regularly in concerts.

Alisa: see Kinchev, Konstantin

Allegrova, Irina: b. 1961 in Rostov; real name Inessa Klimchuk. In 1986 performed with the Elektroklub band. After breaking her vocal chords, her voice became hoarse and smoky. In 1987 she won the Golden Tuning-Fork; from 1992 on, solo career with composer Igor Nikolayev, later with composer Igor Krutoy.

Alsou (Alsu Safina): b. 1983 in the Tatarstan village of Bugulma. In 1991 moved to Moscow and attended musical school. Since 1993 at a design college in London. Her song "Winter Dream" (Zimnii son, 1999) features a clip where Alsou is a Lolita-like character. Contract with Universal. In 2000, represented Russia at the Eurovision Song Contest and took second place, with "Solo." In 2002–2003 released an English album and won the European music award. Studies theater arts at the Moscow Theater Institute. [www.alsou.ru]

Apina, Alena: b. 1967 in Saratov. Apina studied the piano at Saratov Conservatory and played in the local disco band Kombinatsiya (Combination) before coming to Moscow in the late 1980s. She was supported by producer Sergei Lisovsky and later married the manager Alexander Iratov. She performed in the musical *Limits* (Limita), about a girl from the provinces, which was performed only twice but led to an album. Her songs are composed by Arkadi Ukupkin and Oleg Molchanov.

Aquarium: see Grebenshchikov, Boris [www.aquarium.ru] and [http://handbook. reldata.com/handbook.nsf/?Open]

Bashlachev, Alexander: b. 1960 in Cherepovets, Urals. Committed suicide on 17 February 1988. First rocker with authentic poetry, he was discovered by the rock critic Artyom Troitsky in 1984 and brought to Moscow. Bashlachev gave private performances to his own guitar and traveled the country. He married a Leningrad girl to get a residence permit *(propiska)*. In 1985 he toured Central Asia and Siberia. In 1986 started taking drugs and suffered from a writing block.

Butusov, Viacheslav (Slava): b. 1961 in Siberia. In the mid-1970s moved to Sverdlovsk and in 1978 formed Nautilus Pompilius with Dmitri Umetsky. First record "Ali Baba" in 1982, and first album recorded by Alexander Pantykin. Worked permanently with texts by Ilia Kormiltsev. In 1988 Nautilus was disbanded, and Butusov moved to Petersburg, where he reinvented the group in 1990. In 1996–1997, Butusov recorded the album *Yablokitai* in London, with electric music by Bill Nelson.

Atlantida too appeared under the label Nautilus but was created by Butusov. In 1997 dissolved Nautilus and worked with DeadUshki, who compose electronic music. His music features prominently in cinema. **Band Members:** Butusov, A. Beliayev, G. Kopylov, I. Dzhavad-Zade. **Albums:** *The Invisible* (Nevidimka, 1985); *Separation* (Razluka, 1986); *Retreat* (Otboi, 1988); *Prince of Silence* (Kniaz tishini, 1989); *Man without a Name* (Chelovek bez imeni, 1989); *Foreign Soil* (Chuzhaia zemlia, 1991); *Titanik*, 1994; *Wings* (Kryl'ia, 1995); *Yablokitai*, 1997; *Atlantida*, 1997. [www.nautilus.ru]

DDT: see Shevchuk, Yuri [www.ddt.ru]

Galich, Aleksandr: b. in Dnepropetrovsk (Ekaterinoslav) on 19 October 1919. Real name Ginzburg. Galich studied at the Literary Institute, Moscow (1935–1936) and the Stanislavsky Studio (1935–1938). From 1938 to 1941 he was an actor in the Moscow Theatrical Studio. During the war, he was an actor in the theater of the Northern Navy. Galich has written scenarios, plays, prose, poems, and songs. His play *Matrosskaya Tishina* was supposed to open the Sovremennik Theater in Moscow in 1956 but was banned by the Central Committee of the CPSU for the positive portrayal of a Jewish family. The censorship interventions are brilliantly described in Galich's novel, *The Final Dress Rehearsal.* He was expelled from the Writers' Union in December 1971 and emigrated in 1974, living in Oslo (1974), Munich (1975), and Paris (1976). He died on 15 December 1977 of accidental electrocution and is buried in the cemetery of Sainte-Geneviève-des-Bois, Paris.

Gradsky Alexander: b. 1949, Cheliabinsk. Rock-and-roll musician with classical tenor. Gradsky formed a number of student bands in the early 1960s, including Tarakany, with an imitation of Beatles in 1963–1964; Slaviane, 1965–1966; and Skify, 1966. Slaviane and Skify performed in English. From 1966 to 1976 he was leader of a Russian-singing band, Skomorokhi. On the post-Soviet estrada, Gradsky performs solo.

Grebenshchikov, Boris: b. 1953 in Leningrad. Fascinated by the Beatles and playing the guitar, he first sang the Beatles songs in English. BG studied maths. In 1972, together with the absurdist playwright A. Gunitsky, Grebenshchikov formed Aquarium, strongly influenced by Bob Dylan in the late 1970s. After a 1980 concert, he was sacked and excluded from the Komsomol. In the 1980s the band underwent a brief punk phase. In 1981, joined the Leningrad rock club. In the 1980s, attracted famous sax players and the pianist Kuryokhin to the band. From 1985 on, Westernized rock. In 1988–1999, contract with CBS and recording of Radio Silence in London. Aquarium provided the music for Sergei Soloviev's films. Grebenshchikov participated in the alternative art group Mitki and recorded three albums of Mitki songs. 1997, awarded Triumph. Since 1998, solo. **Band:** Seva Gakkel, Andrei (Diushka) Romanov, Mikhail Vasiliev (Fainstein). **Albums:** *Allegories of Count Diffuser* (Pritchi grafa Difuzora, 1974); *On that Side of the Mirror* (S toi storony zerkal'nogo stekla, 1976); *Blue Album* (Sinii al'bom, 1981); *Triangle* (Treugol'nik, 1981); *Acoustics* (Akustika, 1982); *Electricity* (Elektrichestvo, 1982); *Taboo* (Tabu, 1982); *Radio Afrika*, 1983; *Silver Day* (Den' serebra,

1984); *Ten Arrows* (Desiat' strel, 1986); *Equinox* (Ravnodenstvie, 1988); *Kostroma mon amour*, 1994; *Navigator*, 1994; *Snow Lion* (Snezhnii lev, 1996); *Hyperborea* (Giperboreia, 1997); *Kunstkamera*, 1998; *Psi*, 1999; *Territory* (Territoriia, 2000). [www.aquarium.ru]

Ivanushki International: youth project founded in 1995 by Igor Matvienko. [www.matvey.ru] Band consists of dancer and singer Andrei Grigoriev-Apollonov from Sochi, singer and actor Igor Sorin, and Kirill Andreyev. Oleg Yakovlev from the Tabakov Studio Theater joined the group later and took over after Sorin committed suicide. **Selected Albums:** *Naturally, He* (Konechno on, 1996); *Your Letters* (Tvoi pis'ma, 1997); *Tale about Ivanushkis* (Skazka ob Ivanushkakh, 1998); *Pages from Life* (Stranitsy iz zhizni, 1999). [www.matvey.ru/ivanush/]

Kinchev, Konstantin: b. 1958 in Moscow. Lead singer of the band Alisa, which he joined in 1983 upon invitation from the band's founder, Sviatoslav Zaderny. "My Generation" (Moye pokokolenie) became an anthem of the rock movement. **Selected Albums:** *Energy* (Energiia, 1985); *"BlokAda"* (Blockade, but also The Block of Hell, 1987); *The Sixth Forest Warden* (Shestoi lesnichnyi, 1989); *Article 206.2* (Stat'ia 206, chast' 2, 1989); *The End* (Shabash, 1990: memorial concert for Bashlachev); *Geopolitics* (Geopolitika, 1998) with techno, rave, and disco elements; *Solstice* (Soltnsevorot, 2000) with spiritual themes. **Band:** Konstantin Kinchev, Petr Samoilov, Andrei Shatalin, Yevgeni Levin, Mikhail Nefedov.

Kino: see Tsoy, Viktor

Kirkorov Filipp: b. 1967, Varna, son of Bedros Kirkorov. Since 1974 in Moscow. Studied at the Gnesin Institute; graduated in 1988. In 1987 invited to the Leningrad Music Hall and from 1988 to 989 in Alla Pugacheva's Theater. Started a solo career, winning major music awards in 1992 and 1993. In 1994 married Alla Pugacheva, 18 years his senior. In 1997, concert in Madison Square Garden, New York, and Friedrichstadtpalast, Berlin. Produced by Sergei Lisovsky. Kirkorov has appeared in films and on stage, starring in the lead role in the musical *Chicago* (2002). Albums include *Sky and Earth* (Nebo i zemlia, 1991) and *Atlantida* (1992), both of which have been staged as major shows. In the Eurovision Song Contest 1995, won 17th place. [www.kirkorov.ru]

Koroleva, Natasha: b. 1973, Ukraine. Discovered at a competition in Eupatoria by Igor Nikolayev (b. 1960), whom she married. Concert tours to the United States in 1997. Hits include "Little Country" (Malen'kaia Strana, 1995); "Yellow Tulips" (Zheltye tiul'pany, 1995); "Is This Really Me?" (Neuzheli eto ia?). [www.koroleva.ru]

Kuryokhin, Sergei: b. 1954 in Murmansk. Trained as a piano player and then played jazz with Anatoli Vapirov. Kuryokhin played with Aquarium between 1981 and 1984. In 1985, founded his band Popular Mechanics, and from 1988 on, recorded and performed abroad. Kuryokhin wrote scores for theater shows, which were only realized in the 1990s (*Capriccio, Opera for the Rich* [Opera bogatykh]). In 1986 he featured in an episode of the BBC's *Comrades*. He died in 1996 of cancer of the brain.

Leningrad: see Shnurov, Sergei [www.

leningrad.spb.ru] and an unofficial site [http://leningrad.hut.ru]

Makarevich, Andrei: born 1953. While a student of architecture, he became fascinated with the Beatles and formed a band, Atlanty (The Atlants). In 1968 he created the band Mashina Vremeni (Time Machine) as a school band. Time Machine gained popularity during the 1970s, although many bans were imposed on the repertoire. In 1979, he was offered a contract with the state agency Roskontsert and allowed to give official concerts. In 1980 participated in a competition in Tblisi and won the first prize. Makarevich composed music for films, including the theme song for Georgi Daneliya's film *Afonya*. In the New Russia, Makarevich presents the television program *Abazhur* (Lampshade) on musical matters as well as the culinary program *Smak* (Relish). [www.mashina.ru]

Mamonov, Petr: b. 1951 in Moscow. In 1982 began song writing and in 1983 formed Zvuki Mu (1983–1990). The band was sponsored and organized by Sasha Lipnitsky. In 1987 Brian Eno recorded their album for 1989 release. Since 1991, performs with his stepbrother as Mamonov and Alexei. Since 1988, Mamonov has appeared in films: he played the drug dealer Artur in *The Needle* (Igla, 1988); Selivestrov in Pavel Lungin's *Taxi Blues* (1990), and the geologist in Sergei Selianov's *The Time for Sorrow Has Not Yet Come* (Vremia pechali eshche ne prishlo, 1995). In the 1990s, theater performances at the Stanislavsky Theater, Moscow: *The Bald Brunette* (Lysyi brunet, 1991); *Nobody Writes to the Officer* (Polkovniku nikto ne pishet, 1995); *Is There Life on Mars?* (Est' li zhizn' na marse?, 1998).

Mashina Vremeni: see Makarevich, Andrei [www.mashina.ru]

Namin, Stas: b. 1951; real name Anastas Mikoyan. Namin is the grandson of politician Anastas Mikoyan. Namin was the first rocker to join the Union of Composers. While a student at the Suvorov military academy (1965), Namin organized his first band. He transferred to the Institute for Foreign Languages in 1969 and to Moscow State University in 1970, where he formed the rock band Tsvety (Flowers) and had a record released by Melodiya in 1973. In 1974 the band turned professional and was closed by decree in 1975. In 1978 Namin organized the Group of Stas Namin and revived his musical activities. He was engaged in the "rock for peace" campaign. In 1988 he promoted the band Gorky Park. He runs his own musical center cum theater, located in Gorky Park. In 1999 he staged the musical *Hair* with an American and Russian cast.

NaNa: formed in 1994 as boy group by Bari Alibasov (b. 1947 in Charsk, near Semipalatinsk), who had previously managed the jazz band Integral. Modeled on the Beatles, the band consists of Vladimir Levkin (b. 1969), Vladimir Asimov (b. 1968), Vladimir Politov (b. 1970), and Viacheslav Zherebkin (b. 1969). Hits have included "Deserted Beach" (Pustinnyi pliazh) and "Faina."

Nautilus Pompilius (Nau): see Butusov, Viacheslav [www.nautilus.ru]

Nord-Ost: Russian musical. Staged in the House of Culture of Moscow's Ball-Bearing Factory on Dubrovka, where it premiered on 19 October 2001. Based on Veniamin Kaverin's (1902–1989) epic *Two Captains*, a novel covering 30 years of Soviet history. Produced by Alexander Tsekalo and Georgi Vasiliev; libretto written by Alexei Ivashchenko and Georgi Vasiliev (the duo Ivasi). On 23 October 2002 a group of Chechen terrorists held the troupe and the audience of more than 800 people hostage, to press for an end of the Russian military action in Chechnya. On 26 October the building was stormed by special forces after an anesthetic gas had been pumped into the auditorium; more than 100 people died in the course of the liberation of the building. The show reopened on 8 February 2003 but was eventually closed on 10 May 2003. [www.nordost.ru]

Okudzhava, Bulat: b. 9 May 1924 in Moscow to an Armenian mother and a Georgian father. His father was executed during the purges, his mother arrested and released only in 1955. Okudzhava volunteered for the army and served at the front. He was a novelist, member of the Writers' Union, and poet-bard. His first novel, *Good Luck, Schoolboy* (Bud' zdorov, shkoliar! 1961) caused controversy for emphasizing the soldier's fear of death over and above the feeling of heroism and the fight against fascism. Okudzhava died in June 1997.

Pauls, Raimond: b. 1936 in Riga. Pauls studied composition at musical school and conservatory. While a student, he played in a jazz sextet and wrote his first compositions. He joined the Riga estrada orchestra and in 1964 became its head. He has worked with renowned poets, such as Voznesensky, Rozhdestvensky, and Reznik for his songs. In 1981 he wrote "Maestro" for Alla Pugacheva and has also written for Leontiev and Vaikule. He has presented since 1978 a music program on Latvian television. In 1989 he became minister of culture of Latvia and in 1998 was elected to parliament.

Pugacheva, Alla: b. 1949, Moscow. In 1965 appeared in the musical program *Pif Paf*, and toured with VIAs. From 1974 to 1977, with VIA Veselye Rebiata, where she learned her theatrical approach to singing. In 1974 performed the tune for Eldar Riazanov's film comedy *Irony of Fate* (Ironiia sud'by). Her "Harlequin" (1975) gained her stage popularity as a solo singer. Her songs were written largely by Ilia Reznik and Raimond Pauls. In 1985 she began to stage larger shows. Married to Filipp Kirkorov. In 1997 took part in the Eurovision Song Contest with "Primadonna" (placed 15th). Pugacheva's daughter, Kristina Orbakaite (b. 1971, London), starred in Rolan Bykov's children's film *Scarecrow* (Chuchelo) and later had an affair with rock singer Vladimir Presniakov (b. 1968 in Sverdlovsk), with whom she has a son, Nikita (b. 1991). [www.allapugacheva.ru]

Shevchuk, Yuri: b. in 1957 in Magadan. Studied graphic design at Ufa University, where in 1980 he formed his own band. In 1987 moved to Leningrad when the authorities in Ufa forbade performances; he formed the band DDT, which became famous in the rock scene. 1993 awarded the prize Ovation. ***Selected Albums:*** *Pig on the Rainbow* (Svin'ia na raduge, 1982); *Monologue in Saigon* (Monolog v Saigone, 1982); *Thaw* (Ottepel', 1983), English version, 1993; *Actress Spring* (Aktrisa vesna, 1992); *This Is All* (Eto vse, 1995); *Love* (Liubov', 1997); *World Number Zero* (Mir nomer nol', 1999). [www.ddt.ru]

Shnurov, Sergei (Shnur): b. 1973. Formed the techno group Ukho Van Goga (Van

Gogh's Ear) and the hard rock group Alko-repitsa in the 1990s before organizing the band Leningrad in January 1997. Shnurov has appeared in cult films such as Natalia Pogonnicheva's *Drink Theory* (Teoriia zapoia, 2002) and composed the music for Petr Buslov's *Bimmer* (Bumer, 2003) and Andrei Proshkin's *The Play of the Butterflies* (Igry motyl'kov, 2004).

styob: derived from the verb *stebal* (to whip, to lash), it describes the exposure to mockery. Styob is linked to postmodernism because of its parody of socialist culture. Styob may refer to a remake, where the author creates a new myth based on the sacral status of past culture (for example, Chapayev anecdotes, Stirlitz, where the hero of Soviet culture is exposed to laughter and profanation).

Sukachev, Igor (Garik): b. 1959 and graduated from Lipetsk Theater Institute. Musician and actor. Formed the band Brigada S (1985–1993). In 1995–1996 ran, with Alexander Skliar, the project Boatswain and Wanderer (Botsman and Brodyaga) to record old Soviet songs. Since 1993, leader of the band Neprikasayemye (Untouchables). Sukachev has played in a number of films, including *Defence Counsellor Sedov* (Zashchitnik Sedov, 1988) and *The Fatal Eggs* (Rokovye iaitsa, 1995). Acted also in his directorial debut *Midlife Crisis* (Krizis srednego vozrasta, 1997) and directed *The Holiday* (Prazdnik, 2001).

t.A.T.u: Lena Katina (b. 1984) and Julia Volkova (b. 1985), a Russian girl band created in 1999 by Ivan Shapovalov. The duo gained popularity through their scandalous image as two underage lesbians, sporting school uniforms and dreaming of an escape from the society that condemned their love. This image was specially created for them and lasted long enough to promote their songs, compiled on their album, which has also been released in English. t.A.T.u was the first Russian pop band to take first place in the pop charts in several European countries, including the UK. They took part in the Eurovision Song Contest in 2003, taking third place. [www.tatu.ru]

Tsoy, Viktor: b. 1961 in Kupchino, Leningrad. Studied art and woodcutting in Leningrad, when he started to play with various bands: Piligrimy (Pilgrims), Palata No. 6 (Ward 6), Absats (Paragraph), and Garin i Giperboloid (Garin and the Hyperboloid). In 1982 formed a duo with Alexei Rybin and released the album *45*. The group Kino emerged in 1984 with Rybin, Kasparian, Titov, and Gurianov. Tsoy played himself in Soloviev's *ASSA* and Moro in *The Needle*, for which he also provided the sound track. International tours. Died in a car accident in Jurmala in 1990. ***Albums:*** *45* (1982); *46* (1983); *Captain of the Kamchatka* (Nachal'nik kamchatki, 1984); *This Is Not Love* (Eto ne liubov', 1985); *Night* (Noch', 1986); *Blood Type* (Gruppa krovi, 1988); *A Star Called Sun* (Zvezda po imeni solntse, 1989); *Black Album* (Chernyi albom, 1990, posthumous).

tusovka: trend word in the early 1990s, derived from the French term *se tasser; tusovat* means primarily "to shuffle cards." *Tusovatsya* describes the activity of being with friends and having fun, being in one's clique.

Twelve Chairs: after *Nord-Ost*, the second attempt by Tsekalo to create a Russian musical. Based on Ilf and Petrov's satire

(1928), the show was directed by the children's filmmaker Tigran Keosayan and the music composed by song-writer Igor Zubkov. Has played since 7 November 2003 in the Moscow Youth Culture Palace (MDM), but remains a pale reflection of *Nord-Ost*, both musically and in terms of special effects. [www.12stulyev.ru]

Vaikule, Laima: b. 1954 in Riga. At age 14, Vaikule won a prize in a local singing competition. When a student of medicine, she continued to perform as a singer in restaurants and clubs, designing her own choreography for her disco songs. She was discovered by Raimonds Pauls, and her success came with texts and compositions by Pauls and Reznik, beginning with "Night Bonfire" (Nochnoi koster). In 1987 she won the Golden Lyre in Czechoslovakia. Later in her career she performed songs by Igor Krutoy and Yuri Varum.

Vysotsky, Vladimir: b. 25 January 1938, Moscow. He lived with his father, an army officer, in Eberswalde, East Germany, from 1947 to 1949. He graduated in 1960 from the Moscow Arts Theater studio and subsequently worked at the Pushkin Theater and Theater of Miniatures. In 1964 joined the company of the Taganka Theater, where he created his reputation as a stage actor. In 1966 he married (third marriage) the French actress Marina Vlady (Poliakova). From 1966 onward he gave concerts in the Soviet Union, France (1977), and the United States (1979). Vysotsky was addicted to alcohol. He died on 25 July 1980 of a heart failure and is buried in Vagankovo Cemetery, Moscow. [http://vysotsky.km.ru]

Bibliography

Friedman, Julia, and Adam Weiner. "Between a Rock and a Hard Place: Holy Rus' and Its alternatives in Russian Rock Music." In *Consuming Russia. Popular Culture, Sex and Society since Gorbachev*, ed. by Adele Barker, 110–137. Durham, NC: Duke University Press, 1999.

MacFadyen, David. *Estrada?! Grand Narratives and the Philosophy of the Russian Popular Song since Perestroika.* Montreal: McGill–Queen's University Press, 2002.

———. *Red Stars. Personality and the Soviet Popular Song 1955–1991.* Montreal: McGill–Queen's University Press, 2001.

Ramet, Sabrina, ed. *Rocking the State: Rock Music and Politics in Eastern Europe and Russia.* Boulder, CO: Westview Press, 1994.

Ryback, Timothy W. *Rock around the Bloc: A History of Rock Music in Eastern Europe and the Soviet Union.* New York: Oxford University Press, 1990.

Smith, G. S. *Songs to Seven Strings: Russian Guitar Poetry and Soviet "Mass Song."* Bloomington: Indiana University Press, 1984.

Starr, Frederick. *Red and Hot: The Fate of Jazz in the Soviet Union.* New York: Limelight, 1994.

Troitsky, Artemy. *Back in the USSR: The True Story of Rock in Russia.* London: Omnibus Press, 1987.

———. *Tusovka: Who's Who in the New Soviet Rock Culture.* London: Omnibus Press, 1990.

von Geldern, James, and Richard Stites, eds. *Mass Culture in Soviet Russia: Tales, Poems, Songs, Movies, Plays and Folklore 1917–1953.* Bloomington: Indiana University Press, 1995.

5

Popular Entertainment

Russian television serials from *Cops* to *Brigade*, Russian pulp fiction from Akunin to Marinina, and Russian sports from Rodnina to Sharapova all attract a large numbers of spectators and readers and are destined primarily for passive consumption. They provide commercially available entertainment for the masses, and as such they represent genuinely new forms of popular culture. Spectator sports, soap operas, and pulp fiction are expressions of culture that had existed in some rudimentary forms in the Soviet era, when their public consumption was not encouraged by the regime. Detective stories were read widely in the Soviet era, but they had a low print run and were difficult to get hold of. And soap operas were made not for entertainment but for education, although spy thrillers attracted huge audiences in the 1970s. In sports, the Soviet state had fostered the performance of athletes in international competitions but had not encouraged public support (say, in the form of fan clubs). In the post-Soviet era the state-supported system of coaching sportsmen and sportswomen crashed, but sport has become more publicly accessible altogether (both in its active and passive forms). Television serials were influenced by Mexican and Latin American soaps before Russian-made detective and crime series (rather than sitcoms) took off. And in terms of books, the homegrown detective and fantasy stories boom.

Sports

Soviet sports dominated international competitions. It does not follow, however, that since the collapse of the USSR Russian sports have sunk to a low profile. The international sports scene is full of contemporary Russian sports personalities, such as the tennis players Anna Kurnikova and Maria Sharapova, or the hockey stars Pavel Bure and Alexander Mogilny, or the soccer players Valeri Karpin and Alexander Mostovoy. The world, certainly the European Champions League 2003–2004, has had to take notice of the Moscow soccer club Lokomotiv and has not forgotten the popularity of Spartak (Sparta-cus) Moscow in recent years. But all this is trivial when compared to the acquisition of London's prestigious premier league Chelsea Football Club in 2003 by the Russian millionaire and governor of Chukotka, Roman Abramovich. How did Russia manage to become so competitive in the sports market in such a short space of time?

Olympic History

The USSR had always seen sports competition as a way to demonstrate its ideological and political superiority. Winning more Olympic medals than the Americans (which they did most years) was a way of showing to the world the superiority of the Communist system and of reassuring the people at home that the country had adopted the cor-rect and better path—toward the Communist future.

Olympic Glory

The Olympic Games played a crucial role in the official Soviet sports history and in the importance of sports for the Russian people, insofar as the success in some disciplines led to the popularity of that particular sport. The Olympics of the modern era were revived in Athens in 1896 by the Frenchman Pierre de Coubertin. Russia was a founding member of the Olympic Organization but did not partake in the Games in Paris (1900) and St. Louis (1904), making its first Olympic appearance only in London in 1908, followed by Stockholm in 1912. Then World War I interrupted the Games' cycle (1916); in 1924 the Games ac-

Valeri Shantsev (left), vice mayor of Moscow, in front of the Lenin Mausoleum on Red Square, passing the Olympic flame to former hockey player and chairman of Russia's State Committee for Sport, Viacheslav Fetisov, 2004. (Photo by Mikhail Galustov/Kommersant)

quired a winter edition (in addition to the summer games). After the Revolution, Russia, and later the USSR, did not participate in the "bourgeois" competition in sports (as the new regime labeled the Olympics) until 1952, when the country won 22 gold, 30 silver, and 19 bronze medals in Helsinki. In 1956 the USSR participated for the first time also in the winter Games in Cortina d'Ampezzo, where the ice hockey team won a gold medal, beating Canada in the final. In the summer Games in Melbourne, the USSR achieved 37 gold, 29 silver, and 32 bronze medals and by Rome in 1960 they had reached an absolute record of 43 gold, 29 silver, and 31 bronze medals. The Olympic triumph of the USSR continued at the 1964 Olympics in Innsbruck (winter) and Tokyo (summer) and in 1968 in Grenoble (winter) and Mexico (summer). In 1968 the German Democratic Republic (GDR) was for the first time represented as a team competing with the Federal Republic of Germany (FRG), using the Olympics as an arena to demonstrate the GDR's superiority over capitalist regimes. In 1972 the winter Games in Sapporo saw the USSR emerge as the leader in ice skating. The Olympics of Munich in 1972, where Arab terrorists killed the entire Israeli Olympic team, brought for the USSR a new record of 50 gold, 27 silver, and 22 bronze medals. In 1976 the Olympics turned even more into a political arena, when African states boycotted the summer Games in Montreal, because New Zealand, a country that supported the apartheid-ridden South African Republic, was participating. The winter Olympics in Innsbruck remained untouched by politics. In 1980 the winter Olympics took place in Lake Placid, and the summer Games in Moscow became again the place of a political rally. The

United States, West Germany, Canada, Japan, Italy, and the UK (but not France) boycotted the Games because of the Soviet invasion of Afghanistan. In 1984, after the winter Olympics in Sarajevo, the summer Games in Los Angeles were boycotted by the USSR and most Eastern European states in an act of revenge for the 1980 boycott, but also because the United States had allegedly reinforced its assistance for Soviet citizens to defect during the Games. In 1988 the winter Olympics in Calgary were followed by the summer Games in Seoul, not boycotted by the USSR despite calls from North Korea to do so. In 1991 the USSR collapsed; the united teams of the now largely independent republics and the Russian Federation appeared in the winter Games in Albertville and the summer Games in Barcelona in 1992 as the CIS (Commonwealth of Independent States) team, carrying the Olympic, not a national, flag. What was once the ultimate national pride—to participate in and win an Olympic competition—had become a nationless spectacle for the former Soviet sportsmen. In Lillehammer in 1994, after the winter Olympics began to alternate with the summer Games, the team of the Russian Federation made its debut. The Olympics in 1996 Atlanta were doomed by a bomb explosion. In the 1998 Olympics in Nagano, 2000 in Sydney, 2002 in Salt Lake City, and 2004 in Athens the Russian team finally returned to its previous excellent performance, even if not to the former glory of world leadership in the medal count. The Olympics were no longer an arena for proving political superiority through athletic achievements, or the battle ground for political disputes, but had become again what they were once conceived to be: athletic competitions. For the

Olympic Games in 2004 Russia sent 472 sportsmen and -women to Athens, who won 92 medals; there were no major scandals over medals (as in Salt Lake City in 2002, see below), and only one major embarrassment when the shotputter Irina Korzhanenko tested positive in a drugs test and had to return her gold medal, which she had already, hastily perhaps, dispatched to Russia. Russia seems to have settled within the framework of international sports competitions. This is further enhanced by Moscow's bid (alongside London, New York, Paris, and Madrid) to host the 2012 Olympics.

Sport, Soviet Style   The concept of a healthy mind in a healthy body (*mens sana in corpore sano*), the harmony of mind and body, dominated in socialist thought. Therefore, sport was seen first and foremost as a way of keeping fit; physical education (PE) was intrinsically linked to health, almost taking the role of preventive medicine. The Soviet regime perceived competition as "bourgeois," but after a party resolution of 1925, competition on a national level was considered appropriate. Instead of Olympic competition, national Spartakiades (*spartakiady*) were organized from 1928 on. Only in the 1930s could sport become a leisure activity, once the first Five-Year Plan had been fulfilled and workers had more time.

It was not until the victory in World War II, however, that the USSR deemed it worthwhile to demonstrate to the world its superiority in sports. Indeed, Stalin only agreed to sending teams to the Olympics in 1952 in those disciplines where medals were "guaranteed"; he had thought of sending a Soviet team to the 1948 Olympics but had been dissuaded by his advisers, as not enough medals were certain. Spartakiades were held again after 1956 in the year before the Olympics as a testing ground for international competition.

Sport had played an important role in military and army training since 1918. The Vsevobuch (Vseobshchee Voennoe Obuchenie, General Military Training) included skiing, wrestling, and fencing. This led to the formation of CDRA/CDSA (Central House of the Red Army, then Soviet Army) and CSKA (Central Army Sports Club), used by the staff of the Ministry of Defense and the army. In 1923 the club Dinamo (Dynamo) was founded by Felix Dzerzhinsky for the staff of the interior services (Secret Service and Ministry of the Interior). The party held control over other sports clubs, mostly voluntary sports organizations associated with the workplaces. Such sports organizations associated their names with the workers' organizations: Burevestnik (Stormy Petrel) for state trade, later for students; Lokomotiv for railway workers; Spartak for cooperatives; VVS (Voennovozdushnye sila, Air Force) for the air force; and Krylia Sovetov (Wings of the Soviets) for trade unions. By 1938 there were about 100 clubs. In 1936 a football league was formed, and teams were set up in almost every town. Stadiums were designed, recognizing sport as a mass spectacle; many were built only after the war, however.

In 1945 monetary prizes were introduced as an incentive for performance. All sportsmen were employed in the military, or they held fictitious jobs in factories, or they were students. Sportsmen had no need to earn a living elsewhere, a principle called "shamateurism," where the state masks a professional as an amateur. After the war, clubs were organized on a territorial principle. New sports disciplines were encouraged in the 1950s and 1960s during the growing engagement with the Olympic movement. Exceptions were karate and yoga, both deemed to be nonsocial sports that turn the individual away from society. Moreover, facilities such as arenas, pools, and ice rinks were constructed, without, however, providing a suitable infrastructure including restaurants, ticket offices, and proper public access. The introduction of the sports lottery in 1964 served to finance the development of sports facilities and the Olympic travel of USSR teams.

Although sports became of interest to the masses from the 1930s onward, during the Soviet era they never reached the popularity of cinema, literature, and the theater. Television transmissions of matches further took their toll of spectators away from the clubs and the fields in the 1970s. Only hockey continued to attract huge interest. The focus by both the party and the media on Olympic sports only ceased in 1985, when Gorbachev made possible wider coverage of non-Olympic sports. The emphasis shifted clearly to hockey and football. Sports may have been controlled by the party, but that did not mean that fairness and transparency pervaded Soviet sports. There were rigged games, bribed referees, hooliganism, and bought players, and in this sense the Soviet sports world was no different from sports elsewhere. Soviet sportsmen were paid by the party and state and played for the glory of the country, but they also had self-interest at heart.

Television coverage was led by Nikolai Ozerov, an actor of the Moscow Arts Theater. He was a most formidable commentator, always displaying a certain degree of sympathy for the Soviet teams, as is common for sports commentators. The chief sports commentator on radio was Vadim Siniavsky, and the most prolific sports journalist Vladimir Pereturin. In 1988 the Soviet media were able for the first time to send their own journalists to the Olympics to obtain live coverage of the events, although still relying on the images of the Korean hosts. During the 1988 Olympic coverage, the first advertisements (Pepsi Cola) were shown on Russian television, opening the path for a commercialization of sports. The leading journal *Soviet Sport* broke up in 1991 to form *SportExpress*, which is now partly owned by the French *L'Equipe* and reaches a circulation of almost one million. *SportExpress* covers national and international sports, as well as Formula One. In total, there are around 35 journals dealing specifically with sports, including journals on motor sports, an area where Russia has hardly any active role. On television, sports coverage has always usurped a lower percentage of airtime than in other European countries; television devoted a mere 900 hours per year to sports, radio 700 hours per year (averages for the 1990s). For a while, sports disappeared almost entirely onto the paid cable network, but the coverage on the national channels has risen since 2000, and the formation of a sports channel in 2002 (Channel 6) bears further evidence to the growing interest in sports.

After the collapse of the Soviet Union, the republics of Georgia and Lithuania immediately formed their own leagues in football and basketball. At the same time in Russia the interest in football had been waning: in 1987 an average of 27,000 spectators came to a game, dropping to 6,000 by 1992, and picking up only after 1996. This coincided with the "brawn drain" in the mid-1990s when around 300 soccer players, 700 hockey players, and 100 basketball players were on contracts abroad and made it difficult for Russian teams to perform well, until Russia too began to hire and buy foreign players. In the late 1990s, salaries began to rise as sponsorship increased and investors could be found on the Russian market for football and hockey, but less for other sports. The state largely pulled out of sports support, which became independent and now relies on ticket sales, sponsorship, and advertising deals. The Russian team for the Olympics in Atlanta was sponsored by Reebok; other main sponsors at Russian football and hockey games include the Italian dairy giant Parmalat, the German beer company Holsten, and Samsung, which are all strong on the Russian market. Russian sportsmen also appear in advertising clips for products: the hockey trainer Viktor Tikhonov was one of the first sportsmen to do this, appearing in a spot for Vicks cough drops.

Post-Soviet Russia only gradually returned to active sports. Much of the sports facilities belonged to the above-mentioned clubs, and new facilities in Moscow and Petersburg were expensive to use. The new private sports clubs in Moscow are for members only, with fees reaching US$2,000 a year, when the average monthly income was just under US$200 in 2004. Aqua parks and saunas are also expensive, but some cheaper pools remain open. Tennis courts and golf courses are part of luxury hotels or clubs, accessible only to the upper and (upper) middle classes. Open-air sports are still available for the masses: skiing and skating on snowy plains and hills, on frozen rivers and lakes remain as popular as swimming in the sea (Black or Baltic), in the numerous lakes, or in rivers. People play games in parks or courtyards. The high pollution in the big cities makes joggers and runners a rare sight.

Team Sports

Football (Soccer)   The game of football, as soccer is called outside of the United States, originally came to Russia in the form of the Georgian game of *lelo* and the Russian game of *shalyga*. Russia joined the world and European football leagues only after World War II, but the formation of national leagues began in the early twentieth century. Indeed, matches took place between the Russian and the English teams in Petersburg, formed by the colony of British people living in Petersburg in 1907. The first Russian championship took place in 1912. Football clubs were formed in the 1920s, and most sports clubs of the large industries and workers' organizations had their football team in major cities. The club Dinamo had teams in Moscow, Kiev, and other cities.

Once the USSR entered international competition, victory was meant to demonstrate superiority over capitalism. The Soviet performance in the World Cups, however, left a great deal to be desired. The USSR team reached the quarterfinals in Sweden in 1958 and in Chile in 1962. Then the Soviet team disappeared from the international arena until it featured in the quarterfinals in 1982. On the European level, the national team fared somewhat better. In 1956 the USSR won the European Cup in France; in 1964 it lost to Spain in the final; in 1968 it took fourth place; in 1972 it lost to Germany in the semifinal. In the following years (1976, 1980, 1984) the Soviet team did not qualify and returned to the European arena only in 1988, losing the final to Holland. In the late 1990s Russian clubs un-

Disciplined soccer supporters watching a match at the Dinamo Stadium in Moscow in the early 1950s. (Hulton-Deutsch Collection/Corbis)

successfully participated in the UEFA (Union of European Football Associations) Cup (1996, 1998, 2000). In the absence of a strong international performance of Russia's national football team in the World Cup and Russian football clubs in the UEFA cup, it is not surprising that hockey was much more popular as a spectator sport than football. Nevertheless, football too had its followers, especially on a local and national level.

The Dinamo stadium in Moscow is one of the oldest sports venues; it was built in 1927 with a capacity of 20,000–35,000, which has been extended to up to 55,000 after restoration. In the postwar period, outdoor and indoor pools as well as an ice rink and a small arena were added. It is not

roofed, and the southern stands is usually occupied by the club's fans, the Dynamites. Dinamo stadium has its own metro stop outside the front entrance. In order to accommodate the "mass" spectatorship for football and hockey, the Soviet leadership planned grand new arenas in the 1930s, but most of the large stadiums were built only in the 1950s. The Luzhniki Stadium was built in 1956, with a capacity of over 100,000. After the reconstruction in 1997, it remains the largest arena in Moscow. It is located at some distance from the metro, however: the station Leninskie Gory (Lenin Hills, later renamed Sparrow Hills [Vorob'evye gory]) was closed until 2002 after the bridge on which the station is located proved in need of major repair work

Moscow's Luzhniki Stadium, built in 1956, with a capacity of over 100,000. After the reconstruction in 1997 it remained the largest arena in Moscow. (Bettmann/Corbis)

in the 1980s. People have to walk from the metro stop Sportivnaya. Luzhniki is the home of the Torpedo and Spartak teams, and it is a comfortable, modern stadium, which also includes a smaller arena, a gym, a sports hall for indoor events, and a hockey pitch. The Olympic Games in Moscow in 1980 equipped the city with further facilities, including the Olympic Stadium on Prospekt Mira, with indoor seating for 35,000 spectators and two pools, designed by Mikhail Posokhin in the building materials popular in the 1970s, concrete and steel. The roofed Olympic Stadium hosts the Kremlin Cup, Russia's largest tennis championship, established in 1991. The CSKA has a basketball arena, a hockey stadium seating 5,500, and a football pitch in the north of Moscow. The Sokolniki Sta-

dium is one of the training grounds for Spartak, seating 5,000 spectators and also hosting the Russian championships in figure skating on its ice rink. The sports arena at Krylatskoye in the west of Moscow was built in 1979 and has a modern velo-track. In Petersburg the largest stadiums are also in the north of the city: the sport palace Jubilee and the Petrovsky Stadium.

Historically, the Moscow football teams always dominated the national league tables (rankings), and among the Moscow teams, there has always been a rivalry between Dinamo and Spartak. Dinamo was the team favored and formed by the Ministry of the Interior and the NKVD/KGB and distinguished itself by a disciplined and rigorous approach to play. The Spartak team was formed by the workers from the public

Political Football: Stalin versus Beria; Winner Starostin

During Stalin's purges of the 1930s, many people, including sportsmen, were arrested and exiled. The situation for Spartak was worsened by their rivalry with Dinamo, the team sponsored by the NKVD (Secret Service) and its chairman, the Georgian Lavrenti Beria. Beria disliked Spartak for being better than the Dinamo team. But even worse, the Spartak team beat Dinamo Tbilisi (Georgia) in a semifinal in 1939. Beria was so outraged that he ordered a replay of the semifinal after the final had been played and won by Spartak, who fortunately also won the semifinal second time round. Beria's attempts to arrest Nikolai Starostin were hampered on several occasions by the fact that Starostin's daughter went to school with Prime Minister Molotov's daughter, and Molotov refused to sign the order for arrest requested by Beria. In 1942, however, Nikolai Starostin and his brothers Andrei, Alexander, and Peter—all footballers—were arrested for contact with foreigners, which had occurred during the matches abroad in the 1930s. Nikolai Starostin was sent to a labor camp in the north. He was awaited there with great eagerness, however, and instead of hard labour he was "sentenced" to coach Dinamo Ukhta. Then he was transferred to Khabarovsk in the Far East, where he served on similar terms. All this was entirely unknown to Beria. In 1948, while still exiled from Moscow, Starostin was brought back to the capital by Stalin's son Vasili in order to train the VVS (air force) team. Because his return to Moscow was illegal, Vasili Stalin had to accompany Starostin during all public appearances to prevent Starostin from being arrested by Beria. Starostin was caught out, however, and sent to Alma-Ata for the remainder of his exile, where he trained the Kairat Alma-Ata team. In 1955 he was officially allowed to return to Moscow and managed Spartak.

sector (trade) and excelled in a more improvised style of play. Popular sympathies therefore lay with the Spartak team, which was the better team already in the 1930s. Indeed, in 1934 Spartak, with such players as Nikolai Starostin and Mikhail Yakushin, scored a win against the Basel football club (5:2), the first major international win of a Soviet football team. Spartak subsequently went on a tour through several Czech cities. In 1937, Spartak beat the Basque national team, which was visiting Russia, after a disputed penalty. By 1945 Dinamo took the lead, however, and played Chelsea and Arsenal in London, gaining a win over Arsenal. From 1945 to 1951, the CSKA dominated the national league. In the 1950s Spartak recaptured its former glory when Nikolai Starostin returned to the team. On the basis of the Spartak team, he formed the Olympic team that won the gold medal in Melbourne in 1956 with the legendary Abkhazian striker Igor Netto (1930–1999), who was captain of the Soviet team for the World Cup in 1962.

When football matches were watched in the Soviet period, cases of hooliganism were not uncommon, even if the sophistication of fan clubs and the paraphernalia available to express their support did not reach Western levels until the 1990s. The Soviet Union was not immune to disasters either. On 20 October 1982 Spartak Moscow played the Haarlem team in the Luzhniki stadium. At the score of 1:2, with Spartak clearly losing and only minutes of the match to go, many disappointed Spartak supporters started to head for the exit. At

Supporters of Spartak Moscow at a match of their team against Saturn in July 2003. (Photo by Dmitry Azarov/Kommersant)

that point, the police closed three of the four exits. When Spartak scored a goal, the fans tried to return to the stadium and were met by the crowd trying to leave through the one open gate. In true Soviet fashion the media hushed up the event, refused to blame the police for not opening the gates, and the state organ *Izvestiya* admitted 61 dead. Unofficial Western sources suspected 340 casualties; other sources give figures of up to 700. The exact number of victims has never been officially confirmed. In order to avoid crowds clashing in the stadium, the soccer match between Russia and Japan on 9 June 2002 that took place in Luzhniki was translated live onto a large screen built on Manège Square in central Moscow, where no riot police were in place. Hooliganism in the crowd escalated toward the end of the match, and the fans caused serious damage to shops, cars, and public spaces in central Moscow.

In the 1990s, paraphernalia for fans were gradually introduced: imported goods mass produced in England or items handmade in Russia. Spartak Moscow fans wear red and white, the CSKA colors are red and blue, Dinamo sports blue and white, Torpedo Moscow is black and white, and Lokomotiv Moscow carries the colors green and white. Football fans all sport black "bomber jackets" with orange linings as well as black military boots. The Spartak fans are the most aggressive and largest contingent, numbering around 9–10,000. The CSKA team has about 7–8,000 fans and Dinamo 4–5,000. On 30 August 1997, fights took place in Petersburg before a match between Zenit Petersburg and Spartak Moscow; further fights between fans flared up

The team Lokomotive, Moscow, February 2004. (Photo by Dmitry Azarov/Kommersant)

in Moscow on another occasion of a Zenit versus Spartak match. The number of spectators for the sport is not large, as the interest dropped significantly in the latter half of the 1990s when football was increasingly seen as a game for the working class and youth gangs. The CSKA stadium and Luzhniki (Dinamo) were filled to less than a third of their capacity; Krylia Sovetov and Spartak's Sokolniki Stadium to less than half; non-Moscow stadiums, however, managed to fill up their arenas to capacity. The numbers of both fans and spectators are indicative of the low standing of football in Russia when compared with other European countries.

In the early 1990s a few good players from Russian and CIS teams transferred to foreign clubs, among them Alexei Mikhailichenko from Dinamo Kiev, who joined the Glasgow Rangers in 1990, and Andrei Kanchelskis of Shakhter, who moved to Manchester United in 1991. The Ukrainian player Sergei Rebrov (b. 1974) transferred to England's Tottenham Hotspurs in 2000 for a transfer fee of almost $U.S. 20 million; since 2004 Rebrov had played for West Ham United. The highest transfer fee for a Russian player was for Sergei Semak, who transferred from CSKA Moscow to Paris for $u.S. 4 million in 2005.

In 1996 the company owning the Luzhniki Stadium bought Torpedo Moscow, and the new general director, Vladimir Aleshin, and the coach, Alexander Tarkhanov, conducted a mass dismissal of long-serving staff. CSKA was taken under the wings of Mezhprombank in 1996 and has been sponsored by Oneksimbank since 1997. Spartak has found a sponsor in LukOil and includes

Football players Marat Izmailov (left) and Fabio Cannavoro (right) during the match between Lokomotiv and InterMilan. The match was held in the Lokomotiv stadium and finished with a 3–0 score. (Photo by Dmitry Azarov/Kommersant)

a great number of foreign players. Control through targeted crime to eliminate adversaries was common not only in Russian politics and business but also in sports in the latter half of the 1990s. Spartak's president, Lidia Nechayeva, was murdered in 1997 in a dispute over television rights.

In 2003–2004 the Spartak and Torpedo teams, although both declining in fortunes, paradoxically played at the huge Luzhniki Stadium. Spartak's player Yegor Titov was disqualified from UEFA matches until January 2005 for the use of illegal substances.

The coach, Oleg Romantsev, long-time trainer for the national team from 1994 to 1996 and 1999 to 2002, who had been with Spartak since 1989, was dismissed and moved to Saturn (Moscow Region) in 2003; he was replaced by the Italian coach Nevio Scala. This followed the decline of Spartak, the Russian champions from 1996 to 2001, to third place in 2002 and to tenth place in 2003. At the same time, Lokomotiv's fortunes have been rising with cup wins in 1997–1998 and 1998–1999. Lokomotiv was in the Champions League 2003–2004, with

Arsenal, Inter Milan, and Dinamo Kiev. After winning the Russian Cups of 1996, 1997, 2000, and 2001 and the Russian Premier League in 2002, Lokomotiv rose to the Champions League in 2003–2004. Lokomotiv can boast the best Russian players in its club, many of whom returned after contracts abroad, enriched with the experience. Their goalkeeper, Sergei Ovchinnikov, joined the team in 1991 but played in Portugal for several seasons before returning to Lokomotiv in 2002. The players Oleg Panchin and Vladimir Maminov hold Uzbek passports, as they played for Uzbekistan in the FIFA (Fédération Internationale de Football Association) qualifying match in 2002, but both have been one-club players and have been with Lokomotiv since the early 1990s. Marat Izmailov is probably the finest player in the Russian league and a shooting star since his debut at the age of 19. Dmitri Loskov from Rostov is the most prolific striker in the team. The team also includes two players from Georgia, Mikhail Ashvetia and Malkhez Asatiani, the latter the son of the football legend Kakhi Asatiani. Lokomotiv is internationally the most successful Russian football club and is gaining support nationally. Football in Russia is not as strong as other sports, however.

Hockey   Hockey may have been invented in the mid-nineteenth century in North America, but it was played in Russia, albeit with a ball rather than a puck (*shaiba*), as a popular game in Peter the Great's times. It was the Canadians who formed a hockey association in the late nineteenth century, however, and whose governor, Lord Stanley, sponsored the Stanley Cup in 1893. The Canadians also developed the rules of the game as it is known and played today. In 1920 the first world championship took place, and since 1966 there have also been European championships. The NHL (National Hockey League) is the most prestigious association, offering top wages for players in North America.

Hockey became accessible to mass spectators around the world when arenas were built in the 1930s. In 1956 the USSR team won Olympic gold and World Cup medals in ice hockey, a discipline until then dominated by North American teams. In 1957 the world championship took place in Moscow's Luzhniki Stadium. In the years 1957 to 1962, however, the teams of Sweden, the United States, and Canada regained superiority over the USSR. In 1963 the Golden Era of Soviet hockey began: between 1963 and 1971, the USSR won nine world championship and consistently held the Olympic gold medal between 1964 and 1988. They were also world champions for most years between 1973 and 1990. The "golden" Soviet team was coached by Anatoli Tarasov (1918–1995), who had himself played from 1945 to 1953; by the Dinamo player Arkadi Chernyshev (1914–1992), and finally by the former CSKA coach Viktor Tikhonov (b. 1930). Then the Soviet team collapsed with the Soviet Union, and the Russian team returned to its former lead with an Olympic silver medal in 1998, the world championship in 2000, and an Olympic bronze medal in Salt Lake City in 2002. Tikhonov resigned as CSKA hockey coach in April 2004 to concentrate on his work with the national team.

In hockey, the CSKA team had always been a strong leader nationally and served as a basis for the national team. In 1989 a conflict flared up between the CSKA coach Viktor Tikhonov and the players Viacheslav Fetisov, Igor Larionov, Alexander Mogilny,

Russian ice hockey star Pavel Bure at a training session at the Winter Olympics 2002 in Salt Lake City. (Photo by Dmitry Azarov/Kommersant)

and Vladimir Krutov, who wanted to play in the NHL. They were refused the army commission papers that they needed to leave the USSR (they were playing for an army team and their "professions" were major, lieutenant, and so on). Fetisov's papers were unnecessarily delayed in 1989, leading Mogilny to defect in order to play in the NHL. Subsequently, all CSKA players were freed from their army commission in May 1989. Pavel Bure emigrated through a fictitious marriage to a Canadian. The rift in the Soviet hockey team was intensified after the Olympics in Albertville, where the team had won the gold medal. The national team split and two teams were formed, one coached by Tikhonov, the other by Boris Mikhalkov. In addition to the players' emigration ("brawn drain"), a fight for leadership in the hockey association started

when the party replaced the Hockey Association's president Vladimir Petrov with Vladimir Sych in 1995. In 1997 Sych was shot during a dispute over the right to tax-free imports of tobacco for members of the Sports Federation. Alexander Steblin became the new president. The brawn drain had left the Soviet team without its best players. Dmitri Khristich went to the Washington Capitols, Andrei Lomakin to the Philadelphia Flyers, and Sergei Nemchinov to the New York Rangers.

Between 1993 and 1995, the CSKA experienced a first taste of capitalist management in the sports. The Pittsburgh Penguins tried to invest in CSKA, but the team's performance dropped and investors (including Disney) pulled out of the deal, ending the romance between a U.S. and a Russian club. The CSKA hockey team later folded completely. Dinamo's coach Vladimir Yurzi-nov coached the Olympic team, including the forwards Alexander Makarov, Igor Larionov, and Vladimir Krutov, with Viacheslav Fetisov and Alexei Kasatonov as defense and Vladislav Tretiak in the goal.

After emigration became possible in the 1990s, a mass exodus or "brawn drain" began after the CIS team had won the gold medal in Albertville. Most players of the Olympic team stayed with NHL teams. Viacheslav Fetisov and Sergei Fedotov went on to win the Stanley Cup with the Detroit Red Wings in 1997 and 1998; Igor Larionov also joined the Detroit team; Alexander Mogilny joined the Buffalo Sabers, after having defected during the 1989 world championships in Sweden. Pavel Bure, the "Russian Rocket," married a Canadian in order to play with the Vancouver Canucks, then joined the Florida Panthers in 1999 for a substantial transfer fee. The goalkeeper Tretiak coaches the Chicago Black Hawks. They all continue to play for the Russian national team. It may have taken time for Russian players to adapt to training conditions in the West, but North American teams were also stunned by the much lower level of discipline that some of the Soviet players demonstrated. Soviet sportsmen had lived in the secure and protected shell reserved for a privileged elite, who could enjoy the luxuries of Western life and not bother about everyday life problems such as taxes, shopping, and insurance.

Hockey is a popular spectator sport, but it is also widely played on the open air pitches in Gorky Park and Izmailovo Park or on the numerous ice rinks in the major cities.

Basketball, Volleyball, and Handball

The ancient game of basketball was re-invented in Canada by James Neismith (1891) as a college sport. It was brought to Russia in the twentieth century and gained popularity among factory workers in small industrial settlements. In 1909 the first official match took place, and by 1923 there were even Russian championships. In 1936 basketball became an Olympic discipline, and in 1976 women's basketball was recognized as an Olympic sport. Throughout Olympic history, the U.S. basketball teams have been most successful. Twice only could the USSR score a victory, in 1972 and 1988, but really they drew their support from the Baltic states, especially Lithuania, which had always boasted strong basketball teams. Indeed, today's top players are Lithuanian: Arvydas Sabonis (b. 1964), played for Žalgiris Kaunas from 1985 to 1987 and joined Real Madrid in 1990, then the Portland Trail Blazers in 1996. He ensured the USSR national team's victory at the European championships in 1986 and played on the Lithuanian national team that won Olympic bronze in 1992 and 1996. In 2004, new coaches were appointed for the national team: Sergei Babkov from Lokomotiv Novosibirsk and the CSKA player Yevgeni Pashutin. It was, however, the women's team that won a bronze medal in Athens.

Volleyball was invented by William Morgan at Mount Holyoke in 1895 as a college game. It reached the USSR in the 1920s as a popular game. Only in 1947 was an International Volleyball Organization formed, and since 1964 volleyball has been an Olympic discipline. Until then, it was not a sport promoted by the Communist Party as a competitive sport. An unofficial discipline, it was popular among artists and actors in Moscow in the 1920s and 1930s. It was played by students of the arts and film colleges as well as by the famous actors Boris Shchukin and Ivan Moskvin. Once it had become a competition sport, the USSR strove for, and finally achieved, dominance in this sport (Olympic gold in 1980 and 1988). Russia won a silver medal in Sydney 2000 for both the men's and women's teams, and a silver medal for the women's team and bronze for the men's team in Athens 2004.

Handball became an Olympic discipline in 1936. The USSR men's team won a gold medal in the 1976 and 1988 Olympics and the women's team in 1976 and 1980. The CIS and Russian teams also won several medals at the Olympic Games in Barcelona (1992), Sydney (2000), and Athens (2004).

Individual Sports

Golf and Tennis   Golf was neither a competitive discipline nor a leisure activity in the Soviet era. The Soviet Union had one golf course near Vyborg, until the first golf club opened in Moscow in 1987, and the sport spread largely as a form of leisure occupation for the upper classes. In 1992 the first golf tournament was held in Russia, and only in 1996 did Russia venture onto the international arena. The largest golf club in Moscow is in the southwest of the city, on the Lenin (Sparrow) Hills.

Tennis, the kings' game, was invented in eleventh-century France and spread across Europe and North America in the mid-nineteenth century. In France, Australia, and the United States it became part of the school curriculum. The relationship between tennis and the Olympic movement is complex, however: between 1896 and 1924 men's singles were an Olympic discipline; then the sport was removed from the Olympics until the 1988 Games in Seoul.

Tennis player Yevgeni Kafelnikov during the Kremlin Cup at the Olympic Complex, October 2003. (Photo by Dmitry Azarov/Kommersant)

Therefore, achievement in tennis is measured in the four Grand Slam competitions (Wimbledon, Australian Open, Flushing Meadows, and Paris Open) rather than the Olympics, as well as in the Davis Cup, where the USSR has participated since 1962. In the Davis Cup, the Soviet team reached a semifinal only in 1976, but the match was canceled since the team was recalled when having to play against Chile, a country that was condemned for the Pinochet regime. The Russians made a comeback to the Davis Cup in 1993; they reached the finals in 1994 and lost to Sweden. In 1995 they were again in the finals after overcoming the German team with Boris Becker and Michael Stich in the semifinals, when Andrei Chesnokov scored

Tennis star Anna Kurnikova during the Kremlin Cup at the Olympic Complex, October 2001. (Photo by Dmitry Azarov/Kommersant)

a victory over Michael Stich after the latter made a double fault at 15:40. In the finals, however, Pete Sampras beat Yevgeni Kafelnikov, and the U.S. team won the cup in Moscow. In 1998 the Russian team again reached the semifinals in Brisbane, but here the Australian team took the upper hand. Overall, Russian tennis has asserted itself forcefully in the international arena after years of neglect by a Soviet regime that favored collective sports. Indeed, the tennis history of the USSR is not as glamorous as that of other sports disciplines. The sport was popular among actors of the Moscow Arts Theater. Vsevolod Verbitsky was a national champion in 1918. Some players were artists: Nikolai Ozerov was the son of an opera singer, and Anna

Dmitrieva the daughter of a theater designer. Only two Soviet women have ever played at Wimbledon: in 1959 Dmitrieva was the first USSR tennis player at Wimbledon, and in the 1970s Olga Morozova reached the women's finals three times. In the 1960s, Alexander Metreveli was the first seeded player and the first Soviet Wimbledon winner.

In the New Russia, Andrei Chesnokov was the first professional player who had a contract with a Western firm, and he was twice ranked among the top ten players and participated in seven major competitions. In 1992, the 18-year-old Yevgeni Kafelnikov won the Open Italian Juniors. In 1994 he showed his great skill during a three-hour match against Pete Sampras in the Australian Open. By 1995 he was ranked sixth in the world. In 1996 he won his first Grand Slam tournament with the Paris Open and was ranked number three. His performance since has been uneven, although by 1999 he had returned to the first rank after winning the Australian Open and Olympic gold in 2000. The tennis player Marat Safin was 20 years old when his ranking rose to third after a victory over Pete Sampras; in 1999 he scored a victory at Flushing Meadows. Igor Andreyev is another rising star of Russian tennis; he has trained in Spain since the age of 14.

The star of "new" Russian tennis—although not necessarily an outstanding player—is Anna Kurnikova. Trained at the Nick Bolletieri Tennis Academy in Florida since the age of 11, the 16-year-old played a semifinal in Wimbledon in 1997. In 1999 she won the women's doubles in the Australian Open with Martina Hingis. Kurnikova is not a winner, however; instead, she has made a fortune by posing as a model for various sports journals and glossy magazines. In 1999 Yelena Dementieva (b. 1981) entered the tennis arena and won Olympic silver in Sydney in 2000. In the Paris Open of 2004, Dementieva was the first Russian woman to qualify for a Grand Slam final in thirty years, where she was beaten by another Russian player, Anastasia Myskina (b. 1981). Vera Zvonareva, Nadia Petrova, and Svetlana Kuznetsova also performed well in the Paris Open in singles and doubles. The real heroine of Russian tennis celebrated victory in Wimbledon on 3 July 2004, however, when Maria Sharapova was the first Russian to ever win Wimbledon, beating Serena Williams in two sets. Sharapova, born in 1987 in Niagan, has trained for more than ten years at Nick Bolletieri's tennis school in Florida.

As for the active interest in tennis, contemporary Russia knows a growing number of tennis clubs and courts can be found at a number of holiday resorts and in the sports centers (Luzhniki, Dinamo, Olympic complex, CSKA). The Russian Tennis Association has a club in Altufievo in the north of Moscow. Like golf, however, tennis remains a sport for the privileged and the high earners.

Athletics   Athletics are the oldest form of sport, originating in ancient Greece. In 1908 the first championships were held, but only in 1946 was an international federation for athletics formed. Although Russian sportsmen and sportswomen have always performed well in Olympic disciplines, it is in athletics that they have maintained most easily the record level of Soviet times.

In walking (*skorokhod*), the first Soviet Olympic champion was Leonid Spirin, who won in 1956 in Melbourne over 20 kilometers. The first world title was not won until 1976, however, when Veniamin Soldatenko achieved his over 50 kilometers. In 1987 Irina Strakhova was the first Soviet woman to win a world championship title. After the collapse of the USSR, Irina Stankina in 1995 became the youngest world champion, aged 18 years. Yelena Nikolayeva won Olympic gold in 1996 over 10 kilometers, and in the new millennium Olimpiada Ivanova became world champion (2001) and won a silver medal in Athens. It is clearly the Russian women who dominate in this discipline internationally. Among the sprinters (*gladkii beg*), Svetlana Masterkova won two Olympic gold medals in 1996. Valentina Yegorova won the silver medal in the marathon. In hurdling (*baryerny beg*), the former sprinter Irina Privalova won a gold medal in Sydney.

In jumping, particular mention must be made of the Soviet coach Vladimir Diachkov, who developed a special and successful technique for the pole vault in the 1950s, before the flop technique replaced his method in the 1960s and took the lead away from the Soviet team. In the high jump (*pryzhok v vysotu*), Igor Kashkarov won Olympic gold in 1956. Yuri Stepanov established a new world record in 1957, which marked the first time that the world record was not held by an American sportsman. In the 1960s, Valeri Brumel several times set a world record in the high jump, making the "cosmic jump" of 2.26 meters in 1962, claiming Olympic gold in 1964. After sustaining a leg injury in an accident, Brumel had to retire. In pole vaulting (*pryzhok s shestom*), the first world record for the USSR came in 1981 when Vladimir Poliakov jumped 5.81 meters. In the 1990s, the Ukrainian-born Sergei Bubka reached 6.14 meters (1994). Maxim Tarasov won Olympic gold in 1992, bronze in 2000, and became world champion in 1999 with 6.05 meters. The long jump (*pryzhok v dlinu*) is a discipline that has not brought the USSR great triumphs, but it is worth bearing in mind that in over 100 years, the 18 world records have been set by only 12 jumpers. Igor Ter-Ovanesian set one such new world record in 1967, with a jump of 8.35 meters, which later earned him Olympic gold. During the Athens Olympics the Russian women gained several medals in high jump, pole vault, triple jump, and long jump. The athlete Tatiana Lebedeva, who had already secured a silver medal in Syndey and had set an indoor world record in Budapest in 2004, deservedly received a gold medal.

In the discus (*metanie diska*) and javelin throw (*metanie kop'ia*), the Soviet teams scored occasional victories in the 1970s and 1980s. The javelin thrower Alexander Makarov won Olympic silver in 1980, and his son, Sergei, took the Olympic bronze in Sydney in 2000. The first Russian champion in weightlifting in the pre-Revolutionary era was Alexander Zass (1888–1962) from Vilno (now Vilnius), called the "Iron Samson." Zass sustained an injury in World War I and later worked in the circus, where he gained fame for carrying two lions on his shoulders, a number that he modeled on his war experience, when he had carried his injured horse. Yuri Vardanian set five world records in the 1980s. Yuri Zakharevich won three Olympic gold medals in Seoul, and his fellow countryman Andrei Chemerkin, Olympic winner of 1996, is recognized as the strongest man in the world. Other heavy-athletic disciplines, such as judo and karate, were not widespread in the Soviet Union outside competition sports, but with the emergence of clubs in the New Russia, and Russia's president actively practicing karate, these sports have gained popularity. In judo, Alexander Mikhailin has won a world championship.

Ever since the former USSR entered the world arena of wrestling competitions in 1953 with Boris Gurevich, the first Soviet world champion in wrestling, the country led infallibly in the various categories of the discipline. The Greco-Roman wrestler (130 kg) Alexander Karelin (b. 1957 in Novosibirsk) was the longest reigning world champion (1989–1999), and the only athlete who won three Olympic medals for his country under three different flags: for the Soviet Union in 1988, for the CIS in 1992, and for Russia in 1996. After being defeated in Sydney by Rulon Gardner, he defended his doctorate in sports at the Lesgaft Institute in Saint Petersburg (2002) and was elected a Duma deputy (for the party "Edinstvo," Unity) by his Novosibirsk constituency (1999). The wrestlers won ten of the 92 medals won by Russia in the Athens Olympics.

Boxing, so popular in the United States, was part of army training in the Soviet period, and as such, it was a recognized and supported form of sport. The boxer Boris Lagutin (b. 1938), who won Olympic bronze in 1960 and gold in 1964 and 1968, is probably one of the best-known boxers, if not sportsmen, of the Soviet era. In the New Russia the welterweight boxer Oleg Saitov has popularized the sport with a gold medal in the 1996 Olympics, world and European championship titles, the Barker Cup, and two further gold medals at the Sydney Olympics. He achieved another third place in the Athens Olympics in 2004. In 2001, Konstantin Tsiu entered the ring, winning the world championship; Alexander Lebziak won Olympic gold in Sydney in the heavyweight class.

Russian three-time Olympic champion in Greco-Roman wrestling Alexander Karelin fights during the 2000 Summer Olympics in Sydney. (Photo by Dmitry Azarov/Kommersant)

Gymnastics   Gymnastics were, first and foremost, a health exercise introduced to Russia in the late nineteenth century by Doctor Petr Lesgaft from Petersburg, who was sent to Europe with the mission of studying health exercises. Lesgaft founded a school in Petersburg, which became the Lesgaft Institute of Physical Culture after the Revolution.

When Soviet gymnasts entered the Olympic arena, the sport was no longer a health exercise but a highly competitive discipline. It was here that the Soviet teams scored a range of medals at the Olympics. Larisa Latynina won eighteen Olympic medals in the 1950s and 1960 for gymnastics and was world champion in 1962. Then, however, the Japanese took the lead in gymnastics, until in 1970 Liudmila Turishcheva (b. 1952) won the world championship. She gave a remarkable performance at the European championship in London in 1973, when she completed an exercise on parallel bars after one of the bars had broken. Turishcheva, who remains a legend in contemporary Russia, was swept aside on the international arena by Olga Korbut (b. 1955, Grodno/Belarus), who at the age of 16 won Olympic gold in Munich in 1972, showing a loop on the parallel bars and a backward salto. It would soon become common for teenagers rather than mature sportspeople to enter international gymnastics competitions, such as the 11-year-old Romanian Nadia Comaneci (b. 1961), who first appeared at the age of 14 in European championships, where she won four gold medals. She went on to win Olympic gold in Montreal in 1976 with a "perfect" score of 10 for her performance on the uneven bars and gained several medals in Moscow in 1980, competing along with the Korean-born Russian Nelli Kim (b. 1959).

Although it was generally expected that the level of discipline needed for gymnastics could not be maintained without party discipline in post-Soviet Russia, and considering that this sport was not a mass spectator sport, Russia scored surprisingly high in gymnastics competitions in the 1990s. Svetlana Khorkina began her career in 1994; she was European champion (1998, 2000) and world champion (1997, 1999), and won medals in the 1996, 2000, and 2004 Olympics. In Sydney she showed a great sense of team spirit when she let her junior colleague Lena Zamolodchikova (b. 1982) do the jump instead of her, thus giving Zamolodchikova a chance of demonstrating her ability and ensuring the women's team a gold medal. Zamolodchikova also won two gold medals for individual performance on the vault in Sydney, and Khorkina brought in the gold medal on uneven bars. Yulia Barsukova became European champion in 1999 and won Olympic gold in 2000. In 2003 she was cast as the White Cat in the Russian Ice Stars' UK touring production of *Sleeping Beauty*, leaving competitive for

Athlete Svetlana Khorkina receiving a silver medal at the Athens Olympics in 2004. (Photo by Ilya Pitalev/Kommersant)

commercial sports. Alina Kabayeva was European champion in 1999 and 2000 and world champion in 2001; she won Olympic bronze in Sydney and gold in Athens. Among the men, the Belarusian Vitali Shcherbo took six Olympic gold medals in Barcelona in 1992. Alexei Nemov (b. 1976), who became captain of the Russian team for the 1996 Olympics, won gold and silver medals in Sydney for his performance on the horizontal bar, pommel horse, and parallel bars as well as floor exercises.

Water Sports   Rowing was a competitive sport in the Soviet Union but not associated with universities as in the United Kingdom. In 1956 the USSR made a strong debut in the Olympic Games at Melbourne with two gold and three silver medals. After 1991 the performance and interest in the sport dropped, but by 1996 the Russian team was again among the medalists: in Sydney, Maxim Opalev won a silver medal. The former USSR coach Valentin Mankin, who trained the national team from 1988 to 1990, went to Italy and coached the Italian national team that won gold and silver medals in Sydney. Yachting was relatively popular in the Soviet Union: with around a hundred clubs, the sport had 30,000 members.

Swimming was a physical exercise introduced by a swimming school in Petersburg in 1825. By the late nineteenth century, pools could be found in most steam-houses (a steam-house is a *banya*), and in 1895 even the famous Sandunov Baths in Moscow had a small pool. Saunas or steam-houses are still very popular, with Finnish and Russian saunas being an integral part of urban and provincial life. The Russian sauna is a steam sauna, heated up to 60°C, where people beat each other with birch tree twigs (*veniki*). The Finnish sauna is a dry sauna that heats up to 100°C, and it is also common in Russia. The steam-house formed part of provincial life, however, where it provided the bathhouse in areas without sanitation, and it remains an integral part of Russian culture.

Although swimming became a popular exercise, both in the *banya* pools and in rivers and lakes, the USSR did not fare very well in the Olympics. Instead, Johnny Weissmuller, who continued to play the part of Tarzan, conquered the hearts of Russian sports spectators and cinema audiences in the 1950s. The 16-year-old Galina Prozumenshikova was the first Soviet swimmer to win an Olympic gold medal, in Tokyo in 1964.

Swimmer and champion of the 2000 Olympics Alexander Popov prepares for the World Championship in the Olympic Sports Complex, Moscow, in 2002. (Photo by Dmitry Azarov/ Kommersant)

The New Russia has a lot more to offer in terms of competition success. The swimmer Alexander Popov held the world record in 50 and 100 meters and won Olympic gold in 1992. He then trained in Australia and again won Olympic gold in 1996, followed by the European championship in 1997 and a silver medal in Sydney. Roman Sludnov won the world championship in 2001. Among the women, Maria Kiselyova excelled in synchronized swimming in the Olympics in 2000; in 2004 the Russian team won two gold medals in synchronized swimming.

A number of pools can be found in the major cities. The famous open-air pool Moskva, which from the 1960s to the 1990s took up the space where the Cathedral of Christ the Savior stood until 1931 and again stands since 1994, was an extraordinary sight in its time with swimmers in the heated pool at outside temperatures of minus 25° C. All the major sports clubs (Luzhniki, Olympic, Krylatskoye, CSKA) have their indoor pools, and the Seagull (Chaika) in the south of Moscow is the major public pool. Many fitness clubs also have small pools, and there is a growing number of aqua parks.

For the common people, water sports such as diving and waterskiing are available at a great number of Russian holiday resorts on the Black Sea. Swimming is possible in the summer seasons in lakes and rivers, even in the Moskva river, which has a famous beach near Serebrianyi Bor (Silver Forest). There are numerous lakes in the Volga region, north of Moscow, and north of St. Petersburg. Diving is popular, but very expensive because of the special equipment required. A basic course of six hours can cost between $150 and $250.

Other Sports   In fencing, the USSR Olympics team first performed in 1960 and obtained a gold medal; it repeated this success in 1964, 1968, 1976, and 1980, asserting the USSR's superiority in this team sport. In the post-Soviet era, individual fencers gained international awards, first and foremost Stanislav Pozdniakov, who won Olympic gold in 1992 and 1996 and was world champion in 2001. His teammates Alexander Beketov and Pavel Kolobkov also won Olympic medals in 1996 and 2000. In Sydney the women's épée team and the men's saber team won gold medals; in Athens the women's épée team repeated their gold medal, while the men's team took only bronze in foil and sabre.

Darts only entered Russia in the 1990s as a foreign import. In the 2000 world championship in London, however, Anastasia Do-

bromyslova won a bronze medal, becoming the first Russian to gain any awards. The sport remains of limited interest for competition, but facilities are available in clubs and pubs. Paintball reached Russia in 1993. There are a number of carting and bowling clubs that are fairly popular.

In equestrian terms, the Caucasian republics always had a strong presence in horseback riding. The Djigits performed in many circuses. In Soviet Russia, equestrian sports were not very popular. The best racing performance was in 1961, when a Russian jockey participated in the Grand National and reached the tenth hurdle. Horse racing was not a sport sponsored in the USSR; neither was betting, considered to be an utterly bourgeois pastime. There were few clubs or stables where individuals could keep horses. With the collapse of the USSR, it therefore took a while for equestrian sports to establish themselves. Horse racing is still not a mass spectacle, although there are a few races and arenas, most notably the hippodrome on Begovaya in Moscow, which even has a couple of bookmakers (*bukmeikery*). There are horseback-riding clubs in Bitsa, Izmailovo, and Nagornoye where people can hire horses and take riding classes. Interest in the sport is on the increase as the first international successes are visible: Nina Menkova won the bronze and silver medals in the world championships between 1989 and 1991 in the dressage exercises on her horse Dixon. However, such successes remain isolated.

In biking, Russia always lagged behind Europe. The first cyclists in Russia were referred to as "satan riding on the devil" (*chert na diavole edet*); the bike was considered a silly and dangerous Western invention. In 1883 the first bicycle race took place in Moscow, but the bicycle never really gained wide popularity in Russia, neither as a means of transport nor as a piece of sports equipment. There have, however, been occasional record attempts: the electrician Gleb Travin cycled along the borders of the USSR in 1928, an exercise that covered 85,000 kilometers and took three years and 14 days, starting from Petropavlovsk-Kamchatsky and going across the Arctic Circle. The cyclist Viacheslav Yekimov won gold medals in Seoul and Sydney, and Olga Sliusareva took the gold medal in points race and silver in road race in Athens in 2004, but no Russian cyclist has taken part in big international events such as the Tour de France or the Giro d'Italia.

Mountain climbing was not a popular sport in the Soviet era, but an exercise of achievement. Yevgeni Abalakov's conquest in 1933 of Pik Kommunizma (Communism Peak, 7,495 meters) in the Pamir range, the highest mountain of the USSR, was one such achievement. Mountain climbing became a popular sport in the 1990s, when military helicopters were used to transport people to remote locations in the Caucasus for climbing. Other forms of extreme sports, such as bungee jumping, are gaining in popularity among the prosperous "New Russians."

Formula One and other motor races were not part of spectator or competitive sports in the Soviet era, and the interest in Formula One races remains a passive one. Formula One is covered extensively on television and in the print media, indicating an interest in the races as a spectator sport.

The noncompetitive sports of fishing and hunting have long-standing traditions in Russia, and—although they are exclusively male sports—they are extremely popular and widespread.

Winter Sports

The first skis were used in Russia in 1894. By 1910, the first Russian championships took place in Moscow. Bearing in mind the Russian winter, the country was clearly predestined for skiing, and it remains a very popular sport and almost a way of moving through the countryside during the winter.

Soviet downhill ski teams joined international competitions in the 1950s, and here women have always been better skiers than men. In 1956, Vladimir Kuzin won Olympic gold in Cortina d'Ampezzo; Viacheslav Vedenin won silver in Grenoble in 1968 and gold in Sapporo in 1972. The women led more consistently: between 1958 and 1966, Alevtina Kolchina was three times world champion and won Olympic gold in 1964. Galina Kulakova became USSR champion in 1967; she held the title of world champion five times and four times participated in the Olympics. Raisa Smetanina participated in seven world championships and five Olympics. Such long-term champions were no longer on the ski slopes in the 1990s.

In cross-country skiing, the Russian teams have demonstrated their strength: Liubov Yegorova was world champion from 1992 to 1994 and took Olympic gold. Larisa Lazutina was world champion in 1995 and again in 2001, with three gold medals in Nagano. Yelena Vaelbe had, by 1995, won five gold medals in world championships. Among the newcomers are Olga Danilova, Nina Gavriliuk, and Julia Chepalova, making their medal debuts at the 2001 world championships. Indeed, the training opportunities for cross-country skiing are widely accessible, so that the lead in this area is not surprising.

Ski jumping saw only a few Soviet sportsmen win, but the biathlon was another Soviet-dominated discipline. In the 1960s and 1970s Vladimir Melanin, Yuri Kashkarov, Renat Safin, and Alexander Tikhonov were multiple world champions and led in Olympic competitions. The former skier Anfisa Reztsova scored success for Russia in the biathlon in the 1990s.

Skiing remains a very popular leisure activity. There are numerous ski resorts in the Caucasus and Central Asia, now separate republics, but also in the Urals. The resort of Krasnaya Polyana near the Black Sea resort of Sochi has been expanded, since it is President Putin's favorite resort. Many Russians can afford the quite cheap package holidays to Austrian and Swiss, Italian, and French ski resorts. Quite a few ski jumps are available in major cities, with the most famous jump descending from the Sparrow Hills toward the Moskva River.

Ice Skating   Skates were first brought to Russia by Peter the Great, and the first competitions were in speed skating in the nineteenth century. Alexander Panshin was the first Russian world champion in speed skating, taking advantage of the facilities in Petersburg's Yusupov Gardens. He was followed by a whole host of Russian speed skaters, including Boris Shilkov (1954 world champion), Boris Stenin (1960 world champion), Viktor Kosichkin (1962 world champion), four times world champions Inga Artamonova, Klara Guseva (Nesterova) (1960), and Lidia Skoblikova.

The end of the 1960s saw the end of a string of Soviet speed skaters dominating the discipline. At that point in history, figure skating became the domain of Soviet hegemony, and the USSR and Russia have dominated this discipline in all its four variants to the present day. Figure skating is therefore very popular in Russia, but also because skates are relatively cheap and icy surfaces abound in the Russian winter, making the sport a family leisure activity.

The first figure skating competitions took place in Vienna in 1872 and included pair and single skating. In 1908, ice skating first featured in the Olympic program. At the London Games, Russia was represented by Nikolai Panin-Kolomenkin, a finance inspector. Since 1922 there have been European and world championships, which now also include ice dance as a fourth form. As figure skating developed, it encompassed a number of compulsory elements and jump combinations: loops, flips, toe loops, and death spirals. Some new elements were invented and named after the skaters who first performed them: the salchow was named after the Swedish skater Ulrich Salchow; the axel was named after Axel Paulson, who performed it at the 1908 Olympics; the lutz was named after the Italian skater Tomas Lutz; and one of the most recent elements, the Bielmann spin, was first shown by the Swiss skater Denise Bielmann in the 1980s.

The USSR took great pride in its figure skaters, a tradition begun in the 1960s. Men's figure skating has never been quite as strong as that of the Soviet pairs, however. Among the European and world champions of the 1970s were Vladimir Kovalyov, the Leningrad skater Igor Bobrin, and Yuri Ovchinnikov. Alexander Fadeyev showed a fine free skating program based on Russian folk dance and won the world and European championships in the 1980s. He first landed a quadruple toe-loop. The Ukrainian Viktor Petrenko won a gold medal for the unified CIS team in Albertville (1992). Alexei Urmanov received a gold medal in Lillehammer. He has since shown excellent free programs, without, however, winning medals. Ilia Kulik took the gold medal in Nagano.

Yevgeni Plushchenko first won a bronze medal at the world championships in 1998, aged 15; he took the world title in 2001. Plushchenko first performed the combination of a quadruple, triple, and double jump. Russia has been best represented by Alexei Yagudin, who won Olympic gold in Salt Lake City in 2002, relegating Plushchenko to the silver medal. The Petersburg skater Yagudin (b. 1980) excelled with a free program set to "Man with the Iron Mask," but he made Olympic history by achieving the highest total score for individual skating (106.6 out of 108 points).

In women's skating the United States held the lead, and in the 1970s and 1980s the GDR skaters trained by Jutta Mueller, including Katerina Witt, took the limelight. Kira Ivanova was the first and only woman to win an Olympic medal for the USSR in Sarajevo in 1984. Anna Kondrasheva gained a silver medal in the 1984 world championship. Yelena Vodorezova (b. 1963) achieved a European title in 1982. Her pupil, Olga Markova, became a European medalist in 1994 and 1995. In the 1990s, Russian women finally reached the steps of the Olympic pedestal more frequently. The Ukrainian Oksana Baiul (b. 1977) was the youngest Olympic champion, winning a gold medal in Lillehammer in 1994, but her career has been hampered by alcoholism. Irina Slutskaya became European champion in 1996, 2000, and 2001, winning a silver medal in the 1998 world championships and in the Olympic Games in Salt Lake City. Marina Butyrskaya won the world championships in 1999 and European championships in 1998 and 1999, at the mature age of 27. Russian women certainly

Figure skater Irina Slutskaya performing a Bielman spin during the 2002 Olympics in Salt Lake City's Delta Center.
(Photo by Dmitry Azarov/Kommersant)

are back among the leading skaters with solid artistic and technical performances.

The greatest success has been recorded in pairs skating, which has also enjoyed widespread spectator popularity in Russia and abroad. In 1958 the USSR joined the leadership race in figure skating, when Nina and Stanislav Zhuk won the silver medal at the European championship in Bratislava, which they subsequently defended in Davos in 1959 and in Garmisch Partenkirchen in 1960, eventually crowning their career with a sixth place at the Olympics in Squaw Valley. They were soon overtaken, however, by Liudmila Belousova and Oleg Protopopov, who took Olympic gold in Innsbruck in 1964, winning the first Olympic medal in the discipline. They have become, like their successors, national heroes. Their free skate set to Liszt's "Love Dreams" demonstrated their athletic competence in a lyrical and romantic presentation, probably least expected from the disciplined Soviet camp. They defended their medal in Grenoble and reigned as European and world champions between the two Olympics. Since the times of Belousova and Protopopov, the USSR has never lost Olympic gold in pairs figure skating; they surrendered the world championship only seven times and the European title only three times. The coach Igor Moskvin trained his wife, Tamara Moskvina, who skated with Alexei Mishin and won a world championship silver medal in 1969. From this pool of skaters the schools and training camps developed that dominated, and still rule, the sport. Figure skating became a massively popular sport, where the competition was not only between nations but between "camps" of skaters trained in Moscow or Petersburg, by Zhuk or Moskvina.

In 1969 Irina Rodnina (b. 1949) and Alexei Ulanov made their debut at the world championship. They held the European title between 1969 and 1972, when they won Olympic gold; the silver medal went to Andrei Sureikin and Liudmila Smirnova. After the Olympics, Ulanov decided to skate with Smirnova, whom he had married in the meantime, leaving Rodnina without a skating partner. Her trainer, Stanislav Zhuk, paired her with the relatively unknown skater Alexander Zaitsev. Although Smirnova and Ulanov won world championship silver in 1973 and 1974, Rodnina and Zaitsev rose to Olympic gold in 1976 and 1980. They held the title of world champion ten times between 1969 and 1978 and the European title 11 times (1969–1978, and 1980), interrupted only in 1979 when Rodnina had her baby son.

It was impossible to imagine in those days that anyone could overtake the pair of Rodnina and Zaitsev, whose "Kalinka" free skate program became their trademark. The coach Stanislav Zhuk knew, however, that he had to raise a new generation of skaters. In his choice of pairs, Zhuk always chose a small woman and a tall man and peppered the programs with decisive and forceful moves, tending more toward the athletic than the artistic side. Marina Cherkasova and Sergei Shakhrai performed well in the late 1970s but were clearly not challengers for the Olympic gold medal. Yelena Valova and Oleg Vasiliev won several European and world titles between 1983 and 1988, with an Olympic victory in 1984. They were, however, coached by Tamara Moskvina, who insisted on a program that included a variety of jumps, emphasizing overall more the artistic composition. Zhuk's pair of Yekaterina Gordeyeva and Sergei Grinkov, who made their debut aged 14 and 16, soon demonstrated their superiority over the Moskvina pair and held the European and world titles between 1986 and 1990, with Olympic gold in 1988 and 1994. Their free program in Lillehammer to Beethoven's "Moonlight Sonata" was a memorable and truly golden performance. In 1998, Grinkov died of cardiac arrest at the age of 28. Moskvina trained Natalia Mishkutionok and Artur Dmitriev, who quickly ranked among the top skaters and won Olympic gold in Albertville. In Nagano, Dmitriev skated with a new partner, Oxana Kazakova, and won another gold medal. Yelena Berezhnaya and Anton Sikharulidze

Yelena Berezhnaya and Anton Sikharulidze
during their free program at the Winter
Olympics 2002 in Salt Lake City's Delta Center.
(Photo by Dmitry Azarov/Kommersant)

rose to the top three pairs in the world in
the late 1990s, winning silver in Nagano and
gold in Salt Lake City, although they had to
share it with the Canadian pair Jamie Sale
and David Pelletier. After Berezhnaya and
Sikharulidze were awarded the gold medal
on 12 February 2002, it transpired that the
French judge Reine-Marie Le Gaugne had
been pressured to award higher marks to
the Russian pair than they deserved; her
vote was discounted and Sale and Pelletier
had their silver medal exchanged for gold,
while the Russian pair kept their gold medal
also. The rising stars, who are apparently
being prepared for the 2006 Olympics, are
Marina Totmianina and Maxim Marinin, already successful in the European and world
championships since 2002 with a program
set to Sergei Rachmaninoff's "Paganini."

Many contemporary Russian skaters
have Russian coaches but practice in the
United States, where facilities are deemed
to be better.

Ice dance was introduced into international competition rather late, in 1948. The
first world championships were held in
1952, and the first European championships in 1954. Liudmila Pakhomova (1947–
1986) and Alexander Gorshkov were the
first Soviet Olympic ice dance champions.
Their career was hampered by Gorshkov's
undergoing heart surgery in 1975. They won
Olympic gold in 1976, and under their
coach Yelena Chaikovskaya, they took a
number of European and world championship medals in the 1970s. Natalia Lini-
chuk and Gennadi Karponosov succeeded
the pair of Pakhomova and Gorshkov, winning the world championship in 1978 and
Olympic gold in 1980. Irina Moiseyeva and
Alexander Minenkov were coached by
Tamara Tarasova and became world champions in 1975 with their program to "West
Side Story." For the first time, a pair used
one tune for a miniperformance rather than
a mix of tunes in a special arrangement.
Moiseyeva and Minenkov gained Olympic
silver in 1976 and bronze in 1980. Their experiment was ahead of its time, however,
and not rewarded by the judges with the
gold medal they deserved for their artistic
performance reminiscent of classical ballet.
Natalia Bestemianova and Andrei Bukin,
also trained by Tarasova, reigned at the European and world championships in 1985–
1988 and won Olympic gold in 1988 with
their extravagant and challenging style.
Their expressive dance inspired the famed
French pair, Isabelle and Paul Duchesnay.

Marina Klimova and Sergei Ponomarenko followed as world and European
champions between 1989 and 1992 and as

Olympic winners in Albertville. Maya Usova and Alexander Zhulin took the lead for a brief time in 1993–1994. Oxana Grishuk and Yevgeni Platov showed a splendid rock and roll program that won them Olympic old in 1994 and 1998. Anzhelina Krylova and Oleg Ovsiannikov were world champions in 1998 and 1999. Indeed, the Russian dominance in ice dance climaxed in Albertville, when three Russian pairs stood on the Olympic steps: Klimova and Ponomarenko, Usova and Zhulin, and Grishuk and Platov. At the end of the 1990s, Irina Lobacheva and Ilia Averbukh emerged as top skaters. After the Salt Lake City Olympics, a new generation began to emerge in preparation for the next Olympics. Tatiana Navka and Roman Kostomarov impressed at the European championships in 2004 with a dance set to "The Pink Panther." Ice dancers tend to perform in competitions for shorter terms, turning to professional careers after five or six years in order to earn money.

Chess

Russia's most popular game, and indeed sport (the one with most club members), has been chess. International championships had existed since 1851, but most chess masters of the twentieth century were Russian. Indeed, chess has always been popular in Russia, and among the world's top twenty chess players in history there are eight Russians. Garri Kasparov was the youngest player to become a grandmaster and had at the age of 26 achieved the highest rating. Millions of fans watched his matches, especially those against computers, where he was victorious in 1989 and 1996 but lost to an International Business Machine (IBM) computer in 1997.

Chess player Garri Kasparov ponders his next move during the match held to mark the ninetieth anniversary of Mikhail Botvinnik, the patriarch of the Soviet chess school. The match took place in the Pillar Hall of the Unions' House, Moscow, in December 2001. (Photo by Dmitry Azarov/Kommersant)

The first Russian chess master was Alexander Alekhin (1892–1946), whose mother took drugs and left the family and whose father was a gambler. Alekhin himself was an alcoholic. From a well-off merchant background, Alekhin suddenly had to work to provide for himself after the Revolution. A law graduate, he found a job as a police investigator. He emigrated to France in 1921, however, claiming that he had lost seven years of chess practice because of World War I and the civil war. The reigning chess champion had been, since 1921, Jose Raul Capablanca; in 1927 Alekhin challenged and defeated him.

Alekhin defended his title three times, in 1929, 1934, and 1937.

After the war Mikhail Botvinnik followed Alekhin on his throne, gaining, and then defending, the world title between 1948 and 1961, losing only to Vasili Smyslov in 1957.

The dominance of Soviet chess players was regained in the 1970s. Anatoli Karpov won the title in 1978 and 1981 (over Viktor Korchnoy); in 1984 and 1985 and then again in 1996 and 1998, Karpov defeated Garri Kasparov. Kasparov, on the other hand, defeated Karpov three times between 1985 and 1987 as well as in 1990 and held the title in 1993 and 1995. The matches between Kasparov and Karpov always attracted a great deal of attention, as they represented chess games between two equally talented and intelligent players. Alexander Khalifman beat Vladimir Akopian in 1999, and Vladimir Kramnik defeated Kasparov in 2000. All these matches were dominated by Russian players, showing the clear dominance of the USSR and Russia in this field. Chess remains a most popular sport in Russia, as indeed does reading.

Pulp Fiction

Books were always a "deficit" (a product in insufficient supply). Although there were thousands of books in the shops and in the libraries, they were not the books people wanted. The Russian classics were more or less readily available, but contemporary literature was not, and foreign literature in translation was a great rarity. Literary journals with the latest prose fiction were handed around privately, just like the samizdat—typewritten illegal dissident literature multiplied by the use of several lay-

ers of carbon paper. Foreign literature, especially adventure and detective stories, was in high demand. Writers such as Arthur Conan Doyle, Jules Verne, and Jack London were on the "wanted" lists as well as the works of Valentin Pikul and Alexander Dumas's *Queen Margot*. These were bait on the list of books people could purchase if they would hand over books and papers (20 kilograms) for recycling (*makulatura*) to overcome the paper shortage, a system introduced in 1974. Such rare editions could also be purchased at high prices on the black market. Another way of acquiring those much-wanted books was the *beriozka* (birch tree), the hard-currency shop where foreigners could buy all sorts of souvenirs, deficit goods (coffee, detergents, toothpaste, electrical goods), and books. The beriozka on Kropotkinskaya Street (now Ostozhenka) specialized in books.

Publishing

Books were, above all, not regarded as a commodity in Soviet Russia. Whereas in the West the discrepancy was cultivated between high art with a mission of civilizing the people and low, popular culture with no value but revenue, the USSR published books not according to demand, but to need—issuing what the party and ideologues thought to be of educational value. Books had a value as a sign of culturedness and were an essential decor of Soviet flats. The official canon of Russian literature is therefore misleading. Although the nineteenth-century classics are read and known by a wide range of Russians, neither their novels nor the official Soviet literature were best sellers. The most widely read authors were Valentin Pikul, whose historical novels had print runs of more than one million, and Yulian Semyonov, who sold more than 35 million copies of his 60 or so titles. Neither of them features on any higher education syllabus in the West, nor are they widely translated. Thus, the West went along with the official image presented by the Soviet Union as a nation that loved its classics, Russian and Soviet.

The 1960s saw a reading boom: the level of education had increased, and the school curriculum included a great deal of classical literature, so that most Soviet children were widely read and had a taste for literature. According to a survey by Klaus Mehnert undertaken in the 1970s, which was groundbreaking in its time, the most popular writers in the stagnation period were Konstantin Simonov, who had become famous for his war novels in the late 1940s; Georgi Markov, who had written an epic novel set in Siberia; and Yulian Semyonov with his Stirlitz spy thrillers set during the war. It is interesting to note, though, that all three writers had their works turned into films, which reached mass audiences and achieved huge popularity. The league table was followed by the Kyrgyz writer Chingiz Aitmatov; Viktor Astafiev, who wrote chiefly about the war and labour camps; and Yuri Bondarev and Alexander Chakovsky, both famous for their novels about the war. Many of these novels were published in the series Novel-Paper (Roman-gazeta), an edition reserved for very popular works, with a print run of two million copies.

In the Gorbachev period, most previously banned novels were published in the literary journals in the first instance, which explains the massive rise in their print runs in those years. Once the flood of material delayed by censorship had ceased, the journals returned to their preglasnost lev-

els of print runs. This kept prices for books low while at the same time leaving no margin for profit for the bookshops. Then the book trade experienced a drop in light of the unstable economy and a sharp rise in print costs in 1993. If, until 1993, the number of titles and the print runs had been increasing, then after 1993 the time for cheap books was over. The number of bookshops halved in the 1990s, whereas the need for specialized shops arose after 1993 to cover intellectual demands.

Once it had become possible for new publishing houses to register and start business (1991), the book market changed rapidly. If in the mid-1990s the majority of bookshops were still run along the lines of books on display behind a counter and out of reach, where the book had to be paid for at a till before it could be collected with the receipt, then by the end of the 1990s most bookshops, such as Moskva, Dom Knigi, and Biblio Globus had changed to self-service systems with books on open display and payment made to a cashier. By 1994, some 7,000 publishers had registered, although copies went down from 1,553 billion in 1990 to 422 million in 1996. During this period, as in the present, publishers remained largely based in Moscow and a few in Petersburg. Books acquired hardcover and paperback editions, and at last also a dust jacket. By 1997, seven main publishers remained. In 1990 the Russian Association of Bookpublishers (ASKI, Assotsiatsiia knigoizdatelei Rossii) was set up.

Moreover, around the same time books were in great demand: first and foremost children's books, followed by reference books and literature. In children's literature the publishing house Rosmen, founded in 1992, took the lead, producing beautifully illustrated books largely by Russian, but also

The writer Boris Akunin (left) and his colleague Vladimir Sorokin (right) in conversation before the concert of the Finnish group Salvation Army Band in Kinotsentr, Moscow, 2003. (Photo by Dmitry Lebedev/Kommersant)

by foreign, authors. Rosmen also specializes in educational literature.

Publishers of the leading detective fiction writers Alexandra Marinina, Boris Akunin, Daria Dontsova, and Polina Dashkova soon discovered the paperback as a worthwhile addition to the hardback. Detective and crime fiction is published by Eksmo Press, a huge publishing house established in 1993 that produces over 55 million books and 50,000 titles per year, including reference works and dictionaries. Boris Akunin publishes his novels exclusively with the publishing house Zakharov. Olim Press and Astrel also publish popular

crime novels; so does Vagrius, which specializes, however, in prose and memoirs. Olma Press prints encyclopedias, special editions, children's literature, and some crime fiction. The publishing houses Ad Marginem (founded in 1991 by the Institute of Philosophy) and OGI (Obedinennye gumanitarnye izdatel'stva; United Humanities Publishers) publish experimental literature, literary criticism, and art. OGI is a unique setup launched in the late 1990s, where affordable restaurants and clubs (attracting mostly students and intellectuals) were combined with bookshops. Ad Marginem opened its private shop in 1993, complementing the specialized shops of 19 October and Eidos.

Although Eksmo is clearly the largest publishing house, in terms of genre, there are differences. Detective fiction leads clearly with Dontsova, Tatiana Poliakova, Marinina, and Akunin listed as best sellers for 2003. Eksmo has 60 percent of the market share in the print run, followed by AST (short form of Astrel') with 10 percent and Olma Press with 8 percent. Between 2001 and 2003, the print run for detective stories rose from 15,000 to 19,000 while prices went up from 15 to 30 rubles. Most detective fiction is published in series. In fantasy there are about 1,000 titles listed with average print runs of 10,000; here the market is dominated by AST (30 percent) and Eksmo (40 percent). There are some 1,500 to 2,000 titles in this section, with prices rising from 50 to 80 rubles and print runs remaining stable at 8,000. Eksmo leads this sector (17 percent) marginally, before Olma Press (12 percent) and AST (9 percent). Overall, the rating for publishers lists Eksmo, AST, and Olma at the top, followed by Rosmen among the top ten and Akunin's publishing house, Zakharov, in 32nd place (data are for 2003).

The term *best seller* is tricky in the context of the Russian market, where information on film budgets or publication is a well-guarded business secret. Information on the exact print runs is hard to come by, as most publishers reprint a work several times according to demand, in low print runs at a time. As Russia loves ratings and rankings of all sorts, one way to assess popularity is to study the sales rates of bookshops. Here, Pelevin's *Generation P* was a clear hit. The works of Dontsova, Dashkova, Marinina, Akunin, Daniil Koretsky, and Tatiana Ustinova and other crime fiction are clear best sellers. Television and film stimulate the demand for books. Dostoevsky's *Idiot* ended up in the best seller lists after the television serial by Vladimir Bortko had been broadcast in 2003, and Marinina's novels were reprinted after the television serial *Kamenskaya* had begun.

As far as foreign authors are concerned, the times of Dumas and Jack London have long passed. Paul Coelho, Haruki Murakami, Milorad Pavic, and Patrick Suesskind lead on the Russian market just as they do on the European market. The book market responds best, it seems, to the demand of the reading public, yet it is dominated by "pulp" fiction and trash novels.

Best Sellers

After the collapse of the Soviet Union, the State Prize, associated with political correctness and deemed ideological, rather than merit-based, lost in prestige. Especially in the literary world the need for a prize was felt, and in 1992 the Booker Prize was awarded in Russia, administered by a joint Russian and British team, with an international jury member involved and advice taken from literature scholars outside Russia. The first Booker Prize went to the previously unknown writer Mark Kharitonov for his novel *Lines of Fate, or Milashevich's Trunk*. Each year the Booker was surrounded by secrecy, scandals, and great expectations: was the jury objective, and who was on the short list? In subsequent years the award went to rather established writers, such as Vladimir Makanin, Bulat Okudzhava, and Georgi Vladimov, until in 1996 Andrei Sergeyev won the award for *Stamp Album*, which was a memoir in the guise of fiction and created some queries about the genre. In 1999 Smirnoff took on the sponsorship, which had run out from the UK, but only for two years; then Smirnoff was forced to pull out of business in Russia (a dispute over the right to the label Smirnoff/Smirnov). Since then the foundation Open Russia (run by Yukos) administers the Booker award, without sponsorship. In 2001, Liudmila Ulitskaya won the long-deserved award for *Kukotsky's Case.* A scandal occurred in 2003 when a non-Russian-born writer was awarded the Booker: Ruben David Gonzales Gallego for *White on Black* (Beloe na chernom). The winner of the Booker Prize certainly gets media attention and sales are boosted, but Russian readers more often go by the bookshop's choice of the best seller of the week or the month in their choice of titles.

The Anti-Booker Prize was established by the *Nezavisimaya gazeta* in 1995 and was awarded in three categories (poetry, prose, and drama) until Boris Berezovsky (shareholder in *Nezavisimaya gazeta*) was forced out of business in 2000. The award was a counterattack on the Booker, and its value exceeded the Booker by one dollar. The award winners included more popular authors, such as Dmitri Bakin, Andrei Volos, and Boris Akunin. In poetry the award honored the best-known poets of the 1990s, Sergei Gandlevsky, Timur Kibirov, Mikhail Amelin, and Bakhyt Kenzheyev. In drama, the award was important for the emergence of new young writers: Ivan Saveliev, Oleg Bogayev, Maxim Kurochkin, Yevgeni Grishkovets, Vasili Sigarev. The last three playwrights subsequently made a career in national and international theater.

High or Low: Postmodernist Best Sellers

A recent and strange phenomenon is the best seller status attributed by major Moscow and Petersburg bookstores to some authors of "highbrow" literature, in particular to those associated with postmodernism. Viktor Pelevin and Vladimir Sorokin are two tremendously popular authors, widely translated into a variety of European languages, whose works rank among the most popular in Russia. After Pelevin had written several novels and short stories, read widely but largely among educated readers, his novel *Generation P* (1999) turned into a best seller. Pelevin is a postmodernist writer but achieved massive popularity through using the parodic form with a popular twist. While incorporating nonliterary historical or cultural parody, he mocked manifestations of popular and consumer culture. The title alluded to Douglas Coupland's *Generation X*, about yuppie culture in the United States. Here the title *Generation P* lends itself to a number of interpretations (P for Pelevin), but the most pertinent of them is the reference to Pepsi Cola (also on the cover of the original edition). During the Brezhnev era, a license for Pepsi was acquired, so that the soft drink could be manufactured in the Soviet Union. The "generation that chooses Pepsi" (*pokolenie, kotoroe vybiraet Pepsi*) was a common phrase used to describe the generation of those who exchanged (Soviet) high culture for commercial Western values and manifestations of culture, such as jazz music and jeans. Effectively, Pelevin's novel dealt with the commercialization of Russia in the 1990s. The cover showed Che Guevara wearing a cap that advertises Nike and Adidas, set against an American flag that is divided in the middle to foreground an advertisement for Pepsi on the one side and Coca Cola on the other. The dominance of advertising is central to the novel. Since the collapse of the Soviet empire, advertisements have merely replaced the empty political and ideological slogans, a theme frequently alluded to in sots-art works such as in the collage of McDonalds with Lenin's portrait above the slogan "McLenin's: Next Block" by Alexander Kosolapov (1990). In *Generation P* the protagonist, Tatarsky, is a poet who graduated from the literary institute and, as so many literati, is without work after perestroika. He is hired as a copywriter for advertising spots, including the cigarette label Parlament. Pelevin mocked the media language and exposed it to mockery and styob. He also parodied the new phenomenon of PR and image making, leaving politicians as mere reflections (or simulacra) of themselves. Ultimately, Tatarsky realizes that the entire world around him consists merely of mirrors, reflections, and simulacra and that even President Yeltsin is only an animated and simulated figure created in a film studio that Tatarsky visits. Although very much a product of an art that parodies Socialist Realism and Soviet culture (sots-art), Pelevin's novel contained different layers of plot and could be read in different ways (political parody, anecdotal discussion of advertising, critique of commercialization), so that it appealed to different groups and generations of readers.

A similar phenomenon happened with Vladimir Sorokin: a conceptualist who dealt in his early novels and plays with the deconstruction of language, his novels *Blue Lard* (Goluboe salo, 1999) and *Ice* (Led, 2002) were best sellers, although both were published by the relatively small publishing company Ad Marginem, with whom Sorokin had worked earlier. Sorokin was widely read by scholars of postmodernism, thus appealing to an elitist readership with his cynical and mocking comments on Soviet culture and language. Yet he was also one of the few Russian writers who were popular in Germany and France. In his later novels, Sorokin combined utopian and science-fiction elements with his notion of the destructive effect of the totalitarian past on the individual. In *Blue Lard* he explored the theme of an experiment where, through genetic manipulation, text is produced from the cells of great writers, which is weighted by the side product of this creation: lard. Although remaining within the convention of an epistolary novel, Sorokin invented an entire range of words that are explained (or rather unexplained) in a glossary, making clear once more how useless language is as a means of communication.

Such writers as Sorokin and Pelevin, and perhaps also the postmodernist writer Liudmila Ulitskaya, are exceptions, however, in the contemporary book market in Russia. On the whole the demand has risen for sentimental novels, adventure, and fantasy, all those genres that had been in short supply in the Soviet era.

In the first half of the 1990s most works in these genres were translated, but the second half of the 1990s saw a rise in homegrown thrillers and crime fiction, which took a lead in the market. This was followed by love stories and historical novels as well as fantasy. In 1996, crime fiction contributed 38 percent of books published.

The move to the homegrown detective story after 1995 was partly due to large license fees but also because the reality of Russia was so different from that of Western Europe, and crime was taking up the minds of so many ordinary citizens in a period of ruthless Mafia killings, violent street crime, and open media coverage of atrocious criminal offences committed in the country, such as those of the serial killer Andrei Chekatylo, who had sexually abused, mutilated, and killed more than 50 children. Indeed, crime figures were on the rise in Russia, where 750,000 crimes committed in the USSR in 1965 rose to almost 3 million in 1990.

Love novels have not found a large resonance among Russian writers and are published in their majority as translated works. Another genre that has seen excessive growth in the Russian book market is children's books, particularly J. K. Rowling's *Harry Potter*, but also Harry Potter's parodic counterparts of Russian creation, Dmitri Yemets's *Tanya Grotter* and Igor Mytko's *Porri Gatter*.

Detective Stories

When looking at American spy thrillers and detective novels set in the Soviet Union, the amount of incorrect detail is striking. This is one of the reasons why the spy thriller and detective story were far more difficult to import than, say, the sentimental romance. The *detektiv*, the detective story, offered an idealized view of the criminal investigator, underscoring the trustworthiness of the system. Later in the 1990s and into the new millennium, the action thriller (*boevik*) became equally prominent. In a climate of growing inefficiency and the inability of the police to catch the criminals (especially the Mafiosi), the system was no longer seen to be superior, but society was "saved" by the superman-cum-hero figure, often an ex-policeman, who takes the law into his own hands (an example is Danil Koretsky's *Anti-Killer*).

Moreover, it could be argued that detective fiction had a long-standing tradition in Russian literature, if Dostoevsky's *Crime and Punishment* is considered as a detec-

tive story. Indeed, Raskolnikov commits a crime and receives punishment. In that classical novel of the nineteenth century, Dostoevsky also laid the foundation for the composition of the detective story: the reader knows from the start who committed the crime but explores the reason for the crime in the character's psychology and the investigator's strategy to make the criminal confess. Indeed, confession plays a particularly important role not only in Russian crime fiction but also in the judicial system.

After the Revolution, the detective story (à la Pinkerton) was decried as a bourgeois phenomenon, and it was decreed that Soviet literature needed "Red Pinkertons," in an original new Soviet variant of the detective genre. The only such novel, however, was written by Marietta Shaganian and turned into a film, *Miss Mend* (1925); both the novel and the film were considered unsuccessful. During the Stalin years, detective fiction ceased completely, and Conan Doyle was removed from all Soviet libraries. The genre of detective fiction upholds social order but singles out deviance, and such an approach was deemed inappropriate for Soviet fiction, which ought to attribute crime to a social cause. Thus, Raskolnikov's crime was not condemned outright in Soviet interpretations of the classic (Raskolnikov kills an old pawnbroker and her sister to assert his own self and advance to the class of a Nietzschean superman, a concept seen by the writer as incompatible with orthodox faith that assumes meekness and submissiveness as man's superior traits of character). Schoolchildren who studied the novel on the syllabus were led to interpret Raskolnikov as a man who wanted social justice (kill the pawnbroker as a bourgeois-capitalist element) and who redistributed the loot. One pupil went as far as commenting in a school essay: "Raskolnikov was right to kill the old hag; a shame he got caught."

In the postwar period, detective stories were largely written in the guise of adventure stories for children. In the 1960s, Yulian Semyonov created his Soviet spy Maxim Isayev, who, under the name of Max Otto von Stirlitz, takes a key role in Hitler's control center in Berlin during World War II. The brothers Arkadi and Grigori Vainer created the police investigator Znamensky. Agatha Christie novels were widely translated and read between 1966 and 1970, with over 15 works appearing in literary journals. It was not until the émigré writers Edward Topol and Friedrich Neznansky published (abroad) their spy thrillers *Red Square* (1984), *Deadly Games (*1985), *Red Gas* (1987), and *Red Snow* (1988), however, that the way was paved for a new generation of detective writers to emerge, who would explore politically motivated crime. At the same time established writers such as Valentin Rasputin, Chingiz Aitmatov, and Viktor Astafiev exposed crimes of the past in their perestroika novels. Finally, by the mid-1990s, Russian detective series were launched by major publishing houses such as Eksmo and AST.

Indeed, there was not much scope for crime in Soviet fiction, as criminal offenses occurred largely within a family, as there were not the property issues and class differences that explain a large proportion of crime in capitalist societies. The criminal code changed only in 1997. The Russian legal system distinguishes between intentional murder and murder "committed in a heightened emotional state" to differentiate manslaughter from murder. It dwells on the confession of the criminal, thus reduc-

ing the relevance of evidence for the investigation and shifting the focus onto the psychological motivation for the crime. A case can only be brought before the prosecutor if the criminal has confessed and the case is watertight. Therefore, the genre of the courtroom drama is not pertinent to the realities of the Russian legal system and to Russian crime fiction and film.

In the early days of Russian detective fiction, the works were largely written by male writers. They test the masculinity of their protagonist in a situation where social values have collapsed. With the collapse of all values in the New Russia in the mid-1990s, the detective novel became a testing ground for the moral value system and raised questions about the borderline between good and bad and about the acceptability of certain forms of behavior. Crime fiction delineated the current moral and social values, pointed at the violation of such values and their transgression, thus creating a framework for the new society and the old (Soviet) values within it. Therefore in most novels the issue is not about who commits the crime but why it is committed and how the culprit is caught. Detective fiction thereby stresses the need for the individual to subordinate himself to the interests of state and society in order to avoid a "lawless" society. Indeed, one of the crucial areas of the detective novel is to explain why a certain form of behavior was considered "wrong" in the Soviet era and "right" in the New Russia: what the Soviet system condemned as speculation (selling things and being creative) became entrepreneurship; what Soviet society considered as greed (accumulating personal property) turned to ambition; and whereas the Soviet man would be told to bear in mind the benefits for society, capitalist

Russia seems to focus exclusively on the benefit for the individual. At the same time, the Soviet values were fraudulent: it was impossible in the Soviet Union to satisfy the demands of the state (and fulfill the plan) without cutting corners, without procuring spare parts in an illegal way on the black market and from people who sidelined state property (the same spare parts) to make money. Thus, while fulfilling state demand, people undermined the system or flatly robbed the state. This explains why still today, in the New Russia, there is some hostility to property and material possession, which occasionally go hand in hand with villainy (the rich man is the murderer or a criminal).

Another major difference between Russian crime fiction and the Western detective novel is the relative absence of sex. Indeed, neither Soviet nor Russian law has a clause that makes prostitution illegal. Only coercion and sex with minors are described as "crime."

Supermen   Russian culture has a tradition of the "good criminal" redistributing the goods from the rich to the poor. The legendary characters Emelyan Pugachev and Stepan Razin are examples of this tradition that led eventually to the hero of the *boevik* (action thriller): the male war veteran who takes the law into his own hands. The supermen are often veterans of the Afghan or Chechen wars, loners without family, orphans. They are decisive, show no weakness, and neither smoke nor drink. Viktor Dotsenko created such a figure with his protagonist Saveli Govorkov, a returnee of the Afghan war, who fights the Mafia in the manner of a superhero or Rambo. His character Beshenyi (rabid) in *Rabid Love* (Beshenaia liubov') takes money from the

Chechen leader Dudayev in order to give it to the Russian government, represented by the then prime minister Chernomyrdin. The Russian superhero ensures that the state is treated fairly. He is loyal, but his methods do not correspond to the official law, which clearly fails in the face of social and political injustice and chaos. Koretsky's protagonists often specialize in the martial arts and act in self-defense while establishing order where the state fails to do this.

Many writers of detective novels are former policemen and investigators. Alexander Kivinov, the author of the series *Cops* (Menty), turned into a television serial under the title *Streets of Broken Lights* (Ulitsy razbitykh fonarei), is a former investigator of the Petersburg police. His crime squad displays some sympathy for the criminals, and the police officer get away with peccadilloes. A criminal is allowed to have sex in the office before being sent to prison; another has a blind eye turned on him when he goes into withdrawal, and the police officers leave the room so that he can inject himself. There is also a sense of disillusionment with the job: the crime squad investigators resort to a supermarket to arrest some petty thieves so that the statistics of "crimes solved" will look good. At the same time they could be doing more important jobs that would, however, not have such an immediate result. The police officers are essentially kind, but they have human flaws and break the law. Often they have to cut corners in order to catch criminals and combat the chronically underfunded police apparatus. Kivinov's position on the side of the police force is quite obvious in his works. Andrei Konstantinov is also a former police officer, but he dealt with organized crime in

Criminal Petersburg (Banditskii Peter-burg), which has also been turned into a television series.

Alexander Belov comes from the other side of the fence, as he fictionalized in his crime series *The Brigade* (Brigada), also turned into a television series, the fate of himself and his friends of the perestroika years. He explores why they became criminals and offers a gripping account of their criminal adventures.

Boris Akunin is the pen name of the critic Grigori Chkhartishvili, who published in 1998 the first of his historical detective novels that revolve around the police clerk Erast Fandorin and are set in the last 20 years of the nineteenth century. Akunin's novels were extremely popular, since they combined historical settings, romance, and suspense in a well-written text. The first of his novels, *Azazel*, leads Fandorin to London and eventually allows him to reveal the criminal activity and conspiracy of an English lady who uses a charitable institution as her guise. *The Coronation* weaves political history into the cases of Erast Fandorin. *Azazel* (*The Winter Queen* in English) has been turned into a rather unsuccessful film version, and the film rights to other Akunin novels have been acquired by Mikhalkov's studio and also by a U.S. film studio. Another series centers around the nun Pelagiya and her adventures.

The best-known and most prolific former police investigator who turned to crime fiction is Marina Alexeyeva, better known under her pen name Alexandra Marinina. Between 1995 and 2001, Marinina wrote 23 novels, which have altogether sold 30 million copies. She was the most successful crime writer of the Yeltsin era and the first woman detective writer to gain such a reputation. Her novels are published by Eksmo

Crime fiction writer Alexandra Marinina takes part in an awards ceremony for "Russian Women of the 20th Century" at the New Manège in March 2001. (Photo by Dmitry Lebedev/Kommersant)

Press in the series Black Cat. Her new works are usually released with a first print run of 250,000, which is exceptionally high in the Russian book market.

Women Detective Writers   Marinina offers a new view on society. Her heroine Nastia Kamenskaya works in Petrovka 38, the police headquarters in central Moscow, which is an essentially male-dominated world. Kamenskaya is thus inside the system (an officer) while being an outsider (a woman) at the same time. This status enables her to offer a distanced and gripping view of the police system. Marinina herself worked in the Crime Investigation Department (CID) as a special analyst for crime, investigating psychic anomaly and serial crime. The psychopath as a criminal confirms the norm and the "right" social values by his deviant behavior. The criminal may be a product of the system, but this aspect is not investigated; instead, Kamenskaya analyzes personal traumas that motivate and explain the deviant or criminal behavior.

Kamenskaya's team is led by Gordeyev, who defends his colleagues to the outside world while challenging his team intellectually. Ultimately, Kamenskaya works within a system that remains anonymous and becomes dangerous when the individual has no knowledge of its mechanisms. The underlying fragmentation of Marinina's novels bears witness to the complexity of the situation. Kamenskaya relies entirely on her own analysis to piece together fragments that offer no linearity. The reader is also denied an overview, so that ultimately the mechanisms are never seen through. The complexity of the crime requires complex analytical skills. Marinina stipulates that there is always an ulterior reason or motive for people's actions, and in order to find out what this is, Kamenskaya places herself inside the murderer's brain and psyche. This closeness to the victim often places her in danger. Kamenskaya is, in a sense, a synthesizer: she pulls together the threads that initially make no sense to her, nor to the reader.

Coincidence (Stechenie obstoiatel'stv) was Marinina's first novel, in which she detailed the transformation of her heroine, Nastia Kamenskaya, from a mousy character who pays little attention to her appearance, wearing jeans, a sweater, and sneakers, to a femme fatale who uses her appearance as a mask. She turns herself into the bait for a hit-man in order to catch the criminal who is behind the murder of an operative in the Ministry for Internal Affairs. The novel emphasizes the danger of police work, as does *Underlings Die First* (Shesterki umiraiut pervymi), where the operative Platonov has to hide when he deals with an investigation into the illegal export of precious metal. He finds himself too close to the truth—and on a hit list.

In *Away Game* (Igra na chuzhom pole), Kamenskaya goes to a resort to cure her bad back. She encounters a group of perverts who pay money to have a film made about their lust for destruction that culminates in the partner's death. A criminal gang pays for girls and for the film to be made. As Kamenskaya tries to investigate, she encounters a local Mafia boss who controls the police and ensures order. He, not the police, helps Kamenskaya solve the crime, stressing once again the corruption of the police apparatus. The head of the criminals is a woman pianist, who was suppressed under Stalin because she is a Jew and a cripple. The profit from the films is invested into the training of talented young pianists. Her personal trauma determines the role she has taken in this crime. Similarly, in *Unwilling Killer* (Ubiitsa ponevole), the general Vakar commits a series of murders. The reason for his crime lies nine years back, when today's victims killed his talented son and he now takes revenge. In *Posthumous Icon* (Posmertnyi obraz), a filmmaker who has been rejected by his mother in his childhood meets an actress, who is frigid because of molestation in her childhood. He helps her free herself from the trauma, and when she dumps him, he takes cruel revenge. In *Death and a Little Love* (Smert i nemnogo liubvi), a photographer takes revenge for his rejection long ago by the police service. In *The Stylist*

(Stilist), Marinina tackled the issue of authorship. A translator rewrites the author he translates and becomes a commodity for the publisher, who conceals the print run in order to cheat both author and translator.

The role of women in contemporary society is clearly an important issue in the novels. Marinina's heroine is not very feminine, has no interest in domestic matters, and although she has a relationship with the mathematician Alexei Chistiakov, whom she later marries, she seems to be asexual. Kamenskaya knows five languages and translates fiction in her free time. Kamenskaya has a mother who lives in Sweden, and a stepfather who is also in the police and who is her mentor. Her half-brother is a businessman and banker. Her entire family is protective and supportive of her work and accept her as a workaholic.

Kamenskaya's colleague and counterpart Tomilina in St. Petersburg not only prioritizes human values (she lets an accused, who is also a witness, escape to get him into safety), but she is also feminine and maternal. When pregnant, she is exposed to threats and danger, and eventually she resigns because she will not expose the baby to threats.

Irina Zarubina created a different kind of inspector in Klara Dezhkina of *Mrs. Inspector* (Gospozha sledovatel'), who has an unemployed husband and yet manages to be an efficient investigator and a housewife and mother. Polina Dashkova has no experience of police work. Her heroines are ordinary women who, in the absence of a competent police force, take it upon themselves to investigate. In *Flesh for Sale* (Prodazhnye tvari), a student and aspiring actress investigates the sale of women to serve in harems in the Caucasian regions. She encounters the military intelligence (GRU), whose staff are bribed and paid as informants by the Chechens, so that she can expect no help from the official organs in her search. In *No One Will Weep* (Nikto ne zaplachet), a translator and single mother is allocated the telephone number of a swindler and turns to self-help in the absence of any other support. In *Place under the Sun* (Mesto pod solntsem), a ballerina whose husband is killed meddles in the crime investigation and almost becomes a victim herself. She is saved by a new friend with whom she falls in love, however, so that the detective plot also harbors a romantic ending. In *Golden Sand* (Zolotoi pesok), the protagonist marries a politician who turns out to be a criminal, and she needs to resort to self-help. Similarly, in *Image of the Enemy* (Obraz vraga), a woman on vacation in Israel sees her ex-husband, believed dead, who is a terrorist. He is also the father of her son. While hunted by a number of secret services at once, she ultimately has to rely on herself to escape. Dashkova thus implicitly suggests the inefficiency of the police system while also creating the model of the independent woman who goes about solving her problems, and crimes, on her own.

Another enormously popular variant of the *detektiv* is the "ironic" detective story, a genre first represented in the Russian market by translations of the Polish novelist Johanna Khmelnitskaya. Daria Dontsova is the Moscow representative of the ironic detective novel, and Marina Vorontsova from Petersburg is promoted as the Petersburg "Dontsova." Vorontsova turned to writing after suffering from depression (she is a doctor by profession), and her heroine is Alexandra Alexandrovna Voroshilova.

Dontsova has created four characters who engage in private investigations, with-

Detective fiction writer Daria Dontsova arrives at the Olympic Sports Complex to attend the Muz-TV pop music awards ceremony, June 2004. (Photo by Vasily Shaposhnikov/ Kommersant)

out calling themselves detectives. Indeed, none of their "investigations" amounts to any significant result, but rather they are dabbling in detective work without hindering the police but also without contributing to the police investigation. They are crude amateurs who think of themselves as great detectives. Dasha Vasilieva is the first of these "detectives": she bears a number of features from Dontsova's biography (the name Vasilieva is Dontsova's maiden name). Dasha is a teacher of French, who lives, after perestroika, in rather impoverished circumstances with her son Arkadi and her younger daughter Masha (the names of Dontsova's children). Dasha's best friend, Natasha, marries the rich Frenchman Jacques. During their first visit to Paris, Jacques is killed and Dasha helps find the murderer. Ultimately, she stays with her children at Natasha's mansion inherited from Jacques, and only later in the series do they return to Moscow, where they acquire a house in a new elite suburb.

Evlampia (Lampa) Romanova is a spoiled rich girl, who is pampered by her artist parents. She turns out to be a bad harp player but is married off to a rich husband before her parents die. Her husband betrays her and she flees, running in front of a car driven by the surgeon Katia, who picks her up and takes her home. Lampa then stays with Katia and her children, dogs, and cats; runs the household; and learns painstakingly how to shop, how to cook, and how to survive. While searching for her documents she finds a murder victim, and her husband turns out to be a criminal. At the end of the first novel, she stays with Katia and the children and continues to investigate a murder when a neighbor, dying of poison, calls her, dialing the wrong number. Lampa is a clever "private eye" who can actually assist the police friend who solves the crimes.

Viola Tarakanova (*tarakan* is a cockroach; Viola is a brand of soft cheese) was born to alcoholic parents and her father was also a petty criminal. He, however, reintegrates into society after several terms in prison and joins her in Moscow, where he marries her neighbor. As a teenager, Viola lived largely with her best friend, Tamara. When the latter's parents died in an accident, the two young women decide to stay together. Both are married in the first episode: Tamara marries a rich businessman from the Urals, whose daughter Kristia is exposed to danger and saved by Viola in several episodes. Viola marries

Kuprin, a police investigator. Viola has no higher education, but she gives private tuition in German. In one of the episodes Viola is involved in a crime connected with fake paintings. Viola is quite clever but overwhelmed by a number of other chores that stop her from focusing.

The only man among the "private investigators" is Ivan Podushkin (*podushka* is a pillow), a 40-year-old bachelor whose mother, Nikoletta, is an extravagant actress who dictates his entire life. He lives, however, in the apartment of his boss, Eleonora (Nora), whom he serves as private secretary for the charitable fund Mercy (Miloserdie) that she runs. Ivan checks the claims of people in need. In the first episode, Nora's granddaughter disappears, and the solution of the disappearance involves an unknown twin sister. As Nora has chosen for herself the role of Nero Wolfe, she casts Podushkin in the role of Archie for her "cases." In another series he explores a murder for which Nora's best friend, Sonia, has been arrested. Podushkin is the most incompetent and dim of the four "investigators."

They are all ironic because they grope in the dark and follow leads that they cannot piece together until the professionals (police friends) intervene. Viola is married to an inspector, the inspector Maxim is Nora's friend, and Katia also knows a police inspector.

Soap Operas

During the early 1990s, Brazilian and Mexican soap operas drew audiences to television sets. Their overdone melodrama enhanced by the Russian voice-over and the grotesquely overemotional acting attracted viewers. The serials served as an emotional outlet, where it was possible to show compassion for others' suffering as the world around the television viewers collapsed and turned to chaos. Russia could not offer such emotional hype. Instead, the country was ridden with crime.

Crime Serials and Serial Crimes

The rise of the detective genre in television serials coincided with the rise of detective fiction. The interest in crime was not only linked to the rise in crime in post-Soviet Russia, however. Such spy and crime serials as *Seventeen Moments of Spring* (12 series, 1972) about the Soviet spy Stirlitz in Hitler's Germany and *Sherlock Holmes and Mr Watson* (directed by Igor Maslennikov, 2 series, 1979) as well as *The Meeting Place Must Not Be Changed* (5 series, 1979) about the work of a Moscow police station had always enjoyed great popularity with the masses. In the New Russia it was cheaper to acquire serials than to produce them, however. Only after the financial crisis of 1998 did prices and production costs drop, whereas foreign acquisitions became unaffordable. Serial production rose in Russia from 1998 onward, and the production of crime serials flourished. The crime serial simulates patterns of positive behavior, thus projecting a new identity for Russia, showing Russia's capacity for "normalcy" in the mirror of the fragmented life that surrounds it. This projection of an identity without recourse to a varnished reality makes the crime serial extremely popular in contemporary Russia.

In the late 1990s many filmmakers abandoned feature films for television serials, where funding was available. Many scripts for television were adapted from popular crime writers such as Boris Akunin, Alexandra Marinina, Daria Dontsova, Danil Koretsky, or Alexander Belov. The spectacular rise of the Russian television serial, almost knocking its foreign competitors off the screen, is the most striking and significant development in the Russian television and film industry of the twenty-first century.

By 2002, the highest ratings were achieved for Russian serials, especially by the channel NTV, which had the privilege of using the films commissioned by KinoMost, such as *Cops* and *Black Raven* and *Agent of National Security.* In 2002, 800 hours of serials were produced, in 2003 this rose to 1,200 hours, and the tendency is still rising. *Poor Nastia* (Bednaia Nastia) was the first international television serial coproduction with Columbia Pictures, which is indicative of the potential for Russian serials, especially when they are produced to Western schedules (one series shot per day). Several companies have been formed for serial production, such as New Russian Serial (Novyi Russkii Serial) as part of the NTV group; on RTR and ORT, the two experienced filmmakers Valeri Todorovsky and Dzhanik Faiziyev are responsible for film production.

Streets of Broken Lights (1997–1999) was the first Russian-made serial, which to date has generated over 130 episodes. It was released on video under the title *Cops* (Menty). The series is based on the detective fiction of Alexander Kivinov, a former crime investigator. All the episodes are set in a Petersburg police station, where the chief, Petrenko (nickname "Mukhomor"), played by Yuri Kuznestov, heads the team of inspectors: Larin (Alexei Nilov), whose competence lies in crime records; Kazantsev (Alexander Lykov), who is a notorious womanizer; Solovets (Alexander Polovtsev), a Sherlock Holmes type; Dukalis

(Sergei Selin), a simpleton; and Volkov (Mikhail Trukhin), who displays the most nonsensical conduct. They all struggle in their work due to the lack of proper administrative and financial support (broken cars, no petrol, no office space) and have to resort to unorthodox methods to solve their crimes. Their inventiveness and their ability to arrest the culprits despite all odds, and still maintain a sense of humor, make them loveable and realistic. The first series were directed by Alexander Rogozhkin, a master of the ironic and absurd, who set the tone for the subsequent episodes.

Rogozhkin's involvement in the creation of one of the first crime series *Cops: Streets of Broken Lights* was an important move for its launch in 1997. Rogozhkin directed the first and second episode, thus ensuring a sound and professional start for the series. In "Nightmare on S-Street" (Koshmar na ulitse S), Rogozhkin developed an episode where the investigation is led by Vladimir Kazantsev, also known as Kazanova, and Andrei Larin, played respectively by Lykov and Trukhin, both well-known Petersburg theater actors. They investigate the murder of a taxi driver; it turns out that the murderer is an ex-prisoner, hired by the secret police. The film reveals the duplicity of all enterprises: as the crime squad investigates, the secret service FSB is overhearing all their conversations. In "Best Wishes, Larin" (Tseluiu, Larin) the squad investigates a brutal shooting at a New Year party; in the meantime, a drug dealer dies, leaving a trace that leads to the arrest of the main heads of the drug-smuggling ring.

Streets of Broken Lights portrays the hard work of the crime squad, whereas the important parts of the job (arrests, control, PR) are always done by the special forces.

The squad suffers from a lack of resources: a radio transmitter is used as lie detector; they occupy not an office block, but a shabby, old apartment. Reality is unveiled in its most shameful aspects: the brothel is run by an ex-cop, old people are forgotten (when Larin is sent to look at the dead body of an old woman, he finds her covered in yellow and white dust in a desolate flat, still alive). The behavior of the citizens, who bother the police with trivial concerns—from a stolen hat to an alleged theft of $10,000—is as inadequate as are the police responses: Kazantsev unplugs the phone before making calls to close off roads and airports; Larin administers vodka to the old woman whose hat has been stolen, to calm her down. Larin leaves a police informant under arrest alone in his office and allows him to say farewell to his girlfriend. The investigators are "normal" people, not heroes; they are good-natured, and they love beer. The eccentric behavior of the investigators is explained by the circumstances under which they work: insufficient resources, bribery, alcoholism, petty crime, lack of social services all make them deal with issues that are outside of, or beneath, their jobs. Kazantsev is stabbed in the first series, Larin resigns in the second: Petersburg police squads do not make the setting for heroism.

The serial *A Crushing Force* (Uboinaia sila, 2000) continues *Cops* in that the episodes are also based on Kivinov's novels and set in the same crime squad, involving the same actors. In the first part of the series, "Official Conformity" (Sluzhebnoe sootvetstvie), directed again by Rogozhkin, the investigators are shown with human foibles: enthusiastic, they still dream of heroism. They are prone to errors and human flaws: they may gamble, have sex with a prostitute. It is the police reality and society that force them into these acts in order to succeed in life. The police squad continues in this series to be portrayed as insufficiently equipped. Crime thrives, but the investigators are good people and could improve the world—if paid properly and given the resources. The episodes follow the arrest of a drug dealer who holds the key to a series of crimes but is murdered herself. In the meantime, an undercover policeman (Plakhov) acts as a bodyguard for a businessman, who tries to get rid of his surveillance. The fight between organized crime and the ill-equipped force continues in this series.

Kamenskaya (1999–2000, NTV), directed by Yuri Moroz, was based on the detective novels of Alexandra Marinina, whose complex detective novels about big-scale and organized crime were more popular in writing than in the screen version. Three series were made altogether between 2000 and 2003, all starring Yelena Yakovleva as Kamenskaya. The popularity of the novels over the serial also applies to Dontsova's novels with "investigator" Dasha Vasilieva (played by Larisa Udovichenko) and Evlampia Romanova (Alla Kliuka), which remained more popular in print than on screen.

Detective Dubrovsky's Dossier (Dos'e detektiva Dubrovskogo, 1999) is a detective series based on the novel by Lev Gursky, directed by the television director Alexander Muratov and starring the well-known actor Nikolai Karachentsov. Dubrovsky is an ex–Secret Service (FSB) officer who is drawn into a political intrigue, during the course of which he can rely only on himself. He is suspected by the FSB of murder, hunted by money forgers, and—a true gentleman—defends a woman. With a good sense of humor, Dubrovsky stumbles from one crime to the next, in a plot that is almost as complex and confused as the novels of Alexandra Marinina. Dubrovsky tries to solve a case of author's rights for his lady client and accidentally discloses money forgers, who prosecute him. When his former colleague Khromov helps him, Khromov mysteriously disappears. It transpires that Khromov was no longer with the FSB but owed money to the bosses of a pyramid investment scheme, which collapsed. Dubrovsky is suspected of Khromov's murder and forced by the criminals to repay Khromov's debt. In an attempt to recoup his lady client's manuscript, Dubrovsky unveils the documentation relating to the pyramid scheme. Then the chief prosecutor is killed, and a maniac killer released to kill the "double" of the criminal boss, but Dubrovsky eliminates the maniac and discloses all the illegal activities at the end.

Hunting Cinderella (Okhota na zolushku, 1999–2000) is a film about a killer-machine, Nikita. The gray mouse and film graduate, Eva (Amalia Mordvinova-Goldanskaya), has an accident and suffers from memory loss. This makes her extremely suited for the criminal underworld as a killer, whose biography can be reinvented with every case. The agent Nikita can be a hacker in a computer firm, an expert on old rare books, or a computer expert stopping a banking system from being broken.

Other crime serials followed suit. *Bourgeois's Birthday* (Den' rozhdeniia Burzhuia, 1999) consisted of 15 episodes. At the center of the series is an orphan, Vladimir Kovalenko, whose nickname is "the bourgeois." He becomes a successful businessman, when he finds himself targeted by people who threaten him with dis-

closure of his parentage. *Criminal Petersburg* (2000) is a six-part series (with five–ten episodes each) about a gangster clan in Petersburg, based on the novels of Andrei Konstaninov. Antibiotik is the Mafia king who runs the country and sets social values. The Mafia structures are viewed as an alternative to the weakened and feeble structures of the state and society. The replacement of a mechanism to ensure order through criminal structures, explaining rather than legitimizing them, is enhanced by drawing on well-known Soviet actors who play those characters that provide moral guidance. In this serial, the past is used to explain why people have ended up in the criminal world. *The Truckers* (Dal'noboishchiki, 2001) is a road-movie serial, which follows the experienced trucker Fedov (played by the popular actor Sergei Gostiukhin) and the young trucker Sashko on their journeys. They are brought together by the difficulties they encounter on the road. *The Brigade* (Brigada, 2003) was based on a novel by Alexander Belov about four lads from Moscow who try to make money in the early 1990s and end up in the criminal world. *Ice Age* (Lednikovyi period, 2003) is set in the Moscow of the 1990s in the special section of the police force, which faces the task of investigating moles in the police apparatus. *Steep Turns* (Krutye povoroty) explored the fate of a taxi driver who penetrates the criminal world. *Moscow, Central District* (Moskva, tsentralny okrug) was set in a regional police station. *Key to Death* (Kliuch ot smerti) follows Stas Severin, who leaves the police force and becomes a private investigator.

The Agent of National Security (Agent natsional'noi bezopasnosti) is a Russian version of James Bond. Alexei Nikolayev (played by Mikhail Porechnikov) is able to transform himself into a beggar, an art historian, or a computer specialist with great ease to solve crimes: the theft of a Stradivarius violin, the kidnapping of a politician's child, a media incident where Russia is accused of collaborating with Arab terrorists, or the fake Filonov paintings in the Russian Museum in St. Petersburg. *Secrets of the Investigation* (Tainy sledstviia) is based on the novels of the former investigator Yelena Topilskaya. The protagonist is also a woman investigator, Masha Shvetsova, who sees the case of the murderer of the businessman Chvanov reopened and connected to an explosion that kills a duma deputy. She also has to investigate the murder of a businessman's wife. The role of the investigator was played by Anna Kovalchuk, a young Petersburg actress, whose role was rewritten to accommodate her pregnancy.

Crimeless Serials

Gradually, as the social and economic situation appeared to be more stable, noncriminal serials also emerged: it seemed that life had, at least partly, become "normal." *An Ideal Pair* (Ideal'naia para, 2001) is an adventure comedy about Anna and Genrikh, who cheat people. The ten-part series was filmed by the comedy director Alla Surikova. *Black Raven* (Chernyi voron, 2003) is a suspense serial that proceeds from the 1940s to the present. In the present there are two women, both called Tatiana, born of the same father. After the war Alexei had returned to his uncle, whose wife Ada had no children. Ada's mother, a witch, and Ada herself, were anxious to have a baby girl in the family to whom the skill of witchcraft could be passed on.

Lines of Fate (Linii sudby) was directed by the filmmaker Dmitri Meskhiev. The serial captured audiences with the fates of provincial people who come to Moscow to find happiness and success. Roza Vialskaya lets rooms of her large apartment to a number of people who all try to sort out their lives. There are a young couple, a doctor who is suspended from duty and turns into a fortune-teller, a market trader, a ballerina, and a journalist. And there is Katia, whose husband is a former army officer who received an apartment as a reward for his heroic service in the Caucasus. Their fates are linked through the apartment, and each plot line is taken to a solution over the course of the series. Despite the voices that warned filmmakers from making serials rather than art-house films that prophesied the death of Russian cinema at the end of the twentieth century, Meskhiev demonstrated that he was capable not only of making a good and gripping television serial that did not involve crime but also of making a high-quality film: *Ours* (Svoi) won the main award at the Moscow International Film Festival 2004 and was praised by the jury chairman, Alan Parker, as one of the best films he had seen in the past ten years.

A to Z

Akunin, Boris: b. 1956. Real name Grigori Chkhartishvili. Chkhartishvili studied history and specialized in Japanese studies. He worked as a translator of fiction from Japanese and English, as well as producing literary criticism, such as in his book *Writer and Suicide* (1999). Since 1998 he has written under the pseudonym B.

Akunin (read Bakunin, the name of the nineteenth-century anarchist), creating primarily crime fiction set in provincial Russia and preferably in the nineteenth century. The Fandorin series was published by Zakharov Publishing from 1998 to 2001; it comprises *Azazel, Turkish Gambit, Levithian, Achilles's Death, Coronation*, and others. The Provincial Detective series deals with the eccentric nun Pelagiya and comprises *Pelagiya and the White Bulldog; Pelagiya and the Black Monk; Pelagiya and the Red Cockerel*. A new series of the adventures of Nikolas Fandorin has been launched also. [www.akunin.ru]

Anti-Booker Prize: Established by *Nezavisimaya gazeta* in 1995, discontinued 2000. Winners were 1995: Alexei Varlamov (prose); 1996: Dmitri Bakin (prose), Ivan Saveliev (drama), and Sergei Gandlevsky (poetry); 1997: Dmitri Galkovsky (prose, rejected), Oleg Bogayev (drama, *Russian Post* [Russkaia narodnaia pochta]), and Timur Kibirov (poetry); 1998: Andrei Volos (prose, *Hurramabad*), Maxim Kurochkin (drama, *Steel Will* [Stal'ova volia]), and Mikhail Amelin (poetry); 1999: Yevgeni Grishkovets (drama, *Notes of a Russian Traveler* [Zapiski russkogo puteshestvennika]); 2000: Boris Akunin (prose, *Coronation*), Vasili Sigarev (drama, *Plasticine* [Plastillin]), and Bakhyt Kenzheyev (poetry). [www.ng.ru/about/anti.html]

Booker Prize: Modeled on the British Booker Prize, the Russian Buker was established in 1992 under British lead to reward the best work of fiction. Initially, novels had to be published in literary journals to be considered; later fiction already published in book form was also taken into consideration of the jury, always composed of Russian critics and representatives of international Slavic scholarship. After 1999, when the British support expired, the prize was sponsored by the vodka label Smirnoff, but from 2001 on, after Smirnoff was forced to pull out of the Russian market, it has been run by the fund Open Russia, a subsidiary of Yukos. Winners have included Mark Kharitonov, *Lines of Fate, or Milashevich's Trunk* (Linii sud'by ili sunduchok Milashevicha, 1992); Vladimir Makanin, *The Baize-covered Table with Decanter* (Stol pokrytyi skatert'iu i s grafinoi poseredine, 1993); Bulat Okudzhava, *The Closed Theater*, also known as *The Show Is Over* (Uprazdnennyi teatr, 1994); Georgi Vladimov, *The General and His Army* (General i ego armiia, 1995); Andrei Sergeyev, *Stamp Album* (Al'bom dlia marok, 1996); Anatoli Azolsky, *The Cage* (Kletka, 1997); Alexander Morozov, *Another's Letters* (Chuzhie pis'ma, 1998); Mikhail Butov, *Freedom* (Svoboda, 1999); Mikhail Shishkin, *The Conquest of Izmail* (Vziatie Izmaila, 2000); Liudmila Ulitskaya, *The Kukotsky Case* (Kazuz Kukotskogo, 2001); Oleg Pavlov, *The Tale of the Last Days* (Karaganda Karagandinskie deviatiny, ili Povest' poslednikh dnei, 2002); Ruben David Gonzales Gallego, *White on Black* (Beloe na chernom, 2003). [www.russianbooker.ru] and [www.open russia.into/booker/]

Bure, Pavel: b. 1971. Hockey player. Played for CSKA between 1989 and 1991. Since 1991, striker for Vancouver Canucks. Played for Russian Olympic team and silver medalist in Nagano, 1998. In 1999 joined the Florida Panthers in a 50-million-dollar deal. Best striker of the year, 2000. His father, Vladimir, was a well-known swimmer and bronze medalist of the Munich and Mexico Olympics. Bure left Russia after the August coup of 1991 and took up residence in Canada through a fictitious marriage with a Canadian citizen. Great-grandson of Pavel Bure, whose company, founded by Swiss watchmaker Eduard Bure, made precious watches for the Russian tsars after 1815; business revived in 1996. In the 1920s the watches were a sign of respectability and are even mentioned in Ilf and Petrov's *Twelve Chairs*.

Dinamo Moscow: Sports and football club founded in 1923 by Felix Dzerzhinsky, head of the Secret Service, for workers of the Ministry of the Interior and of the Secret Service. Dinamo has branches in all major cities of the former Soviet Union. The logo of the club is a D embossed in blue on white, the first letter of the club and also the initial of Dzerzhinsky. The Soviet government was always very protective of the club, which was the first to own its own stadium with an adjacent metro stop. There has always been a great deal of competition between Dinamo and Spartak: the Dinamo team adopted a more disciplined approach to the play than the Spartak team, which relied on improvisation and chance. Dinamo remains one of the top football teams in Moscow and Russia, with its fans, the "dynamites," displaying more discipline too than Spartak's fans. Top players, however, are with Lokomotiv. [www.fcdynamo.ru]

Dontsova, Daria: b. 1952. Real name Agrippina Arkadievna Dontsova. Née Vasilieva, born in Moscow to a writer and a music manager. From 1969 to 1974 studied journalism at Moscow State University. She was married for three weeks and has her son Arkadi from the marriage. She then worked for two years in the Russian embassy in Syria as translator from French. In 1976 she married again and worked as section editor for the paper *Vecherniaya Moskva*. In 1983 she met the psychologist and university professor Alexander Dontsov, whom she married; in 1986 she had her daughter, Masha. In 1998 she was diagnosed with cancer and turned to writing. In August 1999 Eksmo Press signed her up, changing her first name to Daria (Dasha). [www.dontsova.ru]

Fetisov, Viacheslav: b. 1958. Hockey player. Played defense for the CSKA hockey team, then for New Jersey Devils and Detroit Red Wings. USSR champion 1975, 1977–1989; world champion 1978, 1981–1983, 1986, 1989; Olympic champion 1988. Canadian Cup winner 1981. In 1997 and 1998, winner of the prestigious Stanley Cup. Since 1998 trainer of New Jersey Devils, which in 2000 won the Stanley Cup.

Kafelnikov, Yevgeni: b. 1974 in Sochi. Tennis player who was coached by Valeri Shishkin, and after 1991 by Anatoli Lepeshin. Kafelnikov won the Paris Open in 1996 and the Australian Open in 1999. In 2000 he was a finalist in the Australian Open. Kafelnikov ranked the world's number one for six weeks in 1999.

Kasparov, Garri: b. 1963 in Baku. Chess champion. Thirteen times world champion in chess since 1985. His mother, Klara, is also his manager. Allegedly father of a child (Nika, born 1987) by the Moscow star actress Marina Neyolova, 16 years his senior.

Kurnikova, Anna: b. 1981, Moscow. Tennis player. Started playing tennis at the age of five; from 1981 to 1989, coached by Larisa Preobrazhenskaya. In 1992 Kurnikova moved to Florida with her mother and trained at Nick Bolletieri's Tennis Academy in Bradenton. In 1995 she won the Italian Open juniors and was a Wimbledon junior semifinalist. Kurnikova has been a professional tennis player since 1995. In 1998, first Russian female to be seeded at U.S. Open since 1976. 1998, defeated several top players; 1999 won Australian Open (doubles). Advertising contracts with Adidas, Omega, and Lycos: one of the highest-paid female tennis players. Cover girl (*Sports Illustrated* June 2000).

Lokomotiv Moscow: Football club formed in 1923 for railway workers. The club participated in the first national competition in 1936, taking fifth place. The team ranked among the top ten football clubs until the 1950s, when the former CSKA coach Boris Arkadiev joined the Lokomotiv team and remained its coach until 1967. The team could not hold a position in the top ten and was soon demoted to second division. Since 1991, Lokomotiv has consistently played in the first division; it has ranked among the top three teams since 1998 and won the champion title in 2002 from Spartak Moscow. It has four times won the Russian Football Cup since 1995. Lokomotiv is playing in the UEFA champions league.

Marinina, Alexandra: b. 1957. Real name Marina Alexeyeva. Marinina lived in Leningrad until 1971, when she moved to Moscow. She studied at an English special school and in 1979 graduated from the Law Faculty of Moscow State University and joined the Academy of the Ministry of Interior Affairs, where she worked from 1980 on. Her work consisted of the study of the psychology of criminals, especially psychic anomalies and serial crimes. In 1986 she defended her master's degree. She resigned from police service in 1998. Since 1991 she has written detective stories. "Six-winged Serafim" was published in the police journal *Militsia* in the autumn of 1992, written with Alexander Gorkin. From there stems the pseudonym: Alexander and Marina. In 1992–1993 she wrote "Coincidences," published also in *Militsia* in autumn 1993. In 1993–1994 she wrote *Away Game* (Igra an chuzhom pole) and *Stolen Dream* (Ukradennyi son). In January 1995 she was approached by Eksmo Press and offered publication in the series Black Cat (Chernaia koshka). In 1999 Rekun Film acquired the rights to make a television series based on her novels. Overall, more than 30 million copies of her books have been sold. Novels: *The Seventh Victim; The Apparition of Music; Requiem; I Died Yesterday; Men's Games; The Victim's Name Is—Nobody; The Radiant Face of Death; The Illusion of Sin; The Stylist; Don't Hinder the Executioner; Someone Else's Mask; Everything Has to Be Paid For; Posthumous Icon; The Black List; Death and Some Love; Underlings Die First; Death for Death's Sake; The Unwilling Killer; Stolen Dream; Away Game; The Coincidence of Circumstances.* [www.marinina.ru]

Menty **(Cops):** television serial. Released on video as *Cops*, but shown on television under the title *Streets of Broken Lamps* (Ulitsy razbitykh fonarei), based on the novels by Andrei Kivinov and produced by TNT, then First Channel (ORT) since 1998. The series explores the work in a Petersburg police station, with the boss Mukhomor-Petrenko and the investigators Larin, Kazantsev, Solovets, Dukalis, and Volkov.

Some members of the team continue their work in the serial *The Crushing Force* (Uboinaia sila), also written by Kivinov.

Pelevin, Viktor: b. 1962. Pelevin attended aviation college. He has been a professional writer since 1991. *The Blue Lantern*, a collection of short prose, received the Little Booker in 1993. His work belongs to postmodernism and is characterized by fragmentation. Its outstanding characteristic is the concern with hyperrealities. Works: *Life of Insects* (Zhizn' nasekomykh, 1993); *Omon Ra* (1992); *Generation P* (1999). *Chapayev and Pustota* (1996) is a parody on the Soviet civil war hero Chapayev, in whose regiment the hero and poet Petr Pustota serves. This action is set against a contemporary axis, where Kawabat, Schwarzenegger, and the stars of the soap opera *Simply Maria* meet with the hero. [http://pelevin.nov.ru]

Publishers: There are about half a dozen publishing houses, all Moscow based, which dominate the book market. Eksmo Press is a publishing house of detective and crime fiction; established in 1993, it produces more than 55 million books and 50,000 titles per year, including Marinina, Dontsova, and other detective stories. Olma Press publishes encyclopedias, children's literature, and crime fiction. The group AST unites 50 publishers, including Astrel for crime fiction and sci-fi, and lists more than 10,000 titles. Rosmen is a major publishing house for children's books. Vagrius Press specializes in contemporary prose fiction and memoirs.

Rodnina, Irina: b. 1949. Figure skater (pairs) and Olympics Gold medalist 1972, 1976, 1980. After her debut on international ice in 1969, she skated with Alexei Ulanov until 1972, when Ulanov married the skater Liudmila Smirnova and formed a team with her. Rodnina then skated with Alexander Zaitsev, whom she later married. She is ten times world champion, and it was only in 1979 that the European championship was not hers, since she gave birth to her son, Sasha. Rodnina was trained by Stanislav Zhuk, later by Tatiana Tarasova. After ending her career as skater in 1980, she went to the United States as a trainer, then returned to Moscow to run her own training school sponsored by Luzhkov in the late 1990s.

Russian Football League: Teams in the Upper League in 2004 include Alanya Vladikavkaz, Chernomorets (Krasnodar), Rostov, Rotor (Volgograd), Rubin (Kazan), Shinnik (Yaroslavl), Uralan (Elista), and Zenit (Petersburg) as well as the Moscow clubs CSKA, Dinamo, Torpedo Moscow and Torpedo Metallurg, Lokomotiv, Krylya Sovetov, and the Moscow regional club Saturn. For comparison, the Upper League in 1974 included the following (clubs in now independent republics are italicized): *Ararat Yerevan*, *Dinamo Kiev*, Dinamo Moscow, Spartak Moscow, *Dinamo Tblisi*, *Shakhter Donetsk (Ukraine)*, *Zarya Voroshilovgrad (Lugansk, Ukraine)*, *Dnepr Dnepropetrovsk (Ukraine)*, *Kairat Alma-Ata*, CSKA, Zenit Leningrad, *Pakhtakor Tashkent*, Torpedo Moscow, *Karpaty Lvov (Ukraine)*, *Chernomorets Odessa (Ukraine)*, and *Nistru Kishinev*. It is evident that football was much stronger in Ukraine and in the Central Asian republics than in central Russia, which is represented in the 1974 league only by three Moscow clubs and Zenit Leningrad, all of which were still in the league in 2004.

314 POP CULTURE RUSSIA!

Other Russian clubs were not as strong as clubs in Ukraine, however, and this explains to some extent the low performance of Russian football in the post-Soviet era.

Russian National Football Team: The team, formed for international competitions only, was coached by Oleg Romantsev in 2002. The squad included the star players Valeri Karpin, who ranked 24th in the world in 2004, and Alexander Mostovoy, both playing for Celta Vigo; Yegor Titov of Spartak; Marat Izmailov of Lokomotiv; and Yuri Nikiforov, who plays for Eindhoven. Romantsev clearly prioritized the Spartak and CSKA teams in his choice of players. Romantsev was not reappointed as national coach for 2004. The national team for the 2004 European Cup was coached by Georgi Yartsev. Russia's football team ranked in 24th place in the world in 2002.

Sharapova, Maria: b. 19 April 1987 in Niagan. Tennis player. Sharapova left Russia with her father when aged seven, with her mother to follow later. She trained at Nick Bolletieri's School in Florida. First Russian woman (seeded 17th) to win Wimbledon, 3 July 2004, beating Serena Williams in two sets.

Sorokin, Vladimir: b. 1955. Postmodernist writer. Graduated as chemical engineer from Moscow Oil and Gas Institute, then worked as graphic artist and designer. He engaged in the conceptualist movement. He is married, with twin daughters. His works remained unpublished until the 1990s. Works include *The Queue* (Ochered', 1988); *The Norm* (Norma, 1991); *Roman* (1994). He parodies totalitarianism and deconstructs the past and present, creating an unpleasant sense of reality. [www.srkn.ru]

Spartak Moscow: Sports and football club formed in the 1920s for cooperative workers. Spartak's hockey team has always been a top team in the national ice hockey league, along with CSKA. The Spartak football team first appeared in 1922 in the Moscow league. Spartak was the first team to play international matches in the 1930s, and in 1936 it rose to national champions. The team attracted the envy of the head of the Secret Service (NKVD) Lavrenti Beria for beating his home team, Dinamo Tblisi in 1939. Several Spartak players were arrested during the great purges. The Spartak team emerged as one of the strongest Soviet teams after the war, largely forming the Soviet national team that won Olympic gold in Melbourne in 1956. Spartak Moscow often gained top places in the national championships during the Soviet era, and between 1992 and 2001 it did not once lose the champion's title. In 2002 and 2003 it fell to tenth place. Spartak fans are considered to be the most aggressive, with a number of skinheads and politically motivated youths among the fans. The Spartak colors are red and white. The team practices at Sokolniki stadium, although major matches are played at the huge Luzhniki stadium. [www.spartak.ru] and for the soccer club [http://rus.spartak.com]

Bibliography

Edelman, Robert. *Serious Fun. A History of Spectator Sports in the USSR*. Oxford: Oxford University Press, 1993.
———. "There Are No Rules on Planet Russia: Post-Soviet Spectator Sport." In *Consuming*

Russia. Popular Culture, Sex and Society since Gorbachev, ed. by Adele Barker, 217–242. Durham, NC: Duke University Press, 1999.

Lovell, Stephen. "Publishing and the Book Trade in the Post-Stalin Era: A Case Study of the Commodification of Culture." *Europe-Asia Studies.*50, no. 4 (1998): 679–698.

Mehnert, Klaus. *The Russians' Favorite Books.* Stanford, CA: Hoover Institute Press, 1983.

Nepomnyashchy, Catharine Theimer. "Markets, Mirrors and Mayhem: Aleksandra Marinina and the Rise of the New Russian *Detektiv."* In *Consuming Russia. Popular Culture, Sex and Society since Gorbachev*, ed. by Adele Barker, 161–191. Durham, NC: Duke University Press, 1999.

Olcott, Anthony. *Russian Pulp.* Lanham, MD: Rowman and Littlefield, 2001.

Riordan, James. *Sport in Soviet Society.* Cambridge: Cambridge University Press, 1977.

Schultze, Sydney. *Culture and Customs of Russia.* Westport, CT: Greenwood Press, 2000.

Shneidman, Norman. *The Soviet Road to Olympics.* London: Routledge, Kegan Paul, 1979.

6

Consumer Culture

With the displacement of cultural objects such as books and art posters by consumer products in the aftermath of the reforms of 1991, freeing up prices that had so far been fixed by the state, a new consumer culture emerged. Vendors appeared on every street corner, offering goods cheaper than in the shops; underground passages converted into trade centers; prices rapidly escalated and inflation rose. Cultural objects became luxury goods, and foodstuff and other consumer goods replaced the cherished fetishes of the intellectuals. Almost overnight Russian society turned into a society of consumers, a transformation that trashed anything that was no longer functional or necessary. The impact that consumer culture had on the urban landscapes of major cities, especially Moscow and Petersburg, has already been discussed. Another phenomenon that changed the cityscape was the advertising billboards.

Advertising

The concept of advertising would appear to contradict the spirit of the Soviet economy, which excluded branding and competition. There were advertisements during the NEP (New Economic Policy) period (1921–1928) when a free market was introduced temporarily to remedy the economic crisis in the aftermath of the civil war and the Revolution. Many avant-garde artists and poets pledged their service to the Revolution and helped create advertisements: the poet Vladimir Mayakovsky wrote slogans, the artist Alexander Rodchenko designed posters, and they even received awards for their work at the international exhibition in Paris in 1925. Since the introduction of five-year plans, there had been no advertisements in the proper sense of the word. Rather, advertisements functioned as educational spots to explain new products, introduce new inventions, and guide the viewer. They did not have the function of selling a product—those products that were in demand tended to be in short supply. Moreover, printing facilities for posters were rather limited due to poor-quality paper, and most posters for concerts or shows were hand

Moscow, 1992. A street seller selling souvenirs on the Old Arbat Street in Moscow. (Photo by Andrey Golovanov/Kommersant)

painted or hand printed. Journals were subsidized and did not rely on revenue through advertising. Some products, however, were advertised—for example, products that were in sufficient supply, but expensive (Pacific fish). Electric lighters for gas stoves were advertised in order to explain how to use them when there was a shortage of matches. Milk and dairy products, fruit and vegetables were advertised as a "healthy diet," since people did not eat enough of these. More significant is the fact that 73 percent of food goods were sold unwrapped (for liquids, customers often had to bring their own containers; no cling film or carrier bags were available in the shops). The absence of packaging meant that there was no space for brand-

ing. Only a few goods, such as television sets, some electrical products, perfumes, and chocolates, had brand names.

Advertising entered Soviet culture with Gorbachev. The first ad featured Michael Jackson advertising Pepsi Cola (17–23 May 1988). Pepsi Cola hardly needed any advertising to the Soviet consumer, so the spot was rather of symbolic value: advertising was viewed as part of the images of Western culture that were becoming available in the media. This is also true of the first advertising clips on television, which were synchronized versions of Western clips for Western products. They revealed to the spectator (not consumer) the full extent of the dream world of Western consumerism. Full-blown advertising started after the fixing of prices by the state had ceased on 1 January 1992. Advertising ranged from newspaper ads to billboards in the streets; from banners across the street to advertisements on buses, in the metro, on escalators, on houses, and in other public spaces; and from television ads to movie trailers. Companies and traders began to bid for customers' attention, but Russian companies had no previous experience of supply and demand or the stimulation of consumer dreams, whereas Western companies had no idea of the realities of life in post-Soviet Russia.

The best example is the reception of the massive advertising campaign of Procter and Gamble, competing in the Western world over customers in the cosmetics sector. The Always advertisements for *prokladki* (the collective term for pantyliners and sanitary towels) bombarded the Russian spectator with product information— as if she or he had never heard of feminine hygiene before. The problem was exactly that: people had heard about such prod-

Advertising on a tram, which has just left a stop, with the advertising board reading "This space is for rent." Moscow, 2002. (Photo by Alexey Myakishev/Kommersant)

ucts, but they had not been available in Soviet times. Now they were on the market, but people could barely afford them. The same is true for the much-sought-after tampons or disposable diapers. The advertisements were doubly absurd: by their frequency they seemed to suggest an "indoctrination" with a product that was known, and yet they were showing the consumer the world of the West, distancing the—now available—product from the Russian context.

The advertisements for antiperspirants and deodorants played on the notion of sociability, completely misunderstood in the advertising campaign. One spot featured a woman in an elevator; everybody else runs away to avoid the odors of her perspiration, leaving her on her own in the elevator. When she uses Rexona, her colleagues join her in the elevator (and congratulate her on her birthday): she is no longer alone. A parody of the advertisement shows the way in which it was understood in Russia: A man enters an elevator, having used a "perfume" that emits a stench. Everybody gets out of the elevator, and the man has it to himself. In a society where crowded trolleybuses and crammed apartments were reality, private space, space for oneself, was a sought-after treat, not a sign of isolation. The Rexona advertising campaign ignored the habits of the Russian consumer. The slogan was parodied: "When you boarded the metro train, everybody else got off. Rexona never lets you down."

Similarly, the advertising campaign for the cat food Whiskas bluntly ignored the circumstances of Russian life and was most unsuitable for the Russian consumer. The slogan "*Vasha koshka kupila by Viskas*" (Your cat would buy Whiskas) for the Western consumer implied that the cat made a choice, ridiculous enough as a concept. But on the Russian market, the imported product cost more than the average person could spend on pet food, so never mind what the cat would buy. The advertising campaigns for Western products created by Western ad agencies clearly ignored the realities of post-Soviet Russia, where on top of rising inflation, communal charges were introduced for electricity, gas, and water. The ads created a parallel world: a world that Soviet citizens had dreamed of, that Russians could reach and touch, but that was beyond the financial scope of the ordinary citizen. Advertising therefore showed a dream world; as such, it replaced the ideological propaganda of Soviet times with "propaganda" for Western consumer goods, replacing the socialist value system with a value system of achievement of a different type: consumerism and capitalism.

The Mars chocolate corporation launched a campaign for its products, which took up 87 percent of advertisements for sweets in 1993; this went down to 63 percent in the following year, only because Cadbury's claimed its share of the Russian market. Mars, Snickers, and Twix, along with a whole range of other choco-late bars, entered the media. The advertising for the "protein-laden roasted peanuts, soft caramel and a wonderful milk chocolate," which became "more and more tasty with every time" (*s kazhdym razom vse vkusnei i vkusnei*)—in short, the Snickers bar—dominated the media in more than one way. The Snickers chocolate bar, a product of a foreign company, became the symbol for political and economic reform, representing the invasion of foreign products on the Russian market, which was met with huge hunger by the population. The advertising campaign became a point of discussion for the political parties of Vladimir Zhirinovsky and Gennadi Ziuganov in the 1995 parliamentary and 1996 presidential electoral campaigns, when both leaders promised to remove American trash (advertising and films) from Russian television.

When President Putin announced during his electoral campaign in March 2000 that he would not—like his predecessor Yeltsin—market his image between advertising spots for Tampax and Snickers, he thereby made an important policy statement. On the one hand, he distanced himself from the mass media, from the campaigns both the Moscow mayor Yuri Luzhkov and Yeltsin had conducted in the run-up to elections through "their" television stations (the Russian state owned a majority of shares in ORT and RTR, and NTV's head was part of Yeltsin's electoral campaign team; Luzhkov owned TV6). Putin not only dissociated himself from the mass media and their powerful influence upon public opinion, but he also defined himself neatly between advertising production and advertising placement companies. In this way, he detached himself from those figures that ruled the advertising market, which is one of the most powerful economic structures in Russia, as well as from the "oligarchs." In this respect, Putin's campaign against the mass media embodied by Boris Berezovsky and Vladimir Gusinsky was not wholly unexpected. On the other hand, he distanced himself from Ziuganov and Zhirinovsky, who took advertising seriously enough to make it an item in their political agenda.

The Snickers advertisements not only dominated the advertising time for sweets on television in the early days of advertising and featured on almost every other billboard in central Moscow but also created the first ever product-verb in Russian with its slogan: "*Ne tormozi, snikersni*" (Don't stop, Snickers). In fact, this was not the first infiltration of foreign words and product names into the Russian language. Words for products that had not been previously available, such as *printer*, *konditsioner* (air conditioning), *iogurt* (yogurt) and others, were abundant in the first half of the 1990s.

Product Advertising

Vodka and Other Booze   Advertising spots for alcohol and cigarettes were still allowed in the early days of television; they would be withdrawn later. The advertisements for alcohol, and vodka in particular, were hugely popular, to the extent that one campaign inspired a filmmaker to make a series of films on "the peculiarities of the Russian national character." Most of these advertisements glorified the delirium tremens induced by excessive alcohol consumption. This pattern applied to one of the earliest vodka advertisements on Russian television: the clip for Smirnoff vodka. The clip is set during a ball, in which the

A bottle of Putinka vodka presented at the Leaders of Russian Alcohol Market 2003 awards ceremony in the President Hotel, Moscow. (Photo by Sergey Mikheev/ Kommersant)

"product representative," a middle-aged man, is seated at the table on his own, drinking vodka while the other guests dance cheerfully. The lonely individual, alienated from society (a common character of the Russian advertising world) takes to the bottle. And once he has (almost) emptied it, he looks through the bottle glass and the clear spirit and begins to perceive the party guests as wild beasts, with animal features that expose their real natures. In fact, the clip-maker here drew on the device of intellectual montage, exemplified in Sergei Eisenstein's *The Strike* (Stachka, 1924). When the man looks again at the bottle, he sees his own face distorted in the same way; thanks to Smirnoff he has become part of the social group in which he had previously been isolated.

The vodka label Rasputin featured the mystic's image on the bottle. Grigori Rasputin is animated, speaking from a ghostly world that becomes crystal clear and comes alive. Alcoholic intoxication makes communication with the lost past possible. Moreover, the world of ghosts seems clearer and more real than reality. White Eagle (Belyi orel) had three clips created by the famous clip-maker and film-maker Yuri Grymov. The first was set in Chicago during the Prohibition period, where some men engage in the illegal trade of alcohol. A Native American chief arrives, claiming he is White Eagle (the label they trade with) and collapses—presumably having drunk himself to death. The second clip was set in Russia in the seventeenth century, when a man tries to construct wings to fly toward the sun (Russia as a player in ancient mythology). The man climbs onto a church tower and falls, crashing onto the soil, while three Russian men sit in the field and drink vodka. "How can he manage to fly," one of them comments, "without fuel." He raises his glass, drinks, and floats up into the skies. The third clip portrayed a man asleep and snoring during a performance of *Swan Lake* in the Bolshoi Theatre. He is elbowed, and woken from his sleep, by his rather fat and unattractive wife. This leads him to engage deliriously in the performance: he imagines himself on stage as a disheveled ballerina, who is reprimanded by the conductor. He is the "white eagle" among the swans. The advertisements for White Eagle are appallingly appealing: they are beautifully designed, esthetically perfect, as they advocate the beauty of the world seen under alcoholic intoxication and depict reality as chaotic, boring, and doomed by the all-powerful Russian matron. White Eagle is the Russian man's escape from her commanding voice.

Vodka is Russia's national drink. The label Flagman makes use of the national pride associated with the drink in its slogan "There is something to be proud of" (*Est chem gorditsya*). The poster shows a bottle with its logo in the shape of the order of the star, with beams radiating to the side of the bottle over the dark blue background. The advertisement draws on Russia's pride, clearly lost in the flood of consumer products from the West. The television clip alludes also to the drink's ability to discern between good and evil in the criminal world.

Vodka is a drink that allows the consumer to see reality for what it really is and makes man part of the chaos, the facade, and the criminal world that surrounds him. Vodka has also been widely used to convey an image and enhance the market value of contemporary cinema. After having been awarded an Oscar for *Burnt by the Sun* (1994), Nikita Mikhalkov launched his own vodka brand, KomDiv—the divisional commander he had played in the film featured on the label. This would be followed by the label Russkii Standart (Russian Standard), reflecting the high demands placed on the cadets who star in his epic *The Barber of Siberia* (Sibirskii tsiriul'nik, 1999). The association with vodka, then, is an added value to any film, but it also facilitates the double existence in two realities simultaneously, cinematic and economic.

Beer is a relatively new acquisition of the Russian market. A whole host of Russian

Bottles of different brands of beer in a kiosk display and an announcement "Beer not for sale!" Moscow, 2004. (Photo by Alexander Miridonov/Kommersant)

beer labels appeared in the 1990s. Interestingly, Russian advertisers perceive beer as a soft drink, almost a replacement for breakfast. In an early advertisement for beer and soft drinks, the popular singer and producer of musicals Alexander Tsekalo was depicted in a bathtub filled with beer: it is so cheap that you can bathe in it, but so good that you won't sell it. It speaks of availability and volume rather than taste.

The brand names of beers betray their indigenous Russian character: Afanasy is a man's Christian name; Klinskoye, Ochakovskoye, and Ostanskinskoye refer to place names; Krasnyi Byk (Red Bull) is a parody on the alcoholic drink of the same name; Tolstiak (Fatty) and Tri Medvedia (Three Bears) allude to Russian folk tales. Bochkarov (*bochka* is barrel) is the "right beer" (*pravil'noe pivo*). Staryi Melnik (Old

Miller) and Sibirskaya Korona (Siberian Crown) draw with their names on ancient Russian heritage, which the products clearly do not have.

Baltika has its brand name prominently displayed across the legendary monument to Stalinist architecture in the center of Moscow, the Hotel Moscow. It is Russia's "golden" beer, referring with its brand name to the Baltic states, once the Soviet Union's most Westernized republics, just as Nevskoye (Neva-Beer) refers to the river Neva of the northern capital Petersburg. Zolotaya Bochka (Golden Barrel) has the "golden taste that you deserve" (*zolotoi vkus, kotorogo ty dostoin*). Beers tend to advertise themselves with reference to their color and therefore largely use a beer glass or the bottle as illustrations of the advertisements on a sumptuous dark green or blue background. The private brewery Tinkoff (Petersburg) advertises its products as unique and singular: one of the most impressive ads is a double page in a magazine, with a bottle of Tinkoff on the far left, leaving the entire page white; on the bottom of the right side appears the text: "only he's like that" (*on takoi odin*), emphasizing the uniqueness of this brand. The pronoun *he* also personifies the bottle.

"The Health Ministry Warns—Smoking Is Dangerous for Your Health" Smoking in Russia is a widespread habit. Tobacco is often of inferior quality (*makhorka*), but even Western brand cigarettes are of a different price and a different quality when purchased on the Russian market. A number of new Russian cigarette brands have emerged in recent years, while many Soviet brands have been revamped. The cigarettes Belomor-kanal are the old style *papirosy* with a filter that consists of half of the cigarette and has to be folded before smoking. They have always been the cheapest and most affordable cigarettes.

Although there are advertisements for Western cigarette brands, the Russian brands offer a rather curious advertising campaign. They draw on Russia's past, and the Soviet past, to give their products clout and a pseudo-history that their Western counterparts can genuinely boast of. Russkii Stil (Russian Style) is a brand that uses packaging in the color of the Russian flag (blue and red packs, white for the light cigarettes) and golden ornaments and embossed crests on the package. The slogan "If you shine, then do" (*blistat' tak blistat'*) comments on the brilliance of the golden logo. The slogan "style determines quality" (*stil' opredeliaet kachestvo*) is used on a series of billboards showing a modern inte-

A girl smoking in front of a publicity screen for Russkii stil cigarettes with the warning "Smoking is dangerous for your health." (Photo by Alexey Kudenko/Kommersant)

rior with abstract red and white shapes as the classical and richly patterned cigarette pack features in a corner. The poster emphasizes that the question of style is not between modern and classical, but that quality matters. Another paper advertisement features three packs of the brand in blue, white, and red next to each other (making up the colors of the Russian flag). Or the blue and red packs feature in a picture on the side, with a golden cigarette case (this is a product not for the poor), whereas on the other half of the page a young couple is shown against the backdrop of a Stalin skyscraper, the university: the brand is for the young and successful business people. "Life in the style of perfection" (*zhizn v stile sovershenstva*) is another slogan for the cigarettes, which this time are placed on a red leather working surface of a desk, next to an open book and a golden clock. This is the habitat of the successful and rich, with distinctive style; the golden cigarette case and the crystal ashtray testify to wealth. A magnifying glass is placed over the filter to highlight this innovation. The cigarette brand Fabergé uses a similar method: it appeals to the consumer's "passion for perfection" (*strast k sovershentsvu*), showing two packets, lavishly decorated with ornaments and a golden double-headed eagle, set against the backdrop of a Fabergé egg. The texts praise the special sepiolite filter of the brand.

Yava, an old, Soviet cigarette brand, addresses a younger, more urban consumer with its appeal that it is "newer than you think" (*novee chem ty dumaesh*), detaching itself from its Soviet past, further enhanced by the use of images of New York. The brand appeals to younger smokers. Although using a historically laden brand name, Peter I is produced by R. J. Reynolds. It appeals to a younger consumer with its slogans "life in pleasure" (*zhizn' v udovolstvie*), or the very plain billboard showing half a face of a man (or a woman) against a black backdrop with the slogan "look ahead" (*smotri vpered*). The poster featuring the phrase "always first" (*vsegda pervyi*), showing a young man on a boat holding a pair of binoculars, alludes with the sailing theme to Peter I's favorite pastime and features the Liube singer Nikolai Rastorguyev.

Although beer, vodka, and cigarette advertisements have now been banned from television, they still feature on billboards and in the print media. The majority of print ads concern these products and the above-mentioned chocolates. There are also some advertisements for mobile telephones and networks, usually laden with information on tariffs; some advertisements for radio stations and a few newspapers.

Idylls of the Past   A widespread tendency in advertising for Russian products is the return to nineteenth-century (or earlier) Russia. The chocolate Rossiya (made by Nestlé, a foreign corporation) runs with the slogan "Russia, the generous soul" (*Rossiya—shchedraia dusha*). In a television advertising campaign, the company used period costume and reverted to the traditions of the pre-Revolutionary period in its clips featuring a nineteenth-century ball scene and a duel, which is called off when a chocolate block is found in the pistol case. Several milk and dairy products, such as Milaya Mila (Dear Mila), Lianozovskoye Moloko (Lianozov Milk), Doyarushka (the Milkmaid), and Domik v Derevne (House in the Village) heavily rely on folk themes and the memory of an idealized past for their campaigns. Life in the countryside is idealized but never presented as a modern experience.

Numerous advertising campaigns draw on the golden Soviet years when advertising products that clearly were not available in those days. The advertisements for Savinov sweets were created by a team of young animators and draw on the experience of renaming places, so common in the post-Soviet period. They view this process as something positive: the village Gorkoye (Bitter) becomes Savinovo. The advertisement for Indian Tea (Indiiskii chai) draws exclusively on memories of the Brezhnev years brought on by the consumption of the tea, although the brand was not widely available in the Brezhnev period. The slogan "the same taste, the same tea" (*tot samy vkus, tot samy chai*) also gave rise to a parody, in which two ants are nibbling away at a dead elephant. The story mocks both how long this tea has been around and how bad it tastes. Ten years later they are still at it, and one comments that it's still the same taste. The other replies that it's still the same elephant. Particularly comic here is the fact that the tea wrapper features colorful images of Indian elephants. The insurance group Rosno not only features the solar eclipse of 1999, but their slogan is a paraphrase of the pioneer song "Let there always be sunshine" (*Pust' vsegda budet solntse*). The advertisement for Hershey Cola taps into this nostalgia for a Soviet past. The clip reminisces about the days when the schoolboy Sidorov, a redhead sporting jeans, was an outsider in his class. The advertisement for Sprite comments on the facade that was created in the Soviet era: a fashion clip is being filmed on Red Square, with a male and female model dressed in Russian-style garments. The voice-over comments that nothing is what it seems: her eyes are not blue, her hair not blond, her breasts false, the young man is gay. The only thing they want is Sprite. Russia is facade only, what it really wants are Western consumer goods.

Overall, there is a strong tendency to draw on memories of the past to market Russian food products as if to create a fictional product history. The world of advertising replaced the West: the formerly inaccessible Western world had lost its exotic varnish, and the unaffordable products shown in the world of advertising took over the function of the utopian world, the world of the ordinary Russian citizen's dreams. Advertising also offered stability in a period of chaos: the state control had

gone and left anarchy to reign over the ordinary citizen's life. Advertising laid the blame for the social chaos at the feet of the state. It proposed a way of—virtually—spending money to offer an escape from everyday life and the surrounding poverty. It invited money to be squandered rather than spent sensibly.

Investment and Banks
Banks commissioned the first major televised advertising campaigns in Russia. Some were competing for customers; other just wanted to create an image. The MMM campaign (1992–1994) is probably the most significant single advertising campaign in Russian history. A/O MMM (Joint Stock Company MMM) was a pyramid scheme invented by Sergei Mavrodi, based on the principle that the first investors would be paid out with the deposits of later investors while share prices were growing constantly. The outcome is quite clear: when shares become too expensive, no more investments are made and the pyramid collapses. The scheme is safe as long as the invested money is withdrawn in time. For many Russians, inexperienced in stock markets, unfamiliar with dividends, and uncertain about banks in general, MMM became a sort of wizard system that dished out unexpected goodies. The success of MMM was created exclusively through its advertising campaign, which featured the fictional characters Lyonia (diminutive of Leonid) Golubkov; his wife, Rita; and his brother, Ivan. Lyonia Golubkov, an unassuming man, small, uneducated, lower in social rank than any likely spectators, and as such very much an Ivan-the-Fool character, was elevated to the status of a hero in the best socialist tradition: the working-class man turned hero. Golubkov was no

intellectual and no New Russian, but a simple man, at a time when most product advertisements were aimed at the upper classes, the "New Russians," the young and successful.

The author of the clips, Bakhyt Kilibayev, deliberately drew on working-class people and created a whole series of clips, telling a full-blown story of the impact of MMM on three generations. MMM drew on soap opera, creating a miniseries of everyday life with normal, everyday characters. They suddenly make money, but this does nothing to their lifestyles or their personalities. Apart from Lyonia and Rita, there were the student couple, Igor and Julia, to represent the young generation and the elderly couple, Nikolai Fomich and Yelizaveta Andreyevna, to represent the older generation. There was also a single woman, the middle-aged Marina Sergeyevna, who—thanks to MMM—finds her man, Volodia. MMM provides help for those who cannot be properly looked after by the state: the young, the old, and singles.

In the first set of clips, Lyonia talks with his brother Ivan about making money without doing anything for it. Marina Sergeyevna dreams about happiness. Nikolai Fomich and Yelizaveta Andreyevna have acquired a dog. Igor and Julia have taken a loan they need to repay. The introduction presents the protagonists, representatives of three generations (students, pensioners, married working people, and single woman) with their present state of affairs, which is far from satisfactory. But they neither complain nor act. Part two has the protagonists confess their dreams, and they confess to the star of the Brazilian soap opera, *Simply Maria:* Rita wants a child; Nikolai Fomich and Elizaveta Andreyevna take pride in their grandchildren; Marina

Sergeyevna likes Volodia. The appearance of the Golubkovs' family tree stresses the need to think about the future, about children. MMM will facilitate the realization of dreams and invest in the future. The third set of ads gets more specific and outlines how the protagonists would use additional funds: Nikolai Fomich and Yelizaveta Andreyevna would top up their pensions; Lyonia would buy boots for his wife; Igor and Julia would top up their student grants. The advertisements here point out the state's inefficiency and inability to provide for pensioners and students and to allow people to buy not luxury goods, but essentials.

The fourth part shows the results of the investment, the first "harvest": Marina has trusted the scheme; Igor and Julia will do it again; Rita has new boots, and now would like a fur coat. In the fifth part, Rita has acquired boots and a fur coat and begins to think of other major purchases, such as furniture and a car. Marina looks better; Nikolai Fomich and Yelizaveta Andreyevna advise the young "to do what parents advise," and Igor and Julia worry that they might be reprimanded. The scheme has inspired trust, the results are there, and doubts that it won't continue are dispersed. MMM has brought material well-being. In the final part, personal happiness is achieved because of the scheme: Marina and Volodia marry; Igor and Julia are in love; Nikolai Fomich and Yelizaveta Andreyevna feel much better; and Lyonia and Ivan invest more. On this happy ending the soap opera concludes, following the pattern of Socialist Realist plots where commitment to the right cause it rewarded by personal happiness.

A further socialist principle used by MMM was that of partnership: everybody rejoices in the profit and happiness of others, Lyonia does not just want to gain money (without working, *na khaliavu*) for his own sake but to buy his wife a pair of boots and a fur coat and to invest in an excavator (with a view to later buying a factory with his brother Ivan), and he needs a growth chart to plan what to do next with his wealth (in a scene that features the television soap-opera star Victoria Ruffo of *Simply Maria*). The legitimate reasons for seeking profit in MMM shares are the collective social good that Lyonia will bring to others and society at large: they are not "lazy bones, but partners" (*ne khaliavshchiki, a partnery*).

MMM was soon in trouble for tax evasion, and its subsidiary MMM Bank was closed in 1993; Invest Consulting, another MMM arm, had a tax debt of 49.9 billion rubles. In July 1994, Mavrodi threatened to close MMM, and by 29 July 1994 shares had dropped from 115,000 to 950 rubles. Yet people continued to support MMM and Mavrodi, who compared himself in the press and on the final television ad for MMM to a saint and a martyr, who had tried to help the poor and was now a victim himself. In the final "farewell" clip, he associated himself with another popular hero surrounded by a similar myth, the actor and bard Vladimir Vysotsky, whose music accompanied the five-minute spot. MMM was presented as the target of a political campaign, as a force fighting against the state. Popular support for Mavrodi went as far as his election to the state duma in October 1994 (which he used to gain political immunity). Mavrodi had created for himself the image of a popular force against the state and as such appropriately identified himself with the dissident voice of Vysotsky. Mavrodi has since been found to be behind an Internet scheme of the same kind, with its head office in the offshore Dominican Republic, and is sought after by Interpol.

The disaster with MMM, the August crisis of 1998, and the bumpy curves of the ruble exchange rate did not exactly inspire trust in the Russian banking system. The advertisement for Hermes Credit suitably drew on this mistrust by offering a fireproof bank. In another ad, Hermes Finance used the slogan "*Vashi pribyli*"—"your profits"; however, the noun *profit* in Russian only has a singular form, and this phrase therefore means "your people have arrived."

Most interesting, though, is the first bank to advertise itself on television, Bank Imperial, with its series *World History* (Vsemirnaia istoriia, 1993–1997), created by the filmmaker Timur Bekmambetov. The bank had no dealings with the public at all (it is a business finance corporation) and used advertising merely for decorative purposes. The advertisements reflected the wish to return to a stable past, not Soviet, but pre-Revolutionary, and to draw on the past's moral superiority to enhance the standing of the bank and its relation to customers. The advertisements drew on figures of world history, all rather absolute rulers, who appeared in these ads as people of power but endowed with wisdom, humor, and benevolence. The Russian empress Catherine the Great featured in one ad, hosting a dinner at the palace. One of her guests, General Suvorov, is not eating: he observes the rules of Lent. When asked by the empress why he is not eating, he points out that it is Lent (a hidden criticism of the others, who do not adhere to Lent) and that he must not eat before a star rises. Catherine thereupon asks for the "star of order" to be given to Suvorov, who raises his glass to her and joins the dinner. Another ad features Alexander II in 1861, the year of the emancipation of the serfs. His manservant reports that the serfs are leaving and troops will hold them back. The emperor demands that the wings of his swans should not be clipped but to prevent them from flying away they should be well fed. The swans fly away for the winter, but a voice comments that 1861 was the year when the first metropolitan line opened in London, while in Russia the serfs were freed.

In other nations' history, dictators are proven weak by the humanism of their victims. The Inca live in the land of the sun and of gold until the Spaniards—in black and white—invade their golden lands. The Inca chief will be killed, but he forgives his executioner. In Germany, Konrad III orders the release of all the women taken into captivity and allows them to take with them what they can carry. One woman carries her injured man on her back. The warrior Tamerlane tells each soldier to lay down a stone before going to battle and collect it on return, so he can see how many warriors he has lost. He then mourns every warrior by holding each stone. The cruelty of history is juxtaposed to humanism.

The advertisements for Alfa Bank were created between 1993 and 1996 by Bekmambetov. They marketed the bank as a modern enterprise, with a splendid interior design. When a young backpacker marches into the bank and admires the design, he is treated in a friendly and welcoming manner by the "New Russian" bank manager in an elegant suit, showing him around as a "serious client." The advertisement is designed to take away the fear of modern banking from the young—the target audience that least needs to be won over by banks. Another spot shows a birthday party for a bank employee being prepared as a customer is quizzing her at the end of

the long working day. Nevertheless, she kindly replies to his queries, until the manager phones the customer, who is invited to join in the party. A spirit of collectivity governs the bank, where the customer is part of the bank's team. The bank cares for individuals, both clients and employees, not profit. The 2002 campaign for Alfa Bank, created by Bekmambetov's Bazelevs studio, was based on the slogan "with each client we find a common language." The clips are set at bank counters, where the employees of Alfa Bank competently handle a range of customers: an Eskimo (eternal subject for anecdotes); a young man using street jargon; a pseudo-professional, who really sells ice cream; a young New Russian girl with her pet dog; and a locksmith using such coarse language that every other word is bleeped out. The bank's employees speak all these languages, and in the final clip the employee's response has every word bleeped, signaling that the bankers speak the same language as their customers.

Bank Moskvy (Bank of Moscow) uses some print advertisements, mainly to publicize its special offers. "Collect serial numbers" (*soberi kollektsiiu seriinykh nomerov*) advertises deposit accounts with the image of a magnifying glass on the serial numbers of some U.S. banknotes. Confidence in the ruble is not great. The bank also advertises the "favorite cards" (*liubimye karty*), lining up its credit cards with a picture of the wife and the car keys. Another poster advertises the "keys to all continents": a purse, a passport, and credit cards. Sberbank (Savings Bank), too, markets its credit cards: "the best frames of the summer season" (*luchshie kadry letnego sezona*) appear on three stripes (or a roll) of photo negatives, mixing summer holiday pictures with credit cards. The campaign appeals to those who are better off, who can travel abroad. The print advertising campaigns are both held in the color schemes of the banks (red for Bank Moskvy, green for Sberbank). The function of these ads is twofold: on the one hand, they are designed to boost confidence in a particular bank and create its credentials, which is particularly important after the August 1998 crisis. On the other hand, they make the customers aware, Soviet-style, of a product they are unfamiliar with and bring to their attention the credit card and bankcard.

Social Advertising

Very rapidly, two other domains of advertising were discovered: social advertisement and political advertisement. Political advertising has been dealt with above; social advertising was in theory closest to Soviet propaganda. Therefore, social ads tend to use rather old-fashioned, and ineffective, tactics. Advertising campaigns that encourage a certain social behavior appeal largely to the individual as a member of society. In Russia, such advertisements use a technique of pleading rather than demanding (or threatening punishment). Advertising agencies appeal to the audience for support of the Russian economy.

The best-known campaign is that of the tax police: one set of advertisements was made with the slogan "Pay your taxes and live in peace" (*Plati nalogi, zhivi spokoino*), showing people in situations where they are unable to perform, because their consciences (concerning unpaid taxes) trouble them. A hit in this campaign was the spot where a man is sitting on the bedside at night, his wife asleep, and clearly unable to sleep (or have sex?) be-

cause of his bad conscience. Another campaign was targeted at the danger of illegal alcohol consumption and the detrimental effect that illegal production of alcohol has both on the health system and on the state, which loses tax income. A third campaign of cartoons referred to world history for a legitimization of tax collection, asserting that there has never been an escape from tax. It is worth noting the individual, social, and global framework for these three simultaneous campaigns.

The recourse to the Soviet past is reaffirmed by slogans in street advertisements, encouraging the purchase of Russian produce and emphasizing the state's need for support: "VVTs (Exhibition Centre)—continuation of tradition"; "The Russian producer is the future of the fatherland" (*Rossiiskii proizvoditel'—budushchee otechestva*), "Nobody will help Russia if we don't do it ourselves" (*Nikto ne pomozhet Rossii krome nas samikh*), "Buy Russian—help Russia" (*Pokupat' rossiiskoe—pomogat' Rossii*), and "Let's support the Russian producer" (*Podderzhim rossiiskogo proizvoditelia*). An advertisement for the chocolate Korkunov taps into this vein: "Buy Russian and help Russia: Buy what is made in Russia (*Pokupat' rossiiskoe, pomogat' Rossii: Pokupaite chto sdelano v Rossii*). The underlying principle of Russian advertisements is not to emphasize the quality of the product but to ask for help and support of the economy; not to deduct tax at source but to appeal to the individual to pay; not to act against illegal alcohol production and video piracy but to plead for help with the Russian industry. The pleading manner, imploring and begging rather then demanding for tax payments, is summarized beautifully in another parody of the advertising campaign:

"We have deceived you in 1991 and shot at you in 1993; we thrust you into the arms of MMM and vouchers; we betrayed you in 1996 and 1997; we took your last possessions in August 1998; but we've run out of money again. So please pay taxes."

Needless to say, the result of such pleading campaigns is nil. If people buy Russian products, they do so not because they are better, but because they are cheaper. If people pay taxes, they do so anyway, or because they are caught by the tax police, but not because they can't sleep. Yet the underlying mode of most advertisements for Russian products (except for food) remains the technique of appeal and pledge rather than seduction and temptation.

The New Russia still lacks confidence to boast of its products and its industry; the economy is not presented in a way that indicates the strength of the state. Instead, the New Russia advertises itself as a society that will respond to pleading rather than seduction and that prefers to reinvent the past rather than look at the present or dream of the future.

Leisure

In the leisure sector, tremendous changes have taken place since the collapse of the Soviet Union. If in the 1980s international hotels could not even be accessed by Russian citizens and were at the same time the only place that had half-way decent restaurants, then the number of restaurants and cafés that have sprung up since is impressive. The service that most of them offer can easily compete with Western standards, but many of these venues have Western prices too, making them unaffordable for the "ordinary" Russian with a monthly salary of US$500–1,000. Some parks have been turned into entertainment centers, whereas others have retained their old-world charm as gardens. Many *dacha* settlements have been turned into housing for the New Russians. And Russian holiday resorts have been abandoned by Russian holidaymakers, who prefer foreign destinations. Above all, the pattern of celebration and holiday-making has changed along with the holidays themselves.

Restaurants

Many of the large international hotels offered excellent catering in the Soviet era. In the New Russia, the large hotel chains still boast expensive restaurants, and many new restaurants, from culinary to fast food, have appeared in the cities. In Moscow the Hotel Prague (Praga) has one of the most luxurious restaurants, with nine rooms for dining. Restaurants specializing in a national cuisine were once a way of showing the integration and diversification of Soviet culture, with the famous Uzbekistan, the Georgian restaurant Aragvi, and the Budapest in the hotel of the same name. The restaurant in the writers' and journalists' clubs (House of Writers and House of Journalists) were good dining places for a visitor in the Soviet period and offer some of the most expensive menus and an exquisite setting in the New Russia.

Most Russians used to dine at home or in the canteen, however, and this still remains the case for the majority of people who cannot afford eating out. The first signs of change were cooperatives, such as the co-op restaurant on Kropotkinskaya Street, or joint ventures, especially with Irish enterprises, such as the Shamrock bars or other Irish bars (as on the New Arbat). It is, incidentally, also a Russian-Irish joint stock company that runs the airport duty free shops and the catering at Sheremetievo II airside.

Moscow Restaurants   In the Soviet era, the most fashionable restaurants were the Seventh Heaven (Sed'moe nebo) on the top floor of the Moscow Hotel, closed for "refurbishment" and then demolished in 2004, and the Ostankino Restaurant, closed after the fire on the television tower in 2001. Instead, a range of new restaurants has emerged, making eating out in Moscow both fun and pleasure.

National cuisine dominates a number of restaurants in Moscow. Exotic settings dominate such restaurants as the Limpopo, an African restaurant with fountains and an artificial hippo and crocodile in an interior bordering on kitsch, or the Amazonia, offering a tropical interior with straw mats. Caucasian cuisine has always been popular in Russia. Noah's Ark (Noev kovcheg) is an Armenian restaurant with an orchestra, where waiters dress in traditional costumes. The Aragvi is an old Georgian restaurant, not known for its service but rather for its central location on Tverskaya Street. Its interior contains a balcony and frescoes depicting the Caucasus mountains. The restaurant has a legendary reputation as the favorite restaurant of Stalin's "henchman," the Secret Service chief Lavrenti Beria, who—like Stalin—came from Georgia. The Genatsvale on Kropotkinskaya Street is a more expensive Georgian restaurant, and Mama Zoya offers cheap and excellent food and has become a popular Georgian restaurant. Mama Zoya began in a basement flat of an apartment block and now has a proper restaurant on Frunze Street.

Italian restaurants have become increasingly popular in Moscow in recent years. There is a range of small and expensive restaurants but also pasta and pizza places such as Patio Pizza and Sbarro. It has to be said, though, that pasta and pizza have not really conquered the hearts and palates of Muscovites.

Theme restaurants became immensely popular in the late 1990s. They refrained from imitating Western and foreign themes, however, drawing instead on their indigenous popular heritage. The Traktir na Piatnitskoy (Pub on Piatnitskaya Street) is named after the film of the same title. It is a cheap snack restaurant with a homely atmosphere. The Balaganchik (Fairground Booth) is named after Alexander Blok's symbolist play. The restaurant is located in a separate house on Trekhprudnyi and Mamontov Lane next to the Moscow Youth Theater (MTYuZ), using a carnival decor for its interior design. The restaurant is popular among actors and the theatre community. The Grand Opera in Petrovsky Lines is a more expensive restaurant designed in opera style. The restaurant Mesto vstrechi (the Meeting Place) is named after a popular film of the 1960s. This restaurant is located in the basement of a building on Tverskaya Street but does not offer any particular ambience or menu. Unlike this, the restaurant Kavkazskaya Plennitsa (Prisoner of the Caucasus) is a Georgian cuisine restaurant on Prospekt Mira, set in the ambience of Leonid Gaidai's famous comedy of the same title. Beloye Solntse Pustyni (White Sun of the Desert) is a similar enterprise run by the same company, themed along the style of 1960s Red Westerns and offering Uzbek cuisine. The restaurant is part of the former Uzbekistan, which still occupies the other half of the building on Neglinnaya and offers more sophisticated dishes. Also themed around

The restaurant "White Sun of the Desert" is themed along the lines of Vladimir Motyl's 1969 film of the same title. (Photo by Yury Martianov/Kommersant)

popular films of the 1960s are the restaurants Pechki-Lavochki, with fairy tale and film characters as part of the decor, and the restaurant Pokrovskie Vorota (Pokrovsky Gates), echoing the atmosphere of the mid-1960s.

Classical Russian literature informs the design of the restaurant Pushkin on Tverskoi Boulevard, with an old oak library as part of the restaurant. The Pushkin attracts the elite of politics and business, with its halls expanding over five levels. The Oblomov is named after Ivan Goncharov's novel and divided into two halls after the principal characters, Oblomov and Stoltz, with waiters dressed up as Zakhar, Oblomov's manservant, offering a pensive and well-paced service. Khlestakov on Frunze Street, named after the main character in Gogol's comedy *The Government Inspector*, is owned by Sergei Gazarov. Gazarov made a film with star actors based on Gogol's play.

Zapasnik (the Store) is a small restaurant off Maroseika, offering a range of dishes named after paintings and art styles. The restaurant U Petrovicha (at Petrovich's) is located in a basement off Miasnitskaya Street. The dishes contain references to the patronymic Petrovich, and the walls and tables carry inscriptions parodying and mocking the common patronymic.

The Central House for Literature was one of the most famous restaurants in the Soviet era, when access to it was restricted to members of the Writers' Union and their guests. The Oak Hall has now been restored, and the restaurant is open to the public; it is no longer for writers, but the newly rich. The Spets-bufet No. 7 (Special

Buffet No. 7) is located in the basement of the House on the Embankment, the gray concrete building opposite the Kremlin that Stalin had built for the Party elite. The menu cites politicians and political slogans of the 1920s.

The United Humanities Publishers (Obedinennye gumanitarnye izdatel'stva; OGI) was started by two scientists who began publishing, combined with restaurants at affordable prices. They first opened a restaurant-club with a bookshop on Potapov Lane (near Chistoprudnyi Boulevard) in the mid-1990s. As it was cheap and open late, the place became very popular among students and intellectuals. The Project OGI was followed by PirOGI (*pir* is *feast*, but *pirogi* means *pastry*) on Novokuznetskaya, which closed in 2002 and moved to Dmitrovka Street. Ulitsa OGI (OGI Street) is located off Petrovka Street and combines a gallery with a restaurant that is slightly more expensive than the other OGI venues and has been designed with a modern glass-metal style by the architect Alexander Brodsky. A shabby trailer-type entrance belies the interior of the restaurant. The PirOGI and the Project OGI also have bookshops, and they occasionally offer concerts.

After an invasion of Pizza Huts and other American and Western restaurant chains that were too pricey for average Muscovites and too unsavory for Russian taste, a number of Russian self-service and service restaurant chains started up in the late 1990s, with menus that catered for Russian eating habits: soups and salads, meat and fish for the main course, with potatoes and vegetables as optional. MuMu (pronounced moo-moo), with its typical black-and-white-cow pattern, is a typical chain of Russian cuisine self-service restaurants. Drova

(Firewood) is a chain of restaurants with a buffet service, running with the slogan "eat as much as you can." The first typically Russian restaurant chain with waitress service is Yolki-Palki (*yolki-palki* is the equivalent term for oh-dear-me). Luzhkov's answer to McDonalds was the formation in 1995 of a chain called Russkoye bistro (Russian Bistro), offering instant soup, a variety of pastries (*pirogi*), and salads.

Haute cuisine is available too in a number of Moscow restaurants. Le Gastronome is an expensive restaurant set in a luxurious interior in the high rise on Vosstanie Square. Red Square No. 1 is set in an interior of the period of Ivan the Terrible with vaulted ceilings. Its chef, Alexander Filin, offers a menu composed of historical recipes. Kumir (Idol) on Trekhprudnyi Lane is run by the French chef Michel Truargot.

One of the more clubby restaurants is the Labardance, owned by the actor Maxim Sukhanov and located in the basement of the Mayakovsky Theater. The menu lists all its dishes, spelling them back to front. Another is the Serebrianyi Vek (Silver Age), situated in the former central baths, which preserves the design of the early twentieth century.

Japanese restaurants are growing in number and popularity: the GinoTaki offers a fast service, replicating a fast-food chain in other South East Asian countries, as does the Yakitoria, with restaurants on Arbat and Tverskaya Street. The American fast food chain McDonalds was the first to conquer the Russian market, and the chain has expanded significantly across Russia. It was followed by Pizza Hut, Louisiana Steakhouse, Fridays, and other fast-food chains.

A number of coffeehouses have sprung up in Moscow in the new century. Kofe

Inauguration of the fast food restaurant chain Russkoye Bistro in 1995. (Photo by Dmitry Dukhanin/ Kommersant)

Khaus (Coffee House) is a chain that operates across Russia. Coffee Bean is another chain that styles its interiors in old venues, such as the old Fillipov Bakery on Tverskaya Street or a second-hand bookshop on Kuznetskii Most. Zen Coffee offers a modern coffee culture. Two new Russian coffee networks are the Shokoladnitsa (Chocolatesse) and Coffeemania. The Kofe-In with its Viennese chairs and free newspapers creates the atmosphere of a continental coffeehouse on Dmitrovka Street, not unlike Donna Clara on Malaya Bronnaya Street. The Alexandria is a special teahouse on Tsvetnoi Boulevard. The Café Tun on Pushkin Square is one of the largest and most central cafés in Moscow. It is located next door to Arkadi Novikov's Pyramid, a restaurant with the design of Luc Besson's 1997 blockbuster *The Fifth Element*, the front of which is a famous meeting place for biker clubs. The old Artistic Café used to be a gay meeting place in the days when homosexuality was illegal. The Café des Artistes is now an artistic café, whereas gay culture has moved to other venues. The American Starbucks has not yet arrived on the Russian market, and neither have the Italian chains Café Nero, Costa, and others.

Eating Out in Petersburg   The city on the Neva offers a similar range of restaurants and styles as Moscow, albeit on a smaller scale. Exotic restaurants include the Kongo (Congo) with an interior made of black wood and straw mats; the Vasabi, a Japanese restaurant with waitresses in kimonos; and Le Paris, a French gourmet restaurant. The Afishka (Playbill) is a student restaurant near the Theater Institute and European University.

National cuisine can be found in such restaurants as La Strada (Italian), La Cucaraca (TexMex), Karavan (Caucasian), and the Tblisi (Georgian). In the Uzbek restaurant Kalif, diners can smoke the hookah and watch belly dancers. Theme-based restaurants in Petersburg include the Dvorianskoye Gnezdo (Nest of Gentlefolk) in the Yusupov Palace; the restaurant Zolotoi Ostap (Golden Ostap), named after the figure of Ostap Bender from the 1920s satire *The Twelve Chairs;* Zov Ilyich (Ilyich's Call), with Soviet and anti-Soviet propaganda posters and objects for its interior; and the Idiot, a restaurant with bookshelves and an early-twentieth-century interior, located on the Moika canal. The SSSR on Nevsky boasts an exclusive high-tech-style interior design as the "new Soviet" style. The Landskrona restaurant is situated in the Nevsky Palace Hotel and offers a view over Petersburg. There are also numerous restaurants on boats. Petersburg restaurants have also made good use of old locales: the Camelot, situated in a basement on Bolshaya Koniushnaya, offers a medieval setting with stained glass decor and heavy oak chairs. The Senate Bar is located in the cellars of Senate House. The Metropol is the oldest restaurant in town, founded in 1847 and situated in its original premises on Sadovaya Street. Koniushnyi Dvor is located in an old stable, and Staraya Tamozhnia occupies the old Customs House; the restaurant is run by a French chef.

Coffeehouses also abound in Petersburg. Particularly noteworthy are the Abrikosov coffeehouse on Nevsky 40 and the Nord (formerly Sever [North]) patisserie, which is famous for its cakes and gâteaux. The Idealnaya Chashka (Ideal Cup) is Petersburg's American-style coffeehouse chain. Zhili-byli (Once upon a time . . .), located on Nevsky, is one of the trendiest coffeehouses, and the Lavka Smirdina (Smirdin's Store, Nevsky 22/24) is famous for its ice creams. Most popular among children is the Sladkoyezhka (Sweet-eater) cake shop on Sadovaya Street.

Petersburg can also boast of two famous beer restaurants. The Chaika (Seagull) is owned by the German brewery Jever and was one of the first cooperative restaurants to open on Leningrad's Griboedov Canal. Tinkoff is a genuine Russian brewery offering filtered and unfiltered beer; the restaurant is located in the brewery off Kazan Square.

Most other cities in Russia have undergone a similar development, with a number of Russian and home-based restaurants competing with national or international chains.

Eating and Drinking

Russian food and drink differ in substance from Western European products; moreover, eating and drinking habits vary greatly. Russians have a substantial breakfast, often consisting of a form of porridge (kasha), followed by bread with sausages or meat and often peas. They lunch between 2 and 3 PM, and this is the main meal of the day. Lunch commonly consists of three courses: soup, a main dish, and a small dessert with tea. Dinner follows after dusk and may consist of a hot main dish or a lighter dish. On holidays such as Easter or Christmas, special meals are cooked; these are dealt with elsewhere in this book.

Russian Specialties: Food   There are Russian variants of most dairy products.

Russian cheeses traditionally come from Kostroma or Vologda, regions to the northeast of Moscow that are well known for dairy products (also butter, milk). The most common breakfast cereal is kasha: this may be made from oats (*ovsyannaya kasha*), from corn (*kukuruznaya kasha*), or from buckwheat (*grechka*).

Russian soups are usually made from meat or fish. *Solyanka* is based on meat or fish, whereas the soup *ukha* is made from fish only. *Shchi* is based on vegetable stock and consists largely of cabbage, whereas *borshch* contains cabbage and beets but is made with meat (beef) stock. The *okroshka* is a cold soup popular in the summer, made on a *kvas* or *kefir* basis and containing some fresh greens as well as sausage. A meal often starts with *zakuski* (appetizers), including pickled vegetables and mushrooms as well as salads, such as the popular Olivier (named after an eighteenth—century French chef) or Vinaigrette, which accompany the vodka toasts. A variety of breads is offered with each meal (usually at least comprising one sort of white bread and rye bread).

Main dishes often consist of fish or meat, and vegetarian dishes are not common in Russia. Beef Stroganoff is probably the best known Russian dish, but there is a variety of other meat dishes. Pasta and rice are less common than potatoes. Mushrooms are popular in all forms, as soup, pickled, or roasted. Vegetables are usually scarce with a Russian meal. A *butterbrod* (from the German word for sandwich) is a common evening dish, as are *pelmeni* (filled with meat) and *vareniki* (filled with potatoes or cherries or cream cheese), which are the Russian version of the Italian ravioli but served with *smetana* (sour cream) instead of tomato sauce. Pastries (*pirogi*) with a variety of fillings, from meat to cabbage, potatoes to cream cheese, are a common side dish. Regional popular dishes include the Caucasian dishes *chebureki* (pastry with meat), *lavash* (flat bread), and *khachapuri* (cheese-filled pastry).

Chocolates and sweets were of high quality in the Soviet period, when the state standard (GOST) specified a higher than usual cocoa content in chocolate, making Russian chocolates very rich. The leading chocolate factories Krasnyi Oktiabr (Red October), Babayevsky (Babaev), and Rotfront are thriving, continuing their traditional chocolates such as the praline range Vecherniy zvon (Evening Bells), the chocolate bars Alyonka, and sweets of all kinds (*karamel*). They have found competition from the company Rossiya with the slogan "Russia, the generous soul," which is, however, owned by Nestlé. Another competitor on the praline market is Korkunov, which claims a long-standing tradition in chocolate-making that goes back to pre-Revolutionary years and makes exquisite chocolates at prices that match those of Western chocolatiers such as Lindt.

Beverages à la Russe   Dairy products offer a greater variety and diversity than in many other countries. There is milk, cream (*slivki*), and sour cream (*smetana*); *ryazhenka* is a milk drink with wheat supplement; *sgushchennoe moloko* is condensed milk with sugar; *tvorog* is a firmer form of yogurt made from boiled milk, which is drained (similar to the French fromage frais or the German quark); *kefir* is a liquid sour milk product.

Kvas is a popular drink that is an alcohol-free fermented beerlike drink, made from fermented rye bread. Several regional branches of the eleven Coca-Cola factories set up in Russia to provide the population with the once sought-after Western drinks (Coca Cola, Sprite, and Fanta) have switched to producing *kvas* in an attempt to recoup the losses as Coca-Cola fails to sell as well as traditional beverages. One Coca-Cola plant has even resorted to producing the cheaper and more traditional Soviet era beverages Tarkhun and Buratino, both variations of lemonade. Tarkhun has a distinct green color, as it contains woodruff extract. Indeed, in the aftermath of the August default (1998), many Russians on the one hand could no longer afford expensive Western brands, while on the other hand the excitement with the once-forbidden and inaccessible Western products had dwindled and made way for a return to more homegrown tastes. Coca-Cola's sponsorship of the arts also ceased after 2000, as the coffee label Nescafe stepped into that niche. *Kisel* is a starched fruit juice often made from sour berries such as the cranberry, containing vitamins that are in this way preserved for the winter in drinks liked by children. *Mors* remains a very popular berry juice made from red berries with sugar and water. Typical Russian drinks that have lost their popularity are the egg-flip (*gogol-mogol*) and the *sbiten*, a drink made of honey and a variety of spices.

The most popular drink in contemporary Russia is beer, even if this is often imported beer. Russian-brewed beer is cheaper than Coca-Cola and has outdone the U.S. beverage in popularity. The old Soviet beer factory Trekhgornoye competes with a number of new Russian beer brands, such as the Petersburg labels Tinkoff and Baltika, Sibirskaya korona, and others, which are dealt with in the section "Vodka and Other Booze."

Vodka is an extremely popular drink, and many people continue to distill their own (illegal) *samogon*, or add fruit to the vodka to create a *nastoika*. The vodka business, which had always been in state control, was privatized in the 1990s and brought back under state control after a threat of arrest against the vodka magnate Yuri Shefler in August 2002. Shefler had managed the company Soyuz-plodo-import, converted to Soyuz-plod-import (SPI, dropping the "o" in the second syllable of the acronym) in 1997, with the production of 43 brands, including Stolichnaya and Moskovskaya. The business, with a value of $1.5 billion annual revenue, was renationalized, although Shefler's Swiss SPI export outfit remained in control of vodka exports. The distillery Kristall also produces a variety of vodka labels, including Russkii standart.

Armenian cognac is world famous, even if it had to relinquish the name cognac, which is reserved to French distillers, and resort to the label brandy. The same applies to the Russian sparkling wines of the Crimea, no longer available as *shampanskoye* but as *igristoe vino* (sparkling wine). Wines from Moldova, Georgia, and Armenia can easily compete in quality with French and Italian wines.

Clubs and Bars

The Soviet Union cherished cultural activities such as theaters and cinemas, but even though the Moscow and Leningrad metro would run until 1 AM, there was no nightlife to speak of other than cultural evenings and parties at home. Nightlife was a new activity for post-Soviet youth. Many music clubs emerged from the underground rock and jazz movement of the 1980s and engaged the former subculture of dissident intelligentsia, maybe closest to the 1968 generation in the West. Rock and jazz clubs offered live music and catered for a mixed audience. These clubs are relatively inexpensive and continue the rock movement of the 1980s. Examples are the OGI clubs or the Bunker with cheap food, performances, and concerts. Other newer popular clubs among students and young people are the Club na Brestskoi, Ministerstvo, and Propaganda in the center of Moscow.

During the latter half of the 1990s the number of expensive restaurants grew, and so did the number of clubs for the New Russians, such as the Palkin restaurant, casino, and club in Petersburg on Nevsky Prospekt 47. There are also clubs for the richer classes. The English Club is a reminder of the tsarist era, located on Chistye Prudy Boulevard and destined for rich businessmen, with an annual fee of US$7,000. Luzhkov offered to enter all club members on the mayor's list for the duma elections. The club published the journal *Litsa* (Faces) that served to put a spotlight on the rich and famous. There are also branches of the Rotary Club and Monolith in Moscow and Petersburg. The Automobile Club is sponsored by Slaviya Bank, and membership includes a discount on repairs and the service of driving a member home when drunk after partying. Political clubs exist, such as the parliamentary club that convenes after duma plenary sessions on Wednesdays and Fridays, organized by Gennadi Burbulis in 1994. There are also professional clubs for lawyers, oil magnates, and other business groups.

At the same time the young generation that had grown up after the rock movement of the 1980s and that was not yet part of the new Russian business world looked for entertainment and chose dance clubs or nightclubs. Many of these grew out of dance parties, playing "house" music presented by DJs. The young generation, both "ravers" and trendy young people, frequented night clubs that encouraged an atomization of society, generating isolation instead of reinforcing the Soviet sense of a collective. The most popular hop and youth magazine is *Ptiuch*, which has been going since 1995 with a print run of about 80,000. The Metelitsa (Blizzard) complex in Moscow is one of the most popular nightclubs, despite its expensive entrance fee of US$40. Prostitution is a part of its services. The club life offers a meeting place for groups with the same interest or behavior, mostly to dance to loud music in a reaction against Soviet conventions. Often spaces for special events are hired, such as sports arenas and old palaces or cinemas. Such venues are rented on a nonofficial contract basis, which is overseen by the Mafia (*krysha*), taking a share of the profit in return for ensuring that the agreement between a venue manager and the event organizers is kept. The nightclubs largely cater for a restless young generation and are busiest after midnight, offering loud music, stroboscopic light, and tight security. Some clubs organize fashion shows or present revues of animal dressage and children's entertainment. Some also offer prostitutes.

Moscow Clubs The Yar in the Hotel Sovetskaya is one of the oldest night clubs, operating since 1848, when its revue was frequented by nineteenth-century businessmen. The variety show *Moscow, Golden Cupolas* is a historic landmark in the club. The Manhattan Express in the Rossiya Hotel attracts mainly foreign tourists.

The Pilot club, owned by Anton Tabakov, the son of Moscow Art Theater director

The Metelitsa night club, here pictured in 2001, is one of the most popular nightclubs despite its expensive entrance fee of forty U.S. dollars. (Photo by Alexey Kudenko/Kommersant)

Oleg Tabakov, is located on Krasnaya Presnya in the former Zuyev Culture House, near the Trekhgornaya Beer Factory. The interior reflects the aviation theme, with a model cockpit and the wings of an aircraft. The Bunker was first founded in Prague in the 1980s, and in 1993 it opened in Moscow near Riga Station. Later the club moved to a basement on Tverskaya Street, and in the new millennium Bunker 2 opened on the Garden Ring (Sadovoe kol'tso), with a larger stage for performances and concerts. The club offers cheap lunches and reasonably priced entrance fees for its events, targeting largely an audience of students and intellectuals. The Kitaisky letchik Dzhao Da (Chinese Pilot Jao Da) was established by Alexei Paperny and uses a wing of an aircraft as the bar. The history of the Chinese pilot Jao Da is dis-

played in prints on the walls, recounting episodes from his life. The club is mainly frequented by the media and the artistic elite. The Dom Kukera (Cooker's House) is often visited by the father of rock music, the DJ Artyom Troitsky; it is located near Lubianka. The Studio club on Tverskaya Street is frequented by pop singers Alla Pugacheva and Filipp Kirkorov as well as the extravagant designer Andrei Bartenev.

The club Ot Zakata do Rassveta (From Dawn to Dusk) opened in 1997 and was inspired by Quentin Tarantino, not only in terms of its design but also in the criminal connections of its guests. The club's prices are extortionate, and strippers perform for the guests. Moscow had and has a number of erotic clubs and strip bars. The Hungry Duck (which later closed, and then reopened under different management) near

The pub and restaurant Kitaisky letchik Dzhao Da (Chinese Pilot Jao Da) was established by Alexei Paperny. The wing of an aircraft forms the bar. (Kommersant)

Lubianka opened in 1995 as a den of drink and drugs. It was owned by the Canadian Doug Steele. The Hungry Duck offered a show of male strippers, attracting a largely female audience—after all, Moscow had never been exposed to striptease, not to speak of male strippers. Men were admitted to the club only after the striptease, and numerous stories and reports bear witness to acts of sex under the restaurant tables.

This open flaunting of sexuality was unknown and unheard of in Soviet Russia. Indeed, the NTV program *Pro eto* (About That), hosted by the Russian, but exotically dark-skinned Yelena Khanga, explored issues of sex and assisted largely in the creation of a sexual discourse, encouraging people to verbalize their experiences after a taboo on sexual terminology in the Soviet era. Papers such as Speed-Info, begun as

an information bulletin about venereal and sexually transmitted diseases including acquired immunodeficiency syndrome (AIDS [SPID]), has turned into a "speed" informational outlet, which claims to supply express information while promoting sex as pervading all aspects of everyday life. The first Russian pornography magazine, *Andrei* (1991), distinctively used a more medical vocabulary while avoiding the obscene language of its Western equivalents, making its task to verbalize, not stimulate, sex. It was duly followed by a host of men's journals of Russian and foreign provenance, including *Playboy* and *Men's Health*. Nightclubs with erotic shows abound. The Rasputin is an expensive club with an erotic theater. The Garage offers business lunches and turns into a strip club at night. The Nochnoi Polet (Night Flight) is a central nightclub under Swedish management on Tverskaya Street and a central venue for prostitutes. It opened in 1992 and caters largely for a foreign clientele, offering women at US$200 per night. Male prostitution is also common and offered to single women in many nightclubs. The Tsentralnaya Stantsiya (Central Station) is a club with a travesty show.

Although homosexuality was prohibited by law until 1993, a number of gay clubs have now surfaced. Krasnaya shapochka (Red Riding Hood) is one of the many gay clubs that sprang up in Moscow in the late 1990s; another is the Kazarma, which applies face control and admits members only, offering tables in separate chambers and male prostitutes. The Elf is the oldest gay bar, located near Kursk railway station.

Discos are also common in Moscow. Some of the most eccentric are the Biblos, with different national rooms as interior design themes. The XII and Papa John's are discos that change their décor once a week. Their select elite audiences can often be found relaxing in the summer on Ibiza.

Nightlife in Petersburg   The nightlife in St. Petersburg has a slightly different history and context than the Moscow scene. In the late perestroika years, Timur Novikov (1958–2002), the guru of the youth scene, shared his experience of foreign travel with his compatriots and squatted in a derelict building on Fontanka 145, using the premises for parties between 1989 and 1991. In the "parties," he experimented with music, fashion, and art. From here the DJs begin to emerge in the St. Petersburg music scene, which had hitherto known only the Latvian DJ Janis. Novikov invited foreign DJs to the Fontanka parties before they moved out to the observatory (plane-

tarium). Later the organizers went to the Pavilion of the Cosmos in Moscow's VDNKh (Vystavka dostizhenii narodnogo khoziaistva, All-Union Agricultural Exhibition) for the Gagarin Party (named ironically after the Soviet cosmonaut Yuri Gagarin) on 14 December 1991, followed by the Gagarin Party II in spring 1992. Both events were privately produced and attracted more than 2,000 people, creating the first mass events not controlled by the state. Indeed, nightlife evaded state control. The parties used the Soviet symbols of Gagarin and cosmic walks in a play with Soviet iconography. Further large events followed. These early parties were known for their use of hallucinogenic "magic" mushrooms (a mushroom that grows in the northern forests and contains psilocybin).

The River Club (*rechniki*) members were anarchists and squatters, who in 1994 squatted on a trawler and transmitted radio programs from there. They made furniture from discarded metal. The art critic Timur Novikov had founded the New Academy of Fine Arts in 1991 and coined neoacademism, an art form that combines classical grandeur with technology and junk. Novikov died in May 2002 after an illness that left him blind during the last years of his life.

Petersburg, like Moscow, had known clubs and cabarets before the Revolution, which had seen their heyday in 1912–1915. The Brodiachaya Sobaka (Stray Dog) was a famous artistic cabaret and club, which was closed in the late 1920s. The basement of the now reconstructed building has been preserved and operates a literary and artistic café. The Internet café Tetris and the Sobaka (*sobaka* is *dog* but also the word used to describe the character @) are popular venues.

Exploiting the attraction of the setting, the Tunnel was founded in 1993 by Alexei Haas, using a former fall-out shelter near a factory as premises for his club. Fischfabrik is an old underground club on Ligovsky Street. Numerous erotic nightclubs occupy the Petersburg nightlife scene, such as the Golden Dolls or the Maximus, offering a strip show in a Greek and Roman interior. The Money Honey offers dance to music played by DJs in Apraxin Yard. There is also a Hollywood entertainment complex on Nevsky Prospekt. The Hulli Gulli is a cabaret, often offering erotic shows, with the presenter Roman Trachtenberg. The Magrib is a nightclub and restaurant with belly dance located on Nevsky Prospekt. Petersburg nightclubs thus offer the variety of entertainments that would be found in most European and U.S. capital cities.

Games

Gambling, like betting, was not encouraged in the USSR. Card games and dominoes were condemned in the Soviet period, although these have now gained a certain amount of popularity. Even today there are few bookmakers. People have stopped trusting lotteries and pyramid schemes after a number of economic and financial debacles. A number of popular games, especially children's games in the open, continue to be played, however.

Children's and Adults' Games The old games *gorodki* (a kind of bowling, where the players try to knock out figures with the help of a stick) and *lapta* (a form of baseball or cricket) were turned into "proper," competitive disciplines. There are also numerous open-air games that are known in many countries, but under different names, such as hide and seek (*igra v* *priatki*), cat and mouse (*koshki-myshki*), or blind man's buff (*igra v zhmurki*). Children in Russia also play hopscotch (*igra v klassiki*), tags (*salki*), and skittles (*kegli*). The game breach (*proryvaty*) is played by two teams, each of which forms a line. At the words "Tary-bary give us Max," the person (called Max) must run across and try to break the chain formed by the other team. If Max breaks the line, he can pick one of their players to join his team; if not, he has to stay with the "enemy" team. Cossacks and robbers (*kazaki-razboiniki*) is a form of hide-and-seek; only when the robber is spotted by a Cossack can he run and hide again. When the robber is caught, he is brought home and becomes a Cossack, until no robbers are left.

Indoor games include the well-known checkers (*shashki*), the Japanese game go, and the English game backgammon (*nardy*). Rough sea (*more volnuetsia*; similar to musical chairs) is a game where all the players sit on their chairs, which are positioned with the backs against each other in a row. When the leader says "the sea is rough," all the players walk around the room. Then the leader calls "the sea is quiet" (*more utikhlo*), and each player has to try to find a chair. The player who remains standing has to take the lead and steer the boat.

Billiards, pool, and snooker are gaining in popularity as more facilities are available in hotels, restaurants, and bars. Billiards in particular was reserved for the party elite in the Soviet period but has grown in popularity in the New Russia. Russian billiards has traditionally been played with five balls, whereas the French version known as *carambole* in Russia is played with 15 balls. The most widespread games are American billiards, with eight balls that have to be placed in the pockets, and pyramid, where the player has to score 70 points. There are a number of billiards clubs in the cities, many of them attached to restaurants.

The fifth wheel (*Piatoye koleso*) is an intellectual game where the players have to mark the odd one out of a group of five items. In order to jog their memories, children play lotto, and such games as adding on words to a list of items: "I went to the shop and bought . . ." (*Ia khodil na bazar i kupil*). Black and white (*cherny i bely*) is a game where one player asks questions, and the second player must answer without using the words *white*, *black*, *yes*, and *no*.

Paper games include crosses and circles (*Krestiki-noliki*) and hangman (*Palach*), where for every letter placed in a word to be guessed, the team comes closer to being "hanged." Forfeits (*igra v fanty*) is a very common game, where a *fant* (a sweetwrapper) is used, or a piece of paper, to write down a wish. The wrapper is then thrown into a hat. The players then pull out a wrapper each and read the wish as if it were now his/her own, picking another player to fulfill the wish.

Video and computer games are hugely popular in Russia, especially since the mid-1990s when pirated copies of major computer programs and games were easy prey for the—in those days not-so-well-off—customers.

Gambling   Casinos abound in Russia. There are casinos in most major hotels. In Moscow there is also a row of clubs and casinos on the New Arbat near the globe that decorates the end of the shopping mile between the Hotel Prague and the Garden Ring: they include the casino-clubs Metelitsa, Korona, and Arbat. In Peters-

burg numerous clubs are located on Nevsky Prospect, the city's main artery. All of these venues offer blackjack, poker, roulette, and a variety of games. The Shangri-La on Pushkin Square is a central casino below the Pushkin Cinema. Entrance fees vary around $200 in chips for the most popular casinos. There are also gambling machines, such as one-arm-bandits and others, which have been located in public spaces of the halls of the Moscow Games Systems chains Jackpot since 1999 and Vulcan since 1991.

Relaxation and Holidays

The ways and locations of relaxation and holidays have changed significantly since the collapse of the Soviet Union, when travel to foreign destinations became possible, but not always affordable. Traditionally parks had offered respite in the big cities, alongside the dacha (summerhouse), mostly located on the outskirts of the cities.

Gardens and Parks   Parks were an important aspect of urban planning throughout the twentieth century. Green spaces were deliberately dotted around Moscow and Leningrad, as well as other large cities, and these parks also had an important social function: to provide a breathing space for the healthy urban population and offer collective and publicly accessible (and controllable) leisure time activity. Most parks have ponds that form ice rinks in the winter and can be used for boat rides in the summer. In the 1980s luna parks were introduced, offering the attractions of an amusement park on a Western models. Not all parks have mechanical attractions, but most of those that did were in need of maintenance and repair in the 1990s, when commercial exploitation of these attractions began.

The Gorky Park in Moscow is one of the oldest in the city, set up on the embankment of the Moscow river in the late 1920s. The park is probably better known for its setting of the spy thriller *Gorky Park* by Martin Cruz-Smith than for its attractions, which contain swings, merry-go-rounds, a Ferris wheel, and some children's entertainment. The park leads onto the rather charming and wild Neskuchny Garden with some eighteenth-century buildings. The park in Sokolniki (named after the tsar's falcons, *sokoly*) has a more nostalgic atmosphere, with a fountain in its center, from which several alleys lined with elms and birches radiate. There are some ponds and dachas in the park. The park in Fili, created in the area of a nature reserve in the 1960s, also preserves much wilderness. The park of the All-Union Agricultural Exhibition (VDNKh), renamed the Russian Exhibition Center (VVTs) in the 1990s, contains sales pavilions alongside entertainment attractions such as bouncing castles and a hill for tobogganing, as well as a Ferris wheel. The park in Izmailovo is partly used by the *vernissage*, the weekend sales exhibition of Russian crafts and antiques that is held at the western end of the park. The park itself covers a forest area and is, with more than 1,000 hectares of space, one of the largest in the world. The park in Bitsa in the south of Moscow is also known for art exhibitions, painting in particular. Kolomenskoye is an open-air museum with a church and the tsar's wooden summerhouse in a park with deep slopes toward the Moskva River; it is located in the south of Moscow. The Delphinarium and the zoo offer further respite and entertainment for children. Park Pobedy (Victory Park) was planned in 1958 to mark the victory in World War II. The plans were implemented only in 1983, however, when the obelisk and the museum were built and then completed under Mayor Yuri Luzhkov in 1995 with input from the sculptor Zurab Tsereteli. The memorial chapel is located on the top of Poklonnaya Gora. The ensemble of monuments also contains a statue of the patron of Moscow, St. George.

Tourism: The Russians on Holiday   In the Soviet period, financial support of the trade unions made it possible for most people to have a three-week holiday in a holiday resort. The trade unions would issue vouchers for hotels and sanatoriums that belonged to the unions, making holidays very cheap and extremely affordable; travel was subsidized by the state, and both rail and air travel were cheap. The agency Intourist looked after foreign tourists, and it was KGB-controlled so that the movement of foreigners could be monitored.

With the collapse of the Soviet system, Intourist was no longer the sole agent for offering package tours to foreign operators, opening the market and making prices soar. Simultaneously, hotels were noticeably lacking standards of service when compared with other countries, and as the political and economic climate was more and more destabilized in the 1990s, tourism to Russia dropped sharply. The internal scheme for vouchers for trade union resorts gradually crumbled, as the funds for maintaining sanatoriums and hotels were dwindling, membership contributions were no longer sufficient, and travel became increasingly costly as well. By the mid-1990s, numerous travel agencies came onto the Russian market, offering package tours to foreign destinations such as Spain,

People carrying advertising boards for last-minute holidays on Pushkin Square, Moscow, in 2001. (Photo by Alexey Kudenko/ Kommersant)

Turkey, and Egypt for prices that were almost the same as those that people would have to pay for a holiday within Russia. Therefore foreign tourism increased significantly, despite the visa requirements. Certain tourist destinations have remained extremely popular, such as Croatia, the Red Sea, and Egypt (Sharm el Sheikh and Hurgada) as well as Spanish resorts.

By the mid-1990s, tourism revived: more than 5 million foreigners visited Russia and more than 8 million Russians traveled abroad. Nevertheless, the influx of tourists represents only 1 percent of tourist movement worldwide. By 1995, more than 8,000 firms and travel agents with licenses had established themselves in Russia to sell package tours as well as airline and rail tickets.

The resorts on the Black Sea are restricted, as Yalta and the Crimea now belong to Ukraine. The once-famous resort of Pitsunda now belongs to Abkhazia. Sochi and adjacent resorts have developed, with new international hotels built (Radisson Lazurnaya) and Russian-owned hotels developing. The city of Sochi has also invested in an aqua park for leisure time activity and a number of seaside activities. On the Baltic Sea, the once-popular resorts have also fallen to Lithuania, Latvia, and Estonia: the peninsula of the Kurische Nehrung with the village of Nidden (once the domicile of Thomas Mann), the Latvian resort of Jurmala, and the bay of Tallinn are no longer "internal" destinations, and the resorts on the Russian shore are too far north to offer any real opportunity for swimming in the sea.

The areas of the meandering river Volga and the lakes north of Moscow, the lakes north of Petersburg, and the region of the Baikal offer, however, multiple opportunities for holidays for local residents, and these facilities are being expanded all the time.

Hotels in Russia   In most Russian cities, except Moscow and Petersburg, there is a variety of former Soviet hotels, some restored, others not; the first are usually affordable for the Western traveler, the latter are cheap and often substandard. Most large cities also have a growing number of international hotels, depending on the city's location and its interest for businesses and industries.

In Moscow many hotels have been refurbished and correspond to high international standards. The old pre-Revolutionary hotels nowadays all form five-star hotels. The Savoy is a hotel that has preserved its old interior and antique furniture in all of its 84 rooms. The Metropol was originally built in 1850, restored in 1905, and again refurbished during 1986–1990. The hotel was built by the Scot William Walcott with assistance from Lev Kekushev; the ceramic panels on the facade were designed by the famous Russian artists Alexander Golovin and Mikhail Vrubel in the style of art nouveau. None of the 367 rooms is identical. The Metropol can boast of a restaurant where the opera singer Fyodor Shaliapin once performed. It belongs to the Intercontinental chain. The Hotel Nationale has 221 rooms and is part of the Meridien chain. The hotel, designed by the architect Alexander Ivanov, is more than 100 years old and furnished with furniture made of Karelian birch. Winston Churchill resided here during his visit to Moscow. The hotel Sovetskaya is a historical hotel on Leningrad Avenue with 75 rooms. The Ararat Hyatt, located on Neglinnaya Street, is an old hotel with its 219 rooms entirely refurbished.

Only a few old, Soviet-style hotels have remained open without undergoing major refurbishment: the Ukraina, located in the high-rise opposite the White House, has 1,000 rooms. The hotels Belgrade and Golden Ring are located in two post-1960s towers on Smolensk Square. The Intourist was built in 1970 on Tverskaya Street near Red Square; it was pulled down in 2003. The hotel Minsk was built in 1963, offering cheap and central accommodation until its closure in 2004. The 27-floor semicircular concrete construction of the hotel Cosmos was built jointly with a French company for the 1980 Olympics. It is located opposite the VDNKh. The famous hotel Moscow,

with an asymmetrical facade designed by Alexei Shchusev, was built in 1932 and closed in 2002 for major reconstruction work. The Pekin on Mayakovsky Square is also in a 1950s Stalinist building, but most of its rooms have been refurbished. The Izmailova overlooks the park and consists of five 30-floor towers built in 1979–1980. Finally, the Rossiya is the largest hotel in Europe, with 3,000 rooms, and probably the cheapest and most central hotel that remains open. It was built on an area where several small buildings and churches were demolished. The space was supposed to be used for an administrative complex, but the construction work was frozen under Khrushchev, and when reactivated, the much lower building of the hotel was erected here. After its completion, many of the sixteenth- and seventeenth-century buildings and chapels on Varvarka Street were restored.

New hotels built in the 1990s include the Sheraton Palace with its 200 rooms on Tverskaya Street. The Marriott Grand Hotel on Tverskaya Street with 391 rooms opened in 1998 and was built in Luzhkov style that imitates Stalinist classicism in architecture. The Marriott Aurora Royal has 230 rooms in a reconstruction of the original building on Petrovka Street. The Marriott Tverskaya is a modern building with 162 rooms. The Balchug Kempinski with a Berlin-style Café Kranzler has 202 rooms and is situated across the Moskva River from Red Square in a reconstructed building. The Radisson Slavianskaya is a modern 400-room hotel and conference center near the Kiev Railway Station. The Mezhdunarodnaya (International) Hotel adjacent to the World Trade Center was built in the 1980s to offer office space and accommodation to international firms. The Presi-

The Hotel Balchug-Kempinski in central Moscow, 2004. (Photo by Alexey Kudenko/Kommersant)

Façade of the Hotel Europe in St. Petersburg, 2000. (Photo by Sergey Semyenov/Kommersant)

dent Hotel on Yakimanka Street is a modern building with 200 rooms. The Renaissance (formerly Olympic Penta) has 500 rooms and is located near the Olympic stadium on Prospekt Mira.

Overall, there is very little affordable accommodation in Moscow. Most new or refurbished hotels aspire to five-star accommodation that remains affordable to only a select few, as hotel prices in Moscow rank among the highest in the world.

The situation in Petersburg is somewhat similar to that in Moscow: most hotels have refurbished their rooms and facilities to gain the highest possible ranking and charge extraordinary prices. The Astoria Hotel, built in 1910 by Fyodor Lidvall, has 223 rooms; it is connected with the adjacent Hotel Angleterre that reopened in September 2003 with 193 rooms designed by Olga Polizzi. The two hotels share some facilities for their guests and are owned by the Rocco Forte group. The Grand Hotel Europe with its baroque facade by Carlo Rossi of 1875 and its famous art-nouveau interiors has 301 rooms and is one of the classiest and oldest in Europe. The Radisson SAS on Nevsky Prospect is a new hotel built behind an old facade, with 164 rooms. The Nevsky Palace Corinthia has 282 rooms and was also built behind an old facade of apartment blocks.

The Soviet-era hotels are the St. Petersburg, formerly the Leningrad, on Pirogov Embankment with 710 rooms and the Hotel Moscow near Alexander Nevsky Monastery with 777 rooms. The Sovetskaya is an 18-story building of modern architecture with 1,000 rooms. More recent hotels are the 1980s buildings of Pribaltiiskaya on the Finnish Gulf with 1,200 rooms and the Pulkovskaya (near the airport) with 840 rooms. The Oktiabrskaya was built in the mid-nineteenth century near the Moscow Railway Station, and some of its 563 rooms have been renovated and upgraded. Apart from such large hotels, however, Petersburg has—unlike Moscow—a number of bed and breakfast places and smaller hotels, both central and peripheral, that offer good-value accommodation.

Dachas: Living in the Country   Since the eighteenth century, wealthy Russians have had a summerhouse that they owned or rented in order to avoid the heat in the cities. In the Soviet era, summerhouses persisted, and many Russians owned a plot of land with the appropriate wooden house outside the cities. Most summerhouses had neither heating nor electricity nor indeed any facilities, with water available often only from a well or a rivulet. The dacha nevertheless has remained a favorite occupation of many city inhabitants, both for growing vegetables and plants and for fresh air. At the same time, many New Russians have begun to build brick houses in former dacha settlements, using the car to get in and out of town and making the out-of-town villas their permanent domicile, preferring this to a city apartment.

There were entire dacha districts near Moscow and Leningrad/Petersburg. Most dacha settlements are located near a major railway line: Kuskovo, Malakhovka, and Udelnaya on the Kazan Line; Kuntsevo, Serebrianyi Bor, Zhukovka, Nikolina Gora, and Zvenigorod on the Smolensk Line; and Pushkino, Abramtsevo, and Sergiyev Posad on the Yaroslavl Line. The village of Tarusia is a prominent dacha and summerhouse region. In Petersburg the dacha settlements of Repino and Komarovo toward the north, as well as the Lake Ladoga region, are very popular.

Dachas and garden plots around Moscow. The dachas are summer residences, and gardens are used to grow fruit and vegetables. (Wolfgang Kaehler/Corbis)

The dacha was a given, donated plot of land handed out by the tsar in an act of grace. It served as a retreat during the Revolution and the civil war. In the 1930s, new dachas were built for factory workers and the party elite, but dacha regions lacked a proper infrastructure so that the use of suburban settlement for permanent accommodation was impossible, although living space was badly needed in the cities during the drive on industrialization. Party echelons had their own dacha settlements in Malakhovka, Serebrianyi Bor, and Nikolina Gora, and the writers settled in Peredelkino, where a dacha colony was established to encourage creativity. The dacha was often received as a reward from the party or obtained by using connections within the party hierarchy (*blat*). Many dachas were private properties (owned by cooperatives); others were owned by the state or rented. By the 1980s it was common for people to have a dacha. The dacha plot was used to grow vegetables and potatoes during and after World War II, and despite shortages of seeds and tools, the *ogorod* produced fresh vegetables that could partly be sold. As people left the countryside, many village properties, which had been built with brick and were equipped with some facilities (heating, electricity), were purchased for summer relaxation during the 1970s. The land reform of October 1993 meant that land could be bought, and New Russians began to build their cottages and brick houses next to the old dachas; most of these cottages are used as permanent domiciles.

Housing Developments in the City

New accommodation has been built and is being built not in central Moscow, but

A couple skating during Christmas celebrations at Sokolniki Park, January 2003. (Photo by Pavel Smertin/Kommersant)

mostly on the outskirts. It is apparently assumed that most people who can afford property in the new apartment buildings have a car to travel (along the overcrowded roads) to work. Such new areas are often situated in former dacha regions, where new villas sit next to old wooden summerhouses and shacks. The Triumph Palace, a monumental piece of Stalinist architecture on Leningrad Prospect, is the highest apartment building in Europe with a height of 264.1 meters. The complex on Sparrow Hills near the embassies and Mosfilm studios consists of seven buildings and represents a self-contained village with the appropriate facilities. The Red Sails (Alye

parusa) complex is located on the embankment of the Moscow River with a yachting club attached and a sauna, fitness center, and cinema on site. A new block in Sokolniki overlooks the park and is built in high-tech style in the shape of a semicircle. Elsinor is a business complex with apartments and town houses, copying a European architectural style with gothic forms and facades in the northwest of Moscow.

Celebrations

Although most people enjoy a variety of opportunities for relaxation, leisure-time activities, and holidays, Russian society remains firmly in the grip of rituals and traditions that rule the celebration of anniversaries and public and religious holidays alike. In the Soviet era, religious practice was suppressed by the atheist state, which elevated Communist ideology and replaced God with Marx or Lenin. Political leaders were revered like saints, as is best indicated by the way in which Lenin's corpse was embalmed like that of a saint and displayed in a mausoleum. Indeed, a corpse that did not putrefy was deemed to be saintly.

Public Holidays

Even if the new Soviet regime wanted to abolish religious practice, it soon became clear that celebrations were important for the people: they were a vital element in popular culture and a relief channel for the hardships endured during the civil war. The young Soviet regime therefore decided to introduce a number of secular holidays that subsumed religious holidays and prescribed celebrations that would satisfy the people's need for a release of energy. Choreographed mass celebrations replaced the spontaneous street celebrations of folk rituals. In the first instance, this concerned the celebration of Christmas. The figures of Grandfather Frost (*ded moroz*) and Snow Maiden (*snegurochka*) were pagan enough to remain functional, at least in the children's world, to continue the jobs carried out in Western cultures by Santa Claus: bringing presents and celebrating his arrival with a Christmas tree (*yolka*). Although Christmas was on 7 January, these celebrations took place on New Year's Eve (31 December). The other two important religious holidays, Easter and Pentecost, were scrapped. Easter was sub-

sumed by the May Day holidays, and Pentecost was feebly echoed in the pagan Whitsun celebrations.

As time went by, the Soviet government decreed a number of holidays to celebrate Soviet achievements. International Women's Day, 8 March, was celebrated by men's presenting flowers to women, independent of their relationship. In other words, a factory manager could give flowers to his colleagues, a husband to his wife, a boy to his mother. This way, the holiday combined Mothering Sunday and Valentine's Day in one nonconspicuous holiday. Of course, it was a working holiday, unlike 23 February, which has in contemporary Russia turned into a proper public holiday. In Soviet times it was the Day of the Armed Forces (Defense of the Fatherland)—that is, a men's holiday (to match the women's day two weeks later). The first of May was the classical socialist holiday: International Workers' Day. As 1 May was celebrated widely with official demonstrations and parades, followed by mass walks, and accompanied in Russian style by a lot of alcohol, 2 May was also a public holiday (for recovery). The first two days of May remain public holidays in post-Soviet Russia, but the holiday is called the Day of Spring and Labor (*Den' vesny i truda*). Victory Day on 9 May remains a public holiday with parades of veterans of World War II. The 22nd of August is the Day of the Russian Federation State Flag and is a relatively new public holiday. The first of September is not a public holiday, but the Day of Knowledge marks the beginning of the school year. The seventh of November was the day of the October Revolution (25 October old style) and was celebrated with official parades in grand style during the Soviet era. In contemporary Russia it has remained a holiday, the Day of Accord and Concilia-tion (*Den' soglasiia i primireniia*), al-though no celebrations take place. Holi-days devoted to organizations were noted almost every Sunday: for the police, the army, and the miners and days of theater, cinema, and museums.

In the new Russia, 12 June is a national holiday, Independence Day, when the Rus-sian Federation became independent with the election of its first president, Boris Yeltsin, in June 1991. The 12th of Decem-ber is the Day of the Constitution, which came into force in 1993 (the constitution was approved by parliament on 12 Decem-ber).

Religious Holidays

The New Russia also observes religious holidays. Although Christmas presents are still delivered on 31 December/1 January (*Novy God*), 7 January is a religious holi-day when people usually attend a night mass to celebrate the birth of Christ (*Rozhdestvo Khristovo*). Christmas is the second most significant holiday of the Orthodox church after Easter, which is a flexible holiday that does not normally co-incide with Easter in the Western Hemi-sphere but follows the orthodox (Julian) calendar. The Gregorian calendar was in-troduced in 1918, and the difference is 13 days. A further important holiday is Pente-cost, or Holy Trinity. The time between Christmas and Epiphany (7–21 January) is known as the *sviatki* (Christmas Tide); these are the "holy evenings," when tradi-tionally no work would be done after dark. Before Christmas the revelers (*koliadki*) go around to houses and bless the house-holds and receive small gifts. They are comparable to the *Sternsinger* of Ger-manic tradition.

Easter is the main holiday of the Ortho-dox Church, celebrated in a night mass when people walk around the church three times in expectation of the Resurrection. It follows seven weeks of fasting, or Lent (*ve-likii post*), when many people fast before the Resurrection of Christ, abstaining from meat, fish, and dairy products (and eating only once a day, if following the fast rigidly). Before Lent, however, there is Shrovetide (*maslenitsa*), with street cele-brations and rather fat food, including a Pancake Day, or Shrove Tuesday, when people make pancakes (*bliny*) that have the shape of the sun and recall the pagan holiday from which the church borrowed the festival: the celebration of the sun. At the end of *maslenitsa* stands Forgiveness Sunday (Proshchenoe voskresenie). The strictest week of the 40-day fasting is the week before Easter, Passion Week (Strast-naia nedelia). Easter is celebrated with col-ored Easter eggs and a *kulich*, a round sweet bread with icing. The *kulich* and the eggs are normally taken to church for a blessing the day before Easter. The *paskha*, a cheesecake with raisins, is another popu-lar Easter dish. Pentecost follows 50 days after Easter. Other times of fasting that are not widely kept by people are Peter's Fast-ing (*Petrov post*), which begins a week af-ter Trinity and lasts until 12 July (Peter and Paul); the Fasting of Assumption (*Uspen-skii post*), from 14 to 28 August; and the Christmas fast from 28 November until Christmas.

Orthodoxy was brought to Russia from Byzantium in 988 by Vladimir (remem-bered on 28 July), when the country then called Rus was Christianized. After the fall of Constantinople, Moscow became the Third Rome. Russia's history was ridden with attacks from the Turks, the Mongols,

Orthodox Holidays

Dates that vary from year to year are shown in italics.

7 January: Christmas (*Rozhdestvo Khristovo*).

19 January: Baptism of Christ and Epiphany (*Kreshchenie Gospodne, Bogoyavlenie*). At the age of 30, Christ was baptized in the Jordan by John the Baptist, and the Holy Spirit descended.

15 February: Candlemas (*Sretenie*). Forty days after the birth of Christ, Mary was purified in church.

24 April (2005) Palm Sunday (*Verbnoe Voskresenie*): Jesus arrived in Jerusalem, where his followers covered the road with branches and leaves (*verbnoe* comes from willow).

From Thursday night to Saturday night before Easter darkness reigns in churches.

1 May (2005) Easter, or Resurrection (*Paskha, Voskresenie Gospodne*).

9 June (2005) Ascension (*Voznesenie*). Forty days after the Resurrection, Christ ascended to heaven.

19 June (2005) Pentecost, or Holy Trinity (*Sviataya Troitsa*). Fifty days after Easter, the Holy Spirit appeared among the twelve apostles.

7 July: Birth of John the Baptist (*Rozhdestvo Ioanna Predtechi*), also the pagan festival Ivan Kupala.

12 July: Peter and Paul.

19 August: Transfiguration (*Preobrazhenie Gospodne*).

28 August: Assumption of Our Lady (*Upenie presviatoi Bogoroditsy*).

11 September: Beheading of John the Baptist (*Useknovenie glavy Ioanna Predtechi*).

21 September: Birth of the Virgin Mary.

27 September: Exaltation of the Cross (*Vozdvizhenie Kresta Gospodnia*). The cross, found 200 years after Christ's death in a cave, was erected by the Patriarch Makarius in Jerusalem.

4 December: Presentation of the Blessed Virgin (*Vvedenie v khram Bogoroditsy*). When Mary was three years old, she was taken to the temple by her parents.

---

and the Tatars. Icons were believed to offer protection from the "barbarian" attacks and invasions. In the seventeenth century the Orthodox Church split, when Avvakuum insisted on old traditions whereas Nikon wanted to modernize the church. The Old Believers, a sect still active in Russia today, separated from the Orthodox Church. The Orthodox Church has possessed, since the time of Peter the Great, a very rigid hierarchical structure, at the head of which stand the Holy Synod and the patriarch of all Russia: since 1990 this is Alexei II. The Russian Orthodox Church has always had a strong tradition of paying respect to the *yurodivye*, people who renounce their worldly possessions and lead a life of poverty and devotion in the hope of salvation after death. This view of life as suffering for the reward of life in heaven is an underlying principle of the Orthodox faith. The yurodivye were blessed people, such as Basil the Blessed (Vasilii blazhennyi, 1468–1552), a God's fool under Ivan the Terrible, who earned the tsar's respect and in whose honor the cathedral of St. Basil's was erected on Red Square.

Other religions are tolerated in Russia, and the right to practice them is enshrined in the constitution. A large Jewish constituency in Moscow and other major cities has its theaters, cultural centers, and synagogues. In the southern regions there are many Muslims. Catholics and Baptists are found in central and northern Russia. Shamanism is widely practiced in Sakha (Yakutia) and parts of Siberia. There are also numerous religious sects, but they are not widely supported.

The Russian church and people venerate a large number of saints. On the religious holiday of John the Baptist (birth and death on 19 January and 7 July), the water of the church is blessed, and people also collect tap water in containers, as that water is thought to have special power. Many saints are martyrs who have died for their faith. This is true for the children and wife of Adrian of Rome, Sofia and her daughters Vera, Nadezhda, and Liubov (faith, hope, and love). They were tortured for their Christian faith and died. Their day is marked on 30 September, which is also the name day of all the Veras, Nadias, Liubas, and Sonias. A Roman consul and his daughter Tatiana were burned at the stake for their Christian faith. Tatiana was blinded, given to a lion who did not touch her, then executed in 226. Tatiana's Day (*Tatianin den*) is celebrated on 25 January, and she is the patron of students, because Catherine the Great signed the decree to found an imperial university in Moscow on that day. Boris and Gleb (celebrated on 15 May, 6 August, and 18 September) were the first saints of the Russian church. They were martyrs who died for their faith and showed no resistance to evil.

Other saints have committed important feats for the church or their faith. Sergei of Radonezh (1314–1392) was the founder of the Trinity–St. Sergius Monastery (Troitse-Sergieva lavra, or Troitse-Sergiev mona-

styr') and is commemorated on 8 October and 18 July. Alexander Nevsky (1220–1263) defended the Neva, and his remains are kept in the Alexander-Nevsky Monastery in Petersburg. His nameday is 12 September. Nikolai Mirlikisky is the saint whose legend is similar to Saint Nicholas, and he is remembered on 19 December (6 December old style). Cyril and Methodius are marked on 27 February. Cyril (Kirill) and his brother created the first Slav (Cyrillic) alphabet in 863. Today Cyril and Methodius is also the name of an important online encyclopedia publisher. Georgi Pobedonosets (9 December and 6 May) is the bearer of various legends. He is said to have been a warrior who defended the tsar's daughter, and a saint who died for his faith, a man who fought evil (represented by a snake). His image is a symbol of victory over evil, and in the fourteenth century the figure of St. George became the emblem of Moscow.

Recently canonized figures include the priest Johann of Kronstadt (1829–1908) and Xenia of Petersburg (remembered on 6 January), who chose deliberate *yurodstvo* in the eighteenth century when she became a widow at the age of 26. She dressed like a man and renounced all worldly possessions. Her remains were laid to rest in the Smolensk cemetery in Petersburg, and she was canonized in 1988. The icon painter Andrei Rublev, who lived in the fourteenth century in the Trinity St-Sergius Monastery, became a saint in 1988.

Rites and Rituals

Pagan Practices and Popular Beliefs
Although religious practice and the following of religious rules are increasingly common in Russia, so is superstition. There are

Superstitions of Everyday Life

Do not shake hands over the threshold.

Sit down for a minute before a journey.

If you return home because you have forgotten something, look into the mirror before leaving again.

If a boy sits on the threshold, he won't get married. If a girl sits on the windowsill, she won't get married.

Do not put keys on the table.

If you wipe breadcrumbs off the table with your hands, you'll have no money.

If the blanket falls down from the bed, a guest will arrive soon.

Don't put a ruler on the bed: it means death.

Put out a candle with two fingers; don't blow it out.

Open scissors or an open safety pin means a quarrel.

Do not splash water from your hands; the drops spread little devils.

Don't use somebody else's towel.

Wipe the floor away from the threshold, not toward it.

When you can't find something, tie a kerchief (preferably red) to the leg of the table and call the house spirit for help.

If you give a mirror as a present, the recipient must wipe it with holy water.

When you give somebody scissors as a present, the person must pay a penny.

A broken mirror means disaster

If you wipe your eyes, you will cry soon.

If you have itchy palms, it means money: if the right palm itches you will get money; the left palm means you will give money.

Cross your fingers when praising yourself or wishing good luck.

If you step on somebody's foot, it means trouble. The person should step back on your foot to avoid it.

Only spit over your left shoulder. Over your right shoulder is your guardian angel.

To protect yourself from the "bad eye," wear metal.

A thread on a girl's dress means she will get married.

If a knife falls from the table, a man will come; if a fork falls, the guest is a woman.

If you don't recognize somebody, he'll be rich.

When giving an empty vessel (cup, bowl) as a gift, put a chocolate or a coin inside so as not to give something empty.

Always give an uneven number of flowers.

different types of witches: the *koldunia*, who passes her witchcraft to her grandchild; the *vedma*, who bewitches people; and the *baba yaga*, who appears in fairy tales. Russian folk tradition believes in spirits. The *leshy* is the wood spirit; the *vodianoi* resides in bogs and water; the *domovoi* is the house spirit; and the *rusalka* is the spirit of the water, the unborn child of a maiden. There are also regional spirits, as for example the *shelps*, spirits of the Urals, which bring out the positive or nega-

tive features in any man who encounters them.

People in modern Russia believe in fortune-telling as much as their predecessors did in the nineteenth century. There is a great demand for tarot, crystals, fortune-telling, but also for astrology and horoscopes in newspapers and on television. This is largely owing to the complete absence of any fortune-telling in the country of socialist plans and Communist dreams of party and state. The chain of Third Eye shops, selling anything from aromatherapy and herbs to card and glass balls, prospers across the country.

Names   Many Russian children were given names of Greek origin, such as Anastasia (resurrected), Galina (quiet), Gennadi (benevolent), or Anatoli (eastern). A few names were of Latin origin. In the twentieth century, Slavic names remained extremely popular, such as Bogdan (given by God), Boris or Borislav (brave fighter), Lada (pagan goddess of love), Liubov (love or charity), Liudmila (dear to the people), Nadezhda (hope), Vera (faith), Svetlana (light), Sviatoslav (saintly Slav), Vladimir (ruler over the world). In the last decade of the twentieth century, Russian names that had been popular in the nineteenth century came back into fashion, especially Daria (Dasha) and Glafira (Glasha).

An odd reminder of the Soviet era are the "Soviet" names Vilen (V. I. Lenin), Marlen (Marx-Lenin), Vladlen (Vladimir Lenin), Ninel (Lenin read backward), Dekabrin/a (in honor of the Decembrists), Noyabrin/a and Oktriabrin/a (in honor of the Revolution, October or November). The actress Nonna Mordiukova is called Noyabrina (Nonna); Alexei Balabanov's patronymic is Oktriabrinovich, meaning that his father is called Oktriabrin. Other names were Liutsiya (derived from Revoliutsiya, revolution) and Neya (derived from Energiya, energy). These people have no saints, clearly, and were born at a time when christenings too were replaced by civil (red) ceremonies.

Fashion

As fashion was considered a bourgeois pastime, it had no place in Soviet ideology.

Fashion designers became "costume artists" after the Revolution. Many avant-garde artists tried to bring a new style and new forms into dress conventions; one of these was Popova with her *proz-odezhda*, her industry wear. As with many of her fellow artists, however, her pursuits remained restricted to the "higher" arts, the stage, and never went into mass production. Nevertheless, the 1920s saw some of Russia's most extravagant costumes designed for the silver screen, such as Alexandra Exter's outfits for *Aelita*. One woman has left a remarkable trace on Soviet fashion and made the transition from Russian to Soviet fashion: Nadezhda Lamanova (1861–1941) was the first recognized Russian modelier and designer. She set up her own workshop in 1885 in order to support her sisters after their parents had died. After the Revolution, fashion boutiques were regarded with suspicion, and Lamanova went to work at the Vakhtangov Theater, where she made the costumes for Yevgeni Vakhtangov's legendary opening show of *Princess Turandot*. In 1925 her dresses were shown at the International Exhibition in Paris. In the 1920s and 1930s, Lamanova also made numerous costumes for films, such as *Aelita* (1924) and *Circus* (1934). Her unique method of design on the client rather than on paper, draping textiles around the model, became a widespread innovation. Lamanova's impact on Russian fashion design should not be underestimated, and it is no surprise that the first Russian fashion award established when fashion became again an occupation for designers and not artists was named after her.

After the Revolution, fashion became either an art form or else the production of dress turned into an industrial activity. Design was therefore taught at technical colleges and institutes, from which students graduated as graphic designers, designers, or constructors; or at theater and film schools, where students turned into costume designers (*khudozhniki*). The word *modelier* almost disappeared. This rigid division between art and dress has had a long-term effect on the status of fashion design in Russia today. One comment frequently made about the haute couture collections as well as prêt-à-porter is their unwearability. More and more fashion designers have trained under a new system and gained experience abroad, however, so that gradually Russian designers are producing wearable collections.

Even though the Soviet period witnessed fashion shows and exhibitions, the Soviet style always looked conventional and traditional, strict in form and lacking innovation. Yet what designers presented at these exhibitions never went into mass production. Most people actually wore clothes that were old-fashioned in shape and of poor quality; the exception was the party elite, who had access to better designs. Fur played a peculiar role in Soviet fashion: because of the climate in the Soviet Union, fur coats were no luxury, but a necessity. In the late 1990s a fur coat (not fashionable, not extravagant, but warm) could be purchased for as little as $100. The Soviet Union ran a House of Models (Dom modelei) in Moscow and Leningrad. Natalia Makarova directed the Moscow House of Models on Kuznetsky Most; the Leningrad House was located on Nevsky 21. These houses had designer collectives that prepared collections for shows, but few of the designs went into production. They were for models, not for the people, and fashion was a myth, not a commodity.

The sale of Western clothes through *fartsovshchiki* (illegal dealers, black market traders) was widespread in the Soviet era. Clothes were difficult to come by, and many items, such as Western jeans, the sheepskin coat (*dublenka*), or shoes, were best purchased in this way. And since many people had money, but there was little to buy in the shops, even such things were affordable to many. This explains also the astonishment of people when they encountered the exact inverse in market capitalism: the abundance of goods and the lack of money.

The German-based journal *Burda*, which offers sewing patterns, was a sought-after publication in the late 1980s. Many people could sew and fabric was available, but there was a shortage of designs and a lack of ideas. *Burda* therefore launched a Russian edition fairly early on in the perestroika era. People began to develop a desire to dress well, but they lacked experience in style. Having for decades worn *vatniki* (warm and formless padded jackets), donned *valenki* (felt boots) in winter to plow through masses of snow, and wrapped their heads in *platoks* (head scarves) or worn *ushankas* (fur hats with earflaps), clearly a sense of style did not come easily. In fact, the new sense of style went to the other extreme, in the sense that even today many Russian women wear evening dresses in the street and walk on high-heeled shoes, clearly not suited for everyday wear and tear. They went over to the extreme of dressing in style rather than in what is practical, wearable, suitable, and appropriate. This trend is also echoed in some designer collections.

If Lamanova maintained standards of fashion in the early Soviet era, then a major contribution to the reputation of Soviet dress was made by Viacheslav (Slava) Zaitsev. Zaitsev came from Ivanovo, where he

A model of Slava Zaitsev's collection. Zaitsev is strongly influenced by the Russian style for the accessories of his garments. (Photo by Valery Melnikov/Kommersant)

had trained as a craftsman in printing and painting fabric. In 1965 he joined the House of Models in Moscow and remained there for 13 years, heading the fashion design section. He was disturbed by the fact that the designs did not make their way into production, however, and so he left to found a workshop. In 1979 he also started teaching at the Technical Institute. In 1980 he designed the official uniforms for the Russian Olympic team, and in 1991 he re-designed the Russian police uniforms. When the Moscow Fashion House (Dom mody) on Prospekt Mira opened in 1982, Zaitsev headed it and became its director in 1988; in the same year he became a member of the Maison de Couture in Paris. During perestroika his garments were worn by the intelligentsia and the party elite alike. In 1992 he launched the perfume range Marusia. Zaitsev has worked for European prêt-à-porter (ready-to-wear, as opposed to haute couture) companies. In 1994 he started a competition for young designers under the flagship of the great Russian modelier Nadezhda Lamanova. Since 1994 there have been Weeks of Haute Couture in Moscow, and special Russian Fashion Weeks are held in spring every year. In the first Haute Couture Week (*Nedelia vysokoi mody*), Andrei Sharov and Valentin Yudashkin represented Russia along with Inga Filippova and Irina Selitskaya. In the second competition, Zaitsev won the award, the Golden Mannequin, and Irina Krutikova took the award a year later.

Zaitsev's collections include a variety of theme-based shows, which always indicate his perception of the present (Millennium of the Christianization of Russia, 1988; Russian Seasons in Paris, 1988; Agony of Perestroika, 1991; Recollections of the Future, 1996–1997). Zaitsev's collections are characterized by generous forms, and the decorative element is important. The garments incorporate a classical component while aiming at the business world with trouser suits. Zaitsev usually emphasizes the waistline in his creations, which are essentially modern in form, with a decor element either as accessory or in print that make the garment typically Russian. His black velvet coats were a fashion hit in the early 1990s. His evening dresses integrate Russian folk elements into the design. He also occasionally works for the theater, as for example when he designed the costumes for *The Cherry Orchard* at the Sovremennik, starring the great Alisa Freindlikh and Marina Neyolova.

Couturier Valentin Yudashkin walks along the podium during the final ceremony of the Ninth Haute Couture Week at the Rossiya Hotel in Moscow in 2002. (Photo by Valery Melnikov/Kommersant)

What Slava Zaitsev has done for fashion, Irina Krutikova has done for the design of fur coats, an essential part of Russian dress. She is often referred to as the "fur queen." Having studied in the Soviet era at the Berlin Art School, Krutikova returned to Russia to develop a new technique for the mass production of fur and innovations in the way in which fur was used. In 1967 her first collection was presented at a fashion festival, and it was the first time an author collection was exhibited from the Soviet Union. In 1992 Krutikova, who is a permanent guest of the Frankfurt fur fair, was awarded the State Prize.

Haute Couture

Valentin Yudashkin has his boutique on Kutuzov Prospekt 19. His boutique is not in central Moscow on the main arteries (Arbat, Nikitskaya, Tverskaya, Dmitrovka, Petrovka, Neglinnaya, and Miasnitskaya), which are all inside the Garden Ring (Sadovoe koltso), but across the bridge from the center. Kutuzov Prospekt used to house a number of embassy accommodation complexes and foreign television studios and was the main road to the districts where the party elite had their accommodation.

Yudashkin has been a member of the Syndicat of Haute Couture (Paris) since 1996. His workshop was founded in 1987, and his Fashion House (Dom mody) followed in 1991. Yudashkin tends to present his collections first in Paris, before they participate in the Haute Couture shows in Moscow. As he refrained from opening a boutique in France, he had to drop out of the Paris fashion shows in 2000 and has since demonstrated his collections at the Milan fashion week. Yudashkin's collections are usually centered around a historical theme that inspires the entire collection and signals very clearly style and form as well as color and material. Many of the creations of the early years were acquired by museums in Russia (the Anna Karenina collection was acquired by the Historical Museum) and abroad (among others, in the Louvre). The Fabergé collection (1991) was particularly noteworthy for the dresses made in the shape of Fabergé eggs. Often collections are inspired by contemporary events, such as the Fin de Siècle (1999), the Journey from Moscow to Petersburg (2003) to mark the 300th anniversary of St. Petersburg, or the collection 2001 Night, associating the year 2001 with tales of 1,001 nights and creating the eastern magic of the Arabian nights in richly embroidered dresses. The Moscow–St. Petersburg collection consisted of colorful garments in shiny material, with frills, applications, and embroidery, bordering on the carnivalesque. Corsets (2003–2004) was essentially a black-and-white collection closely following the body contours while leaving large slits or using frilly transparent ornaments at the sides or on the shoulders to break away from the strict lines. The summer collection was in olive and light blue, using parts of bustiers and corsets as decor. In the 2004 Deco collection, dress functions as decor, not garment. Yudashkin received the Golden Mannequin in 1997.

Yudashkin uses exclusive fabrics, including fur, and rich decorative embroidery. He draws on historical Russian themes and is inspired by folk traditions, visual art, and architecture alike for colors and forms. His forms are influenced by European fashion history and trends, however. His Russian bead embroidery is world-famous. He employs 250 staff and has showrooms in France and Italy as well as boutiques in Russia. He creates haute couture and prêt-à-porter collections as well as shoes, accessories, perfume, and jewelry. There is also a new, "young line" under the label VY, and he has begun designing china and silver for a "home line." Yudashkin designed the Olympic uniform for the Russian national team in 1994 and 1996 as well as the staff uniforms for the Ukraina Hotel, Moscow, and for Aeroflot Russian International Airlines. The use of fur in fashion design was boosted in Russia after several designers attended a workshop organized in 1999 by Saga Furs in their international design center in Copenhagen, showing ways of coloring and shaving fur.

Igor Chapurin is one of the most successful Moscow designers. In 1992 he took part in the International Festival of Young Designers and won the competition organized by Nina Ricci. He then turned to making evening dresses for models in beauty competitions, before presenting his first collection at the Metropol Hotel in 1995, called To Russia with Love. In the collection he used a special style of embroidery that combines beads, corals, and gold. The actress Tatiana Vasilieva was among the mannequins presenting the collection, which boosted its profile. In the following year Chapurin was invited to join the Association of Haute Couture (Paris). While working for the Italian fashion house Galitzine, he also presented his own collections and created outfits for television presenters and figures of the artistic world, including the actress Alla Demidova. Chapurin's collections show a compromise between a desire for commercial viability and recognition as well as artistic originality. Chapurin's style is quite European-oriented. He prefers taffeta, linen, and silk and keeps to rather cold hues of pink, green, bordeaux, and blue with a platinum and bronze effect. Chapurin innovated the role of computer design to print on fabric, introducing Russia to a new technology. He characteristically uses unusual materials or combines them in a new way; thus, he combined fur with chiffon and crepe georgette, or straw (1998). Chapurin has a boutique on Myasnitskaya Street and a second one in the Berlin House, a shopping mall on Petrovka Street and Kuznetsky Most. Chapurin twice received the Golden Mannequin, in 1998 and 2002. In his 2002 collection, the colors beige, gray, and black dominated, and feathery parts broke the otherwise straight and classical lines. Chapurin also used rings to string together part of the material.

Chapurin created the dresses for Oleg Menshikov's first independent production of *Woe from Wit* (Gore ot uma, 1999), consisting of almost exaggerated versions of historical costumes of the early nineteenth century. In Menshikov's second production, *The Kitchen* (Kukhnia), based on Maxim Kurochkin's contemporary play with echoes and references to the Nibelungen myth, Chapurin created modern outfits made from leather, wool, and metal that carried a medieval simplicity. His research for this production inspired his later collection, which drew on the wildness of the north and the history of the Vikings. Chapurin also worked on the costumes for the unfinished film *Vocal Parallels* (Vokal'nye parallaly, 1997) with the director and designer Rustam Khamdamov, whose sense of style has influenced many contemporary art-house filmmakers.

In his collection Frenchwoman in the East (2001), Chapurin combined European content with Eastern forms. This collection was largely in brown, beige, and gold tones that reflected the desert; materials included the lightweight fabric organza and suede, combined with local and regional material such as horsehair and muslin. His collection Les Folies Arlésiennes (2001–2002) clearly drew on van Gogh's paintings of the Arles period, bright in colors and using semitransparent materials as well as fur. The collection Serenade of the Sunshine Valley (2002–2003) was inspired by the Hollywood musical and told a tale of jazz music and neoromanticism on the catwalk, accompanied by the tunes of Glenn Miller. The models were all of earthy colors and used the forms and shapes of the fashion styles of the 1940s.

Tatiana Parfionova is an established designer from St. Petersburg. She opened her boutique on Nevsky 51 in 1995 after ten years of practicing as a designer. She produces two seasonal and two mid-season collections. After winning a competition of young designers in 1989 in London, she has designed clothes on a professional basis. More important for her career was the Safron collection (1995–1996) presented in Vilnius, where she received the Golden Button award from Paco Rabanne. In 1996 her collection, Marat's Mountain, was partly acquired by the Russian Museum, which exhibits a unique dress, consisting of 74 parts. In 1997 Parfionova participated in international fashion shows. In the collection Demonstration (1998), she used the red figures of Henri Matisse's paintings of *The Dancers* and embroidered them on fabric with silk thread. Her interest in visual art of the nineteenth and twentieth centuries is a distinctive feature of her pat-

Viktoria Andreyanova and models with her design of new Aeroflot uniforms. (Photo by Vasily Shaposhnikov/Kommersant)

terns for printing and embroidery. She also brought back the silk armband that used to be worn by office workers in the nineteenth century as a fashion accessory. For the 1999 Tourmaline collection, she chose the theme of multiethnicity, combining elements of national Buryat, Tatar, and Chuvash costume in a collection made of silk, cotton, and wool. All fabrics were hand-colored in red terracotta and gold colors and richly decorated with glass beads. The collection Colorist of 2002 used bright colors on silk, creating stark impressions with simple forms. In 2004 her collection was dominated by red, black, and white, as frills were applied to otherwise plain simple forms.

Parfionova has a clearly modern style that shows no nostalgia for the heritage of the city of St. Petersburg, where she works. She makes elegant fashion with a slight hint of hooliganism, eccentricity, the extraordinary. Her collections are made to be worn rather than shown, and many show business figures from Moscow and Petersburg wear garments by Parfionova. She also designed the uniforms for the staff at the Hotel Europe (1998) and the Moscow Kempinski Balchug (1999), where a contemporary, but classical, style was required. Moreover, she designed the costumes for Igor Maslennikov's film *The Winter Cherry* (Zimniaia vishnia) and for Vladimir Bortko's *The Circus Burnt and All the Clowns Have Left* (Tsirk sgorel, a vse klouny razbezhalis'), both made in the late 1990s. She received the Golden Mannequin in 1999.

Viktoria Andreyanova has her boutique on Petrovka 19, where she sells her label

VA. Her early collections were inspired by her knowledge of South Asian fabrics and her visit to Scottish tweed factories, as well as a seminar attended at Saga Furs Scandinavia. Since 2001 she has also made prêt-à-porter collections, and in 2002 she designed the uniforms for the Ararat Hyatt Hotel staff. She debuted as a costume designer in her brother-in-law Alexander Strizhenov's film *Fall Up* (Upast' vverkh, 2001); her younger sister Katia Strizhenova is an actress. Andreyanova also worked on several commercial theater productions and dresses the ORT presenter Andrei Malakhov; the actor Georgi Taratorkin and the clip-maker Yuri Grymov are also among her customers. She was awarded the Golden Mannequin in 2000 and 2001.

Andreyanova's collections are entirely wearable. In the collection The Traveling Aristocrat (1997), she alluded to forms and decor of the 1920s aristocracy in a range of garments made from gray tweed material with traditional fur collars. Snow Woman (1998) was held in beige, white, and black and underlined feminine and flowing forms. Happy End (1999) again remained in black, gray, and white while following the 1950s style with short and plain dress and longer coats as well as tulip-shaped skirts or garments with a diagonal hem line. Careful, a Woman! (2000) was a colorful collection, using straight geometrical forms to create an asymmetry that did not underline feminine forms at all. Census (2002), which reminded of the census that took place in the same year, used printed textiles and focused largely on the black-and-white color range. Her collection South Pole (2004) again used bright colors, such as yellow, orange, and green, combined with flower applications and patterned fabrics.

Fashion Design

Although Yudashkin, Chapurin, and Parfionova are the best-known Russian designers, both at home and in the West, there are a number of other designers who have made an impact on fashion in a more general way.

Andrei Sharov is a painter and theater designer who is probably best known for the costumes he created for the productions of Andrei Zhitinkin, Oleg Fomin, and Sergei Vinogradov. Through the designs in their shows, which were intended for a large audience and created on a commercial or semicommercial basis and involving star actors, Sharov gained a reputation and won the prestigious Seagull (Chaika) award for his costumes for *My Dear Friend* (Milyi drug, 1997). He made the dresses for *The Adventures of Felix Krull*, staged by Zhitinkin at the Tabakov Studio and starring Sergei Bezrukov, as well as Alexander Domogarov in Zhitinkin's *Nijinsky* (1998) and *The Portrait of Dorian Gray* (2000). Sharov, who never graduated from his course at the Moscow Technical Institute, made a career in the fashion world (a boutique in the Smolensky Passage) and now teaches at Slava Zaitsev's school. Sharov created his style with the use of clocks and safety pins.

In his first fashion show Tack Tick (1994), he decorated his dresses lavishly with clocks and safety pins. The collection Queen of Waste (1994) used parts of windows, sugar spoons, metal rings, and door handles for decorations, and the collection Not Everything's That Easy simply used buttons. Sharov used leather and reptile skin, elements of armor and amber on black and shiny materials as well as fabrics of bright primary colors. Sharov's trademark, however, remains the safety pin. His more wearable collection, Taisia (1996), consisted of puffed skirts in aniline colors, complemented with shoes with extra long noses. Great and Small Human Weaknesses (1997) used metal elements such as knives and forks to form the shape or construction of the dress. This Is All for You (1999) was made from material used in Russian crafts, such as birch and Orenburg lace. Zoo-room used animal patterns and such fabrics as ostrich skin and antelope leather. From 2001 on, his collections became more industrial, especially with the launch of Bureau 365, a prêt-à-porter collection made largely from linen, denim, silk, and cotton and using bright colors and simple forms. The collection Bonnie and Colt (2002) was inspired by the Hollywood of the 1940s, combining leather and fur (polar fox and mink) to create the chic of the Chicago-gangster style with its romantic view of the criminal world.

Andrei Bartenev is a fashion designer and performance artist. His performances and displays demonstrate eccentric and extravagant costumes of a challenging and provocative nature that inspire the observer to think about dress. His displays often accompany large public events, such as theater or film festivals. He also created the costumes for the Novosibirsk theater production of Witold Gombrowicz's *Ivonna, Princess of Burgundy* (1996), staged by Oleg Rybkin. His costumes have been exhibited in the Tretiakov Gallery (1993) and the Pushkin Museum (1997) as well as the Victoria and Albert Museum, London (1996–1997). Natasha Naftaliyeva founded a theater of fashion (1989) and has been engaged in her own fashion house since 1992. She creates mainly evening and wedding dresses made predominantly from leather.

Katia Leonovich is a designer who paints her creations; she is based in Italy.

Razu Mikhina (Daria Razumikhina) presented her collection Paradigm in 1999. Having studied in London, she works for boutiques, including Liberty, as well as the Russian fashion chain Podium. She uses Russian materials, such as lace and folk ribbons, and also purchases her silk from the Russian cloth factory Krasnaya Roza. Her 2001 collection Dotted Line combined elements of world religion. Since 2001, her collections have clearly tended toward a country-style look, with No. 5 containing stripes as found in Norwegian sweaters. She uses linen stripes to create patterns, and as the dresses and skirts become longer, there are frills and laces of the Laura Ashley style. Resume (2003) integrated Russian folk patterns into forms of country style in the European manner.

Julia Dalakian has run her own workshop and the label D-Julia since 1996. Her 2000 collection consisted of loose garments, often transparent fabrics. Her 2001 collection All You Need Is Love and Me Again presented loose trouser suits and transparent dresses, blouses with large décolletés, made from materials in black, white, and beige-yellow. In 2004 Dalakian used strings to create a blouse, rings to hold the material together, combined with slit skirts and hot pants. Her collections have a sexy, hippie touch while remaining sophisticated in the choice of fabric and the color schemes.

Irina Selitskaya is a designer who specializes in shoes and works with leather to create accessories. The former art director of the shoe department of the Model House in Moscow founded her own company and a design school after the collapse of the Soviet Union. Her shoe collections are used by Yudashkin and Sharov in their fashion shows. In 1994 she used fish skin for the first time, with a new patent discovered to produce this fabric. Selitskaya also designs fashion.

Liudmila Dobrokhotova from Tula began her career in a knitwear factory. She then created designer collections, before moving from machine knitting to hand knitting and setting up her own company. Although she has international contracts, she remains based in Tula. Dobrokhotova's knitted dress with themes and motifs of Russian life, decorated with bells (1999), received special attention, and in the same year she won the special prize in the Lamanova competition for her collection Mirrorland. She uses thin ribbons of fur or strips of material (silk, linen, chiffon) for her knitting. Her collection Reportage (2001) was made from chiffon strips, sewn together or providing the thread for knitwear in silk, wool, and fur while remaining in white and pale colors.

VASSA is a company with a designer's concept. Vassa studied in Moscow and was sent to Virginia on an exchange program in 1990, before moving to New York, where she worked for Fashion Source International for several years while also studying merchandising. Her first collection was presented in New York in 1996, and it was purchased by Manhattan boutiques. In 1997 Vassa presented her collection in Moscow. After her following collection was shown in the Ministry of Foreign Affairs, she set up the Vassa company and opened Russian branches with Viacheslav Granovsky. Granovsky had worked at Uzbekfilm as a costume designer, before working for Neiman Marcus in the United

States and returning to Russia in 1994. Vassa is one of the most widely available designer brands, sold in more than half a dozen stores in Moscow in a high-tech interior, at affordable prices.

VQ (Vladimir Perepelkin) worked in the textile industry in Europe and North America before setting up business in Moscow. He has worked for the Moscow Youth Theater, creating historical costumes for their performances, as well as working with the Bolshoi, the Helicon Opera, and the New Opera. He uses fur, leather, and fabric. Although his collections of 2001 and 2002 were based on a play with bright and intense colors, his collection Farces (2002) was essentially black, classical in style but using the magic of Eastern forms. Both Vassa and VQ, with their experience of Western markets, create highly wearable and marketable collections. Down the scale from their collections remains the cheap and reasonably fashionable knitwear of Vladimir Zubtsev's Paninter.

Natalia Drigant studied in France and founded her own fashion house with her father, an economist. She offers haute couture, prêt-à-porter, and a young line. Her collections usually reveal the naked body under loose warps and tulle, and longer dresses tend to follow a straight bodyline. She almost seems to bare women's lingerie and corsages to semicover them through her creations. Nina and Donis (Nina Neretina and Donis Pupis) create collections that have an effect of deliberate carelessness, using ribbons. The collection of black dresses with an application of poppies created a storm in the press, not because of the costume but because they sent invitations with poppy seeds, and one paper sent this for an anthrax test. Inga Filippova worked with Slava Zaitsev on the knitwear collection. She also works on graphic design for greeting cards and book design and leads a fashion column in the newspaper *Moskovskaya Pravda*. In 1996 she established her own fashion label. Yelena Makashova set up a label of Shirpotreb (Mass Production), which sells more than 15,000 garments per year. Tatiana Beliakovskaya has worked at Mosfilm on costume design but creates black evening dresses under her own label. Alisa Tolkacheva is a designer and image maker who works for show business people such as Angelica Varum and Tatiana Bulanova. The Kiev-born graphic designer launched her own collections: Wild Swans (2001) used coarse silk and sand grass colors. Irina Zima creates collections made from old materials and dresses. In her 2001 collection she was inspired by Portobello Road in her style of the 1950s and 1960s. In 2002 she used elements of the nineteenth century.

Models   Even if we may want to associate modeling with the Western markets, there were fashion models in the Soviet Union. Indeed, this was a highly prestigious job, as it involved international travel. Film-maker Nikita Mikhalkov's second wife, Tatiana, worked as a model before their marriage, and she remains associated with the fashion world to the present day. The Soviet Union knew no proper cover girls or "faces" for perfume, cosmetic, or fashion labels, however. In 1989, as the consumer industry began to emerge in Russia, Tatiana Koltseva founded the Red Star Model Agency, which later represented Elite Models in the CIS. In 1994 the agency started to prepare models for the Elite Model Look competition, and in the same year Natalia Semanova took first place. She made a ca-

reer as a model, appearing on numerous editions of glossy journals and advertising Escada, Armani, and Yves Saint Laurent. In the following year Irina Bondarenko won second place in the Elite Model Look. In 1996 Diana Kovalchuk gained the first prize. She subsequently adorned international editions of the glossy fashion magazines. The agency represents the highest-rated models, who appear on the covers of Russian and international editions of the glossy magazines and make international careers. They include Liudmila Isayeva, the wife of the hockey player Vladimir Malakhov and model for Guerlain and Escada; and the St. Petersburger Olga Pantiushenkova, who has featured on *Vogue*, *Elle*, *Marie-Claire*, and *L'Officiel* and represented Dior and Shiseido; she is also the "face" of Cacharel's Eden perfume. Red Star collaborated with the Moscow Haute Couture weeks.

Another agency is Modus VivendiS, established in 1992 and headed by Elena Ermolaeva. The agency works with Western clients and provides models for fashion shows. Their models appear more in Russian-language editions of glossy journals, however, such as *XXL*, *Ona/She*, *Yes*, *Oops*, *Krestianka*. Although Modus VivendiS runs a school for models as well, the main "visagiste" (makeup stylist) is Lev Novikov, who has worked with Igor Chapurin and other designers.

Fashion is still very much an art and design business in Russia, rather than an exercise that leads to the creation of clothes for the wider population. It is often still cheaper to buy foreign rather than Russian labels. There is nothing but Pan-inter for mass consumption, whereas Russian designers have worked on haute couture, and only a few have created lines for the consumer. Only the VASSA collection is really affordable at around $100 per item. The gap is with the mass market, where people still purchase inferior-quality garments at markets while beginning to realize that quality clothes last longer.

Consumer Future

The development of consumer culture has changed Russian culture most profoundly. Although it may have been possible to talk about "popular" culture in the Soviet era with reference to those things that were in demand but unavailable or that were not nurtured by Soviet ideology, in the last decade of the twentieth century Russians were exposed to the full range of consumer culture and gradually formed a taste for things they like, want, and desire. Russian culture stood on its head, turning the underground into popular entertainment; trashing Soviet forms of culture through parody, mockery, and anecdotes; and creating new cultural values. These are no longer aimed at raising the level of educatedness but at entertaining, relaxing, and amusing.

A to Z

Andreyanova, Viktoria: Designer (label VA) with her own boutique on Petrovka 19. In 1984 she graduated from the theater school MTXTU (Moscow Technical Artistic-Theatrical Institute, Moskovskii tekhnicheskii khudozhestvenno-teatral'nyi institut), doing her diploma work for a show at the Malyi Theater. In 1989 graduated from the textile academy. Extensive stays in Singapore and Indonesia during 1991. In 1992 she founded the firm Victoria A. Her collections have included Traveling Aristocrat (1997), Snow Woman (Snezhnaia baba, 1998), Happy End (1999), and Careful, a Woman (2000). In 2002 she designed the uniforms for the Ararat Hyatt staff. [www.niv.ru]

Bekmambetov, Timur: b. 1961 in Kazakhstan. Studied art and design and graduated from the Tashkent College for Theater Design (1987). Worked as designer with Tashkent's Ilkhom Theater. Moved to Moscow, where he worked as film director and clip-maker. He directed, with Gennadi Kayumov, the film *Peschawar Waltz* (Peshavarskii val'ts, 1994) about the Afghan war. He made advertisements, among others for Bank Imperial and Alfa Bank. [www.bazelevs.ru] He is the general director of Imperial Film and the film studio Tabbak. In 2000 he made the film *The Arena* (Gladiatriksy). In 2004 he made *Night Watch*, the first Russian blockbuster to reach a box office (more than $12 million in 18 days) that was higher than that of U.S. films. [www.dozorfilm.ru]

Chapurin, Igor: b. 1968. Fashion designer. Boutiques on Miasnitskaya Street (1999) and in Berlin House (2002). Graduated from Vitebsk Technical School and in 1991 from the Vitebsk Technical Institute. In 1992 won competition of young designers in Paris. In 1995 presented his first collection at the Metropol Hotel: To Russia with Love. Since 1996 member of the Association of Haute Couture, Paris. Collections: Chapurin 96, Chapurin 97. From 1996 to 1998 designed for Galitzine (Italy). Costumes for theater productions in Moscow. Since 1999, also jewelry. Collections:

Frenchwoman in the East (2001); Les Folies Arlésiennes (2001–2002); Future through the Present (2003); Serenade of the Sunshine Valley (2003). [www.niv.ru]

Easter (*paskha*): Easter is the main celebration of the Orthodox church. The date of the holiday moves according to the moon calendar and is calculated on the basis of the Julian (not the Gregorian) calendar. Therefore orthodox Easter does not normally coincide with Christian Easter. Easter Dates: 1 May 2005, 23 April 2006, 8 April 2007, 27 April 2008, 19 April 2009, 4 April 2010. The Easter celebrations are preceded by the Great Fast, when people should abstain from meat and dairy products. The resurrection of Christ is celebrated at church with a night service, leading the community round the church and greeting with the words: "Christ has risen."—"He has truly risen." Since Easter is the most important and brightest holiday, the Easter service is one of the most beautiful church services in orthodoxy, when almost all candles and lights in churches are lit. The Sunday is marked with coloured Easter eggs; the *kulich*, a plain cake with raisins; and the *paskha*, a cheesecake with raisins.

Lamanova, Nadezhda (1861–1941): Born in Nizhny Novgorod, she opened her first workshop in 1885 in Moscow. By 1901 she worked for the tsar. In 1919 she began teaching at VKHUTEMAS (Vysshie gosudarstvennye khudozhestvenno-tekhnicheskie masterskie, Higher Artistic-technical Workshops). She married the actor Yuri Kayurov, who later returned to his original career as lawyer. In 1921 she joined the Vakhtangov Theater as costume designer.

In 1925 her models participated in the International Exhibition in Paris. Lamanova made numerous film costumes. She died as the theater was evacuated from Moscow during the war, suffering a heart attack as she was seated on a bench in front of the Bolshoi Theater.

MMM: Pyramid scheme of the early 1990s run by Sergei Mavrodi. The scheme collapsed, leaving many Russians without their pay-out in the early days of free enterprise. The advertising campaign by Bakhyt Kilibayev (b. 1958, scriptwriter for Rashid Nugmanov's glasnost film *The Needle*, 1988) for MMM was one of the first original and most successful for a Russian product.

Orthodoxy: Christian faith is represented in several religions: the Catholic, the Protestant, and the Orthodox Church are three of the main Christian religions. Orthodox faith arrived in Russia in 988, which is the year of the "Christianization of Rus." Russia subsequently had to defend its territory and its faith against "barbarian" invasions by the Mongols and Tatars. Orthodox Christians believe in the protective power of icons as images that, like the words of the Bible, create a direct link with God. The veneration of icons in the orthodox tradition contributed to the split between the Western churches (Rome) and the Eastern church (Constantinople). The Orthodox Church separated from the Old Believers (*staroobriadtsy*), who refrained from modernization. In orthodoxy the church is a space where man comes close to God, and His presence suggests the rich decoration of the church and the abundance of candle light to celebrate this closeness. Certain strands of Orthodox thought also believe in the need for man to lead a humble and meek life, even to renounce possession, in order to be admitted to heaven after death. This is evident in the heroes of Dostoevsky's novels and also in the figure of the *yurodovy*, the fool-in-God.

Parfionova, Tatiana: b. 1956. Fashion designer, St. Petersburg. Boutique on Nevsky 51. Studied painting at Serov school and then graduated from Moscow Technical Institute; 1989 competition of young designers, London; 1995–1996 Safron presented in Vilnius; Golden Button from Paco Rabanne. Collections: Marat's Mountain (1996); Lela, Lialia, Liusia (1996); Guards (1997); White Pavilion (1997); A Chinese in the Courtyard (1997); Stepanida (1998); Demonstration (1998); Urban Details (1999); Female Usurper (1999); Another (1999); Tourmaline (1999); Rose and Rose (2001); Mushka (2001); Veratrek (2002), Colorist (2002). She designed the uniform for staff at the Kempinski Balchug (1999) and Hotel Europe (1998). [www.niv.ru]

Mikhina Razu (Daria Razumikhina): Born in Moscow, Daria Razumikhina studied at the Moscow State University and received a master's degree before studying at St. Martin's College, London from 1995 to 1999. In 1999 she presented her first collection of prêt-à-porter, and in 2001 she participated in the Haute Couture Weeks in Moscow. She works for boutiques such as Liberty (UK) and Podium (Moscow). [www.niv.ru]

Red Star: This model agency was founded by Tatiana Koltseva in 1989 and represents Elite Models in the CIS. Since 1994 the agency has run the Elite Model Look, which has produced numerous cover girls for international editions of glossy journals and for Western and Russian fashion and style. [www.redstarsmodels.ru]

Sharov, Andrei: b. 1966. Fashion designer, painter, theater designer. Boutique in Smolensk Passage opened in 2001. Sharov studied at MTI (Moscow Technical Institute) without receiving a diploma. He has worked extensively in the theater with Andrei Zhitinkin, Oleg Fomin, and Sergei Vinogradov. In 1994 he presented his first collection, Tack Tick (dresses with clocks and safety pins). The collections Queen of Waste (1994) and Not Everything's That Easy (1994) followed. In 1995 the collection Joke (Shutka) received third place in the Lamanova competition. Other collections have included Taisia (1996), Great and Small Human Weaknesses (1997), This Is All for You (1999), Zoo-room (2001), Spring Challenge (2001), Leather Summer (2002), Bonnie and Colt (2002), Too Second (2002), and Autumn Challenge (2003). In 2002 he launched the prêt-à-porter label Bureau 365. [www.niv.ru]

VASSA: Fashion label. Vassa studied at the MTI (Moscow Technical Institute) and in 1990 went to Virginia on an exchange program. Then she moved to New York, where for three years she worked for Fashion Source and for Anne Klein, Calvin Klein, and Forecast America. She also worked with Federated, Inc. In 1996 she presented her first collection in Soho in New York City, and the collection was subsequently sold in Manhattan boutiques. In 1997 she presented a collection in Moscow and soon thereafter opened a Russian branch. In 1999 the Vassa Company was set up, and by 2000 there were five shops in Moscow with a high-tech interior design and including a store in GUM. [www.vassatrend.ru]

Yudashkin, Valentin: b. 1963. Boutique on Kutuzovsky 19. Since 1996 member of the Syndicate of Haute Couture, Paris. Founded his own workshop in 1987 and opened his fashion house in 1991. Collections: Early Rus (1987); Peter's Ball (1988); Fabergé (1991); Music (1992); Nature Morte (1993); Frescoes (1994); Catherine the Great (1994); Ballet (1995); Birds of Paradise (1996); Silent Cinema (1996–1997); Russian Moderne (1998); Anna Karenina (1998–1999); Fin de Siècle (1999); Show Me Love (1999–2000); Impressionists (2000); Byzantine (2000–2001); Night (2001); Journey from Moscow to Petersburg (2003); Corsets (2003–2004); Deco (2004). Design of Olympic uniform (1994 and 1996). Design of staff uniforms for the Ukraina Hotel, Moscow, and for Aeroflot International fleet. Young Collection VY.

Zaitsev, Viacheslav (Slava): b. 1938 in Ivanovo. He trained as a craftsman in printing and painting fabric. In 1965 he joined the House of Models in Moscow and remained there for 13 years, heading the fashion design section. He left in 1978 to set up his own fashion label. In 1979 he also started teaching at the Technical Institute. In 1980 he designed the official uniforms for the Russian Olympic team, and in 1991 he redesigned the Russian police uniforms. In 1982 the Moscow Fashion House opened on Prospekt Mira, headed by Zaitsev, who became its director in 1988. In 1988 he became a member of the Maison de Couture in Paris. In 1992 he launched the perfume range Marusia. Zaitsev remains an important designer in contemporary Moscow. [www.zaitsev.ru]

Bibliography

Azhgikhna, Nadezhda. "Russian Club Life." *Studies in Twentieth Century Literature* 24, no. 1 (Winter 2000): 169–191.

Borenstein, Eliot. "About That: Deploying and Deploring Sex in Postsoviet Russia." *Studies in Twentieth Century Literature* 24, no. 1 (Winter 2000): 51–83

———. "Public Offerings: MMM and the Market of Melodrama." In *Consuming Russia. Popular Culture, Sex and Society since Gorbachev*, ed. by Adele Barker, 49–75. Durham, NC: Duke University Press,1999.

Condee, Nancy, and Vladimir Padunov. "The ABC of Russian Consumer Culture." In *Soviet Hieroglyphics: Visual Culture in Late Twentieth-Century Russia*, ed. by Nancy Condee, 130–172. Bloomington and Indianapolis: Indiana University Press and BFI, 1995.

Goscilo, Helena. "Stimulating Chic: The Aestheticization of Post-Soviet Russia." In *Essays in the Art and Theory of Translation*, ed. by Leonard Grenoble and John Kopper, 35–57. New York: Edwin Mellen Press, 1997.

Lane, Christel. *The Rites of Rulers*. Cambridge: Cambridge University Press, 1981.

Ledeneva, Alena. *Russia's Economy of Favours: Blat, Networking and Informal Exchange*. Cambridge: Cambridge University Press, 1998.

Lovell, Stephen. *Summerfolk: A History of the Dacha 1710–2000*. Ithaca, NY: Cornell University Press, 2003.

Matizen, Viktor. (In Russian). "Steb kak fenomen kultury" [Styob as a cultural phenomenon] *Iskusstvo kino* 9 (1993): 59–62.

Ryazanova-Clarke, Lara. "Advertising on Russian Television: Cross Cultural Battle or Cross-cultural Communication?" *Slavic Almanac* 5, no 7/8 (1999): 219–240.

———. "Elements of Persuasion in the Language of Russian Television Advertising." in *Language and Society in Post-Communist Europe*, ed. by John Dunn, 109–134. Basingstoke: Macmillan, 1999.

Salnikova, Ekaterina. "Entdeckung eines neuen Lebens, Fruehe Frensehwerbung in

Russland." in *Kommerz, Kunst, Unterhaltung: Die neue Popularkultur in Zentral- und Osteuropa*, ed. by Ivo Bock, Wolfgang Schlott, and Hartmute Trepper, 301–317. Bremen: Edition Temmen, 2002.

Schultze, Sydney. *Culture and Customs of Russia*. Westport, CT: Greenwood Press, 2000.

Sterling, Bruce. "Art and Corruption." *Wired*, January 1998, pp. 119–140.

Yurchak, Alexei. "Gagarin and the Rave Kids: Transforming Power, Identity and Aesthetics in Post-Soviet Night Life." In *Consuming Russia: Popular Culture, Sex and Society since Gorbachev*, ed. by Adele Barker, 76–109. Durham, NC: Duke University Press, 1999.

Glossary

General

babushka: grandmother.

banya: steam house, sauna.

chastushka: (mocking) ditty, usually in four lines.

chernukha: tendency to portray reality in dark and negative colors (literally, making black).

dacha: summerhouse, usually built from wood.

DK (Dom kultury): House of Culture, usually a stage and auditorium for cultural events that belonged to factories, institutes, and other organizations.

estrada: literally, "raised platform" or stage: popular entertainment, synonymous with "show business" in the Western world.

intelligentsia: a social class that represented the "think tank" of the Communist regime, composed of thinkers, writers, and scientists.

kolkhoz: collective farm.

komsomol: Communist Party's youth organization.

lubok: woodcut or print, usually portraying in a satirical manner a social or historical event and commenting with a slogan or a ditty on the scene.

magnitizdat: "publishing on tape," that is, the (illegal) distribution of music copied from tape to tape.

matrioshka: Russian nesting doll.

propiska: "residence permit." Every Russian (and formerly every Soviet) citizen has his residence registered in his passport. A Moscow "propiska" entitles one to live and work in the city; these permissions are difficult to obtain for migrants from the provinces.

stilyaga: a style hunter. The term was used in the 1950s and 1960s to describe the young people who were paying attention to fashion (tight trousers, large ties, hairstyle).

styob: parodic and satirical tone.

Writers' Union: association, trade union, for writers. Also Composers' Union, Filmmakers' Union. In the Soviet period, union membership was required for an artist to practice his art as a profession (that is, for a writer not to have another job).

History

Bolshevik: member of the Bolshevik Party that led the October Revolution in 1977. Lenin was the head of this faction.

Purges (chistki): Stalin's operation in the 1930s of cleansing the party apparatus and society from "enemies of the people," who were arrested and executed.

Socialist Realism: a concept imposed on the arts in 1932 that required artists to express themselves in a "realistic" way that showed the path of the Soviet Union toward a bright, Communist future.

Politics

Soviet Period:
CC: Central Committee (of the Communist Party) (Tsentralny komitet, TsK).
CPSU: Communist Party of the Soviet Union (Kommunisticheskaya Partiya Sovetskogo Soyuza).
RSFSR: Russian Soviet Federal Socialist Republic, main constituent republic of the Soviet Union (USSR) (Rossiiskaya Sovetskaya Federalnaya Sotsialisticheskaya Respublika).

Soviet Union: constituent republics of Belarus, Ukraine, Moldova, Latvia, Lithuania, Estonia, Kazakhstan, Kyrgyzstan, Uzbekistan, Tadzhikistan, Turkmenistan, Armenia, Georgia, Azerbaijan.

CIS = Commonwealth of Independent States (SNG: Soiuz nezavisimykh gosudarstv): formed in December 1991 as an association of the former Soviet republics, except for the three Baltic republics—Latvia, Lithuania, and Estonia.

Soviet System:

Party	State
General Secretary	Chairman of Council of Ministers
Politburo	Council of Ministers
Central Committee	USSR Ministries
Republics' Party Ministries	Republics' Committee
Regional (Oblast) Party	Regional Administration
City Party Organization	City Administration (Mossovet, Lensovet)

Russian Period:
CPRF (KPRF): Communist Party of the Russian Federation (Gennadi Ziuganov).
LDPR: Liberal Democratic Party of Russia (Vladimir Zhirinovsky).
SPS: Soyuz pravykh sil (Union of Right Forces) (Sergei Kirienko, Boris Nemtsov, Irina Khakamada, Anatoli Chubais).
Yabloko (Grigori Yavlinsky, Yuri Boldyrev, Vladimir Lukin).

Center party formations supporting the prime minister/government in different elections:

- Vybor Rossii (Russia's Choice): (pro-Yeltsin) 1993
- NDR or Nash Dom–Rossiya (Our House–Russia): (Viktor Chernomyrdin) 1996
- OVR or Otechestvo–vsia Rossiya (All Russia, the Fatherland): (Yuri Luzhkov, Yevgeni Primakov) 1999
- Edintsvo (Unity): (Igor Shoigu, pro-Putin) 1999
- Edinaya Rossiya (United Russia): 2003

Constitution 1993:
- President appoints prime minister (PM), who appoints ministers (cabinet).
- 450 Duma deputies are elected by the electorate every four years.
- Duma approves PM.
- Electorate directly votes for president (every four years, maximum two terms).
- President can disband parliament and dismiss the cabinet.

Duma (Parliament): Elections for the Duma are normally held every four years; however, after the first elections in 1993 (which coincided with a vote for a new constitution) the next elections were held after two years to allow for a proper transition to a democratic election system and the formation of political parties.

Duma Election, 12 December 1993 (55 percent participation):

LDPR 23 percent; Vybor Rossii 15.5 percent; CPRF 12.5 percent; Zhenshchiny Rossii (Women's Party) 8 percent; Agrarnaya Partiya (Agrarian Party) 8 percent; Yabloko 8 percent; Edinstvo i soglasie (Union and Accord) 7 percent; Demokraticheskaya Partiya 5.5 percent

Duma Election, 17 December 1995 (65 percent participation):

CPRF 22 percent; LDPR 11 percent; NDR 10 percent; Yabloko 7 percent

Duma Election, 19 December 1999 (62 percent participation):

CPRF 24 percent; Edinstvo (Medved) 23 percent; OVR 13 percent; SPS 8.5 percent; LDPR 6 percent; Yabloko 6 percent

Duma Election, 7 December 2003 (56 percent participation):

Edinaya Rossiya 37.5 percent; CPRF 12.5 percent; LDPR 11.5 percent; Rodina 9 percent. The parties Yabloko and SPS did not reach the required 5 percent necessary for representation in parliament (Yabloko 4.3 percent; mSPS 4 percent).

Index

ABBA (Swedish band), 208
Abdrashitov, Vadim, 91
Abdulov, Alexander, 151, 172
Abramovich, Roman, 44, 63
Abuladze, Tengiz, 78, 87
Acrobatics, 183, 186–188, 191
Adasinsky, Anton, 144, 146, 188
The Adventures of Felix Krull (Mann), 145
Advertising, 11, 27, 41, 47, 56, 296–330
    bank, 325–329
    and cultural misunderstanding, 318–319
    product, 317–325
    and product prices, 317, 318, 319, 325, 330
    products banned on television, 324
    social, 329–330
    television, 317
    and Western companies, 317–319, 320, 324, 325, 337
Afghan war (1986–1988), 7, 30, 212
Afisha (*Billboard*, entertainment guide), 57, 134
Africa. *See* Bugayev, Sergei
Agatha Christie (rock band), 221–222
Agency of Lonely Hearts (television game show), 35
Agent of National Security (television serial), 306, 308–309
Agitprop, Department of, 9
Agutin, Leonid, 242, 255–256
Aguzarova, Zhanna (see also Ivana Anders), 214, 215(photo), 218, 256
AIDS, 340
AiF (newspaper). *See Argumenty i Fakty*
Ainutdinov, Sergei, 101
Aitmatov, Chingiz, 293, 299
Akakievich, Akaki, 36
Akinshina, Oxana, 97
Aksyonov, Alexander, 18, 23
Akunin, Boris (real name Grigori Chkhartishvili), 294, 295, 296, 301, 305, 309–310
Aldashin, Mikhail, 101
Alechenko, Diana, 187
Alekhin, Alexander, 291–292
Alexander Garden, 115
Alexander II (czar), 184
Alexandrov, Boris, 8

Alexandrov, Grigori, 3, 76
Alexeyeva, Marina, 301–303
Alibasov, Bari, 230
Alisa, 224–225
Alive Forever (Rozov play), 5
Allegrova, Irina, 224–225, 238, 256
All-Russian Circus Festival, 191
All-Russian State Institute for Cinematography
    (VGIK), 215
All-Russian Television and Radio Broadcasting
    Company. *See* VGTRK
All-Russian Theater Society (VTO), 138–139
Alsou (Alsu Safina), 235, 256
Amalrik, Leonid, 100
American Center, 74
Amirkhanova, Shakhri, 57
Anders, Ivana (see also Zhanna Aguzarova), 218
Andrei (magazine), 60, 340
Andreyanova, Victoria, 362–363, 367
Andreyev, Igor, 279
Andreyev, Nikolai, 112, 113
Andreyeva, Nina, 53
Animation. *See under* Film
Anthropology (television program), 37
Anti-Booker Prize, 55, 156, 296, 310
Antikiller (film), 71, 72(photo), 98, 298
Antikiller 2 (film), 98
Apartment bombing (Moscow 1999), 29, 30–31
Apartment Question (program), 36
Apina, Alena, 243, 256
APN (Agence Press Novosti) news agency. *See*
    RIA Novosti/RIA Vesti
Apocryph (television program), 37
Aquarium (rock band). *See* Grebenshchikov,
    Boris
Architecture, 105, 112–128, 162, 270
Arefiev, Igor, 191
Argumenty i fakty (*Arguments and Facts*,
    weekly paper), 46, 52, 56, 57, 83–64
Ariupin, Dmitri, 188
Ariya (heavy metal band), 218
Arsenal (jazz band), 207–208
Art, 104–105, 201, 344
    crafts, 105, 107, 108–112, 344
    movements, 105–108
    underground, 7
    See also Modern art; Sculpture; Sots-art
Artistic café (Moscow), 4
Artists, 2, 105–112, 113
    See also Fashion designers

Arzhak, Nikolai (pseudonym), 7
Asatiani, Malkhez, 275
Ashvetia, Mikhail, 275
Askoldov, Alexander, 9
ASSA (film), 214, 215, 224
Astafiev, Viktor, 293, 299
Astrakhan, Dmitri, 79, 128
Asya's Happiness (film), 8–9
Atamanov, Lev, 100
Athletics, 280–281
Auktyon (post-punk band), 224
Autoradio, 48, 49
Avrora (*Aurora*, journal), 62
Avtograf (art-rock group), 217–218
Azazel (also: *The Winter Queen*, Akunin), 301

Babadzhanyan, Ario, 237
Babitsky, Andrei, 30, 31(photo), 32
Babkina, Nadezhda, 237
Bakin, Dmitri, 296
Baklanov, Grigori, 63
Balabanov, Alexei, 79, 93–94, 95, 96, 97, 128–129
Ballad of a Soldier (film), 5
Ballet, 8, 12, 57, 134, 156
Baltser, Grigori, 111
Baltser, Ruslan, 75, 79, 82
Baluyev, Alexander, 98
Banner (journal), 62
Baranovsky, G., 121
The Barber of Siberia (film), 91–93
Bard movement, 4, 199, 202–207, 212
Bardin, Garri, 101, 129
Barnet, Boris, 2
Bartenev, Andrei, 364
Barto, Agniya, 162
Basayev, Shamil (Chechen leader), 43
Basharov, Marat, 172
Bashlachev, Alexander, 312–324
Basic Instinct (television program), 38
Basketball, 267, 277
The Battleship Potyomkin (film), 2, 76
BBC (British Broadcasting Corporation), 47
The Bear's Wedding (film), 2
Beatniki, 200
Bed and Sofa (film), 2
Beer, 337
    advertising of, 321–323
Before and after Midnight (television
    program), 18
Begunov, Vladimir, 222

Behind the Glass (reality show), 36
Bekhtina, Natalia, 48
Bekmambetov, Timur, 327, 367
Bekstein, Viktor, 218
Beliakovich, Valeri, 139, 143
Beliavsky, Alexander, 98
Belov, Alexander, 40, 301, 306
Berezhnaya, Elena, 289–290
Berezovsky, Boris, 13, 28, 41, 43–44, 46, 50, 55, 56, 64, 296, 320
Bering Strait (pop band), 232
Bernes, Mark, 8, 237
Bezrukov, Sergei, 145, 172, 363
Bichevskaya, Zhanna, 8, 237
Biking, 285–286
Billiards, 342–343
Bimmer (film), 71, 98
Bird Market, 117
A Bit of Time (television program), 34, 36, 38–39
Black and White (MTV program), 38
"Black Raven," 3, 306, 309
"Blood Type" (song), 215, 216
"Blue Balloon" (song), 204
Blue Lard (Sorokin), 297
Bodrov, Sergei, Jr., 36, 94, 96, 97, 129
Bodrov, Sergei, Sr., 79, 83, 84, 93, 96, 129
Bogayev, Oleg, 158, 296
Bogorodsk toys, 106
Bolsheviks, 1, 2
Bolshoi Theater, 8, 12, 134
Bolshoi Drama Theater (BDT), 5, 6, 12, 136
Bolshoi gorod (*Big City*, newspaper), 57
Bondarenko, Irina, 366
Bondarev, Yuri, 203
Bonum 2 satellite, 44
Booker Prize, 295–296, 310
Books, 12, 292
Bookshops, 123, 292, 293
Bordovskikh, Julia, 34
Borisevich, Roman, 75
Borok, Alexander, 163
Borovik, Artyom, 33–34, 53, 54
Borzykin, Mike, 225–226
Bouquet in Triumphant Style (sculpture), 106
Bourgeois's Birthday (television serial), 40, 308
Bove, Osip, 120
Bovin, Alexander, 47–48
Bowling, 285, 342
Boxing, 281

Boys bands, 230–232
Bragin, Viacheslav, 25
Brake (film), 101
Brand names, 317, 320, 321, 322, 323, 324, 337
Bravo (rock band), 218
Brecht, Bertolt, 6, 137
Brezhnev, Leonid, 6, 7, 8, 9
    jokes about, 174
The Brigade (television serial), 40, 301, 308
Brill, Igor, 201
Brodsky, Joseph, 4, 7
Bronzit, Konstantin, 101
Brother (film), 79, 94–96, 97
Brother 2 (film), 97, 239
Brumberg, Valentina, 100
Brumberg, Zinaida, 100
Brumel, Valeri, 280
Bruskin, Grisha, 107
Budziovich, Olga, 191
Bugayev, Sergei, 214–215
Bukashka (film), 101
Bulanzova, Tatiana, 243
Buldakov, Alexei, 80, 81, 172
Bulgakov, Mikhail, 62
Bulldozer Exhibition, 7, 105
Burda (German publisher), 60, 357
Bure, Pavel, 263, 276, 310–311
Burglar (film), 214
Burnt by the Sun (film), 27, 87, 88, 89–90, 91
Buslov, Petr, 79, 98
Buto theater, 146, 188
Butusov, Viacheslav, 108, 227–228, 256–257
Butyrin, Yuri, 102
Bychkov, Mikhail, 155
Bychkov, Viktor, 81, 82
Bykov, Rolan, 75
Byt, 158

Cabaret actors, 8
Cannavoro, Fabio, 274(photo)
Cannes Film Festival, 5, 90, 93
The Captain's Daughter (film), 90
Car World (journal), 60
Carandache (Mikhail Rumiantsev), 188
Carnival Night (film), 5, 77
Cartoons, 50, 102–104
    heroes as puppets, 162
Castling (television game show), 36
Cathedral of Christ the Savior, 114, 115, 123, 124(caption), 129–130, 284

Catholics, 354

Cats theater. *See* Teatr Koshek

CDs. *See* Compact discs

Censorship, 8–9, 26, 54, 138, 293

Center for Drama and Playwriting, 158

Center Plus (*Tsentr Plius*, newspaper), 56

Central Television (Soviet), 24, 41

Cerceau (Slavkin play), 142

Chachalev, Sergei, 191

ChaiF (rock band), 222

Chakovsky, Alexander, 293

Chapayev, Vasili Ivanovich, 192

Chapayev (film), 3

    character in, 181, 245

Chapurin, Igor, 360–361, 367–368

"Chattanooga Choo Choo" (Miller), 200

Chavro, Yuri, 187

Chechnya, 20, 29, 30–32

    and journalists, 29–30, 43

    war film, 83–85

Checkers, 342

Checkpoint (film), 84–85

Chekasin, Vladimir, 201

Chekatylo, Andrei, 298

Chekhov, Anton, 137

Chekhov, Michael, 136

Chekhov Arts Theater, 139

Chelnokov, Anton, 191

Chelnokov, Nikolai, 191

Chernenko, Konstantin, 212

Chernobyl nuclear explosion (1986)

    and media, 20–21

Chernyshev, Arkadi, 275

Chesnokov, Andrei, 278, 279

Chess, 291–292

Chicherina, Julia, 235

Chizh and Co. (pop band), 108, 231

Chkhartishvili, Grigori (see also Akunin), 301

Chliants, Sergei, 75

Chocolate, 336

    advertising for, 319, 320, 324

Choocha (film), 101

Choreographers, 185, 186–188, 192

Chubais, Anatoli, 28

Chukcha, jokes about, 178

Chukovsky, Kornei, 100, 162

Chukhrai, Pavel, 5, 79, 91

Chuprinin, Sergei, 63

Churches, 114, 115, 123–125, 129–130

Churikova, Inna, 151, 154, 172

Chusova, Nina, 155

Chuvikha (female version *stilyagi*), 200

The Cigarette Girl from Mosselprom (film), 2

Cinema. *See* Film

Cinema Center (KinoTsentr), 74

CineMax (film producer), 74

Cinescope (television program), 34

Circus, 134, 135, 182–186

Circus (film), 3, 76, 356

Cirque du Soleil, 190–191, 192

The Clown (film), 100

Clowns, 142, 144, 156, 183, 185, 188–190, 191

Coincidence (Marinina), 302

Collective farm, 4, 8

Comaneci, Nadia, 283

Comic Trust (clowns' theater), 144

Commercial culture, 11, 12

The Commissar (film), 9

Commonwealth of Independent States (CIS), 75

Communism, 2, 7, 10–11

Communist Party (Russia), 27, 29

Communist Party of the Soviet Union, 3, 8, 11, 23

    hardliners, 4, 9

    reformers, 4, 9, 15

Compact discs (CDs), 32, 50, 82, 117, 217

Computers, 49, 117

    games on, 343

    software piracy, 32, 217

Conceptualism, 12, 104, 105, 107

Conclusions. See Itogi (journal)

Congress of People's Deputies (CPD), 23–24

Consumer culture, 10, 11, 12, 200, 316–370

Consumerism, 3

Cops (television serial), 39, 153, 300, 306, 312–313

Copyright, 32

The Coronation (Akunin), 301

"Cosmopolitans." *See* Jews

The Country and the World (television program), 34

Coup [putsch] (August 1991), 24–25

The Cow (film), 101

The Cranes Are Flying (film), 5

Crematorium (rock band), 218–219

Crime and Punishment (Dostoevsky), 298

Criminal Petersburg (Konstantinov), 300–301, 308

Criminal Petersburg (television serial), 40

The Crushing Force (television serial), 40, 307

Crystal, 111
CTB (film producer), 75
CTC (Network of Television Stations), 32–33
Cuckoo (film), 82, 84, 85
Cupolas, 116, 118
Czechoslovakia, 7

Dabizha, Natalia, 101
Dacha, 343, 348–349
Dalakian, Yulia, 364
Dance, Western as suspect, 199–200
Dance Floor (MTV program), 38
Daneliya, Georgi, 8
Daniel, Yuli, 7
Darfilm (studio), 165
Darts, 285
Dashkova, Polina, 294, 295, 303
Day in the Life of Ivan Denisovich
    (Solzhenitsyn), 4, 62
Day of Knowledge (September 1), 351
Day of the Armed Forces (February 23), 351
Day of the Constitution (December 12), 352
Day Watch (film), 99
DDT (rock band), 226, 227
De la Mothe, Vallin, 120
Dead Souls (Gogol), 112
Dementiev, Andrei, 48
Dementieva, Yelena, 280
Demichev, Peter, 9
The Day (*Den'*, newspaper), 54
Derevo (mime group), 144, 146, 192
Detective Dubrovsky's Dossier (television
    serial), 40, 307–308
Deutsche Welle (German radio), 47
Diachenko, Tatiana, 28, 50
Dialogues with Animals (television program),
    38
Diary of a Killer (television serial), 40
Dibrov, Dmitri, 35, 37
Dinamo stadium, 269
Directing Myself (television program), 36
Discos, 341
Discus throwing, 281
Disinformation, 16
Dissent movement, 7, 9, 11
    and film, 78
DJs (disc jockeys), 48, 341
DMB (film), 82
Dobrodeyev, Oleg, 41, 44
Dobrokhatova, Liudmila, 365

Doctor Zhivago (Pasternak), 4
Dodin, Lev, 151–152, 192–193
Dog Show (television program), 36
Dolina, Larisa, 238
Dom Kino, 75
Don't Even Think (film), 75, 79, 82
Dontsova, Daria (Agrippina Arkadievna), 294,
    295, 303–304, 306, 307, 311
Dorenko, Sergei, 29(photo), 30, 34, 43, 64
Doronina, Tatiana, 139
Dostal, Vladimir, 74, 75
Dostoevsky, Fyodor, 90, 112, 151, 295, 298
Dosug v Moskve (*Leisure in Moscow*,
    newspaper), 61
Dotsenko, Viktor, 300
Double Self-Portrait as Pioneers (sots-art), 106
Drigant, Natalia, 365
A Driver for Vera (film), 91
Drozdova, Olga, 172
Drubich, Tatiana, 215
Druzhba narodov (*Nations' Friendship*,
    journal), 62
Dubov, Yuli, 13
Dubovitskaya, Regina, 36
Dumas, Alexander, 292
Dunayevsky, Isaak, 76, 186, 251
Durov, Anna, 185
Durov, Vladimir, 185
Durov Circus of Animals, 185
Durov's Theater of Beasts, 185
DVDs (digital video discs), 117
Dykhovichny, Ivan, 88, 239
Dylan, Bob, 216
Dzerzhinsky, Felix, 113
Dzusova, Olga, 243

East-West (film), 97
Edelman, Robert, 11
Efros, Anatoli, 5, 136–137, 138
Eggert, Konstantin, 2
Eisenstein, Sergei, 1, 2, 76, 112
Ekho Moskvy. *See* Radio Echo Moscow
Ekran I stsena (*Stage and Screen* magazine),
    61
Ekspert (Expert, newspaper), 46
Electrification, 46
Elephant (film), 93
Emigration, 7
    jokes about, 177
Eppelbaum, Ilia, 165, 166(photo), 167

Erdman, Nikolai, 100, 183
Ernst, Konstantin, 32, 33(photo), 75, 171, 241
Estrada, defined, 168–169. *See also* Music, pop
The Eternal Call (television serial), 16
Europe Plus (radio), 46
Everything Will Be OK (film), 79–80
Exter, Alexander, 356
Extra M (newspaper), 56

Fadeyev, Max, 243
Farces (theater), 144, 146
Fashion, 356–357
    boutiques, 119, 121
    costume, 356, 357, 358, 362, 363, 364
    designers, 2, 50, 119, 224, 239, 356–366
    haute couture, 359–363
    models, 366–367
    Western, 200, 357
Fatherland—All Russia (OVR political party),
    29, 43
Fedorova, Oxana, 38
Feklistov, Alexander, 156, 172
Fellini, Federico, 100
Fellowship of Taganka Actors, 139
Fencing, 285
Fetisov, Viacheslav, 264(photo), 275, 276, 277,
    311
Fifth Wheel (Leningrad television program), 19,
    67
Filippov, Ivan, 121
Filippova, Inga, 365–366
Film, 2–3, 8–9, 14, 39, 71–104
    actors, 9, 80, 81, 83(photo), 88(photo),
        95(photo), 96, 98, 99, 151, 156, 215
    actresses, 3, 76–77, 88(photo), 97, 151
    American, 2, 5, 74, 98
    animation, 99–104, 108
    avant-garde, 2
    awards, 71, 75, 86, 90, 101
    blockbusters, 3, 71, 74
    box office revenues, 71, 98
    comedy, 8, 77, 79, 82
    commercial 12
    crime thrillers, 82, 98–99
    directors, 1, 2, 3, 5, 8, 9, 13, 27, 53, 71, 79–90
    educational, 38
    festivals (Russian), 75
    historical, 90–93
    language in, 179–180
    multiplex theaters, 71, 75, 76, 119

musical comedy, 3, 5, 76
NTV, 32
and pop music, 243
and privatization, 75
production and distribution, 73–76, 165
reality, 178–179
and rock music, 214–216
Russian, 39, 74, 75, 78–86
and sound, 4
Soviet, 71–74, 76–78
of Stalinist era, 86–90
on television, 32, 34, 74
and the Thaw, 4, 5
theaters, 74, 75
on video, 74
war, 83–86, 97
Western, 9
A Film Is Being Shot (Radzinsky play), 8
Filmmakers' Union, 62
Finansovye izvestiya (*Financial News,
    Izvestiya* supplement), 57
Finger puppets, 162
First Channel television (formerly ORT), 33, 41
Fishing, 286
Fisson, Vadim, 144
Florensky, Alexander, 107
Flowers (rock band), 209
The Fly on the Grater (art), 105
Fokin, Valeri, 145, 153
Folk songs, 3, 8, 199, 237
Fomenko, Nikolai, 154, 172
Fomenko, Petr, 152–153, 156, 193
Fomina, Yelena, 191
Football. *See* Soccer
The Forbidden Drummers [Zapreshchennye
    barabanshchiki] (pop band), 232
Formal Theater (Formalny teatr), 146
Fortune-telling, 355–356
The Forty-first (film), 5
Fourth wall, 3
Foxtrot, 199–200
Frankfurt School, 10
Freedom of the press, 45–46
Friendly Troops. See Us
Frunze, Mikhail, 113
FSB (Federal Security Agency), 31
Fund of Legal Reformers (film series), 101
Fundamental Lexicon (sots-art), 107
Funny Business, Family Business (television
    serial), 40

Furniture, 122
Fyodorov, Leonid, 224

Gabriadze, Rezo, 164, 167–168
Gaft, Valentin, 154
Gaidai, Leonid, 8, 9, 77
Gakkel, Seya, 209
Gala (journal), 60
Galich, Alexander, 202–203, 206–207, 256
Galkin, Maxim, 35
Gambling, 342, 343
Games, 342–343
Gandelevsky, Sergei, 296
Ganelin, Viacheslav, 201
Garden of "fallen statues," 113
Garkalin, Valeri, 154, 172
Garmash, Sergei, 172
Gazarov, Sergei, 172
Gazmanov, Oleg, 239
Gazprom, 13, 44, 45, 49
    Media, 44, 46, 57
The General (sculpture), 106
"Generation of Janitors" (song), 211
Generation P (Pelevin), 295, 296, 297
Gergiev, Valeri, 134
Germanova, Yevdokiya, 145
"Get out of Control" (song), 226
Gherman, Alexei, Jr., 71, 78, 85–86
Ginkas, Kama, 158
Ginne, Karl, 184
Giordano (rock opera), 239
Girl bands, 229–230
Glasnet (ISP), 50
Glasnost (openness), 10, 15, 18, 20, 52, 63, 138, 142
Glass, 110–111
Gliukoza. *See* Ionova, Natalia
Globa, A., 162
"Glossy" journals. *See* Magazines
Glove puppet, 161, 162
Gneushev, Valentin, 185, 186–187, 188
Gogol, Nikolai, 36, 100, 112, 165
Gogol Theater, 158
Golden Gramophone (song competition), 49
    as television program, 241
Golden Lion (Venice film award), 71
Golden Mannequin (fashion award), 362
Golden Mask (theater award), 164
Golden Telecom (U.S.-owned), 50
Goleizovsky, Kasian, 183

Golembiovsky, Igor, 55, 56
Golf, 268, 278
GOMETs (Soviet Central Administration of
    State Circuses), 161, 183
Good Night, Kids (television program), 38, 100
The Good Person of Szechwan (Brecht), 6, 137
Goodman, Benny, 200
Gorbachev, Mikhail, 9, 10, 11, 21, 24, 136
    and Chernobyl, 20
    and coup (1991), 24
    jokes about, 174–175
    and literature, 293
    and Lithuania, 22
    and music, 212
    and newspapers, 52
    and radio, 47
    resigns (Dec. 1991), 25
    and television, 15–16, 18, 40, 41
    and Yeltsin, 23
Gorbacheva, Raisa, 16
Gorbunov House of Culture, 217
Gordeyeva, Yekaterina, 289
Gorky. *See* Nizhny Novgorod
Gorky, Maxim (Alexei Peshkov), 113
Gorky Film Studio, 72, 74
Gorky Moscow Arts Theater, 139
Gorky Park (rock band), 209
Gorodok (*Little Town*, television show), 36
Gorsky, Alexander, 183
Goskino (Department for Cinematography), 73,
    74, 78
Gostinyi Dvor (shopping mall), 130
Gostiuk, Leonid, 185
Govorukhin, Sergei, 30
Govorukhin, Stanislav, 30, 32
Gradsky, Alexander, 207, 208(photo), 257
Grammatikov, Vladimir, 74
Graph of History (art), 105
The Great Solder (Dubov), 13
Grebenshchikov, Boris (BG), 108, 209–212, 214,
    257–258
Gribkov, Sergei, 75
Griboyedov, Alexander, 156
Grigoriev, Igor, 60
Grigoriev, Oleg, 107
Grimailo, Alexander, 192
Grinkov, Sergei, 289
Grishin, Viktor, 9
Grishkovets, Yevgeni, 155–156, 158, 193, 296
Grozny (Chechnya), 30

Gubenko, Nikolai, 139
Guelman, Marat, 104
GUM (department store), 119, 120, 130
Gurchenko, Liudmila, 77, 154
Gurevich, Boris, 281
Gusinsky, Sergei, 81
Gusinsky, Vladimir, 13, 28, 29, 41, 42, 43, 44, 55, 56, 64–65, 320
Gus-Khrustalnyi (crystal manufacturer), 111
Gymnastics, 282–283

Hammer and Sickle (film), 86–89
Handball, 278
Hand-Made (television show), 36
Hands Up [Ruki vverkh] (dance band), 231–232
Hard-currency shop [Beriozka], 292
Hermès, 92
Hermitage Museum, 12
Hippies (Soviet), 207
Hockey, 263, 268, 275–277
Hoffmann, Ernst Theodor Amadeus, 100
Holidays
    public, 351–352
    religious, 352–354
    See also Tourism
Homosexuality, 341
Horse racing, 285
Horseback riding, 285
Hotels, 118, 345–348
The House at the End of the World (film), 101
House of Cinema (see also Dom Kino), 74
House of Leningrad Trade (DLT), 120
House of Models, 357, 358
House of Culture (DK), 142
Hungary (1956 uprising), 4
Hunting, 286
Hunting Cinderella (film), 308

I Myself (television program), 37–38
Ibragimbekov, Murat, 71
Ibragimov, Yevgeni, 164
Ice (Sorokin), 297
Ice Age (television serial), 40
Ice skating, 268, 287–291
Icons, 124, 125–128
Idiot (Dostoevsky), 90
    as television serial, 295
Imperial Alexandrinsky Theater (St. Petersburg), 1
In Search of Joy (Rozov play), 5

In the Animal World (television program), 38
In the First Person (radio program), 48
Independence Day (June 12), 352
Independent Media, 57
Independent Television (NTV), 13
Intelligentsia, 11
Interfax (independent news agancy), 15, 66
International Trade Center, 115
International Women's Day (March 8), 351
International Workers' Day (May 1), 351
International Youth Festival (1957), 4, 216
Internet, 46, 49–51
    cartoons, 50, 103
    providers (ISPs), 50
    search engines, 50
Investigative journalists, 19–20, 22, 24, 30, 32, 34, 38
Ionova, Natasha (Gliukoza), 236
Is It Easy to Be Young? (film), 214
Isayeva, Liudmila, 366
Israel, 7
ITAR-TASS (Information Telegraph Agency of Russia) news agency, 15, 46, 66
Itogi (*Conclusions*, journal), 46, 60, 65
Itogi (*Conclusions*, current affairs program), 33, 34, 41, 42, 44
Ivan Vasilievich Changes Profession (film), 241–242
Ivanushki International (pop group), 230, 231(photo), 258
Ivanov, Anatoli, 16
Ivanovna, Anna (empress), 160
Ivanov-Vano, Ivan, 100
Izmailov, Marat, 274(photo), 275
Izosimov, Oleg, 191–192
Iz ruk v ruki (*From Hand to Hand*, advertising paper), 56
Izvestiya (*News*, newspaper), 46, 51, 53, 55, 57, 65
    online, 50

Jacques. *See* Zhakevich, Vadim
Javelin throwing, 281
Jazz, 5, 199–201
Jesus Christ Superstar (rock musical), 248
Jewelry, 111, 122–123
Jews, 3, 9, 206, 353–354
Jigalov, Andrei, 189, 192
Jim and Dollar (puppet play), 162
John, Elton, 207, 259–260, 261–262

Jokes, 173–182
Jolly Fellows (film), 76, 77, 200
Jordan, Boris, 44, 56, 57
Jouravel, Vitali, 191
Journals, 57–63
"glossy" (*see* Magazines)
"thick" (*see* Literary journals)
Judo, 281
Jumping, 280–281

Kabakov, Ilia, 105, 106(photo)
Kachanov, Roman, 82, 100
Kafelnikov, Evgeni, 278(photo), 279, 311
Kakuchaya, Olvar, 24
Kalatozov, Mikhail, 5, 90
Kalinin, Mikhail, 113
Kalish, Alexander, 61
Kalugin, S., 119
Kamburova, Yelena, 202
Kamenskaya (television serial), 307
Karachentsov, Nikolai, 40, 151, 153, 172
Karate, 281
Karavan (journal), 46
Karpin, Valeri, 263
Karpov, Anatoli, 292
Kaseyev, Dana, 186
Kashkarov, Igor, 280
Kasparov, Garri, 291
Katina, Lena (t.A.T.u), 261
Kaverin, Veniamin, 250
Kee, Viktor, 191
Keft, Valeri, 191
Kenzheyev, Bakhyt, 296
KGB, 10, 22, 113
Khabensky, Konstantin, 99, 153, 154, 172
Khakassian Puppet Theater, 164
Khalifman, Alexander, 292
Khamatova, Chulpan, 154, 155, 172
Khamdamov, Rustam, 361
Kharitonov, Mark, 295
Khasbulatov, Ruslan, 25
Khavtun, Yevgeni, 218
Khazanov, Gennadi, 171, 193
Khitruk, Fyodor, 100
Khlebnikov, Velimir, 224
Khmelnitskaya, Johanna, 303
Kholodov, Dmitiri, 32, 52
Khorkina, Svetlana, 283
Khoroshev, Andrei, 34–35
Khrenov, Anton, 34

Khristich, Dmitri, 276
Khrushchev, Nikita, 3, 4, 136
and art, 201
jokes about, 174
on Stalin, 86
Khrzhanovsky, Andrei, 100
Khvostenko, Alexei, 224
Kibirov, Timur, 296
Kinchev, Konstantin, 224, 248
Kino, 223–224
KinoPark (journal), 61
Kinoshok (film festival), 75
Kinostsenarii (*Film Scripts*, magazine), 62
Kinotavr Sochi Open Russian Film Festival, 75
Kirkorov, Filipp, 238, 239, 240(photo), 248–249,
258
Kirov (Mariinsky) Theatre, 8, 12, 134
Kiselyov, Dmitri, 17
Kiselyov, Yevgeni, 13, 34, 41, 42, 44, 45, 57, 65
Kiselyova, Maria, 35
"Kitchen sink drama" realism, 6
Kivinov, Alexander, 300, 306
Kiziakov, Timur, 35
Kliaksa (terrier), 188
Klein, Roman, 121
Klimenko, Vladimir, 147
Klimov, Elam, 9, 78
Klimova, Marina, 290–291
Klinsky, Yuri, 222
Knebel, Maria, 136
Kobzon, Iosif, 8, 14, 237
Kodak Cinema World, 74
Kokh, Albert, 44
Koliada, Nikolai, 157–158, 193
Koliada Teatr, 158
Koltseva, Tatiana, 366
Komar, Vitali, 106
Kommersant (newspaper), 13(caption), 46, 53,
57, 65
Komsomolskaya pravda (*Komsomol Truth*,
newspaper), 32, 46, 51, 52, 53, 57, 65
online, 50
Konchalovsky, Andrei, 8
Konchalovsky, Yegor, 79, 98
Konstantin, Andrei, 300–301
Korbut, Olga, 283
Koretsky, Danil, 98, 295, 298, 306
Kormiltsev, Ilia, 189
Koroleva, Natasha, 242–243, 258
Korotich, Vitali, 52

Korzhakov, Alexander, 28
Kosmachevsky, Vladimir, 147
Kosolapov, Alexander, 107
Kovalchuk, Diana, 366
Kozak, Roman, 172, 193
Kozlov, Alexei, 208
Kozlov, Grigori, 165
Kramer, Viktor, 143–144, 188
Kramnik, Vladimir, 292
Krasnopolskaya, Maya, 165, 166(photo), 167
Kravchenko, Leonid, 24
Krestianka (*The Peasant Woman*, magazine), 57
Kristall (distillery), 91
Kriuchkov, Vladimir, 22, 24
Krokodil (*Crocodile*, magazine), 4, 52, 173, 207
Krutikova, Irina, 359
Krutoy, Igor, 237, 238
Kudashov, Ruslan, 165
Kuklachev, Yuri, 188
Kukly (*Puppets*, NTV program), 31, 34, 35(photo), 43, 44
Kukotsky's Case (Ulitskaya), 296
Kuksenaite, Irena, 214
Kuleshov, Peter, 35
Kultura (Culture television channel), 34, 37, 38, 42, 46
Kultura (*Culture*, weekly newspaper), 61
Kulturnost (culturedness), 10
Kurkova, Bella, 19, 20
Kurmangaliev, Erik, 149
Kurnikova, Anna, 263, 279–280, 311–312
Kurochkin, Maxim, 156, 159–160, 193–194, 296
Kursk (submarine), 29, 43
Kuryokhin, Sergei, 201, 210, 258
Kutsenko, Gosha, 72(photo), 98, 154, 172
Kuvayev, Oleg, 50, 102
Kuznetsov, Terenti, 111
Kuznetsov, Yevgeni, 185
Kvas, 336–337
Kvasha, Igor, 172
Kvint, Lora, 239
Kyrgyzstan, 113

Ladynina, Marina, 3, 76
Lagutenko, Igor, 232
Lamanova, Nadezhda, 356, 357, 368
Lacquer boxes, 12, 108–110, 112
    production centers, 131, 132
Larionov, Igor, 275, 277

Larkina, Yelena, 188
Larsen, Tutta, 38, 42
The Last Hero (television program), 36
The Last Train (film), 71, 85
Latynina, Julia, 48
Latynina, Larisa, 282
Lavrov, Kirill, 139
Lazarenko, Vitali, 183
Lazarev, Alexander, 172
Leap Year Summer (Visokosnoye leto, rock band), 209
Lebed, Alexander, 28
Lebedev, Artemy (Artyom), 51
Lebedev, Nikolai, 85
Lebedeva, Tatiana, 281 Lebedev-Kumach, Vasili, 76
Legat, Kirill, 34
Lel', Katia, 243
Leikin, Leonid, 191
Leisure, 330, 350–352. *See also* Games; Nightlife; Parks and gardens; Tourism
Lenfilm (studio), 72, 74
Lenin (Ulianov), V. I., 2, 10, 14, 17–18, 113
    and film, 71
    jokes about, 173
    monument to, 113
Leningrad (now St. Petersburg), 113
    rock music, 222–228
    theater, 142–144, 146
Leningrad (rock band), 12, 98, 232. *See also* Shnurov, Sergei
Leningrad Institute for Music, Film and Theater (LGITMiK), 163, 164
Lenkom Theater, 172
Leonovich, Katia, 364
Leontiev, Avangard, 172
Leontiev, Valeri, 8
Lepin, Anatoli, 77
Lerner, Oleg, 141
Leshchenko, Lev, 237
Lesnovsky, Dmitri, 75
Liberal Democrats (LDP) (political party), 27, 30
Liberalization, 9–10. *See also* Thaw
Ligachev, Yegor, 9, 15, 18, 23, 53
Lilikan Theater, 165, 166(caption)
Liling, Song, 149
Limonov, Eduard, 54
Limonovka (newspaper), 54
Linda (pop singer), 243

Lindenberg, Udo, 216
Lines of Fate (Kharitonov), 295
Lingerie, 121
The Lion with the Gray Beard (film), 100
Lisovsky, Sergei, 28
List of People Who Have the Right to Receive (art), 105
Listiev, Vlad, 17, 32, 35, 60, 61(photo), 65
Literary ("thick") journals, 7, 10, 57, 62–63, 158
    online, 50
Literature, 4, 8
    action thriller, 300–301
    banned, 293
    best sellers, 295–298
    children's, 293, 294, 298
    detective and spy, 4, 8, 9, 11, 263, 292–295, 297–301, 305–309 (*see also* Film, crime thrillers; Television, and spy and detective programs)
    educational, 294
    foreign, 292, 295, 299
    and *glasnost*, 10
    historical, 8, 11
    postmodern, 12
    romance, 297, 298
    rural, 7
    science fiction, 8, 297
    sex in, 300
    on television, 37, 305–309
    war, 293
    Western, 4, 8, 10
    See also Books; Publishers/publishing; Reading level; Television, soap operas
Lithuania, 20, 22
Literaturnaya gazeta (*Literary gazette*, newspaper), 51, 52
Lithuanian Popular Front (Sajudis), 22
Litsa (*Faces*, monthly journal), 54
Litsedei (clown and mime group), 142–143, 146, 189–190, 194
Little Red Devils (film), 2
Little Vera (film), 53, 77, 214
Liube (pop band), 229
Liubimov, Alexander, 17, 34
Liubimov, Yuri, 5, 6, 136, 137–138, 152
Liutkevich, A., 102
Living and Dead (film), 5
Livnev, Sergei, 74, 88
Liza (women's journal), 60
Lokhov, Dmitri, 164

Lomakin, Andrei, 276
Lomakin, Sergei, 17
Lomonosov Porcelain Factory (LFZ), 110–111, 130
Long Farewells (film), 9
Loshak, Andrei, 34
Loskov, Dmitri, 275
Lubok (woodblock prints), 107
Lukianenko, Sergei, 71, 99
LukOil, 44, 55
Lungin, Pavel, 13
Luxury, 3
Luzhkov, Yuri (Moscow mayor), 29, 30, 41, 42, 43, 56(photo), 105, 114–115, 116, 319, 344
Luzhniki Stadium, 269, 270(photo)
Lysenko, Anatoli, 17
Lysenkov, Alexei, 36

Magazines ("glossy" journals), 55, 57, 59(photo), 60–62. *See also* Literary "thick" journals
Magnetic Storms (film), 91
Magnitizdat (tape recording distribution), 4, 202
Magomayev, Muslim, 237
The Maids (Genet play), 150
Makanin, Vladimir, 295
Makarevich, Andrei, 209, 217, 230, 259
Makariev, Artur, 48
Makarova, Natalia, 149, 357
Makovetsky, Sergei, 172, 194
Malashenko, Igor, 28
Malikov, Dmitri, 238
Maltsev, Igor, 60
Mamonov, Petr, 172, 215, 219, 250, 259
Mamontov, Savva, 108
The Man Who Flew into Space (art), 106(photo)
Manège art exhibition (1962), 4
Manège Square (Moscow), 115, 118, 130–131
Mariinsky Theatre. *See* Kirov Theatre
Marin, Alexander, 145
Marinina, Alexandra (Marina Alexeyeva), 40, 295, 305–306, 307, 312
Marionettes, 160, 163, 165
Markov, Georgi, 293
Markova, Maria, 191
Mashina Vremeni (band). *See* Makarevich, Andrei
Mashkov, Vladimir, 145, 156–157, 194
Masiania (cartoon), 103–104, 131

Masiuk, Yelena, 30, 43

Mass, Vladimir, 183

Mass culture, 1, 9

Matrioshka, 104, 108, 109(photo), 131

Matvienko, Igor, 230

Mausoleum (Red Square), jokes about, 175

Mavrodi, Sergei, 325, 327

Maximov, Anatoli, 75

Maximov, Andrei, 34, 37

May Day Parade (1990) and media, 21

Mayakovsky, Vladimir, 1, 100, 201, 316

Mazayev, Sergei, 217

MediaMost (NTV parent company), 44, 45(caption)
    and radio, 48

Medved (*Bear*, magazine), 60

Medvedev, Sergei, 24

Medvedev, Yuri, 191

The Meeting Place Cannot Be Changed
    (television serial), 16

Megapolis Ekspress (newspaper), 56

Mehnert, Klaus, 293

Meladze, Valeri, 102

Melamid, Alexander, 106

Melkumov, Sergei, 75

Melodiya (Soviet record label), 208, 216, 236

Menshikov, Oleg, 83(photo), 96, 156,
    157(photo), 194, 361

Menshov, Vladimir, 36, 77

Menshova, Julia, 37, 155

Merezhko, Viktor, 34

Meskhiev, Dmitri, 86, 309

The Messenger (film), 97

Mestechkin, Mark, 184

Method acting, 3

Metro (musical), 248

Metro (newspaper), 32, 42, 56

Metropol (almanac), 7

Mexican soap operas, 39

Meyerhold, Vsevolod, 1–2, 3, 6, 135, 183

Mezdrich, Boris, 141

Middle class, 11

Mik and Mak (buffoons), 189

Mikhalkov, Nikita, 27, 75, 87, 88(photo), 89, 91,
    93, 131, 321

Mikhalkov, Sergei, 162

Mikhalkova, Anna, 38, 88(photo)

Milgram, Boris, 154

Miliutin, Yuri, 251

Miller, Glenn, 200

Mimes, 142–144, 146, 188, 192

Miracle Field (television show), 35

Mirror (television program), 34

Mirzoyev, Vladimir, 147–148, 194

Mishin, Alexei, 289

Mitki (art group), 107–108

Mitkova, Tatiana, 17, 22, 41, 44, 65

MMM, 325–327, 368

MNVK (Moscow Independent Broadcasting
    Corporation), 41, 42, 44

Modern art, 4, 7

Mogilny, Alexander, 263, 275, 276

Moguchy, Andrei, 146

Moiseyev, Igor, 8

Mokeyev, Mikhail, 147

Molchanov, Oleg, 238, 239, 243

Molchanov, Vladimir, 18

Molodaya gvardiya (*Young Guard*, journal),
    62

Molotov-Ribbentrop Pact (1939), 22

Monasteries, 124

Mongol Shuudan (rock band), 219

Monuments, 112–114, 115, 116

Mordvinova, Amalia, 40

Morrow, Colette, 191

Moscow, 114–116
    churches, 123
    department stores, 119, 120–121
    850th anniversary (1998), 115
    hotels, 118, 345–348
    housing, 349–350
    malls, 118
    markets, 117, 121, 131–132
    metro stations, 113
    museums, 344
    night clubs, 338–341
    parks, 344
    restaurants, 330–334
    retail space, 120
    rock music, 216–222
    street names, 113
    zoo, 114

Moscow (journal), 62

Moscow Arts Theater, 135, 139, 154, 156, 172,
    194
    School, 5, 52, 57, 65–66

Moscow Does Not Believe in Tears (film), 77,
    78–79

Moscow Institute for Theater Arts (also Theater
    Institute, GITIS/RATI), 164, 184

Moscow International Film Festival, 75, 86
Moscow News (*Moskovskiye novosti*, weekly), 25, 52, 57, 65–66
Moscow Parade (film), 88
Moscow State Circus, 8
Moscow State University Theater "Nash Dom," 139, 148
Moscow Times (English-language newspaper), 57
Mosfilm (studio), 72, 74
Moshkov, Maxim, 50
Moskovskaya pravda (newspaper), 51, 55
Moskovskii komsomolets (newspaper), 46, 51, 53, 55, 66
Moskovskii nabliudatel (*Moscow Observer*, theatre magazine), 61
Moskvichka (*The Muscovite*, women's magazine), 55
Moskvina, Tatiana, 81
Mostovoy, Alexander, 263
Motor races, 286
Mountain climbing, 286
MTV (Music Television), 32, 36, 38, 42
Mukhina, Vera, 113
Mukusev, Vladimir, 17
Murashov, Petr, 102
Muratova, Kira, 9, 78, 79
Museum of Architecture, 163
Museums, 163, 344
Music, 4, 5, 8, 108
    American, 200
    composers, 17, 98, 102, 151, 164, 186, 200, 208, 229, 238, 239, 242–243
    conductors, 134
    disco, 208
    pop, 229–236, 241–243
    pop (estrada), 5, 8, 10, 14, 32, 48–49, 138, 169–171, 199, 200, 236–243
    pop singers, 8, 237–243
    radio, 47
    records ("on the bones"), 201, 208–209, 217
    rock, 12, 108, 199, 200, 201–202, 207–229, 241
        (*see also* Rock opera)
    rock musicals, 207–208
    Soviet, 241
    Soviet pop, 199
    taped, 4, 47, 202, 217
    underground, 207, 241
    Western, 48–49, 199, 201, 207, 211, 241
    See also Bard movement; Jazz

Musicals, 246–255
Muslims, 354
Muz TV, 240
Muzykalnaya zhizn (*Musical Life*, magazine), 57
My Cinema (television program), 34
"My Generation" (song), 224, 225
Mytko, Igor, 298

Nadezhda (radio station), 48
Na dne (*Lower Depths*, newspaper for homeless), 54
Naftaliyeva, Natalia, 364
Names, 356
Namin, Stas, 209, 248, 259
NaNa (band), 230, 259
Nash sovremennik (*Our Contemporary*, journal), 62
Nasyrov, Murat, 243
Natalie (women's magazine), 55
Naumenko, Mikhail "Maik," 222
Nautilus Pompilius, 227, 229
Nechayeva, Lidia, 274
The Needle (film), 215, 219
Negoda, Natalia, 53
Nemchinov, Sergei, 276
Nemov, Alexei, 283
Neoclassical Academy, 104
Neoclassicism, 115
NEP (New Economic Policy, 1921–1928), 316
Neretina, Nina, 365
Nesting dolls, 108, 109(photo)
Neva (journal), 62
Nevzorov, Alexander, 19
New Drama (festival), 157
New Russia, 10, 11, 12, 326, 330, 352–353
New Russians, jokes about, 181–182
News agencies, 15, 46, 66
News of the Week (television program), 34
Newspapers, 13(caption), 46, 51–57, 58(table), 61
    and coup (1991), 24, 25
    English-language editions, 57
    foreign, 53
    free, 56, 57
    and internet, 50
    journalists, 32, 56
    paper for, 54
    printed abroad, 54
    Russian, 54, 55–57

Newspapers (*continued*)
   Soviet, 51–54
   tabloid, 55, 56
   weekly, 52
Neyolova, Marina, 172, 358
Nezavisimaya gazeta (*Independent Gazette*, newspaper), 46
   online, 50
Neznaika in Sun City (film), 102
Neznaika on the Moon (film), 102
Neznansky, Friedrich, 39, 299
Night clubs and bars, 337–342
Night Flight (television program), 37
Night Shift (television program), 37
Night Watch (film), 71, 75, 99
"Night Watch" (song), 202, 203
Nijinski, Vaclav, 156
"Nika" (film award), 75
Nikitin, Akim, 184
Nikitin, Dmitri, 184
Nikitin, Nikolai, 184
Nikitin, Petr, 184
Nikitsky Gates (theater), 139, 144
Nikolai, Aldo, 172
Nikolayev, Igor, 243
Nikulin, Mikhail, 185
Nikulin, Yuri, 185, 186, 187(photo), 189
Nizhny Novgorod (formerly Gorky), 7
Nobel Prize, 4, 7
Nord-Ost (musical), 249–250, 251, 252–253, 254, 259–260
Norstein, Yuri, 100, 131
Nosik, Anton, 50
Nosov, Nikolai, 100, 102
Novikov, Timur. 104, 214
Novozhenov, Lev, 36
Novy mir (*New World*, literary journal), 7, 62, 63, 66
Novye Izvestiya (newspaper), 46, 55, 56
NTV (television channel), 28, 29, 30, 33, 34, 35–36, 42–43, 44, 46
   journalist, 45(photo)
   online, 50
   parent company, 44
   film production arm, 32, 46, 75
   takeover, 44, 45, 46
Nugmanov, Rashid, 215

O Happy Man (television quiz show), 35
Obraztsov, Sergei, 162, 163, 195

Obshchaya gazeta (*Common Gazette*, newspaper), 24
October (film), 112
October (journal), 62
October Revolution (1917), 1, 113
   celebration, 351–352
Ogonyok (*Little Flame*, current affairs journal), 46, 52, 57, 60
Ogorodnikov, Valeri, 85, 165, 214
Oil (film), 71
Okhlopkov, Nikolai, 1
Okhotny Riad (Hunters' Row), 131–132
Okudzhava, Bulat, 202, 203–204, 207, 260, 295
The Old Man and the Sea (film), 101
Old Songs about the Main Thing (television program), 32, 241
Oleinikov, Ilia, 36
Oligarchs, 13, 40, 42, 320
Olympic Games, 264–266, 267, 268, 280, 281, 282, 287–291
   boycott (1980), 7, 265
   stadium, 270, 278
   uniforms, 358, 360
Opekushin, Alexander, 112
Open Radio, 49
Open Russia (Yukos-supported fund), 57, 296
Opera, 134, 149. *See also* Rock opera
Operation "Happy New Year" (film), 80
Opposition parties, 11
Orbakaite, Kristina, 102, 240
Orlov, Boris, 106
Orlova, Liubov, 3, 76
Orpheus and Eurydice (rock opera), 207
ORT (Russian Public Television), 28, 29, 30, 32, 33, 34, 35, 36, 37, 38, 40, 41, 43, 46, 67, 71
   and film production, 75
   and Russian Radio, 49
   and Soviet films, 32
   See also First Channel television
Orthodox Church, 352–353, 354, 368–369
Ostalsky, Dmitri, 55
Ostrovsky, Alexander, 113, 135
Otdokhni (*Relax*, journal), 60
Ours (*Nashi*, television program), 20
Ovcharov, Sergei, 100, 132
Ovchinnikov, Sergei, 275
Overcoat (Gogol), 100
OVR. *See* Fatherland—All Russia
Ozerov, Nikolai, 267

Paintball, 285
Pakhmutova, Alexandra, 8
Palace of Soviets, 114
Palme d'Or, 5, 90
Panfilov, Gleb, 90
Panin, Andrei, 172
Panova, Yelena, 187
Pantiushenkova, Olga, 366
Paper games, 343
Paper recycling, 292
"Paper Soldier" (song), 203, 204
"Parasitism," 4
Parfionova, Tatiana, 361–362, 369
Parfyonov, Leonid, 34, 171
Parkhomenko, Sergei, 48
Parks and gardens, 334, 343–344
Parliament, 25–27
Pasternak, Boris, 4, 51
Patrioshka, 104, 108, 109(photo)
Pauls, Raimond, 237, 238, 260
Paulson, Andrew, 57
Pavlenko, Nikolai, 187
Pavlov, Vladimir (prime minister 1991), 24
Peculiarities of National . . . (film series)
    Bath-house, 80
    Fishing, 80, 81–82
    Hunt (in Autumn), 79, 80, 81, 82
    Hunt in Winter, 82
    Politics, 80
Pelevin, Viktor, 12, 295, 296–297, 313
Perchance (*Juno and Avos*, rock opera), 40
Perepelkin, Vladimir (VQ), 365
Perestiani, Ivan, 2
Perestroika, 11, 47, 77
Performance art, 104, 358
Perfumes, 92, 121
Peter the Great (czar), 114, 115(monument
    photo)
Peterburg Radio, 48
Petersburg. *See* St. Petersburg
Petersburg (film), 100
Petersburg Theater Institute (SPATI), 152
Petersburg Theater Journal, 62
Petersburg Times (English-language
    newspaper), 57
Petkun, Viacheslav, 38
Petrosian, Yevgeni, 171
Petrov, Alexander, 100–101, 132
Petrov, Vladimir, 276
Petrushevskaya, Liudmila, 100, 148–149

Petrushka (trickster/rebel puppet), 161
Pevtsov, Dmitri, 151, 172
Pharaoh (film), 100
Pharmacies, 123
Photographers, 2
Piatigorsky, Leonid, 200
Pichul, Vasili, 53, 77
Piekha, Edita, 237
Pikhienko, Olga, 191
Pikul, Valentin, 8, 11, 292
Pilot (animation studio), 101
Pilot Brothers (film series), 101
Pivovarova, Natalia, 229–230
Planet Earth (television program), 38
Plasticine (Sigarev play), 154, 158
Platonov, Andrei, 164
Playboy (Russian edition), 60
Playwrights, 1, 5, 100, 135, 154, 157, 158, 172,
    183, 296
Plisetskaya, Maya, 134
Poetry, 105, 201, 214, 296
Poets, 1, 4, 7, 147, 151, 201–202, 224
Poliakova, Tatiana, 295
Polishchuk, Liubov, 154, 172
Political asylum, 13
Political parties. *See* Communist Party of the
    Soviet Union; *under* Russian Soviet
    Federated Socialist Republic
Politkovskaya, Anna, 32, 63(photo)
Polunin, Slava (Viacheslav), 100, 142, 146, 186,
    189–190, 195
Pomerantsev, Alexander, 120
Ponomarenko, Sergei, 290–291
Ponomaryov, Alexander, 147
Poor Nastia (television serial), 306
Pop singers. *See under* Music
Popov, Alexander, 284
Popov, Gavriil (mayor of Moscow), 21, 41
Popov, Oleg, 8, 188–189, 195
Popova, Liubov, 356
Popova, Yelena, 192
Poptsov, Oleg, 41, 42, 56
Popular culture
    defined, 1
    post-Soviet, 11, 12
    underground, 7, 9
    Western, 10
Porcelain, 110, 111, 130
Porgy and Bess (jazz opera), 200
Pornography, 340

Posokhin, Mikhail, 114, 115
Posters, 2
Postmodernism, 12, 296
Potanin, Vladimir, 56, 76
Potudan Theater, 164–165, 195
Pozner, Vladimir, 18, 21, 34, 67
Pozner and Donahue (U.S television show), 20
Pravda (*Truth*, newspaper), 51, 52–53, 54, 67
Premiere (magazine), 61
Presniakov, Oleg, 154, 158–159, 160, 195
Presniakov, Vladimir, 154, 158–159, 160, 195, 240
Press, jokes about, 176
Press Law (1990), 53, 54
Prigov, Dmitri, 105, 147
Primakov, Yevgeni, 29, 30, 43
Princess Turandot (Gozzi play), 135, 356
Prisoner of the Mountains (film), 83–84, 96
Privatization, 41–45, 75
Profil (journal), 60
Prokhanov, Alexander, 54
Prokofieva, Sofia, 162
Proletarian fashion, 2
ProMedia, 46, 49, 76
Proof of Quality (television program), 36
Psychological realism, 3, 5, 135
Publishers/publishing, 46, 56, 292–295, 297, 313
Pugacheva, Alla, 8, 14, 171, 237, 238, 239, 240(photo), 269
Pugo, Boris (minister of the interior, 1991), 24
Pulp fiction, 263, 292, 295
Pupis, Doris, 365
Puppets, 101, 157(photo). *See also* Kukly; *under* Theater
Pushkin, Alexander, 90, 100, 115
Pushkin Cinema (formerly Rossiya), 74
Pushkin Square, 112
Pushkin Square (publisher), 56
Pushkin Theater, 172
Pushkina, Oxana, 38
Putin, Vladimir, 10, 29
    and Chechen conflict, 29
    at icon, 127(photo)
    as nesting doll, 109(photo)
    presidential campaign, 29–30, 319
    and state control, 45
    and television, 41, 319–320
Pygmalion (film producer), 75

Quarenghi, Giacomo, 116, 120
Queen Margot (Dumas), 292

Rabid Love (Dotsenko), 300
Rabotnitsa (*The Woman Worker*, magazine), 57
Radio, 4–5, 23, 38, 41–49
    cable, 46, 47, 48
    jamming, 17, 47
    joint venture, 47
    jokes about, 177–178
    journalists, 30
    music, 47, 48–49
    Russian, 47–49
    Soviet, 46–47
    stations, 46–47
    See also Privatization
Radio Chanson, 49
Radio Dinamit, 49
Radio Echo Moscow, 45, 46, 48, 49, 64
Radio Europa Plus, 47, 49
Radio Liberty, 30–31, 47, 49
Radio Maximum, 38, 49
Radio Mayak (Lighthouse), 47, 48, 49
Radio Moscow, 4–5, 17
Radio Moscow Speaking, 48
Radio Nostalgie, 49
Radio Russia, 23, 47, 48, 49, 67
Radio Yunost (Youth), 47, 48, 69
Radzinsky, Eduard, 8
Raikin, Arkadi, 8, 14, 38, 168, 170, 171, 195–196
Raikin, Konstantin, 153
Rambler (search engine), 50
Ramstore (market), 120
Rasputin, Valentin, 299
Rastrelli, Bartolomo, 116
Rastorguyev, Nikolai, 229
Razu, Mikhina (Daria Razumikhina), 364, 369
Reading level, 8, 293
Recreation. *See* Sports
Red Sky (film), 85
Red Star (model agency), 366, 369
Red Waves (Soviet rock album), 216
Reed, John, 6
Reformers. *See under* Communist Party of the Soviet Union
Religions, 352–354
REN-TV, 75
Repentence (film), 78, 87

Reshetov, Petr, 18, 22
Resorts, 345
Restaurants, 330–335
    Western, 333
The Return (film), 71, 72, 75
Reviakina, Maria, 141
RIA Novosti/RIA Vesti (news agency), 15, 46, 66
Riazanov, Eldar, 5, 8, 77
Robin Hood (film), 2
Rock opera, 40, 208, 239, 245
Rodchenko, Alexander, 2, 316
Rodnina, Irina, 289, 313
Rogozhkin, Alexander, 39, 79, 80, 81, 82, 84, 132, 172
Rokashkov, Natalia, 192
Rokashkov, Sergei, 192
Romanov, Andrei (Diushka), 209
The Romanovs (film), 90
Room, Abram, 2
Rossi, Carlo, 116
Rossiiskaya gazeta (*Russian Gazette*, newspaper), 46
Rowing, 283–284
Rozov, Viktor, 5
Rozovsky, Mark, 136, 139, 143, 144, 207
RTR (Russian Television and Radio) channel, 17, 22, 23, 24, 25, 26, 28, 29, 32, 33, 34, 35, 36, 39, 40, 41, 42, 43, 44, 46, 56, 67–68
    film production, 75
    online, 50
Rubinstein, Lev, 147
Rublyov, Andrei, 124
Rudinstein, Mark, 75
Run, Lola, Run (film), 82
Rusalka (film), 101
Russia. *See* Russian Soviet Federated Socialist Republic
Russian (language), 243–245
    dictionaries, 243–244
    and foreign terms, 320
    prison slang, 244
    swear words, 246
    youth slang and jargon, 244–246, 247
Russian Association of Book-publishers (ASKI), 293
Russian Filmmakers' Union, 75
Russian food, 335–337
Russian Football League, 313–314
Russian Media Group, 49

Russian (Russkoye) Radio, 49, 68
Russian Soviet Federated Socialist Republic (RSFSR), 12, 23, 26, 41
    Communist Party (KPRF), 27, 29
    Congress of People's Deputies, 23
    constitution, 26
    coup (1993), 25–27
    political parties, 26–27, 29
    presidential election (1966, 2000), 27–30
    See also New Russia
Russians, jokes about, 178–179
Russia's Choice (political party), 27
Russkin, Sergei, 81
Rutskoy, Alexander, 25
Rybin, Alexei, 223
Rybnikov, Alexei, 151, 208, 247
Rymbaeva, Rosa, 230

Safin, Marat, 279
Sagalayev, Eduard, 17, 25, 47, 68
St. Petersburg, 112, 113, 116
    hotels, 347(photo), 348
    markets and shops, 117, 119–120, 123
    night clubs, 341–342
    restaurants, 334–335
Sakharov, Andrei, 7, 18
Salamonsky, Albert, 184, 185
Salim-Meruet, Erik. *See* Kurmangaliev, Erik
Saltykov, Viktor, 238–239
Samizdat (self-publishing typescripts), 7, 244, 292
Sarnatsky, Alexander, 189
Sarnatsky, Lada, 189
Satire Theater, 184
Satirikon Theater, 153
Sauer, Derk, 57
Saulsky, Yuri, 201, 208, 212
Saveliev, Ivan, 296
Saxophones, 200
Sazonov, Pavel, 161
Scandals of the Week (TV6 talk show), 37
Schnittke, Alfred, 17
School of Contemporary Play (theater), 155
School of Scandal (television program), 37
Sculpture, 106, 112, 113
Seagull (theater award), 363
"Second economy," 7–8, 11, 217
Secrets of the Investigation (Topilskaya), 309
Segodnia (*Today*, newspaper), 55, 68
Sektor Gaza (rock band), 222

Selianov, Sergei, 75

Selitskaya, Irina, 364–365

Sem' dnei (*Seven Days*, journal), 60

Semanova, Natalia, 366

Semyonov, Yulian, 5, 8, 11, 17, 53, 293, 299

Sense and Sensibility (television program), 38

Serebrennikov, Kirill, 40, 154, 155, 158, 159, 160(photo), 196

Sergeyev, Andrei, 295

Sergeyev, Viktor, 74

Seventeen Moments of Spring (television serial), 9, 16, 180, 305

Sex education, jokes about, 176

Sexually transmitted disease, 340

"Shadow economy." *See* "Second economy"

Shadow theater. *See* Teatr Ten'

Shagin, Dmitir, 107

Shakhet, Boris, 183

Shakhnazarov, Karen, 74

Shakhrin, Vladimir, 222

Shakurov, Sergei, 98

Shamanism, 354

"Shamateurism," 266

Shapiro, Adolf, 145

Shar (animation studio), 100

Sharapova, Maria, 263, 280, 314

Sharnin, Andrei, 189

Sharov, Andrei, 363–364, 369

Sharovatova, Irina, 230

Shatrov, Mikhail, 151

Shcharansky, Anatoli, 7

Shchedrin, Rodion, 212

Shcherbakov, Boris, 172

Shefler, Yuri, 337

Shenderovich, Viktor, 34, 43, 45(photo)

Shepitko, Larisa, 78

Shepotinnik, Peter, 34

Shevardnadze, Eduard, 18

Shevchuk, Yuri, 226–227, 257, 260

Shifrin, Yefim, 171

Shinkarev, Vladimir, 107

Shnurov, Sergei, 98, 232, 260–261

Shoigu, Igor, 29

Shopping malls, 115, 118–120

Shops, 116–123

Short Encounters (film), 9

Shtatniki (American style *stilyagi*), 200

Shtein, Alexander, 5

Shuidin, Mikhail, 189

Shumiatsky, Boris, 2–3, 76

Sigarev, Vasili, 154, 158, 159, 160, 196, 296

Sikharulidze, Anton, 289–290

Silver Rain (radio station), 49

Simonov, Konstantin, 293

Simonova, Yevgeniya, 172

Simple Truths (television serial), 40

Siniavsky, Andrei, 7

Siniavsky, Vadim, 267

Sisters (film), 97

Sitkovetsky, Alexander, 209, 217

600 Seconds (television program), 19–20

Skiing, 286–287

Skliar, Alexander, 219

Skoroded, Valeri, 219

Skyscraper (sots-art), 106–107

Slaviane (rock band), 207

Slominskaya, Julia, 161

Slovo (film studio), 75

Slutskaya, Irina, 288(photo)

Smekhova, Alika, 35

Smirnova, Dunia, 37

Smith, Martin Cruz, 209

Smoking, 323–324

Smoliakov, Andrei, 145

Soap operas. *See under* Television

Soccer, 263–264, 267–275

   teams, 270–275, 311, 312, 314

Sochinushki (film), 100

Socialism, 12

   and culture, 1–2, 3

Socialist Realism, 2, 3, 4, 10, 105, 106

Sokolniki Stadium, 270

Sokov, Leonid, 107

Sokurov, Alexander, 78, 79

Soloviev, Sergei, 215

Soltan, Marcella, 188

Solzhenitsyn, Alexander, 4, 7, 62

Sold Out (talk show), 36–37

"Song about Five Minutes," 77

"Song of the Motherland," 3, 4

Songs, 3, 4, 49, 76, 77, 108, 199, 203–206, 210, 218, 219 (*see also* Bard movement)

Sorokin, Vladimir, 294(photo), 296, 297, 314

Sorokina, Svetlana, 26, 41, 45(photo), 68

Sotheby's (Moscow), 104, 107

Sots-art, 12, 104, 106–107, 132

Sovershenno sekretno (*Top Secret*, newspaper), 53, 56

Sovetskaya kultura (*Soviet Culture*, newspaper), 52

Sovetskaya Rossiya (*Soviet Russia*, newspaper), 52, 53, 205
Sovetskii balet (*Soviet Ballet*, magazine), 57
Sovetskii ekran (*Soviet Screen*, magazine), 57
Sovetskii tsirk (*Soviet Circus*, magazine), 57
Soviet Army Ensemble, 8
Soviet foreign policy, 7
   jokes about, 175–176
Soviet Union collapse (1991), 11, 24–25
Soviet Unions of Composers, of Artists, of Cinematographers, of Theater Workers, of Writers, 2, 7, 9, 10, 74
Sovremennaya dramaturgiya (journal), 62
Sovremennik (Contemporary) theater, 5, 6, 136, 138, 155, 172
SPATI (St. Petersburg Academy of Theater Arts, formerly LGITMiK), 164, 165
SPEED-Info (AIDS-Info, SPID-Info, newspaper), 46, 56, 57
Sport FM (radio station), 48, 49
SportExpress (magazine), 267
Sports, 11, 263–292
   commendations, 267
   equipment and facilities, 112, 268, 269, 284–285
   and military training, 266
   under Soviets, 271
   See also individual names
Spotlight on Perestroika (television program), 19, 67
Spy thrillers, 263. *See also* Television, and spy and detective programs
"Stagnation" period, 6–9
Stalin, Josef, 3, 4, 10, 27, 86, 113
   and film, 73, 76, 78
   jokes about, 173–174
Stalin and Hitler (art), 107
Stalin and Marilyn (art), 107
Stalingrad. *See* Volgograd
Stamp Album (Sergeyev), 295
Stanislavsky, Konstantin, 3, 5, 6, 135
Stanislavsky Theater, 148, 172
The Star (film), 85
Star Factory (television program), 36, 241
State Emergency Committee (GKChP, 1991), 24, 25
State Puppet Theater, 162
Steblin, Alexander, 276
Stepanov, Yuri, 280
Stepanova, Masha, 103

Stepanova, Varvara, 2
Stirlitz (character in spy literature), 4, 16, 53, 180–181, 196, 293
Stick/rod puppets, 160–161, 162
Stilyagi (style hunters), 200
Stites, Richard, 11
Stolper, Alexander, 5
Storming of the Winter Palace (directed by Yevreinov), 1
Stoyanov, Yuri, 36
Strategic control, jokes about, 176–177
Street Watch (television crime program), 34
Streets of Broken Lights (television serial), 39, 300, 306–307
Streltsov, Alexander, 187
Strider: The Story of a Horse (Tolstoy), 6, 136
Strok, Oskar, 200
Strugachev, Semen, 81
Strugatsky, Arkadi, 8
Strugatsky, Boris, 8
Styob (parody of socialist culture), 245, 261
Subsidized culture, 12, 317
"Suburban Moscow Evenings" (song), 4
Submarine accident, 29, 43
Subway terrorist attack, 29
Sukachev, Igor (Garik), 220, 261
Sukhanov, Maxim, 148
Sukhorukov, Viktor, 98
Summer Garden (pop group), 243
Superstition, 354–356
Suslov, Mikhail, 212
Suteyev, Vladimir, 100
Svanidze, Nikolai, 34
Sverdlov, Yakov, 113
Sverdlovsk (now Yekaterinburg), 113
Sviridova, Alyona, 239
"Sweet N" (song), 222, 223
Swimming, 268, 284–285
Sych, Vladimir, 276

Tabakov, Oleg, 140, 141, 145, 158, 171, 196
Tabakov Theater, 142, 155, 198
Taganka Theater of Drama and Comedy, 4, 5, 6, 9, 136, 138, 139, 203
Tale of Tales (film), 100
Tango, 199, 100
Tape recordings, 4
Tarasov, Anatoli, 275
Tarasov, Vladimir, 201
Taratorkin, Georgi, 172

Tarkovsky, Andrei, 8, 78
Tarzan (film), 5
TASS (Telegraph Agency of the Soviet Union)
  news agency, 15
TASS Is Authorized to Report (television
  serial), 16
Tatarsky, Alexander, 101
t.A.T.u (girl band), 199, 232–235, 285
Tayekin, Sergei, 191
Tchaikovsky, Pyotr, 113
Tea, advertising for, 324–325
Teatr (*Theater*, magazine), 61, 138
Teatr Koshek, 188
Teatr Ten' (Shadow Theater), 161, 165–167,
  196–197
Teatralnaya zhizn (*Theater Life*, magazine),
  57, 61–62
TEFI (television award), 33, 36
Tele-Special-Force (television program), 34
Television, 4, 8, 12, 13–46, 240
  and American influence, 27
  and American programs, 32, 38, 39
  awards, 33, 36
  cable, 14, 32, 41, 42
  channels, 14–15, 17, 23, 25, 28, 32, 34
  children's, 38
  crime programs, 34
  current events programs, 33–34
  educational, 38
  and game shows, 14, 16, 17, 32, 35–36
  history programs, 34
  independent, 16
  live, 15
  movies on, 32, 34, 41
  and music, 4, 18, 240–241
  and news, 14, 15, 16–32, 33
  news anchors on, 17, 22, 29
  producers, 32
  propaganda and ideology, 15, 45
  and public opinion, 14
  reality, 36
  Russian, 15, 16, 17, 18, 25
  satellite, 14, 18, 32–33, 42
  serials, 16, 39–40, 75, 295, 309
  sets, 14, 72
  soap operas, 39, 78, 305–309, 326
  Soviet, 14, 15, 20, 23, 40–41
  space bridges, 13, 20
  and sports, 15, 45
  and spy and detective programs, 16, 39–40

talk shows, 36–38
  and timeliness, 15
  tower, 14
  and Western programs, 15, 39
  and women's programs, 37–38
  youth programs, 18
  See also Investigative jounalists;
    Privatization
Televizor (rock band), 225–226
Ten Days that Shook the World (Reed), 6, 137
Tennis, 263, 268, 278–280
Terts, Abram (pseudonym), 7
Thaw (liberalization), 3–6, 18, 47, 86, 91, 136
Theater
  of the Absurd, 142
  author's, 6
  avant-garde movement, 135
  awards, 160
  boulevard, 171–173
  children's, 136, 147
  commercial, 12
  directors, 1–2, 3, 5, 6, 135, 137, 141, 147,
    151–153, 154, 156, 172
  experimental, 2, 3, 8, 10, 135, 140–141
  festivals, 187
  Russian, 153–160
  Soviet, 135–141, 151
  Stalinist, 3
  and television, 34
  underground, 7
  and unions, 10
  See also Actors/actresses; Circus; Clowns;
    Mime; Opera; Playwrights
Theater of Europe, 153
Theater of Nations, 139
Theater of Satire, 183
Theater of the Lenin Komsomol (Lenkom), 136,
  151
Theater South-West, 143
Theater Workers' Union (STD), 139, 141, 146
Theaters, 1, 2, 4, 5, 6, 116, 136, 139–140, 141,
    143, 144, 146, 147,148, 153, 155, 158, 184
  puppet, 135, 160–168
  puppet productions, 162, 163–166
  studio, 139–142
  workshop, 146, 147, 152
Theatrical Management Association (TMA),
  160
Theatrical Monday (television program), 34
"Thick" journals. *See* Literary journals

The Thief (film), 91
Three Sisters (Chekhov), 137
Tikhomirov, Alexander, 19
Tikhonov, Viktor, 275, 276
Tikhy, Sasha, 147
"Time for Little Bells" (song), 213
Timeliness, 52
Times Square (sots-art), 107
Tiurin, Yevgraf, 123
TNT (television satellite channel), 32, 46
Tobacco. *See* Smoking
Today in the World (television program), 15, 42, 54
Todorovsky, Valeri, 75
Tolkacheva, Alisa, 366
Tolstaya, Tatiana, 37
Tolstoy, Lev, 6, 136
Tolstunov, Igor, 75
Ton, Konstantin, 114
Top Line (film producer), 75
Top Secret (television program), 33–34, 68
Topilskaya, Elena, 309
Topol, Edward, 299
Toropov, Igor, 219
Total (television program), 34
Total Show (MTV game show), 36
Tourism, 343, 344–345
Tovstonogov, Georgi, 5, 6, 136, 138
Toys, 107, 108
Trade unions, 51
"Train on Fire" (song), 211
"Trash" culture, 8, 11, 12
The Tree with the Golden Apples (film), 101
Tretiakov, Vitali, 55
Tretiakov Gallery, 12, 113
Trezzini, Domenico, 116
TriTe (film producer), 75
Troika, 49
Troitsky, Artemy (Artyom), 216, 218
The Truckers (television serial), 40
Trud (*Work*, newspaper), 55, 57, 68
Trukhin, Mikhail, 153, 172
Trushkin, Leonid, 154, 171
Tsereteli (Tsulukidze), Zurab, 114, 115, 118, 124(photo), 133
Tsfasman, Alexander, 200
TSN (Tele Service News), 17, 22, 25
Tsoy, Viktor, 214, 215, 222–224, 261
TsUM (Moscow Central Department Store), 120–121

Turishcheva, Liudmila, 282
Tusovka, 261
TV Park (journal), 60
Tvardovsky, Alexander, 7, 8, 62
Tver, 113
TVS (Television Spectrum), 44, 45
TV6, 32, 34, 36, 37, 38, 41, 42, 46, 69
    parent company. *See* MNVK
TVTs (Center Television, TV-Center), 30, 38, 43, 42, 46, 69
Twelfth Floor (television program), 18, 47, 64
Twelve Chairs (musical), 253–254, 255, 261–262, 335
Twentieth Party Congress (1956), 3
Twenty-fifth Party Congress (1976), 8
Twilight Watch (film), 99
Twists of the Times (radio program), 48
Two Captains (Kaverin), 250–252
The Tycoon (film), 13
Tyorkin in the Other World (Tvardovsky), 8

Udarnak Theater, 74
Ufimtsev, Ivan, 100
Ulanov, Alexi, 289
Ulianov, Mikhail, 98, 139
Ulianovsk (formerly Simbirsk), 113
Ulitskaya, Liudmila, 296, 297
Umetsky, Dmitri, 227
Union of Composers, 212
Union of Right Forces (SPS), 11
Unions, 2, 7, 9, 10, 138, 146, 161, 212
Unity (political party), 29, 30, 43
Uspensky, Eduard, 100
Ural (literary journal), 158
Urban planning and design, 105, 112–123
Us (film), 86
Ustinova, Tatiana, 295
Utesov, Leonid, 200

Vaikule, Laima, 238, 262
Vakhtangov, Yevgeni, 135, 356
Vapirov, Anatoli, 201
Varum, Angelika, 242
Vasilevsky, Andrei, 63
Vasiliev, Anatoli, 140, 141, 142
Vasiliev, Georgi, 3
Vasiliev (Fainstein), Mikhail, 209
Vasiliev, Sergei, 3
Vasilieva, Tatania, 154, 172, 360
VASSA, 365, 369–370

Vecherniaya Moskva (*Evening Moscow* newspaper), 46, 51, 55
Vedomosti (*Information*, newspaper), 57
Venediktov, Alexei, 48
Venetsianov, Georgi, 185
Venice International Film Festival, 71
Vereshchagin, Leonid, 75
Versions (television program), 45
Versty (newspaper), 56
Vesti (RTR news program), 23, 33, 44
Vetlitskaya, Natalia, 238–239
VGTRK, 23, 42, 46, 69
VIA (vocal instrumental ensemble), 217, 218
Video recorders, 74
Video-piracy, 32, 74, 217
Viktiuk, Roamn, 147, 148–151, 86, 197
Vilnius (Lithuania) independence movement (1991), 22, 30
Virsky, Pavel, 8
Vishnevskaya, Galina, 115
Visual culture, 11
VJ (video jockey), 42
Vladimov, Georgi, 295
Vlast (*Control*, journal), 60
Vodka, 91–92, 337
    advertising for, 320–321
Voice of America (VoA), 47, 201
Volga-Volga (film), 76
Volgograd, 113
Volleyball, 277–278
Volos, Andrei, 296
"Vote or you'll lose" (election slogan), 28
VOTM (Creative Workshops), 146–147, 148
Voznesensky, Andrei, 151, 208
VQ. *See* Perepelkin, Vladimir
Vragova, Svetlana, 140, 142
Vremechko (see *A Bit of Time*, talk show)
Vremia (television program), 15, 17, 20–21, 24, 33, 34, 36
Vse dlia vas (*Everything for You*, advertising paper), 56
Vuchetich, Yevgeni, 113
Vyrypaev, Ivan, 158, 159(photo)
Vysotsky, Vladimir, 9, 14, 16, 98, 113, 138, 202, 203, 204–206, 207, 212, 222, 244, 262, 327
Vzgliad (television program), 17, 18, 19, 47, 69, 96
    journalists, 47

Walking, 280

War (film), 97
Wargnier, Regis, 97
The Weakest Link (television game show), 35
Weightlifting, 281
Western culture, 4
While Everybody's Still at Home (television program), 35
Who Wants to Be a Millionaire (television game show), 35
Window on Europe (film festival), 75
Wine, 337
"Wings" (song), 228, 229
Wintour, Charles, Award, 160
"Wolf Hunt" (song), 98, 205–206
Women's View (television program), 38
Woodcuts, 107
World and Youth (television program), 18
World Circus Festival, 191
World in a Week (radio program), 47–48
World of the New Russians (shop), 111–112
World War II (1939–1945), 3, 5
Wrestling, 281, 282(photo)
Writers, 7, 8, 12, 13, 16, 37, 39, 40, 98, 100, 102, 162, 216, 250, 292, 293, 295, 296, 298
    women detective, 301–305

Yabloko (political party), 11, 27
Yachting, 284
Yakov, Valeri, 56
Yakovlev, Alexander, 9, 15, 25
Yakovlev, Yegor, 52
Yakovleva, Yelena, 37, 40
Yakubovich, Leonid, 35
Yakunina, Masha, 103
Yanayev, Gennadi (vice president), 18, 24, 25
Yankovsky, Oleg, 75, 151, 172
Yarbusova, Francesca, 100
Yastrzhembsky, Sergei, 31
Yatsuro, Yelena, 75
Yavlinsky, Grigori, 27
Yazov, Dmitri (defense minister, 1991), 22, 24
Yefremov, Oleg, 5–6, 136, 139
Yeltsin, Boris, 9, 10
    and censorship, 26
    daughter (*see* Diachenko, Tatiana)
    and Gorbachev, 23, 25
    health, 28
    and parliament, 25–26, 27
    as president, 25, 26, 27–32,
    as presidential security boos, 28

as puppet, 34, 35(photo)
and radio, 27
and television, 15, 16, 23–24, 27, 28, 41, 319
Yemets, Dmitri, 298
Yepifanova, Irina, 218
Yeralash films (Gorky studios), 38
Yermolaeva, Elena, 366
Yerofeyev, Viktor, 37
Yershov, Stanislav, 75
Yeryomin, Yuri, 147
Yevreinov, Nikolai, 1
Yevteyeva, Irina, 100
Your Game (television program), 35
Youth Café, 207, 208
Yudanova, Yelena, 229
Yudashkin, Valentin, 239, 359–360, 370
Yunost (*Youth* journal), 60, 62
Yurievich, Andrei, 128

Zaderny, Sviatoslav, 224
Zadornov, Mikhail, 197
Zaitsev, Viacheslav (Slava), 357–359, 370
Zakharov, Mark, 10, 17. 151, 152, 172, 197

Zakharov, Vasili, 9
Zakhoder, Boris, 100
Zakutsky, Valeri, 35
Zalygin, Sergei, 63
Zamolodchikova, Lena, 283
Zarubina, Irina, 303
Zavtra (*Tomorrow*, newspaper), 54, 55(photo)
Zemfira (Ramazanova) (rock singer), 235, 236(photo)
Zdorovie (*Health*, magazine), 57
Zhakevich, Vadim (Jacques), 147
Zhdanov, Andrei, 200
Zhirinovsky, Vladimir, 27, 30, 49, 319, 320
Zhitinkin, Andrei, 145, 197–198, 363
Zhurbin, Alexander, 207
Zhvanetsky, Mikhail, 8, 170–171, 198
Zimianin, Mikhail, 9
Ziuganov, Gennadi, 27, 28, 29, 32, 49, 319, 320
Zoopark (rock band), 222
Zorin, Leonid, 5
Zudina, Maria, 145
Zviagintsev, Andrei, 71

About the Author

Birgit Beumers is senior lecturer in the Russian Department at Bristol University. After completing her PhD at St. Antony's College, Oxford, she taught for two years in the Slavonic Department at the University of Cambridge before moving to Bristol in 1994. She specializes in contemporary Russian culture, especially cinema and theater. Her book publications include *Yury Lyubimov at the Taganka Theatre 1964–1994* (1997); *Burnt by the Sun* (2000); and *Nikita Mikhalkov: Between Nostalgia and Nationalism* (2005). She edited *Russia on Reels: The Russian Idea in Post-Soviet Cinema* (1999).